SPEAKING BEING

SPEAKING BEING

WERNER ERHARD, MARTIN HEIDEGGER, AND A NEW POSSIBILITY OF BEING HUMAN

BRUCE HYDE AND DREW KOPP

AFTERWORD BY MICHAEL E. ZIMMERMAN

Dear Saby,
May this work
Continue to speak to
you and support your
ongoing transformation.
♡ — Lamar

WILEY

Cover design: Tom Greensfelder
Cover image: © Ralf Hiemisch/Getty Images

Published by John Wiley & Sons, Inc., Hoboken, New Jersey.

Published simultaneously in Canada.

For general information on our other products and services or for technical support, please contact our Customer Care Department within the United States at (800) 762–2974, outside the United States at (317) 572–3993, or fax (317) 572–4002.

Wiley publishes in a variety of print and electronic formats and by print-on-demand. Some material included with standard print versions of this book may not be included in e-books or in print-on-demand. If this book refers to media such as a CD or DVD that is not included in the version you purchased, you may download this material at http://booksupport.wiley.com. For more information about Wiley products, visit www.wiley.com.

ISBN 9781119549901 (paper)
ISBN 9781119550211 (ePDF)
ISBN 9781119550204 (ePub)

SPEAKING BEING: Werner Erhard, Martin Heidegger, and a New Possibility of Being Human, written by Dr. Bruce Hyde and Dr. Drew Kopp, includes material and ideas originally developed by Werner Erhard and owned by Landmark Worldwide, such material and ideas which the authors have juxtaposed with the thinking of Martin Heidegger in an effort to illuminate both thinkers. The views and arguments expressed in this book in reference to the material and ideas are the sole responsibility of the authors and were not written by, nor are they endorsed by, Landmark, its affiliates, or its predecessors.

LANDMARK and LANDMARK WORLDWIDE are registered trademarks of Landmark Worldwide LLC ("Landmark"). The 1989 Forum, The Landmark Forum, and other programs presented by Landmark, its affiliates, and its predecessors are proprietary to Landmark and protected by international intellectual property laws. Materials and quotations from such courses in this book are the copyright of Landmark, are used with permission, and may not be reproduced without the prior written permission of Landmark.

Landmark wishes to make the materials, concepts, and information that constitute its programs, as well as the way in which these are assembled and presented, available to academics for examination, study, research, and comment. As such, academics are invited to quote from the Landmark material, with attribution to Landmark, and are not required to have Landmark's prior written permission to do so

Printed in the United States of America

V10011546 062219

To the students in my Communication Studies classes at St. Cloud State University, who for the past twenty-five years have been my partners in the play and mystery of ontological inquiry; and to my wife Susan Saetre, my constant guardian angel.

BRUCE

To my friend and writing partner, Bruce Hyde (1941-2015), who blazed a trail with his unrelenting commitment to communicate the unsaid. What a gift to have worked with a man of such brilliance, humor, and courage, even unto death, and with this book, Bruce will continue to speak to each reader willing to take up the call to enter the conversation this book is but a fragment of. I also dedicate this book to my students, ever my co-experimenters in the inquiry of what it means to be a writer and a reader; and to my wife Cindy, and my children, Tristan and Cassidy: I dedicate the fruits of my labor to your future.

DREW

CONTENTS

ABOUT THE AUTHORS

BRUCE HYDE (PhD, University of Southern California, 1990) was a Professor of Communication Studies at St. Cloud State University until his death on October 13th, 2015 (1941-2015). His primary interests as an educator were with the ontological dimensions of language and communication, and with dialogue as a non-polarized and non-polarizing form of public discourse.

DREW KOPP (PhD, University of Arizona, 2009) is an Associate Professor of Writing Arts at Rowan University. His research interests focus on the theory and history of rhetorical pedagogies, and he has published articles in journals in the field of rhetoric and writing studies, including *Rhetoric Review* (2013), and *JAC: Rhetoric, Writing, Culture, Politics* (2012). He has also contributed a chapter to the edited collection *Disrupting Pedagogies in the Knowledge Society* (2011).

PRAISE FOR *SPEAKING BEING: WERNER ERHARD, MARTIN HEIDEGGER, AND A NEW POSSIBILITY OF BEING HUMAN*

From the Afterword:

I regard *Speaking Being* as an enormously important contribution to understanding Heidegger and Erhard. The latter has received far too little serious academic attention, and this book begins to make up for that lack. Moreover, the book's analysis of Heidegger's thought is among the best that I have ever read. I commend this book to all readers without reservation.

MICHAEL E. ZIMMERMAN, *Professor Emeritus, University of Colorado, Boulder*

This book is powerful, imaginative, frustrating, amusing, threatening, and enlightening—all at the same time. It also has the power to transform your life.

JONATHAN D. MORENO, *University of Pennsylvania Professor of Ethics, author of* Impromptu Man

The profound impact of Werner Erhard's work on culture and society is a manifestation of an incredible insight, the experience of *being*, presented in this book through a comparative analysis of a transcript of a 1989 Forum led by Erhard alongside Heidegger's reflections on the meaning of "being there." The authors have drawn amazing parallels between these two extraordinary thinkers and have demonstrated the intersections of Heidegger's language with Erhard's ontological rhetoric of transformation. Erhard has at times described aspects of his method as *ruthless compassion*, and like all forms of compassion, evident here is a fundamental motivating desire to alleviate the suffering of others.

JAMES R. DOTY, MD, *Founder and Director, The Center for Compassion and Altruism Research and Education, Professor of Neurosurgery, Stanford University School of Medicine, and Senior Editor of* The Oxford Handbook of Compassion Science

Speaking Being is not a book. It is a multimodal *tour de force* of ontological rhetoric that hails its reader into an event and in so doing performs as an event, rather than what is commonly rendered as a book between two covers. Its status as an event is performed on every page wherein the "showing" of *Being* is enacted via its remarkable design. Kaleidoscopically, Bruce Hyde and Drew Kopp have drawn their readers into a dazzling display, where the participants in dialogue with Werner Erhard in a specific Forum in 1989 are put into dialogue with Martin Heidegger. The result is arguably one of the most astounding academic interventions into both Erhard's methodology and Heideggerian thought. Citing David Farrell Krell, Hyde and Kopp remind us that "to be on a woodpath means to be in a *cul-de-sac*, a path that leads nowhere and has no exit." *Speaking Being* puts its readers in a dizzying *cul-de-sac* within which they may never leave, but rather transform into one of the glittering particles of this rhetorical kaleidoscope.

CYNTHIA HAYNES, *Professor of English, Clemson University, author of* The Homesick Phone Book: Addressing Rhetoric in the Age of Perpetual Conflict

Theory and Practice: Ways of seeing what one claims to be the truth of some intended object of consciousness and ways of applying this truth to one's everyday existence in order to cultivate wisdom, goodness, self-realization, and justice. The dialogical teachings of Werner Erhard speak to the importance of this relationship and its ontological significance. Professors Hyde and Kopp, scholars of rhetoric and communication who had observed and participated in programs designed by Erhard, provide comprehensive and detailed conversations—what they term "ontological rhetoric"—that took place in Erhard's 1989 Forum, and they demonstrate how Erhard and Heidegger can be read together for the benefit of both. This book is a major achievement in the scholarship of Erhard and Heidegger studies. A much-needed moment of enlightenment.

MICHAEL J. HYDE, *University Distinguished Professor of Communication Ethics, Wake Forest University, author of* Perfection: Coming to Terms with Being Human

In *Speaking Being* the reader discovers two original thinkers—Werner Erhard and Martin Heidegger—two intellects who independently reached linguistic, ontological, and phenomenological philosophies that illuminate each other.

Authors Hyde and Kopp accomplish the formidable task of masterfully presenting Erhard and Heidegger side by side in a readable, lively, and illuminating text. There is nothing quite like it!

JERONIMA (JERI) ECHEVERRIA, *Professor of History and Provost Emerita, California State University at Fresno, former Executive Vice-Chancellor for Academic Affairs of the California State University System*

Educational research confirms that without a significant intervention, students who become teachers are likely to replicate the pedagogical approaches their teachers used with them. Practicing Erhard's approach to ontological inquiry—presented in print for the first time in this book—provides such an intervention. It equips students, teachers, academics of any field to critically examine their dispositions and access more effective ways of being and acting. *Speaking Being* is a must read for scholars of social foundations of education, teacher education, and frankly, for members of any field of study.

CAROLYNE J. WHITE, *Professor of Social Foundations, Department of Urban Education, Rutgers University Newark*

A different you and a different me must show up each day if we are going to tackle the world's most vexing problems. This book talks us through a process of transformation by showing us what it means to be an authentic human being in an inauthentic world, and what it means to take a stand for a world where everyone matters and where everyone can make a difference.

WILEY "CHIP" SOUBA, MD, SCD, MBA, *Professor of Surgery, Geisel School of Medicine at Dartmouth, former Dean of Medicine and VP for Health Affairs, Dartmouth College*

This engaging study of Erhard's counter-discursive approach to transformational education—and how this approach aligns significantly with Heidegger's thinking—

might serve as a starting point for a deeper Indigenous philosophy. Rooted in a more non-hierarchical epistemology, such an Indigenous philosophy promises to move us away from a colonized and deeply problematized way of thinking, toward embracing the power and mysteriousness of presence, and making possible a place-based, non-anthropocentric interconnectedness. This is the next essential step we must take if we are to survive as a species.

FOUR ARROWS, AKA DON TRENT JACOBS, PHD, EdD, *editor of* Unlearning the Language of Conquest, *author of* Point of Departure *and* Teaching Truly

While some readers of *Speaking Being* may be familiar with The Landmark Forum, most don't know its connections to the philosophical tradition. Hyde and Kopp have woven together concise explanations of Heidegger's notoriously difficult thinking with an actual transcript of Erhard's Forum—by turns moving, funny, and shocking. This juxtaposition draws the reader into the experience and powerfully illuminates the teachings of these two thinkers.

DAVID STOREY, *Associate Professor, Boston College, author of* Naturalizing Heidegger

Speaking Being presents an ontological play between Erhard, Heidegger, the participants of a Forum delivered in 1989, and the reader, who is summoned to the scene to dwell in compelling questions and distinctions, the living of which make available the invention of a life that is experienced as authentic. The relentless commitment of authors Hyde and Kopp to communicate the unsayable, *Being,* opens up new directions for a rhetoric of emancipation that goes beyond traditional critical theories. *Speaking Being* speaks a new relation to language, one that honors the unexplored ontological power of language to create a new freedom to be, to live with existential courage.

MARGARIDA GARCIA, *Vice-Dean, Research and Communications, Faculty of Law (Civil Law) and Professor, Faculty of Law (Civil Law) and Faculty of Social Sciences, University of Ottawa*

Many academics in cultural studies accept postmodernity and content pedagogy as unquestionable facts of the world, but with a paltry understanding of how these ideas undermine our intention to produce morally conscious, action-oriented citizens. In their lucid exposition of Werner Erhard's methodology, Hyde and Kopp offer a cogent roadmap out of such a paralyzing paradigm of knowledge and subjectivity. Brilliantly, the authors use Martin Heidegger's writing to illuminate Erhard's work and The Forum's compelling impact on participants. Readers will discover for themselves, based on the contexts they bring, a powerful pedagogy of transformation grounded in an ontological inquiry into human being that leads students to discover their own paths of social agency and initiative. Highly recommended!

TRYSTAN T. COTTEN, *Associate Professor, Gender Studies, University of California, Stanislaus, founder and managing editor of* Transgress Press

Speaking Being presents, perhaps for the first time, a complete transcript of an actual Forum led by Werner Erhard, allowing the reader to directly observe and experience the unique power of dialogue as a tool for human transformation. Furthermore, authors Hyde and Kopp provide an intellectually satisfying correlation between the philosophical ideas of Martin Heidegger and the *out-here-in-the-world* work of Werner Erhard, revealing their surprising complementarity. I congratulate the authors on achieving this *tour de force*.

MICHAEL LESLIE, *Associate Professor, Journalism and Communications, University of Florida*

Introduction

In 1971, the television debut of *All in the Family* tickled an American public who was also celebrating the successful moon landing, and safe return home, of two Apollo space missions. In the same year, much smaller audiences took note of Igor Stravinsky's death and the birth of Calvin Broadus Jr. (aka Snoop Dogg/Lion); a marketing phenomenon was born in Seattle with the opening of the first Starbucks; Idi Amin ousted Milton Obote to become the dictator of Uganda; and in the new academic field of composition and rhetoric, a movement to elevate the status of process began to stir. Meanwhile, in October of that year in a meeting room of San Francisco's less-than-swank Jack Tar Hotel, Werner Erhard assembled some two hundred participants for the debut of the *est* Training. Given this timing for the emergence of the *est* Training, media at the time characterized it as a part of the human potential movement, but scholar Jonathan Moreno has more recently called *est* "the most important cultural event after the human potential movement itself seemed exhausted" (*Impromptu Man* 247).

Infamous for its rigorous ground rules and confrontational methods—elements Erhard says were necessary in the liberated, let-it-all-hang-out, "new age" ethos of the time—the *est* Training (Latin for *it is*, and an acronym for Erhard Seminars Training) grew in popularity throughout the 1970s because of the impressive benefits participants reported having received, including better relationships and a greater sense of "aliveness." Trainees experienced being "at cause" in the matter of their lives, and having a new sense that their lives could make a difference in the world. They felt "free to be." This new sense of responsibility and freedom allowed for breakthroughs in communicating with others, and enabled them to produce results, both personal and professional, that they would previously have seen as unlikely.

At the source of this educational enterprise was an experience Erhard had undergone earlier that year, although he later said it was "not in itself so much an *experience*, as a shift in the context in which he held all process, including experience" (Bartley 168). In some traditions, such an event might be referred to as an individual's having undergone *enlightenment*; Erhard has called it a *transformation*. He was, at this point in his life, a highly successful sales manager and trainer for a large publishing company. Further, he had devoted much of the previous decade to the rigorous exploration of various systems of enlightenment and personal development, from Zen (the essential one, he says) to the Dale Carnegie course and Mind Dynamics. But one morning in 1971, as he was driving across the Golden Gate Bridge en route to his office, he suddenly realized that he knew nothing. As he related the incident to his biographer, William Bartley:

 All the things I had ever heard, and read, and all those hours of practice, suddenly fell into place. It was so stupidly, blindingly simple that I could not believe it. I saw that there were no hidden meanings, that everything was just the way that it is, and that I was already all right. . . . I realized that I was not my emotions or thoughts. I was not my ideas, my intellect, my perceptions, my beliefs. . . . I was simply the space, the creator, the source of all that stuff. I experienced Self as Self in a direct, unmediated way. I didn't just experience Self; *I became Self.* Suddenly I held all the information, the content, in my life in a new way, from a new mode, a new context. . . . I am *I am.* (Bartley 167–168)

In other words, an experience of being. The insight Erhard derived from that experience subsequently became what thousands of *est* trainees would spend two weekends and several hundred dollars to "get" for themselves.

Discussing his work later, Erhard addressed the challenge he had confronted in attempting to communicate what seemed essentially incommunicable: "You can't do this in the ordinary sense of communication: I can't have it and give it to you. But I can communicate in a way so that you get an opportunity to realize that you have it yourself already. Essentially, this is what the *est* Training was developed to do. It provides a setting in which this kind of sharing takes place" (Bartley 169).

From the outset, the language of *est* was central to both its pedagogical process and its public image. A fundamental tenet of the *est* Training, as well as its successor program, The Forum, has been that *transformation lives in language,* and that participants keep the program's results available in their lives by communicating those results with others. At the same time, Erhard's enterprise has consistently eschewed traditional advertising. The only way people have become aware of his work has been through hearing about it from their friends, family, or associates. The resulting symbiotic relationship—the program survives only when participants communicate about it with family and friends, and it is through communicating about it that participants keep the benefits alive in their experience—has served the work well through four decades. By 1985, when the *est* Training was discontinued and replaced by The Forum, word-of-mouth had brought a half-million people to see for themselves what this transformation was all about. As of 2019, another 2 million people have graduated from The Forum, either the four-day Forum of Erhard's time through 1991, or the current iteration of the course, the three-day Landmark Forum (www.landmarkworldwide.com).[1]

Erhard's influence on the culture has made itself felt in another way as well. During the 1970s, when it sometimes seemed that every fifth person in San Francisco was an *est* graduate, you could generally detect that element of the population by their use of the program's language, which in casual use began to be heard as jargon. Erhard's use of this terminology, however, was highly purposive, and many of those words and phrases made their way into the public sphere, some to lasting effect. An example has been the shift in the popular understanding of the term *sharing.* Before *est*, people shared a cookie or a bench in the park; what was shared was *divided,* and in the process one's own share was inevitably diminished. But in the *est* Training, participants *shared their experience,* and through sharing, that experience was augmented. To share, in the world of *est*, was to communicate in such a way that one's *self* and not merely one's story was made available, leaving the other touched rather than merely informed. This meaning of the word, we assert, is now common in our culture. Likewise, the term *coaching*, borrowed by Erhard from the sports arena in the early eighties to identify the style of his pedagogy, has since become ubiquitous in the field of management, human resources, and executive coaching. And the ubiquitous Mastercard catchphrase, "Master the possibilities," was born in the mind of an *est* graduate for whom the term *possibility* had acquired a new level of meaning; however, through overuse in the media, this new level of meaning has diminished.

The move to discontinue the Training in 1985 and replace it with The Forum arose from Erhard's perception of a shift in the culture's way of responding to the Training; he wanted to design a course that was responsive to that shift. At this point, while Erhard's success during those years had been greeted by considerable media curiosity, scholarly interest was moderate. Several studies of the *est* Training attempted to measure its effects using a psychological model; while he considered such efforts valuable, Erhard has asserted that this approach is inappropriate for

analysis of his work. His work, he says, is not psychological but *ontological*: his concern is the *being* of human beings ("Heart of the Matter" 1984). He has also consistently emphasized that the focus of his work is the development of the language in which it is articulated. Yet no significant scholarly work dealing either with Erhard's language use, or with the nature of an ontological methodology, has been published, even in the academic fields most likely to be deeply concerned with such matters—rhetoric and writing studies, business management, philosophy, and communication studies. This book aims to begin to correct that omission.

Before proceeding, we offer this statement of authorial stance: The authors have engaged extensively, both as participants and as scholars, in numerous programs designed by Werner Erhard. The senior author took the *est* Training for the first time in 1973, and we have each participated a number of times in The Forum, both during Erhard's tenure in the organization and following his departure. Our doctoral dissertations (University of Southern California, 1990; University of Arizona, 2008) consisted of rhetorical and philosophical analyses of The Forum. Based upon this considerable study and experience, our assessment of Erhard's work is unequivocal: we have found this work to be pedagogically effective and intellectually significant in all of its historical iterations. Our intention in this book is to stimulate its serious consideration by the academic community, as well as by others in the culture at large.

It is also important to note that our approach as participant observers has its limits. To carry out the design of the book, we have precluded a number of approaches that readers may wish to see addressed, and we beg those readers to indulge us. Before any significant and critical treatments could be viable, or even possible, from a number of disciplines—including philosophy, communication studies, rhetorical criticism, and so on—the phenomenon must be first made available. We present this book as a way into the phenomenon in question, and consequently, we invite members from a range of academic disciplines to enter the conversation we are seeking to initiate.

Evolution

This is an historical document. It presents an account of one moment—albeit a significant one—in an ongoing project for the development of human being. The first iteration of this project, the *est* Training, was designed to communicate to people living in the cultural environment of the 1970s. As Erhard saw it, considerable logistical rigor was required for the course to achieve its purpose, and thus the format included demands for which *est* soon became notorious, including lengthy sessions

---

[1] Landmark describes The Landmark Forum as a personal and professional development program, based on the discipline of applied ontology and phenomenology. Erhard created the work in the early 1970s and continued its development until in 1991 Landmark took over its ongoing development as expressed in The Landmark Forum and other Landmark programs. As of the writing of this book, the material and structure of The Forum have continued to be developed during three decades since the 1989 Forum presented in this book. The Landmark Forum of today (circa 2019) is less time (three days and an evening and each day ends by 10:00 pm), it incorporates the use of PowerPoint displays and videos that enhance the participants' experience of and access to what is being presented, and there is no use of profanity on the part of the program leaders.

with limited bathroom breaks, a highly confrontational interaction style—with the use of explicatives—and the surrender of all wristwatches at the door. These demands were modified when The Forum replaced the Training; and in subsequent years, as the communication paradigm of the culture has continued to shift, the delivery of The Forum has altered accordingly.

On the one hand, of course, The Forum conversation inevitably challenges participants' familiar way of seeing things. Ontological inquiry—pedagogy such as The Forum, that aims to get beyond mere conceptual knowledge—is of necessity rigorous and sometimes uncomfortable. In Martin Heidegger's words, authentic inquiry into Being always "has the character of doing violence, whether to the claims of the everyday interpretation, or to its complacency and tranquillized obviousness" (*BT* 359). But while the conversation in the current Landmark Forum remains rigorous, participants will find a presentation that can for the most part be described as gentler, and more user-friendly, than the one presented in this book.

A further aspect of this difference, of course, has to do with Werner Erhard's personal style. In his delivery of both the Training and The Forum, Erhard's communication was edgily playful and relentlessly purposive. He called his approach *ruthless compassion;* and it included a profound sense of humor and Socratic irony implicit in the human condition. To communicate the humor as well as the compassion, he often provoked and insulted participants, using language generally considered inappropriate for such a setting (in a parody of one of his favorite epithets, graduates of the Training were sometimes referred to as "estholes"). Yet, as this book shows, those participants who initially resisted these intrusions inevitably got the message. Erhard has related this confrontive aspect of his communication to his 1971 experience of transformation: "On the bridge," he said, "all of a sudden I could be 100% responsible for everything in my life, and at the same time none of it had any significance. At that point you are free and fearless" (Erhard, interview with authors). Erhard's communication style, and his humor, remain on full display in this book; the authors see them as important and entertaining aspects of the historical account we are presenting here.

Erhard Encounters Heidegger

Despite the shift we have cited here in The Forum's style and tone, a central thesis of this book is that from the first offering of the *est* Training in 1971, through its replacement by the Forum in 1985 and its current iteration as the Landmark Forum, the process at the heart of this pedagogy has retained its transformational dynamic. This dynamic, as we will show, arises in the *unspoken ontological realm* of The Forum conversation as it proceeds, and has been the essential element of the course through all of its terminological variations.

During the transition to The Forum, Erhard excised many of the *est* Training's more meditative exercises and incorporated into the course a new vocabulary and redesigned procedures, with the stated intention that participants would have an enhanced experience of creating a new realm of *possibility* for themselves and their lives. At about this time, through colleagues, he was introduced to the work of the twentieth-century German philosopher Martin Heidegger. Erhard was taken with the way Heidegger's thinking reverberated with his own, and he consulted with several Heideggerian scholars on the subject. Two of them—Hubert Dreyfus of University of California, Berkeley and Michael E. Zimmerman of Tulane—provided formal assessments of the *est* Training's effectiveness, and noted its consistencies with elements of Heidegger's thought. When Erhard's revised technology emerged in The Forum and other redesigned courses, significant Heideggerian terminology was included in its rhetorical mix, and Erhard occasionally read passages from Heidegger in his presentations.

Most significantly, Erhard saw that Heidegger's ideas and his own were communicating from the same *unspoken* realm, and that the *specifications* of the two vocabularies could be merged to communicate that realm more powerfully: "I learned from Heidegger," said Erhard, "*nuances* of what I had been saying that clarified and made more potent what was there" (Erhard, interview with authors).

What was there was Erhard's technology of language for the communication of being, and its ability, in both the Training and The Forum, to consistently and powerfully evoke an experience that participants found transformative. The evocation of that experience has remained The Forum's essential element; Erhard's encounter with Heidegger enriched the vocabulary in which he could see into it more profoundly and communicate it more effectively.

Technology

The form of this study will be *comparative analysis*: we will demonstrate that the work of Werner Erhard is aligned in significant ways with the philosophy of Martin Heidegger, and that a comparison of their work illuminates the thinking of both men. We will show that The Forum's dialogic form introduces a performative dimension of Heidegger's ontological vocabulary in a way that Heidegger himself, working within a restrictive academic and political culture, was unable to do. We propose that The Forum conversation is *ontological rhetoric*: purposive speaking that communicates and makes present a context of meaning that, if left unexamined, shapes and limits our way of being. However, this context of meaning cannot be spoken directly. It becomes present by virtue of what *is* said.

The dynamic of Erhard's technology of language responds directly to issues raised by Heidegger in his 1954 essay, "The Question Concerning Technology" (*Basic Writings*). Technology's essence, proposes Heidegger, is its relentless demand that all of nature, including human beings, be placed in *standing reserve*, on call for the uses of technology itself. The way of being evoked by this development (i.e., that we ourselves function as "calculable material" in a cybernetic system designed to serve ourselves) poses the danger that we may become lost in the profound reflexivity of that system, and, most fatally, may forget that anything has been lost. Surrender to technology "threatens man with the possibility that it could be denied to him to enter into a more original revealing and hence to experience the call of a more primal truth" ("QCT" in *BW* 333). Such surrender, however, seems inevitable: the technological epoch is where we have landed, the only way of being we have been provided, and resistance is as futile as surrender is fatal.

But Heidegger suggests a middle path, a "comportment toward technology which expresses 'yes' and at the same time 'no'" (*DT* 54). Further, he proposes that "essential reflection upon technology and decisive confrontation with it must happen in a realm that is, on the one hand, akin to the essence of technology, and, on the other, fundamentally different from it" ("QCT" in *BW* 340). We suggest that Werner Erhard's work provides such a realm. It is both a manifestation of the technological epoch and a subversive appropriation of its impulse, a thinking which reaches beyond the technological paradigm by reaching *through* that paradigm.

In Academia

For half a century, postmodern and poststructuralist theories across many disciplines have theorized a new freedom from the constraints of the Cartesian model of human being. Human subjectivity has been decentered; the self is no longer understood as the fixed and self-certain *cogito* but is open to creative reinvention; language does not merely re-present a preexisting world of objective meanings, but in fact generates the meanings that constitute that world.

These theoretical assertions concern *being.* But their effective communication in the universities has been hindered by our epistemologically-based academic tradition, which assumes that the central dynamic of education is *knowing.* This has given rise to a pedagogical model in which the ontological domain must always remain merely conceptual, because *being is not apprehended by knowing*. The book's thesis is that the work of Werner Erhard makes available the ontological domain of language, so that the decentering of subjectivity and the reinvention of the self can be experienced as possibilities rather than merely considered as theory.

We recognize that this pedagogical model is in many ways a radical one, given the strength of the assumptions embedded in our tradition; but Heidegger says that an experience with language in the ontological domain always requires "*a leap.*" As our educational institutions struggle increasingly to generate an opening for the human in the face of the advance of the technological, we argue that the situation is critical, and that a leap of this kind is in order.

The Plan of the Book

The central text for this book, located in the left and right columns on either page, is the combination of two sources: notes taken by the senior author while observing a Forum in San Francisco led by Werner Erhard in December 1989, and a transcription of the video of the same four-day event made available to the junior author on location at Landmark Worldwide's archives. While the transcript provides comprehensive and detailed conversations of the actual 1989 Forum, there are important alterations that must be accounted for. First and foremost, all names have been altered except for Werner Erhard, and actual names have been used only for those participants who speak more than once or twice with Erhard or the other two individuals leading the course ("Kipp" and "Wes"). In addition, some conversations have been edited out, or summarized, for the sake of space. For instance, all discussions dealing with the Six-Day Course, discontinued in 1990, have been removed. Also missing from the transcript is the Evening Session of the 1989 Forum: there was no extant video recording of that event. However, that omission can be rectified for interested readers if they were to attend an evening session of The Landmark Forum, where participants will share their experience of the course for guests they themselves have invited.

We call the text that accompanies the transcript either "sidebars" or "intervals." Sidebars occur in the central columns between the far left and right panes that house the transcript of The Forum, and the intervals occur between sessions of the course, and at the conclusion of each of the four days. In the sidebars and intervals are relevant ideas from the thinking of Martin Heidegger. Sometimes the connection between a sidebar and the transcript it accompanies may be apparent; sometimes it may be intended obliquely, as a hint at the background. Intervals are more often oblique in this way due to the focus on Heidegger's thinking in its wider arcs, for instance, the central theme of "the forgetting of Being," which has eight parts. Our purpose in this book is not to explain The Forum, or Heidegger's philosophy—although there are moments where we do provide analysis—but rather, we primarily aim to engage the reader in thinking Erhard's and Heidegger's ideas for themselves.

For readers who have previously participated in The Forum, we believe the confluence here of Heidegger's thinking with Erhard's will enrich the way those readers hold their Forum experience. This has been true for the authors, and it is likewise consistent with the experience of Werner Erhard, for whom exposure to Heidegger's thinking provided profound insights (Erhard, interview with authors). We intend that this book, in a dialogue with its readers, will evoke such insights.

Martin Heidegger once cautioned his students not to focus too closely on the concepts in his lectures, but rather to follow the "movement of showing" (*OTB* 2). The Forum conversation, we assert, is a carefully designed movement in language for the showing of being. In this book, we will show that showing. Our goal—Heidegger's, Erhard's, the authors'—is the unconcealment of a powerful aspect of human being with which we are, for the most part, unfamiliar.

While it may go without saying, reading this book will not provide an experience of The Forum. We intend to hint at that experience, and we encourage readers for whom our hints are provocative to seek out the experience for themselves. The Forum occurs essentially as a *dialogue*; ontological inquiry demands interactive play, and needs "the widest sphere in which to swing" ("DL" in *OWL* 27). In written form, Heidegger warned, "the movement of the questioning that is called for here might too easily *congeal*" ("DL" in *OWL* 50).

Nonetheless, as we undertake this project, the authors stand in the open question: *What is the possibility of communicating being*? This is not a questioning that seeks an answer; rather, the inquiry it generates persistently reflects the question itself back upon the questioner, undermining comforting and limiting assumptions. Thus we see it as a transformational question. We invite the reader to join us in this inquiry.

Acknowledgments

It is impossible to list all those who have contributed significantly to the composition of this book; to do so with full integrity would mean naming all who have risked what it means to hear the unsaid in what is said. In particular, our gratitude goes to several extraordinary individuals without whom our work would have failed to move beyond the planning stages, including first, Barbara Stevenson and Sheryl Burke, who, beyond their tireless support, have gathered together a generous reading group. To the group, composed of Allan Cohen, Joe DiMaggio, Bruce Gregory, Michael C. Jensen, Sigurfreyr Jonasson, David C. Logan, Nicholas Merton, Daniel Rogerson, Steve Zaffron, and Michael E. Zimmerman—we want you to know our immeasurable joy when we received feedback that could only come from the deepest appreciation. For granting access to Landmark Worldwide's archives to allow for the production of an accurate and complete transcript, we thank Harry Rosenberg, Mick Leavitt and Landmark Worldwide staff. To the Wiley team, including Shannon Vargo, Sally Baker, Peter Knox, Deborah Schindlar, and Jocelyn Kwiatkowski: thank you for taking a risk on this project—given its untraditional scope, design, and size—and for taking such great care throughout all stages of bringing this book into the world. To Lou Agosta, Jeff Bineham, Richard Doyle, Charles Guignon, Michael J. Hyde, and Carolyne White—together with the members of Lecole book club—thank you for reviewing and responding to the early versions of the manuscript; we hope your thoughtful attention presages serious study of this rich rhetorical phenomenon within such academic fields as rhetoric and writing studies, education, philosophy, and communication studies.

Last, Bruce and I together stand in ovation to the man who has made, and will continue to make, the difference for both of us and countless others—the difference for all those who have had the opportunity, the gift, to be and speak with him—for in the very act of speaking being we create possibility for ourselves and our lives. Werner Erhard: Thank you for providing a way to say what otherwise remains forever unsayable.

SPEAKING BEING

DAY ONE

FORUM DAY ONE:

SESSION ONE

PRELUDE

More than 700 people were assembled in the ballroom of the Hyatt Regency Hotel in San Francisco on the morning of December 27th, 1989. This was the first day of The Forum, and the occasion was unique in several ways. The first was that this Forum was to be led by Werner Erhard himself. Although he had created the technology of language that constituted The Forum, since 1973, to accommodate growing demand for the program across the United States and in Europe, the course had increasingly been led by members of a growing body of *est* Trainers, and later Forum leaders, a group of men and women trained by Erhard. As of 1989 there were forty-three Forum leaders, ten women and thirty-three men.

A second unique aspect of this four-day event was that it was an exceptionally large Forum composed of various groups in addition to the 502 regular participants (the usual number ranged from 100 to 250). Forty Forum leaders were also present as part of their training; during breaks in the procedure, they met with Erhard for debriefing sessions that the senior author attended as part of a special program for Forum graduates called Openings, a group of approximately 100 participants who were permitted to observe without actively participating. Also in the room were a number of invited observers who occupied a visitors' gallery and whose number varied during the course of The Forum. Last, a large contingent of staff and assistants (volunteers) performed logistical duties throughout the four days.

Due to the efforts of the assistants, the ballroom set-up remained consistent across all sessions of each of the four days. Regular participants and Forum leaders were seated in rows, theater-style, before a raised platform which stretched across most of the width of the room, and included a runway section extending well into the center of the audience area. Arranged on the platform were three chalkboards, two bar-height director's chairs, a music stand, and a large table which held a water pitcher and glasses, tissues, and writing materials. Openings participants and other observers were seated on risers at the rear of the room. Also at the rear of the room was an enclosed translators' booth: among the participants in Openings were twenty-five observers from Japan, seminar leaders and staff members in the Tokyo office of Werner Erhard and Associates. They listened to the proceedings in simultaneous translation through earphones connected to the translators' booth. Finally, three television cameras were placed strategically around the room to record the event, and several television monitors were placed so that most participants could watch the proceedings on video if they chose.

THE FORUM BEGINS

At 9:00 am, unannounced, Werner Erhard walked onto the platform. His manner was relaxed and casual. He wore dark tan slacks, a white shirt open at the collar, and an olive sweater vest. He greeted the participants in a friendly way, welcomed guests, and asked for questions while late arrivals were completing their paperwork. He asked if there was anything about the television cameras that needed clearing up, and he explained the presence of the Openings participants and the observers seated in the Gallery. Someone asked about the people wearing earphones, and he explained about the translators and participants from Japan. "That's a good question," he said. "Questions like that . . . what about, what if?"

Participants who raised their hands were asked to stand and wait until they were given a microphone; an assistant was stationed on each aisle to deliver one. After Erhard responded several questions about the various colors of name tags worn by people in the room, one participant raised her hand. Erhard called upon her to stand, and she asked about Erhard's use of language.

ERHARD

You need a language that gives you access to the kind of detail that you need to be a brain surgeon... The language you and I are going to use in here is also a specific language. It's designed to let you get at something you can't get at without that language. Surgeons generally confine that kind of speaking to the operating room, and so do I. I don't use that language when I'm out to dinner. For the most part it's unseemly to use special language when you're with people who don't share in that language.

Erhard asked for more questions. After he called on someone, he explained the reasons for standing up and for calling on multiple people ("to allow time to get microphones to them"). She asked about logistics. Erhard said it would happen later. She sat down.

BLAKE (*after receiving a microphone from an assistant*)

I don't know whether The Forum started yet, but I wanted to get through my apprehension of speaking before the group.

ERHARD

I suggest that those of you who have a fear of speaking take the same opportunity as Blake did. In The Forum no one is required to stand up and speak, though it is in your interest to do so, especially if you are reluctant to stand and speak.

Erhard also discussed the schedule of the course, pointing out that the daily ending time would be sometime between 11:00 pm and 1:00 am, adding that

ERHARD

Nobody guarantees you that schedule. You want to be clear about that. We're going to do this as long as it takes to get it done.

In addition, he said, The Forum would not be complete until the completion of the evening session, which would be held on the following Thursday evening—simultaneously in several cities, since many participants in this Forum had traveled to San Francisco for this event. Participants were encouraged to bring guests to their respective evening sessions.

As the conversation proceeded into the second hour, it gradually became clear, without transition, that the serious business of the course had begun. A participant named Ruth rose to say that she was pessimistic about getting the results of The Forum. Erhard began his response by acknowledging the validity of her doubt.

Talking about Being

One of the similarities between the work of Werner Erhard and Martin Heidegger is that both are *designing a language* for a specific purpose: the evocation of Being. Since the debut of The Forum in 1985, Erhard has regularly incorporated Heideggerian terminology into his vocabulary, and has quoted Heidegger extensively in his courses. It is the primary thesis of this book that Erhard's work is aligned in significant ways with the philosophy of Martin Heidegger. Even the *est* Training, the beginnings of which predate Erhard's encounter with Heidegger (circa 1980), already was aligned in significant ways with Heidegger's thinking. This alignment allowed Erhard to creatively incorporate Heideggerian language in the delivery of what would become The Forum.

Heidegger's language, on first encounter, is notoriously difficult; he regularly invented new German terms for his ideas, and translators have struggled to capture his meanings. Erhard likewise uses words in unconventional ways, and calls his work a "technology of language" in recognition of that fact. It is the experience of the authors that a comparative inquiry into the two bodies of work illuminates the thinking of both men, and helps to clarify the linguistic complexity of Heidegger's writing. In this book, we intend gradually to *unconceal* (a Heideggerian term Erhard has used) that clarity (*IM* 116).

This is not to say that either body of thought ever reaches the kind of logical understandability that we generally expect in what we read and hear. "If you walk out of here understanding," Erhard tells The Forum participants at one point, "that's the booby prize." Both Heidegger and Erhard are attempting to communicate something that, on that familiar level, cannot be communicated or grasped. This is new territory for communication, and requires both a new language (or, as Erhard says, new "languaging") and a new way of listening.

We request, therefore, that the reader join us in embracing the atmosphere of questionability that must surround this entire project. There is a sense in which *we don't know what we are talking about,* and the emphasis in that sentence should be placed on the word "know," as implying a secure conceptual grasp. Talking about Being is challenging and sometimes feels, to use the vernacular, weird. Being is both pervasive and evanescent. It is elusive, vanishing even as it appears.

In his writing about Being (and all of his writing is about Being), Heidegger celebrates the ambiguity surrounding the topic. This is "something which every thinker has to see afresh each time, else he is not a thinker: that everything that lies before us is ambiguous" (*WCT* 201). However, this does not mean fuzziness at the expense of rigor:

 This multiplicity of possible interpretations does not discredit the strictness of the thought content. For all true thought remains open to more than one interpretation—and this by reason of its nature. Nor is this multiplicity of possible interpretations merely the residue of a still unachieved formal-logical univocity which we properly ought to strive for but did not attain. Rather, multiplicity of meanings is the element in which all thought must move in order to be strict thought. (*WCT* 71)

► **NOTE:** Erhard believes that Heidegger's use of the word "thought" leaves people misled about what Heidegger means in the following way: Perhaps the word "thought" is valid for what is written down for people to consider, but it did not come from "thinking"—by which most people will understand "figuring it out"—it came from something like "looking," or "just being with," and is pointed to by the word "wonder" (Erhard, interview with the authors).

ERHARD

Very, very little in life turns out the way it was promised. So I remember my mother told me if I was a good boy everything would be great in life. I tried it for one day and it didn't work. People are told that when they graduate life will be wonderful, life will be easy, and it didn't turn out that way. When you get married it'll be great but it doesn't turn out that way. People say when you get divorced it'll be all right but it doesn't turn out that way. Most things don't live up to their promises.

RUTH

And what about the promises of The Forum?

ERHARD

Based on surveys, most people who've done this work say it turned out better than they expected. For you that'll be easy, because you have a pessimistic view about how things'll turn out. We've got your six hundred dollars. You're not going to get it back. Given that conversation's over, it'll turn out however it turns out. You know, I've never been wrong about that.

(To Ruth)
I could say a lot of things to reassure you, and that would be a mistake. Your pessimism *is* you.

(raising his voice, he turned to the group)
Listen up! If you haven't noticed, The Forum has begun. See, you and I think that our mood, our internal state, the way we are seeing things; we think *that* is a product of the circumstances. So I look at something and I like it, or I look at something and I don't like it. I think if I like it, it's the fault of the thing I'm looking at, and if I don't like it, I think it's the fault of the thing I'm looking at. That's the kind of thing that generates in me: "like"; and that's the kind of thing that generates in me: "don't like." You and I think that our way of being is a product of what's over there. As you will see as we do The Forum together a lot of what is going on with you and me is something we already always are. It's something I am before anything happens. I'm kind of a pessimist waiting for life to happen, or I'm an optimist waiting for life to happen. About certain kinds of things I'm a pessimist before I even look at them, and then when I look at them, it's hard for me to recognize that the pessimism isn't generated out of the thing I'm looking at, but it's something I brought with me. Kind of like I was already always pessimistic and then this thing came along. So it's good that you're pessimistic, and if you're not pessimistic, that's good too.

(to Ruth)
If you find yourself being that way, don't try to change it. What's good is whatever you are, because that's what you want to bring into The Forum. If you deal with that pessimism which you are in a certain way, you'll have a choice about being pessimistic when it is appropriate. Pessimism is not a bad idea, and if you didn't have pessimism I would give it to you, because one of the things you're going to find in here is that we ask you not to believe anything that's said in here. We'll talk more about that later. At any rate, the point that

ERHARD (*continuing*)

I want to make now is that whatever it is that you're feeling, or whatever it is that you're thinking, or whatever your mental state is, or whatever your perception is, the way you are viewing things—that's exactly the way it ought to be. I'm going to probably have to say that to you ten times, because you won't remember that.

(*to the group*)

Another way you already always are is stupid about yourself. If that sounded a little bit like an insult, you got it right. You may not be able to see that about yourself, but you'll be able to see it about others. As I said: not you, but other people.

(*laughter*)

There are ways of being with yourself that are disempowering and disenabling. You lose power and you lose ability. Whatever way you find yourself now, and whatever ways you find yourself variously throughout The Forum or in the evenings, or on the breaks: that's the way you're supposed to be—whatever way that is. One way to disempower or disenable yourself is to question whether you are being the right way... You'll get a lot more out of The Forum a lot faster if you let yourself be the way you are.

(*pausing*)

There's a lot of this you're not going to get. Some of it won't make any sense. You're not going to get the whole Forum. The questions we're asking in here are too powerful to get it all. The Forum leaders are still getting it. So am I. But there are parts when you need to get it. In those parts, put up your hand if you don't. There will be a lot of repetition in here, too. For the fourth time: you should be the way you are! However you feel, that's the way it ought to be. The way I know that is, that's the way it *is*... The only right way to do The Forum is to be the way you're being. If you say you shouldn't be pessimistic, you're getting in your way.

A participant complained that she was distracted by and resentful about the physical set-up for this Forum—the cameras, the observers, etc.

ERHARD

What you want to get out of that is that life is upsetting because it isn't the way you expected it to be. The Forum will be that way also. What you want to get out of that is that you're already upset. You're already always upset at any change, at anything that violates your expectations. You think you're not upset until something violates your expectations. I said this strange thing: you are already always upset. You *live* upset. I know you don't believe that and I'm not asking you to. You're an upset waiting to happen. You'll see that more clearly as we proceed.

LYNETTE

I'm often upset.

ERHARD

You're always upset, and sometimes you notice it.

Nevertheless, despite its challenges, we assert that Being is also the most important thing that one could talk about, since talk that evokes Being has the ability to transform talk about everything else.

A fundamental difference in this arena is the distinction between *ontological* and *ontic* inquiry. Ontological inquiry is concerned primarily with Being. Therefore all of Heidegger's writing, and all of the dialogue of The Forum, is ontological in nature. Ontic inquiry is concerned with beings, and with facts about them. Therefore all of our everyday conversations—everything from political discourse to casual social chat—may be seen as ontic.

This is not to dismiss ontic inquiry as unimportant, or to equate a discussion of religion or physics with coffeeshop banter. We are not claiming that ontological inquiry is better, but that it is essentially different. And in the experience of the authors, it is profoundly interesting because of its transformational possibilities. In this book, we will illuminate the nature of ontological inquiry.

A prefatory note: people who write about Heidegger's work differ as to whether the term *Being* should be capitalized. This is, of course, a choice for translators and not one that confronted Heidegger, since in German all nouns are capitalized. It is a problematic choice because capitalization tends to reify or even deify, suggesting to some scholars that Being is "an eternal metaphysical foundation or eternal principle," while for Heidegger it was "the *event* in which an entity reveals or shows itself" (Michael E. Zimmerman, *Heidegger's Confrontation with Modernity: Technology, Politics, Art* xxii). Others feel that capitalization is important so that what it *means* to exist (Being) is not confused with the entities that exist (beings) (Richard Polt *Heidegger: An Introduction* 3).

In print, Erhard himself did not capitalize the term: a 1985 Forum brochure states that the purpose of The Forum is to provide participants with "direct access to the domain of being itself." In his more recent work, such as documents outlining his development of an ontological/phenomenological model of leadership (https://papers.ssrn.com/sol3/ cf_dev/ AbsByAuth. cfm?per_id=433651), he continues to employ the lowercase.

In this book, we will employ capitalization in those instances where it clarifies the word's meaning in a specific sentence. We raise the point here to emphasize the unique nature of the issues that arise in any discussion, oral or written, of this subject. Being/being, as an ontological phenomenon, defies grammatical categorization. ◼

▶ **NOTE:** As of 2019, Landmark Worldwide's Forum leader faculty included more than 60 people, representing a diversity in gender and race, and hailing from countries including the United States of America, India, Japan, Australia, New Zealand, the United Kingdom, Canada, Israel, the Netherlands and Switzerland.

LYNETTE

Do you have any more advice about how to get the most out of this?

ERHARD

I do and we'll go over that this morning.

TRENT

I hear there are Forum leaders here.

ERHARD

Forum leaders are here as part of their job.

TRENT

Four consecutive days instead of two weekends?

ERHARD

We've done this using odd schedules in different settings, for instance, in prisons.

BLAKE (*who expressed reservations about speaking*)

Continuing what you were saying as far as upset is concerned, and always being with you. My barrier is the fear of revealing who I am. I should accept that.

ERHARD

Whatever you think is in the way, especially those things you think are part of the circumstances—for instance, you don't get along with your boss and it's quite clear to you that's because you work for a jerk—bring that in here. Blake is clear that it's something he carries around with him; it doesn't come out of the circumstances. That's easy. It's the stuff you think is a product of the circumstances. So if there are circumstances in here, for instance, because there are people observing—that sounds like it is a product of the circumstances.

CHRISSY

You talked about being in The Forum whatever way you are being. What about outside The Forum?

ERHARD

Let yourself be like you are in those parts of The Forum that are outside The Forum, for homework assignments during the breaks, etc. If that's your mood at the moment, don't try to change it. You want it there because if it isn't there it's not going to get dealt with—particularly those things you think are part of the circumstances: bring that in here. Most of what you do outside The Forum in the next four days is going to be inside The Forum. If you do something to avoid that, then you've successfully avoided that once more. See, there's a lot of this you're

ERHARD (*continuing*)

not going to like. You're sitting there now with a whole bunch of assessments and conclusions. We've done this a lot. I can even tell you what your assessments and conclusions are.

A participant asked whether, based on all of this, he should keep his specific issues and concerns foremost in his mind.

ERHARD

You don't need to have something you're kind of holding in place. We will hook what's there in you that's appropriate to be hooked and pull it up to the surface. So you can kind of relax about that. A lot of stuff you won't even think about will get handled in here.

Another participant asked about the history of the organization.

ERHARD

We've been doing this work since 1971 and it was at the end of 1984 that we finished a four-year process of developing The Forum, and we've been offering The Forum since 1985 all over this country, and in lots of other countries around the world.

At this point, a man named Jake rose to complain about the purpose of the evening session, to which participants had been encouraged to invite guests.

JAKE

Isn't that more for Werner Erhard and Associates to hustle more members?

ERHARD

You know that you are a hustle waiting to happen, right?

JAKE

I said I feel like I'm being hustled.

ERHARD

I said you are a guy who is being hustled waiting to happen.

JAKE

I don't mind being hustled.

ERHARD

I said you are a guy who is being hustled waiting to happen.

JAKE

I don't see it that way.

Erhard came down from the stage and sat on the edge of the platform near him.

Dasein

At the outset, it is important to introduce a term that is central in Martin Heidegger's work, and will therefore begin to come up here almost immediately.

Dasein is Heidegger's word for *the Being of human beings*, and is one of the few terms in English editions of his writing that consistently remain untranslated from the German. In fact, the 2014 *Dictionary of Untranslatables*, published by Princeton University Press, calls the word "a paradigm of the untranslatable," and devotes six double-columned pages to a struggle to explain it (Adam Gopnik, "Word Magic," *New Yorker*,. May 26, 2014, 37).

A problem with translating this term, of course, is that term is central in Heidegger's most important work, *Being and Time*, in which he presents his ontological model of human beings. The specific elements of this model will be discussed in further detail as we proceed. For now, it is sufficient to note that Dasein will be spoken of as if the term indicates an individual; but since it indicates the Being of that individual, it refers at the same time more broadly to the collective Being of human beings.

ERHARD

You're oriented around being hustled. You would see hustle where other people wouldn't be smart enough to see it.

JAKE

I could go along with that.

ERHARD

You are a guy who is being hustled waiting to happen. Remember I said people are upset waiting to happen? You're hustle waiting to happen.

JAKE

I'm still not getting it.

ERHARD

Okay good, then we'll keep doing it until you do get it.

JAKE

In front of all these people?

ERHARD

Sure. You see hustle where others don't. You are already always being hustled. You are waiting for it to happen. You wake up that way in the morning, you just don't have the circumstances to express it yet.

JAKE

I think I see that... I am. I'm on the watch-out. I watch my bucks.

ERHARD

I've already got your bucks, don't I? Before this is over I'm going to get some more of your bucks.

JAKE

That's a challenge.

ERHARD

With you, I'd almost bet on it.

He remained seated on the edge of the platform as this interaction modulated from confrontational to friendly.

ERHARD (*continuing*)

That by the way was meant as a compliment. I'm going to offer you an opportunity to do this for the rest of your life, because I'm clear that you're going to get a lot of value out of this and I'm going to offer you the opportunity to get more value. You will always have the power to decline. I want you to know that's there in the relationship between me and you. I have no reluctance to hustling you, because you always have the power to decline. Is that clear?

JAKE

Yeah, I got it.

The first morning of The Forum continued as a dialogue with the group as Erhard responded to participants' questions. One woman expressed a concern that the content would go "over her head."

ERHARD

Most of what I say is not designed for your head. Understanding is not the problem in life. If you took a four-day course in how to be a tennis player and you left the course as a great tennis player without understanding a word of it, the difference would be your being a great tennis player. We don't promise you any understanding. You're welcome to understand. I like this stuff, so I enjoy understanding it. That's a quirk in me. We do this so that there's a freedom to be. If you walk out understanding, that's the booby prize. You walk out of here with the freedom to be that you didn't have when you walked in here, then you got something for your money. Speaking in here is designed to create the freedom to be... You don't understand what that means. What interests me is the freedom to be. You'll be interested in that too before this is over. I've done The Forum before so I know it works out.

A woman stated that she was already always nervous.

ERHARD (*to the group*)

How many people in here are already always nervous?

(*most raising their hands*)

You understand that the things that are going on with you are going on with everybody? You're like a rainstorm. You've got to get that there's nothing personal about a rainstorm—that is, that it waters the little flowers. You think that the rainstorm is worried about life on earth. You think that it rains *so that*... it rains *in-order-to*. It's true that life is sustained by the rain, but it's not true that it rains in-order-to.

SAL (*standing up, receiving a microphone*)

You're just arguing semantics.

ERHARD

No, it's not semantics. Or the other answer to that is, yes it's semantics, but so is everything else in the universe.

Two Theses

The first thesis of this book, which will be addressed directly in the text, is that the work of Werner Erhard is aligned in important ways with the thinking of Martin Heidegger. Our purpose is to show this alignment through a comparative analysis of their work, an analysis that not only illuminates the thinking of both men, but sheds light as well on the nature of their shared central concern.

The second thesis, equal in importance to the first, cannot be addressed directly in the text. We have indicated it with the term *Being,* since unless we indicate it we cannot talk about it—as Heidegger puts it, "one cannot get by in public without rubrics" (*OWL* 29). But the term serves merely as a place-holder, since what it indicates cannot be thought, or even thought about, in our usual way of conceptualizing. Think "freedom" and a conceptual barrage is evoked; think "Being" and the mind's resources are few.

Our second thesis, since it eludes capture in concepts, can only be *hinted* at. It exists always as a background, in a domain of language that remains always unspoken. Unspoken, it is the unexamined context that shapes the way we understand everything else; unspoken, it is made present as the transformational background in the dialogue of The Forum; unspoken, it is hinted at persistently in Heidegger's writing and in his lectures. Our second thesis, then, *is* this unspoken domain of language, formally referred to as the *ontological* realm.

In this book, to show what Werner Erhard and Martin Heidegger are doing in their work, the authors are called upon to say—to hint at—the unspoken shared dynamic at the center of that work. Inevitably, an element of mystery attends this topic; but nothing here is devious or arcane. While ontological communication makes rigorous demands on our everyday understanding, Erhard's work is a practical pedagogical methodology, demonstrating that education beyond the merely epistemological is a real-world possibility.

The authors intend that our second thesis will be communicated in the background as we proceed through this book, leaving the reader with a hint of its nature as it emerges in The Forum.

One aspect of this background communication is that unfamiliar terms or concepts may not be fully defined at the point of their first appearance. Rather, they will be *distinguished* gradually as they appear and reappear in the text. A definition specifies conceptual limits; a distinction opens a space for thinking and acting, and the space is expanded each time the distinction is encountered. The goal of the inquiry, then, is never an answer, but the opening of a question from which to experience the world. We invite the reader to embrace the freedom that this background of questionability gives: at play in the question, you don't need the right answer. ∎

SAL

I believe that when it rains it rains in order to sustain life.

ERHARD

Okay, let's stay there. Anybody else in that ballpark with Sal? Stand up if you are. Stand up if it rains in-order-to.

(a number of people rose)
If you're not standing and you are an in-order-to, you're interfering with your participation in The Forum. These people who are standing are not silly. They've got their foot nailed to the floor someplace. This will happen to all of you a lot of times during The Forum.

(to Sal, indicating the director's chair on the platform)
Are the legs there to hold up the chair? We know that the legs do hold up the chair. For the legs, is there any in-order-to? Are the legs in-ordering-to?

(pausing)
It's too hard that way... let me try something different. Is the wall standing in order to hold the ceiling up?

SAL

Yes, in my opinion.

ERHARD

Does the lightning lightning in order to start forest fires?

SAL

No.

ERHARD

Where is this organ of intentionality in the rainstorm?

SAL

The spirituality of the universe.

ERHARD *(to the group)*

He just told me where his foot's nailed to the floor. He's got something he believes so he can't think about it.

(to Sal)
You think there's an intentionality in the rainstorm. You said it's your belief that matter was invaded by spirit in some way. Does it rain in order to produce floods?

SAL

No.

ERHARD

So the intentionality organ is not operating when it produces floods?

SAL

No, that just happens.

ERHARD

But it doesn't just happen that when it rains life is sustained? Remember, Sal, there's no question between you and me that water does sustain life. The question is: does it rain in-order-to? Or does it just happen, and by the way, it sustains life?

At this point Sal seemed to see Erhard's point, and sat down.

ERHARD (*to Sal*)

Okay. Now, just something personal between you and me. I've done this a lot. There's something I appreciated about you in this conversation. You were *open* in the conversation.

(*to the group*)

Nobody's ever going to win with me in here. Because this is my game, and only an asshole would try to win in another guy's game. You and I had a discussion where we *got* something together. Rain is impersonal. We weren't talking about a higher order of things. I don't want anybody to believe anything I say. And I'm not interested in sustaining anything you believe.

BLAKE (*recalling what had happened up to this moment in the conversation*)

I know that there was some sequence and I missed it. I mentioned that I was nervous, that I didn't like it, and then we were talking about the rain.

ERHARD (*to the group*)

He just demonstrated not knowing, being clear he didn't know. That's different from being confused. This is one of those things to get. There's a difference between knowing that you don't understand, knowing that you didn't follow something; knowing something didn't make sense and being confused are very different. You didn't invent being nervous. Even though the rain is impersonal, you do personally get wet. The same thing goes for being nervous. Being nervous is part of being human. Being human doesn't belong to you; you belong to it. You didn't invent being human. You were late for the party. Being human is an already always way of being that you walked into. It's like a rainstorm, and it's true you personally got wet. You are a human

Ontological Dialogue

A striking aspect of Erhard's method, one which appears again and again throughout The Forum, is his persistence in pressing any interaction or any topic of discussion through to completion. *Complete*, for Erhard, does not mean simply finished, but rather whole, and lacking none of its essential parts. Repeatedly, after he has been engaged on a particular point with an individual, he requests that others in the room who are not clear on that point stand, and works with each participant individually until all of them have "gotten" it for themselves. Erhard often uses the term "flatten" in the same sense, as in "Let's get that one flat before we move on." To get something flat, in an ontological dialogue, means that the item in question has been moved beyond a purely conceptual level of understanding, and has been distinguished as an ontological possibility, at least in a preliminary sense. The distinction will continue to be teased out as The Forum proceeds, ultimately becoming a clearing for Being; but the first step in that process is to flatten the concept, so that its ontological possibility can be heard.

Of course, "getting it" and "being complete" might be read as "having surrendered to Erhard's point of view." Erhard himself seemed to support this interpretation, telling one Forum participant Blake, "Nobody's ever going to win with me in here. Because this is my game, and only an asshole would try to win in another guy's game." During a debriefing session with The Forum leaders regarding their role in the dialogue, Erhard again referred to the process in agonistic terms: "You've got to have some appreciation for the advantage you've got there," he said. "And yeah, you're going to use the advantage, that's part of the game."

The game in The Forum is the evocation of the presence of Being, and The Forum leader's opponent is the way of being that we in the technological age have been born into (the way we wound up being). Clearly, there is a certain direction which must be maintained in The Forum dialogue if its purpose is to be achieved. The maintenance of this direction in the face of participants' resistance might appear, to the everyday understanding, as motivated by a need on The Forum leader's part to win the game, so that The Forum's perspective is shown to be the true one. However, accepted in The Forum is that The Forum leader's responsibility is maintaining the ontological character of the conversation. "My job," said Erhard, "is to manage the dialogue." This management is not a matter of winning, but of keeping the way in view. In a recent conversation with the authors, Erhard put it this way: "I used this way of speaking to deal with people who are resisting in order to resist, rather than functioning in a dialogue."

Any discussion of dialogue as pedagogy must always consider the question of mutuality, and this is especially delicate when the dialogue's purpose is the presencing of Being. The Forum leaders' rank in The Forum dialogue is given by their ability to listen to the conversation from a certain perspective. As Erhard told The Forum leaders, "You've got to know that an authentic dialogue is going to generate clarity. You've *also* got to watch you don't get hooked. What hooks [you] is when someone says something that you think puts you at a disadvantage." Being hooked, for a Forum leader, means being drawn into argument or commiseration with participants' stories about their lives, rather than maintaining the transformed perspective given by The Forum's ontological distinctions. It is The Forum leader's job not to get hooked.

This balance between mutuality and directedness in an ontological dialogue is an important matter. Obviously, there is a thrust to such a dialogue—a movement of the conversation in the direction of its ontological intention. In his dialogue with the Japanese scholar in *On the Way to Language,* Heidegger points to the nature of true dialogue when he states that "we may

being, but you didn't make up human being. You didn't invent being nervous. You didn't invent having a barrier to expressing yourself. That doesn't belong to you. That's not yours. That's in the already always being of human being. It doesn't belong to you; you belong to it.

(forcefully)
It owns you! You don't own it. Being nervous owns your life. You don't own being nervous. The metaphor is that there's nothing personal about a rainstorm. It just rains, and I, you, personally get wet. But the rainstorm didn't rain in order to get me wet. Being nervous is already always there in the being of being human. And you and I walk out into that rainstorm and get wet... In The Forum, you get back the power to say something about your own way of being. Now you can only report on it. But you can't say "I'm not nervous" and have it make any difference. After The Forum you will be able to.

BLAKE

I'm not as nervous as when I first stood up. I am here to make a change, find a new occupation, to get up in front of people. What it requires is getting up.

ERHARD

Not necessarily.

BLAKE

Well, I don't know.

ERHARD

That's right. And I do know.

BLAKE

That's why I'm asking you.

ERHARD

I want to get it settled because you're going to keep saying those stupid kinds of things: what you have to do and what you don't have to do for this to work. And the answer is you don't know. So I'm gonna tell you: what you have to do is what you do. So you'll always know what you have to do because you're doing what you're doing. To do something you're not doing: that's bad. If you do what you do it'll all work out. One of the things that you are doing is thinking you have to stand up. That's fine for you to think that. You wanna know why I think it's fine for him to think that? Because that's what he's thinking.

BLAKE

You're right. At some point you broke through whatever was in the way and now you're up there doing what you are doing.

BLAKE (*pausing*)

It's really hard for me not to be funny.

ERHARD

Yeah. You're already always funny.

BLAKE

And I don't want to be silly or you're going to get mad at me. It's just a temptation to always be funny.

ERHARD

It's the way you avoid dealing with what you don't want to deal with, which is being anything but funny. That's what you don't want to deal with. You learned how to deal with being funny. You got that down very well and the rest of it you're a little nervous about. But you're not nervous about being funny, are you?

BLAKE

No.

ERHARD

And you're not nervous about whatever your racket is either. You're just nervous about the rest of it. I know you don't understand half of what we're talking about, but that's all right. Just the first couple hours.

BLAKE

I don't want to be nervous anymore.

ERHARD

Somebody write that down for me.

BLAKE

I'm not a dictator and so I have to live with the things I'm not comfortable with, and when I'm uncomfortable, other people are uncomfortable. I don't like that.

ERHARD

Thanks... The next subject. Everybody ready for the next subject?

A participant named Charles, who was still concerned with the conversation about the rain, rose.

CHARLES

I'm with "it rains so that life is sustained."

confidently entrust ourselves to the hidden drift of our dialogue. . . *as long as we remain inquirers*" ("DL" in *OWL* 30, emphasis added). In true dialogue—which always has an unspoken ontological intent—the dialogue itself can be trusted to move us along if we, as participants, continue to be a certain way. Notice the reflexive nature of the process: simultaneous surrender and evocation. In The Forum, the maintenance of this delicate balance is The Forum leader's task.

A central element of The Forum's effectiveness is the inclusiveness of its conversation: interactions between The Forum leader and those participants who actively engage in the dialogue are conducted in front of the entire group, so that even those participants who are listening and observing are able to derive the benefits of those interactions.

For both Heidegger and Erhard, a shared tendency of human being underlies all of our diverse individual and cultural concerns. The assumption of The Forum's methodology is that a skillfully managed dialogue between two people can affect the ontological insight of others who are listening to that dialogue, and who share the tendency of being that generates it.

A participant whose concern is her relationship with her employer can recognize, in another participant's discussion of his problems with his mother, the same existential structure that is at the source of her own problem. Thus The Forum leader regularly exhorts participants to "listen from your own concerns." ∎

ERHARD

What we were discussing is this in-order-to. I say the rain has no intention to do anything. There's nothing there that could intend. It just rains when it rains. There's no intention in the rain. Look, Charles, I'm doing something in the conversation which is designed to allow you to take a look at your own beliefs. I'm asking questions which reduce your thesis to an absurdity. If I ask if it rains in order to destroy life, you have to say yes if you believe that it rains in order to sustain life, and so it makes you reexamine your theory. If you can consider the possibility that there is no intention in the rainstorm, then you are no longer stuck with what you used to believe.

CHARLES

I'll keep looking at it.

ERHARD

We have to go quickly now or there won't be any fifth night. There'll be a twelfth night.

Someone raised a question about why participants were not allowed to take notes in The Forum, a policy that had been communicated when they registered for the course.

ERHARD

Because we don't want you to retain information. So you don't get stuck trying to remember something. You think Bjorn Borg remembers how to hold the tennis racket? This is no different than the conversation about the rainstorm.

(loudly)

You have this superstition that you do things because you remember how to do them! You don't drive your car, play tennis, or live life powerfully and effectively out of anything you remember. If Joe Montana had to remember how to throw the football when he's back in the pocket, he'd get killed every Sunday.

A woman named Doris rose with a question about the rainstorm:

DORIS

What about the role of ultimate being in natural events?

ERHARD

I don't like to discuss ultimate being with people who don't know their ass from a hole in the ground.

DORIS

I find that response pretty offensive.

DORIS (*stammering slightly*)
Are you inferring that I don't . . .?

ERHARD

No.

(*pausing*)
We don't know yet.

DORIS

I assure you I do.

ERHARD

Really? We'll see. You either do or you don't, so there's nothing to be nervous about. Then we could discuss ultimate being.

(*pausing*)
I want you to get that *I am not a guy in a diner.*

He moved toward the back row where Doris was standing:

ERHARD (*continuing*)
When I was growing up on the east coast, my family took trips to visit people. And we would drive home, oftentimes very late at night, oftentimes when it was raining or snowing or nasty. And diners, as far as I knew, were places where you stopped to get a cup of coffee so you could stay awake while you were driving. And at my age I couldn't let anybody do anything without my being there, so I always had to go in with them. And I learned about guys in diners. Guys in diners, late at night like I'm describing to you, are usually fairly lonely, because they don't have anybody to talk to. And they just *love* for somebody to stop in because then they've got somebody to talk to. And you know, you go in, and you're the only person there, and you sit up at the counter, and you have your cup of coffee and whatever else. And you find out that this guy in the diner—the guy behind the counter—knows everything about everything. There is nothing about which he does not know. He knows what the president ought to do about the deficit, he knows what the country ought to do about international relationships, he knows what you ought to do about your marriage, he knows what kind of work you ought to do and how whatever kind of work you are doing how you could do it better, he knows something about everything. Most people are like a guy in a diner. Goddamned near everybody knows everything about everything. So in here—at least in The Forum—I question everything. *Everything*—including whether or not you know your ass from a hole in the ground. And whether anyone is qualified to discuss ultimate being. I didn't say you weren't. That's the way I do The Forum.

(*to Doris*)
Okay?

Being-in-the-world: Being-in

An important term that Werner Erhard often employs in his work, and one which is central in the thinking of Martin Heidegger is Being-in-the-world. To indicate clearly that a human being in his model of things is not a self-contained Cartesian subject, separate from an objective world "out there," Heidegger never presents Dasein's Being as disconnected, either from others or from the world. Dasein's Being is *Being-in-the-world*. This indicates "a *unitary* phenomenon" which "must be seen as a whole" (*BT* 78).

However, while "Being-in-the-world cannot be broken up into contents which may be pieced together," the constituent parts may be "brought out for emphasis." One of these parts is *Being-in*.

Being-in articulates an essentially different relationship from the one we usually have in mind when we say something is "in" something. If we say "the water is in the glass," for example, the two phenomena being related have a prior and individual existence in space: the water was there, and the glass was there. We have simply put one in the other. Further, as Heidegger points out, we can easily extend such relationships outward: the glass is on the table, the table is in the kitchen, the kitchen is in the house, and so on, until finally we can say that the water is in "world space" (*BT* 79).

Objects such as the glass and the table are, in Heidegger's vocabulary, "things occurring 'within' the world" (*BT* 79). Therefore they have a different kind of being from Dasein. The table and the glass are *whats*; their characteristics are *categorical*. While the table and the glass can have a *location-relationship* within the world, the water is not in the glass in the same way that a human being is in-the-world.

Dasein, on the other hand, is a *who*, and its characteristics are *existential*, which define an existence structure quite different from that of a table. This is, of course, on one level obvious. But Heidegger, remember, is languaging a view of the world that is very different from our everyday way of understanding things. Therefore he is rigorous in setting out the terminological differences between states of being.

A chair can be next to the wall, but the chair can never *touch* the wall, "even if the space between them should be equal to zero" (*BT* 81). Heidegger is not making a sensory distinction but an ontological one. *To touch* is *to encounter meaningfully,* and such meaningful encounters are possible only for entities with meaning. In Heidegger's vocabulary, a table and a chair are *worldless*.

Werner Erhard can be seen as distinguishing worldlessness early in The Forum, in his interactions with participants on the subject of whether the rain falls in order to water the flowers. In doing so, he is beginning to create an understanding of *meaning as a human characteristic*, rather than an aspect of the things out there in the world. This distinction will be further developed later

DORIS

Okay.

She sat. A man rose to object to Erhard's earlier assertion that our ways of being, such as nervousness, own us.

FOSTER

I understand that being nervous is a human quality. Why don't I own being nervous? Isn't that a quality of *me*?

ERHARD

Where is this quality?

FOSTER (*pointing to his heart*)

Here, and it's pounding!

ERHARD

My dog's heart pounds. You and I explain things about people by assigning qualities to them. But this may not be effective if what you want to do is have access to the things you're explaining. The language we use every day is designed to explain things. The language we use in here is designed to *gain access* to things. So it's a different language. Explanations give no access to power. If you want power and access, we're going to invent such a language in here. I'm not limited to merely reporting the way I am. I'm an anti-quality-ist. You ain't got any qualities inside you. Qualities are an explanatory principle. It won't hold up on closer examination.

Erhard was now in the aisle, moving among the participants. One rose to defend the importance of having what he called self-beliefs.

RAY

How does one hold beliefs about oneself and about reality in a way to be powerful and creative?

ERHARD

One of the ways is to not have any beliefs. Does anyone need to believe that the floor is there? You don't need to have any belief about the floor and it works just fine. And if you didn't have any beliefs about gravity it would work just fine. You only need to believe in things that you doubt. The only problem with belief is that you can't *think* about anything you believe.

RAY

I have an interpretation about myself, and how do I hold that interpretation?

ERHARD

As an interpretation.

RAY

Thank you.

Shortly before the first break of the morning, Erhard introduced a new topic:

ERHARD

The next subject is the matter of your being here. At the upcoming break, you will be given an opportunity to leave and have your money refunded. You want to listen up! I'm going to give you the opportunity not to be here. You shouldn't be here if you didn't put yourself here. The Forum won't work for you anyhow, so you're wasting your time here. You shouldn't be here if you're here because you were threatened. We don't allow people to participate in The Forum who were coerced or threatened. You may have been here on that basis up till now. You can leave now and you'll get all your money back. And if you'll get in trouble with whoever you're here for, I'll write a note that says that you begged and pleaded and tried to stay here and I threw you out. If you're here because you were pressured into being here, would you stand up please?

(one participant stood)
Anybody else?

(another long pause as another stood)
I'm going to say "Anybody else?" five more times.

Eventually several people stood in response to his request, and he began to interact with them individually. The interactions varied strikingly in their tone. With the first participant, a teenager named Kathy, Erhard's manner was quite gentle. He moved closer to her, standing at a distance of about four feet. Before beginning the conversation, he asked her if she was willing to interact with him in front of the group, acknowledging that it might be "scary" for her to do so. He then reiterated his assertion that pressure, like embarrassment and hustle, was a clearing she was bringing to the circumstances:

ERHARD *(continuing)*

I know that if you're here because somebody pressured you to be here, that that's an issue in your life. The only people who experience being pressured about The Forum are those for whom pressure is an issue. I'm giving you the opportunity to make a choice. Now that I've given you the choice, would you like to leave or would you like to be here? There will be no bad results from you leaving. You'll get your money back.

KATHY

That's good. I feel like I have the opportunity to choose now, whereas, before, I didn't feel like that.

on the first day when participants' *stories* about the events in their lives are distinguished from the events themselves.

Human beings exist in a world of meaning, and their relationship with that world is fundamental. *In-ness* is an aspect of Dasein's existence from the ground up. Consider: a human being never exists as a (meaningful) human being until she exists in-the-world, and when she leaves the world (dies), she ceases to exist (as a human being). Heidegger's German term for the Being-in relationship (*Sein bei*) carries the implication of what we would call *being at home* (BT 80, note 3). Dasein is at home in the world, *Being-with* others. "Being-with" is examined in the first sidebar of Session One of Day Two, and we address the "world" of Being-in-the-world at the beginning of Session One of Day Four. ∎

ERHARD

I only do this work with people for whom it's going to be successful, so I'm not willing to do this work except on the basis that people chose to be here. What's your choice?

KATHY

I choose to be in The Forum.

ERHARD

No coercion? That's your choice? Made freely?

KATHY

Yes.

ERHARD

Thank you for going through the process in front of all these people.

Along with Kathy, two other people sat down. The only participant who remained standing was a young man in the front row named Bill, who spoke as soon as an assistant got a microphone to him:

BILL (angrily)

I think there's kind of a thin line between choice and being compelled to do something because someone cared enough to continuously call me up and get me here.

ERHARD (moving in to a face-to-face stance with Bill)

You're an asshole, and somebody...

BILL

Your language is bad.

ERHARD

It's much worse than you think it is. You don't want to fuck with me.

BILL

You don't scare me.

ERHARD

You're in my game, my friend, you don't want to fuck with me.

BILL

Someone should use language to try to clear a point.

ERHARD

I understand what you believe. I'm not interested.

BILL

That's quite obvious.

ERHARD

Now do you have something to say that's thoughtful? Because I'm not interested in your beliefs.

BILL

You're competing with me in your lack of thoughtfulness in the terminology that you use on a regular basis, my friend.

ERHARD

Really?

BILL

Yes. Thoughtfulness is as thoughtfulness does. To be thoughtful I would expect a mutual kind of communication.

ERHARD

You got a mutual kind of communication. You got bullshit for bullshit.

BILL

Thank you very much. You are quite impressive.

ERHARD

Thank you. Are you here because you were pressured into being here?

BILL

I drove here.

ERHARD

I understand. Were you pressured into being here? I know you're not here because you were pressured into being here. I can take one look at you and know that wasn't true. I know you're up there to fuck with me.

BILL

Now...

ERHARD

Hold on, let me talk for a while. So you're going to tell me the story about people called you a lot of times and people kept inviting you and kept saying you were supposed to. Understand? That's the story you're going to tell me and I already know the story. You won't be the first person with that story. This is a story I've heard a lot of times. Now why was I bad with you

MOOD

Heidegger's masterwork, *Being and Time*, presents a model of human being that focuses on our lived, everyday experience. This "average everydayness," he says, has been generally disregarded in attempts to understand our nature. It is so apparent and well-known to us that we fail to recognize the ontological significance of its elements. One of these elements is *mood*.

Mood, or *state-of-mind* (*Befindlichkeit*) is a manifestation of the moment-to-moment way one is automatically *attuned to the world.* My mood provides a context—a background environment—in which I move; it pervades and colors my relationship to whatever I am up to at any moment, for instance, when Erhard says "your pessimism is you." In bad moods, "Dasein becomes blind to itself" (*BT* 175). And while we may not notice it, says Heidegger, a human being always has some mood, even when its specific nature is elusive:

 The pallid, evenly balanced lack of mood, which is often persistent and which is not to be mistaken for a bad mood, is far from nothing at all. Rather, it is in this that Dasein becomes satiated with itself. Being has become manifest as a burden. Why that should be, one does not *know*. (*BT* 173)

Furthermore, "when we master a mood, we do so by way of a counter-mood; we are never free of moods" (*BT* 175). Mood is the persistent background of our lives. Our moods *come over us*, and our cognition cannot reach their source: "The pure 'that it is' shows itself, but the 'whence' and the 'whither' remain in darkness" (*BT* 173).

This last point will be seen as significant as The Forum approaches its climax: we are always brought before ourselves in our moods, but we tend to turn away from what they might reveal. In moods, we find ourselves, but "in a way of finding which arises not so much from a direct seeking as rather from a fleeing" (*BT* 174). In our assured, everyday way of speaking, we dismiss a state-of-mind, or rather, an attunement, as "just a mood I'm in." But in doing so, we evade a more primordial disclosure, an understanding which stares us in the face "with the inexorability of an enigma" (*BT* 175).

At this early point in the proceedings, Erhard is making two important moves. First, he is suggesting to the participants that the nature of their moods is not what they have taken them to be. They are not a product of the circumstances, but are instead an aspect of their own way of being. Second, he is urging the participants not to attempt to avoid or transcend their moods, however uncomfortable they may seem, but rather to allow them, and to bring them into The Forum so that they can be part of the process. As The Forum proceeds, these suggestions will be seen as crucial to the development of the ontological dialogue. ■

just now? Because I want to get this story up. There's a lot of people with that story here and I want to get that story killed. I got people's attention here. I got your attention too, but more important: I got their attention.

(to the group)
I know you've got a story about how you got here. That's your story. I don't know what the truth is. I know Bill was a pain in the ass.

BILL
Thank you.

ERHARD
You were, and you probably are most of the time. Do other people in here know you?

BILL
I'm not sure.

ERHARD
If I had a group of your friends here and asked them, "can Bill be a real pain in the ass?" what would they say?

BILL
Well I imagine if they pushed me to extremes...

(laughter)

ERHARD *(shaking his head)*

Wait, wait. That's not what I mean. I mean, if I said to your friends, "can Bill be a real pain in the ass?" what would they say? I would bet they would say "yes." More than infrequently.

BILL
What about your friends?

ERHARD
Let me explain something to you.

BILL
You put me on the spot, why can't I put you on the spot?

ERHARD
I didn't pay to be in here, you did. Because you invested $625 to come to my seminar. But if I leave here and I'm still an asshole, I didn't lose anything. If you've got a seminar that keeps you

ERHARD (*continuing*)

from being an asshole, send me a flyer, and I will decide if that's the seminar that'll handle my being an asshole.

BILL

You know I have to say something. The only value I've gotten so far is entertainment from your cynicism.

ERHARD

You remember when I said you would be sitting there with your judgments and assessments?

BILL

Believe me, I'm here with an open mind.

This interaction, which was in its early moments the most belligerent of the entire four days, gradually became playful. Bill began to smile, and the dialogue assumed the character of good-natured sparring.

ERHARD

Back to the issue of pressure. Did you get a lot of phone calls?

BILL

From one lady in particular. During the process I was trying to prospect her into something and in the end she prospected me into something.

(*laughter*)

ERHARD

I'm not going to ask what you were prospecting her into. But at any rate there was a lady who called you a number of times.

BILL

She's married, Werner.

ERHARD

It's hard to have this conversation with you with your foot nailed to the floor. How many times did she call?

BILL

I don't know. A half dozen to a dozen times. Perhaps more.

ERHARD

And what did you say to her when she called to talk about The Forum?

BILL

I appreciated her concern about my welfare.

ERHARD

Did you really, or were you bullshitting her?

BILL

No.

ERHARD

So you never told her "no," right?

BILL

Never directly "no."

ERHARD *(turning to the group)*

I'm revealing the nature of pressure. That's what Bill and I are having this conversation about. Nobody does The Forum because they were pressured into it.

(Erhard placed his hands on Bill's head and pushed down)
That's what pressure is. But what had the people from the Center done? They called you. They spoke to you. What else did they do? They stayed engaged in the conversation with you because you never said no.

BILL

They called me every day.

ERHARD

Every day?

BILL

Well, maybe every other day.

ERHARD *(to the group)*

You all have a story, and your story is as full of shit as Bill's. And I'm using language that's clear enough for everybody to understand.

(to Bill)
Bill, because you've been carrying this load for everyone, you can leave now whatever your reason.

ERHARD *(pausing)*

You've got a story called pressure. You've got a story and then there's what happened.

BILL

I just want to say that I was disillusioned by the salesmanship involved in getting me into the program...

ERHARD *(interrupting)*

What is this salesmanship?

BILL

Let me finish my sentence!

ERHARD

I'm not interested in your finishing your sentence when it's bullshit.

BILL

Bullshit flows both ways.

(laughter)

ERHARD

What is this salesmanship you're talking about? You wouldn't have been called any more if you'd said no. You said "Call me some more."

(turning to the group)

If you think you were pressured, I want you to stop lying about it and tell the truth about what happened or get out of here.

BILL

Why don't you look at me? These people aren't interested in being entertained by you on my eccentricities.

ERHARD

Bill, I'm more likely to know what they're interested in than you. Are you able to make a choice about being here now that you've got a choice?

BILL *(stammering)*

Some of what you've done is offensive to me. I might get something. I don't know.

ERHARD

Would you make that choice for me?

Hesitantly, Bill sat down.

ERHARD

Do I take that to mean that you've chosen to be here?

BILL

Yes.

(to the group)
All Bill's doing is doing you a favor. He's letting you see yourself. That's an extraordinary gift, to see yourself.

(turning back to Bill)
I want to apologize to you for saying things that you found offensive. Do you accept my apology?

BILL

Yes, I do.

ERHARD

I'm not clear you're here because you chose to be here.

BILL

Yes. But I'm not clear if I'll get the results.

ERHARD

And you won't be. How The Forum works is you learn nothing. And then you learn more nothing. And then you learn it all at once. It's an all of a sudden phenomenon.

(pausing)
What we just went through is very important. I brought something to that conversation that's designed to leave you in a different place about those conversations. I predict that when The Forum is over you'll tell me this was the most important experience in your whole life. We'll see. There's a bit of a risk here, and I accept that.

Erhard finally left Bill, and addressed the group, moving among them.

ERHARD

Nobody participates in programs that I lead because they were pressured. A lot of people are here because they've got reasons to be here. And I want you to know you're not here because of your reasons. *You* put yourself in that chair, and not your reasons. You've got a story called force, and what actually happened was somebody spoke to you. If you live in a story called force, your life will look like a response to force. See, most of you live in response to a story you made up. You live in a sea of reasons. But I want you to be clear, you put yourself in that chair,

---

▶ **NOTE:** Please see the final conversation Erhard has with Bill near the close of Session Three of Day Four.

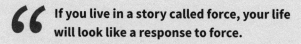

If you live in a story called force, your life will look like a response to force.

ERHARD (*continuing*)

not the reasons, nobody else and nothing else. And you have reasons. That's what I mean by people don't know their ass from a hole in the ground. People don't know what put them in that chair. If you're stuck with this idea that you were pressured, I want you out of here. I'm going to say a lot of things in here and you're only going to get them almost. I know that today you're going to get almost nothing I say, because you're going to put it in the language in which *you* dwell. Like "should." I don't dwell in the language of should. It's patently obvious here. I'm asking you who's buried in Grant's Tomb. This is not hard. *You* put yourself here.

A participant raised a question about a friend he wanted to do The Forum. He described the man.

PARTICIPANT

Would he feel pressured?

ERHARD

Yeah, because he's an asshole.

PARTICIPANT (*laughs*)

Yeah, that's true.

ERHARD

You see, you can't pressure people who are straight. They give clear answers, like "no," or "don't call me." I *invite* people. I want to be clear what I mean by an invitation. An invitation for me always carries with it the power to decline.

Erhard mounted the platform, and announced a break. However, he said, "in The Forum there are no breaks," so he gave the participants an assignment.

ERHARD

The assignment during the break is to sort out your "story" from "what happened." Most people live in the story and don't live in the what happened. And there's something disempowering about living in the story instead of living in the what happened. The problem is that you are *thrown*—that's like *already always*—you are thrown to the story. You are addicted to the story. "People don't like me" and "being insulted" never happen. I'm going to demonstrate insulting. I'm going to insult you: *I insult you*. For the first time in your life you've now been insulted *as a what happened*. All the other times, someone said something, and you *got* insulted. People have said you're a jerk. But that's somebody saying "You're a jerk." The *insult* was a story.

Having given the assignment, Erhard called Julie, The Forum Supervisor, to the podium.

ERHARD

Julie's the person who keeps this organized enough so that it can happen. So your cooperation with her is in your interest.

After Erhard left the room, Julie requested that due to the size of the group all participants should be respectful of the hotel. She pointed out the assistants who could direct participants to pay phones and bathrooms. "We request that you don't eat on this break," she said. "If you must eat for medical reasons, please see Wes," one of the two Forum leaders who were assisting Erhard. Finally she introduced the other four Forum supervisors who were working with her, and who were available to answer their questions. Finally, as she would before every break, she read the names of participants who had received telephone messages during the session.

The Forum adjourned for a break at 12:40 pm.

SESSION ONE INTERVAL

Hints: Ontological Distinctions

The Forum achieves its result through the development in dialogue of what Werner Erhard calls *distinctions*. In traditional education, based in an epistemological model in which the goal is to increase or enhance what is known, information—concepts, ideas, processes—are communicated through definition and explanation. The Forum, however, develops an *ontological* model of education, in which the goal is not an increase in knowledge but an experience of Being. In this model, the elements of the course content are *distinguished*.

The nature of distinctions will be addressed at length by Erhard later in The Forum. But here, early on the first morning, the development of distinctions is already under way. Erhard is beginning to employ an aspect of his methodology that, according to Martin Heidegger, is central to ontological communication: the use of *hints* to communicate what cannot directly be spoken, thereby providing access to the content as lived rather than as merely understood.

Heidegger introduced the idea of hinting as a way of communicating Being in his 1959 essay, "A Dialogue on Language" (in *OWL*), which provides an account of his conversation with a Japanese scholar who shared his interest in ontological inquiry. The interaction, presented in the form of a transcript, occurs as a stately conversational dance, a linguistic minuet. Each move is made with great care, so the interaction proceeds at times with excruciating deliberateness. At one point Heidegger (referred to in the account as the Inquirer) poses a question—"Do you have in your language a word for what we call language?"—to which the scholar arrives at a tentative answer only after twenty-three pages of thoughtful circumnavigation in and around the topic.

In response to a remark by the Japanese about language's "essential being," Heidegger refers to his often-quoted characterization of language as "the house of Being." The phrase, he says, "gives a hint of the nature of language" ("DL" in *OWL* 26). As the two men's dialogue continues, the extraordinary attentiveness given to each word reveals a respect for the nature of hints. Hints, Heidegger observes, "belong to an entirely different realm of reality. . . . They are enigmatic. They beckon to us. They beckon *away*. They beckon us *toward* that from which they unexpectedly bear themselves toward us" ("DL" in *OWL* 26).

In his conversation with the Japanese scholar, Heidegger is *distinguishing* hinting, which is to say that he is hinting at the nature of hints. The Forum's development of distinctions is likewise a process of hinting.

In hinting, words are spoken in such a way that "each word in each case is given its full—most often hidden—weight" ("DL" in *OWL* 31). What is not spoken, but communicated in the background, is allowed to reverberate. In this way a *space* is allowed to develop around each utterance:

> [*Inquirer*]: **Hints need the widest sphere in which to swing. . .**
>
> [*Japanese*]: **. . . where mortals go to and fro only slowly.**
>
> [*Inquirer*]: **This is what our language calls "hesitate." It is done truly when slowness rests on shy reverence. And so I do not wish to disturb your hesitation by urging you on too rashly.**
>
> [*Japanese*]: **You are more helpful to me in my attempt to say the word than you can know. ("DL" in *OWL* 27–28)**

Further, although each distinction has a rubric for its topic—in this dialogue, the topic is the nature of language—in developing distinctions the aim is not to arrive at a correct verbal articulation of the rubric. On the contrary, the goal is to *avoid* such a resolution:

> [*Japanese*]: **We Japanese do not think it strange if a dialogue leaves undefined what is really intended, or even restores it back to the keeping of the undefinable.**
>
> [*Inquirer*]: **That is part, I believe, of every dialogue that has turned out well between thinking beings. As if of its own accord, it can take care that that undefinable something not only does not slip away, but displays its gathering force ever more luminously in the course of the dialogue. ("DL" in *OWL* 13)**

In this conversation, Heidegger and the Japanese scholar may be seen as enacting the methodology of The Forum: the dialogic development of distinctions through a process of hinting. Being cannot be verbalized. Being is in language, but it is not in the words that are spoken. It lives in the unspoken background, and in a conversation for Being, that background must be made present. Hints are an appropriate form for bringing a background to presence because they direct our attention toward something we had not noticed, something which they at the same time bring forward to meet us.

Ontological hinting is not an easy form of communication to master, and by characterizing it here as an element of The Forum's "methodology," we have fallen prey to one of its pitfalls. When Heidegger says to the Japanese scholar that calling language "the house of Being" gives a "hint of the nature of language," the scholar immediately recognizes the danger: "I fear that to call your 'house of Being' a hint might tempt you and me to elaborate the notion of hinting into a guiding concept in which we then bundle up everything" ("DL" in *OWL*). Heidegger concurs, but adds that this error can "never be prevented in the sense of being totally excluded," since "the mode of conceptual representation insinuates itself all too easily into every kind of human experience" ("DL" in *OWL* 25).

A relevant observation by the senior author: during my years of participation in Erhard's work, the distinguishing of distinctions has remained a source of fascination, challenge, and even mystery for me. I have observed conversations between Forum leaders—people for whom the development of distinctions is central to their professional practice—in which the speaking occurred to me as a kind of short-hand. Elements of everyday interaction—details, transitions, connections—seemed to be missing. On one occasion, a statement by one Forum leader elicited this response from another: "You're explaining it. Distinguish it." I found myself struggling to recognize the difference being referred to.

An extensive hint at the nature of distinctions is found in Heidegger's later work, where he turned his attention increasingly to the ontological possibilities of art, and specifically of poetry. Poetry, he said, is *projective saying*—that is, a kind of saying which *projects a clearing for Being* by speaking the unspoken. "Projective saying is saying which, in preparing the sayable, simultaneously brings the unsayable as such into a world" ("OWA" in *PLT* 71). But such saying is not limited to the speaking of the poet, because "Language itself is poetry in the essential sense" ("OWA" in *PLT* 72). Indeed, "everyday language is a forgotten and used-up poem, from which there hardly resounds a call any longer" ("L" in *PLT* 205).

The thinker, says Heidegger elsewhere, confines his thinking to a *single thought* (*PLT* 4). Heidegger's single thought was the question of Being. A similar single-mindedness characterizes the poet, and so Heidegger's description of the poet's relation to the unsayable is useful:

 Every great poet creates his poetry out of one single poetic statement only. . . . The poet's statement remains unspoken. None of his individual poems, nor their totality, says it all. Nonetheless, every poem speaks from the whole of the one single statement, and in each instance says that statement. ("LP" in *OWL* 160)

Therefore all of Heidegger's writing and all of Werner Erhard's work, as well as all the poetry of Dickinson or Rilke or Wallace Stevens, may be seen as bodies of hints for the Saying of what is essentially unsayable.

During the forty-minute break, statements had been written on two of the chalkboards. On one: "Promise of The Forum: You can have anything out of The Forum that you are willing to stand for having gotten." On the second: "The commitment of the work is Transformation: bringing forth a breakthrough in the possibility of being for human beings."
As The Forum resumed, Erhard began with a question.

ERHARD

What happened when you were considering the difference between your story and what happened?

PARTICIPANT

I found that I didn't want to confront my stories.

ERHARD

It's possible to live in a kind of unconsciousness that we don't ordinarily call unconsciousness because we're not knocked out. It's an unconsciousness which appears as *not being there*. What you can't be with prevents you from being. If you mash up the what happens and the story, it kind of keeps you a little unconscious, because you don't have to *be* with it. But when you start to distinguish the story from what happened, you begin to see the story as a story, and it's not very attractive that way, is it? And it's something one would mostly avoid being with. There will be a lot that will come up in here that you don't want to *be with*. It's useful to be with what you don't want to be with. What you've already learned to be with and survive with--that's not going to be very useful in here, it's the part you've avoided being with here. Anything else? Thanks very much.

As participants responded to this question, Erhard contextualized their contributions by expanding the distinctions he had introduced earlier in the day.

JOHN

I've never really liked my wife's version of the story of how we got married.

ERHARD

When you can recognize a person's story as their story, you begin to have access to their version of the story, so that you're not stuck with, you don't have to resign yourself to, their version of the story. You have access to different possibilities within the story, but not when it's mashed up with what happened.

JOHN

I got so upset, I left the room, and while I heard the story from another part of the house, my upset turned toward wanting to get out of my marriage.

ERHARD (*interrupting*)

You didn't invent thinking about getting out of your marriage. That's already always in the culture of being for human beings. You think, "oh well, this happened and that made me think I

> " When you can recognize a person's story as their story, you begin to have access to their version of the story, so that you're not stuck with, you don't have to resign yourself to, their version of the story.

should quit or leave." That's not the way it works. It's a rainstorm. Leaving, getting out of things, quitting—owns your life. It's true you have the conversation with yourself personally. But that's like getting wet in a rainstorm.

(with emphasis)
I'm not thinking that. That is thinking me.

(pausing)
I'm starting to talk like people don't talk, because I want *access* to what concerns me that people don't have. So you and I are starting to invent a language that gives us access to the things that are interesting, or important, that concern us in life. It's not your thought. I want you to start to think that *it thinks you*. You have the thoughts like you get wet in the rainstorm. I'm just asking you to begin to think in a way you haven't thought before. The kind of person you are is given by that thinking, which isn't your thoughts or your thinking.

JOHN

What I noticed was that each of us have different stories about how we got together.

ERHARD

You can't ask questions like "True?" about people's stories. There's no such thing as "true stories." "True" and "story" don't go together. A story's a story. People get into trouble in life because they start believing their stories. Even worse, you start believing someone else's story— makes you a spear-carrier in somebody else's opera. This is not a good way to live.

JOHN

We did what we did and got married.

ERHARD

Who is not clear about choosing to be married? The conversation about why you're in The Forum could apply as well to you in your job, or your marriage. Almost nobody thinks they are anyplace because they put themselves there. But *everybody* puts themselves there. Then you get the story about why you're there. There's no power in the story... You live in a story about being married. *I accuse you* that you live in a story about being married, and the quality of being married reflects that it in part is generated by a story. I didn't say you don't have a good marriage. But it's limited to a certain box, a certain space or quality, when it's a story. What happened? You got married. Then there's this whole story. And they're *distinct* from one another. The same thing is true about everything in life. See, you and I have the kind of lives that people would have if they lived out of a story. And mostly the story is constituted mostly by your reasons. But *you* got that job. That's what happened.

JOHN

Normally I know that, but I wasn't clear about that last night. It's so easy to forget.

Philosophy as Rhetorical Evocation

We propose that The Forum is an instance of ontological rhetoric. We emphasize at the outset that this is not the everyday understanding of rhetoric as "mere rhetoric," that is, language that is superficial and disconnected from serious purposes. *Rhetoric* as we use the term is any use of language that is intended to produce a real-world result. Ontological rhetoric communicates in the unspoken realm of language to provide its listeners with access to the realm of *Being*.

Recognition of the value and function of ontological rhetoric is found in the later writing of Henry W. Johnstone, Jr., founder of the journal, *Philosophy and Rhetoric*. Early in his career, Johnstone believed that the role of the philosophical rhetor was "to treat his audience as an object," and that his goal

ERHARD

That's why we don't give you anything to remember. You just have to *be*.

HANNAH

There's a new babysitter watching the baby while I'm here and I got a note at the break to call and I immediately felt terror because six months ago there was an accident that threatened his life.

ERHARD

You understand that the terror is of no value to her? You sympathize with the terror. When you leave here you'll be a little more ruthless than you are now. You'll be concerned for what empowers people, not for sympathizing with their weaknesses. No empowerment in terror.

HANNAH

I had lost closeness with him. It was more about clinging, and I saw that it was more about terror.

ERHARD

Major issues like parenting or confronting death generate the most persistent stories. The things that are real close to us are hard not to be stupid about. It's hard to *be with* that people do die. And you are going to die. And that's hard to be with. The more dramatic the soap opera is the easier it is to get drawn into it and not be able to distinguish the story from what happened.

MAX

I'm here because I want my life to stop being an emergency, in my personal and professional life. I am an upset waiting to happen.

ERHARD

Some of you are an argument waiting to happen. You're waiting for the occasion to act out the argument.

MAX

Turning away from my story to what happened is like becoming an arbitrator. It helps me get away from my guilt.

ERHARD

If guilt were useful, I would say have a lot of it. *Listen up here*! This is another one of those things you want to get. Feeling guilty makes it all right that you did something. If you didn't feel guilty you'd be a bad person. That's not terrible to be a bad person. No, it's all right to do something as long as you feel guilty about it. Guilt is the salve we put on something that we did so that we don't have to be responsible for it. But you don't know what I'm talking about because you don't know the difference between guilt and responsibility at this point. Max?

was "to manipulate his audience so as to secure agreement" ("Persuasion" 19). But a "turn" in Johnstone's thinking led him to acknowledge by 1978 that "the distinction between finding the truth in philosophy and finding the proper rhetorical devices for propagating it cannot be maintained" ("Truth" 74). In other words, "truth" is always and already rhetorical, never severed from its communication, and thus finding the "truth" requires holding up a pretense that rhetoric is merely a convenient accessory that can be dispensed with.

Johnstone's new perspective of the philosophy–rhetoric relationship was based in the concept of *evocation*: "My present view is that a successful argument in philosophy is one that is intended to evoke, and does evoke, a response of a certain kind in the man to whom it is addressed" ("Truth" 75). Johnstone cited Heidegger as evidence for this view, and his description here of Heidegger's language use is consistent with our understanding of both Heidegger's and Erhard's thinking:

 If I am correct in arguing that Heidegger conceives philosophy as basically rhetorical, some revision in our conception of rhetoric is called for. . . its purpose is not to incite its hearer to action—even the action of adopting some specific belief. Instead, rhetoric totally reorients the hearer; if he listens to it he is in a position to abandon an inauthentic life in favor of an authentic one. ("Rhetoric" 68)

On this view, the truth of philosophy is intimately infused with its *communicability*: "discovery, communication, and rhetoric all collapse into a unitary philosophical act" ("Truth" 76). Further, communicability is manifested as evocation: "The only way to tell whether what I have is a truth or a falsehood," said Johnstone, "is to contemplate its *evocative power*." And rhetoric, he added, is "the art of evocation" ("Truth" 76).

Finally, Johnstone's discussion of Heidegger raises a third issue which will be particularly relevant in our analysis of The Forum: that is the question of the appropriate rhetorical *style* for addressing an untransformed audience whom one intends, through one's rhetorical transactions, to transform. Johnstone stated the problem this way:

> **Heidegger's entire position is specifically committed to the task of awakening philistines from their ontological slumber . . . . *Das Man* [the "they," the philistine, the untransformed] expects to be told in plain English what he can in fact come to understand only by being awakened. But because Heidegger's entire thrust is *toward* the awakening of *das Man* he cannot reject as a mere philistine the man who fails to understand him. In Heidegger's own terms, he is not successful until he has reached the philistine. Hence in a sense there are no philistines at all for him. ("Rhetoric" 68)**

How does one awaken people from a debilitating slumber if they resist the process which is necessary for their awakening? This question, as we will show, is a central one for the rhetorical process of The Forum. ■

> **Only what I say that doesn't fit with stuff you think, that provokes you to think and see things in a new way: that's what's valuable.**

MAX

The story is that I joined the service, and went to Vietnam. And my welcome home isn't what I expected. What happened was, I went to war and came back alive. Same as any other war, there's...it's cleared up a lot of issues to look at it as what happened rather than my story in relation to my coming home.

ERHARD (*with emphasis*)

Listen up! Vietnam's a great, great story. Lot of people badly, badly fucked up by the story. Notice I didn't say by what happened? Lots of people profoundly disabled by the story. Lot of freedom for people to start to distinguish the story from what happened. Thanks Max.

Erhard shifted his tone, calling attention to the process they had been engaged in: they had developed a number of distinctions as *tools for their inquiry*.

ERHARD

We're going to get these tools sharpened up as we proceed. Your questions are useful. You notice I've done most of what I've done out of people's speaking. This is not a lecture, that's why we call it The Forum. This is a *dialogue*. My job is to manage the dialogue, not to lecture. I have no pipeline to the truth. No one is asking you to believe anything that is said in here. But I'm asking you to think about it. That's different from "reject" or "accept" it. Instead, see what the world looks like standing in that idea. It doesn't matter whether you agree or not. To tell the truth, I'm not that impressed with you yet, to care whether you agree or not. I do want to hear what you have to say. I'm not interested in your agreement or approval, or endorsement. I am interested in you looking at what we're saying here, to think about it yourself. And the way I'd like you to do that is to not judge it or evaluate it to see if it fits with what you already think. If I say anything that fits with what you already think, you shouldn't be here. You can forget all that. Anything I say that fits with what you already think: that's not The Forum. Only what I say that doesn't fit with the stuff you think, that provokes you to think and see things in a new way: that's what's valuable. But this isn't the truth either. I don't know about the truth. I know how to talk so that people have new possibility in their life. If you talk with me, you can bet that you'll walk away with a new possibility in your life.

Now he introduced a new way to address what has already been the subject of the discussion.

ERHARD (*continuing*)

We're going to talk about *existence*. That's what we've been talking about. It's hard to talk about. It's hard to pick yourself up by your own bootstraps. It's got to exist to talk about it. If you're going to question existence—talk about existence—it's got to exist to talk about it. The word for a concern for existence is *ontology*. And the reason I bring up that fancy sounding word is I want you to know The Forum is not psychological. Most people can't tell the difference. Psychology is pervasive in our culture. The structure for interpretation for most people in this culture is psychological. We're all amateur psychologists. You see everything through a psychological lens.

ERHARD (*pausing to wake a participant who was nodding off*)
It's okay to sleep in here if you can do it bolt upright with your eyes open.

(*returning to his topic*)
Ontology is the difference between knowing how to play tennis and being a tennis player. They don't teach this in school for the most part, and when they do, they do it badly for the most part. An ontological approach—that is to say, a *concern-for-being* approach—has got a lot of room in it because it's something we haven't engaged in very much. The point is, there's a lot of room in a new realm. The psychological approach is one we've pushed really hard. And I want to be clear I'm not denigrating it. And that's not our approach.

(*moving to one of the blackboards*)
So far, we've distinguished two realms of existence. A phenomenon can exist in the realm of *story* and it can exist in the realm of *what happened*.

Erhard drew two circles on the board: in the left circle he wrote the word "Story," and in the right he wrote "What Happened."

ERHARD (*indicating the left circle*)

Max gave us a good example. There's the story of Vietnam and that's *here*. And there's what happened, and that's *here*.

(*indicating the right circle in which he wrote "what happened"*)
We're going to see what happens when you begin to distinguish these two. You're going to see the impact it has on your ability and state of being to distinguish Vietnam "the story" and Vietnam "the what happened." You can apply the demonstration anywhere. We need to talk about thinking. Listen up. This is hard. Human beings have the notion that they think. Or—I might as well introduce this—they *are* that they think. They *be* like they're thinking. And there is something happening. You and I call that "I think." Here's an exercise to tell if you're thinking. I'm going to shut up and you're going to stop thinking.

(*pausing for about fifteen seconds*)
You didn't make it, did you? Nobody ever does, because it's not you thinking. If you were thinking then you could stop thinking. *It* is thinking, and you are having the thoughts it thinks. Which is true? The old way of saying it or the way I said it? That's not the point. I told you, I don't know the truth. I'm saying there's something empowering about this, in the recognition that you don't think. Like: "Hmm. I'm not thinking. It's thinking, and I'm having those thoughts." What comes up when you think this way is the possibility of actually *thinking*. Thinking is a process independent of those thoughts. Thinking is something like sitting with, or more precisely something like *dwelling* in. It's not like figuring it out. You see, I asked you to dwell in the possibility that it's not you thinking.

(*pausing again to address a number of people in the room who were getting sleepy*)
It always happens about now. Thinking *about* thinking puts you to sleep. *Thinking* wakes you up. Thinking is when you have to break your mind—though not all of that is thinking. Some of it is bullshit.

> " *It* is thinking, and you are having the thoughts it thinks.... Thinking is something like sitting with, or more precisely something like *dwelling* in. It's not like figuring it out.

(turning to The Forum Supervisor)
Julie, would you ask Eric to get the Heidegger books out of my room.

(returning to the blackboard, and pointing to the circle labeled "story")
I want to take back making this bad. What's disempowering is not the story, what's disempowering is when you *collapse* "what happened" with the "story" and you can't distinguish the story from what happened. You can't distinguish because you've got this mush, this mess, this swamp of what happened and the story mixed together. The two need to be distinct. What does distinct mean? It means existing then on their own, being there of themselves. It's possible for Vietnam to exist as a story and it's possible for Vietnam to exist as a what happened. They're two distinct realms of existence. Sometimes the story is appropriate, sometimes what happened is appropriate. What's never appropriate is when these two distinctions get collapsed.

As this conversation developed, Erhard added other terms to his blackboard model. In the right circle, below "what happened," he wrote "presence" and "I'm late." In the other, below "story," was written "concept" and "reasons."

ERHARD

Confusing what happened with your story about it is like ordering steak and then mixing the steak with the menu. Most people think life is sour because they've been eating the menu for so long, they don't recognize reading the menu. You should not say "I love you" to people. You should say, "I live with the *concept* 'I love you.'" Love as a concept is sometimes important, but it isn't the same as love as a presence. What falls out of my mouth when I say "chair" is a concept. It's not a chair—but it's useful. Just separating the two domains of existence in any area of your life will leave you with more power in that area. For this to work, try it on in your own life. This is not the truth. Try it on. If it works, good; if not, throw it away.

At this point, The Forum Supervisor brought Erhard a copy of Heidegger's *What is Called Thinking?* (1968, pages 76-77). He spent a minute looking for the passage he wanted, and finally turned back to her.

ERHARD

This is the wrong copy. This is not the copy I can find things in. I have two marked copies and I can find things in one and not the other.

Julie brought up the correct copy.

ERHARD *(beginning to read)*

"People still hold the view that what is handed down to us by tradition is what in reality lies behind us—while in fact it comes toward us because we are its captives and destined to it."

(pausing)
We think we're out in front of tradition on the leading edge. He's talking about where the rubber meets the road. This is not some fancy talk.

ERHARD *(loudly)*

He's talking about your future. He's saying you've got no future. Your future is constituted by the past. Listen up! This is not a guy in a diner, by the way.

(shifting tone)
Where's the person I had that conversation with?

Doris, with whom he had earlier discussed whether she knew her "ass from a hole in the ground," stood.

ERHARD

Did I leave you insulted, by the way?

(Doris looking hesitant)
Can I withdraw the insult? Will you forgive me?

(nodding, she then sits)
Thank you.

(continuing to read)
"The purely historical view of tradition and the course of history is one of those vast self-deceptions in which we must remain entangled as long as we are still not really thinking. That self-deception about history prevents us from hearing the language of the thinkers. We do not hear it rightly, because we take that language to be mere expression, setting forth philosophers' views."

(to the group)
Some people are actually thinking, and *speaking* their thinking. That's different from "saying what you've got on your mind." But the thinkers' language tells what it is. And hearing it is in no case easy. Hearing it presupposes that we meet a certain requirement, and we do so only on rare occasions. So there's a requirement to be able to hear thinking. And you can bet your hat, ass, and overcoat that the same requirement exists for thinking. And here's the requirement.

(continuing to read)
"We must acknowledge and respect it. To acknowledge and respect consists in letting every thinker's thought come to us as something in each case unique, never to be repeated, inexhaustible."

(to the group)
You will notice that everything that has been said in here today you have associated with something else. In order to have it live by itself, you have to *think*. Association happens anyhow, because you're not doing it. *It's* doing it.

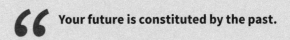
Your future is constituted by the past.

(continuing to read)
"—and being shaken to the depths by what is unthought in his thought."

(to the group)
It's like what is unsaid, but there by virtue of what is said. Anything that's going to make a difference will be unsaid. Did you ever care about speaking in such a way that what you didn't say was present? Probably not. But that's where making a difference lies.

(continuing to read)
"What is unthought in a thinker's thought is not a lack inherent in his thought. What is *unthought* is there in each case only as the un-*thought*. The more original the thinking, the richer will be what is unthought in it. The unthought is the greatest gift that thinking can bestow."

(to the group)
Listen up real good to this part!

(continuing to read)
"But to the commonplaces of sound common sense, what is unthought in any thinking always remains merely the incomprehensible. And to the common comprehension, the incomprehensible is never an occasion to stop and look at its own powers of comprehension, still less to notice their limitations. To the common comprehension, what is incomprehensible remains forever merely offensive..."

(to the group)
Where Heidegger uses the word "offensive," I say "it's bullshit." It's a little clearer the way I say it, isn't it? It's more rigorous the way he says it, but it's a little easier to get the way I say it.

(continuing to read)
"—proof enough to such comprehension, which is convinced it was born comprehending everything, that it is now being imposed upon with an untruth and a sham. The one thing of which sound common sense is least capable is acknowledgment and respect."

(to the group)
The distinction I'm developing between the story and what happened is not the commonsense understanding. Love as a concept is what you and I live with most of the time, not love as a presence. If you uncollapse the domains, you can have presence and story. It's not worth a damn if you don't map it onto your own life. Take something you're concerned about—and by *concern* I don't mean something you're worried about. Take something you *care* about.

As the time for the second break of the day approached, Erhard moved to another topic.

ERHARD *(continuing)*
We're now going to talk about promises. There are certain promises you must make in order to participate in The Forum. You didn't know that. This is a change! An occasion for upset! It's very hard to talk about promises to people who don't know what a promise is. Who you are is a

> **Did you ever care about speaking in such a way that what you didn't say was present? Probably not. But that's where making a difference lies.**

ERHARD (*continuing*)

person who goes around pretending you're going to do what you say you'll do. Isn't it true that you present yourself as someone who'll do what you say you'll do? But isn't it true that maybe you'll do it and maybe you won't? And you always justify it. Everybody does what they can't justify *not* doing. Why is that?

PARTICIPANT

If justification equals doing it, when you don't have a justification for not doing it, then you have to do it.

ERHARD

That's a little sophisticated for us today.

ANOTHER PARTICIPANT

Because I want to be right.

ERHARD

You do what you feel like, or what is convenient, but you justify it so you can be right.

(pausing)
Diogenes looked for an honest man. I want to find someone who is *late*. I'm fifty-four years old and I've never found anyone who's *just late*. It's always "I'm late" *plus* the reason. By the way,

(pointing to the "what happened" circle)
here's "I'm late"...

(pointing to the "story" circle)
...and here's the reason. Being late is in a totally different realm than the reason for being late. And the two are not related. "I'm late" and the reasons arise in different realms of existence. They're apples and oranges. They don't go together.

(to a drowsy participant)
Remember the rules about sleeping. You've got to do it bolt upright. You may make it before the week is over.

He tossed the chalk he was holding at another participant, who remained seated during the following exchange.

ERHARD

Only bolt upright can your eyes be closed.

PARTICIPANT

They weren't closed.

> " Isn't it true that you present yourself as someone who'll do what you say you'll do? But isn't it true that maybe you'll do it and maybe you won't?

ERHARD

I apologize.

PARTICIPANT

Yeah, sure.

ERHARD

Is that like "fuck you"? Do you mean "I don't *feel* apologize"? I'm not my feelings. I'm my mouth. You're not your mouth. You say "okay" when you mean "Fuck you."

PARTICIPANT

Not always.

ERHARD

You did that time.

PARTICIPANT

That's true.

Throughout this interaction Erhard's style was relaxed but direct.

ERHARD (*to the group*)

The truth is that whether you keep your word depends on how you feel. Create this possibility: that you present yourself as someone who keeps your word, but in fact does or does not depending on whether you feel like it. Try on that possibility. "Honor your promise" means something like keep them *in spite of* the circumstances. Try on this possibility: that you present yourself as someone who keeps your word, but in fact are someone who does or does not keep your word depending on whether you feel like it. Try that on. I say that if you do that you will have the freedom to honor your word. I know more about lying than most people in this room. I've lied more than most people in this room, and I know the kind of life it gives. And it's my observation that you're never going to be able to honor your word until you can be with yourself in the way in which I just accused you of being. I say that until you can be with that, you can't honor your word. By the way, I want to introduce a phrase here: that would be called *being authentic about being inauthentic*. Who doesn't get this?

MARY

I know that sometimes I won't keep my word.

ERHARD

But you don't present yourself as that.

MARY

No, I do what I do.

ERHARD

You say, "Hey Werner, I'm going to meet you tomorrow at noon..."

MARY

And I'll get there at two.

ERHARD

But you don't say, "But Werner, I may show up and I may not."

MARY

No.

ERHARD

That's the inauthenticity. If you went around saying to people, "Look, I'll give my word, and maybe I'll keep it and maybe I won't." Nothing inauthentic about that—that's quite straight.

MARY

And I'm right about that.

ERHARD

We'll discuss more about that later. You get what I mean about that being inauthentic? Anybody who can't see that?

JAKE

I make the best effort to... I don't understand.

ERHARD

Let me tell you how I listen. I just told you that one and one equals two. And I asked you if you got that, and you said you're confused. So I think you've got something going on in this area.

JAKE

That's one of the reasons why I raised my hand.

ERHARD

You're not confused; you've got something going on.

JAKE

I've got something going on.

Getting It and Losing It

The Forum content is communicated through the gradual development of a series of distinctions. These distinctions offer access to a certain way of being; they are *ontological clearings*, contexts of meaning. They shape the way the circumstances of life occur so that a new way of being with those circumstances arises naturally. The new way of being becomes a possibility when the distinction is "gotten"—in Heideggerian terms, in a moment of *Augenblick*, or ontological insight. Thus the purpose of The Forum is to have participants "get" the distinctions deeply enough during the course of the four days that they leave The Forum *dwelling* in those distinctions. As Erhard told The Forum leaders during a debriefing, "What makes a difference is that there is a conversation generated that distinguishes the distinction, and that they're *dwelling* in the conversation," that is, they are "used by" the distinction rather than caught up trying to remember a piece of information as a precondition to being able to apply it.

The Heideggerian notion of "dwelling" is central to the way in which The Forum material is to be assimilated. Dwelling, for Erhard, is synonymous with "coming from"—that is, to *dwell* in a context is to *come from* that context into one's life, or to allow oneself to *be given being* by that context. Heidegger called *dwelling* "*the basic character* of Being in keeping with which mortals exist" ("BDT" in *PLT* 158). Dwelling, for Heidegger, designates that ontological state in which we attain our essential relatedness to the world, so we must "think for the sake of dwelling" ("BDT" in *PLT* 159).

However, a point that we will introduce here and to which we will return throughout this book, is that *Being withdraws*. The ontological communication of The Forum, the speaking of Being, occurs always in this precarious context: it *wavers* on the brink of concealment. Thus the process of dwelling-in-a-distinction consists of repeatedly "*getting*" and "*losing*" that distinction. Erhard consistently tells his audiences that if they "got it and it went away," that is the appropriate way to assimilate ontological communication: "That's the way it's supposed to happen," he says, "getting and losing and getting and losing and getting and losing" ("Beyond the Winning Formula"). This is an essential aspect of the ontological rhetoric whose nature we are developing here, and it is consistent with the authors' own experience of having participated in Werner Erhard's programs: the insights that we have attained in the process have occurred waveringly.

As we have participated over the years in courses and seminars based in Erhard's work, something would often be said which *in that instant* produced an illuminating insight, but which seemed, a moment or an hour later, to be simply words, or even incomprehensible jargon. *Longitudinally*, however—over the years of our participation in this work—we are aware of a parallel development: a gradually increasing *dwelling-in the way of being* that has been opened up by the distinctions which we are simultaneously getting and losing. Further, this ongoing dwelling-in has, over the years, become more salient than the getting and losing. That is, we notice that we increasingly act *from* the

ERHARD

What have you got going on?

JAKE

I'm one of those people who stood up that said I'm a person of my word.

ERHARD

And you're not. Isn't that true? You do what you say you're gonna do?

JAKE

I damn well try.

ERHARD

Very good. "I am a person who will do what I say I am going to do, when in fact, I am only a person who will try to do what I said I will do, and what I mean by try is, given the way I see things, which will be generated by my feelings, my mood, if I can see that I can't do it, I won't do it. But I'm not gonna tell you that. I'm going to tell you that I'm a person of my word."

Erhard sat on the edge of the platform facing Jake.

ERHARD (*continuing*)
Try to sit down.

(*Jake sat*)
No, you sat down.

(*Jake stood*)
I didn't say sit down. *Try* to sit down.

(*again he sat*)
No, you're sitting. I said try to sit.

JAKE

I'm not getting it.

ERHARD

You're getting it. You don't like it. Trying to sit down looks a lot like standing up. You're just a bullshit artist. That's not a bad thing to be, by the way. It's just a thing with no power.

JAKE

I'm getting that, but I don't see the point. What is it worth?

ERHARD

Let me tell you something, my friend. You're not going to get anything out of here you can do something with. Do you think I'm going to give an asshole tools? What you walk out of here with will give you freedom. You won't use it. It will use you. I have read all the books, and I've gotten value; but that's not transformational.

JAKE

I don't know where you're coming from with this asshole stuff.

ERHARD

It's not because you are one. I don't call you an asshole because it's an apt description. I call you that because it has an impact. If I wanted to call you the right name I'd call you Jake.

JAKE

I'm doing a good job as I listen to you, as we talk about keeping your word and things like that. I'm aware of the burden I inflict on myself with trying to keep my word.

ERHARD

And you see, when you walk out of here, you will be free to be your word. There will be no burden in your word. Not bad. It's worth something isn't it? But you haven't the remotest clue about how to get there. You couldn't get there in a billion years. Now we need you to get there, but you're stuck in this area. So that's my business.

(laughter)

If I need someone in your business to do something, I don't come to me, because I'm an asshole in your business. You aren't going to know when this is working and when it's not working. You wouldn't know if we were there if we fell over it, because you look for the wrong kind of evidence. Stop worrying about whether it's working. That's my job. I don't mean to attack your sincerity. Your sincerity is not worth attacking, because it's worthless.

JAKE

That almost sounded like an apology.

ERHARD *(looking out at the group)*

Your sincerity is worthless because you're still standing when you try to sit down. Now, I've got to live with your standing, not with your trying. This is like a cult of assholes.

JAKE

It sounds like you're condoning being a real sloppy person about your word.

ERHARD

That's what hooked you, isn't it?

way-of-being made available by the distinctions of Erhard's work; that way-of-being is the ontological "place" we *come from* into the encounters of our lives.

Two significant qualifications must be added here. First, we have generalized what has been produced by our participation in Erhard's work as "a way of being." This is of course a gloss on an existential phenomenon that defies capture by words. On the one hand we sense, in our recent experiences in the seminars of Landmark Worldwide, what we might call reverberations that are harmonic with our earliest experiences of Erhard's work. At the same time, since each of us *is* the way of being whose evolution we are addressing, we obviously have no place to stand outside that evolution from which to address it.

Second, these years have included years when we have participated regularly and frequently in Erhard's work, and years when we have not participated at all. Our assessment of this process is that our experience of life has been enhanced during those periods of participation. Certainly there have been ups and downs in every period; but the phenomenon that Erhard calls transformation does indeed live in language, and it is our experience that regular participation in the conversation keeps it alive. And for us, even in the nonparticipating periods, the development of the distinctions remains ongoing just in the process of life itself.

Thus the purpose of The Forum is to communicate the distinctions repeatedly and at sufficient length such that participants can move, as far as possible, from *getting* them to *dwelling* in them. "Why we're going on and on down there," Erhard told The Forum leaders during a debriefing session, "is so that the distinctions are transferred from something people *get* to something they *come from*."

Therefore, we request that readers consider this possibility in approaching the ideas in this book. If something we say seems, at one moment, to make sense, but upon further reflection doesn't, that may be the way it should be assimilated.

For the senior author, the point which Erhard was making at this particular juncture of The Forum—that I present myself as someone who keeps my word, whereas in reality I keep my word when I cannot justify not keeping it—wavers for me as I consider it. I see its validity: I do keep my promises and adhere to my agreements, but only until I see some overriding justification for breaking them. I obey most laws—my social contracts—except for certain laws which I justify not keeping: for example, I cannot personally justify cheating on my income tax returns, but I often justify exceeding the speed limit. The classic ethical dilemma—whether one would tell an axe murderer the "truth" about the location of his innocent quarry—can be seen as a variation of this same point: I tell the truth until I can justify not telling it.

And yet I notice my resistance to accepting this when it is put so baldly. Protestations of my "honesty" leap to mind: it is not that I keep my word depending on how I feel about it, it is that I always keep my word except when there is some overriding reason not to. But—and here is the point Erhard is driving toward—isn't that simply the same "what happened" with a different "story" attached to it? Isn't it true that I either keep my word or I don't, and then I add a story, a justification of some nature for whichever action I take? Doesn't the "what happened" remain unaltered, regardless of the explanation or justification I attach to the event? ■

JAKE

Yep.

ERHARD

It sounded like I was attacking one of your sacred beliefs. You couldn't *tolerate* being a guy who said he would do it and didn't do it. You couldn't listen to the rest of what I said, and got confused. You can't live with being a guy who doesn't keep his word.

JAKE

I think I have good reasons for not doing it.

ERHARD

I didn't say it wasn't a valid story. I love everybody's story. But you can't ask about it, "true" or "false"? Is it really true that you *couldn't* do it? What's true is that you *didn't* do it. Sometimes a cigar is just a cigar, as Freud said. Listen, you can't be with that. You can't be with the possibility of not being your word. And you know what? Something happened, when you were a kid, and you couldn't be that anymore.

JAKE

This is something I value.

ERHARD

I know. You're nutty about it.

JAKE

Yes I am a nut about it.

ERHARD

And anything you're nutty about you have no freedom with.

JAKE

What's the value in being two hours late just because you want to be two hours late?

ERHARD

I never said anything like that. You said that. You're so nutty you're hearing voices. That's part metaphorical and part literal.

JAKE

No, somebody did say that.

MARY

I said that, but I didn't say I wouldn't try.

ERHARD

You have no idea: she struggles with being on time.

MARY

Yeah.

ERHARD

So now it's okay with him.

(laughter)

JAKE

I believe that people's intentions are important. Let's take a poll.

ERHARD

If we took a poll 100 years ago, somebody in here would be burned as a witch.

JAKE

That's true.

Another participant, Paul, spoke up while remaining seated.

PAUL

In some languages making promises sometimes involves using a special tense that says you might not arrive.

ERHARD *(laughing)*

When I arrive, if I do...

PAUL

It's characteristic of other languages. In Spanish there's all these subjunctive tenses. You can say: "When you do this for me, then I'll do that." It's subjunctive, it's something we don't recognize in our language. It's recognized as theoretical. Maybe that's what you're getting at.

ERHARD

No it's not, but what you've said is useful nevertheless for what I am getting at: that you will present yourself as a person who will do what you said you will do, and you don't do what you say you will do. In fact maybe you will do it and maybe you won't. That's inauthentic.

PAUL

Well, I wouldn't agree.

ERHARD

Why don't you stand up for a while?

PAUL *(standing and receiving a microphone)*

To me being inauthentic is to say you're going to do something without fully intending to do it. That's inauthentic to me.

ERHARD

Try to keep in mind I've been discussing this for seventeen years with people almost as smart as you are. And I'm still saying this thing. I haven't met the person, although I haven't met anyone as smart as you...

PAUL

Nor have I met anybody as smart as you.

ERHARD

You don't know that.

PAUL

I know I don't, but neither do you know what you are saying.

ERHARD

Oh, you're going to do your program with me, right?

PAUL

Oh no, I'm just...

ERHARD

Wait, wait. I don't know a word for that except "asshole."

(laughter)

If someone pays $625 to come in and take my course and they take the time to do their course with me for free, that's an asshole.

PAUL

You're playing with words.

ERHARD

What isn't playing with words?

PAUL

Well anything nonverbal is obviously not playing with words.

ERHARD

Really? Are you a linguist?

PAUL

Yeah, I speak three languages.

ERHARD

I didn't ask if you speak three languages, I asked if you understood language. Is that your business? Is language your business?

PAUL

No, but I speak several languages.

ERHARD

How many people in this room speak several languages?

(many hands raised)
I have a lot of respect for people who speak several languages. I don't mean any disrespect, but it doesn't mean you know shit about language.

PAUL

Well, language encompasses a pattern of thought, a process of thought. It's contained within the language you think within. Like I was referring to with Spanish, you have within the language incorporated a structure for dealing with the fact that some things are hypothetical, some things are real...

ERHARD *(to the group)*

You want to listen to this very carefully, because otherwise you're going to stand up and do this. And I'm going to let him do this long enough that you can see what it looks like. Go on Paul.

PAUL

The point is, I agree, that to be inauthentic is to, you're saying that it is to, to do something, to say you're going to do something and, nobody knows, I could say I'm going to walk over here, and the world may end before I get there.

ERHARD

That's not my point. That's not what I said.

PAUL

Well, what is the point?

ERHARD

The point is, to present your self in one way and be another way is inauthentic.

PAUL

Yeah, that's true.

ERHARD

That's what I said from the beginning. It's like I said one and one is two, and then you say, "Well, not always..."

PAUL

But that doesn't account for intention. There are some things within one person's realm of control and other things that aren't.

ERHARD

You're nutty about this too.

(pointing to Jake)
I want you to listen here. We'll get this now. I don't know if he'll get it, but you'll get it.

PAUL

I'm trying to clarify the distinction.

ERHARD

Hold on. I understand. See, look: I didn't say anything about intention. You brought that up, actually it was Jake, but in this conversation, you brought that up.

PAUL

Yes.

ERHARD

I said that "inauthentic" was to present yourself in one way, and be another way. That's pretty goddamn simple, isn't it?

PAUL

Sure, yeah.

ERHARD

And is that inauthentic?

PAUL

Yes, if that is your way of being.

ERHARD

That is what I said. I said if you present yourself in one way, and you're actually being another way, that's inauthentic. Right?

PAUL

Sure, if you're mindful of the fact that you're that other way.

ERHARD

Well how about if the moon comes up blue with pink polka dots?

PAUL

Well...

ERHARD

How about if the world ends in 30 seconds? My question is: Why are you coming up with these little things about intentionality, when what I'm saying is very simple?

PAUL

Well, because it implies will.

ERHARD

It doesn't imply anything. If you present yourself one way, when in fact you are another way, that's inauthentic. If it says gold stamped on a thing and it's not gold, that's inauthentic.

PAUL

No.

ERHARD

It's when you present yourself one way, and you're another way—that's inauthentic.

PAUL

Well, I don't agree, but still. I think that's the wrong word.

ERHARD (*to Jake*)

Do you get that he doesn't agree with that?

JAKE

Can I respond to what you're saying?

ERHARD

Did you get that he doesn't agree with that?

JAKE

We're not exactly aligned.

ERHARD

I understand that. Jake, you're not exactly aligned from exactly the same place.

(addressing the two men)
You're both nutty about your word. He's coming from the same thing. If you *thought* it was gold and you stamped gold on it, then it's really gold. You hear how stupid that sounds?

JAKE

Yeah.

ERHARD

That's what you said.

JAKE

I didn't say that.

ERHARD *(indicating Paul)*

That's what he said. Pretty stupid what he said, isn't it? If you *thought* it was gold and you stamped gold on it, then it's really gold. That's what really counts, what you intended. Right?

JAKE

It doesn't make it authentic, but it doesn't make me dishonest. It doesn't make me a liar either.

ERHARD *(to the group)*

I'm taking all this time with this bullshit because I want to accomplish something. No matter what I bring up, somebody will have a thing about it. Somebody will be nutty about it. No matter what they're saying, it's obvious these two guys are intelligent. But they've got their foot nailed to the floor, so it's like talking to stupid people. Being stuck makes you stupid. There's no power available where you've got your foot nailed to the floor. All this conversation regarding intention, in response to my simple statement about authenticity, indicates that there's some nuttiness there. The point is, at some point, you will be that person.

(to Jake)
And to settle this conversation: I ask you to stand in—that a person who presents himself one way, and in fact acts another way, for any reason, is inauthentic. That's not true. It's a "take the case that" I'm asking you to stand in. Is that clear?

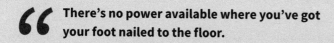

There's no power available where you've got your foot nailed to the floor.

Jake nodded and then sat down.

ERHARD *(to Paul)*
Did you get what I said to him?

PAUL
Yeah, so, what you're saying is that specific instance you didn't do what you said, you're inauthentic, and I would agree with you there, but...

ERHARD
I don't want your agreement. I want you to create this square.

(drawing an imaginary square on the floor in front of Paul)
Inside that square is a different world. Inside that world, when you act one way and present yourself another way, that's inauthentic.

PAUL
Specifically, or generally?

ERHARD
Generally. Just in that world. It's not true in the rest of the world. Can you handle that?

PAUL
Yeah. I'm not sure what it applies to, but...

ERHARD
It doesn't apply to anything. Can you handle that?

PAUL
Yeah.

ERHARD
Stand in that square and listen to what I say next. Because only standing there will what I'm about to say make any sense. All right? You ready to stand in that square?

(to Paul)
You ready? So in that little square, I know it's not true, and it's not that way in the rest of the world, and for those for whom one and one is two, when you pretend to be one way and act another, that's called inauthentic. When you own up to this, that's being authentic about your inauthenticity. Anybody not get that? That's the beginning of authenticity. *Authenticity does not*

AUTHENTICITY

Here Erhard provides a counterintuitive, but very Heideggerian premise: authenticity is possible only with the development of an authentic relationship with our own inauthenticity. Here authenticity is an act of ownership, of owning the calculative clearing which we are, of accepting the particular gift of Being whose sending characterizes our epoch. Heidegger introduced this idea in *Being and Time*, where he employed the term "resoluteness" to characterize Dasein's state of having-appropriated; he described this resoluteness as an empowering authenticity toward one's own inauthenticity:

 Resoluteness appropriates untruth authentically. Dasein is already in irresoluteness, and soon, perhaps, will be in it again. . . . The irresoluteness of the "they" remains dominant, notwithstanding, but it cannot impugn resolute existence. (*BT* 345)

This idea lies at the heart of the appropriative event: in the context of having appropriated one's inauthenticity, that inauthenticity, which persists, is nevertheless transformed. It is an idea which defies our usual thinking: ontically, such a "transformation" can only be seen as blatant self-justification, a philosophically sophisticated rationalization for accepting one's worst nature. Ontologically, however, appropriation justifies nothing. Appropriation appropriates; it gives Being. Resoluteness, then, is "the opening up of human being, out of its captivity in that which is, to the openness of Being" ("OWA" in *PLT* 67). Much of The Forum is devoted to developing the possibility of a non-justificatory event of appropriation. ∎

begin with being authentic. Authenticity begins with being authentic about your inauthenticity. If you're ever going to have any degree of authenticity the only way to get there is to start with being authentic about your inauthenticity.

(to the group)
I'm not interested in your belief systems, I'm not interested in your values, I'm not interested in your principles. So no more conversations like I just had with Jake and Paul. I don't mean don't say anything, I mean don't preach. I'll do all the preaching in here, and if I'm any good, I won't do any either. All I'm asking when I talk to you about the things I'm talking about is: build a square, stand inside of it, look out at life and the world and see what you can see standing in that square and standing in that possibility. If it empowers you to stand there, keep it. If it doesn't empower you to stand there, destroy it. Simple.

BELLA

You said to someone else that something happened when they were a child. I remembered. My father was a liar, and I decided I could never be that. I had to be honest. I've had no freedom to keep my word.

ERHARD

You can't be anything you're forced to be. Anything you are forced to be, you aren't.

BELLA

I couldn't stand the feeling.

ERHARD

Yeah.

(to the group)
Who couldn't stand being a liar?

(several raise their hands)
You think a truth teller would find lying absolutely abhorrent? For the person who tells the truth you don't have any problem with a lie, it's only somebody down in the swamp, in the bottom of the Valley of the Shadow of Death, who is afraid they might be a liar. I know you know better.

BELLA

I am a liar.

ERHARD

Yeah. You are a liar. That's being authentic about being inauthentic. And that's the beginning of authenticity—and the beginning of the freedom to tell the truth.

> **All I'm asking when I talk to you about the things I'm talking about is: build a square, stand inside of it, look out at life and the world and see what you can see standing in that square and standing in that possibility.**

ERHARD *(to the group)*

I know most of you don't get that, but never mind. Just listen. What today and tomorrow is about mostly is about being authentic about being inauthentic. So there are a couple of things to get. One: you present yourself as someone who keeps your word, but in fact you are someone who does or does not keep your word depending on whether you feel like it. Is that the truth about you? I told you I don't know the truth. See if it's empowering—like trying on a robe. Two: when you can wear that robe, that's called being authentic about your own inauthenticity. Always, the beginning of authenticity is being authentic about your own inauthenticity. I want you to treat the promises in here differently from usual. I want you to say *"regardless."* When it's all over, maybe you will, maybe you won't. Sincerity is pure story. I'm asking you to engage in these promises as a matter of integrity, not sincerity. As a matter of fact, standing in the background is always the possibility that you may not. But then you won't, and that's that.

At 3:12 pm, The Forum adjourned for a second break.

SESSION TWO INTERVAL

Dasein: Meaning and Mineness

Dasein is Martin Heidegger's name for the central figure in his 1927 *magnum opus, Being and Time*. The term is one of the few in Heidegger's writing that consistently remains untranslated from the German: the most literal translation of *Da-Sein* is *being-there*. Scholar Hubert Dreyfus suggests that the best way to understand Dasein is to think of "our term 'human being,' which can refer to a way of being that is characteristic of all people or to a specific person—a human being" (Hubert L. Dreyfus, *Being-in-the-World* 14).

But the term *being-there* itself indicates the essential characteristic that distinguishes humans from other beings. Dasein is being-*there* because it is the only being *for whom its Being is an issue.* Humans are the beings who reflect upon themselves, and the only ones who exist in a world of *meaning*. We dwell in a meaningful "*there*," and we *bring our "there" along with us when we show* up. Other beings inhabit the earth; human beings live in a world.

This is a challenging and essential aspect of the thinking Heidegger is developing here, and a distinction that emerges persistently over the four days of The Forum. The meanings of the things in our world are *not properties of the things themselves.* Non-human beings are "entities whose kind of Being is of a character other than Dasein's," and therefore they must be understood as "*unmeaning, essentially devoid of any meaning at all*" (*BT* 193). When Heidegger says that "*only Dasein can be meaningful or meaningless,*" he is saying that *other beings can have or lack meaning only when they are encountered by Dasein and are thereby disclosed as meaningful or not* (*BT* 192–193). Consider: a dog may not be "a dog" for another dog, nor may the dog see "beauty" in a sunset. Dasein is the only being in whose world there is meaning. Only for human beings do things show up as the things they are.

Further, Dasein is the only being for whom existence is always an issue, and the issue for each Dasein is always fundamentally its *own* existence. Heidegger calls this human characteristic *mineness:* the Being of human beings, while it characterizes the ontological nature of the collective, always occurs as the Being of *a particular* human being. Therefore, while Dasein is not a person, we have to talk about it as if it were: "Because Dasein has *in each case* mineness, one must always use a *personal* pronoun when one addresses it: 'I am,' 'you are'" (*BT* 68).

Each Dasein relates to this existential situation in a particular way. "Mineness belongs to any existent Dasein, and belongs to it as the condition which makes *authenticity and inauthenticity* possible" (*BT* 78, emphasis added). That is, my

Dasein is always mine, but whether or not that relationship is authentic—as Werner Erhard would put it, whether I *own* the condition of mineness, or whether it owns me—depends upon an act of existential choice. The purpose of The Forum is to bring participants face-to-face with that choice, thereby making available the possibility of authentic existence.

FORUM DAY ONE: SESSION THREE

The Forum resumed at 4:00 pm. Erhard was not present for this session. During the first half-hour, The Forum Supervisor, Julie, oversaw a procedure that took place in every Forum (but is currently not practiced in The Landmark Forum): participants raised their hands, section by section, to request rides or places to stay during the four days of The Forum, and other participants responded with offers. This process having been completed, Kipp came onto the platform. He introduced himself and Wes as the two Forum leaders who would be leading The Forum with Erhard, and then turned to the next order of business: the promises and requests of The Forum, which Erhard had mentioned earlier in the day. Julie, the Course Supervisor, came forward.

JULIE

We're asking you to give your word—to make certain promises—and to keep your word—to keep the promises.

The required promises:

(1) Regarding speaking in The Forum: Raise your hand, speak into the microphone. Don't talk to each other during The Forum.

(2) Wear your name tag at all times. Get the name on the tag correct.

(3) Take no notes. No tape recorders or cameras, no busy work at your chair, no food/drink in the room. Exception: Forum leaders may take notes.

(4) You agree to maintain the confidentiality of The Forum. This includes names of participants and their remarks. Keep in mind that confidentiality in a group of this size cannot be guaranteed.

(5) Regarding videotaping: if you didn't earlier sign a video release, sit in the no-video section.

(6) No resale agreement. All materials in this program are the property of Werner Erhard and Associates, in some instances protected by copyright. You agree not to resell, modify, package, and deliver in a seminar, training program, workshop, consulting, or similar business activity. This protection extends beyond the copyright law.

(7) Informed consent. The Forum is not therapeutic in design or intent. Forum leaders are not trained mental health professionals. A series of questions was included about participant's status with regard to therapy. If you're in therapy and winning, advise your therapist. If not, or if you've been hospitalized for drug or alcohol abuse, we recommend you don't take The Forum. In the form you signed earlier there is a list of emotions which may come up during The Forum; if you find them threatening, don't take the Forum. If you have a problem dealing with stress, don't take The Forum. Certain medical conditions and certain drugs are also listed in this category. This informed consent is intended to have legal significance.

KIPP

Are there any questions regarding the ground rules?

PARTICIPANT

What are the reasons for the rules?

KIPP

Everything that we design is not meant to suppress you. It's meant to provide maximum possible benefit for you from The Forum.

PARTICIPANT

I'd like to know why we're spending so much time on logistics. I'm angry.

(applause from some of the group)

KIPP

So you have no question? Thanks.

Following the required rules, an opportunity to leave was announced. No one did.

KIPP

Your sitting in your chair is a promise, and we will relate to you on the basis that you have given your word.

JULIE *(continuing to read the recommended promises)*

(1) Be present for all sessions. We recommend that you be on time in the morning and back from breaks. If you miss any part of any Forum session, you forfeit the right to expect the results of The Forum.

(2) Do not consume drugs and medications—including alcohol, aspirin, marijuana, but not including those prescribed by your doctor—before the end of the fourth day of The Forum.

(3) Stay awake during The Forum. Staying awake is easier if you don't slouch or slump in your chair. If you get sleepy, we recommend that you sit straight in the chair with your eyes open.

KIPP

A distinction has started to open up in the room: *I'll try* vs. *I'll keep my promises*. This distinction was not merely about words. We're not asking you to speak a certain way. We're showing you a distinction of an empowering way to be with promises.

JULIE *(continuing to read the suggested promises)*
(1) Eat only during the one announced meal break. Eat a big breakfast.
(2) Don't sit next to someone you knew before The Forum started.
(3) Advise us of the phone number where you're staying this week.

Assistants distributed phone information cards.

PARTICIPANT

Is gum chewing forbidden in The Forum?

KIPP

How many drops of pee does it take to spoil the stew?

PARTICIPANT

One.

KIPP

Get it?

PARTICIPANT

I know I should say yes. I know the group is the stew. Am I the pee?

KIPP

You're at a moment of choice now.

(to the group)
What are some reasons for being in The Forum?

PARTICIPANTS *(several calling out)*

So my speaking is a possibility for people; Because I know there's more out there; etc.

KIPP

Now let's hear some things you could *fix* from being in The Forum.

Again, people called out answers, a series of standard benefits similar in quality to the first group of responses.

KIPP

Neither of these provide you with what work The Forum has for you. A reason for being here, or something to fix, won't provide you with what you need to be in The Forum. So we're going to have to think of being here in a new way, a way you're going to have to invent rather than discover. Namely, *what you're willing to put at stake*. You can't ever find something at stake. You can only invent it, create it. It's a creative act, it's a self-generated challenge which you create for yourself. And that's who you are for The Forum. Some of the tools you need for this we haven't developed in here yet. The first place you will look is at what's wrong with you. Let that be. This is confusing because it requires real thinking. Your reasons got you here but they are no longer sufficient. During the meal break, I invite you to create what you're willing to put at stake.

(pausing)
This works. We're not wondering anymore whether The Forum works. We're promising you that you can have anything you are willing to stand for having gotten in The Forum. And the access to that is your willingness to put yourself at stake here in The Forum. This requires *speaking*. You *speak yourself* in the matter. The first action which it requires is speaking, speaking what you're putting at stake. And the second part is to promise to *be your word*. Have a conversation with others at dinner about this: if your life were an *expression*, what would that expression be? The Forum won't provide you with what's possible out of a reason for being here. At-stakeness is something that exists the moment you create it as a possibility. What we're asking you to do is to begin to create your life. What you're willing to stand for in here is what you have at stake.

PARTICIPANT

What's the difference between The Forum and positive thinking?

KIPP

Remember that "stop thinking" exercise we mentioned earlier? Try to make all those thoughts positive. It's a difficult thing to do, trying to make something you have nothing to do with positive. Like, "Oh my God! There's a bad thought! It's supposed to be positive!"

(to the group)
During the meal break, you are to create what you are willing to put at stake like a possibility. Have a conversation with another person and with who you are going to have dinner with.

Following this discussion, Julie came onto the platform and announced a meal break at 6:20 pm.

SESSION THREE INTERVAL

Yankelovich Study Results

Prior to the delivery of The Forum presented in this book, Werner Erhard and Associates (WE&A) commissioned a study by noted social scientist Daniel Yankelovich, wherein he analyzed the results reported by graduates of the course. By the time the results of the study were published, circa 1991, Erhard had sold WE&A to his employees, and that company today is called Landmark. Here is the summary of those results and Yankelovich's analysis.

An Analysis of The Forum and Its Benefits
A Yankelovich (DYG, Inc.) Study

Summary

Internationally recognized social scientist Daniel Yankelovich surveyed more than 1300 people who completed The Forum during a three-month period. Prior to their course, people were asked what they expected to achieve in the course; after their course, they were asked about the benefits they actually received.

The study explored four areas: the value of The Forum, the profile of participants, satisfaction levels after The Forum, and unexpected benefits that were experienced. A few of the findings include:

- More than 90% of participants report practical and enduring value for their life — well worth the time and cost.
- More than 90% of participants report a better understanding of relationships and their role in them.
- Nearly every participant received unexpected benefits — ranging from achieving personal and professional goals.

"Several of the study's findings surprised me quite a bit, especially the large number of participants for whom The Forum proved to be 'one of the most valued experiences of my life.' This is not a sentiment that people, particularly successful, well-educated people, express lightly. I can understand why people recommend The Forum to their associates, friends, and relatives."

Daniel Yankelovich, Chairman
DYG, Inc. (public opinion analyst)

Daniel Yankelovich, Chairman of DYG, Inc., a noted social scientist and public opinion analyst, as well as a leading researcher of values and future trends who has been conducting these kinds of studies for more than 30 years, did an analysis of the survey.

The following charts indicate the value reported from The Forum, the benefits most often cited as a result of their participation, and their level of satisfaction.

Daniel Yankelovich is a leading interpreter of trends shaping American society and the global economy. He is the author of 10 books and chairman/founder of three organizations: Public Agenda; DYG, Inc.; and Viewpoint Learning. His pioneering work has earned him numerous awards in the field of public opinion research.

"More than 7 out of 10 found the course to be one of their life's most rewarding experiences. To me, this suggests that it addresses many of people's most profound concerns — to improve their personal relationships, how to be a more effective person, how to think productively about their lives and goals."

Value of The Forum

The degree of value to which participants felt the course had in the areas listed below:

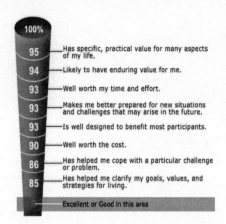

100%
95 — Has specific, practical value for many aspects of my life.
94 — Likely to have enduring value for me.
93 — Well worth my time and effort.
93 — Makes me better prepared for new situations and challenges that may arise in the future.
93 — Is well designed to benefit most participants.
90 — Well worth the cost.
86 — Has helped me cope with a particular challenge or problem.
85 — Has helped me clarify my goals, values, and strategies for living.

Excellent or Good in this area

Satisfaction Levels

The degree to which The Forum fully met the expectations of those attending for these reasons:

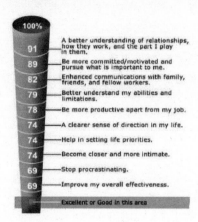

100%
91 — A better understanding of relationships, how they work, and the part I play in them.
89 — Be more committed/motivated and pursue what is important to me.
82 — Enhanced communications with family, friends, and fellow workers.
79 — Better understand my abilities and limitations.
78 — Be more productive apart from my job.
74 — A clearer sense of direction in my life.
74 — Help in setting life priorities.
74 — Become closer and more intimate.
69 — Stop procrastinating.
69 — Improve my overall effectiveness.

Excellent or Good in this area

Unexpected Benefits

Nearly every participant in the Yankelovich survey reported receiving some entirely unexpected benefits from The Forum. These benefits ranged from specific educational to business goals. Unexpected benefits were most frequently noted in nine areas:

1. Greater confidence and self-esteem
2. A new ability to express thoughts and feelings, both publicly and privately
3. Job is more enjoyable and satisfying
4. Better relationships with co-workers
5. More comfortable and at ease with others
6. Less concerned with the approval and opinion of others
7. Better relationship with parents and family members
8. Overcame a fear or anxiety
9. Have more fun in life

Profile of Participants

These charts indicate the distribution of participants by age, educational level, and occupation. The greatest number of participants are in their mid-twenties to mid-forties. On the whole, they are very well educated, with 87% indicating some college work, well over half having completed college, and 20% holding postgraduate degrees. Participation is distributed fairly evenly between women and men, and among married, single, and previously married adults.

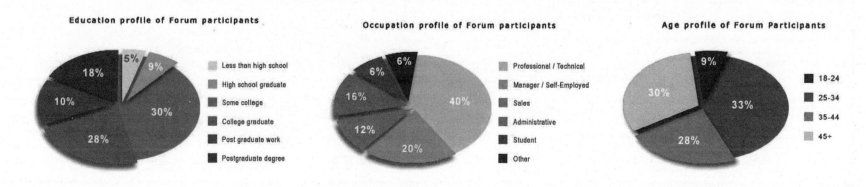

Education profile of Forum participants
- 5% Less than high school
- 9% High school graduate
- 18% Some college
- 10% College graduate
- 30% Post graduate work
- 28% Postgraduate degree

Occupation profile of Forum participants
- 6% Professional / Technical
- 6% Manager / Self-Employed
- 16% Sales
- 40% Administrative
- 12% Student
- 20% Other

Age profile of Forum Participants
- 9% 18-24
- 33% 25-34
- 28% 35-44
- 30% 45+

Areas of Greatest Impact

Before attending the workshop, we asked participants to indicate areas where they felt they needed improvement. Very few people felt they needed a great deal of improvement in many of the 68 areas we questioned. Yet after the workshop, many participants realized that they could improve themselves and their job performance dramatically in ways they hadn't considered before the workshop. The ranking below shows the areas where the workshop had the greatest impact.

Pre-Workshop results represent the percentage of participants saying, "I feel this is an area that needs a great deal of improvement." These percentages were obtained by combining the top 2 points of a 5-point scale.

Post-Workshop results represent the percentage of participants saying, "The workshop has made a dramatic and positive difference in my intention to take action in this area." These percentages were obtained by combining the top 2 points of a 5-point scale.

Being able to acknowledge mistakes fully and do what is necessary to correct them.
8%
84%

Being fully committed to my company's success.
1%
76%

Having high standards of quality for myself and the people who work with me and for me.
5%
66%

Confronting difficult situations head-on instead of avoiding them.
15%
75%

Always listening carefully and attentively to other people at work.
16%
75%

Being as concerned with the performance of my department/division and the company overall as I am with my own performance.
14%
69%

Always being responsive to the concerns of those who work for me.
13%
67%

Being quick to give recognition to others for the work they do.
9%
62%

Welcoming constructive criticism from others.
18%
70%

Being very effective in communicating work related issues with my co-workers.
18%
69%

Being good at letting other people get all the credit they deserve.
7%
58%

Feeling free to be frank and open with those who report to me.
12%
62%

Top Benefits Received

After completing the workshop, we asked participants to assess its impact on 68 specific areas having to do with responsibility, performance, communication, leadership, and job satisfaction. The ranking below reports the top benefits received.

"The workshop has made a dramatic and positive difference in my intention to take action in this area"

These percentages were obtained by combining the top 2 points of a 5-point scale, where "1" represents "The workshop has made a dramatic and positive difference in my intention to take action in this area" and "5" represents "The workshop has made no difference in my intention to take action in this area."

Being able to acknowledge my mistakes fully and do what is necessary to correct them.

84%

Being fully committed to my company's success.

76%

Having a clear understanding of the vision, objectives, and strategies of my company.

75%

Being as fully productive as I am capable of being.

75%

Confronting difficult situations head-on instead of avoiding them.

75%

Always listening carefully and attentively to other people at work.

75%

Endorsing the vision, objectives, and strategies of my company.

74%

Always seeking out ways to improve my performance.

71%

Endorsing the goals and priorities of my department/division.

70%

Being confident in my ability to be innovative at work.

70%

Welcoming constructive criticism from others.

70%

Being as concerned with the performance of my department/division and the company overall as I am with my own performance.

69%

Being very effective in communicating work related issues with my co-workers.

69%

Top Benefits Received - By Category

Participants in the workshop reported receiving many benefits. Below is a ranking of the top benefits received in each of the five categories: Responsibility, Performance, Communication, Leadership, and Satisfaction.

"The workshop has made a dramatic and positive difference in my intention to take action in this area"

These percentages were obtained by combining the top 2 points of a 5-point scale, where "1" represents "The workshop has made a dramatic and positive difference in my intention to take action in this area" and "5" represents "The workshop has made no difference in my intention to take action in this area."

RESPONSIBILITY

Being fully committed to my company's success.

76%

Having a clear understanding of the vision, objectives, and strategies of my company.

75%

Endorsing the vision, objectives, and strategies of my company.

74%

PERFORMANCE

Being able to acknowledge my mistakes fully and do what is necessary to correct them.

84%

Being as fully productive as I am capable of being.

75%

Confronting difficult situations head-on instead of avoiding them.

75%

COMMUNICATION

Always listening carefully and attentively to other people at work.

75%

Welcoming constructive criticism from others.

70%

Being very effective in communicating work related issues with my co-workers.

69%

LEADERSHIP

Always being responsive to the concerns of those who work for me.

67%

Developing excellent relationships with those with whom I work.

65%

Being able to impart to others a larger purpose to the work we do.

62%

SATISFACTION

Feeling that I am a valued part of the company.

59%

Being very enthusiastic about taking on new projects.

59%

7:50 pm: Erhard's manner was light and casual as he opened this session, interrupted by a number of people who were returning late from the meal break. The first participant to stand shared that in looking for issues to put at stake, he found that his issues were already big enough and did not feel he needed to invent new ones. Erhard noticed an empty seat and began to manage people missing.

ERHARD

I made up my mind not to call you assholes any more, but I want you to know it's very hard. Speaking about issues and what you can have at stake...

(drawing a large circle on the chalkboard)
Let that circle represent everything there is to know. Everyone in The Forum is successful. We know from independent studies of The Forum that participants are above average in their ability to succeed. So a certain amount of what is in this circle you know, and you know that you know.

(drawing a small wedge in the circle)
What we do to be successful and able is we put what we know to use. That's what common sense tells us to do with what we know that we know. But there is also some stuff that we don't know, and know that we don't know.

(adding a larger wedge)
The older I've gotten, the more I know I don't know. Common sense tells us that to find out what we know that we don't know, we need to go to school, read a book, take a seminar. I'd like you to see that you really fit that. The rest of the pie is what you don't know that you don't know. What does common sense tell you to do about that? Nothing. Common sense is silent on that subject. What The Forum is about is what you don't know that you don't know—what's behind you that you can't see. The purpose of The Forum is to provide access to what you didn't know that you didn't know. In independent surveys, people have reported that The Forum is the single most dramatic learning experience in their life.

(drawing a point on the second chalkboard)
When you take a point, which has zero dimensions, and extend it into the first dimension, you get a line.

(drawing a line extending from the point)
You don't get a bigger and better point. Then, when you extend the line into the second dimension, you don't get a bigger and better line: you get a plane.

(drawing out from the line to form a square)
And when you extend a two-dimensional plane into the third dimension, you don't get a bigger and better plane, you get a three dimensional figure, in this case, a cube.

(building from the square, Erhard drew a cube)
Almost invariably, the results of our life are results from extending ourselves on the same dimension. But adding a new dimension is an exponential leap. *You want to listen up here and get this!* The Forum doesn't push out on the dimensions of living already available to you. What

FORUM DAY ONE: SESSION FOUR

it does is *add* a dimension. So there's an exponential leap in the possibility of Being. And that's maybe why there are these outrageous claims people make about what they got from participating in The Forum.

PARTICIPANT

Couldn't you add a fourth slice to the pie? Intuition? What you know but don't know that you know.

ERHARD

Yes, that's very legitimate. You didn't get the point about dimensionality?

(adding it to the model on the board)
In a *point*, you have no degrees of freedom. In a line, one dimension, you get one degree of freedom, and so on, and we simply expand on that one degree of freedom. The Forum adds a new dimension. You get an exponential leap of possibility.

PARTICIPANT

It's what you don't know that you don't know.

ERHARD

Exactly.

PARTICIPANT

How do you get there?

ERHARD

You're in here four days and one evening. You'll see how it's done by the end of the third day. Anybody else here not get this dimensionality?

PARTICIPANT

Could you say that what The Forum does is to "unconceal" a new dimension?

ERHARD

Yes, that's a technical term for it. It's called unconcealing. What begins to get you into this domain of "don't know that you don't know" is to dwell in the power of the question. We're hungry for answers, addicted to answers. People hate being in the question; they want the answer. You don't get answers. Light gets shed on what you are concerned with. That's not the way you and I are usually. The way you and I are is hungry for answers. What do I do about it? The beginning of gaining access to what you don't know that you don't know, the beginning of establishing a new dimension for being, a new dimension for living, is to start to dwell in the question, develop the courage and the stamina and the wherewithal to orient yourself around

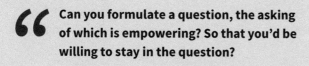

Can you formulate a question, the asking of which is empowering? So that you'd be willing to stay in the question?

ERHARD (*continuing*)

questions the asking of which makes a difference. There are certain questions, just the asking of which impacts people's ability in life. See, you and I don't look for those questions, we look for answers, which you can only find in what *you know* that you don't know. This is about developing questions the asking of which gives access to what *you don't know* that you don't know about your life, about other people, and about living. The Forum is about developing a certain muscle for asking questions the mere asking of which makes a difference.

Here Erhard read a passage from Heidegger's *On the Way to Language* (page 13), in which Heidegger recounts his dialogue with a Japanese scholar:

ERHARD (*reading*)

"Japanese: We Japanese do not think it strange if a dialogue leaves undefined what is really intended..."

(*to the group*)

That's not very familiar to most of us, is it? In our dialogues we want to get definition very quickly. We want it explained.

(*continuing to read*)

"...or even restores it back to the keeping of the undefinable.
Inquirer: That is part, I believe, of every dialogue that has turned out well between thinking beings. As if of its own accord, it can take care that that undefinable something not only does not slip away, but displays its gathering force ever more luminously in the course of the dialogue."

(*to the group*)

That means putting it back into "don't know that you don't know." It's a harmonic with what I read you earlier about the unspoken. See, what you're looking for here is light, not answers. Insight you can't create by the numbers. What you want if you're going to create is light, not answers. Listen up, goddammit!

(*continuing to read*)

"Our dialogues with Count Kuki probably failed to turn out so well. We younger men challenged him much too directly to satisfy our thirst for handy information."

(*to the group*)

You're here listening for answers. You're listening for what we call "tips." Nothing worthwhile in life can be gotten there by ten steps. Or twenty steps. You can't dance knowing where to put your feet.

(*continuing to read*)

"Inquirer: Thirst for knowledge and greed for explanations never lead to a thinking inquiry. Curiosity is always the concealed arrogance of a self-consciousness that banks on a self-invented *ratio* and its rationality."

(*to the group*)

What that all means is that this greed, this thirst, the question, "How am I going to use this?"— that's a product, according to this guy, of a concealed arrogance, an arrogance that everything

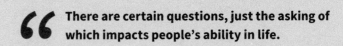

There are certain questions, just the asking of which impacts people's ability in life.

in life that's worth knowing is merely an extension of what I already know. But the truth is that everything worth knowing is going to violate what you know.

(continuing to read)
"The *will* to know does not *will* to abide in hope before what is worthy of thought."

(to the group)
I think all there is, is having thoughts. But there are certain things that if you stand in front of them in a certain way, give you thinking. If you stand in front of things worthy of thought you get thinking. Thinking is a dance with that about which you are thinking. When you stand in front of questions worthy of thought, you get thinking. Now that's tough, because we're in the rainstorm called "I think." We're all Cartesians. No one's had an original thought since then about thinking—at least not one that has gotten to you or me. You and I are still Cartesians. But there are possibilities beyond Descartes. And they give you access to a new way of being that you can't get to—being the kind of person you already always are. We're going to be thinking. That's the way The Forum works. It goes backwards.

PARTICIPANT

What about disciplines that promise "inner transcendence"?

ERHARD

Inner transcendence. That's what California is about. I don't want to insult your pet project, but I am not a guy in a diner about getting someplace. And you aren't going to get there leaping over being human. There's no possibility of being beyond what you already always are until you own what you already always are. Californians don't like that. Californians have this magical bullshit they believe in. That's not the way The Forum works. The Forum's got two pieces to it. The first is an inquiry into the already always being of human being. What kind of an opening are you for life? What's the color of the clearing you are for life? To say that more rigorously: what is the already always condition of being for human beings? What did you get yourself into here? Not your individual version of being human. That's the question of ninety percent of The Forum. That's called going backwards. It's about owning yourself as you already are. Being authentic about inauthenticity is particularly frightening for Californians. We don't want to be inauthentic. Why? Because it looks bad. And I don't like looking bad. And your life is about looking good. This is moving backwards to own what I already always am. This is not individualistic except that each of us has his or her own version, we got wet in this rainstorm called human being. *What is it to be a human being?* See, people don't ask that question. They want to be thinner, younger, sexier. Those questions don't give thinking. Because it is a question worthy of thought it creates the possibility of thinking.

(pausing)
The Forum is two questions. The first: what is the already always being of human beings? Being human owns you. It gives you your life. The second half of The Forum is another question. The second question is, what is the *possibility* of being for human beings? What's possible beyond what I was given to be? I did what's called in Zen the low road. In the low road you must do *everything* that doesn't work. So I'm not a guy in a diner about the low road. Most people want

> **There's no possibility of being beyond what you already always are until you own what you already always are.**

ERHARD (*continuing*)

to start with the second question. But you can't get to the possibility until you own what you already always are. The pathway—concrete, authentic, real—is to embrace what you already always are.

(*pausing*)

The problem is that if you move forward from where you are, all you're doing is *changing*. The medium in which you create may be something, but the source of creation is *nothing*. I had the privilege of having a relationship with Dick Feynman, the physicist. He took one note the whole time I knew him: "There are certain things you can only know by creating them." As a matter of fact, when he died that note was on his blackboard. That was just my best moment.

(*pausing*)

When I use the term *possibility*, I mean stuff in the dimension of "don't know that you don't know." So that's what The Forum is about. In the first question, you move backwards. And it begins with being authentic about your own inauthenticity. To the degree that you're not able to be with your own inauthenticity, to that degree you are unable to be. Where's Jake? I want to identify the conversation we were having. He's a fine guy. And yet, I'm saying that there's something possible in that area he has a lot of interest that is denied to him because he can't be "I don't do what I said I would do." I didn't say that was true about him. That's not important. What's important is that he can't be there yet. Whatever you're not able to be with won't let you be. So the degree to which you are not able to be with your inauthenticity, to that degree you are prevented from being. You're stuck being this, so there's nothing else you can be. Or you're stuck not being that, so there's nothing else you can be except not that. You're like a Johnny one-note "not-that." *Not-that* is way more attached than *have-to-be-that*.

PARTICIPANT

I get this as a dance. I'm uncomfortable. I don't know where to put my feet. It's extremely uncomfortable to be in that "don't know that you don't know."

ERHARD

So "don't know that you don't know" is uncomfortable. Ever jumped out of an airplane? It's uncomfortable. It's also a lot of fun.

PARTICIPANT

I'm starting to ask myself, "what is worthwhile?"

ERHARD

That's a great question: A question to live with. If you live with that question for the rest of your life, your life will have a quality that it won't have without it. You ask the question for the light the question gives.

> To the degree that you're not able to be with your own inauthenticity, to that degree you are unable to be.

CONCERN

In introducing the distinction *concern*, Erhard is articulating another hint at the realm of Being the Forum is designed to evoke. As with his earlier conversation about moods, he is relocating the source of participants' problems from their own agency to the contextualizing background.

In *Being and Time*, Heidegger makes a similar move when he says that "Being-in-the-world has always dispersed itself or even split itself up into definite ways of Being-in." To develop this point, he provides a list of examples, such as having to do with something, producing something, attending to something, undertaking, and considering. "All these ways of Being-in," he says "have *concern* as their kind of Being" (*BT* 83).

Heidegger also distinguishes a category that he calls *deficient modes* of concern, in which "the possibilities of concern are kept to a 'bare minimum'" (*BT* 83). Deficient modes include leaving undone, neglecting, renouncing, and taking a rest.

In everyday use, the word "concern" can have several meanings. The most common in our current usage is apprehension, as in "I am concerned for the success of our project." But Heidegger and Erhard have used the term in another way, as a term for an *existential* characteristic of human beings, "a possible way of Being-in-the-world."

Just as human beings are never not in-the-world, they are likewise never not concerned, since *they are concern essentially.* Consider: you cannot locate yourself outside of your concerns, since the very attempt to do so is itself a manifestation of concern. Like lightning, which exists only in flashing, a human being exists always and only as a body of concerns.

With this distinction, both Heidegger and Erhard are undermining our everyday understanding of the meanings in our world. In so doing, they are preparing the way for the final transformational leap, the evocation of the Nothing. ∎

PARTICIPANT

That's just life.

ERHARD

It's life in the fast lane. "The more things change the more they remain the same." That's true. And we'll look at why that's so.

PARTICIPANT

There's fun in engaging with this even though I don't know what I'm doing.

ERHARD

I don't know what *I'm* doing. Would you want to dance knowing what you're doing? But in our culture, you're not allowed not to know. It's shameful not to know. It's the way we already always are. There's an opportunity to develop a certain relationship with not knowing in here that will give you a more powerful access to what is worth knowing. With me? Thanks.

(pausing)
I'm not going to call on anybody for a while. We're going to introduce a new what-you-call subject. We're going to introduce a new what-I-call *distinction*. When this is all over, you'll call it that too. The distinction is *concern*. The usual meaning of concern is "worried about." When I use the word concern I use it in a broader sense. You and I are constituted by a body of concerns, kind of like what we attend to.

Erhard drew an X on the chalkboard.

ERHARD *(continuing)*
X is a symbol that represents one of your concerns. X could be "being related."

(responding to a participant asking for clarification)
It could be said that human beings are constituted by a body of concerns. The word *constitutive* means something more than "is a part of." It means something like "gives the thing itself." It's like your concerns give you your *self*.

PARTICIPANT

It gives the essence of my self...

ERHARD

You've got to watch because I'm going to say "no" to damn near everything you're going to say, and everything you say is good, but it's not quite it. We're not going to get this nailed down and I'll show you why in just a second. You're in the right ballpark. You're fine.

(pausing)
So X represents one of your concerns. Let's just say this represents the concern for being related. Everybody's got this concern. A hermit expresses this concern by saying "I'm not related."

ERHARD (*continuing*)

You've got a concern for being related otherwise why would you be concerned about not being related? Clear?

(*pausing*)

What is our access to what concerns us? Our access to what concerns us is to get at what concerns us in its aftermath. After the thing happens, in hindsight, we can understand. You can't even see it before it happens, can you? The already always access that human beings have to their concerns, the access you inherited, is something like this...

To the right of the X Erhard listed *description, definition,* and *explanation.*

ERHARD (*continuing*)

...All of which, will lead to understanding.

(*adding "understanding" to the list*)

And out of understanding you derive prescriptions, which gives you guidance for how to deal with what concerns you: *ten steps to...* Now, you haven't *articulated* all your prescriptions, have you? Because a lot of your prescriptions are contained in the way you *are.* They're set in you. *You want to get this!* This is one of those things you have to get. This conversation's got to be there for the whole Forum.

(*pausing*)

So you've got, for example, golden rules about relations, such as "keep them happy," "do something so they're attached to you," et cetera. You and I have got great prescriptions. And what you can predict out of that is that you and I will get better and better at that. A rat can learn how to negotiate a maze by finding a piece of cheese, but will choose a new tunnel if the cheese is moved. The difference between a human being and a rat is as follows: a human being will go down the tunnel with no cheese *forever.* You know, you've been doing the same shit year after year after year, hoping for a different outcome. What you care about is being in the *right* tunnel, regardless of whether there's cheese or not. Doing the same thing over and over again expecting different results. That's the definition of insanity.

(*turning to the chalkboard and indicating the empty space to the left of the X*)
Nobody looks over here, *before* it happens.

(*writing the word "source"*)
That's where it's generated, that's where it's created. *You want to listen up to this next part. Wake up! Wake up!* When you get to the *source* of something you are no longer limited by it. That, by the way, is a part of how this works: by getting to the source of things.

(*to Wes and Kipp*)
I promise that tomorrow I will give them one answer—*the* answer to what those guys on mountaintops in Tibet are looking for.

(*pausing*)
We're going to get at concerns from the source side. You don't get description, definition, explanation, and prescription—you just get power. You don't get a PhD out of here. Plato and Socrates killed that kind of research anyway. They tried it and found out it didn't work. You read

Lee Iacocca and Al Newheart's books? They would give everything they've got if they could give what they've got to you. Why can't they?

(pointing to the right of the X on the chalkboard)
Because they write the book in this language, the language of description, definition, and explanation. Because people don't buy books they can't understand. That's why we took your money before you got in here. When I talk about power I'm talking about something like the freedom to be, not force, which is the negation of power. I saw a film of a Japanese Judo master, and never once saw that man stop to think. And I watched the film over and over. The guys he was fighting stopped to think and got thrown. He was acting out of *being* something. His opponents, on the other hand, were acting out of knowing the answers. You see, you can't throw somebody unless they're set some way.

(moving away from the board)
We're going to talk about another critical thing: *the listening that you are.* I know you've got questions and comments, and I know some of it didn't go clunk for you yet. That's all right. We'll get there. I talk in a language designed and crafted to give access to what concerns you at its source. Now I want to talk about the *already always listening* that you are. What is the listening you already always are? For the moment, in this conversation, what you *are* is a listening. In the normal course of events, I talk to you like you're an empty vessel. That isn't the way it is. The vessel's already full, up to the top. It only admits certain things and it expels other things. It changes certain things. You and I are an already always listening.

(pausing)
When I got this distinction already always listening—not a concept or an idea, but a distinction; I'm teasing you with that word and you'll find out about it tomorrow—I began to look at what is my already always listening. It was very clear to me. The already always listening I was, was "I know." I was even a bigger pain in the ass in those days, and a smartass to boot. The only thing I ever heard was what I already knew. You *wake up* a certain listening. Your job on this break will be to discover the listening which you already always are.

(pausing)
Who can see already what your listening is?

PARTICIPANT
The already always listening which I am is that I understand you completely.

ERHARD
Very good.

PARTICIPANT
I'm not good enough.

ERHARD
A lot of us share that one: "The listening I'm going to provide for you is 'I'm not good enough.'"

Already Always Listening

This is a core distinction of The Forum, a hint that works together with other distinctions (e.g., mood and concern) to relocate participants' understanding of the source of meaning in their lives. It asks participants to consider that the way they hear (and see) events and people in their lives is a function of their listening, rather than being sourced by the people and events themselves.

It would be possible, of course, to engage in a similar conversation using a more familiar psychological model. Such a conversation would assert that one's perceptions are shaped by one's attitudes. This way of framing things would be immediately accessible to anyone whose understanding has been shaped by the Cartesian paradigm of an "internal" subject in an objectively meaningful world.

But locating the source of meaning in one's *listening* rather than in one's mind situates the process *in the world* rather than "in the heads" of participants. This furthers the development of the Heideggerian model of human being as Being-in-the-world. Participants in Werner Erhard's work are frequently coached to "stay out of your head," and to "get present." In Erhard's vocabulary, "in your head" is equivalent to "in the past." This is where the nature of one's already always listening is determined: one makes decisions about people based on past events ("he's untrustworthy," "she's controlling," "they never listen to me"), and these decisions shape the way life occurs in the future.

Erhard has used the analogy of yellow sunglasses, worn for an extended period of time: eventually, you forget that the sunglasses

PARTICIPANT

I'm going to figure out what you're saying wrong.

ERHARD

There's a lot of crap in school. I don't want to put the school system down. I have a lot of respect for teachers. But one of the things you find out in school is that you're either smart or dumb. However, there's no such thing as dumb. I did some work in a school for the disabled. One student, Jesse, was considered "uneducable." It was decided, however, that he was educable enough to be sent to a school to learn to wash cars. On the day I was there, I was told that Jesse had stuffed a teacher in a trash can. As a consequence, he got sent back to the home for disabled students, where he could sit around, be friendly, and play. Stupid is a way to survive in school. Stupid is an act, a racket.

PARTICIPANT

The already always listening that I am is "I don't want to and you can't make me."

ERHARD

You want to get this. A lot of people listen through "life is hard." A lot of people listen through "life is a burden." My dentist told me about his experience as a Boy Scout. No matter what the scoutmaster had suggested—hiking, swimming, going home—the Scouts always had the same response: "OH NOOOOOO!" You *are* this listening. That's the clearing you are in which life happens.

PARTICIPANT

Mine is "How can I use this?" "How can I get better?"

ERHARD

Almost everybody's like that: "How can I use this?" Almost all the power in the world can't be used. People don't use power. Power uses people.

PARTICIPANT

"What are you going to tell me new that I don't already know?"

ERHARD

Great.

PARTICIPANT

My already always listening is "How can I help you? Do you like me now?"

ERHARD

Beautiful.

are the cause of the world's yellowness. Like the sunglasses, one's way of listening remains invisible because it is always and already determining one's point of view, making the way a situation appears become the way things are. The aim of this inquiry is for participants to notice these already always ways of listening in as much specificity as possible. The Forum proposes that the fundamental elements of human listening are widely shared, even across cultures; Erhard asserts that there is a "culture of human being" that transcends national boundaries. All human beings, for example, listen for positive assessments of themselves, and for evidence that they are right in their beliefs about the world. But individuals develop specific variations, and in this part of The Forum dialogue participants are encouraged to discover their own. In this way, the dialogue continues to turn participants toward themselves in an intensely reflexive process. ■

PARTICIPANT

My already always listening is "I'm very clever and I'll prove it to you."

ERHARD

See, there are times when "I'm very clever and I'll prove it to you" is a very workable listening. But if you're already always "I'm very clever and I'll prove it to you," there are a lot of occasions that doesn't match.

PARTICIPANT

I have several of these. My listening is that "I'm not good enough."

ERHARD

"I'm not good enough" almost always has got another listening, which is "I'm better than you are." "I'm not good enough but I'm better than you are." You want to listen up. These guys are being authentic about their own inauthenticity. These are not nice people. They are cold, calculating, conniving people. They are out to get you to like them. And it's not *them*. They didn't invent that. And if this is the opening that I'm providing for the world to occur in, it's not surprising how the world shows up. We have done some work facilitating meetings between American and Soviet representatives. We discovered that the already always listening of the Americans is "You can't be trusted for your word; now let's talk." This made the results predictable.

PARTICIPANT

My always already listening is "I'm too smart and too quick, and I better not let anyone know that."

ERHARD

It's the "already always way of listening." I keep losing why the order is important, but there's some significance to the order. What is the already always listening that gives you being the way you are? Believe it or not, the way you are is given to you by your listening.

PARTICIPANT

"You're boring."

ERHARD

We're going to take a break. I want you to consider that the way you are is given to you by your listening. I'm inviting you to get down to the already always listening, you know, as deep as you can, however deep that happens to be. Clear?

The Forum adjourned for the final break of the day at 10 pm.

SESSION FOUR INTERVAL

Jargon

Erhard's influence on the language of Western culture has been significant. His terminology, like Heidegger's, has always been unusual and highly purposive, and many of these words and phrases made their way into the public sphere, some to lasting effect. But that language, in its casual use, began to lose its power. Heidegger detailed this process of devolution in *Being and Time*:

> **In the language which is spoken when one expresses oneself, there lies an average intelligibility; and in accordance with this intelligibility the discourse which is communicated can be understood to a considerable extent, even if the hearer does not bring himself into such a kind of Being towards what the discourse is about as to have a primordial understanding of it. We do not so much understand the entities which are talked about; we already are listening only to what-is-said-in-the-talk as such. What is said in the talk gets understood; but what the talk is about is understood only approximately and superficially. . . . Idle talk is the possibility of understanding everything without previously making the thing one's own. . . . Thus, by its very nature, idle talk is a closing-off, since to go back to the ground of what is talked about is something which it *leaves undone*. (*BT* 212–213)**

Erhard's comments in a 1986 interview, discussing the evolution of his own language use, echo Heidegger's account of the process by which terms lose their originative power. Many of the words he had used in his work, Erhard said, "eventually drifted into popular use." They "lost the creative intention behind them and degenerated into a kind of jargon." Outside their original context, as Heidegger put it, the terms no longer reached out into the "totality of involvements" in which their significance was grounded (*BT* 200).

This was the fate of the term "transformation," a central term to which Erhard had assigned "an extremely precise meaning." Today, he said, "you hear it everywhere. You read about it in business journals. It's 'hot.' So, to some degree, it's lost its potency." He continued:

> **I hardly use the word "transformation" at all any more. . . . because while it once was a word that people had to think about, struggle to grasp, work on, that's just not true anymore. The word no longer wakes people up. Now, when you say "transformation," the word puts them to sleep—like they know what it means—they stop thinking, looking, inquiring.**

Instead, he said, as his ontological inquiry has developed, "the notions keep getting said differently" (Simon, "Quarterbacks and Coaches: Tossing It Around with Werner Erhard," *Family Therapy Networker*, March–April 1986, 30–39).

Heidegger addressed his own confrontation with this situation in his essay "A Dialogue on Language," a transcript of his conversation with a Japanese scholar. At one point Heidegger (referred to in the transcript as the Inquirer) mentions two of the ideas that were central in his early work, hermeneutics and phenomenology.

> **[*Japanese*]: I am all the more puzzled that you have meanwhile dropped both words.**
>
> **[*Inquirer*]: That was done, not—as is so often thought—in order to deny the significance of phenomenology, but in order to abandon my own path of thinking to namelessness.**
>
> **[*Japanese*]: An effort with which you will hardly be successful. . . .**
>
> **[*Inquirer*]: . . . since one cannot get by in public without rubrics. ("DL" in *OWL* 29)**

What is essential in both Heidegger's work and Erhard's is what is unspoken and therefore essentially nameless. Much of Erhard's work during the four decades of its evolution may be seen as the development of new rubrics (distinctions) to replace those that have devolved into jargon, such that what is said makes present what cannot be said in words.

FORUM DAY ONE: SESSION FIVE

The Forum resumed at 10:30 pm. Erhard began by inviting questions from the participants. One participant, reviewing The Forum, shared that his already always listening had altered as a result of that experience.

ERHARD (*addressing the group*)
He's got a possibility beyond his thrown listening. He got it by owning his thrown listening. There's something called *getting off it*. This is a sacred thing. To get off it is sacred. Now, what does getting off it mean? It means he's not constrained to entertain that listening. He can hear himself listening and *get off that listening*. When his already always listening comes up, he is able to own it, to embrace it, to be responsible for it. In the normal course of events, if I found out my already always listening was disempowering I would try to stop it. He didn't change it. That's the big secret. Because when you change it, nothing changes.

(*shifting tone*)
This is a "you-gotta-get-this." So listen up.

At the chalkboard, Erhard placed the chalk on the surface and moved it, so that the chalk ended in a different place but a line remained indicating the path of its movement.

ERHARD (*continuing*)
Change persists. When you're different, what persists? That which you're different than. So when you're different you're the same, because the thing from which you're different is still there. The more difference, the more persistence. If you're *really* different, the thing you're different than has a big persistence. If I'm a nice guy as a solution to a problem, the problem for which being a nice guy is a solution stays in place. About ninety-nine percent of what you are, you became as a solution to a problem. Education is a solution to being stupid. When you solve a problem, what persists is the problem.

(*to the participant*)
So your listening that altered hadn't solved the problem of your already always listening.

(*to the group*)
He had embraced it. He was able to *be with* the problem.

(*drawing two tangent circles on the board*)
Can you imagine putting two solid objects in the same place at the same time? If you did that, what would happen? They would disappear. Push them into

the same space—the space between them—and they will disappear. Anything you can let be will let you be. There are no accidents of being. You've got to be there for it, open for it, available for it.

DAVID
I wanted to recognize that I haven't really been listening.

ERHARD
Recognition is the beginning. When you recognize your own already always listening, you're on the field. The game's not over, but you're on the field.

DAVID
What do I do with my realization?

ERHARD
Nothing. It'll do something with you. It'll give you something you didn't have before. Most of you ought to be able to map what David said onto your own listening.

Here Erhard called Kipp to the platform to conduct the next exercise; Erhard remained nearby, interrupting occasionally to reinforce a point.

KIPP (*to the group*)
Your job is to sit in your chair, and when I say "now," describe to yourself whatever's happening right now.

(*pausing*)
Now.

(*a minute of silence*)
Okay, plenty of data. Let's have a few people report what they are experiencing now.

PARTICIPANT
I'm bored and I don't want to be here.

PARTICIPANT
I'm analyzing a lot.

ERHARD
It's not you analyzing, it's *it* analyzing, because you can't stop it.

PARTICIPANT
What am I supposed to do now?

PARTICIPANT

I noticed I was really exhausted.

KIPP

So what you just did was unconceal a fundamental condition that human beings are. I asked you to sit in your chair and think about what's happening *right now*, and what did you do? By the time you get around to describing what's happening right now, it's gone. Yet everybody stood up authentically, honestly, and described what happened *then* but said it was what is now. There's *no description* available for now. So you've got to have the *representation*. But what's present is clearly distinct from the representation. And what it is to be a human being is not to have that distinction. This is what happened at the party before you got here. The domains of presence and representation got collapsed. The moment you say what *was* happening is what *is* happening, the representation starts to shape the presence.

ERHARD

What's the difference between now and your representation of now? You can never describe presence because there's no description in the realm of presence. If this isn't making sense, don't worry. The valuable stuff in here will not make sense. But it's valid. "Make sense" means "fits with what you already know." To get what doesn't make sense requires thinking. What Kipp is trying to get you to get is that you don't make any distinction between love as a presence and love as a story. Is there anybody in the room who can't see that existence as a presence is different from existence as a concept or representation?

(pausing)
Life exists in the world of concepts and life exists in the world of presence. But that's misleading, because the two get collapsed. Something happens, like a "what happened." And that devolves into a concept. What happened back then is never present like a presence. But that's not clear to you. You think you're dealing with what happened when what you're really dealing with is your story about what happened. One is not better than the other. The problem is when they get mixed together. This creates a *vicious circle*: the concept of your previous experience now becomes a filter for your next experience, which is now a little less free because it is conceptually shaped. The conceptually shaped experience reinforces the concept; the reinforced concept more fully shapes the experience. I'm trying to drive out this seventies bullshit that there's something wrong with your head. I'm an anti-human potentialist. I'm not saying that you're stuck in the concept. I'm saying that you're stuck in the vicious circle. I don't want questions. I want to know: "Did you get that?"

(pausing)
Good. Everybody got that. So now we're going to demonstrate what happens when you've got that distinction. Once you get a distinction, it uses you. *Three distinctions to get*: one is the realm of existence called presence. The second is the realm of existence called concept or representation. The third is the vicious circle. The vicious circle is constructed by a collapse of the first two domains.

(pausing)
We're going to play a new game. We're going to do a survey. How many of you are tired?

(a majority of participants raised their hands)
How many of you have a headache?

(calling on a young woman named Diane)
Would you be willing to participate in a demonstration? Then please come up here onto the platform.

Diane sat in the second director's chair that an assistant placed alongside the first.

ERHARD

Would you be willing to have your headache disappear?

DIANE

Yes.

ERHARD

And would you be willing to not know *why* it disappeared?

DIANE

Okay.

ERHARD

Please close your eyes. How long have you had your headache?

DIANE

Since before the dinner break.

ERHARD

How big is it?

(hesitating, she holds hands outstretched)
Where is it located?

(pointing to her left temple)
What color is it?

DIANE (*hesitating*)

Brown.

ERHARD

If it had a geometric shape, what would it be?

DIANE

Triangular.

ERHARD

How much water would it hold?

DIANE

About a pint.

ERHARD

On a scale of one to ten, where is it?

DIANE

Six and a half.

ERHARD

Why do you have it?

DIANE

Because it's been a long day.

ERHARD

Headache and long day live in different realms. You have collapsed them. So, why do you have a headache?

DIANE

Because I've been sitting still.

ERHARD

So you've got two domains collapsed. Every time I ask you that stupid question "Why?" it collapses the two domains.

(*repeating this series of questions several times*)
How's your headache now?

DIANE

It's a four.

ERHARD

How much water would it hold?

DIANE

Still a pint.

ERHARD

It's critically important that you get it. The headache *now* and the headache *a moment ago* are collapsed together. When she says the headache is "*still*" a pint, I know she has collapsed the headache now with the representation of the headache then.

(*continuing to question her regarding the headache's shape, color and location right now*)
Do you have a headache?

DIANE

No, I don't.

ERHARD (*to the group*)

What happened was, I asked her questions which in order to answer she had to be in the presence of her headache like a *presence*.

DIANE

I focused on it.

ERHARD

No! What happened was you got the domains uncollapsed. All that happened was that the headache, instead of showing up in the vicious circle, showed up distinct in the domain of presence. You looked at your headache. You were present to the headache. There are no reasons when the headache is like a presence.

A second demonstration followed with Patricia, a participant who said she was tired. She sat in one of the director's chairs; Erhard sat on the arm of his, facing her.

ERHARD

How tired are you on a scale from one to ten?

PATRICIA

A four.

ERHARD

Do you know why you are tired? Notice I didn't ask you "do you *think* you know why?" I asked if you know why you're tired.

PATRICIA

No.

ERHARD

What's the relationship between the reasons you have for being tired and being tired? There isn't any. The reasons are valid. In other words, in the world of reasons every reason you have is a valid reason. You don't have any nutty reasons.

(turning to the group and speaking in a loud voice)
There's no such thing as tired! That's a concept!

(back to Patricia)
Where in your body are you experiencing what you used to call being tired?

PATRICIA

My arms.

ERHARD

And where else in your body?

As Erhard repeated the question, she responded each time by identifying a tired area of her body.

ERHARD

Nothing much conceptual about this, is there? It's all presence.

PATRICIA

My arms are still tired.

ERHARD

For a while there you were really looking. But then you got to thinking about it. Whenever you say "still" or "also"... See how easy it is to collapse the domains?

(continuing to question her)
You were at a four when you started this. Where are you now?

PATRICIA

Three.

ERHARD

Good. We're going to leave you at three.

(returning to her seat as the group applauded)
For how many people in the room is something starting to move?

(many hands raising)
For how many people in the room is nothing starting to move?

(more hands)
How many people are at maybe, can't tell?

(still more hands)
You know where you should be? Where you are?

(pausing)
I'm going to give you an assignment which will determine how much you get out of The Forum. I got your money. I can't lose. You can lose. The point is: you have a chance to enhance what you get out of here. *Bring your life in here tomorrow.* Don't bring the face you brought today—the "I've got it all together" face. Bring in the face that's authentic about your own inauthenticity. What has it cost you in life to collapse those domains? What you're bringing in tomorrow is your inauthenticity.

(pausing)
We didn't talk about looking good today, did we? We're going to do it in thirty seconds. *You have a major concern for looking good.* For some people looking bad is looking good. So when you come in tomorrow, be able to talk about where in your life are you used by looking good. Looking good owns your life.

(pausing)
The four-day format of this Forum is both an asset and a liability. The liability is that there aren't five days between the weekends for you to be back in your lives and talk about your experience. You have got to communicate what's happening for you here. You have got to be articulate in this conversation. Tonight you've got to talk about this to other people. You've got to begin to be able to generate the conversation. You've got to be able to *speak* this. You don't have to explain it. You want to be in communication about this like an experience, like a presence. I know a lot of people who understand this and don't live it.

PARTICIPANT

It is very late and I am tired.

ERHARD

Do you think I give a shit that you're tired? We're talking about the rest of your life and you're sitting there complaining about being tired. That's disgusting. You are disgusting.

(pausing: to the group)
Now that I've got your attention. . .

(repeating the assignments)
Let me leave you with a reminder. I have already gotten everything I need out of this Forum. You have not. You need to be twice as powerful tomorrow. The way to be twice as powerful is to do these assignments. You gave your word to be here on time tomorrow. Is that clear? You gave your word to be on time tomorrow regardless of the circumstances, is that clear?

(to a participant who was standing at the back of the room preparing to leave)
What are you doing at the door with your hat and coat on? You need to be back in The Forum so we can end The Forum.

The participant returned to her seat in palpable silence.

ERHARD

Thank you.

The first day of The Forum ended.

END OF DAY ONE INTERVAL

Reflexion: The Cartesian Deficiency

At the outset of *Being and Time,* Martin Heidegger makes a point that might otherwise be dismissed as obvious: any inquiry into the nature of Being—such as Werner Erhard's project, or Heidegger's own—must always be conducted *by human beings,* who as far as we can tell are the only beings who have a concern for the matter, as well as the only ones who are capable of inquiring. Humans are therefore involved at multiple points in the inquiry—as the beings who are questioning, as the beings *of whom* the question is asked, and as the beings *about* whom the question is asked.

This point is important because of its implications for the inquiry: it will be characterized throughout by *reflexion.* Reflexion, or self-referentiality, is an important idea in the work of both Heidegger and Erhard. The term designates a state in which we are turned *toward* our selves, as when confronting a reflection.

Reflexion requires, first of all, self-consciousness. To say that human beings are the only beings for whom their being is an issue, is to say that human beings are the only beings who are self-conscious—or, to say it more simply, *we are the only beings who have a self.* While the consciousness of other animals is likely always to remain a mystery at some level, it is generally agreed that dogs do not reflect upon their existence. Here, Heidegger emphasizes the centrality of such reflection to human awareness:

> " **Consciousness is self-consciousness, and self-consciousness is ego-consciousness or "we"-consciousness. The essential thing in this is the re-flexive, and in it the "I," "we," "self," the presentation-to-self and *self-production.* (*EP* 64)**

Two points in this passage should be noted. The first, like many points that arise in an ontological inquiry, can seem at first both apparent and trivial: one's consciousness always includes consciousness of one's self. That is, in being aware of my world, I am always at some level aware of my self as the center of my awareness. It is worth taking a moment to notice this, because the nature of the self, and the quality of its *presence* in human awareness, will become a central topic as The Forum proceeds. Clearly, there are moments in life when one's self-consciousness becomes intensified, resulting in either pleasure or discomfort, depending upon the circumstances. There are also moments when we experience freedom from self-awareness. The difference between these two states is relevant to our inquiry here. Where does the self live when it is not alive in our awareness?

This leads to the second point made here by Heidegger, one which is generally less apparent than the first: self-reflection is at the same time self-production: "The essential thing is 'I will myself'" (*EP* 64). The human self is not like the human elbow: it is not a ready-made part of the package that accompanies an infant's arrival in the world. What *is* included in the package, although not immediately functional, is language, which provides the material with which we are eventually able to *produce* a self. But in a world of beings with selves, questions about the nature and stability of the self arise persistently, and recent advances in the study of the human brain, as well as child development, have informed the inquiry but have not answered the questions. Therefore we note the point here as a question to be kept open as The Forum proceeds.

Regarding the phenomenon of reflexion, Heidegger says further that it is "Man's settling down in one of his essential places," and he notes with emphasis that it is characterized by "certainty, certainty" (*EP* 60). That is, for the most part, human beings are made both secure and comfortable by the condition that their self-knowledge provides. While many of us spend considerable time tinkering with the details of our identities in the interest of self-improvement, on the whole those identities give us security. On the whole, we are *at home in ourselves.*

This, at least, is the way of things in the current paradigm. This interpretation of the self, however, while *self-evident* to most of us, is an artifact of a particular way of understanding human being. Indeed, it has been the dominant understanding for several centuries; and while it is increasingly questioned among people who think actively about these matters, such as philosophers and other scholars, it remains the operative understanding for most people in the world—not as something they bring to mind, or could articulate, but as a way of functioning in their everyday lives.

This particular way of understanding the world, and our place in it, is generally known as the Cartesian paradigm. It is so called in recognition of the man in whose thinking the model was crystallized, the seventeenth-century French philosopher and mathematician Rene Descartes. As a philosopher, Descartes' job was to engage in thought experiments; and in one of those experiments—which turned out to be significant for all of us—he decided that he would place everything in the world *in doubt.* His purpose in doing this was to discover what, if anything, was *indubitable:* what in the world, in the face of committed skepticism, could retain a quality of absolute certainty?

The outcome of this experiment led him to the formulation that has come down to us as his most famous statement, one familiar to almost every university undergraduate although generally without a clear idea of its implications: *I think, therefore I am* (or in Descartes' original Latin, *Cogito, ergo sum*).

That is: if I doubt everything, the only thing of which I can be certain is that I am the doubter. I can know nothing with certainty except *myself,* as the one who is thinking. Further, since I am the only certainty, I am also the inevitable arbiter of what counts as real. In the Cartesian model of human being that emerged from this experiment—the model that today we inhabit unthinkingly—the *cogito,* the "I," the being who thinks, is the grounding certainty at the center of things. It is the *subject* (Latin *subjectum,* what lies beneath), while *out there,* independent of the subject, is a world of o*bjects (objectum,* over against). For humans, Being-in-the-world demands that we determine the true meanings of those objects. Heidegger scholar Michael E. Zimmerman describes the situation this way:

 Although Copernicus had only recently shattered man's illusions about being the center of the physical universe, Descartes established man as the *ontological* center: henceforth, the reality of the real was what *man* asserted it to be. . . . "To be" meant to be conceived by and through the subject. . . . Everything got determined and evaluated from the *standpoint of man.* ("Beyond 'Humanism': Heidegger's Understanding of Technology" 222)

It is this paradigm, of the fixed and self-certain human subject, that both Heidegger and Erhard are placing in question through their work. As Heidegger *points out,* Descartes arrived at his conclusion by accepting as given the nature of the *sum*—Being, the "I am." But Heidegger proposes that the nature of "I am" has never been fully worked out in the history of Western philosophy, so that behind Descartes' conclusion "there lies hidden a failure to master the basic problem of Being" (*BT* 127).

The Cartesian model itself was the result of an experiment in reflexive thinking. The heart of the subject–object distinction is "I think something" (*EP* 62) a premise that turns thinking back upon itself, toward the "I," and thus toward "the presentation-to-self and self-production" (EP 64). Presentation demands production, since the "I" is not there to be reflected upon. In reflecting upon my self, I create my self.

But in the Cartesian model, the subject is self-certain—that is, certain of itself as an entity that persists. The clearing for creation has been occupied. Therefore Heidegger proposes that self-consciousness, which has in Descartes' model bent back far enough to see its "I," must now bend back further and confront the *context* in which the "I" stands essentially, a context that puts its self's certainty in question.

As we will show, the culminating event of The Forum—the unconcealment of Being—is accomplished through the evocation of a profound bending-back, revealing not only the context of the "I," but in a masterful moment of existential rug-pulling, the context of that context as well.

SPEAKING BEING

DAY TWO

FORUM DAY TWO:

SESSION ONE

The day began at 9:00 am, with Julie, The Forum Supervisor, leading the participants through the process of filling out the Graduate Records form. Before the forms were collected, she asked the participants to stop writing, and Kipp mounted the platform (T-shaped, with stairs at the end of the center runway) and led a conversation about the Six-Day Course.* Following this hour-long conversation, Wes replaced Kipp on the platform to invite participants to share what they encountered when doing the assignment given at the end of Day One.

WES
Good morning. We're going to begin with sharing. Would someone repeat the three assignments Werner gave you last night?

MAC (a participant in a wheelchair)
You're one of the leaders of this Forum. This program has been going on for seventeen years with hundreds of thousands of people, which means you have had many hundreds of Forums. To keep us here to one o'clock means for me that after doing my homework I wasn't able to get to bed until a quarter till three. I request that you organize yourselves, as we must organize ourselves, so that we can leave here by eleven instead of one o'clock.

WES
I got your suggestion.

MAC
But are you going to do anything about it?

WES
The Forum will probably end between eleven and one am.

---

*▶ **NOTE:** The Six-Day Course originally was included as part of what was called the Ten-Day Teen Training, first delivered in June 1973. In addition to the four-day est Training, six days were devoted to various physical challenges such as riding zip-lines and repelling cliffs.

The Six-Day Course that Kipp discussed here at the beginning of Day Two of The Forum was first delivered in March 1977 for adult graduates of the est Training, and continued to be delivered through the transition to The Forum in 1985, up until June 1991 when the last Six-Day was held.

Some elements of the course were included (though significantly revised) in what became the Landmark Advanced Course, first delivered in 1991. This course still (as of 2019) serves as the second of four parts of Landmark's Curriculum for Living, the other two parts of which are The Landmark Forum in Action ten-session seminar series and The Landmark Self-Expression and Leadership Program.

MAC

So you're not going to do anything about it.

WES

No, we're not going to follow your suggestion.

MAC

Well at least I got it off my chest.

WES

There's something at stake here which is much more important than an hour or so of sleep.

MAC

For some of us, sleep is important to function.

WES

Yeah, yeah, it'll get worse.

(laughter)

Who can repeat the assignments?

(some raising their hands)

Who cannot repeat them?

(others raising their hands)

Now, who can repeat the assignment and share about it?

SIENNA

Share your experience with someone in The Forum. Bring areas to work on, inauthenticities. And look at areas of your life where looking good uses you.

WES

Look at the possibility that looking good has used your life. Which one do you want to share about?

SIENNA

I want to share about looking good, and the way I look good goes back to the already always listening. I have a presence that is an act about knowing, about knowing it all.

WES

Without this distinction you are dealing with, we tend to put our knowledge and our information in a box, and we don't see that we use that box for something, we make the box itself right,

> ▶ **NOTE:** See the beginning of Session Three of Day Four, where Mac comes forward to share what he had gotten out of the course.

and we don't see how we use the box to be right, which makes us very ineffective, by the way. Whatever power knowing has, whatever power information has, the power becomes displaced by the motivation behind the gathering of it.

SIENNA

What I do then is spend a lot of time judging whether they are acting as if they know, or acting as if I know, even when I don't know, which makes it very upsetting for me yesterday and this morning, that there's a piece of me that knows that what's critical for me, you know Werner said to focus on where you were upset or confused. And I'm attracted to that area in the circle that I don't know that I don't know. And when I'm in my act of having to know, it is so critical to my success that I'm willing to say that I know when I don't. And then I miss the opportunity to create solutions when I'm in my act "I already know."

WES

Brilliant. She's creating "creativity," and she knows she can't step into that domain, because the very thing that keeps her from stepping into that domain is this thing, that she's "*got* to know." But if you're going to create something, you can't know what you're going to create. That's the area of creativity: you can't step into it unless you're willing to give up what you previously knew. This is a major issue people have a breakthrough with in the creativity seminar.

(to Sienna)

That's great.

SIENNA

There's another thing about the act and inauthenticity, which I have become very sophisticated in. I decided at some point about people who are assholes, who stand up and challenge authority, and I decided all that stuff was inappropriate. And yet one of my inauthenticities is that I walk around knowing that I know a lot more than anyone else. But if I said that, that would mean being an asshole: and so I've cloaked it. But it's worse because it's indirect. And then I walk around worried that people will find out what I don't want them to find out about me. It's silly because it's probably written all over me.

WES

They won't acknowledge it because the unspoken agreement with your friends is that you won't call them on their inauthenticity and they won't call you on yours. That's what it means to have a friend. You'll let that slip by. The other agreement is that your friends are willing to listen to your racket. Today you'll find out about your racket.

(to the group)

She is sharing an aspect of her racket. It's a technical term. I don't know if we mentioned it yesterday, but here's how to listen to people sharing in here. You should listen to the participants' shares like that's you in some way speaking. Even if the person sharing is female and you're male. The Forum is not about men and women as men and women as much as it is

WES (*continuing*)

about human beings. And I'm inviting you, like a possibility, to see your humanness in anybody speaking, and let something open up for you. So who can see an aspect of themselves in what she just shared?

(*many people raising their hands*)

SIENNA

I'm also, when I'm in this place of knowing and acting that way, and not being willing to say I know more than you do, that I'm very insulated about sharing with people, like yesterday, like I didn't want to talk. And I felt very separated from everyone. I didn't want to see as far as seeing that my already listenings were similar to other people's in the room, but I didn't want to see that it wasn't even them and me. I always felt like those things were always kind of special, like the chosen few and not just being human, like everybody. And that separates me, in a way that means that I don't share when I'm confused, and people don't really know what's going on with me. It's like I'm missing all that. I'm both missing something about being related to people, and I also see how I'm stuck there, and that it is important, unless I want to stay here being stuck. I can't have both.

WES

Thanks. Very useful. Look around the room. You should notice that in a Forum of about 500 people, there are probably around 20 or 25 hands up. Hands down. Here's something you want to get off of real quick. It's called participating in The Forum. It's called sharing in The Forum. The first thing you should know is The Forum isn't real. This is not real life. Now, we're going to sit here for four days, kind of in this artificial environment. What's the point? The point is what goes on after in your life. This is *coaching for your life*. But you've got to begin it here. And the way you begin it here is to start participating, start sharing. It's okay if you kind of mess it up a little in here, you see, this isn't real. But there's something at stake in here. You have to confront what's at stake for you in here. She just shared something that few people ever see about themselves, that their life is about knowing something so as to look good. And the few people who get that ever, get that it's killing their life. So here's a woman who shared something that's going to open up her life. That's what's happening in The Forum. Are you willing to participate? Okay, who's willing to participate?

(*calling on five people who stand*)

PHOEBE

I was sure that with all these people putting their hands up I wouldn't get picked. But I got picked.

WES

Yes.

PHOEBE

It was safe to do what everyone else was doing. Also, part of my act for looking good is to be very appropriate.

Being-in-the-World: Being-With

Werner Erhard emerged into public attention during a period characterized by some as a decade of Narcissism, a period when the culture's emphasis on self-understanding and personal empowerment led to the emergence of what has been called the "Me" generation. As a result, Erhard's work was sometimes tarred with that brush.

For the authors of this book, however, a significant element of The Forum experience has been the atmosphere of affinity and connection with others that inevitably emerges among participants as the course moves toward its conclusion. Certainly, individual empowerment is a significant element of the transformation that The Forum makes available. But this empowerment is consistently accompanied by an experience of profound relatedness to others, which then encourages a commitment to community contribution. To use a metaphor often employed by Erhard, the individual empowerment and the sense of connection are as symbiotic in their emergence as the front and back of a hand.

In *Being and Time,* Martin Heidegger locates the source of that connection in the nature of Dasein's Being-in-the-world.

As noted previously, Dasein, as the clearing for Being-in-the-world, frees other beings to be the beings they are (see the sidebar "Being-in-the-World: Being-in" in Session One of Day One, as well as the Interval "Dasein: Meaning and Mineness" at the end of Session Two, Day One). A dog can be a dog only for a human being; only for a human can a sunset be beautiful. But also among the entities freed by Dasein to be in the world are other human beings—entities which are "like the very Dasein which frees them, in that *they are there too, and there with it*" (*BT* 154).

These terms—*with* and *too*—are to be understood *existentially*. That is, Being-there-too does not mean merely that the Others are present-at-hand in the world, available to be encountered. Heidegger is not describing a situation in which beings are located alongside each other in world space; rather he is distinguishing integral elements of the beings themselves. *Withness* is a part of Dasein's Being—my own Dasein, and the Dasein of Others. The "too," says Heidegger, means a "sameness of Being" (*BT* 154).

Heidegger makes precise use of hyphenation in languaging the ontological world-structure he is proposing. Early on in *Being and Time,* he specifies that Things—substances, equipment, objects of nature—are *within the world*, a location-relationship that he indicates by the absence of hyphenation (*BT* 91). Here, he posits a further specification:

 Thus Dasein's world frees entities which are not only quite distinct from equipment and Things, but which also—in accordance with their kind of being as Dasein themselves—are 'in' the world in which they are at the same time encountered within-the-world, and are 'in' it by way of Being-in-the-world. . . . So if one would want to identify the world in general with entities within-the-world, one would have to say that Dasein too is 'world.' (*BT* 154)

So because Dasein—mine and the Others'—are in-the-world existentially, we can be encountered "in" the world environmentally.

Once again, we call attention to the deeply reflexive nature of Heidegger's ontological distinctions. His languaging repeatedly turns thinking back upon itself, since his goal is to have us bend back to see ourselves from a new perspective.

(referring to Sienna)

What she said, I felt I could identify with and so I felt that I had nothing to contribute. But for me to really get something out of being here, I really need to say it out loud. I seem to have the answer for myself and everyone, and I'm so busy looking good that I'm not getting my..., that having all the answers has killed off the possibility in my life.

WES

Like maybe you've killed your life.

PHOEBE

Yeah, that I'm so smart and that I've got it so figured out, that I have the answer and no possibility. And I noticed when we did our homework, last night and this morning, that all that kept coming up was lots of answers and no new stuff, which is what I think I got out of yesterday, the possibilities of what my life could be about. That's what I don't have is possibility in my life.

WES

Got it. Great. Thanks.
(another participant stands)

ROSS

I've been waiting for the right time to get up here and say something profound and so this is the right time, but it isn't anything profound.

WES

The wrong time is when it is profound, so you don't have to worry about it. How many are waiting for something significant, profound, before you're going to get up to share?

(many raising their hands)

We don't want your crummy shares! If you really listen you'll find that the most powerful shares are some of the simplest and dealing with the most ordinary aspects of our life. From the power and insight of The Forum to shed light on the ordinary aspects of our life, you'll find some of the most powerful things you've listened to. Thanks for acknowledging that.

ROSS

What happened for me yesterday and last night and I'm convinced, also while I was sleeping, was just the continuous looking again at all the beliefs, a lot of the things that I've been working on in this area, and opening up different possibilities for it, and starting really, one of the reasons why I came to The Forum was that I wanted to take a look at what the barriers were for my success. I've been successful in the past, I've been able to create the things that I've wanted, and then they slipped away, for whatever reason, and I really want to take a look at what those barriers were and what's been happening. All yesterday and last night, and this morning is, let's take a look at the distinctions. They're really starting to separate. I find that I spend a lot of time and energy in the story, and very little time dealing with what's happening.

WES

Yeah.

ROSS

And in the short time that I've been doing this, I've already noticed some openness come into the picture.

WES

Yeah, what if you lived your life totally in a story? Just consider that as a possibility. Now I know you can always find exceptions, but you know the exception only shows the rule. So don't look at the exceptions. Stand in the possibility that your whole life is a story. And as you get the distinction "story versus what happened," you might notice that life is passing by, and that you're in a story about life. You're not in life.

ROSS

There were lots of things that I took a look at last night and the major thing that I'd like to share with you is integrity... is probably one of my major inauthenticities, at least there's a possibility for that. And I'm real quick to pick it up in somebody else. Actually as a result of yesterday I've been able to look at some of the possibilities where I am not in integrity. I did an exercise with my daytimer, and I realized that all the things that are really important to me just didn't get done. And so there's one major commitment not kept, which I really felt to be important to me having accomplished.

WES

Great. Thank you.

MARSHA

Last night when I went home, I guess things were starting to get uncovered because I was so angry. My normal thing is to be the cheerleader and get up in the morning and get things done and extend myself so far wide that there's nothing left for me. It is starting to wear on me physically, and what I got last night was that I am so angry, so angry: at me. It came across at first last night, being so angry at Werner. I did the training 15 years ago, but if I saw Werner out in the parking lot last night I would have run him over. I was so angry. I chewed off my sister-in-law's head last night. It has never been expressed like this before, because it has been so important to me to express, to get across, "you don't like me and I'm going to make you like me," and that has taken a tremendous amount of energy, and what is underneath that is just a lot of anger.

WES

And anything underneath that?

MARSHA

I don't know yet. I'm just really into the anger now.

In Heidegger's account of Being-with, we find "world" pervaded by relatedness. The presence of Others is embedded in all of our everyday activities. When we are at work on a project, the Others for whom the project is being performed are encountered in the work. If we walk along the edge of a field, the field "shows itself as belonging to such and such a person." If I am at leisure, the book I am reading "was bought at So-and-so's shop and given by such-and-such a person, and so forth" (*BT* 154).

Heidegger is not making the obvious point that the book belongs to someone, but is emphasizing the degree to which the presence of my relatedness to Others imbues my existence. Others whom I encounter in these objects and activities are a part of my world and in the same way I am a part of theirs.

 By reason of this *with-like* Being-in-the-world, the world is always the one that I share with Others. The world of Dasein is a *with-world*. Being-in is *Being-with* Others. Their Being-in-themselves within-the-world is *Dasein-with*. (*BT* 155)

I am a clearing for the Other, at the same time that the Other is a clearing for me. Others make it possible for me to Be, a situation that persists even when no Other is present.

 Even Dasein's Being-alone is Being-with in the world. The Other can *be missing* only *in* and *for* a Being-with. Being-alone is a deficient mode of Being-with; its very possibility is the proof of this. (*BT* 156–157)

Thus Heidegger has distinguished in *withness* an extraordinary existential possibility for human relatedness, a possibility which we see as an essential element of The Forum transformation. Here he specifies another aspect of this connection:

 Being-with is such that the disclosedness of the Dasein-with of Others belongs to it; this means that because Dasein's Being is Being-with, its understanding of Being already

implies the understanding of Others. This understanding, like any understanding, is not an acquaintance derived from knowledge about them, but a primordially existential kind of Being, which, more than anything else, makes such knowledge and acquaintance possible. (*BT* 160–161)

Of course, says Heidegger, the factical development of my relatedness with another human being will always depend upon how well I have come to know myself. And here he makes a point that is significant for our understanding of The Forum dynamic: *self-knowledge, he says, arises from relatedness to Others:*

 Of course it is indisputable that a lively mutual acquaintanceship on the basis of Being-with, often depends upon how far one's own Dasein has understood itself at the time; but this means that it depends only upon how far one's essential Being with Others has made itself transparent and has not disguised itself. And that is possible only if Dasein, as Being-in-the-world, already is with Others. (*BT* 162)

We propose that the transformation that occurs for participants in The Forum is not an individual experience, but that the self-knowledge it makes available arises mutually with an understanding of others.

This is the function of The Forum's dialogic structure, in which even participants who do not participate overtly in the conversation are able to *find themselves in the sharing of others.* Forum participants are repeatedly exhorted to listen to others' sharing "like that's you in some way speaking." As the sharing continues, The Forum leader persistently deconstructs each participant's story about his or her experience, and frames the experience instead in the language of the distinctions being developed. The distinctions gradually reveal the ontological structures underlying the experiences, structures common to all of the experiences despite the differences in their details.

WES

You're present to your anger.

MARSHA

I'm very present to my anger. And I am not a nice person. I'm really getting that I'm, a couple people looked around here and "oh boy, what a bitch she is." And I'm saying, I am the biggest flaming bitch. And I've covered that up for a long time.

WES (*to the group*)

Consider the possibility that you are a "covering-up." I did not say you have a covering-up. I said consider the possibility that you are a covering-up. See, when she deals with herself, deals with the covering up; cheerleader on top of angry woman, but that's who she is.

At this point (10:30 am) Erhard appeared at the back of the room, and spoke in response to the conversation about covering up. His attire remained the same throughout The Forum: today the sweater-vest was olive-green, the slacks brown.

ERHARD

The way it works operationally is—it's something you're afraid you might be—is angry. There's always a something happened—always, always. However it is that you are, there's always a "something happened" that caused that. And almost nobody knows that because they come at the way they are from the conceptual side, from the descriptive side, from the explanatory side. When you get to the source of the way you are, there's always a "something happened." You put yourself together, fashioned yourself as you were growing up. We pay attention, particular attention to various aspects of what we call our selves, or what we might call, more accurately, your identity at various eras of our growing up. In a certain era of your growing up, you were building a certain part of your identity. And at another era you built another part of your identity. And then sometimes you go back and put the finishing touches on something you built earlier. But I want you to begin to be able to think that people are manufactured. You and I are constructed. Whatever it is that you're referring to when you say "I think," whatever the "I" refers to, you call that your self, or your identity—sometimes you'll call it your personality. But whatever is being referred to when you say "I think," "I feel," "I believe"; and it gets put together out of "what happened"; and there's a "what happened" for every piece of you. A lot of who you are, of how you got to be the way you are, and a lot of what maintains your identity is a product of what you're afraid you might be. Something happened in Marsha's life, and she decided it was wrong to be angry, or she shouldn't be angry, or only bad people are angry, or something like that.

(*Marsha is weeping; Erhard addresses another participant*)
Don't help her. Thanks.

(*continuing*)

And she decided that was wrong or bad or something she shouldn't be, and then she got to be afraid that she might be that, and so she had to keep that down in the swamp, at the bottom of the Valley of the Shadow of Death, and it's been there for years, and it runs her life: what she's afraid she might be. See I don't even know that she is angry. I don't know that the truth about

ERHARD (*continuing*)

Marsha is that she's an angry person. I know that's what's running her life. Once she's able to be with being angry, once she's able to give *being* to being angry, she might find out she's not angry at all. But "not being angry" is going to run her life until she's able to be angry. I know you don't get all that yet. You're starting to get it. As you go along today you will get it. Before you get out of here, you will get at the source of your identity. What happens if you get at the source of your identity, somebody with a yellow name tag?

Participant (*who is wearing a yellow name tag, i.e. someone doing The Forum for the first time*)

It doesn't own you anymore.

ERHARD

Yeah. It's that simple. This is something almost nobody knows. You're now one of the few people in the world that knows this. What everybody else in the world knows is that you've got to fix what's wrong with you, you've got to avoid what's bad, in you or in life. What you now know is any time you get at the source of something, you are no longer limited to it. Most people would be afraid to do what Marsha has done. They find anger so abhorrent, that they are afraid they might find out that they are angry. And they can't tolerate that, they can't be with that, and so they never get to the being angry like that's a possible way of being; they fight against being angry, they reject it. In the 70s you were supposed to let it all hang out. That's indulging anger, that doesn't work either. When you felt angry you were supposed to spray it all over the place on people. That's indulging the anger. That's as much bullshit as suppressing the anger. There's a thing called responsibility. As I told you yesterday you don't know what that means yet, but we'll get to it before we're done here. Something close to owning something, being able to be with it. So you want to take a look down in the swamp down there at what you're afraid you might be or hoped you weren't, or don't want to be. That's where the monsters are. The green slimy monsters of what you're afraid to be are running your life. Most of us would be afraid to get at it, because we're afraid we might *be* it. When you own that, at its source, it no longer owns you. We're afraid to get at it for fear that we might be it. What you're afraid of owns you. Marsha, what did you notice in there?

MARSHA

I notice that I'm angry at everybody and everything in this world.

Erhard (*to the group*)

You want to get the courage in that. She's angry waiting to happen: already always angry. It's all over the place. It colors the clearing in which the world occurs for her. And only to the degree she is willing to be with that, standing in front of 800 people and starting to communicate it, you're starting to be with it. That's a lot different than hoping you're not that. You were saying?

MARSHA

There isn't one person in this world that I'm not angry with.

ERHARD

And that's sad for you.

Through this process, as people in the room hear their own concerns repeatedly expressed in the speaking of others, not only do they gain a new way of understanding their own situation, but at the same time, through the mutuality implicit in the Forum's dialogic structure, the *witness* of Being-with-Others is gradually brought to presence. The dialogue of The Forum thus unconceals the possibility of a profound *relationship of Being* among human beings. This relatedness, we propose, is at a deeper and more fundamental level than the differences—of race, ethnicity, religion, or politics—that occur for us as persistent barriers to cooperation in all aspects of our lives. Erhard's work, and its expanding manifestation in the current programs of Landmark Worldwide, create the possibility for transcending those barriers. ∎

So you want to take a look down in the swamp down there at what you're afraid you might be or hoped you weren't, or don't want to be. That's where the monsters are. The green slimy monsters of what you're afraid to be are running your life. Most of us would be afraid to get at it, because we're afraid we might be it. When you own that, at its source, it no longer owns you.

MARSHA

Yeah, because I want relationships with people, and I can't get close.

ERHARD

Listen up here, because most of you are not going to have the courage for this. So you need to get it from those who do have the courage. That there's something sad for her about being angry—that's why she's afraid she might be angry, then it's all mashed in with being close. Convoluted in a knot.

MARSHA

My whole life has been an act about being happy and cheerful, giving and caring, getting everybody to like me, and they do. The truth is that I don't have an enemy in the world.

ERHARD

Hold on for a second. So if you're a person who has the skills that Marsha has, the skills of being related to people well, and somehow that's not nurturing her deeply and profoundly; that's not leaving her full of joy, because it's there in order for her not to be angry! Do you hear the in-order-to? In order not to be angry?

Marsha remained standing while Erhard worked with several other participants.

ERHARD

So if I'm nice in order not to be angry, what persists? You've got to get clear on this. Who's not clear on this?

A participant named Mike stood.

ERHARD

So Mike, if I relate well, in order not to be angry, when I relate well, what's always there is being angry. It's being there as something I'm resisting.

Erhard approached another participant, and did a demonstration in which each man grasped the other's hands and attempted to push the other away.

ERHARD

So if I'm resisting something, I'm attached to what I'm resisting. All this relating-well dances around anger, is attached to anger. I never have any profound sense of being related, because what persists under being related is being angry all the time. I don't have a deep sense of fulfillment out of relating well, because what persists is being angry all the time. See, I'm not related well in order to be related, I'm related well in order not to be angry. You ever notice that real nice people, when you crack their shell a little bit, there's a lot of dissatisfaction and sadness? You know, there's a lot of real nice people in here; all you got to do is crack the surface and then there's dissatisfaction. Is it starting to be clear?

MIKE

Just a bit. I see you pushing against this gentleman over here, and I'm understanding something about anger. You're saying, pushing it away, it's still there. Kind of fuzzy.

ERHARD

When I push him away, am I not attached to him?

MIKE

You're touching him yes.

ERHARD

No, attached to him. I can't get away from him as I'm pushing him away, can I?

MIKE

No you can't.

ERHARD

So in a sense I'm attached to him, am I not?

MIKE

And you're doing the attaching.

ERHARD

Never mind who is doing the attaching.

Erhard returned to the other participant and had him hold Erhard's shoulders.

ERHARD

So, he's got me now, right? And I can't get away. He's holding on to me, right?

MIKE

Right.

ERHARD

What's the difference between that and this?

Erhard pushed the participant as he did in the previous instance.

ERHARD

In terms of being attached? Whether John is holding on to me, *or* I'm pushing him away, we are equally attached.

MIKE

Okay.

ERHARD

So, whatever it is you're resisting, it's exactly the same in its end result as what it is you're indulging. If I'm addicted to anger, I'm no more or less attached to anger than if I was resisting anger. Clear about that part?

MIKE

I am clear about that part.

ERHARD

Good. Let's go to the next part. By virtue of not being angry... You see, what being effective at relating is about for Marsha, it's about not being angry. So what's the result of relating effectively?

MIKE

I'm lost.

ERHARD

You're not lost. You're intelligent. You're *clear* that you don't understand what I'm saying. Saying you understand when you *don't* is "lost." Clear?

MIKE

I want to say yes, but... go ahead.

ERHARD

Is it clear that you aren't lost?

MIKE

It's clear that I don't know what you are talking about right now.

ERHARD

Yeah. That's pretty clear isn't it? So you're not lost. You're clear.

MIKE

I got that.

ERHARD

Good. Now we're going back to this business about "if I relate well in order to avoid anger," what is the result of my relating well?

MIKE

I'm avoiding the anger.

ERHARD

Perfect. Is there any satisfaction in that? Is that going to leave you whole?

MIKE

It'll delay confronting the anger.

ERHARD

It might do that but that's not my point. My point is that being well related with somebody ought to be a source of fulfillment and satisfaction, yes?

MIKE

That's a presupposition.

ERHARD

Yeah: A fairly safe one. If you and I are well related, there ought to be a sense of being fulfilled by that.

MIKE

Okay.

ERHARD

But if you and I are well related in order to avoid being angry, the result of being well related is not satisfaction and fulfillment: it is avoiding being angry. So you can be well related all over the place and it's not going to leave you full of joy or profoundly satisfied. It's going to leave you having avoided anger. You won and they gave you the booby prize. Is that clearer?

MIKE

Yes.

ERHARD

There are accomplished people who are not nurtured by their accomplishments, because they are accomplished in order to not be something they're avoiding being.

(to Mike)

Do you get that?

MIKE

Partially.

ERHARD

Okay, let's get it completely clear.

MIKE

Okay.

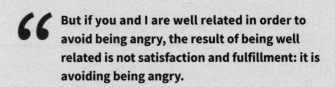

But if you and I are well related in order to avoid being angry, the result of being well related is not satisfaction and fulfillment: it is avoiding being angry.

ERHARD

This is a room full of highly accomplished people. And you know accomplished people?

MIKE

Sure.

ERHARD

And they are not necessarily profoundly satisfied, are they?

MIKE

No they're not.

ERHARD

And they're not full of joy.

MIKE

No they're not.

ERHARD

There's something wrong there. When people see that, like you and me, we start to come up with these stupid conclusions. "Well, life isn't worth it after all. You get all this stuff done and so what?" "Is that all there is? I got to be the president of the company," or "I raised a wonderful family. Success is shit. Do what you want." People give up accomplishment: all these weird solutions. Accomplishment doesn't work for people because they do it in order not to be something. Clear?

MIKE

I get the theory.

ERHARD

Once you get what you call the theory, you want to stand in that theory and look at life. People who get married in order to not be lonely, even when they are successful in the marriage, simply end up being not lonely, while still being attached to "lonely." This whole big possibility of being married or being related, they're not there. They're in "lonely." Clear?

MIKE

That part is clear.

ERHARD

Which part isn't clear?

MIKE

I'm just trying to digest everything.

▶ **NOTE:** This is a "hint" toward the conversation near the end of Day Three called "There's something wrong here."

ERHARD

Don't try to digest everything. What I want you to do is stand in it and look out in life.

MIKE

How do I do that?

ERHARD

Tell me how to walk. And then I'll tell you how to do that.

MIKE

Lean forward.

ERHARD

Tell me how to lean forward.

MIKE

Bend your back.

ERHARD

Tell me how to bend my back.

(silence)

The truth is, you don't know how to walk. You walk, but you don't know how to walk. You don't walk out of "knowing how." Even if you studied anatomy and knew every single muscle I needed to use, and understood the operation of all the parts of the body, and all the neural pathways impulses had to be sent down, you wouldn't know how to generate them in the first place, besides which, you couldn't keep all that in mind to lift one leg up, let alone to walk, right? The fact is you don't know how to walk. You just walk.

MIKE

I guess I never looked at it from that point of view.

ERHARD

You never looked at it from that point of view. You don't need to guess about it. Who you are is an "I guess." You don't know how to walk, do you?

MIKE

I can walk.

ERHARD

Yes. That's not in discussion.

Giving and Reflexion

In his use here of the word "*gives*," Erhard is employing a term that was central in Heidegger's efforts to say the relationship of language to Being.

For anyone who has participated in the work of Werner Erhard, and has experienced the way that a particular combination of words can make available a new perspective on the world, a primary delight in reading Heidegger is surrendering to his precise and profoundly reflexive languaging. Its frequent circularity is consistent with its purpose, which is not to take us anywhere new, but to bring us "back to where we already are," which, he warns, is "infinitely harder." His task is to "think Being without beings"—that is, to bring Being to language as distinct from beings, a distinction that has been lost to our metaphysical tradition. He wants to *say Being;* his task is therefore "unceasingly to overcome the obstacles that tend to render such saying inadequate" (*OTB* 24).

The Being of Language

One of these obstacles he confronts in undertaking this task is found in the nature of language itself. Language was increasingly the focus in Heidegger's later writing, and his most well-known statement is his assertion that "Language is the House of Being" ("LH" in *BW* 217). But what about the Being of language itself? Here Heidegger articulates the conundrum:

> **We speak of language, but constantly seem to be speaking merely *about* language, while in fact we are already letting language, *from within* language, speak to us, in language, of itself, saying its nature. ("NL" in *OWL* 85)**

Heidegger's characteristic response to this *aporic* puzzle is to problematize it further, beginning with a line from the German poet Stefan George, which reasserts his own view of language: "Where word breaks off no thing may be." He teases us into the paradox created by this statement: if without language things cannot be, then things *are* only when the word already *is*. But is a word a thing? On the one hand, it seems so: "if the word is to endow the thing with being, it too must be before any thing is—thus it must

MIKE

Yes, I know how to walk.

ERHARD

Okay, tell me.

MIKE

No, I don't know how to walk.

ERHARD

Okay good.

(to the group)

You've all got a lot of stupid notions. You're a bunch of thoughtless people. You've given very little thought to anything of significance. You have a lot of thoughts, but you don't *give* thought. So in here, you and I are going to give thought. Like most of the other people on the planet, Mike never stopped to look at whether he knew how to walk: wasn't too important to his walking, so why bother? But in here, some of the things you take for granted, we won't take those things for granted. See, it's common sense that if a person walks they know how to. But Mike and I just reduced the idea of knowing how to walk to an absurdity. Maybe knowing how is not the pathway. You can't produce art by the numbers. So getting back to this standing in a possibility: you think it, not believe it or agree with it. You think it. You think: "people are accomplished in-order-to." So what they get is avoiding the "order-to." But avoiding the "order-to" is the same as being attached to the "order-to." Stand in there and take a look at life from there and think that, generate it as a possibility. Speak to yourself or others. Clear?

MIKE

Yes.

ERHARD

Thank you. That was a very useful conversation.

MIKE

Thank you.

(applause)

ERHARD *(returning to Marsha)*

So Marsha, you were saying?

MARSHA

I'm angry at everyone in the world, because what I know about each person in the world is that they don't like me. I'm angry at them.

ERHARD

So, "I am 'they don't like me' waiting to happen." The already always listening I am is "you don't like me, so what was that you were going to say?"

MARSHA

I am already always "you don't like me." I'm angry at that.

ERHARD *(to the group)*

Yeah. And something happened when Marsha was a little girl. And when somebody didn't like her, getting angry worked for that little girl. Now the little girl is running the mature woman with a lot of relational skills being put to use by a little girl who gets angry because people don't like her. There's a little girl mashed in with a mature and competent woman. And the mashing is that the little girl is in charge, calling the shots. And the mature competent woman keeps her in charge by being afraid she might be angry, and not wanting to be. And see, the people who can see Marsha now want to make her feel better. I don't want to make her feel better. I want her just like she is, because what she is doing is growing up. She's getting to the source of what she's afraid she might be. When she's completed that, she'll have a freedom to be that she didn't have before this conversation. She won't *know* better how not to be angry. There'll be a freedom that wasn't there before. She'll be related to people effectively in order to be related to people effectively. That's fulfilling. The thing in itself. Anything else?

MARSHA

I suppressed anger starting in the fifth grade.

ERHARD

What happened?

(to the group)

Listen through the distinctions we developed yesterday. "People don't like me" never happens. It's a story about what happens. "People don't like me" can't happen. If you can't see that, stand up?

A participant stood up and takes a microphone.

ERHARD

Lisa, I said, "people don't like me" never happens.

LISA *(smiling)*

I get it now.

ERHARD

It never happens, it's always a story isn't it? It's a story about what happened. Larry said you're a jerk. He might even have said, "I don't like you." That's what happened, and you told the story "people don't like me." "People don't like me" can't happen, can it?

inescapably be itself a thing" ("NL" in OWL 86). But can a thing then give being to another thing? If things cannot be without the prior existence of words, the inevitable conclusion is that "word and thing are different, even disparate" ("NL" in OWL 86). But what could be the nature of that difference?

Words can be said, but can the word for a word ever be said? A dictionary is filled with terms, but no words, since "a dictionary can neither grasp nor keep the word by which the terms become words and speak as words." When we try to think this, Heidegger proposes, we seem to arrive at the conclusion that "saying has no being." But then another question presents itself: we say a thing *is* when a word is available. But what about the "is" itself? "The 'is' cannot be found anywhere as a thing attached to a thing." Indeed, "It belongs no more among the things that are than does the word" ("NL" in *OWL* 87).

At this point in our thinking, we may throw in the towel; or, says Heidegger, if we will follow him for one more step, we may be struck by something we had not noticed. While we have reached no answers in our inquiry—it has raised neither the word nor the "is" nor the relation between the two to the status of thinghood—it has pointed us toward something "thought-provoking and memorable." It has suggested the possibility of "what is there and yet 'is' not."

 The word, too, belongs to what is there—perhaps not merely "too" but first of all, and even in such a way such that the word, the nature of the word, conceals within itself that which gives [B]eing. If our thinking does justice to the matter, then we may never say of the word that it is, but rather that it gives—not in the sense that words are given by an "it," but that the word itself gives. ("NL" in *OWL* 87-88)

Out of the unspoken background, the word gives a context of meaning for human action.

Thus we have dug down to the essential simplicity: *es gibt* (it gives). Heidegger is languaging the Being/being relationship that is also the heart of his important term, *appropriation*. As we will show later in this book, the nature of appropriation is absolutely central to the ultimate rhetorical move of The Forum.

Werner Erhard, who found in Heidegger's vocabulary a way of expanding the value that his own work made available, discussed the nature of *giving* in a 1989 satellite telecast from New York City.

> **A distinction *gives*. It comes into existence by giving. . . . You've got to be able to think something coming into existence in the act of giving existence. Distinguishing arises in the act of giving—hard for us to think about because we can only think serially. I'm asking you to think of a new kind of relationship called giving. . . . This is getting to the essence of Being. There's no such thing as Being. You can't separate Being from the world, therefore there's no such *thing* as Being. . . . Being arises in the act of giving. ("Beyond the Winning Formula")**

Reflexive languaging demands that thinking bend back on itself. Such languaging is inherent in thinking about Being; note how that very phrase tickles the mind.

While Heidegger's writing is often considered to be highly complex, he suggests an alternate view: "What is strange in the thinking of Being is its *simplicity*. Precisely this keeps us from it" ("LH" in *BW* 263, emphasis added). Heidegger teases out this idea further in his "Letter on Humanism." At one point in the letter, when considering the role of language in Being, he calls attention to a specific instance of its simplicity:

> **But just now an example of the inconspicuous deed of thinking manifested itself. For to the extent that we expressly think the usage "bring to language," which was granted to language, think only that and nothing further, to the extent that we retain this thought in the heedfulness of saying as what in the future continually has to be thought, we have brought something of the essential unfolding of Being itself to language. ("LH" in *BW* 263)**

(Lisa shakes her head)

Clear?

LISA
Yes.

ERHARD
Anybody else not get this?

(another participant stands)

MASON
So you're saying it's never possible that it's people in general? It could be one person?

ERHARD
There's no such thing as "people" happening.

MASON
So it could be Frank doesn't like me.

ERHARD
Yeah. "People don't like me" is always a story, isn't it?

MASON
I got that.

ERHARD
"People don't like me" never happened. "Nobody liked me" never happened. Always a story, right?

(to Marsha)
What happened?

MARSHA
What happened is, from Kindergarten through fourth grade was fun. In the fifth grade girls were developing, noticing boys, but I was still in pigtails...

ERHARD
Hold on. You wanna start being able to be with people here. Whatever you were yesterday isn't going to work today. You have to be powerfully with people. You've got to be up on the edge of your chair when this woman is giving you a gift you ain't going to get again. You're going to

ERHARD *(continuing)*

go back out of here three days from now, and nobody's gonna talk this straight to you. You're going to go out and have those chicken shit conversations with people. So you want to get what you can out of this. And you aren't going to be able to see this in yourself until you can see it in Marsha. All that sadness of the fifth grader is there right now. Marsha's got a fifth grader running her life. This is a mature, attractive, confident, accomplished woman with a fifth grader calling the shots.

(to Marsha)

You were saying?

MARSHA

Suddenly there was a distinction. It was not okay with the other girls that I was not growing up. They starting getting in like a clique. And...

ERHARD

Talking behind your back and excluding you, and no longer was there that kind of loose easy sense of being with people. Now it was a drama to be with people: a kind of plot; a kind of strategy.

MARSHA

What I saw worked a little bit was to start getting happy, bubbly.

ERHARD

So this is pretty intelligent for a fifth grader. It makes very good sense for a ten-year-old girl to say the answer to this is to be happy all the time. You got to remember this is Marsha inventing Marsha. This is Marsha inventing her identity. She has happiness as a way to push away sadness. Then what happened?

MARSHA

As we grew up, they were the attractive ones, the cheerleaders; the boys were interested in them...

ERHARD

Listen up here, because this is about to get really stupid. Here is a really attractive woman who's going to tell you she was not in with the girls who were attractive. Stupid in the sense that this is not logical.

MARSHA

Up until the fifth grade I was called ___, after my ninety year old aunt who was an "old maid."

ERHARD *(to the group, lightly)*

How come men are bachelors and women are called old maids? I don't get it.

In considering reflexive languaging, one is immediately reminded of *koan* meditation—the process in which a Zen student is assigned a single problematic phrase upon which he or she meditates until its embedded ontological hurdle has been made. The paradigmatic *koan* is the question, "What is the sound of one hand clapping?" Heidegger's paragraph above, considered carefully, pulls one toward *koan*-like thinking.

Michael E. Zimmerman has likened Heidegger's use of *aporia*—unresolvable problems—to the existential puzzles found in *koans*. As an example, he cites the *aporic* conceptual dilemma, central to Heidegger's thought, that Being is inconceivable except as a being, and yet no being can *be* a being without a prior experience of its Being. As Zimmerman points out, the solution to such *aporia* is beyond the capabilities of rational thought; and this is precisely the *power of reflexion*, that it turns the thinker's thinking reflexively in upon itself, demanding a different *kind* of thinking and thus a different thinker: "Before one can speak about the difference between Being and beings, it is crucial that one put oneself in the position of being able to experience that difference" ("Heidegger and Heraclitus on Spiritual Practice" 100). Participants in The Forum have put themselves in that position.

The experience of engaging one's mind with a profoundly relexive idea may be imagined as the process of revving an engine so hard that the torque sends it flying off its mounts. This image calls to our minds the way participants in The Forum "get it" after several days of struggling to understand it conceptually.

Reflexive languagings, and the thinking they demand, are central in the work of both Heidegger and Erhard. Erhard distinguishes thinking from having thoughts, and he hints at the difference using such languaging as "This statement is false," "I always lie," or "A superstition is a superstition only when it isn't a superstition, and a superstition isn't a superstition only when it is a superstition." Such statements *call* for thinking, call for the movement of thought through the structure given in language. ■

MARSHA

That's when I changed my name to Marsha. I wouldn't answer to that other name any more. And by the time I got to high school, there was a new group. The act was down great. It worked. I was class vice president. I became popular on a different...

ERHARD

Not quite right, though, still popular; popular enough to avoid being unpopular. Your identity got built when the issue was popularity.

(to the group)

You got put together for the purpose of dealing with issues like popularity.

MARSHA

As years went by, I got it down good that I won homecoming queen in college; student body president; president of the sorority: everything.

ERHARD

She's now one of those kids you couldn't be that you thought had it all together. She was the popular kids: the in-crowd; the one who whispered behind your back. These were the people who were really happy, not like you.

Erhard stopped to address a participant sitting down, who remained seated, without a microphone, and who shook her head in response to each of Erhard's questions.

ERHARD *(continuing)*

Is this hitting close to home? Popularity wasn't your thing? What did you care? You have a chip on your shoulder? If I asked your friends if you had a chip on your shoulder, what would they tell me? I know you can't think for them, but what do you think they would say? Think about it. I'll be back.

(laughter; to Marsha)

You were saying?

MARSHA

I've got six children, a wonderful husband: I arrange everything.

ERHARD

You generate the family. You source the family.

MARSHA

But I am so thin and my body can't do it anymore.

THE THEY-SELF

Throughout his work, Werner Erhard has proposed that the fundamental purpose for human beings in our current Cartesian paradigm—their *design function*—is the survival of the self; and that just as survival for a biological organism requires food and water,

ERHARD

Listen carefully. What Marsha's telling you doesn't belong to her. That bullshit is all over the place. It's a rainstorm. It's all over the place: that bullshit about being stretched too thin. You ain't ever going to be big enough to operate in a way that doesn't leave you unnurtured and too thin. You're going to die disappointed, because you aren't ever going to accomplish enough to be fulfilled when accomplishment is there *in-order-to.* All you're doing is building dissatisfaction that accomplishment is designed to avoid. It looks like a big pile of satisfaction. I mean, here's a woman who was successful as an older child; successful in college. Extraordinarily successful raising six children, married to a great guy: and it's making her "thin." It makes you thin when those accomplishments are in-order-to. It ought to be making her "thicker" not "thinner." They make you thinner when they're not fulfilling, when they're not enlivening, when they're a strategy.

(to Marsha)

What else?

MARSHA

Here I am today.

ERHARD

You're in the right place.

(applause)

You aren't going to be around that much honesty for the most part. What you and I did yesterday was put together a structure in which it is possible to be honest. You need to develop a language for honesty. You can't be honest in everyday language. It's not designed for honesty. You and I have been building a structure of distinctions designed for honesty. So you and I have been building a language, a set of distinctions, building a structure where it is possible to be honest. You've got to be a big person to be authentic about your inauthenticity. Being authentic about your inauthenticity gives you being big. There's no "big" inside of Marsha. No qualities in there. What you and I describe as "qualities" arise in the moment of action. Someone who is authentic about their own inauthenticity is giving themselves being big. Is that clear to you?

(returning to participant who remained seated without a mic)

There are no big people in here, because people are neither big nor small. They're just people. And when you're authentic about your inauthenticity, it gives you being big. If she already had the quality in there, that would be like being tall. If big were inside us, there wouldn't be anything very interesting about that, would there? Big arises in the acting. On the common sense view, what would it occur to you to do with your inauthenticity? Hide it. Stamp it out. Change it. Fix it. Repair it. The way you already always are about your inauthenticity is something across the spectrum from fix it, not-be-it, shove it down, across the spectrum to hide it. The idea to share it would never occur to you. The idea to dump it on others might occur to you because of the idea you've got called "friends." It's pure crap, what you tell your friends, pure crap. Because what do you tell your friends? The story. They have no respect for you so they sympathize with you. They think you're crap, just the same as you do, and that's sad. And the appropriate

for an ontological entity, such as a human identity, the essential survival requirements are *being right and looking good,* which together justify and maintain whatever way we wound up being.

Both of these elements are addressed here during the second day of The Forum. Being right is proposed as one of the primary payoffs in the structure of a racket; and the discussion of looking good grows out of the assignment given at the end of the first day, when participants were told to locate the places in their life where they were being "used by looking good." Both of these distinctions are essential elements of the model Erhard is creating in order to deconstruct our Cartesian understanding and reveal the clearing for a new possibility of being human.

Heidegger has likewise proposed a structure for understanding human Being (Dasein) in terms of its domination by a concern for the opinions of others. His rubric for this structure is *das Man.* In the standard translation of *Being and Time,* this phrase is rendered as *the "they,"* and here Heidegger describes the situation:

 [Dasein] itself *is* not; its Being has been taken away by the Others. . . . These Others, moreover, are not *definite* Others. On the contrary, any Other can represent them. What is decisive is just that inconspicuous domination by Others which has already been taken over unawares from Dasein as Being-with. . . . The "who" is not this one, not that one, not oneself, not some people, and not the sum of them all. The 'who' is the neuter, *the "they."* (**BT 164**)

Hubert Dreyfus proposes that to translate *das Man* in this way suggests that *I* am to be distinguished from *them.* But the point is that the "they" has taken *me* over, so that in being dominated by the "they" I am one of them. Therefore Dreyfus prefers the translation "the One"; that is, we don't conform to the norms because "they" do it, but because "it's what one does" (*BITW* 151–152). Says Heidegger: "In this inconspicuousness and unascertainability, the real dictatorship of the 'they' is unfolded" (*BT* 164). As a result, Dasein loses itself in the ways of Being of the "they," and the Self of everyday Dasein becomes the *they-self.*

Heidegger specifies other characteristics of the "they" which thereby become aspects of our everydayness. First, because we generally encounter others in the context of our everyday concerns—the competitive environment of the workplace, as well as the social and political realms—we experience "constant care as to the way one differs from them, whether one's own Dasein has lagged behind the Others and wants to catch up in relationship to them, or whether one's Dasein has priority over them and sets out to keep them suppressed" (*BT* 164–165). As this complex of concerns takes Dasein over, the *withness* of Being-with-Others is interrupted:

> **The care about this distance between them is disturbing to Being-with-one-another, though this disturbance is one that is hidden from it. If we may express this existentially, such Being-with-one-another has the character of *distantiality*. (*BT* 164)**

Further, since the "they" is everyone and no one, it is characterized as well by *averageness*:

> **Thus the "they" maintains itself factically in the averageness of that which belongs to it, of that which it regards as valid and that which it does not, and of that to which it grants success and that to which it denies it. In this averageness with which it prescribes what can and may be ventured, it keeps watch over everything exceptional that thrusts itself to the fore. Every kind of priority gets noiselessly suppressed. Overnight, everything that is primordial gets glossed over as something that has long been well known. Everything gained by a struggle becomes just something to be manipulated. Every secret loses its force. This care of averageness reveals in turn an essential tendency of Dasein which we call the "levelling down" of all possibilities of Being. (*BT* 165)**

response to that is sympathy. Awww, you poor thing. Marsha, thank you very much. And you want to be clear that when Marsha sits down some of what didn't resolve for her while she was standing up, although she was pretty complete about that, the rest of that will resolve for her. See it's like a house of cards: when you take one of the cards out, the whole thing falls down. That whole thing that's tied together begins to break apart. There's more attached to that, that Marsha didn't tell us. She hasn't looked all the way through it, and doesn't want to be up there for a half hour telling the whole thing. She already gave you one insight. Anger was related to "people don't like me." And "I'm angry at people for not liking me." So you find the anger and see that what's attached to that is "people don't like me." And what's attached to that is I've got to be likeable, and then you get really good at being likeable. Not in some cheap sense, not with smoke and mirrors; earned like. She produced the results, earned the contribution. Put out the energy. And she's gotten really good at it.

(moving among the participants on the floor)

The problem is that when it's there in order to avoid not being liked, about which I'm angry... Accomplishment doesn't leave you nurtured. That's why they have happy hours after work. The way people relate to their job, accomplishment in their job doesn't nurture them.

(turning to a participant who had been standing the entire time)

JODIE

Interesting how much things have changed since I stood up.

ERHARD

Amazing, right?

JODIE

Looking good rules my life: completely and utterly.

ERHARD

If you haven't seen yet that looking good owns your life... if you haven't seen that yet... I promise you that that's the case. You may not have seen it yet. So you don't know that it is the case. Like I said, I don't know the truth, but I'm also not a guy in a diner about this, not a guy with an opinion. If you haven't seen this you want to be listening up. Like Mike and I were saying, you want to listen to this like a possibility...that when Jodie's finished, you want to stand in the possibility that you don't own your life, that your life doesn't belong to you. Yeah, you've got this arrogant façade that you run your life and call the shots. Listen to Jodie's sharing out of this possibility: to see how your life is shaped by looking good. And the quality of your life is that of a life devoted to looking good. Your actions are limited to the span of action being given by looking good. Stand in that possibility when Jodie is finished.

JODIE

What also came up from yesterday when you talked about concept and experience and reinforcing each other, my whole life is, that I've got to look good and if I don't look good it doesn't

JODIE (*continuing*)

come off well, and that reinforces that I've got to look good. And it just goes around and around.

ERHARD

So when you don't look good, it reinforces looking good, and when you do look good, that reinforces looking good.

JODIE

And that there's been times in my life where, that looking good prevents me from expressing what I want to express. I could go home to my intimate relationship and I could go home alone and say "okay, at least I look good."

ERHARD

Yeah. Listen. Your little $625, that's chicken shit compared to what you just got from her. You can't buy that kind of honesty. That's more insight than most people are ever going to have in their entire life. What she told you is that you don't own your life. *Looking good owns your life.* And life is not about self-expression. You now know why there's no satisfaction in your success. Looking good is gratifying, but not fulfillment. You notice it's never enough. Nothing is ever enough. Nothing. Nothing leaves you whole and complete, nothing leaves you full of joy. Because that's not the name of the game. The name of the game is looking good. It's the only game in town. You are not living life. You are looking good. Of course, some people look good by looking bad. A lot of people look good by being the victim. For example, if you screw up someplace when you're a kid and get a lot of attention. People who are *unable*. It's a way of life. There's an organ for some people called dealing with electrical things, and they don't have that organ, you see.

(laughter)

Not long ago they burned women to death in Scotland as a favor because their souls were possessed. The best people in the community applied the tests to see if a woman's soul was possessed by a devil. A lot of what you know to be true is in the same order as what those Scots knew that led them to burn women to death. One of those things that isn't true is that you own your life, because you don't. One of those things that isn't true is that you're free, but you're not. You're owned by looking good.

JODIE

For me what happened was I was unattractive as a child. I was 5 feet 8 inches at 12 years old. I always stood out in a crowd, was gawky and all that. Always popular with the girls and never with the boys. Unattractive all the way through high school. And when I was 17 the transformation took place. I lost 35 pounds, got contact lenses and a professional haircut. All of a sudden men liked me. What showed up for me was that when I was young men didn't like me.

Collectively, these ways of being—distantiality, averageness, and levelling down—constitute what Heidegger calls "Publicness," which

> **controls every way in which the world and Dasein get interpreted, *and it is always right*—not because there is some distinctive and primary relationship-of-Being in which it is related to 'Things,' or because it avails itself of some transparency on the part of Dasein which it has explicitly appropriated, but because it is insensitive to every difference of level and of genuineness and thus never gets to the 'heart of the matter.'** (*BT* 165, emphasis added)

Finally, although all of this would seem to paint an unrelievedly bleak picture for Dasein's possibility of Being-in-the-world, there is one more element that, at first glance, might seem to provide some relief, and might (initially at least) be called "the upside of the they-self." In Werner Erhard's model, it is in fact one of the "payoffs" in the structure of a *racket:*

> **[B]ecause the "they" presents every judgment and decision as its own, it deprives the particular Dasein of its answerability. The "they" can, as it were, manage to have 'them' constantly invoking it. . . . It 'was' always the "they" who did it, and yet it can be said that it has been 'no one.' . . . .Thus the particular Dasein in its everydayness is *disburdened* by the "they." Not only that; by thus disburdening it of its Being, the "they" accommodates Dasein if Dasein has any tendency to take things easily and make them easy.** (*BT* 165)

And what Dasein wouldn't want to make things easy? Avoidance of responsibility for one's situation, and off-loading of blame onto someone or something else whom you can make wrong, is a significant payoff of one's racket, a distinction that has been mentioned several times but will not be distinguished until the next session.

Aside from the payoff, the structure of a racket has another element: the cost. And here Heidegger names it: "[B]ecause the 'they' constantly accommodates the particular Dasein by disburdening it of its Being, the 'they' retains and enhances its stubborn dominion" (*BT* 165). Through its surrender to the domination of the "they," Dasein has embraced the Cartesian security of being right in its averageness; but it has at the same time sacrificed its freedom and power. As The Forum participant Jodie states, "looking good rules my life."

In these "characters of Being," says Heidegger, we find "the 'constancy' of Dasein which is closest to us" (*BT* 166). Certainly, the attitudes and behaviors he has presented here are familiar to all of us—and if we can't quite recognize them in ourselves, we can certainly recognize them in others, or in the culture at large. And we must feel some discomfort in acknowledging that his descriptions are so apt.

But straight talk about the way things look now is the essential first step in gaining a new perspective; and in The Forum, the creation of a new possibility must be preceded by a hard look at our present way of Being. Heidegger takes us through the steps one at a time.

 Neither the Self of one's own Dasein nor the Self of the Other has as yet found itself or lost itself as long as it is in the modes we have mentioned. In these modes one's way of Being is that of inauthenticity and failure to stand by one's Self. (*BT* 166)

Confronting the reality of the they-self responds to the first question of The Forum: "What is the Being of human being?" Authenticity and taking a stand become available when the second is addressed: "What is the possibility of Being for human being?" ∎

ERHARD

Now is that true? Did that ever happen? "Men don't like me?" Is it true "I'm not attractive"? Is that true? Could that be true? Who said yes? "Not attractive" could happen? Stand up. I want you to tell me how that could happen.

SAM

I could make it up that I'm not attractive.

ERHARD

Oh, that's a story. "Not attractive" can't happen. Did you ever wonder, "that guy is so unattractive. How did he ever get that woman? She must be blind." Do you know that attraction is the weirdest stuff in the universe? Everybody's attractive. A lot of people don't troll their bait, that's all. So if your story is that "I'm tall and gawky and not attractive," you don't have your bait out. I would be willing to bet that there isn't anybody for whom there are no fish, given what I've seen. You begin to live out of a story that you're not attractive. Don't tell me there are no fish if you're not trolling.

(to Jodie)

You were saying?

JODIE

So I got attractive. And I know that I can walk into a room and every man will look at me. That's happened for me.

ERHARD

Nothing's changed about being tall, right? Tall is now attractive. Same stuff. I want to get this clear with you. You gotta get this.

Erhard walked to the blackboard, and drew two circles. One circle he labeled "attractive," one he labeled "not attractive." He wrote "tall" in both.

(continuing)

The way things are is not determined by the way things are. That's hard to think, so that's what I'm asking you to think. The way things are is determined by the *context* in which things occur. I'm wanting you to begin to see that *this* part—the circle, the context—is critically important. I'm saying that the circumstances *never* produce problems. I don't care what happened in your life. That's not the problem. I don't care if you were raped when you were a little girl or you were molested when you were a little boy. I don't care who's sitting there with cancer. I know you think that did something bad to you. I'm saying no. The circumstances never are the problem. Tall occurs as not attractive in one context, in one domain of existence, and tall occurs as attractive in another domain of existence. Anybody not get that? It's never what happened that's the problem. I don't care what's happened in your life. That is not the problem. The problem is the context in which "what happened" occurred.

(to Jodie)

Yes, you were saying...

JODIE

When I was a child, I was not liked by boys. That's my story...

ERHARD

Or boys didn't say certain things to you. That's what happened. And boys didn't act in certain ways with you. There's a thousand possible stories: "I was so awesome that those twerps didn't have the balls to say to me what they said to those little girls."

JODIE

That's what I say now.

ERHARD

All I'm trying to point out is that a story is just a story. The "what happened," that's what's true or not. It did or it didn't. Mostly true. Because she wouldn't have even noticed boys not saying or acting a certain way unless her listening was "boys don't like me." If your listening is that somebody doesn't like you, everything they say is an expression of not liking you. If we pushed Jodie hard enough she could go back and remember that "oh yeah, one of them was trying to be nice to me once." Something like that.

JODIE

So I got attractive and, men asked me out. What I find now is that as an adolescent I believed that men didn't like me, so when I got attractive it was like a shell I was putting on.

ERHARD

This is good. I got to stop you because they are listening like this is a soap opera and they need to listen deeply.

(to the group)

If you're attractive to make up for not being attractive... if who you really are is unattractive, but they don't know that, every time you are attractive, what you are left with is being unattractive. When you change unattractive to attractive, what persists is unattractive. It's a con game, underneath which is unattractive. There's no object that has the quality "attractive." There's no being fulfilled in being attractive. There's stuff in my house I think is wonderful, the dog walks right by.

JODIE

When someone tells me "You're really beautiful," what comes up for me is "but you don't really know me." When I go home I take this off and there's the real me and you won't like that person.

ERHARD

Here's what you want to get: nobody wants to know that about themselves. Nobody wants to get that really underneath it all they're really unattractive. That's why you paid $625. Because in here, it's structured so you can get at that—to the degree that Jodie can be with this, and she

All I'm trying to point out is that a story is just a story. The "what happened," that's what's true or not. It did or it didn't. Mostly true.

> **What you begin to see here is that when the name of the game is looking good, there is no self-expression. None. So whatever there is, whatever quality life would have, if life were self-expression, it doesn't have that when life is looking good. And life is looking good.**

doesn't screw it up by trying to fix it. If all she does is just be with it, there will be a whole new possibility in attraction. It'll be a different thing for her. That will not be the limit of attraction.

JODIE

I've buried me. I've buried it so much, I don't even know what's there anymore. I don't want to take it out and look at it.

ERHARD *(to Jodie)*

That's really very beautiful, what you saw: really extraordinary. It took me about ten years to get what you got overnight. What you begin to see here is that when the name of the game is looking good, there is no self-expression. None. So whatever there is, whatever quality life would have, if life were self-expression, it doesn't have that when life is looking good. And life *is* looking good.

(to the group)

You aren't going to get any clearer than she gave it to you. I'm going to talk about it a lot. But she gave it to you real clearly.

(to Jodie)

What else?

JODIE

It all comes down to wanting to be liked. And what shows up for me in relationships and especially work relationships, I put on this story: "I don't care if I'm liked, I want to be respected."

ERHARD

Anybody who tells you that is full of shit. What they really mean is that they're not sure about being liked. They don't know whether they can play that game. They got more confidence about being respected. Everybody wants to be liked. It's nothing personal about you. It's a rainstorm called the already always being of human beings. And it is in the nature of being of human beings to have a powerful concern for being liked. And there are endless strategies for dealing with this powerful addiction to looking good. People who say they don't care about being liked: if you don't care then why are you telling me? You didn't say you didn't care if I blink my eyes. Why did you go out of your way to say you don't care if I like you? "Methinks the lady doth protest too much." It's not personal. Can we get that flat now? It's not personal. You don't have a fucking thing to do with it, nothing. You didn't make that up. It belongs to the already always being of human being. You just happened to walk into the rainstorm called being a human being, and as such you got wet by that rain. You personally want to be liked, have to be liked, need to be liked, are addicted to being liked. But it's nothing personal, and treating it personally is stupid and it will make you stupid. Some people are guilty about wanting to be liked. You're guilty of being a human being, that's all. You need to know it's an ontological phenomenon, a phenomenon of being. And it doesn't belong to you personally, it belongs to being human, as you do.

While Jodie remained standing, another participant, Max, who had the story about Vietnam, stood to speak.

MAX (*visibly shaking*)

I'm stuck. I'm afraid I won't get it. I want to pay my money and have you give it to me. I don't want to have to work at it. I'm really controlled by looking good. I know it controls my life. I'm living my life for everybody else, not myself. I'm stuck and I don't know what to do with that right now. I'm pissed off at myself when you asked if there was anybody who didn't get authenticity...

ERHARD

About being inauthentic.

MAX

I'm stuck on that. I don't know where to go with it. I don't understand it.

ERHARD

All right. I got it. You're in the right place. Relax. I mean, I know you won't relax, but you're in the right place. I just read your thermometer. You're all right.

JODIE

I'm really concerned about people liking me, but it's not me that I'm portraying for them to like anyway. There's this big catch 22. I really want you to like me, but it's not the real me anyway so if you don't like me, I already have an out.

ERHARD

Right. It's very illogical. Very nutty. What's that thing about lies and webs? "Oh what a tangled web we weave, when first we practice to deceive." You have no idea how tangled it is. It starts with the first lie, and the first lie is: the story is true. Very powerful contribution. Thanks.

Jodie sat to applause. Wes then replaced Erhard on the platform and directed participants to engage in a few minutes of "paired sharing—sharing with the person seated next to you what you have been seeing in The Forum so far today." Following this, he gave the group an assignment for the upcoming break.

WES

Have a conversation, like an inquiry, with at least one other person about your *racket*. I want you to consider the possibility that you are a candy store with a *racket* in the back. Rackets have a cost and a payoff. What are yours? Get some insight into your racket—what the payoff is and what it costs you. There's a point to it that gets you something from other people and from life, and what does that kind of way of being cost you? Get some insight into your racket. That's the opportunity of the break.

The first break of the day began at 12:35 pm.

SESSION ONE INTERVAL

Hermeneutic Phenomenology

Heidegger's analysis of Dasein in *Being and Time* is based in two philosophical orientations: phenomenology and hermeneutics.

Heidegger's introduction to phenomenology as a philosophical method came by way of Heidegger's mentor and colleague, Edmund Husserl, who summarized the approach with his famous exhortation, "To the things themselves!" In Heidegger's characteristic reformulation of this approach, phenomenology means "to let that which shows itself be seen from itself in the very way in which it shows itself from itself" (*BT* 58). Both statements point to phenomenology's fundamental purpose: to set aside all previous theoretical and philosophical constructions (Husserl called this "bracketing"), in order to bring the phenomena fully into the light.

Of course, Heidegger acknowledges, this purpose may be seen as "abundantly self-evident," since it states "the underlying principle of any scientific knowledge whatsoever" (*BT* 50). And certainly phenomenology, as both a philosophical orientation and a method of inquiry, is sufficiently flexible to have been subjected to widely varying interpretations (see, e.g., www.phenomenologyonline.com). (Note: Although at the time of this 1989 Forum Werner Erhard did not present his work using the term "phenomenological," his later projects, as well as the recent work of Landmark Worldwide, have employed this term.)

But regardless of the term's inexactness, Heidegger is adamant that a rigorous phenomenological inquiry can penetrate the layers of appearance and semblance which normally impede our access to things. Heidegger's goal in the inquiry is *aletheia*, or unconcealment, which for the early Greek philosophers was the truth of "pure sensory perception," prior to any judgment or covering-up. Phenomenology perceives things "just by looking at them," thereby (in a phrase employed by both Heidegger and Werner Erhard) "letting beings be."

Since Heidegger's inquiry is concerned with the meaning of Being, his phenomenology has a specific character:

> " What is it that by its very essence is *necessarily* the theme whenever we exhibit something *explicitly*? Manifestly, it is something that proximally and for the most part does *not* show itself at all: it is something that lies *hidden*, in contrast to that which proximally and for the most part does show itself; but at the same time it is something that belongs to what shows itself, and it belongs to it so essentially as to constitute its meaning and its ground. (*BT* 59)

"Proximally" is a term Heidegger uses frequently in *Being and Time* to characterize our most obvious and everyday experiences. These experiences, he says, do not include a perception of Being, which remains hidden, even though it constitutes the meaning and ground of what shows itself. Therefore, when defined by its subject-matter, "phenomenology is the science of the Being of entities—ontology" (*BT* 61). For Heidegger's phenomenology "the thing itself" (which of course is not a thing at all) is Being.

A further complication for the phenomenological approach is that for Heidegger it must always be recognized as *hermeneutical*. Hermeneutics is the study of *interpretation,* the process by which we develop an understanding of a phenomenon. We can never get to "the things themselves," says Heidegger, since perception is always mediated by the understanding of the human being doing the perceiving, and that understanding has always been arrived at by a process of interpretation. Thus by defining his phenomenological method as hermeneutical, Heidegger is including his recognition that whatever understanding he arrives at will never be the "final" one: "For in such an inquiry, one is constantly compelled to face the possibility of disclosing an even more primordial and more universal horizon from which we may draw the answer to the question, "What is *Being*?" (*BT* 49).

This lack of closure that characterizes a hermeneutical phenomenology is important for both Heidegger and for the work of Werner Erhard. Heidegger's stated goal is to let Dasein "*put itself into words for the very first time, so that it may decide of its own accord whether, as the entity which it is, it has that state of Being which is disclosed in this interpretation*" (*BT* 362). But really, isn't it more accurate to say that the words into which Dasein is being put are Heidegger's words (and likewise, Erhard's words)? Heidegger is creating his own hermeneutical vocabulary here. Why should we accept these terms as valid?

Heidegger is not arguing that we should. He is not proposing a final truth, but a step on the way, and he asks that we—as ourselves Dasein—decide "of our own accord" whether we find value in his interpretation. This is always the way that thinking advances—through the development and testing of new vocabularies. In the field of psychology, Freud invented a vocabulary to describe the behaviors he observed in his work. He did not "discover" the ego and the id, but invented them, and for decades they demonstrated their validity through their use by generations of psychotherapists. More recently, they have been largely supplanted by other vocabularies, or by psychotropic drugs; and many of Freud's terms have taken their place in our everyday usage, where excessive neatness is routinely characterized as "anal" behavior, and an inflated ego is considered as natural as a sore elbow.

Werner Erhard regularly frames his work as a new vocabulary to be considered. "We ask you not to believe anything that's said in here," he tells The Forum participants at the outset of the four days. Instead, he says on numerous occasions, "consider the possibility," or "stand in that theory and look at life," or "try it on."

¥

In the passage below, taken from an audiotaped 1986 seminar, we present an example of Erhard's phenomenological approach that is quite different from that demonstrated in The Forum. This seminar is a working session, in which he is interacting with Forum graduates to develop distinctions on the subject of leadership, a subject that Erhard has continued to develop in subsequent years into what is now called the Being a Leader and Exercising Leadership Effectively Course: An Ontological/Phenomenological Approach. His method here is often framed in a sports metaphor, in which the ideas to be "bracketed" are characterized as the comments of observers ("up in the stands"), while "the things themselves" are the events as they are experienced by those engaged in the game ("down on the court").

ERHARD

What's on the court when you're on the court, rather than what's on the court when you're up in the stands? What's actually there like a presence? Peter?

PETER

Me watching somebody else.

ERHARD

Okay, very good. So if we stand back from the whole thing, there was you in the stands watching somebody else. Now, you notice something down with the people you were watching, which is the comment of an observer giving an account. When you were giving that account, what was the guy and the gal on the court . . . what was present?

PETER

(Silence)

ERHARD

Now let me give you a little clue about how to do this. One of the things that I imagine was present was *somebody*. Is that true? There was actually somebody there. . . . You don't get leadership on an empty court. . . . So this is kind of obvious, but at least it's a place to start: that leadership as a presence is people. Okay. So what else is there, like a presence? People, we got that much. What else, like a presence, is present?

PETER

There's action.

ERHARD

Okay, but what action? Okay, let's just stay with that. There's action. So leadership as a presence presences itself as action. People in action. . . .

PETER

So all I have is a description of it, an observation.

ERHARD

Good. Now I want you to get down there on the court and tell me what's there. So far what you've got down there is people in action.

PETER

So there's . . . commitment.

ERHARD

No. Can't see commitment. It's not a presence. I don't mean you can't see it, therefore it's not a presence, but I'm trying to kind of engage you into: how do you inquire into presence? So is commitment ever present? No, that's always a conversation, an assessment about what's going on there. . . . What's actually going on there?

PETER

I don't know.

ERHARD

Try this: something about unrestrained action? Maybe something like unrestrained action, maybe something like consistent action? Maybe something like repetitive action, maybe something like action powerful enough to meet a resistance? I don't know. See, I don't know, and I don't care about the answer! What I care about is establishing ourselves in the domain of leadership as a presence. That's what this is all about. It's a trick. This is not really to get the answer. We're not going to give you a test to see if you got the answers right afterwards. . . .

PETER

It's action without concern.

ERHARD

Okay. Good. Now, what does concern mean? See, no matter what he says, I'm going to have a question, aren't I? Why? Because I don't care about the answer!

PETER

Anything I can think of is a description.

ERHARD

Yeah, it's okay. That's right. And every time you say it, I'm going to say that's a description, and what's underneath that? Why? Because—you know, I'm going to say this a thousand times today, I can feel it coming—because it's the inquiry where the power is, not the information you derive from the inquiry. Look, we've invented a new technology. We've invented a technology called ontological inquiry. Really, that's wrong. We've invented a technology called ontological design. The way you do ontological design is like Peter and I are doing it: "Maybe it's this. But how could it be that? What's underneath that? Well, underneath that is this. Okay, but how could it be that? What's underneath that?" And somehow, if Peter and I are doing it correctly, when we're all done, neither of us will know anything we didn't know before, but life will be an opening for that into which we've inquired. So Peter and I will find ourselves, not remembering what to do to be leaders, or not remembering what property we need to have to be leaders, but rather we will find ourselves *being leaders*. . . . Because I say that a well-designed, rigorous inquiry, while not leading to answers, while not leading to information, while not leading necessarily to understanding, leads to an opening, like a possibility, like a clearing, for that into which I'm inquiring.

Erhard was on the platform as the second session began at 1:15 pm.

ERHARD

So I'm willing to tell you The Answer now. You're not going to like the answer. What you get after sitting on a mountaintop for twenty years—what you get is—the answer is that there isn't any answer: and that is *The* Answer. Somewhere on the third day that will fall into place for you. What we want to do is distinguish a racket. The problem is that you don't know what distinguishing is. First we need to distinguish *distinction*. When you and I distinguish something, it's not the same as defining it. Distinguishing and defining are two different operations. And distinguishing is not describing. When you distinguish something you are not describing it. What is it that defining does? When you define something, what does that do for you?

PARTICIPANT

You set up a boundary, or a limit.

ERHARD

Right on. When you define something, what you do is to take a mass of undefined stuff, and you draw a kind of line that divides what you're defining from what you're not defining. Also, defining indicates something with reference to something else, something you're not familiar with in relation to something you *are* familiar with. Distinguishing doesn't work like that. Defining objectifies something. When you define something you turn it into an object. Defining gives it a form, a location in space and time, turns it into a thing. And we're all comfortable with things. When you distinguish you don't turn it into an object. And that's why distinguishing makes people uncomfortable. Because while it exists by virtue of being distinguished, it doesn't exist as a thing.

(pausing)

So we're going to take a little bit of a look at what distinguishing might be. Defining identifies; distinguishing sets up a *realm*. You don't need to understand that yet. Just have it like, "He says distinguishing sets up a realm." 2, and 9, and 74 are numbers. But *number* is not itself a number. It's a realm in which numbers can happen. Number distinguishes a realm of possibility.

Erhard called on a participant to stand up.

ERHARD (*to participant*)

How many loops in one square foot of rug?

PARTICIPANT

A couple thousand.

ERHARD

You know exactly how many: a lot. If I take one loop away, how many are there? The exact same number. The number is called *a lot*. We can't distinguish between that number and that number minus one. A lot minus one is still a lot. You have no way to see the difference between a lot and a lot minus one. *Conceptually* they're different, but conceptually the world is flat. We're talking about the way the rug occurs for you. Similarly, we're told that there are cultures, societies, in which the number system goes up to seven.

(*holding up eight fingers*)
That would look like *many.*

(*holding up nine fingers*)
So would that.

(*to the group*)
You've got to get this, you see. *This is one of those things you've got to get.* Now we're going to talk about two... like t-w-o. Pretend you're in a culture with no numbers at all. You've got only none, one, and many.

(*holding up two sheets of paper*)
If I said that was two, you'd say, "All right."

(*holding up two rulers*)
If I said that's two, you'd say, "okay."

He continued, holding up two erasers, then two fingers, each time responding with increasing certainty as the imaginary tribesperson—until he held up one ruler and one eraser.

ERHARD (*continuing*)
Can you see that you'd say, "I don't know"? Two *different* things would not occur for you as "two." However, after a few examples of different things as two, you would eventually get that.

(*holding up two things in one hand and one thing in the other*)
A *new* level to get, which would again require demonstration by examples. Then another new level.

(*holding up one finger*)
A set and an empty set. You'd never get this as two. No set of examples, however large, ever distinguishes two. It only describes or defines two. You can't invent new twos when you've just got a definition of two. When you distinguish two, what you do is create a *realm of possibility* in which things can occur, arise, as two. You can't ever invent without a distinction. Definitions limit, distinctions open up. What you are doing when you are distinguishing is creating, opening up a context in which what you are distinguishing can occur, can happen. Is that starting to get clear? What you're doing now is very different. You are *distinguishing distinction.* That's a little bit like putting your hands underneath your feet and lifting yourself up.

PARTICIPANT
How *would* you distinguish two?

THINKING

The kind of thinking that Martin Heidegger was distinguishing in his writing has not been available for human beings. We can't think this way because this way of thinking has not yet been thought as a possibility, and therefore it is none of the things which already-thought ideas always are: understandable, consistent within themselves, or consistent with our other thoughts. It is not yet already-available for assertion or evaluation. It must first be unconcealed.

Heidegger's first step in bringing forth this unthought thinking is to distinguish our current thinking *as* "our current thinking" rather than simply as "thinking." Essential to an inquiry into the possibility of thinking, Heidegger says, is an inquiry into what thinking is for us now: what we presently think about thinking, what we presently define as thinking, and—since our thinking gives us our being—what we *are* that thinking is (*WCT* 17). We must begin to think the difference between the possibility of thinking and whatever it is that we are doing now in the name of thinking, so that the difference becomes the opening for the possibility. The development of this distinction—a new way of thinking—is central to Werner Erhard's work, as it is to Heidegger's; therefore we will mention here several of the ways in which Heidegger characterizes the thinking he is attempting.

ERHARD

We'll get to that. Here's what I want you to get first. Distinguishing establishes a domain of possibility, is making possible, not giving form to, but making form possible; very important to get that difference. Be in this conversation: distinction or distinguishing is an operation unlike defining, explaining. It does not lead to understanding. You do not understand two when you have distinguished two. Distinction is an action which leads to power, because it creates possibility, which is freedom.

PARTICIPANT (*Forum leader*)

What is the difference between occurring and distinguishing?

ERHARD

Occurring happens in a realm distinguished. There are cultures in which, we are told, if you show people a photographic image they don't see it. These people, by the way, survive an environment you would die in, so they're probably not stupid. There's no image on the paper or in your brain. These cultures have never generated the possibility "photographic image," and so they see splotches on the paper. If you explain it to them, they don't see an image but a representation of an image. Where does the image happen? It happens *in the distinction "photographic image."* In that domain of possibility arises "photographic image."

PARTICIPANT (*Forum leader*)

I would like you to tease this out for me a bit more. Using the example, when you're distinguishing two with any objects, and then it now occurs as two. So when you give me examples of that, the occurrence now is determining how it occurs for me.

ERHARD

No. The definition is determining its occurring.

PARTICIPANT (*Forum leader*)

So it's a concept.

ERHARD

Yeah. And what you get is a conceptually driven occurring. And isn't that the way you learned mathematics? You weren't creative or generative in mathematics. Mathematicians learn math at the level of distinctions, not at the level of definition. Consequently, they invent numbers. They are not limited by arithmetic; they are freed by arithmetic, because arithmetic is constituted by distinctions not by definitions. Arithmetic is not conceptual for them. Art is conceptual for most people. Artists don't generate art conceptually. If they do, that's not art. That's handicraft, not art. You can't create out of concepts, definitions. Dancers don't dance out of explanations of dance. They generate it out of a domain of possibility in which they can invent forms. What's present when a dancer is dancing is an occurring allowed by the possibility, not an occurring allowed by the conception. You start doing the same thing over and over again when your art is reduced to a concept. That's painting by the numbers.

Fundamentally, this thinking is a response to an *appeal*. The appeal arises from the wavering in appearance of Being, from its tendency in the act of appearing to disappear. "Nature loves to hide," says the common translation of a fragment of Heraclitus, the pre-Socratic Greek thinker (Wheelwright 70), which Heidegger retranslates to emphasize his reading of *physis* (pronounced *foo'-sis*): "Being (emerging appearance) intrinsically inclines toward self-concealment" (*IM* 126). Thus the essential—Being, that which must be thought—*turns away*. Being withdraws. And although Heidegger acknowledges that for contemporary humans this withdrawal is now almost unnoticed, nevertheless as beings, we *are*. Therefore at some level we are always turned toward that missing aspect of our existence:

> What withdraws from us, draws us along by its very withdrawal, whether or not we become aware of it immediately, or at all. Once we are drawn into the withdrawal, we are drawing toward what draws, attracts us by its withdrawal. And once we, being so attracted, are drawing toward what draws us, our essential nature already bears the stamp of "drawing toward." (*WCT* 9)

This is the exigence in the background of our lives. We are drawn toward the ongoing concealment of Being, and in being so drawn we find ourselves *pointing* in its direction: "*We are who we* are by pointing in that direction—not like an incidental adjunct but as . . . an essential and therefore constant pointing toward what withdraws" (*WCT* 9, emphasis added).

The *way* to draw toward that which withdraws is through thinking, since "Being in general gets interpreted on the basis of thinking" (*IM* 129), but not in the ordinary way we understand thinking. To think is "to lend a hand to the essence, the coming to presence, of Being" ("TT" in *QCT* 40). When we are thinking we are looking and drawing toward what withdraws: "Whenever man is properly drawing that way, he is thinking—even though he may still be far away from what withdraws, even though the withdrawal may be as veiled as ever" (*WCT* 17). Therefore Heidegger says of Socrates: "All through his life and right up to his death, Socrates did nothing else than place himself into this draft, this current, and maintain himself in it. That is why he is the purest thinker of the West" (*WCT* 17).

The relationship of thinking to Being is easily conceived in familiar Cartesian terms: "Being is the objective, the object. Thinking is the subjective, the subject. The relation of thinking to Being is that of subject to object" (*IM* 150). Such a conception, however, keeps us stuck in one of the primary dualities of metaphysical thought. Heidegger finds an alternative view in a fragment from the Greek thinker Parmenides: *to gar auto noein estin te kai einai*, which has been translated, traditionally and (says Heidegger) inadequately, as "thinking and Being are the same" (*IM* 152). In fact, the relation between thinking and Being is much subtler than simple "identity," and it is the development of the nature of this relation which is at the center of Heidegger's later thought. In Werner Erhard's work, this relation is explored persistently in the dialogue of The Forum.

Heidegger emphasizes that the way to thinking is not thinking *about* thinking, a practice that has flourished in the West as "logic" (*WCT* 21). Nor, even more fundamentally, is it the kind of thinking which Nietzsche called "blinking," the formation of ideas which "present and propose of everything only the glitter, only the appearance of surfaces and foreground facets" (*WCT* 82).

Merely having thoughts, for Heidegger, is "idea forming," and not at all what is involved in true thinking: "We understand, of course, and consider it the most obvious thing in the world, when someone says, 'I *think* the matter is such and such,' and with it has in mind, '*I have such and such an idea* of the matter'" (*WCT* 45). But we have not yet really thought what is involved in idea-forming. That is, we have thought of "idea forming" as "thinking," but we have not yet thought of idea-forming as idea-forming, that is, as a distinct *mode* of thinking. Thus we have not thought something which is determinative of our very existence:

PARTICIPANT (*Forum leader*)
So occurrence can be constitutive of distinguishing?

ERHARD
No. The other way around and constitutive is not the right word. Allowed by is better. Occurring is allowed by the distinction in which it occurs. The occurring is possible by virtue of the domain of possibility which you have established. For instance, the photographic image doesn't occur in the brain or in the eyes. Those were operational before. The occurring happens in a "house called possibility." Possibility is a product of an operation called distinguishing.

PARTICIPANT (*Forum leader*)
Thank you.

ANOTHER PARTICIPANT (*Forum leader 2*)
I have a sense that there's an architecture, or whatever word you want to use, so that in order to objectify something, you have to be able to locate it, someplace, sometime, some form, some architecture for definition. Is there an architecture for distinguishing?

ERHARD
I'm not clear about your use of the word architecture.

PARTICIPANT (*Forum leader 2*)
Anatomy or elements.

ERHARD
At one end of the spectrum is design, at the other end is making. Anatomy is at the making end. What's up at the design end, mostly lives in what will remain unsaid. Although present by virtue of... all that...

PARTICIPANT (*Forum leader 2*)
Is it possible to elevate or transform a concept to a distinction, and create a possibility?

ERHARD
That's moving from anatomy to design. When you deal with distinction, with design, there's something inherently satisfying about that. There's something inherently satisfying in mastering something, and mastery and distinction are synonymous.

(*to the group*)
Whatever it is, what are you going to use it for? To look good. The problem is, you can't use distinctions. Distinctions use you, you don't use them. Distinctions *give* you. Not many people own a yellow car, right? Buy a yellow car and see how many yellow cars you see. We're developing *occurring* as a new distinction. You got *is*.

THEODORE

How do you distinguish something without defining it?

ERHARD

Yeah. We're going to get to that.

THEODORE

I got something about looking good. In being here I want this to be successful, and one of my fears is not looking good, going home and seeing that nothing happened.

ERHARD

You're not free and that will keep something from happening. So when you're willing to be with one of the possible outcomes–that nothing will happen–then you're in a place where something can happen to you. You see how strange that sounds? By being willing to have nothing happen you are in a place where something can happen. Thanks.

(*Theodore sits down*)

Distinction is an operation in language. In the normal course of events, you and I think of language as something we use to *report* on something. Language is for talking *about*. It's for *abouting*. Describing and explaining are operations in language called reporting. We think that there's something *out there* that has a particular way it is, and I make a representation of it. And if my representation is accurate, I can make it work. But now we're distinguishing a new kind of operation in language. It's an operation in language called *generating*. It's as though I said "chair" and a chair came out of my mouth. Watch. You're going to see this thing fall out of my mouth as I say it: *I promise*. When I said "promise," what fell out of my mouth was a promise. When I say "I promise," that's a promise, isn't it? What falls out of my mouth when I say "I promise"? A promise. *When I say "I promise," a promise falls out of my mouth.* All I want you to see is there's possibility in language that didn't occur to you, because you hadn't distinguished language as a generative act. So we're sneaking up on the answer to the question: what is the operation by which one distinguishes? Not an operation in language like reporting, but creating. Listen up. Apes are not stupid. But no ape has ever picked up a stick along a path because he needed to knock down bananas. Why not? Because apes live in a world with no possibility; because they live without language. And I don't mean laboratory apes. Laboratory apes are tainted with language.

LOUISE

What about the hundredth monkey?

ERHARD

It's totally false, that example. It's bullshit, and demonstrated to be so. The author has acknowledged that he wrote that to make a point. Lyall-Watson recanted that as scientific evidence. I want to stop hearing that crap about the hundredth monkey.

> **One might say, for instance: "I think it will snow tonight." But he who speaks that way is not thinking, he just has views on something. We must be very careful, however, not to regard this "viewing" as insignificant. All our daily life and all we do moves within what we have in view, and necessarily so. (*WCT* 32)**

That is, idea-forming shapes us, and thus "the *essence* of idea-forming is probably the first thing that must be put into the language of thinking" (*WCT* 55). This is the first step in the *appropriation* of our current way of thinking: the recognition and taking-over of that thinking, which is necessary before we can attain a possibility beyond it.

This aspect of Heidegger's thinking has been central throughout its evolution, emerging in various iterations, from the resoluteness of Dasein in *Being and Time* to the gentler *releasement* of his later work. It is also a central element in Werner Erhard's methodology. Both men posit the paradoxical idea that, rather than resisting those aspects of ourselves that we see as in some way problematic, we *let them be,* and own them, and thereby gain a freedom to think beyond them. The idea is fundamental to the transformation that both men are working to make available. ∎

LOUISE (*continuing to object*)
Apes and dogs have language. So do rocks.

ERHARD
If everything's got language there's nothing to talk about, because nothing's distinguished.

LOUISE
They are different languages.

ERHARD
You're making yourself stupid. You're a fucking Californian. It's that hundredth monkey shit. You denigrate the great mysteries when you turn them into crap. Apes don't have language. It's true that apes signal. But they don't communicate. Rocks bump into each other, and animals have a fancy form of bumping. But animals don't have language, they have signals. Whatever it is we're distinguishing with the word language, it's what human beings do. Apes don't dwell in possibility. To dwell in possibility you've got to have what I call language. I'm asserting something, and you can't prove an assertion. You can disprove an assertion but you can't prove it. You can validate an assertion, and there's a lot of evidence for that one. You can move without language. Rocks move all the time. One *distinguishes* by an operation in language in which possibility is generated. And it's generated by speaking and listening, and by what's present without being said by virtue of what is said. Let me give you an example.

(*addressing The Forum Supervisor*)
Julie, give me some water please? She doesn't come up and throw a bucket of water on me.

(*to the group*)
Where the hell is "in a bucket" or "in a glass"? It's not in your brain. *It's in the conversation.* One of the possibilities in the domain of possibility called language is possibility itself. *Two was distinguished in the conversation we had for distinguishing distinction.*

(*moving to the chalkboard and drawing a series of marks*)
Is this two?

LOUISE
It's two.

(*grouping the marks with two enclosing outlines*)
Now it occurs as two. Two is there if you've got the possibility "two." There's an infinite number of ways to make that "two."

LOUISE
But how do you do it?

ERHARD
It arises in language. Do you know how to ride a bicycle?

> **One distinguishes by an operation in language in which possibility is generated. And it's generated by speaking and listening, and by what's present without being said by virtue of what is said.**

LOUISE
Yes.

ERHARD
How did you learn?

LOUISE
Just started to go and then discovered that my dad was not behind me.

ERHARD
That's the story they say. But let me tell you how it happened. When you first sit on a bicycle all the sensations are the same. They all feel the same: they're all falling. At some point some sensations are falling and other sensations are not. They're the same sensations you had when you first sat on the bicycle, but now some of them occur as falling and some as not falling. That happens when the distinction *balance* is distinguished as a possibility. Now your father told you, "you've got to balance. And balance is up like this." That didn't help. It all still felt like falling. When the distinction balance is distinguished—not conceptualized—then some of the sensations start to occur as balance, as not falling.

(*pausing*)
There are no twelve easy steps to distinguishing. If you're willing to engage in the conversation there's a possibility of distinguishing there. Distinction arises in the conversation. You just can't see conversation. Very useful conversation. Thank you.

ANOTHER PARTICIPANT (*Forum leader 3*)
When you said "I promise," a promise falls out of your mouth; if I had listened to you promise twenty times and not keep your promise, then when you said the word "promise," a promise wouldn't fall out of your mouth, just the word "promise" would.

ERHARD
Yeah. If you don't keep your promise repeatedly, you create a no-possibility listening for promising, so that what falls out of your mouth is the word. So the possibility lives in the conversation.

PARTICIPANT (*Forum leader 3*)
So the sacredness of a promise can only live in a conversation.

ERHARD
Yeah. And one of the things that fucks it up brutally is that bullshit about sincerity. Disgusting. We'll get to that before The Forum is over.

PARTICIPANT (*Forum leader 3*)
The other thing. When I say I hate you, what could fall out of my mouth is hate or...

ERHARD

Watch out or we're going to get too far ahead into The Forum.

ANOTHER PARTICIPANT (*Forum leader 4*)

In mapping this conversation onto an area of my life where I have a rich body of distinctions, things like skiing or leading The Forum, or being with my kids. Looking at my kids' development. It seems like there are three things in the conversation for distinguishing distinction. I wanted to see if I'm tracking with it. One is that it's almost entirely in what is unsaid. What's said is almost only because something needs to be said for there to be an unsaid. The second is that action is a necessary component.

ERHARD

Yeah, that would be misunderstood at this point. You can have an action in language too.

PARTICIPANT (*Forum leader 4*)

The spoken conversation doesn't necessarily need to be about what's being distinguished.

ERHARD

That's right. That's what I read from Heidegger about leaving it the realm of the unsaid. Like in the *Karate Kid*.

ANOTHER PARTICIPANT (*Forum leader 5*)

I had participation as a definition, and it shifted over to a distinction. I started to listen differently. When you talked about being used by a distinction, two things happened. I recalled a movie I saw called *The Gods Must Be Crazy*. There was no Coke bottle for them, but I get that there was no *not*-Coke bottle for me. I'm here for a breakthrough in my commitment in my relationship with my children and my wife. I've used up the context for my family.

ERHARD

Listen up here. You create a possibility for your family and when you use up that possibility, and wonder where the juice went: What's missing may not be more and better content. What's missing may be a new opening, a new possibility.

PARTICIPANT (*Forum leader 5*)

And I could see that the conversation for extending the single dimension. There's a new demand for myself for generating distinction.

ERHARD

Something extraordinary opens up with a new realm of distinction. It's not additive. It's unrelated to what it was before. No persistence of the old.

PARTICIPANT (*Forum leader 5*)

So now this isn't news—the power of distinction—see I had that as a definition distinct from

HEIDEGGER'S PEDAGOGY

Here, despite the affinities we are proposing between the thinking of Heidegger and the work of Werner Erhard, we call attention to a fundamental difference in the nature of their work. This difference lies in the *rhetorical form* of their communication. In The Forum, the model is not orator and audience, a commonplace view of rhetoric. Rather, The Forum's form, elements of which have emerged in the various perspectives expressed in this book, is *rhetorical dialogue*, a strategic transaction which has as its aim the inclusion of the dialogic participants in the disclosive experience itself. Preservation, in this model, stands in a different relationship to disclosure: it becomes the dwelling-within the work by those who have themselves participated in the disclosive and creative act of communication.

PARTICIPANT (*Forum leader 5; continuing*)

distinguishing distinction. And then I saw that there's a particular relationship that I've adopted. I don't see the incident, but I've got an already always listening, a new one I hadn't seen before: "this is theirs, not mine." I can see now that's been using my life. There's an opening.

ERHARD

When you can see "it's theirs, not mine," then there's a possibility beyond "it's theirs, not mine." When you keep avoiding it, there is no possibility.

KYLE

What is the difference between difference and distinction?

ERHARD

Distinction is not dependent upon relationship, and difference is. Something that's different is dependent upon that from which it is different. I don't see photons, I see people, although what's out there are photons. I don't see with my eyes. I see with my mouth. That is to say, I see with language. Things occur as they occur because of language. What distinguishing is, is to take something like an undifferentiated mass and to bring forth from that mass a realm of possibility. Distinction gives existence. It makes existence possible. Distinctions aren't dependent on. They are kind of, of *themselves*. The effectiveness of someone who can deal from the whole—and all that means is having the distinction—is very different from someone who has all the parts.

(*Kyle sits down*)

Why we had this whole discussion: so we can distinguish *racket*—so your racket *occurs* for you as a racket. So that you're not looking around for what fits the definition. I want it to show up for you as a presence. I'm going to distinguish a racket. A racket's got to be something that you're protesting, saying you don't want to be doing or being. Something you wish you weren't doing, or trying not to do it. Like let's say you're being stupid. It's not a racket if you say listen, I'm being stupid on purpose, I get a lot out of being stupid. See when I'm stupid I don't have to be responsible for anything. That's not a racket. A racket is where you are like, "I wish I wasn't so stupid!" That's when it's a racket. A racket has got to be something you're doing or being that you are protesting or resisting or that you don't want to do or be. That's what makes it a racket. And what's driving it is the payoff. You're getting something out of being stupid—that's your racket. Like, "my family walks all over me, and I don't want them to do that." There's a protest there. Then what's the payoff? I get to feel sorry for myself. "Oh I see: that's a racket." What's driving you to be a way that your family walks all over you is the payoff you get for having your family walk all over you. And then there's a cost. There are three elements to a racket. You're doing or being something that you're protesting or resisting, but you're still doing it. It's persisting and you're protesting the persistence. The second element is the payoff. It's the payoff which drives the racket. Rackets are not habits. Take the payoff away, the racket disappears immediately. Being cranky is not a habit. Brushing your teeth is a habit. Pull all your teeth out, you'd brush your teeth about three days. The payoffs are invariant and the costs are also always the same. Someone give me an example.

The scholar John Anderson has observed that throughout his work, Martin Heidegger is "urging his hearers and readers toward a kind of transmutation of themselves. . ." (*DT* 12). Ronald Bruzina locates this transmutation in a surrender to the *direction* of Heidegger's thinking:

 Heidegger is not attempting to formulate a position, but rather to execute a movement. If we realize now that this "movement" he executes is not only always *in language*, but also in a highly original and strange kind of wording, then we are close to seeing that this very *immersion in a wording movement* constitutes thinking. (Ronald Bruzina, "Heidegger on the Metaphor and Philosophy" 197)

Heidegger himself claimed that this direction of movement requires a transformation, which "occurs as a passage. . . in which one site is left behind in favor of another. . . and that requires that the sites be placed in discussion" ("DL" in *OWL* 42).

The critical element in this process was the *passage*. This point was made again at the beginning of the lecture series later published as *On Time and Being,* when Heidegger instructed his students on the way of *listening* they should bring to the lectures in order that the intended transformation might be achieved: "Let me give a little hint on how to listen," he said. "The point is not to listen to a series of propositions, but rather to follow the movement of showing" (*OTB* 2).

At the same time, Heidegger recognized the limitations of the lecture format for achieving the transformation he sought. In concluding this same lecture series, he acknowledged that "the form of a lecture remains itself an obstacle. . . . The lecture has spoken merely in propositional statements" (*OTB* 24). Neither, he suggested elsewhere, is a "scientific dissertation" an appropriate medium for an inquiry into language and Being, since "the movement of the questioning that is called for here might too easily *congeal*" ("DL" in *OWL* 50, emphasis added). Nor, he added, can "a transformation" be "established as the consequence of an accumulation of the results of philosophical research" ("DL" in *OWL* 42). For Heidegger as for Erhard, transformation was a gestalt switch from one site of understanding to another, a leap.

While Heidegger was committed to a transformation of his students' thinking about Being, he did not engage them as individuals in a dialogue about the possibility of this transformation *in their own lives*—that is, in their own Being-in-the-world. Heidegger's student Gadamer has commented in an interview with Ansgar Kemmann that Heidegger's lectures, while astonishing in their effects, were not explicit *exchanges* with his audience. In fact, Gadamer has suggested that Heidegger's relentless dedication to the communication of his ideas, in many ways so gripping, actually worked *against* his ability to engage the students in mutual conversation ("Heidegger as Rhetor" in *HR* 50).

An example of Heidegger's pedagogical inquiry, consistent with Gadamer's observation, is given in Medard Boss's account of Heidegger's 1958 seminars at the Psychiatric University Clinic in Zurich. Says Boss: "Only the participants of those first seminars are able to estimate what endless effort it cost until his medical listeners, trained solely in natural science, began to even suspect what Heidegger was trying to say" (*Heidegger and Psychology* 10). The following exchange is a fragment from the transcript of one of the seminars.

> **Heidegger: What is distance?**
>
> **Listener E: A definition of space.**
>
> **Heidegger: What then is space as such?**
>
> **(Ten long minutes of silence. . .)**
>
> **Listener F: We have never heard such questions and do not know what you regard as important, what you want to hear, what you want to say.**
>
> **Heidegger: I am only concerned that you open your eyes and do not immediately dim and distort your vision once more with artificial suppositions or theoretical explanations. How is it, then, with this matter that you have called an interval of space?**
>
> **(Seven minutes of silence. . .).**
>
> **(*Heidegger and Psychology* 10–11)**

MARY

I don't want to follow the rules.

ERHARD

Are you up front about not wanting to follow the rules?

MARY

Yes.

ERHARD

Then it's not a racket. So, let's say we're going to have a relationship. I'm going to be up front that I'm not going to follow the rules. Fine. No racket.

MARY

Are you saying it's hidden?

ERHARD

It's just not a racket if you're up front about it. So if I say, hey Wes, I want to follow the rules in the relationship, and I try to, but I just can't do it. It's not hidden, just something you're protesting. Something you're resisting. If you're doing what you want to do and saying that you don't want to do it, and you're doing it to get the payoff, that's the racket.

ANOTHER PARTICIPANT

My racket is sitting still, not participating.

ERHARD

And he wants to stand up and participate, except he doesn't, but he wants to. One more example.

ANOTHER PARTICIPANT

I say I am a partner with my husband, but I do things unilaterally.

ERHARD

Right, good. We'll get into more examples, but first I want to talk about the payoffs. If you're unhappy about something in your life, unhappiness is invariably a racket because there's something that you are that you don't want to be. Nobody wants to be unhappy. What's the payoff? "Well there's no payoff, it's just terrible. I'm unhappy." No, no. There's a fucking payoff in there. And the payoff is...

(Kipp writing on the board: the three elements of a racket: Protest Payoff Cost)

You're protesting, but it persists... When you go home tonight and start to run your racket, I want it to be present for you like a racket, not like some fucking soap opera about "you're unhappy"; present for you more like "I'm that way because I'm getting something out of it. And

ERHARD (*continuing*)

it's costing me something." And I want that to arise whenever you run your racket. I don't want you to take some stupid notes and try to remember that. What you do about running your racket is none of my business. My business is that when you leave here and you run your racket, it's gonna show up like your racket. And you and I are gonna have a conversation till we got racket distinguished powerfully enough so that when you run it, it shows up like "this is my racket." Clear? Stand up. Wait for the mic. Relax!

(*laughter*)

ANGEL (*to the group*)
He's assuming I'm not relaxed.

(*to Erhard*)
I am uncomfortable with calling my unhappiness over my divorce a racket.

ERHARD
Yes, you're fucking divorced.

ANGEL
It invalidates the fact that it hurts.

ERHARD
You're fucking divorced.

ANGEL
It's not a racket. It hurts.

ERHARD
You're fucking divorced. It didn't hurt. That is a fucking racket.

ANGEL
The word racket makes it sound like...

ERHARD
No I said fucking racket...

ANGEL
Fucking racket makes it sound like it's not real.

ERHARD
It's as real as any soap opera ever got.

We can assume that the students in Heidegger's philosophy classes would have been more responsive. Yet the transcript suggests that Heidegger, accustomed to the one-way communication form of the lecture, seems not to have been practiced in prompting dialogue. ∎

ANGEL
But when I hurt over it, it's not my decision to hurt over it.

ERHARD
Horseshit! Angel, listen up. When you walk out of here tonight, you are not going to be carrying your divorce around with you.

ANGEL
I've had it for a long time.

(*laughter*)

ERHARD
Wait. Wait. Listen to me.

(*holding a director's chair and dragging it across the stage, to laughter*)
See this is what you look like. And you wonder why are people looking at you funny. "What the hell are they looking at? I don't see anything funny."

ANGEL
But that's not my racket. I already picked out my racket.

ERHARD
Wait. Wait. Wait. You're not a woman, you're a woman who was divorced...

ANGEL
Twice.

(*loud laughter*)

ERHARD
Yeah, when you walk out of here, you won't be carrying around your divorces anymore.

ANGEL
Are you telling me I won't hurt about them anymore?

ERHARD
What hurts about them is carrying them around. Getting divorced does not hurt.

ANGEL
Yes it does.

ERHARD

No it doesn't. And you're a fucking racketeer and you've been carrying those goddamned divorces around, and the pain, for the payoff. And after Kipp gets this distinguished when we get back, you and I will have a little conversation. But we've got the ground established clearly. Do we not? Look, you're so frightened of losing that racket it's got you really upset. You're going to be a real wrong lady when we're done with the conversation. You will have spent years in pain for nothing. You're going to lose that whole justification after being in pain. You'll also lose all that baggage you've been carrying around.

ANGEL

All that pain makes it worth something.

ERHARD

Ahhh. Emerging racket. Listen. There is a payoff. Yeah, you got to justify what happened. That's one of the payoffs. Self-justification. Listen. I want you to be upset. I want you to be bothered. I want you to stay that way until we talk after the break again. And I intend to insult you and make you feel bad.

ANGEL

Thank you.

ERHARD

You're welcome.

(*laughter*)

Yeah, and I'm insulting you and making you feel bad because you *are* your divorces. And I have no respect for your divorces. No respect for the story and no respect for the soap opera. And I can't find any of *you* to respect there. Once we get some of you up, then I'll have some respect. Not insult. I'm insulting that crap.

ANGEL

There are a lot of people who respect me for my divorces, and my story about my divorces.

ERHARD

For certain, or you wouldn't still be doing it otherwise. No one inflicts pain on themselves.

ANGEL

Then why are you accusing me of inflicting pain on myself?

ERHARD

Because you are. You're listening to this like it's your fault. I didn't say it was your fault.

SOLICITUDE OF A FORUM LEADER

In Heideggerian terms, the Forum leader's way of Being-with-The-Forum participants is characterized as *extreme positive solicitude.*

Solicitude is Heidegger's term for Dasein's way of Being-with-Others who are themselves Dasein—that is, other human beings. This is distinct from how Heidegger understands *concern,* which indicates our way of being toward Things, or present-at-hand entities (please see the sidebar "Concern" in Session Four of Day One). Solicitude is an *existentiale,* which is to say, an aspect of Dasein's Being. "Thus in concernful solicitude the Other is proximally disclosed" (*BT* 161).

Throughout *Being and Time,* Heidegger introduces characteristics of Dasein as occurring in various ways or "modes," which indicate that the characteristic generally shows up to a greater or lesser degree, or in some cases not at all. Describing this feature of Heidegger's work, the book's translators, John Macquarrie and Edward Robinson, comment: "It is as if zero and the negative integers were to be thought of as representing 'deficient modes of being a positive integer'" (*BT* 42, note 1).

Heidegger tells us, for example, that solicitude, as a characteristic of Being-with-one-another, maintains itself for the most part in the "deficient and Indifferent modes." "Being for, against, or without one another, passing one another by, not 'mattering' to one another—these are possible ways of solicitude" (*BT* 158).

Because of the prevalence of these deficient modes, Dasein, sensing a need to create factical human connection, has devised ontic structures to correct the problem—empathy and "welfare work" are two that Heidegger mentions. But he also points out that these ontic solutions can never constitute or adequately replace Being-with, since they overlook the fundamental ontological issue: the deficiencies in the dominant modes of Being-with.

But solicitude has a positive mode as well, which Heidegger calls *extreme solicitude.* This mode has two forms. On the one hand, Dasein can *leap in for the Other:*

> **This kind of solicitude takes over for the Other that with which he is to concern himself. The Other is thus thrown out of his own position. . . . In such solicitude the Other can become one who is dominated and dependent, even if this domination is a tacit one and remains hidden from him. This kind of solicitude, which leaps in and takes away 'care,' is to a large extent determinative for Being with one another. . . . (*BT* 158)**

In normal circumstances, a Forum participant might expect to receive that kind of sympathetic response to her circumstances, such as the marital issues being described by this participant. But Erhard's solicitude in The Forum is of the second form:

> **[This is] a kind of solicitude which does not so much leap in for the Other as *leap ahead* of him . . . not in order to take away his 'care' but rather to give it back to him authentically as such for the first time. This kind of solicitude pertains essentially to authentic care—that is, to the existence of the Other, not to a *"what"* with which he is concerned; it helps the Other to become transparent to himself *in* his care and to become *free for* it. (*BT* 158–159)**

We find in Heidegger's distinction here of *extreme solicitude as leaping ahead of the Other* a profound characterization of the role of a Forum leader. ∎

ANGEL
Having this as a racket isn't my fault?

ERHARD
No, the question of fault is... it isn't somebody else's fault either. And it's your responsibility. And as I've said, nobody knows what I'm talking about when I use the word responsibility, so we're not going to talk about that much anymore. Relax until we get back. You've been living with the pain for however many years it's been, another... while people take a break... You know, peeing is very important to people... Peeing is more important to people than their lives. And particularly more important than your life. If it was their life they might not have to pee, but because it's your life, they have to pee. So we'll continue this after the break.

Erhard left the room, and Kipp came onto the platform. He moved to the blackboard and expanded what Erhard had written about the structure of a racket:

right	dominates	justifies itself	win
wrong	avoids domination	invalidates others	lose

KIPP
The payoff expresses itself as: it always dominates, wins, or justifies itself. Till you can get up here on the board, I promise you nothing. The structure for the payoff, what keeps the payoff in place, is what's up there on the board. The first thing it costs you is your self-expression. Second, the cost is any happiness in your life. You're only happy to be right. The next cost is your vitality or your health. And the final cost of having your life be lived by your racket is the possibility of love, of affinity. You cannot put love, affinity, and being right together. If the cost gets bigger than the payoff, you'll give it up in a moment. That's why in a tragedy you'll be heroic: because the cost is right there in your face. Angel has been too generous. She has given you the whole mechanism. If she couldn't be right about the pain what would she have to confront in her life?

Erhard joined Kipp on the platform.

ERHARD
Angel, the pain makes the divorces right. You getting a divorce was wrong, and the pain makes it right. You've got the pain to make yourself right. That's the payoff. What I'm asking you to see is that the pain is not there because you got divorced. The pain is there to keep you from being wrong about having been divorced. It works that way, doesn't it?

ANGEL
Yes.

ERHARD
Never mind why it's there. Forget that for the moment. Too hard to see that. If the pain weren't there you'd be very wrong wouldn't you? You'd be a shallow nobody whose promises didn't

ERHARD (*continuing*)

mean anything, wouldn't you? Yeah. So you need the pain to keep you from being wrong. At least it works that way doesn't it?

(She nods)

Good, that's all I want you to see for the moment. I want you to see how godawful important it is to look good. Now we've gotten looking good a lot more sharply defined. Looking good is constituted by being right. Or having something you identify with as right. And having other people and other things be wrong. Angel would tell you that people who get divorced easily and don't have any pain are wrong. I want you to see that it is so important that you're willing to suffer pain over a long period of time: intense pain over a long period of time that destroys your happiness. Being right is so important, so sacred, that even a lot of pain over a long time is not too much a price to pay to be right. I want you to see that this is not anything that would occur to you normally. It would never ever in a million years occur to Angel that the pain made her right, because that's not the structure for interpretation in which we hold life. You and I have invented a new structure of interpretation for life: *racket.* Getting divorced does not produce pain. Having your child die does not produce pain. Rackets produce pain. What happens never produces pain. If you lose a child and you're sad, that heals the loss, and that's not a racket. Authentic sadness heals the loss, then the loss diminishes, then the sadness, and finally it's complete. But not in a racket: where life becomes about being sad. It's very hard to see this, and that's why you need to distinguish this possibility powerfully so that what was a soap opera, a drama, which is very real and valid, can be seen for what it is, namely a racket. That isn't going to be easy for you to do, so you need to listen up with the distinguishing.

(indicating Angel)

You and I are not finished. After the break.

Kipp set up paired shares. The Forum Supervisor announced the beginning of the break at 3:50 pm.

SESSION TWO INTERVAL

The Forgetting of Being, Part One of Eight: Getting and Losing

In November 2013, while this book was in development, we delivered a presentation about it as members of a panel at the National Communication Association conference in Washington DC. Our thesis was that the ontological discourse of The Forum provides participants with direct access to an experience of Being. Following the presentation, an audience member asked this question: After participants have undergone the experience of Being that The Forum makes available, what becomes of that experience? Does it persist?

This is obviously a central question for any consideration of Erhard's work. From its inception as the *est* Training, there has been a persistent quality of elusiveness, and therefore of mystery, about the transformation this work makes available. People do not leave The Forum having gained the kind of cognitive understanding we generally expect from an educational process. The result, instead, is that by engaging in the conversation that occurs in The Forum, participants have "*gotten it,*" in somewhat the way that one gets a joke. Heidegger characterizes such a phenomenon as *undergoing an experience with language,* which means that language "befalls us, strikes us, comes over us, overwhelms us and transforms us" ("NL" in *OWL* 57).

The process is not linear; Erhard has described it as not getting it for a long time, and then getting it all at once. But there is at the same time a recognition that what you're suddenly seeing is a truth you'd already always known at some level. Heidegger characterized it as "a leap" onto the ground on which we are already standing (*WCT* 233), and Erhard has characterized it in similar terms: "I can't have it and give it to you. But I can communicate in a way so that you get an opportunity to realize that you have it yourself already. Essentially, this is what the *est* Training [and later The Forum] was developed to do" (*Bartley* 169).

Heidegger's German word for this kind of experience is *Augenblick.* The usual translation is *instant, moment, or split second;* but Hubert Dreyfus says that in Heidegger's use, the word is more appropriately rendered as *moment of vision or transformation* (*BT,* note 376; Dreyfus, *Being-in-the-World* 321). In *Being and Time,* Heidegger uses the word to designate the gestalt switch that occurs when a human being takes resolute ownership of his life and an authentic existence becomes possible (*BT* 387).

Since the experience of The Forum is not understood in the usual way, neither is it retained in memory in the way that cognitive understanding is. Being can be communicated, and the results reported by Forum participants give evidence that its communication is experienced as transformative; but a quality of elusiveness persists in the way that transformative experience is retained. Further, according to Erhard, the elusiveness is to be expected. "That's the way it's supposed to happen," he tells The Forum participants. "Getting and losing."

Why the elusiveness? What is it about Being that leads it to withdraw—as it has withdrawn over two millennia from the human experience of existence; and as it withdraws repeatedly during The Forum dialogue as Erhard and the participants struggle to bring it to presence?

Heidegger has provided a response to this question in a series of lectures he delivered at the University of Freiburg in 1935. Published in 1959 under the title *An Introduction to Metaphysics,* these lectures became his first book-length work to be translated into English. He later extended his thinking on the subject in four essays, published in 1975 as *Early Greek Thinking.* In these volumes, Heidegger locates the source of Being's withdrawal at the point of its first emergence. He calls this juncture the *beginning of history*—the moment when the West's first philosophers were beginning to think about the nature of Being, and to understand themselves as world-creators.

But in Heidegger's account, Western thinking, at its very inception, failed to capture the truth of Being in language. As a consequence, Being, and what its experience might make available, has been lost to us, and so thoroughly that even its conceptualization defies our thinking. What does Heidegger see as possible if human access to Being was restored? He says that we would be opened to *the epiphany of a world* (*IM* 69)—our everyday perceptions and experiences would occur newly, in a context of possibility that is not present in our current view of things.

This context of possibility, he says, was available to humans in one brief moment of history. What became of Being? In this series on the forgetting of Being, during Intervals between sessions, we will present Heidegger's account.

The Forum resumed at 4:20 pm. Kipp returned to the platform and called for participants to share what they had discovered about their rackets.

KIPP
We asked you to distinguish *sharing yourself*. The time in The Forum for explaining your life is over.

JODIE
I want a relationship.

KIPP
Are you sharing or talking about?

JODIE
I don't know.

KIPP
My racket is... My payoff is... The way my racket shows up in my life is... Share the juice.

JODIE
My racket is that I want a relationship. And every time one appears I sabotage it, so that it doesn't happen.

KIPP
What's the truth?

JODIE
I'm not in a relationship.

KIPP
No. What's authentic is "if I had a relationship, I'd be wrong. What gets me up in the morning is how I can avoid being in a relationship." And the racket is that you say what?

JODIE
That I want a relationship.

KIPP
Who do you get sucked into the racket? There's a distinction called "on the court." There's another distinction called "up in the stands talking about what's on the court." What your life is about is not having a relationship. How do you feel about that?

FORUM DAY TWO:
SESSION THREE

JODIE

Cheated.

KIPP

That was on the court. You could hear that. Who has to pay for your not having a relationship?

JODIE

Everyone in my life.

KIPP

If you're not cheated, you don't know who to be in life. Maybe there is no being authentic. Maybe the best there is, is being authentic about your own inauthenticity. Being related is much more risky than being unrelated. You've got to be there in the presence of being human.

JODIE

I got it.

KIPP

Don't be so quick to get it. See, I don't think you got it. I don't think you got the dagger in your heart. What's your racket an excuse for? You don't have to reveal yourself. You don't have to create a relationship. What persistent condition do you complain about? A cheated person has to look like a cheated person. You can't have love in your life or you'd be wrong. What today's about is beginning to be in the presence of your own life.

JODIE

I want to get beyond this.

KIPP

There is no getting beyond it. That's more California. The opportunity is to be with it. Maybe there is no getting beyond your racket. Maybe the only dignity is in owning it.

The participant, Mike, who earlier in the day had interacted with Erhard about "knowing how to walk," raised his hand.

MIKE

I don't know what my racket is. I'm lost.

(*laughter*)

KIPP

What case are you pleading?

MIKE
I don't know.

KIPP
Look at your life. What is your life about? What is something that if you could do, you'd do it?

MIKE
I would have everybody like me.

KIPP
But...

MIKE
But if they get to know me, they stop listening to me after ninety seconds.

KIPP
When you are in the presence of another human being, what's there?

MIKE
I look at the ceiling.

KIPP
Do you feel stupid?

MIKE
Yes.

KIPP
What happened when you were young?

MIKE
I tried to get in with a crowd of kids at school. I tried to blend in. A good friend of mine turned away and cut me out of the circle.

KIPP
Any others?

MIKE
When I was sweeping. Ten-years-old. My dad said I didn't sweep well. I wasn't smart enough to sweep.

KIPP

"I'm not smart enough to sweep" never happened.

Erhard joined Kipp on the platform.

ERHARD

Mike, it's something you became. Did "I'm not smart enough to sweep" ever happen?

The tone here was very quiet and still—the interaction was delicate, Mike somehow fragile.

MIKE

I don't understand; I need more clarification. I know that I missed places.

ERHARD

Did it happen that you missed places?

MIKE

Yes.

ERHARD

Did it happen that your father pointed out where you missed?

MIKE

Yes.

ERHARD

Did "I'm not smart enough to sweep" ever happen?

MIKE

I guess not.

ERHARD

What do you mean, you guess? Guess is part of your racket about being stupid. I want you to get something: *you became "I'm not even smart enough to sweep."* You didn't just think it. You didn't just have that thought. You *became* "I'm not smart enough to sweep." You made yourself into "I'm not smart enough to sweep."

Erhard sat on the edge of the platform facing Mike. The room was very still. Kipp sat nearby on the platform edge.

MIKE

I became "I'm not smart enough to sweep."

ERHARD

You made yourself into "I'm not smart enough to sweep." It wasn't true; It wasn't false: Because that's not something that's true or false. It's just something you became.

MIKE

Okay.

ERHARD

What's the payoff in becoming that?

MIKE

I didn't have to try any harder, so I gave up.

ERHARD

One of the payoffs was, you avoided the responsibility of having to produce the result. You avoided the domination of the responsibility for producing. Your brothers and sisters were dominated by the need to produce. You avoided that domination.

MIKE

Correct.

ERHARD

Good. When did you first have this conversation about being stupid?

MIKE

Eight or nine years old.

ERHARD

What happened that that became a conversation?

MIKE

Another time I was sweeping, I missed a spot.

ERHARD

And you became stupid at some point. You've got as much sense as anybody does. You started being stupid when you were eight or nine years old as a way of dealing with what was going on with your dad. It's a way of being you took on. What other payoffs are there?

MIKE

I didn't have to fight my dad back in fighting that I was stupid.

ERHARD
You avoided the domination of your father by giving in.

MIKE
Right.

ERHARD
How much energy did your father put into fixing you?

MIKE
He kept pointing out all the wrong things I did.

ERHARD
So you dominated your dad by getting him attached to your stupidity, right? Like Brer Rabbit. That was his relationship to you, trying to deal with your stupidity.

MIKE
When he was trying to correct me.

ERHARD
What other payoffs did you get out of being stupid? Did you get to be right? Did your father get to be wrong?

MIKE
I got to be right about being dumb.

ERHARD
Did you identify strongly with your father?

MIKE
Yes.

ERHARD
So you made what you identified with right.

MIKE
Correct.

ERHARD
What did it cost you to have a racket called being stupid?

MIKE
I stopped talking with my dad.

ERHARD
So there was a loss of relationship?

MIKE
Yes.

ERHARD
A certain loss of love.

MIKE
Loss of my self.

ERHARD
You lost self-expression. You cut off that avenue of self-expression called intelligence.

MIKE
Okay.

ERHARD
What about happiness?

MIKE
I was sad that I couldn't make my dad happy.

ERHARD
Got it.

MIKE
I still don't understand why the whole crowd was laughing at the beginning.

ERHARD
I don't know. Why were they laughing at the beginning?

KIPP
They laughed when he stood up and said he didn't know what his racket was.

ERHARD
Mike, you've been in here for a little while right? People thought I was insulting when I called them assholes. That was like a "damned with faint praise," not an insult. Asshole is a fairly high level. People are really stupid. Are you tuned in?

MIKE
Yeah.

ERHARD
I want to acknowledge you for not pulling one bit of shit during the two conversations you've had with me. You are an extraordinarily straight guy, who just had one racket: stupid, which you now know is a racket. My business is that when you run the racket you'll know it's a racket. Anything else to complete for you?

MIKE
No.

ERHARD
Thanks.

(*applause as Mike sits*)

(*to the group*)
All you've got to do is get it straight: my racket is, the cost is, the payoff is. That's all you got to get. Just that.

(*looking around*)
Where is Angel? Stand up and tell me what you've made of this so far.

Angel, who had earlier interacted with Erhard about her divorce, rose.

ERHARD
What's your racket? My racket is...

ANGEL
I've had a long time to think about this so I'm supposed to know, right?

ERHARD
You're not supposed to know anything. What do you know? My racket is...

ANGEL
That I'm a victim.

ERHARD
Very good. Yeah. You've got this big stupid soap opera, this stuff. The truth is you're a racketeer. The truth is you've got this racket about being a victim. That's the truth. Not all this soap opera... That's a smoke screen for being a racketeer. Your racket is that you're a victim. Yes?

ANGEL

Yes.

ERHARD

And what is the payoff for being a victim? Take your time and look up there and say what the payoff is.

(*pausing as Angel stares at the chalkboard*)

Puzzling, isn't it?

ANGEL

I don't know what I get to be right about. I get to be right about what?

ERHARD

About being sincere.

ANGEL

And deeply emotional and caring. You forgot about that.

ERHARD

Yeah, you're not deeply emotional and caring or sincere. You're a fucking racketeer. And the racket is being a victim and the payoff is that it makes you right. You've got this bullshit golden calf called being deeply emotional and caring and being sincere. Being emotional and caring and sincere is bullshit. This is not holy or sacred. I didn't say it wasn't nice. So, you've got this racket called being a victim and it makes you right because if you weren't a victim and you weren't suffering, then you would be wrong, you would be invalidated, would you not?

ANGEL

Yes.

ERHARD

You would be invalidated as a caring, deeply emotional, sincere person.

ANGEL

That's why your telling me that I don't hurt over my divorce invalidates and hurts.

ERHARD

I understand. I understand. All I'm doing is getting you, what I call "up on the pike," so we can work together on something. Did you want to say something?

ANGEL

I say that what I want to get out of The Forum is a marriage that would, like, last forever, but obviously what I've been about is making sure that I never can have that.

ERHARD

But you don't care about having a marriage that would last forever. All you care about is what validates you as a caring, sincere, deeply feeling person.

ANGEL

That would do it.

ERHARD

Yeah exactly, but you see, you don't care about being married. You really don't care about being married. You don't. If God came into the room and said, if you dyed your hair purple, that would make it clear to everyone that you are a deeply caring, sincere, feeling person, hell, you'd be out there dyeing your hair purple. To hell with getting married. That's your act. Your act is that you're sincere, deeply feeling, and a caring person. That's an act with you. That's not what you are. Mike is not stupid. Mike has an act called "being stupid."

ANGEL

So his father gave him his act.

ERHARD

No, no. He gave himself his act to deal with his father. Never mind that. Here's what I want you to get: Mike is not stupid. Mike's got an act called being stupid. You don't care. You've got an act called "I care" and you're not deeply feeling. That's an act. And you're not sincere. That's also an act.

ANGEL

I believe he's not stupid.

ERHARD

And you don't care. Now that's not quite accurate. So listen up. It's worse than that. I don't mean that you don't care like "I don't care." I mean you are not caring. That's an act. What you call caring is a fucking act. Why are you afraid of not caring?

ANGEL

It would make me a bad person.

ERHARD

Who didn't care?

ANGEL

It's the opposite.

ERHARD

Who?

ANGEL
Who cares more than anyone I know?

ERHARD
Who's that?

ANGEL
My mother.

ERHARD
Okay. What happened there? We haven't made the connection yet. Did you decide you had to be like your mother to survive? Oh, you didn't care, right?

ANGEL
Right. My mom told me I didn't care.

ERHARD
I got it. And?

ANGEL
And that's what happened. My mom told me I didn't care.

ERHARD
How old were you?

ANGEL
I was five.

ERHARD
Good. So what does a five year old… Take your time. Let yourself be with that. So you were a five-year-old little girl, and your mother told you that you didn't care. Yeah?

ANGEL
Yeah. My mother took in foster children. And I felt unloved because she was giving them her love and attention. She told me I was not being caring because I should care and understand that they need it more than I do, and that I was being selfish.

ERHARD
Isn't that a stupid fucking thing to tell a five-year-old? Listen…

ANGEL
But she was helping somebody who really needed it, who didn't have a mother or father, who…

ERHARD

Horseshit! What do you mean really needed it? That's all horseshit. They're probably 10 times as tough as you are. Probably needed a lot less than you did. But...irrelevant. You think a five-year-old is sophisticated enough to deal with that kind of logic?

ANGEL

I tried.

ERHARD

Is a five-year-old sophisticated enough to deal with that kind of logic? You know what a five-year-old girl looks like?

ANGEL

Yeah, I do, I saw home movies over Christmas. I know exactly what I looked like.

ERHARD

A five-year-old girl is pretty...not very worldly, huh? And also very caring, aren't they?

ANGEL

Yes. But she told me I didn't care.

ERHARD

Wait. We're not back at five now. We're having a discussion up here for a moment and then we'll go back to five. But I want you to look at a five-year-old little girl and see that a five-year-old girl cares very deeply, and is not up to the logic "you don't care" because if you'd care you would know that these other children need more love and attention than you do. So you dealt with it like a five-year-old. What does a five-year-old decide?

ANGEL

She was right.

ERHARD (*raising voice*)

No! She decides she's going to be the most caring person in the whole world!

ANGEL

Yes! Yes! Yes!

ERHARD

Like those magical bullshit fucking things that five-year-old girls do, which is wonderful when you're a five-year-old girl. You know, you decide, "I'm going to be the most caring person in the whole world! No one's going to care more than me."

ANGEL
Right.

ERHARD
You became that like Mike became stupid. It wasn't something you decided, it wasn't something you thought. You became that.

ANGEL
You want to hear something stupid? Being stupid isn't good but being sensitive and caring is good.

ERHARD
But listen up. You didn't quite get what I said. You actually *became,* gave yourself an identity, called caring. Whatever caring you had got buried under that identity. You became a caring machine. You became a caring robot. And whatever authentic caring you had, whatever authentic feeling you had; that got obscured by the robot. You get what I'm saying? You know what it's like to be married to a robot? Not good. This is not a good thing. Being related to a fucking robot. Particularly when the robot looks like they might be good for something else, like a real relationship. Did you hear what I just said?

ANGEL
Yes.

ERHARD
That caring act will get you plenty of relatedness, but it will never fulfill itself.

ANGEL
Right. That's why I could get married a million times, but I can't stay.

ERHARD
Caring is very attractive. The only problem is it's no fun to do it with a robot. And you're a fucking robot. You know, like a doll. Like a caring doll. You push on the button that says "I care." It's a lot of fun for a little while. But after a while it's got to have some substance. You took a very good thing and turned it into a mechanism.

(*referring to Mike*)
You see, he at least took something bad and turned it into a mechanism.

(*laughter*)
He had a little better luck than you did. You took something really good and turned it into a mechanism. So you know, his straightness, his authenticity leaks out around his act. But you took caring and being, like really being there, and turned it into an act, and it obscures your authentic caring and authentic feeling.

ANGEL
So I'm inauthentic about caring.

ERHARD
Precisely. Now you have a great fucking act. It's attractive, like bait.

Erhard sat on the edge of the platform, facing Angel. His tone was more forceful in this interaction than it had been with Mike. Kipp again sat nearby.

ERHARD (*continuing*)
You attract people because you're good at your act called caring. And you're good at your act called deeply feeling. So you get the fish up.

ANGEL
I was so good I believed it.

ERHARD
Exactly. See, underneath there is some kind of caring. I don't know what the hell it is. Maybe you care, I don't know. That doesn't interest me. I'll tell you one thing. You'll never be happy being something you're not, being your act. Ever. You're never going to care enough, feel deeply enough, to be happy, because none of that is who you are. And I don't know what you are. You may be caring. I don't know. Neither do you. You only know what your act is. What there is to get is that it's an act. You've done a very good job of that standing there. And I know it isn't easy. You noticed how a lot of the stupidity for Mike started to go away near the end of that conversation, interesting, right? Yeah. You want to relax for a little while; about this caring shit and about being deeply feeling. You might want to enjoy yourself for a little while, having some fun being shallow.

(*laughter*)

See it doesn't make any difference. This is a really important conversation because most of the acts are going to look a little nasty. But a positive act is as detrimental as a negative one, in fact it's worse. She would have died like that. Shit. All the pain is pure bullshit, pure bullshit, nothing authentic about the pain, not an iota of it. It's all there to make you right. The pain's not so attractive anymore is it?

ANGEL
No.

ERHARD
What happened? You got divorced twice. Okay. That's what happened, right? You got married. Then you got divorced. You got married. Then you got
divorced. That's all that happened. Not, "and I didn't keep my vows, and nah nah nah nah." None of that ever happened.

ANGEL
Right.

ERHARD
When my dog walks up to you, and all he can tell is you smell good. That's the whole story about you for my dog. You're starting to get how brutally stupid it's been to waste your life feeling badly about those stupid divorces. You know, you made a mistake. You know, I had seven children. I never punished my children. I never decided on their punishment. In fact we never talked about punishment. In life you do whatever you want, I've got certain rules. The rules are not for you; they are for me. Don't walk out in the street and get run over, I don't want to see you bloody. When you grow up you can do anything you want. When you're around me don't get run over, I don't want to see you bloody. You get run over there's a consequence. When my kids did something I would say, "You did it, good, now what's the consequence?" "I shouldn't be allowed to eat for a week."

(*laughter*)

"Okay," I would say, "I understand what you said, but we're going to be a bit more lenient than that." Kids are nuts about punishing themselves. And you had a five-year-old running her marriage. You had to be the most caring person in the whole world. So when the marriage didn't work, like when I asked my kids what should happen to you because you did this, I should not eat for a week. You had to make this enormous punishment for yourself.

ANGEL
Like I should not be happy for the rest of my life.

ERHARD
Precisely. Very good. I don't want to see you cry any more about that. I want you to see how stupid that is, how patently, brutally stupid. How old are you?

ANGEL
Thirty-two.

ERHARD
How old were you when you first got married?

ANGEL
Twenty-one.

ERHARD
How old were you when you got divorced first?

ANGEL
Twenty-five.

ERHARD

Okay. How long have you been suffering and unhappy?

ANGEL

From what?

ERHARD

From the divorce. Did it take the second divorce?

ANGEL

Yeah. The suffering and unhappiness was in the marriage.

ERHARD

But you put up with it.

ANGEL

I put up with a lot.

ERHARD

And that was good because somebody who cares more than anybody else in the world will put up with a lot of shit. So it made you right to suffer in your marriage. Made you a good person. You know what doormats attract?

ANGEL

People who step on them.

ERHARD

Exactly. You got it. And you know what? A doormat keeps a person who wants to wipe his feet stuck to the doormat. You dominated him just as sure as I'm sitting on this platform. You dominated him by being the victim. Now, he had his racket as well—two racketeers rubbing up against each other.

ANGEL

We had a great game.

ERHARD

It's disgusting.

ANGEL

I couldn't play without him.

ERHARD

Right.

ANGEL

And so I turned it around in my second marriage, where I was happy, but then I created the divorce so I could be a victim of the divorce.

ERHARD

Watch that word "created"; that gets bandied around by people who have done this work, and they don't know what they're talking about. What happened was: you got divorced. And that left you deeply unhappy.

ANGEL

The same place I was when I was married before.

ERHARD

Yeah. So you've got to get to the point where a fart and having been divorced are on equal levels.

(*laughter*)

ANGEL

There's something very wrong about that. I don't know what it is...

(*laughter*)

Is that really possible?

ERHARD

Yeah it is really possible. They're both just a "*what happened.*"

(*laughter*)

People who get married sometimes get divorced, true or false?

ANGEL

True.

ERHARD

You got married and you got divorced, true or false?

ANGEL

True.

ERHARD

And that's what happened. Like a fart.

ANGEL (*lightheartedly*)
There you go invalidating my um...

ERHARD (*playing an imaginary violin*)
Yeah, your zhuuuuuu.

(*laughter*)
Okay. Your racket is being a victim. And your racket is being righteous.

ANGEL
And being caring.

ERHARD
Right. And it makes you right and the rest of the world wrong. It allows you to dominate and allows you to avoid domination of a gutsy being-related-to-somebody.

ANGEL
Yes.

ERHARD
Don't forget that part. That's an important part of the payoff. And you got to justify yourself. You see, "after all I was a good girl." And what it cost you is, well, my guess is you pay for everything up there.

(*referring to the chalkboard*)
You're so young, maybe you haven't paid with any of your health, I don't know, maybe vitality. Clearly it cost you happiness and love.

ANGEL
Because I thought that was the act of loving someone.

ERHARD
And it is the act, but in that wrong sense. And my guess is that it has cost you some self-expression. See I don't know who you are.

ANGEL
I don't either.

ERHARD
I know who you are not. And that's right, you don't know either. And when you get out of here you can have the fun of finding out. And you'll find out every time you get off it, and you won't

ERHARD (*continuing*)

find out every time you're on it. And for you, on it is caring. And feeling deeply. I've been doing this work long enough that I can see behind people's masks a little bit, and you're a very beautiful person, but not in the way you think. Not in some airy fairy bullshit sense. But in a really gutsy sense. Who knows. I can be full of shit too.

(*to the group*)

There's no finish to this... There's no "And then she stopped being that!" She'll be that act forever. And when she's being that she'll have a possibility beyond being that. When she's running that act there will be no possibility beyond running that act. You got to own being a fake. You've got to be authentic about being inauthentic. Good for you. There ought to be some lightness in that for you.

ANGEL

It's incredible. I can't even describe how it feels to be able to say that I faked caring.

ERHARD

Yeah.

(*long, loud applause*)

(*to the group*)

The important part for you is to get how implausible this is, that being able to be that you're a fake gives you power. That's totally implausible. It's what you're afraid to be that keeps you from being. And the worst thing in the whole universe, the worst thing for the last twenty seven years of Angel's life would be to be a fake. There couldn't be anything worse than that. The nastiest thing she could be. And avoiding being that cost her her life. That's implausible, that doesn't make any sense, and if I told you that yesterday you wouldn't have gotten it. You could not have gotten what Angel just did with herself, yesterday. You're now living in a different structure of interpretation. You're dwelling in a different conversation. So you can tolerate counter commonsensical phenomena: what doesn't make sense normally—like being able to be "I don't care" for a person for whom that is the worst thing you could be—would be a source of power.

(*to Angel*)

Anything else?

ANGEL

No, thank you.

ERHARD (*to another participant*)

Yes?

SOCIAL MOODS

As we pointed out in our discussion of moods in Day One, Heidegger says that moods are not individual "psychical" phenomena, but rather aspects of the way the world is disclosed to Dasein.

He also says that moods can be *public*:

 Publicness, as the kind of Being which belongs to the "they," not only has in general its own way of having a mood, but needs moods and 'makes' them for itself. It is into such a mood and out of such a mood that the orator speaks. He must understand the possibilities of such moods in order to rouse them and guide them aright. (*BT* 178)

In our analysis of The Forum, we are not characterizing Erhard (or any other Forum leader) as an orator, but as a *rhetor,* which is to say simply a person who uses language to some end. Rhetoric does not have the same formal implications as oratory, and the dialogic ontological rhetoric of The Forum is a significantly different mode of communication from the monologic public speaking of an orator.

And yet Erhard, in a debriefing with The Forum leaders during the 1989 Forum, stated that one of the results he had to achieve in leading The Forum was to "produce some effects." We also know from our experience that Forum leaders are acutely sensitive to the mood in The Forum room.

Hubert Dreyfus, in his study of *Being and Time,* asserts that in addition to being public, moods can be *social,* and he quotes this passage on social moods from a lecture Heidegger delivered in 1929:

> " **Moods are *not accompanying phenomena*; rather, they are the sort of thing that determine Being-with-one-another in advance. It seems as if, so to speak, a mood is in each case already there, like an atmosphere, in which we are steeped and by which we are thoroughly determined. It not only seems as if this were so, it is so; and in light of these facts, it is necessary to dispense with the psychology of feelings and experiences and consciousness.** (*Being in the World* 171)

Observes Dreyfus: "Heidegger would no doubt appreciate the fact that we ordinarily say we are *in* a mood, not that a mood is an experience *in* us."

Having participated in, and observed, a number of Forums, we know from personal experience that the process can be seen as a roller-coaster of mood shifts. Erhard tells the participants on the first day that they should bring their current moods into The Forum with them, and not try to fix them; so the moods of the participants are of course at some level individual, though not subjective, with each participant Being-in-his-or-her-own-world.

But in conjunction with our analysis of Being-with (in the sidebar with that title in Session One of Day Two), and in light of our own experience of The Forum, we raise this point about the nature of social moods. We do so to contrast such moods with the collective sense of affinity that inevitably accompanies The Forum transformation.

Heidegger's distinction of the publicness of the they-self is presented as an aspect of Dasein's fleeing its authentic self. Publicness, in that context, characterizes the levelling-down of Dasein's possibilities to the average, in the service of its flight from authenticity. We assert that the general mood in The Forum, through its roller-coaster changes to its ebullient finish, is an aspect of what it means for the authentic self to appropriate its own inauthenticity, and it diverges greatly from the levelling down the publicness

PARTICIPANT

Can you have more than one act?

ERHARD

Yes. I don't say you won't do your old number again. I just say you're left with a possibility beyond your old number. Being related is enormously risky. I don't care what fairy-tale bullshit you bought into. You're going to get hurt being related.

(*to the group*)

There are no answers to being successfully related. And you, assholes, have been looking for the answer to being successfully related. That's why you're assholes. There's a way to be empowered and enabled in the face of the risk that being related is. You can bring power and ability to the risk. You can't bring answers. There are no formulae, no ten easy steps. Okay. We need to do this about three times.

Kipp now took the lead in the interactions with participants, but Erhard remained in the conversation, wandering around at the back of the room and sometimes taking over an interaction that Kipp had begun.

ERHARD

See, you're so thrown to the story that you tell the story about the racket, and that will never give you anything beyond your racket. That's what the structure of the distinction racket is for, to break up the story. You die without knowing who you are if you live your life for approval.

(*regarding one participant's persistent back pain*)

You think people are really built that badly?

PARTICIPANT

My racket is I'm scared of doing it wrong. That doesn't sound right.

ERHARD

That's a very frequent payoff—avoid the domination of being responsible for. That's a very childish concern, but that's where your racket comes from. Kids' rackets are avoiding the domination of being responsible. You are going to be a little boy or little girl until you complete your relationship with your parents. You are not going to grow up until you complete your relationship with your parents. You are not going to get away with it. I happen to have had a mother who never made a mistake... only one. I'll tell you what that was later. This is one that I know about deeply and profoundly. You are not ever going to make it until your parents make it with you. No kidding. You just got to get off it with your parents. I've spent most of my life engaged in this question about what it is to be human. What is it that

ERHARD (*continuing*)

makes you and me the way we are? The standard interpretation as to how you and I got to be the way we are has no power. It gives me nothing to say about it. I can't talk myself into being. A lot of the lack of freedom is constituted in your relationship with your parents. The single most important learning experience in my life was doing programs with teenagers. The ten-day course for teenagers we used to do in the mountains—let me tell you what I found out about teenagers. After ten days, you find out that the single most important thing in your life is that you love your mother and father. And that's no shit. And there's very little structure in a teenager's life to express that. You've got to get that resolved, and if you're smart you'll get it resolved tonight. We'll let you out of here early enough to call your mother, call your father.

(*forcefully*)

You just gotta get off it. You're wasting your time and money in here if you're going to stay on it with your parents.

(*in response to a question about what it means to be complete*)

What I meant by being complete... your parents have got to be all right with you exactly the way they are. Your parents don't owe you a thing. They don't owe you their love. You are not entitled to your parents' love. You owe them. I know, it's a bitch. I don't like it either. I don't like gravity. I don't like being tied down. Gravity doesn't care. It's the way it is. Until you are complete with your parents you can't be yourself. Just loving them isn't enough. You've got to be able to *fully be with your parents the way they are.* You know, I spent most of my life tied to my mother's apron strings. And she had very long apron strings. I deserted my family. They didn't know where I was. Gone for years. I was still my mother's little boy. I didn't grow up till I was thirty something.

Here Erhard acknowledged a nineteen-year-old participant who had shared about his relationship with his parents for being complete with them at an early age.

ERHARD (*continuing*)

I don't know if you can see it or not, but until that happens you aren't anything but your mother's little boy.

Erhard left the room at this point, and Wes took the platform.

WES

We're now in the bonus category. This goes beyond The Forum. Look at your relationship with your parents from the question: "Are they really all right with me?" What do you have to get off with them? Being complete never leaves anybody with something dumped on them. Use the dinner break to complete with your parents. Find a telephone. Reach them. If your parents are not alive, find someone with whom you are incomplete and complete with them. Is anybody unclear?

As Erhard returned to the room, Jane, a teenage participant, rose and spoke, her manner very shy and serious.

of the they-self governs. As participants share and disclose their stories, as they own up to and appropriate the *ways* they *wound up being* (owning their "thrownness"—see the next sidebar), and further, as they grasp and admit the harm that justifying these ways of being has wrought: the "social mood" of profound affinity gets evoked. ■

THROWNNESS

Thrownness is a central Heideggerian term that Werner Erhard uses extensively in responding to the first question of The Forum: What is the Being of human beings?

In *Being and Time*, thrownness is a fundamental aspect of Dasein's existence; Erhard calls it "the default clearing" for human beings (Author notes, Intro to 6-Day LA 1989). "In thrownness," says Heidegger "it is revealed that in each case Dasein, as my Dasein and this Dasein, is already in a definite world and alongside a definite range of definite entities within-the-world" (*BT* 264). Thrownness determines Dasein's options in life, and there are no others: "As something thrown, Dasein has been thrown into *existence*. It exists as an entity which has to be as it is and as it can be" (*BT* 321), and further, "it has been brought into its 'there,' but *not* of its own accord" (*BT* 329).

The word "thrownness" expresses the way we wound up being, the way we find ourselves to always already be: thrownness determines what we automatically are, and it limits our future possibilities (what we "can be"). It is the ontological clearing which Being has sent in our time. "We've got only the possibility which we inherited," says Erhard, "the possibility into which we were thrown—we're thrown to be this particular way, we're thrown into this kind of being that has this particular set of options" ("The Heart of the Matter").

Heidegger says that these options are not objective brute facts about the environment into which we are thrown; that would be the *factuality* of the situation, and we might discover those facts if we looked for them. But Dasein's thrownness "is meant to suggest the *facticity of its being delivered-over*" (*BT* 174). We live in the facticity, the *way* we *wound up being*, and not the factuality; we don't see the raw data of the environment, we see a *story* about the world. This is our facticity: that we are thrown, and that our thrownness is not determined by the things or circumstances "out there." Rather it is characteristic of Dasein's way of Being-in-the-world. Dasein has wound up whatever *way* it *wound up being*, and to perpetuate itself, Dasein must avoid owning up to what it costs to self-justify this thrown way of being. From the point of view of the *way* we *wound up being*, then,

JANE
I don't understand about being complete with your parents.

WES
Are your parents all right with you the way they are?

JANE
Yeah.

WES
So what's the problem?

ERHARD (*gently*)
Jane, there's something going on with you about your parents, isn't there?

JANE (*very tentative*)
I don't know.

ERHARD
Does it feel like there is?

JANE
Yeah.

ERHARD
So what's going on?

JANE
I don't know. Something from the past?

ERHARD
Is there something that feels badly for you?

JANE
Yeah.

ERHARD
What is it?

JANE
The only thing I can think of is my stepmom, the way they brought her into my life.

ERHARD

So let's talk about that a bit. What happened?

JANE

My dad came home with her. He was gone for a while, and he said "this is your mom." That's it. No questions.

ERHARD

And what did you say to yourself?

JANE

Fine.

ERHARD

Did you? Did you stuff it?

JANE

Well I thought that maybe he brought her in so that I would have a mom, 'cause my parents got a divorce, and then two months later my real mom died. And I feel like he brought her into my life.

ERHARD

Is what you're feeling badly about...

JANE

But my mom loves me. I'm glad for half the things she does. But at the time I thought, "she's such a bitch, why is she doing this?" And I wanted to just run away. Now I realize she loved me, and that she wasn't trying to replace my real mom.

ERHARD

Good. It doesn't mean that your mother is not weird. Because we're all weird, right, you've seen that in here. But your mother loves you, and she's weird. With your mother, it's got to be that she's all right just like she is. I didn't say she was right to be the way she is. My mother didn't do the stupid things she did with me because she loved me. She did the stupid things she did with me because she was stupid. And she loved me. It's not that she was right. So you've got a little bit of a ploy in there about making your mother right for the way she is, you all. So, any better sense of what that sadness is? Does it have to do with your mother and father's divorce?

JANE

I don't remember that.

ERHARD

Does it have to do with your mother dying?

ontological inquiry—the kind of speaking that evokes Being—occurs as something to turn away from, to try to leap over.

Indeed, Heidegger is emphatic about the centrality of our facticity in determining our existence. Our mood, our state-of-mind, the way we understand our world—from the phenomenological perspective—those are the facts: "[M]ood brings Dasein before the 'that-it-is' of its 'there,' which, as such, stares it in the face with the inexorability of an enigma." Even if Dasein strives for "rational enlightenment," tries for a detached standpoint, and tells himself that, really, it's just a mood—"all this counts for nothing as against the phenomenal facts of the case" (*BT* 175).

Hubert Dreyfus, in his reading of *Being and Time*, chooses to translate Heidegger's *Befindlichkeit* as affectedness rather than state-of-mind. The latter phrase, he feels, suggests a private subjective mental state, when what Heidegger is distinguishing is Dasein's "being found in a situation where things and options already matter" (*Being In The World* 168). This is an important point. In our thrownness, things are encountered as already and always meaningful:

 Letting something be encountered is primarily *circumspective;* it is not just sensing something, or staring at it. It implies circumspective concern, and has the character of becoming affected in some way. . . . Being-in as such has been determined existentially beforehand in such a manner that what it encounters within-the-world can *"matter" to* it in this way. (*BT* 176)

Heidegger's point is that our moods, like our states of mind, are not the subjective individual phenomena found in a Cartesian model of human being. For Heidegger, a mood "comes neither from the 'outside' or 'inside,' but arises out of Being-in-the-world, as a way of such Being" (*BT* 176).

Our thrown way of being is not one that we could make explicit or theorize. It is not based upon beliefs, and human beings do not, for the most part, subject our everyday actions to analysis. We simply engage in the practices of our inherited traditions, the tradition into which we have been thrown. But our understanding of ourselves remains superficial: "Ontically, of course, Dasein is not only close to us—even that which is closest. We *are it,* each of us, we ourselves. In spite of this, or rather for just this reason, it is ontologically that which is farthest" (*BT* 36).

Dreyfus has proposed examples of the way we inherit elements of this thrownness. A Japanese mother comforts her baby in the manner of her culture, in quiet and soothing ways, while her American counterpart stimulates her baby into more active and vocal behaviors. These parenting choices are, in large part, unconscious on the part of the mothers; they are simply reproducing their cultures' ways of being. Nevertheless, by the time the infants are three to four months of age, they have already learned to *be* Japanese and American infants (*Being In The World* 17). In another example, Dreyfus proposes that all of the implicit but important rules governing nonverbal behaviors, which differ widely among cultures—such aspects of proxemics as the appropriate distance to stand from others, the relative desirability of direct eye contact, or the situational expectations regarding touch—are learned by unconscious observation as we mature within a culture (*Being in the World* 18). These rules become inculcated long before we might explicitly reflect on them, and by then, Dasein's everyday existence is already determined factically, along with the social moods that shape our options for being with others in the world.

It is important here to note that thrownness, like other ideas introduced by Heidegger to distinguish Dasein's existence, should not be interpreted as a *negative* state of Being. Given its apparent limitations, this is counterintuitive, and challenging for us to think. But such paradoxical languaging is crucial to understanding the thinking of both Heidegger and Erhard. Negative conditions naturally lead to the human impulse...to "fix" them, but both Heidegger and Werner Erhard propose a more unorthodox response. ■

JANE
I remember that, but I remember more my stepmom coming into my life. And my mom dying.

ERHARD
Did you love your real mom?

JANE
I don't really remember. I thought I did. I don't remember her.

ERHARD
So is there anything incomplete with your real mother?

JANE
No.

ERHARD
You're okay with her?

JANE
Yeah.

ERHARD
Your dad?

JANE
I'm complete with him.

ERHARD
Your stepmom?

JANE
Yeah.

ERHARD
You notice the almost stupid "not"? She didn't have to be stupid there. Not "I guess." And that's from the beginning because she just showed up and you didn't have a chance to build a relationship. Like here's your mother. Have you built a relationship since then?

JANE
Yeah.

ERHARD
So what's incomplete there?

JANE
I don't know. I have a relationship with her. But I don't know what's incomplete.

ERHARD
How old were you when she became your mother?

JANE
Four, or five, or six.

ERHARD
Did you lose something back there?

JANE
Back when I was a kid?

ERHARD
Yeah.

JANE
Maybe I lost some respect for my dad.

ERHARD
I'm going to tell you a story and I want you to look inside the story and see what's there for you. Children have a bond of belonging and sometimes that gets broken. There's this bond between your parents and you, and then it gets broken. Did that happen for you?

JANE
I don't think so.

ERHARD
Did it happen back then?

JANE
I don't know.

ERHARD
Did you have a bond with your dad?

JANE
Yeah and she broke it.

ERHARD
Okay that's what happened and that's what you're sad about. You had a bond with your father, and just her presence broke that bond. What did you decide?

JANE
That I had to break the bond between them, her and me? Tell her how I feel. And tell her how I felt that she came.

ERHARD
That's not a strange way for a little girl to feel, now is it?

JANE
No.

ERHARD
But for a mature woman, that's clearly not what happened, is it?

JANE
I don't understand.

ERHARD
Looking from your point of view now, did your father's marriage break the bond between you and your dad?

JANE
No.

ERHARD
Can you get off it with your stepmom about breaking the bond between you and your dad?

JANE
Yeah.

ERHARD
So maybe you could say to your stepmom that when I was a little girl, I didn't even realize it until I saw it today, but there's been something in the relationship between you and I. "When I was a little girl and you came into my life, it felt like you had broken my bond with my father, but now I see that that isn't true. So that's not between you and me any more. I can be fully related to you." How does that feel?

JANE
But I'm still sad. I don't know what it's about.

ERHARD

Whatever that's about will come up before we're through. You know you've got to be a big person to have the kind of conversation we just had?

Erhard had been very gentle during this entire interaction, standing very close to Jane. Kipp then proceeded to do the seminar program enrollment.

ERHARD (*to the group*)

For the dinner break there are two assignments. Observe and inquire into the real nature of your relating to other people. What's really going on with you when you're relating to other people? As you're being with people, what's really going on with you? And two, after dinner, I invite you to have a conversation about the seminar program.

The Forum adjourned for a dinner break.

FORUM DAY TWO: SESSION FOUR

The Forum resumed at 9:10 pm, following the dinner break. Kipp was on the platform with Erhard, and asked for questions in response to the break assignment to have a conversation about the seminar program. After Kipp fielded these questions, Erhard came forward.

ERHARD

I know it's possible to turn this into another thing you've done in your life. In independent surveys, most people say it was the most, or a very, significant experience in their life. The way you determine what's possible is by the conversation that you are. This was not designed as another seminar. This was not designed to help you get better. This was not designed to improve you. We could have done that with a lot less time and effort. You want to be here for something extraordinary. You want to be here for the possibility that this could make *the* difference in your life. This was designed to make *the* difference in your life. Now with regard to this seminar business: See, I don't like this conversation. What is so strange about doing something about who you are regularly? I go to the dentist regularly, do something for my teeth regularly. This is extraordinary stuff. If what happened in this room before the break didn't move you, didn't touch you... if that didn't turn you on, this is not a great thing for you to do. But if this speaks to you, this is a very appropriate place for you. So we're going to talk to you about the seminar program. You have the power to decline. This is a very easy conversation to pay attention to if you're clear about the fact that you've got the power to decline.

During this conversation Erhard came down from the platform and moved around among the group.

(continuing)

How many of you have had some major impact in your life out of the two days so far?

A majority of the participants stood.

(continuing)

This is a part of The Forum. You know that form you filled out this morning? That's a part of The Forum.

(indicating Kipp)

He's not like you. He's not hanging out. Kipp is up to something. It looks like we're doing one Forum. We're really doing five hundred different Forums because each person brings something different to it. You don't know what you are. You only know what you were. If you give yourself a future based on what you were, that's not very powerful, is it? We want to give you the power to create a future not given to you by the past.

PARTICIPANT

Isn't that artificial?

ERHARD

Yes, in a certain sense it's artificial, in that you can't predict it. But in a certain sense isn't everything that's created artificial? I have a little rule in my relationships. Don't ever do anything you don't want to do. I've got another rule: ride the horse in the direction it's going. They're the same rule.

(loudly)

Because nobody ever does anything they don't want to do... "I don't want to be here" is a racket. Did you ever see *Karate Kid?* That was coaching. That's what happens in seminars.

At this point Wes moved forward on the platform. Erhard remained in the room, strolling around in the aisles.

WES

We're going to take a deeper look at the distinction *racket.* You have to be listening from the question, what is the distinction racket and what is *my* racket? Try on the possibility that your racket is both something put out there and something covering up.

ERHARD

You don't need to see what happened... Here's all that's important: my racket is, the payoff is, the cost is. Wes is going through the other stuff with people so you can see more of the racket that underlies that. But you don't gotta get what happened in order to gain some freedom from your racket.

(pausing)

Lots of people are trying to get better. And it's a racket. If you're trying to get better, it's all right if you don't produce results. There are certain relationships between payoffs and costs. Avoiding responsibility and stifled self-expression are almost invariably related.

WES

Selfish lives in your mouth. Or, more rigorously, in your conversation... Selfish is in your listening... That's the location of your racket. Your racket is a conversation. The point of the conversation is on the board (i.e., racket payoffs). It's never going to get any better. You're never going to not have your racket. Never. And there's no hope. Nothing in life is so good as being right. As a matter of fact, people will give up their whole lives to be right. How many people on the dinner break called and reached someone in your life and got complete?

About one hundred people raised their hands.

As the second day of The Forum neared its end, assistants distributed homework assignments to the participants.

WES
Here's your assignment for this evening. First, consider inquiring into what's driving your relationship with other people. Second, write a letter to someone you know. Here's the form: I came to The Forum to accomplish...; what I actually am accomplishing is; I plan to use The Forum in... Twenty-five people were late this morning. Cut the crap.

The second day of The Forum concluded.

END OF DAY TWO INTERVAL

The Forgetting of Being, Part Two of Eight: Questioning

The Forum is an *inquiry*. It is a process of asking questions, not providing information. The value of the process arises in the questioning itself. This is questioning of a radically different nature than we are accustomed to. "To pronounce the interrogative sentence, even in a questioning tone, is not yet to question," says Heidegger; he continues:

> If I say to you "Why are there beings at all instead of nothing?" then the intent of my asking and saying is not to communicate to you that a process of questioning is now going on inside me. Certainly the spoken interrogative sentence can also be taken this way, but then one is precisely not hearing the questioning. The questioning does not result in any shared questioning and self-questioning. It awakens nothing in the way of a questioning attitude, or even a questioning disposition. For this consists in a *willing* to know. . . . Questioning is willing-to-know. (*IM* 23)

In this passage Heidegger distinguishes a questioning state of mind, a standing-in-the-question that at the same time wills itself forward into the opening of the question—a *dialogic* engagement in the questioning process, a listening which participates in the questioning advance along with the questioner. This possibility of the listener's thinking-Being along with the questioner will be seen to be an important element of The Forum.

Despite the fact that the question of Being never elicits an answer, the questioning itself—"a distinctive occurrence that we call a *happening*" (*IM* 6)—is a transformative experience. This is because "the question of Being must be asked of Being about Being from within Being" (*BT* 24), and therefore is in its essence reflexive:

> The why-question challenges beings as a whole, so to speak, outstrips them, though never completely. But this is precisely how the question gains its distinction. What is asked in the question rebounds upon the questioning itself, for the questioning challenges beings as a whole, but does not after all wrest itself free from them. . . . It runs up against the search

for its own why. The question "Why the Why?" looks externally and at first like a frivolous repetition of the same interrogative, which can go on forever; it looks like an eccentric and empty rumination about insubstantial meanings of words. Certainly that is how it looks. The only question is whether we are willing to fall victim to this cheap look of things and thus take the whole matter as settled or whether we are capable of experiencing a provocative happening in this recoil of the why-question back upon itself. (*IM* 6)

A body of scholarship has noted the affinities between the thinking of Heidegger and that of Zen (e.g., Steffney (1977), Kotoh (1987) and Storey (2012)). Heidegger's attention here to the possibilities of an apparently tautological question recalls the use in Rinzai Zen of seemingly nonsensical *koans* (What is the sound of the one hand clapping?) to effect a transformation in thinking.

But the locus of the transformation is not the thinking of the questioners; nor are the circumstances themselves altered. Rather, in the questioning itself, every secure foothold is lost (*IM* 32). In that moment, the possibility of new understandings emerges.

This power of the question of Being to undermine foundations is central to the process of The Forum. Erhard's ontological inquiry is constructed upon two fundamental questions: *What is the Being of human beings?* and *What is the possibility of Being for human beings?* The first question undermines the foundation; the second moves toward the creation of new understandings. Both are essential and distinct elements of the same questioning movement. It is this *modulation of questionableness into possibility* that Heidegger addresses here:

> Our questioning just opens up the domain so that beings can break open in such questionworthiness. . . . Yet, it is *this* questioning that pushes us into the open, provided that it itself, as a questioning, transforms itself (as does every genuine questioning), and casts a new space over and through everything. (*IM* 33)

The situation is not changed through questioning; its possibility is transformed. But questioning, according to translator J. Glenn Gray, was not for Heidegger a codified procedure:

> **Putting in question is not primarily a method for him as it was for Descartes and for his teacher Husserl. At least it is not a method in the sense that one uses it as a preliminary to building up a body of doctrine after tearing down earlier systems. No, for Heidegger questioning is a way or path of thinking which each one must clear for himself with no certain destination in mind. (*WCT* xiii)**

The seeking of answers is so basic to the scholarly calling that conceiving such a questioning attitude is problematic, and maintaining that attitude more so:

> **Being able to question means being able to wait, even for a lifetime. But an age for which the actual is only whatever goes fast and can be grasped with both hands takes questioning as a "stranger to reality," as something that does not count as profitable. But what is essential is not counting but the right time—that is, the right moment and the right endurance.**
>
> **For the mindful god**
>
> **Does detest**
>
> **Untimely growth.**
>
> **—Hölderlin, fragment from the period of "The Titans" (*IV*, 218).**
> **(*IM* 229-230)**

SPEAKING BEING

DAY THREE

FORUM DAY THREE

SESSION ONE

Day three of The Forum began at 9:00 am, with The Forum leader, Kipp, on the platform asking participants to share about the assignment from the previous evening: to share their experience of The Forum with someone in their lives.

KIPP
When you talk about what happened, people are left, and you're left, with whatever description gives you. We're going to call that domain of speaking "up in the stands." Does talking to the person next to us about what's down on the court impact the game? Now I'm asking you to get on the court and share from being on the court. Here's how it starts: "Who were you with?" "You said what?" "What did they say?"

Wearing a dark gray sweater-vest with black slacks, Erhard appeared in the back of the room, watching the interaction.

BETTY
I phoned my brother last night, and I told him, in the beginning of him harassing me to make a decision of being here, that I wasn't sure of... that I blamed him...

KIPP
You said you blamed him?

BETTY
I said I blamed him. This is the conversation that we had. "I blamed you Bob for me being here because I didn't want to be here. It's your fault and I hate you for it."

KIPP (*to the group*)
You're right there with her because she's not talking about sharing, she's sharing. You're right there on the phone with her. Then what did you tell him?

BETTY
I told him that I was sorry for how I felt, that I had no right to feel that way, that I was the one who was wrong and selfish.

KIPP
And he said?

BETTY
He said that he loved me, and that the reason that he wanted me here was because it would be good for me. And I told him that I didn't want to see it from his point of view; to see it from my point of view, and it took me to get through yesterday to realize that. I got through that point. I realized it. I'm here. It's great for me. And I told him that I appreciated him for making that decision for harassing me.

KIPP

Whether it's convincing you or harassing you, neither ever happened. In the sense of what happened, your brother spoke to you.

BETTY

In a sense it didn't and in another sense it did.

KIPP

It's called describing it. He spoke to you.

(to the group)

What she just shared with you just about never happens after two days of anything in your life. This isn't a new situation; this is, however, many years between her and her brother and two days. It's hard to be present to that; it's hard to see because it seems like two years.

BETTY

I hated being here the first two days.

KIPP

No you didn't... You had those thoughts. Did you have anything to do with any of those thoughts?

BETTY

No.

KIPP

No. It was like the rain.

BETTY

It was like the rain.

KIPP

Stop identifying with the rain.

ERHARD *(entering the conversation)*

He's making a slightly different point, and it would be useful for everybody to get it. That's not you thinking. The stuff going on in your head is not yours. It doesn't belong to you. You didn't invent it, or generate it. It's thoughts you're having. I want you to be able to think that what's going on when you're thinking is not you thinking. You're *having thoughts*. It thinks. I'm having the thoughts it thinks. In the book, *The Man Who Mistook His Wife for a Hat*—there was such a man—he actually thought his wife was a hat. And you mistake it thinking for *you* thinking. Not you personally. People mistake it thinking for them thinking just like the guy who mistook his wife for a hat. You have to do some thinking to get that. It thinks, and you have the thoughts that it thinks. You want to stop being so entangled in your thinking. You want to be able to

IN-ORDER-TO

Here Erhard is characterizing the current clearing for Being as calculative—as technological—wherein everything is placed in reserve, standing by, ready to be used—everything including our selves (please see the series of sidebars on technology during the third and final session of Day Four). Since we have not recognized the technological clearing as a paradigm, a particular way of being which we have been sent, we see it as simply *the way things—including our selves—are*. The in-order-to of standing-reserve, not confronted as the "it" which we have been sent, becomes "us." The "giant cybernetic system," to use Hubert Dreyfus's phrase, has thereby been set in motion: "We don't produce the clearing. The clearing produces us" ("Gaining a Free Relationship to Technology," Applied Heidegger Conference).

We have become *both* the "it" which acts in-order-to, and, as the they-self/identity, one of those entities which is *subject to* the in-order-to of the "it." Erhard has summarized the result of this system:

> **When you are that you are the identity "I"—when you are that you are that—and you couple that with what "it" is up to, you get a very powerful look into how this what-it's-up-to is translated into our everyday way of Being-in-the-world, into our everyday engagement with our everyday concerns. What "it" is concerned with, once you are that you are it. . . what "it" is up to is making you right. . . and making anything else by contrast wrong. ("The Heart of the Matter")**

In *Being and Time,* the *in-order-to* is also shown by Heidegger to be a central element of the existential structure of Dasein. As we have shown elsewhere, Dasein is always in the world in such a way that it is *concerned* about things—getting them done, producing them, giving them up, considering them, and so forth (*BT* 83–84, 96)—and our understanding of the world is mediated *through* these concerns (see the sidebar "Concern" during Session Four of Day One). Heidegger calls the things we encounter in this way *equipment,* and in-order-to is a characteristic of equipment:

> **Equipment is essentially 'something in-order-to. . . .' A totality of equipment is constituted by various ways of the 'in-order-to,' such as serviceability, conduciveness, usability, manipulability. [. . .] Dealings with equipment subordinate themselves to the manifold assignments of the 'in-order-to.' (*BT* 97, 98)**

stand back a bit and watch it think. You think you're limited to what it thinks. But that's it thinking. It has thought you into a lot of pain and suffering, unhappiness, and dissatisfaction. And it has a purpose, like a machine. It is designed in-order-to. It is not designed in order to leave you with love, fulfillment, and full self-expression. Have you got any idea what it's designed in-order-to? It's designed in order to make you look good. That's its design function.

(*in the aisle among the group*)
And it uses thinking and feeling, interpretations, what you believe to be true, in order to make you look good. It utilizes and organizes those elements and generates those elements in a form designed to make you look good. What does it mean to look good? Well, specifically, it means to make you right and others wrong, to foster your dominating and to avoid the domination of anything else. And it uses your thinking and your feelings, and your perceptions and your interpretations, conclusions, etc., to justify yourself; except yourself and it have become one. You have identified with it. You are an it; you are an anybody. What makes you an *anybody* is you identify with it. You identify with its thinking and its feeling, and that makes you an anybody, and the costs are love, happiness, and self-expression. It thinks and you have its thoughts, and it thinks in order to make you look good, and what it costs you to identify with it is love, happiness, vitality, and self-expression.

BETTY
I think the thing that hit me the strongest was the racket. When I could identify my racket and my reason for allowing things to take place in my life and receive the cost that I received from it, was the identification of breaking through the barrier of all of this. I felt like this ton of bricks was lifted from my shoulders, being able to acknowledge that. And I realize what I was doing...

ERHARD
See—hold on. *It* doesn't think like that. What she's speaking doesn't have anything to do with looking good, does it? As a matter of fact if you were real concerned with looking good you would never say what she just said. You can't say what she just said without thinking, because it might make you look bad. Go on.

BETTY
I realized the cost that I was paying for the racket I was having.

ERHARD
Running. You run a racket.

BETTY
The racket I was running. In allowing myself to be used for acceptance.

ERHARD
Kipp and I may have to go home and let her do this. That's extraordinarily powerful to recognize that your life doesn't belong to you. That it's using your life for its purposes. And its

ERHARD (*continuing*)

purposes are looking good--all that stuff up on the board specifically--that's what looking good looks like: being right, making other people and other things wrong, dominating, avoiding domination, justifying yourself and invalidating others, and other things. When you come to see that that's what your life is being used for, you've gotten pretty close to the source of your self. You've gotten pretty close to the source of your identity. Pretty close to the source of that with which you've confused your self. Go on.

BETTY

He was right that I allow myself to be used for acceptance. That was the cost that I was paying. I didn't enjoy the cost I was receiving. I made them wrong to be right when I was the one who was wrong.

KIPP

Even though she didn't enjoy the cost she was receiving, it was familiar. And what you call comfortable is what is familiar, what you are used to. She doesn't know now how to relate to her brother. She knows how to relate to him before: make him wrong. But now she has to be in the presence of the risk...

ERHARD

She's got to make up a relationship with her brother. That's called "invent." She's got to invent a relationship with her brother. Another word for that is "create": create a relationship with her brother. You want to think about that a little bit: The possibility of living life as a creative act, where you don't have an answer when you stand in front of the canvas. What you've got is an empty canvas, possibility. You create something in the empty space of not knowing how to be there already. Knowing how to be there already is nothing more than the past coming around to meet you in the future. Sure she knows how to relate to her brother that way she's always been. That's comfortable. It's uncomfortable to stand in front of an empty canvas. It's uncomfortable because you're at risk. You might make a fool of yourself. You might be conned. You might get taken advantage of. You don't like that, visit the surgeon and get a lobotomy.

BETTY

It doesn't just stop at my brother.

ERHARD

Obviously it doesn't stop at your brother. Somebody who says "I hate, I hate, I hate"—that is "disgruntled and unhappy" waiting-to-happen. Suppose she doesn't have this as a way to start every morning? Suppose she doesn't have that as a way to walk into work? She'll have to create a way to walk into work, and create a way to walk into her relationships with her family, and create a way to walk into relationships with men in her life—instead of being sour to start with before anything happens.

BETTY

I stay sour constantly.

The pervasiveness of in-order-to thus creates a context of *referentiality,* a frame of reference for our understanding—a "towards-which" for all of our/its dealings in the world. And the primary towards-which, says Heidegger, is always the "for-the-sake-of-which" that Dasein *itself is*: "the 'for-the-sake-of' always pertains to the Being of Dasein, for which, in its Being, that very Being is essentially an *issue*" (*BT* 116–117). My concerns and my actions always circle back to my own Being, always defined by the in-order-to: "In so far as Dasein exists factically, it understands itself in the way its 'for-the-sake-of-itself' is thus connected with some current 'in-order-to'" (*BT* 416).

One of The Forum's central purposes is the unconcealment of the *in-order-to,* which is the design function of the "it"—the calculative thinking which characterizes the technological clearing. Erhard has pointed out that recognizing his *own* thrownness to in-order-to was central in the development of his thinking. During his 1971 experience of ontological insight, from which the *est* Training was generated, he says:

 I realized that I actually didn't know *anything*. Everything that I knew had a tag on it, and the name of the tag was "in order to." So I knew this in order to, I knew *that* in order to, et cetera. Everything was somehow a part of a story about how it was going to advance me or how it could be used, or how it could benefit people, or whatever it might be. Nothing lived on its own. (Simon 37)

As we will show in the closing Interval for Day Four of The Forum, the danger of the technological clearing, for Heidegger, is that we are oblivious to its nature and are thus denied access to the truth of *aletheia*: "Through [the technological destining of enframing] the other possibility is blocked," said Heidegger, that human being "might rather be admitted sooner and ever more primally to the essence of what is unconcealed and to its unconcealment [*aletheia*]" ("QCT" in *BW* 331).

Similarly, for Erhard, it is the in-order-to of the technological clearing which diminishes our experience of truth:

> " . . .if you take something which is true and add to it an "in order to" or even a "because" or a "therefore," you've changed it. And you've changed it so dramatically that it's no longer the truth. It's the truth *used* for something—to prove something, to coerce others, to be right or make someone else wrong. The truth used like that isn't the truth any more. It's closer to a lie—something pretending to be the truth. (Simon, ibid. 38, emphasis added)

Here we find ourselves in another instance of the reflexive thinking that characterizes the work of both Erhard and Heidegger: even *attempts to escape* in-order-to are undertaken *in order to escape in-order-to*. Consequently, much of The Forum is devoted to the distinction of a possibility beyond in-order-to. As Forum leader Roger Armstrong told the Openings participants during this 1989 Forum, "To do *one thing* that's not in-order-to" could be worth the entire four days of The Forum. The paradox—embedded deeply in Heidegger's central distinction, *appropriation*—is that one can get beyond in-order-to only by *allowing and owning* the inevitability of in-order-to. ∎

ERHARD

See, look. If she won the Nobel Prize that would be less important to her life than what she just said. There's nothing more important for her to say. Because once she can own that, there's a possibility beyond that. And until she can own that, there's no possibility beyond that. All there is, is shucking and jiving around that: one ploy after another ploy—trying not to be that way, to finding out you are that way, giving in to being that way, making up your mind to be some other way, trying not to be that way, fixing being that way—it's all a trap like having your foot nailed to the floor and running around real fast.

BETTY

I'm going to fix it.

KIPP

What do you mean by that? Because it's going to be misheard.

BETTY

I'm going to fix it by acknowledging my racket. When my racket goes to swing I'm going to stop it. Because I'm not going to allow myself to pay the costs, just for me to be right and make everyone wrong. Feel what I'm feeling. I'm going to take full control of it.

ERHARD

Most of that's pretty good. A little "fix it" in there; a little "stop it" in there. Most of it is responsibility for it. And to the degree that she can be responsible for it, to the degree she can be with it—be *with it* and *be responsible for it*—these words are synonymous, by the way—to the degree that she can be responsible for it, to that degree she's not limited to it. It's not going to go away. That's who she is. That's the identity she's built for herself. It's gonna be there forever. And to the degree she can be with that, there's a possibility beyond that. We're too far into today now, so I'm going to stop talking like that.

KIPP

What you're present to is the distinction *sharing*. There's no manipulation, no in-order-to. That's what sharing sounds like. This is what The Forum is about. So if you're sitting in your chair, if you're with whatever's happening in her life with yours, if there's a harmony, if it strikes a chord, then you should know that's what this work is about. If you find yourself in her speaking—if you find yourself in *your* life in *her life*—that's what we're doing here. Out of her generosity—the truth is, out of her getting off it—that's what it sounds like when someone's getting off it. She had no life. What she had was hate and resentment and bitterness, and hate and resentment and bitterness were winning. We're going to continue to distinguish this distinction "sharing."

SUSAN

I didn't think you'd call on me.

KIPP

That's what you get for thinking.

SUSAN

Well I called my husband last night, and he's the one I thought had forced me to do it.

KIPP

Let's get a little more rigorous. You *had* the thought...

SUSAN

Right. We were recently married in October. He participated in The Forum a couple of months ago. When he came back from it he was so excited and he was great. He was excited about our relationship—which was wonderful. But what really bothered me was that he said it was because of The Forum. And that bugged me. My husband told me the reason he married me was because of The Forum. That is a bunch of garbage; "You married me because you love me, and there's nobody who is making you marry me." I went to Forum Introductory meetings and didn't like it because they wanted to work on me.

KIPP

No, you didn't like it because you're a creep.

SUSAN

Right. Yesterday I was sitting in here, and all these people have these major problems. I don't see a major problem in my life. And then I said, "my gosh, that's one right there."

KIPP (*to the group*)

That's big. Some of you haven't gotten here yet. Slow group.

SUSAN

As I developed it in my mind, I realized I got to share this, and so I put my hand up. "Now what if he calls on me? I have to make sure I got this all planned out to say it right." Then I realized: I'm terrified.

KIPP

That's the point. The rest was fill. Keep going, please.

SUSAN

The thing that I came into The Forum to accomplish was to have the ability to find the right position. I just moved up here, and I don't have a job yet. I wanted to wait until after the holidays...

KIPP

Wait. What's true is you don't have a job yet.

SUSAN

That's right. I'm afraid I'm not going to find the right position. I told him about my racket, that "I'm right only when it matters to you that you're right. It doesn't matter if either way is okay. But if you're adamant about being right, then I want to be right."

KIPP

It's called new love. It's a new marriage.

SUSAN

Anyway. Very difficult for me.

KIPP

But that's the important part. How difficult it is. Everything that you call yourself is going to fight against it. Every justification in the world is going to be there to shut up.

SUSAN

I was afraid that I would lose footing.

KIPP

That's right. Marriage isn't about loving, about being at risk: it's about dominating and winning.

SUSAN

I thought I didn't want to dominate. I just didn't want to be dominated.

ERHARD (*entering the conversation*)

Thanks for this Susan. Very useful conversation. Dominating and avoiding domination are two sides of the same mirror. It doesn't mean be a patsy either. There's an alternative to dominating and avoiding domination. There's a possibility beyond that. And it's not possible to see that until you see what it costs you to dominate or avoid domination. Most marriages are about dominating and avoiding domination. They're about being right and avoiding being wrong. That's what marriages are really about. They're not about the stuff they put in the fairy tales. And they're always going to be about that because you and I didn't make that up, we inherited that when we became human beings. And it's only to the degree that you can own that, for there to be a possibility beyond that. What you're doing now, looking at that and owning that, taking it on and seeing that that's what owns your marriage: that starts to create the possibility of some power in the marriage.

(*pausing*)

The other thing is, you want to be able to get to the point where you can be with what people say. Otherwise you're going to be manipulated by what people say. See, whatever your husband said about The Forum: stupid. But you couldn't be with it; it took your *being* away from you.

SUSAN

He used a lot of the terminology that you used, and that drove me nuts because he acted kind of smug. You know he had found "it." I hadn't, so I had to go get "it."

> "There's an alternative to dominating and avoiding domination. There's a possibility beyond that. And it's not possible to see that until you see what it costs you to dominate or avoid domination.

ERHARD

Yes. That's the smell of enlightenment. You want to keep your enlightenment to yourself and not let the smell out. What you want to share with people is empowerment, not enlightenment. You want to watch doing enlightenment with people, and it's possible to empower people. If someone says something stupid to you—I'm not telling you how to handle this, I'm just illustrating that there's a way to be with it—if somebody says something stupid to you, you can say, "okay, I understand exactly what you're saying." That gives you much more of an opening than "that's stupid." I don't talk like this outside of here. I don't use all this jargon outside of here. I use it in here because there's a reason to. Now, you're going to be stupid. You're going to use all the terminology inappropriately. And there's not much you can do about it. It's hard not to. If we could take it back before you left here, we would, so you would just be left with yourself. All this stuff in here is not significant. The only thing significant is you. And you can work your way through those things with your husband now that you're hip to what's going on. It's a pretty exciting thing to think about the possibility of marriage beyond the games in marriages.

KIPP

So in sharing with your husband last night, you said?

SUSAN

I said "I'm sorry I was such a twit about signing up."

ERHARD

A twit?

SUSAN

It's softer language for me.

ERHARD

You cleaned it up for television.

KIPP

And he said?

SUSAN

He said "That's all right, I love you."

KIPP

And what was left? What were you then standing in?

SUSAN

Standing in my own decision.

> If we could take it back before you left here, we would, so you would just be left with yourself. All this stuff in here is not significant. The only thing significant is you.

ERHARD

And standing in the love that was there. Not a bad place to stand—talking about power. What you call love is not love: it's love in-order-to; love to keep somebody around; or love to get something out of them; love because you need. That's not love. When you take everything else away, what is left is love. When you take away "I was a twit," and take away him being arrogant, what you're left with is love for each other. And it doesn't mean anything, but it's extraordinarily powerful. And you can stand there and really make something happen in life— like really create something worth creating. Fabulous.

SUSAN

During dinner last night I was expressing things that had bothered me before, and he said, "I think it should be a requirement for spouses, that when one takes it the other should take The Forum."

ERHARD

We like it to get bad first, though. Makes it clearer about what you're up to if it gets bad first.

SUSAN

I know because listening to everybody else yesterday, things they wanted to fix, and I didn't think I had anything--I just haven't lived long enough.

ERHARD

You know, we do this with children. They're as fucked up as you are. They've got all the same stuff as you going on and they're in the process of building their identity. And I'm probably one of the few people in the world who's an expert on teenagers. And I know almost nothing about teenagers. The truth about teenagers is that they're human. People are insulted when I say that. But when you live with a teenager, you're not sure.

(*laughter*)

The truth is that teenagers are adults. That's hard to get, because they're a weird kind of adult. They're adults who don't have their act together well enough to get it bought all the time. And it's very painful to get called on your act. Very painful. Adults are teenagers with their act so well put together that they almost never get called on it. Very simple and very powerful.

SUSAN

I see that as I was looking for a job I was afraid of telling my husband for fear he might make me continue if it didn't work out.

KIPP

Yeah, don't establish a network of support for yourself.

SUSAN

He might force me: "Just in case it doesn't feel good you can jump right out."

ERHARD

Susan brought up something important about living in fear all the time. The truth you're going to find out today is that you live in fear all the time. It's so pervasive that for you it's become ordinary. So it's only when you're overwhelmed by fear that you notice that you're frightened. But the fear is there all the time: "afraid I might get stuck with this"; "afraid I might get boxed in." It's there all the time. This is an experiment to see what it looks like to live in fear and don't call it that. Call it "everyday living." The more forceful you are, the more frightened you are. You're just overcompensating for the fear, so to speak. Why do you suppose it takes courage? The more frightened you are the more courage you need. The more forceful you are the more frightened you are.

SUSAN

I'm not really sure. I keep being confused. My natural tendency is to want to fix it.

ERHARD

No, it's not your natural tendency; it's its natural tendency.

SUSAN

Its natural tendency. I keep looking for something.

ERHARD

Right, to try to fix it. And whatever you try to fix gets permanent-ized.

SUSAN

I can't wait to be able to share equally with my husband.

ERHARD

Well done. Just one point about not sharing in-order-to. Sharing attracts. Looking good ensnares, and sharing attracts. You don't build relationships talking about what you think. You build relationships by speaking yourself, and listening self; listening for the self there, not listening for the story there. If you listen for self, people will speak their selves. If you listen for crap, people will tell you their crap. If you listen for self, people will tell you their crap first, but they'll get around to speaking themselves.

A young man named Andy, wearing a sweatshirt with the logo "Youth at Risk" (a project of Werner Erhard and Associates), rose.

ANDY

I am a lowdown mother-fucking sleeze.

ERHARD

What do you have to do with Youth at Risk?

ANDY

I work there.

ERHARD (*to the group*)
You've got to have advanced training to know that about yourself.

ANDY
My life's been about being a sleaze. The question was "what do you care most about in life?" and I said "I care about making a difference with people." And I see that isn't it. I care about making a difference with young people and I could give a fuck about adults. And my actions show that. So who I am with an adult is a snake in the grass.

ERHARD
That's pretty popular. I'm for this and the hell with everything else. That doesn't give you any power with what you're for.

ANDY (*replaying a conversation he had*)
So she said, "what do you get out of that?" I said, "well, I get to look good. Mr. morality. Mr. right. Look like I'm honest—all the good stuff that goes along with it. It was all fun and games at first." "What's the cost?" "I don't see no cost. Maybe self-expression. Tell people what I'm really thinking because I'm being manipulative." "Well what about love?" "I could give a fuck about love: I've got my family. I got all the love I need." And then she said, "how could you do what you do? You fucking hurt people, you use people, you lie. How would you feel if someone was doing that to you all the time? And that's all you're doing." And it does hurt. It hurts deep inside. I was denying it.

KIPP (*moving closer to Andy*)
You were doing what you've done your entire life.

ANDY
I'm not denying it anymore. I am a sleaze.

KIPP
Being a sleaze is a nice handy phrase that doesn't let you be present to what's there in your life.

ANDY
I don't trust adults.

KIPP
That's a concept. "I don't trust adults" is saying information about it.

(*clapping his hands*)
That sound is present. What's present when you're with adults?

ANDY
I don't know.

KIPP

See, you got hurt, didn't you, when you were growing up?

ANDY

Yeah.

KIPP

See how you said "yeah"? So today your job is to get present to your own life. And you gloss over it by saying you're a sleaze. People aren't interested in things, people are interested in you. We give people things, we don't give them our selves. You're a guy walking around with a chip on your shoulder, and the chip has become your life.

ANDY

Right.

ERHARD (*coming forward*)

Hold on, hold on a minute. A lot of people in here with a chip on their shoulder. How many people in here have a chip on their shoulder? I'm looking around here to see if the right hands are up.

Erhard pointed out a couple of people to indicate that they needed to have their hands raised. He addressed one of them.

(*continuing*)

That costs you your beauty, you know that? You're a beautiful woman. Nobody can see that with that fucking chip on your shoulder; takes your power away from you.

KIPP

Anything more?

ANDY

Just that it is so powerful.

KIPP

Right. The chip on your shoulder uses your life.

ANDY

Like a drug.

KIPP

Thank you.

(*applause*)

KIPP (*to the group*)
I'm inviting you to keep being present to sharing.

XAVIER
I called my girlfriend. I think I'm getting things. I kid myself about getting things, and I don't know shit.

KIPP
Yeah. What do you do in life?

XAVIER
I'm a student.

KIPP
Of course, you have to be a student if you don't know shit... Somebody that doesn't know shit has to be a student—because you can't be present to "I don't know." If you can get that you're reporting when you're reporting—that's worth the four days... "I was talking about rackets" is reporting. "I said I was full of shit" is sharing. And what did your girlfriend say?

XAVIER
That I was just reporting on things.

KIPP
Listen. That's worth his four days. If you can get that you're reporting when you're reporting, it's worth the four days. And?

XAVIER
I said that I am full of shit; I am running rackets all the time.

KIPP
She said?

XAVIER
She shared about how uncomfortable it is to be called on her rackets. It's embarrassing.

KIPP
Being alive is embarrassing. If you don't want to be embarrassed, stay dead.

ERHARD
It's embarrassing to be yourself. Ask any teenager, he'll tell you. That's why teenagers put an act together. It's innately embarrassing to be yourself. That's how you get to be an adult when you're a teenager. You learn not to be yourself. It's true about everybody in the room. You want to get that. It's embarrassing to be yourself.

KIPP

You start participating in your own life, it's going to be awkward and embarrassing for you. It took about three years to train me. I was too embarrassed to be with people.

(*prompting Xavier to keep sharing rather than describing*)
And you said? And she said?

XAVIER

We broke up on Tuesday.

KIPP

Good. Always break up before The Forum. You might get lucky in here.

(*laughter*)
Careful. You're having fun. It might be a shock to your system.

(*laughter*)

XAVIER

I'm sitting here during The Forum having these thoughts.

KIPP

No, the thoughts are having you. And the thoughts say?

XAVIER

I'm a worthless piece of shit.

Kipp crossed the platform to the table, picked up a box of tissues, and used the tissues to demonstrate Xavier's "thoughts" that he was "identifying with," and "being owned by." Kipp did this by pulling a tissue from the box, wafting it through the air, and inserting it into one of his nostrils, and then another in the other nostril, to much laughter.

KIPP (*with tissues in his nostrils, regarding Xavier*)
And you go?

XAVIER

I'll never amount to anything.

KIPP (*filling both ears with tissues; laughter*)
And the next thought?

XAVIER

It's hopeless.

KIPP (*covering his head with a tissue; laughter*)
This is what you've been calling you.

XAVIER
I see the payoffs and the costs, but now what?

KIPP
Two more days, that's what.

Xavier sat down looking considerably lighter than when he had stood up. Another participant, Edna, stood next.

EDNA
When I came in here I had a bag of negatives with me.

KIPP
"A bag of negatives" is a description.

EDNA
I didn't want to be here. I have six children and grandchildren in this Forum. I thought we were all going to do The Forum together. It didn't take me long to realize that they were going to do their Forum and I was going to do my Forum. I kept looking for where in the room my family was. At one point, I saw my son walking toward the door. I feared for his and my looking good. I realized how much looking good had been running my life. It's not anymore.

KIPP
It is anymore. It is there. But you've got some choice now in how it uses you.

(*to the group*)
What you're listening to is a mother whose children became trophies.

ERHARD
Like all mothers: you lose yourself. You become your children. Let me tell you something: you have very little to do with the way your children grow up. Look at yourself. You did it the way you wanted to do it. But everyone has bullshit about "They made me." Kids like to eat. "If you want to eat in this house, do this and this and this. If you don't want to eat, do something else." I told my son, "I don't feed you because I love you. It's against the law not to feed you." You lose yourself and become your children. The single most important thing you have to give your children is your own well-being, and make sure they don't get in the way. They may not use it wisely, but your self is what you've got to give them. The one thing I could never get away from with my mother was who she was. But I forgot everything she told me.

EDNA
They didn't know the reason for me wanting them to look good: so that I would look good.

AWAKENING ATTUNEMENTS

Werner Erhard has consistently denied that his work is appropriately characterized by the term *philosophy*. But he has issued this denial in a cultural context where philosophy is generally regarded as a purely academic pursuit, in which one studies the thinking of great thinkers in order to gain knowledge and perhaps thereby to attain wisdom.

The people who direct this study are professors of philosophy, but are rarely considered publicly to be themselves philosophers; our culture has no clear or official requirements for that designation. The academic process generally entails learning about philosophy, not doing philosophy. This is not necessarily the aim of the professors, but arises from the constricting assumptions of the current paradigm that structures the processes of acquiring knowledge within academic settings. Given this way of understanding the term "philosophy," it clearly does not describe Erhard's methodology.

But certainly, as Erhard has acknowledged, his work does address many of the *concerns* of philosophy ("The Heart of the Matter"), concerns that are likewise central in the work of Martin Heidegger, who is considered as official a "philosopher" as anyone from the twentieth century. In Germany during the prime of his career, between 1920 and the 1960s, Heidegger was immersed in a culture that revered both the academic system itself and in particular the academic discipline of philosophy. In responding to this opportunity, he rose to pre-eminence as an academic and as a philosopher. (Please see Michael E. Zimmerman's Afterword to this

ERHARD

If you were going to design a universe you would not design growing up like people do it. But that's the way it is. It's messy. The single most important issue between parents and children is that they love each other. And that's almost never the discussion. It doesn't make you a better person to clean your room. The point is to have a little straightness in the conversation. It's a difficult process at best. There are no experts on raising children. No one has the code. It's very powerful what Edna is talking about. You've got to keep getting off it with your children too. The interesting thing about kids: if you get off it with them, they'll get off it with you. When you're being straight with them, it occurs to them they might be straight with you. Great, Edna. Good stuff, really good stuff.

(*turning to the group*)
Where's Jane?

The young woman who had spoken the previous day (Day Two, Session Four) about her father and stepmother stood.

ERHARD

What happened to sad?

JANE

I don't know.

ERHARD

Do you really not know, or do you not want to talk about it?

JANE

I think I was sad because… it was all up here. I was scared so much.

ERHARD

What do you mean "I think"?

JANE

I know.

ERHARD

What you're saying is "I was feeling emotional because I was standing up in front of a group of people." What happened that you feel that way? Don't say "I don't know" ever again.

JANE

Something that happened that I don't remember.

ERHARD

Can you remember a time when you stood up in front of a group of people?

book to provide further context concerning questionable political judgments of Heidegger the "man," which put at risk the substantial innovations and contributions of *Being and Time* and of his other writings.)

The contribution and innovation of Heidegger's thinking that is central to our study includes his particular path of thinking, a path that reached beyond the academic context in which he worked and thrived, and into the domain of ontology. Working persistently in this domain for more than five decades, he strove to honor the discipline of philosophy by committing his life to undermining its foundational concepts.

Embedded throughout his many published volumes is a perspective on philosophy, and its relation to language, that strongly resonates with Werner Erhard's approach to ontological inquiry. In the lectures published as *The Fundamental Concepts of Metaphysics,* for example, Heidegger is elusive regarding philosophy's nature. Philosophy is

 not some mere gathering of knowledge that we can easily obtain for ourselves any time from books, but (we know this only obscurely) *something to do with the whole*, something extreme, where an ultimate pronouncement and interlocution occurs on the part of human beings. (*FCM* 4, emphasis added).

He is emphatic on one point: "*Philosophy is philosophizing. . . . It itself is only whenever we are philosophizing.*" Philosophy emerges in acts of languaging; and if it is authentic philosophy, it emerges newly in each iteration, "however much we seem merely to be repeating the same thing" (*FCM* 4). Frequently in The Forum, Erhard calls out the participants whom he hears codifying their experiences as beliefs. Authentic philosophy rips space open newly in every articulation; it is philosophizing that never calcifies into philosophy.

Further, Heidegger suggested the direction that philosophical dialogue should move in the current epoch. The task concerns *attunements,* which are ways of being open to the world. A human being is never just open; we are always open in some particular way.

> **Our fundamental task now consists of awakening a fundamental attunement in our philosophizing. I deliberately say: in *our* philosophizing, not in some arbitrary philosophizing nor even in philosophy in itself, for there is no such thing. It is a matter of awakening *a* fundamental attunement which is to sustain our philosophizing, and not *the* fundamental attunement. Accordingly, there is not merely one single attunement, but several. (*FCM* 59)**

The task that Heidegger proposes is the distinguishing of the fundamental attunements that, unrecognized, generate human thinking. His purpose here is not to *ascertain* these attunements, since that term implies objective knowing (i.e., the stance of a subject whose goal is to learn about something separate from itself), but that I am never separate from my attunements:

> **Perhaps such a thing as the fundamental attunement we are seeking is precisely something that cannot be ascertained in this way by an inquiry. It could be that it pertains to ascertaining an attunement not merely that one has the attunement, but that *one is attuned in accord with it*. (*FCM* 60, emphasis added)**

To *know* an attunement, then, requires *entering* it.

Such inquiry makes a special demand of the inquirer, a demand always present in ontological inquiry, and one that has made scholarly or scientific studies of Werner Erhard's work problematic. Central to The Forum's promise is the possibility of choosing an authentic existence; but participants—even those with scholarly credentials—cannot ascertain whether that result has been produced by hearing about the experiences of others in The Forum, or even by observing their behaviors. In this domain of knowing, the evidence lies in one's own lived experience; and to further challenge scientific inquiry, it is in the nature of one's lived experience that what it means is up to you.

JANE
Last summer at a camp.

ERHARD
What happened?

JANE
Everybody had to say their problem out in the open and I didn't want to do it. They kept asking over and over until I did.

ERHARD
Can you remember a time before that speaking in front of a group of people?

JANE
I didn't.

ERHARD
What about in school?

JANE
I never talked in school. I sat in the back.

ERHARD
When were you frightened about standing up?

JANE
In the fourth grade.

ERHARD
What happened in the fourth grade?

JANE
Well my first year of fourth grade I had to stay back. And most of the people—well this is my story—made fun of me for staying back, and said I was stupid.

ERHARD
How do you do in school?

JANE
Fine. I get good grades.

ERHARD
Are you happy in school?

JANE

No.

ERHARD

Would you like to be happy in school?

JANE

Yeah. Well, I feel if I was happier about being in school I'd get better grades.

ERHARD

Okay. You'd also be happier in life.

JANE

Yeah.

ERHARD

What happened in the fourth grade?

JANE

The biggest thing I remember is I asked people to come to my birthday party, and no one showed up for it.

ERHARD

What did you decide when nobody showed up?

JANE

That no one liked me.

ERHARD

I want you to be right there—back in the fourth grade. You didn't merely decide "nobody likes me." You *became* "nobody likes me." You've been living over top of "nobody likes me." And when nobody likes you, it's threatening to stand up in front of a group. Do you get that?

JANE

Yeah.

ERHARD

Is it true that nobody likes you?

JANE

No.

ERHARD

How old are you when you're in the fourth grade?

The scientific mind boggles; but these principles lie at the heart of a phenomenological approach to knowing, such as those of Heidegger and Erhard: *you* must yourself be fully available for the outcome; and the insight of the transformational *Augenblick* is that the meaning of my life is determined by the stand I take on it. But I must first take a stand.

¥

Attunements are *already always there*. I am never not attuned in some way to the world; there is never a naked "I" which subsequently becomes attuned. We are attuned from inception, but without being *conscious* of our attunement. This is tricky territory.

> **We speak, after all, of the unconscious. In one respect it is at hand, and yet in another respect it is not at hand, namely insofar as it is not conscious. This strange 'at hand and yet at the same time not at hand' arises from the possibility of being conscious of something unconscious. (*FCM* 61)**

Attunements live in the realm that Werner Erhard calls *what we don't know that we don't know*. The Forum functions to unconceal the "blind spots" that constitute this realm.

> **The distinction between not being there [*Nicht-Dasein*] in the sense of the unconscious and being there [*Dasein*] in the sense of what is conscious also seems to be equivalent to what we have in mind by awakening, specifically by the awakening of whatever is sleeping.**
> **(*FCM* 61)**

Therefore Heidegger begins with a proposal that attunements are *sleeping,* and we want them awake so that they can be dealt with, and their influence on our world can be perceived. "Awakening means to make something wakeful. . . . To awaken an attunement means, after all, to let it *become awake* and as such precisely to let it *be*" (*FCM* 60).

But Heidegger quickly pulls us up short here: on second thought (and it is in the pattern of Heidegger's thinking that there are many second thoughts for any proposal), are we really, in awakening an attunement, letting it be? On the contrary, Heidegger suggests that attunements function best as themselves when they are *not* recognized as themselves. If, he asks,

> **we make an attunement conscious, come to know of it and explicitly make the attunement itself into an object of knowledge, we achieve the contrary of an awakening. The attunement is thereby precisely destroyed, or at least not intensified, but weakened and altered. (*FCM* 61)**

Therefore, considering attunements as being asleep, and therefore to be awakened—since it may destroy the very phenomenon to which we wish to attend—may not be the best path for inquiry; so Heidegger proposes another direction for our thinking:

> **How often it happens, in a conversation among a group of people, that we are 'not there,' how often we find that we were *absent*, albeit without having fallen asleep. This not-being-there, this being-away [*Weg-sein*], has nothing at all to do with consciousness in the usual sense. On the contrary, this not-being-there can be highly conscious. In such being absent we are precisely concerned with ourselves, or with something else. Yet this not-being-there is nonetheless a *being-away*. (*FCM* 63)**

A human being can only be *away* because its being has the character of being-*there*. As being-there, "a human being—insofar as he or she exists—is, in his or her being there, also always already and necessarily away in some manner" (*FCM* 63):

JANE

Seven or eight years old.

ERHARD

You've got an eight-year-old running a seventeen-year-old's life. You know that?

JANE

Yeah.

ERHARD

Is it true that nobody likes you?

JANE

No.

ERHARD

You *are* "nobody likes you," even though you know that's irrational. But it wasn't irrational for a eight-year-old, was it?

JANE

No.

ERHARD

If I told you a story like yours to a seventeen-year-old, you'd understand that makes sense for an eight-year-old to think that, right?

JANE

Yeah.

ERHARD

But would you understand that in a seventeen-year-old woman?

JANE

No.

ERHARD

No, it's not the thinking of a seventeen-year-old woman, is it?

JANE

Right.

ERHARD

You want to know about yourself that you put your identity together, you put your *persona* together. You built yourself. Your life will be a compensation for not being liked. And the way

ERHARD (*continuing*)

to get to the possibility beyond that is to really see what happened when you were a seven- or eight-year-old little girl, and you got held back. Look out there.

(*indicating the group*)
What do you see?

JANE

A lot of people staring at me.

ERHARD

You can't see that. You can't see "people." You can see that person and that person and that person. You can't see people. "People" is a story. Look out there and see if you can see persons.

JANE

Yeah I see persons.

ERHARD

What are those persons doing?

JANE (*looking*)

Some are nodding. Mouths open.

ERHARD

Is there anybody out there not liking you?

JANE

No.

ERHARD

Just persons, right? Some of them may not like you. Because there are people "not liking people" waiting to happen. And there are seven- and eight- year-olds like that, aren't they? The other thing: I want to know if you're going to hide the rest of your life. You know you're hiding?

JANE

Yes.

ERHARD

You know you're not expressing yourself?

JANE

Yes.

ERHARD

That's your racket, isn't it?

 Being-away is itself a way of man's being. **Being away does not mean: not being at all. It is rather a *way* of Da-sein's being-there. The stone, in its being away, is precisely *not* there. . . . Only as long as we are-there [*da-sind*] can we be away at all, and vice-versa. Hence being away, or this 'there and not there,' is something peculiar, and attunement is connected in some as yet obscure way with this peculiar manner of being. (*FCM* 64, 65)**

An attunement, then, is not being asleep; nor is it being unconscious. It is more akin to being away while there. But it is never not there, which is the traditional perspective of moods and attunements, as "feelings"—emotional events that come and go as a result of circumstances (*FCM* 64).

We have so far discovered some things that an attunement is not. "Therefore," says Heidegger, "we must now ask: How are we to grasp attunement *positively* as belonging to the essence of man, and how are we to relate toward man himself if we wish to awaken an attunement?" (*FCM* 65).

He beckons us to follow him by suggesting this example:

 A human being we are with is overcome by grief. Is it simply that this person has some state of lived experience that we do not have, while everything else remains as before? If not, what is happening here? The person overcome by grief closes himself off, becomes inaccessible, yet without showing any animosity toward us; it is simply that he becomes inaccessible. . . . Everything remains as before, and yet everything is different, not only in this or that respect, but—irrespective of *what* we do and *what* we engage *in*—the *way* in which we are together is different. (*FCM* 66)

Heidegger is asking us to look closely at the situation. It is not that I myself feel grief; but that the attunement of our being with one another has shifted.

Or consider someone who is always in a good humor and "brings a lively atmosphere with them" (*FCM* 68); or "someone who through their manner of being makes everything depressing and puts a damper on everything" (*FCM* 67). These attunements are "not at all inside in some sort of soul of the Other," nor are they out there at hand in the world in some way (*FCM* 66).

Where and in what way are they, then?

 In positive terms, attunement is a fundamental manner, *the fundamental way in which Dasein is as Dasein.* . . . **And precisely** *those* **attunements to which we pay no heed at all, the attunements we least observe, those attunements that attune us in such a way that we feel as though there is no attunement there at all, as though we were not attuned in any way at all—these attunements are the most powerful. (***FCM* 67–68)**

In attunements, "we first meet ourselves—as being-there" (*FCM* 68). They shape our world, give us our ways of being, and provide the context for our philosophizing. Heidegger says that the task of philosophy is to "awaken" them in some sense, and then . . . well, we correct the situation, of course. This is the usual human impulse: fix the problem by altering or replacing the attunement.

Heidegger and Erhard, on the other hand, are proposing a different response, one distinguished throughout their thinking and most importantly referred to by Heidegger as *appropriation;* appropriation lets the situation be, distinguished as itself.

[A]wakening attunements is a manner and means of grasping Da-sein with respect to the specific 'way' [*Weise*] in which it is, of grasping Da-sein as Da-Sein, or better: of *letting Da-sein be as it is, or can be, as Da-sein.* **Such awakening may perhaps be a strange undertaking, difficult and scarcely transparent. If we have understood our task, then we must now see to it that we do not suddenly start to deliberate** *about* **attunements again or even** *about* **awakening, but inasmuch as this awakening is an acting, we must** *act* **in accordance with it. (***FCM* 68)

JANE
Yes.

Erhard stood very close to Jane at this point, his tone intimate.

ERHARD
Because it's something you do and something you are that you wish wasn't so.

JANE
Yes.

ERHARD
What's the payoff for hiding? Does hiding make you right that people don't like you? It makes you right about the fact that you're not something to be liked.

JANE
Yes.

ERHARD
Who does it make wrong?

JANE
Them.

ERHARD
Yeah. Because they don't like you. And you don't have to be responsible for relating; don't have to be dominated by relationship. Who you are is, "I'm not in the game." Right?

JANE
Right.

ERHARD
How does it have you dominate? It keeps people trying to get in, doesn't it? People around you are puppets trying to get in. They're puppets dangling on the hand of your racket. Right?

JANE
Yeah.

ERHARD
Are you physically attractive?

JANE
No. I'm ugly inside.

ERHARD
What's the "ugly inside"?

JANE
My feelings.

ERHARD
Like worthless. Like being nobody.

JANE
Yeah.

ERHARD
Do you know you made yourself "nobody"? At some point in your life something happened and you became "I am worthless." It's not that you think it. It's that you *are* it. It's not that you are worthless because you think you're worthless. It's the other way around. You are that you are "worthless" and therefore you think it, and you see it, and you listen it, and you smell it, taste it and touch it. You're already always worthless. You're worthless waiting to happen. Did you hear what I said?

JANE
Yeah.

ERHARD
Now, sometime today, or at the worst, tomorrow morning, you're going to find out about this worthlessness business. But all I want you to get right now is that at some point in your life, something happened, and you made yourself worthless. It's not that you are naturally worthless. At some point today you're going to find out what you are at the bottom, and it ain't worthless. It's something else. You made "being worthless." And you're clear there's a payoff to being worthless, right?

JANE
Yes.

ERHARD
What does it cost you to be worthless?

JANE
Love, happiness, self-expression.

ERHARD
Mostly self-expression. Look out there. Does it look different?

JANE
Yes. Just people.

Therefore, early in The Forum, Erhard exhorted participants not to try to fix anything they think is wrong with them, or to lose any "moods" they think may get in their way. *Attunements are us*; they are the raw material of The Forum.

Letting them be is difficult and not as transparent as it sounds. ■

ERHARD
Stick around. It's not over yet.

The Forum leader, Wes, now came onto the platform. Erhard remained in the room.

WES
Good morning. We're going to do the letters now. What do you think the purpose of this assignment was? The results of The Forum are not something deep inside yourself. Here's what's deep inside yourself: gunk, blood, undigested food. There's no place deep inside yourself where life's really happening. It's important to get this because you've got to know where The Forum takes place to have The Forum be effective for you. You need to know where The Forum occurs so you can have it occur powerfully. Okay, here's the hard part: where does The Forum occur?

(*pointing to his mouth*)
The Forum occurs right here. The Forum occurs in languaging. That's where The Forum occurs. It doesn't occur where you thought it occurred. The Forum occurs in a conversation, which becomes you, or it doesn't. How do people keep getting results one to two years after The Forum? Generating the conversation is how you make The Forum effective ongoingly. What you want to master is what occurs in being able to say and listen what The Forum is. Ultimately, The Forum occurs in your ability to say it—to say the possibility which it is. To those who didn't do the assignment, who didn't write the letter: You blew it. Listen to what people share: You could've gotten that.

A Japanese woman, Ayako, rose to share her letter addressed to one of her parents: she had come to The Forum to make a career decision, but found herself discovering that her racket is "being nice," and that this was what was in the way. She stopped reading to explain to Wes the circumstances behind her letter.

WES
You want your letter to be so clear it doesn't need to be explained. You should've put that in your letter.

AYAKO
I'm confused. I'm in the gap between living in the US and having a Japanese background.

WES
You don't sound confused to me. You may be disempowering yourself to call it confusion. Not knowing like a possibility may be a very powerful place to be in life. One of the most powerful places to be in life is to let be "not knowing."

(*to the group*)
I invite you to stop being confused.

ERHARD (*rejoining the conversation*)

"I'm confused" is a racket; always only a racket. It's a way of being from which you can survive when you're threatened. "I know that I don't *know*" is an opening for enlightenment. Nothing shows up in confusion. Confusion is a resistance to knowing, and it's built on a resistance to not knowing. Your resistance to not knowing produces this racket called being confused. Lots of the time when I'm reading I have to read something over again because I don't get it. But I'm not confused. If I'm confused I put the book down and walk away. Not knowing is a very high state of knowing. It's the step next to knowing. But confusion is way down at the bottom. The state before natural knowing is knowing that you don't know. Confusion is a defense mechanism, not an attempt to learn. It's a defense mechanism against fear.

AYAKO

My sleepless nights disappeared the moment I signed up for The Forum.

WES

How many of you had something significant happen out of enrolling?

(*most people in the room raising their hands*)

Why that happens: it was a commitment. Filling out the card, paying the money, created a commitment. It's a stand for something, which itself generates the results.

PARTICIPANT

What I'm in the presence of is the cost of trying to change my racket instead of having it.

WES

You always have a reason for everything. That's what it is to be human. What displaces the possibility of contributing or making a difference is identity.

PARTICIPANT

I was surprised that the person I chose to write the letter to was my mother—surprised that she was the person who would understand—with all the stuff I have going on.

WES

You notice her mother didn't change. This shift in her relationship with her mother came from a realization *she* had. When your racket is running your life, your life isn't happening. Something dead is happening, not living. When your racket is running your life, something is thwarting life.

At this point Wes announced a break, and gave participants an assignment.

WES (*continuing*)

Two questions for the break: What is your fundamental point of view about life? What is the fundamental point of view about life?

They adjourned for a break at 12:25.

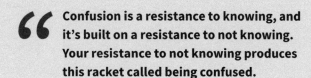

> **Confusion is a resistance to knowing, and it's built on a resistance to not knowing. Your resistance to not knowing produces this racket called being confused.**

SESSION ONE INTERVAL

The Forgetting of Being, Part Three of Eight: Heidegger's Etymologies

Heidegger's project may be seen as a reaction against the development of the metaphysical tradition in Western thinking, and as a corresponding attempt to think a way back to the greatness which was promised at the beginning of Western philosophy. For Heidegger, a significant step in this thinking-back involves tracing the *etymologies* of terms whose meanings emerged with the pre-Socratic Greek thinkers, whose writings mostly exist as fragments. These meanings, and the path of their development over the centuries, have critically influenced the way human beings in Western cultures (and, increasingly, global cultures) experience their world.

The meanings of these terms, Heidegger claims, took an unfortunate turn early in their development, so that today, in our loss of an experience of Being, we suffer the consequences of this *devolution.* Heidegger is forceful on this point: our language, he says, is "worn out." We must therefore "seek to win back intact the naming force of language and words; for words and language are not just shells into which things are packed for spoken and written intercourse. In the word, in language, things first come to be and are" (*IM* 15).

In tracing this historical process, Heidegger has constructed what Richard Polt describes as "a saga in which an original Greek experience of unconcealment degenerated into a focus on correctness, with dire consequences for us all" (*Heidegger: An Introduction* 133). Heidegger's historical perspective on language, and thus Being, is developed throughout his writing, and is therefore complex and varying, especially after the "turn" in his later work. But, says Polt, what remains constant is that the story of Being is a story of decline, "a fall from a promising Greek beginning" (132).

In his attempt to restore the power of Being, therefore, Heidegger proposes to explore the earliest extant written clues to our origins. In his development of these etymologies, Heidegger's readings of the Greek texts are controversial. John Stewart, among others, has raised the question of whether these readings are in fact supported by the texts themselves ("Speech and Human Being" 64); and Richard Rorty has gone so far as to call Heidegger's etymologies "largely fake" (*Contingency, Irony, and Solidarity* 131). Polt characterizes them as "idiosyncratic," and wonders whether, in his selection of Greek texts to deconstruct, Heidegger is "so attracted to

the pre-Socratics because they survive only in fragments whose interpretation can easily be skewed in a Heideggerian direction" (Polt 133).

But Gerald L. Bruns, in his study of Heidegger's later writing, has suggested that in his conversation with the ancient Greeks, Heidegger is musing on "a handful of overtranslated words (*physis, logos, moira, eris, aletheia, hen*)" in order to 'undertranslate' these words, as if to preserve them in their darkness" (*Heidegger's Estrangements 181*). This means taking words in "a sense which is different from what is customary or established or used with reason; it is to take them in a sense which is wandering or ambiguous in the manner of the word rather than fixed in the manner of the term" (*Heidegger's Estrangements* 181). Here we have wandered into a traditional definition of rhetorical figures, both tropes and schemes, which serve to turn us away from the common usage and meaning of sentences (schemes) and words (tropes). Etymology is one such turning away from the current and common to retrieve and make present what has been lost and dispersed; etymology is in essence a form of punning that brings about a shift, an awakening to a sense distinct from the obvious and everyday. Bruns writes that

> **After all, an etymology is, rhetorically, a figure of speech that consists of taking a familiar expression strangely, where the strangeness takes the form of some repressed or forgotten "original sense." But of course there never was such a sense in the sense of a time when etymology determined use. There never was anything but idiom, that is, no time of pristine, undisseminated (fixed) meaning. . . . To imagine a people somewhere actually speaking etymologically is comic theatre worthy of Jonathon Swift or James Joyce—or Woody Allen. (Gerald Bruns, *Heidegger's Estrangements* 134–135)**

While there is no "original" meaning of a word, the tendency to forget the constitutive possibilities of language leaves us to assume there was a time of pristine and fixed meaning from which we have devolved, and back to which the practice of etymology might bring us. Thus, remembering our forgetfulness through etymological punning—if we follow the movement of Heidegger's figure—evokes the "strangeness" of what appears to be an "original sense."

John D. Caputo has proposed a similar justification for these etymologies: Heidegger's goal, says Caputo, is "to effect a 'destruction,' a shaking loose, of Western philosophy in order to gain access to what is really being said in and by it.

For Heidegger . . . the deepest meaning of a text is 'concealed' within it, for what a text has to say is 'unspoken' in it." This is why Heidegger's interpretations appear "outrageous" and "scandalous," says Caputo: Heidegger hears a "primal address," "the power of the first word" (*The Mystical Element in Heidegger's Thought* 170).

It is also useful, given the emphasis that Heidegger's later thinking placed on the generative nature of the language of poetry, to consider this passage from his analysis of the Anaximander fragment, considered "the oldest fragment of Western thinking": "Thinking of Being is the original way of poetizing. . . . Because it poetizes as it thinks, the translation which wishes to let the oldest fragment of thinking itself speak necessarily appears violent" (*EGT* 19).

Thus Heidegger may be seen in his exploration of Greek thinking to be weaving a linguistic and poetic tapestry, threaded throughout with ambiguity, but a tapestry to which his entire thought is devoted: the language of Being, which is already always *in* language. If language is "the house of Being," the question of Being is necessarily implicit in every question and yet at the same time always *beyond* language: "Being remains unthought" ("LH" in *BW* 242).

His etymological discursions should therefore be considered in the same way as his phenomenological proposals regarding Dasein's existential components: we should *try them on*, to consider whether, in the end, they allow us to see something we had not heretofore seen. As Polt points out, Heidegger's etymologies, while idiosyncratic, nevertheless succeed in shedding a new light on the tradition: "Translating *logos* as 'reason' may not be wrong, but it certainly does less to make us think than does Heidegger's rendition of it as 'collecting collectedness'" (*Heidegger: An Introduction* 135).

The Forum resumed at 12:55 pm. Wes was on the platform, and called for participants to share about having called their parents or others in their lives to "get complete."

PRESTON
I think I've had what's called a breakthrough. I will try to contextualize it using the language I am learning here.

WES
Why don't you just share it?

PRESTON
I always feel better after a disclaimer. I was in New Jersey two weeks ago and Werner was there. On the blackboard was written: "I am prepared to be the man I haven't been, and I won't be the man I was." And what came to me as I was settling up with my parents is that I chose to honor the integrity of the process.

WES
What's happening in The Forum could be called coaching. That's the conversation The Forum leaders are committed to. Very few people in life are coachable. Children are uncoachable. Because every time you say anything to them they say, "I know." And very few of us ever grow out of that. Making oneself coachable is an act of generosity.

PRESTON
It was an act of trust. I got that as soon as the floor is raised by one of us, it affects all of us. There's a redundancy of overlap that makes for perfect survival. I felt the mechanism of the floor. My racket is manipulation: When it comes to relationships with women, first I fascinate, then I entice sexually, and then I become emotionally unavailable. But I'm able to be with that now. The boss racket I run is manipulation. The way I am in the world is manipulation. And the way that it is, is that you can have anything in the world as long as it isn't touched by manipulation. The manipulation that I've crafted into a high art turns out to be the only thing that can sabotage what really exists, which is, you can have it, just don't tell a story, have it, go about the steps to have it. I completed with my parents, who are both gone. I see that I've got doubts to meet every situation, but I've also begun listening. I want to acknowledge you all for the privilege.

WES
So you want to hear in people's speaking: The Forum. That's the whole Forum. So now he's going into the bonus land. He got the whole Forum. You don't even have to remember what he said. What you want to see is The Forum working in people's speaking, and allow yourself to be used by it. Joyce?

JOYCE
Yesterday, I was clear that I was complete with my father, who had passed away. Then I looked at my mother, and saw that she is perfect the way she is, and that I was complete with

her. There was nothing else to do. But then I realized that there was something incomplete, which was how I was in the relationship, but not how I presented myself in the relationship. I saw what a shit I was when I was a teenager, and how much damage I had done by leaving. I left home after college and I emigrated to this country alone. I made it on my own. I never completed that I ran away.

WES

She's talking about running away as a solution to a problem. Probably useful for you to look at the things you have left, the people you have left in order to solve a problem. To get the communication you left from their perspective.

JOYCE

Yesterday I saw the damage I had done. I see that I participate, but I don't share. I'm very good at what I do, but I don't put myself in there. And I knew that I had to give that up here in The Forum. I called my mother. I told her. She said "that's great!" I told her about two incidents that were very troubling. I told her that I got how rotten I was in the process of leaving. She said, "yes you were."

WES

And right there was the moment of getting off it.

JOYCE

She said, "thank you for telling me that." She described how I was and it was frightening. I can see what it must have been like for her. I saw what I am like; I can see what a pain in the ass I am for all the people I work with. I have heard it but haven't really seen it. It was very settling.

WES

There's a possibility for being in communication that settles issues.

JOYCE

She told me "hearing this gives me a wave of warmth." I got that I set her free and that I was too.

WES

Great. Thank you.

(*applause*)
I invite you to listen to big people, people willing to set aside their accomplishments, to not use them as an excuse to not participate, as a way for you to put yourself into The Forum.

Jake stood—the participant from Day One who was "hustle waiting to happen" and who also was "nutty" about inauthenticity.

JAKE

I was a shit to my mom when I was nine years old. Our relationship has been the same, and so I apologized to her. I told her I was here and she thought that was neat. She was glad to hear that. I said "let's not be this anymore." I told her that I accept her. She drives me nuts, but I want a relationship with her.

WES

She doesn't drive you nuts. You can have an interpretation that your mother drives you nuts. I know that one very well. When I was thirty-five I visited my mother in Miami and she told me what time she thought I should be home. Drove me nuts. If it was raining out, she would suggest clothes to wear. Drove me nuts: until I got off it and got how much of a creep I was. I got off it and I allowed my mother to mother me. Because that's what mothers do. That's their job. What did you expect your mother to do? Business deals with you?

JAKE

I've got a complex network of anxiety of reactionary being. When I'm that way it destroys what we can't have between each other. We don't have a connection. I told her I loved her and she said something to me. I realized she knew more of what's going on than I thought. She said that she would give me the space to be me. She knows how crazy she is. And she said she was going to stop doing that with me.

WES (*to another participant taking a microphone*)
This is about completing with your parents?

ESME

My twin sister. I saw how I make her wrong. I told her that I loved her, that I had taken things out on her instead of "you," which I mean everyone.

WES

There's a lot more love going on around you than most people are willing to experience.

ESME

I completed with my sister about our competition for our dead father's love. But I still was having an issue with "you" when I overheard a bunch of people asking a woman from Uganda really stupid questions. I realized she wasn't upset about stupid questions, and that I don't have to be. I can be an expert about being a twin.

WES

We've got to move on. But you have a standing invitation to keep getting complete with people in your life. One of the commitments of The Forum is to unconceal the being of human beings—what's giving you who you are. What was there before you were born? If you're a man or a woman, you were born into what it is to be one. If you're trying to carve out a new version, you're doing it against that already always background. The being of human being was decided at a party you weren't invited to and you had to fit into that once you showed up. One of the

Danger: Attunements and Moods

In Heidegger's account of human existence, Dasein—human being—is always being some *way*. Being-in-the-world, that is, is always a particular *way of being*. Heidegger uses two terms for this condition—*Befindlichkeit*, which is translated as *state-of-mind* (Dreyfus translates this as *affectedness*), and *Bestimmung*, translated as *attunement*. Both terms will be found in passages quoted in this book, but we will focus on the latter term, "attunement," since it avoids psychological implications embedded in "state-of-mind," and more powerfully suggests the totality of the situation: I am always attuned to the world in some way, and my attunement at any moment determines what things in the world mean to me—how much and in what way they "matter."

But my options for ways of being attuned to the world have been made available to me in my *thrownness*—that is, they are limited to a certain range of opportunities for understanding, a context of meaning into which I have been thrown, willy-nilly, and over which I have no control (see the "Thrownness" sidebar in Session Three of Day Two). The nature and source of these limits are invisible to me; like water to a fish, this background is so enveloping, so constitutive of everything, that I cannot see it. I simply experience its strictures in my life, and, occasionally, have the vague sense that there might be something more. In another of Erhard's expressions, my thrownness lies in the realm of *what we don't know that we don't know*, and is therefore beyond our grasp. But it colors everything.

Further, there is something primordially threatening about the nature of this context, a danger that leads us to avoid confronting it (though we don't know that this is what we are doing), despite our sense that more might be possible in life. Dasein, at some level, recognizes that it does not want to face up to the inescapability of its limits—what Heidegger calls "the *facticity of its being delivered over*" (BT 174). To avoid this confrontation, we lose ourselves in the distractions of the they-self—averageness, curiosity, ambiguity, and the chatter of the public realm. In certain states of mind, a situation may occur for us with a heightened intensity, but its nature remains obscured: an attunement is the kind of Being in which

> **Dasein constantly surrenders itself to the 'world' and lets the 'world' "matter" to it in such a way that somehow Dasein *evades its very self*. (*BT* 178, emphasis added)**

Attunements disclose thrownness in such a way as to conceal it; thrownness is disclosed *in the manner of an evasive turning-away* (*BT* 175). It's there but we don't want to look.

Closely related to an attunement is a *mood,* which may be seen as the attunement's affective dimension—the ontic manifestation in human experience of an ontological condition that remains in the background. We are never free of moods, whether intense or pallid. But nothing like a mood could occur for us, says Heidegger,

> **if Being-in-the-world, with its state-of-mind [*Befindlichkeit*], had not already submitted itself to having entities within-the-world "matter" to it *in a way which its moods have outlined in advance*. (*BT* 177, emphasis added)**

A mood arises from an attunement. So while we generally ascribe the cause of a mood to the circumstances, Heidegger suggests that we always already have a relationship with the world that evokes our particular moods. Our unwillingness to confront this situation leaves us stuck as the victim of the circumstances. It leaves us going through the motions of a life that is not our own, and thus we are immersed in an inauthentic existence.

But in certain attunements, Heidegger saw the possibility for an authentic human experience of Being. Some moods, he saw, have more significant potential for prompting such a disclosive experience. The prerequisite is that the mood evoke a *shift of focus*: we must become *present to the world,* rather than to those specific things in the world with which we are concerned.

Generally, in our everyday preoccupations, we seem to "cling to this or that particular being." But at some level, says Heidegger, we are always dealing with beings as a whole. This does not mean assuming a detached "objective" stance toward the populace; it is rather an element of our attunements:

commitments of The Forum is to unconceal the entire design of human being. Something very powerful occurs, transformation occurs when you can actually be present to the design: human being. What we want to confront, near the source of the design "human being," is what is your fundamental point of view and relationship to life? Life is really composed of other people. What we're really asking is, what's the fundamental relationship to other people?

At this point, Wes called two participants to come to the chalkboards.

WES
We're going to start with the question, what is the fundamental point of view of human beings for life? Your fundamental point of view toward life occurs in a very simple statement. I'm not interested in your complicated philosophies. Call out, "Life is —"

The group began calling out responses, and as they did so, the two participants at the boards wrote the answers: hard, change, imperfect, me, a problem, survival, dangerous, fun, experiences, etc.

WES
When you're being in life, what's really there?

Various participants called out: "Imperfect. Hard. Quest for knowledge. Change. Problem. Me. Evolvement. Survival. Dangerous. Not fair. Getting by. Threatening. Fun. Continual state of learning…"

WES
A lot of this is bullshit—When you're being in life. "Continual state of learning" is conceptual. That's not you walking down the street having to deal with the street. See, there's you, and there's it… everything else. Isn't that a fundamental division? There's you and then there's "it." I want to know your relationship to "it." When you're present to you and "it," what's there, like a presence?

People continued to call out answers which were written on the board: I'll show it, impressing it, struggle, approval, hide from it, it's fucked and I'll never fix it, separation, dealing with stupid people, life can hurt you, etc.

WES (*continuing*)
Your relationship to "it" is struggle, and "it" is going to win. It will. You don't live like that. "It" is bigger. You're going to die. Your life is about a relationship to "it," to prevent dying, and "it" is going to win. You don't live like that. You know it. People forget how they originated. You're dealing with "it," but in a way that you're going to lose. The fundamental point of view upon emerging into noise and cold and pain at birth: life is about avoiding the threat. *Life is dangerous.* It's threatening. Life is a threat. How do you respond? Survive. Life is about surviving the threat that life is. That's the already always way it is. That's what you inherited. That's what you joined. You didn't choose it. And you *are* it. Some of you are dealing with danger by getting "its" approval. Some of you are dealing with danger by flattering "it." Some

WES (*continuing*)

of you are dealing with danger by being smart. Some of you are dealing with danger by being successful. Your racket is your way of dealing with the danger that life is. I want you to consider the possibility that along with this fundamental point of view there is an experience of living, which is almost never acknowledged by people. It's totally suppressed, but it runs your life. It runs your relationships with other people. Ask yourself, why do I have to have a racket? What's it covering over? What's driving it?

LOTTIE

I'm so tough I don't need anybody. I'm supposed to know and if I don't know then I'm not tough.

WES

What does that cover over?

LOTTIE

That I'm a woman.

WES

What's the experience underneath that?

LOTTIE

That I'm a sexual being; that I'm not supposed to want it.

WES

Are you scared of sex?

LOTTIE (*reluctantly*)

Yes.

WES

You see, she couldn't even say it. Couldn't acknowledge it. And this is a woman who was really trying to say it, but it was horrifying to even acknowledge that she's scared of it—because she's tough. Tough people are never afraid.

LOTTIE

I just about died at the thought that it could be a part of my life.

WES

Got it. Great. Thanks.

(*applause*)

Other participants shared their answers and as they did so Wes indicated the fear that underlay each one: "I'm afraid I'll get taken advantage of"; "I'm terrified of being alone"; "I'm afraid of being

 In the end an essential distinction prevails between comprehending the whole of beings in themselves and *finding oneself* in the midst of beings as a whole. The former is impossible in principle. The latter happens all the time in our existence. ("WM" in *BW* 99, emphasis added)

But for the background to be disclosed, it must become the foreground: our presence to the whole must occur as salient. This shift may happen, for example, in the mood of *boredom*:

 No matter how fragmented our everyday existence may appear to be, [. . .] it always deals with beings in a unity of the "whole," if only in a shadowy way. Even and precisely when we are not actually busy with things or ourselves, this "as a whole" overcomes us—for example in genuine boredom. . . . Profound boredom, drifting here and there in the abysses of our existence, like a muffling fog, removes all things and human beings and oneself along with them into a remarkable indifference. This boredom reveals beings as a whole. ("WM" in *BW* 99)

Why do such moods give a possibility of authentic self-disclosure? Remember, we are questioning after the background, the determinative context for the everyday. Heidegger calls it the *nothing*, but it generally occurs for us as something, and we resist it. If we are moved to seek it, however, where can we look? Heidegger's response:

 If the nothing itself is to be questioned as we have been questioning it, then it must be given beforehand. We must be able to *encounter it*. Where shall we seek the nothing? . . . *The totality of beings must be given in advance* so as to be able to fall prey straightway to negation—in which the nothing itself would then be manifest. ("WM" in *BW* 98, emphasis added)

It is the function of The Forum to make present the totality of beings so that it can be cleared through negation.

From Fearful to Fearsome

In addition to boredom, two other human moods are presented by Heidegger as having special potential for making possible an authentic disclosure of our thrownness.

The first is *fear.* The evocation of the underlying source of fear has been a significant element of Erhard's work since its inception, in both the *est* Training and The Forum.

The second is anxiety. Heidegger draws a fundamental distinction between these two states-of-mind. Fear may of course take various forms, such as alarm, terror, or dread. But in every case the source of the fear remains the same: "All modifications of fear, as possibilities of having a state-of-mind, point to the fact that *Dasein as Being-in-the-world is 'fearful'*" (*BT* 182, emphasis added). This is the element of the human condition that is being distinguished at this point in The Forum. In fear, "that in the face of which we fear is a detrimental entity within-the-world" (*BT* 230). That is, we are always afraid of *something;* something has a significance, and that significance arouses our fear. But fear is not generated by the something.

The exercise being initiated by the Forum leader here—referred to as the Danger Process—is designed to distinguish the nature and source of the participants' fear, and to transform their relationship to life from "life is dangerous" (I am at the effect of life) to "I am dangerous" (I am powerful in life).

Erhard has told the participants that The Forum is designed to "take them down one step at a time," and the evocation of fear at this point is an important step. The structure of the Danger Process first evokes the fearful mood, so that, in Heidegger's words, "fear can then look at the fearsome explicitly, and 'make it clear' to itself" (*BT* 180). But then, in a dramatic example of reflexive rhetoric, *the fearsome is flipped.* The fearful become the fearsome. In this way, participants take an important hurdle, a stretch toward the ultimate leap of their transformation.

Anxiety

What is concealed in the mood of *fear* is *anxiety.* Anxiety, says Heidegger, is "*what first makes fear possible*" (*BT* 230). Fear is, as it were, anxiety with a false cause. Fear arises when Dasein flees the

hurt." This last statement came from a participant who had lived in bed for eight years with back pain.

WES

What's here in The Forum now is a safe place to communicate what's really so for you in your life. We've designed a space in here where you can confront your own fear of being alive, your own fear of other people and of living. I invite you to experience it, not to avoid it; not to sleep through it. Wake up! I don't know who you got out there that you lie to, but the ultimate jerk is someone who lies to themselves. You may have people conned, but the one person you don't want to con is yourself. It turns you into the ultimate jerk. This is a chance to get straight with yourself, to find out what is running your life.

PARTICIPANT

I'm powerfully addicted to approval. If I don't get it I leave.

WES

And what's underneath that is fear.

(*to the group*)

Let it up in your body. At first you'll have to reach for it. You're so dead to it you have to reach for it. The fear is so frightening that you'll find an unwillingness to fully get present for it. Let it up for yourself.

BETHANY

My knees are shaking.

WES

Allow it to be.

BETHANY

I can't let my sons love me. I ask: "what would happen if I let them love me?"

WES

Here's what it's all about. You need to experience your deep and profound fear of being loved by them. What would happen if you let that in, and then left, or they died?

BETHANY

I don't know what I would do, or what it would feel like.

WES

Just let yourself experience what stops you from letting them love you. Very simple. Don't make any decisions. Just acknowledge and experience the fear. We're in a group of exercises. That's what there is to do in this exercise. Just experience that.

Wes continued taking shares about fear, and unconcealing the fear underneath participants' fundamental points of view.

WES

Human beings put "bad" around fear. You can't experience what we called "bad." But it's always there. You're born into fear. If you don't believe me, read the newspapers. Newspapers trade on fear.

PARTICIPANT (*Forum leader 6*)

I've never been present to as much fear as I'm present to right now. I'm afraid if I share myself you'll find out how bankrupt I am, that I'm stupid, uncreative, inadequate, ineffectual, nasty, uncaring, and you'll throw me out of the game. I hate to say this because it's one of my rackets to handle this—to be humorous—I'm too short. I can see where my whole life is generated out of this. I am just terrified. I've done everything to prove that I'm intelligent, creative, effective, productive. I lead The Forum which is a perfect way to avoid being present to the terror, when you're up there with a microphone and drinking out of a cup, it's very insulating. I'm terrified of discovering how worthless I am. I went to an Ivy League university, graduated top of my class, a successful veterinarian, an effective Forum leader, all in an attempt to stop you from seeing that I'm none of the things I'm supposed to be.

WES

Thanks.

PARTICIPANT

I'm terrified all the time. Scared to death of horror movies.

WES

The fear is always already there. Horror movies just bring it up. Those of you who can't be present to the fear raise your hands.

PARTICIPANT

I'm afraid of being alive.

WES

All it takes is being able to acknowledge it. Try on the possibility that you actually are scared to death, and don't know it, and don't know that you don't know it; that your whole life is a strategy for avoiding the domination of life. You're scared of living. It's too confronting. It's all too dangerous. And your whole crummy act is put together as a strategy for making it in a world of danger. Try it on. Don't reject it. Just acknowledge it for yourself.

Here Wes called for paired sharing, where participants sitting next to each other replicated for themselves what others have said before the entire group. Following this, Wes announced an eyes-closed exercise.

disclosure of its thrownness, and turns in its flight toward entities in the world, which it then identifies as the source of the fear.

In *anxiety*, however, the entities in their significance disappear, and the background to all fears is revealed:

> **What is the difference phenomenally between that in the face of which anxiety is anxious and that in the face of which fear is afraid? That in the face of which one has anxiety is not an entity within-the-world. . . . That in the face of which one is anxious is completely indefinite. . . . [In anxiety], the world has the character of *completely lacking significance*.** (*BT* 230–231, emphasis added)

In moments of anxiety, the meanings with which we customarily comfort ourselves, even the meanings that make us fearful, lose their certainty, so that what is disclosed is the context of meaninglessness from which all of the meanings have been distinguished.

> **That in the face of which one has anxiety is characterized by the fact that what threatens is *nowhere*. Anxiety 'does not know' what that in the face of which it is anxious is. . . . it is so close that it is oppressive and stifles one's breath, and yet it is nowhere. . . . [In anxiety] entities within-the-world are of so little importance in themselves that on the basis of this *insignificance* of what is within-the-world, the world in its worldhood is all that still obtrudes itself. What oppresses us is not this or that, nor is it the summation of everything present-at-hand. . . . *Being-in-the-world itself is that in the face of which anxiety is anxious*.** (*BT* 231–232)

But recall: Being-in-the-world, as the Being of Dasein, is not something separate from Dasein itself. In anxiety, therefore, Dasein—the "there" of Being-there, the clearing in-the-world for Being—*comes face-to-face with itself*, and *not conceptually, but directly.* Thrownness is disclosed as what it is—a situation with no significance, a world that we inhabit because that's where we showed up. It has us, and it has no meaning. And that's all there is to it.

> **Anxiety reveals the nothing. We "hover" in anxiety. More precisely, anxiety leaves us hanging because it induces the slipping away of beings as a whole. This implies that we ourselves—we humans who are in being—in the midst of beings slip away from ourselves... In the altogether unsettling experience of this hovering where there is nothing to hold onto, *pure Da-sein is all that is still there. . . .* ("WM" in *BW* 101, emphasis added)**

And when Being-in-the-world is all there is, what gets revealed is that

> **The 'world' can offer nothing more, and neither can the Dasein-with of Others. Anxiety thus takes away from Dasein the possibility of understanding itself, as it falls, in terms of the 'world' and the way things have been publicly interpreted. (*BT* 232)**

In anxiety, the meanings of our everyday reality—the interpretations of the they-self—fall away. "Anxiety reveals the nothing" ("WM" in *BW* 101).

WES
That was the tip of the iceberg. Now we're going to give you the opportunity to experience the whole thing. It's an exercise designed for you to really confront your fear of living and being with people. You may hear people expressing it, crying. Allow yourself to be with your fear of other people. If you really allow yourself to experience it, the depth of it may surprise you. You have to be willing to take on what I'm asking you to consider and stand in it.

The next forty-five minutes were devoted to the Danger Process. Participants were asked to remain in their chairs with their eyes closed and to follow Wes's instructions, as he directed them to surround themselves, in their imaginations with an ever-widening circle of dangerous people. First, he told them to imagine that they were afraid of the people sitting on either side of them. After a few minutes, he said they should imagine—"create"—that they were afraid of the hundreds of people in The Forum room. With each step, participants were urged to create the experience of fear, to "let the experience up," and with each step he allowed time for the fear to be generated.

As he continued, Wes expanded the fearful environment to include the entire population of San Francisco, and then the 250 million people in the United States, and the world (circa 1989). As he exhorted participants to create the experience of fear, people began to respond vocally with screams and shouts. At first these were isolated, but gradually the room became a cacophony of cries and wails. Wes, already using a microphone, had to speak even more loudly to make himself heard over the din, as he persisted in his instruction that people let the fear up, that they continue to create for themselves this fear of other people.

This dramatic expression of fear continued at maximum pitch for some fifteen minutes. As it began to subside, a few laughs could be heard permeating the screams, and Wes spoke.

WES
There's something on the other side of it, something to get. There's a fundamental absurdity about living. All those people you are afraid of? They are, in fact, afraid of you.

At this point he reversed the process and led participants back through the concentric circles, this time pointing out that all of those people they'd been afraid of—the population of the world, the country, of California, of San Francisco, the people in The Forum, the people sitting on either side of them—were "just as afraid of *you* as you are of them. Making you the most dangerous person in the world."

WES (*as the laughter diminished*)
Going through this exercise is about allowing you to be with your fear, not to get rid of it. This may enable you to be compassionate, now that you understand what people are going through, including yourself. This won't make the fear go away, but will allow you to be with it. It'll still be there, but it doesn't have to stop you. Not overcoming it, not in spite of it, but allowing it to be. If you didn't get it, go out on a street away from the hotel, and when someone approaching you is about 3 or 4 feet away, jump out and say boo!

(*laughter*)

Participants who had not yet shared in The Forum were asked to share their experience of the exercise.

PARTICIPANT
I was feeling my body all scared, and I felt like I didn't want to be left alone. I like to pretend like I'm okay when I'm alone.

WES
Do you see a new possibility for yourself?

PARTICIPANT
To let people know I'm afraid.

WES
Powerful people are afraid and have the power to communicate that when it would make a difference. Thank you.

(*applause*)

PARTICIPANT
I've always pretended to not be afraid. I remembered a childhood experience. I didn't want to go to school. I was afraid to do anything. I really am afraid of my children. I always have to be strong. I didn't cry when my dad died. I completely suppressed it. I'm willing to be with my being scared.

WES
Great. Thanks.

(*applause*)

PARTICIPANT
I haven't shared yet because I'm afraid. I got that it's so ludicrous to be afraid of all these people who are so afraid of me. I'm in a different world now. I can see the faces out there, and I couldn't before. That wasn't possible before.

WES
Thanks.

(*applause*)

But now watch closely; something important is happening:

> **Anxiety throws Dasein back upon that which it is anxious about—its authentic potentiality-for-Being-in-the-world. Anxiety individualizes Dasein for its ownmost Being-in-the-world, which as something that understands, projects itself essentially upon possibilities. Therefore, with that which it is anxious about, anxiety discloses Dasein *as Being-possible*... Anxiety makes manifest in Dasein its *Being-towards* its ownmost potentiality-for-Being—that is, its *Being-free for* the freedom of choosing itself and taking hold of itself. Anxiety brings Dasein face-to-face with its *Being-free-for* the authenticity of its Being, and for this authenticity as a possibility which it always is. (*BT* 232)**

Anxiety as the abyss of nothing has morphed into anxiety as a clearing for the freedom of possibility. *This is the essential movement of The Forum,* hinted at persistently and in many iterations throughout the conversation. This is the reflexive rhetorical moment that will be achieved in its fullness by The Forum's conclusion, and for which the Danger Process has greased the slide. In Heidegger's terms, this is the event of appropriation.

In anxiety, we are confronted with the fundamental possibility of our existence, because the people, things, and events which usually have meaning for us are suddenly without significance. Literally, they mean *nothing*: "When anxiety has subsided, then in our everyday way of talking we are accustomed to say that 'it was really nothing.' And *what* it was, indeed, does get reached ontically by such a way of talking" (*BT* 231).

We call attention to Heidegger's use here of the qualifier "ontically," which refers to facts and concepts within the realm of beings. That is, it is *conceptually accurate* to say that what we fear in anxiety is "really nothing"; in saying this, the *concept* of nothing has been reached. But what gives an experience of anxiety its potential for self-revelation is that in such a state of mind *we reach nothing ontologically.* And in this deeply experienced loss of worldly significance there occurs, simultaneously, the possibility of the clearing, the pure Being-openness which is Dasein. As anxiety, the experience is unsettling; beneath and beyond lies the possibility. But do not build up too much hope.

In the Danger Process, we can observe a clear instance of what appears to be a symbiotic relationship between Erhard's work and the thinking of Martin Heidegger. This process was a central element of the *est* Training from its inception, and consistently provided one of its most dramatic components. But in The Forum, when that process is placed within the framework of Heidegger's model of Dasein, it gains a new and empowering context; while at the same time, the in-the-world power of Heidegger's model is illuminated.

We note, however, that despite this affinity between the evocative aims of the two thinkers, on our view it would be inaccurate to say that The Forum evokes an experience of anxiety in participants. That term has denotative power in its use by Heidegger, suggesting the affective extremity of the path to ontological liberation. But the languaging of The Forum employs its own vocabulary of hints, thereby providing an alternate ontological path—equally extreme, but without the inevitable psychological implications that currently accompany the concept of anxiety.

We assert that what distinguishes the transformation of Erhard's work from the majority of personal empowerment programs—those that, in Erhard's words, help people become "more, better, or different"—is its evocation of the Nothing. An authentic experience of Being, said Heidegger, must begin by doing violence to the "tranquillized obviousness" of the everyday interpretation. Therefore The Forum works backward before it moves forward; this is the heart of its genius. ■

PARTICIPANT (*a teenage boy*)
I've always been cracking jokes, always had to have something to say, and now what I'm looking at... is... it's all an act.

PARTICIPANT
I could only get in touch with a little fear.

WES
This is not about liberation. You should experience that suppression. Whatever you experience is fine, really. Just continue to listen to the conversation in the room. And if you continue to listen to the conversation in the room, it will continue to open up for you—what's going on with you. We're a long way until the end of The Forum. Be here, now, in this conversation. The Forum is too simple for complicated minds. The conversation going on in the room is more powerful than your internal dialogue.

(applause)

PARTICIPANT (*Forum leader 7*)
This is the first time I really saw how scared to death I am of people in authority. My father died when I was four years old, and my mother was a very strong and powerful woman. That's the bitch I can never get away from. If we did not do what she asked us to do, she would tie us up and beat us with a stick, or with words. I saw that I can never be myself around people in authority, because I am always afraid of being beaten or yelled at. And so I turn into a weasel around authority and I can't make straight requests, because when I asked my mother, I knew it wouldn't be accepted. And I couldn't say no to her, ever. None of us could, there were three of us. And the other side of it, that being able to see, really, that she was scared to death of me, that she was scared to death that I would not do what she asked if she didn't use force. Later on, when you spoke about compassion, and I felt such deep compassion for all people in authority who use force, because they're really scared that if they don't use force, you won't do what they are asking you to do. I'm standing in this huge possibility of really being with people who use force and really being there and really acknowledging my terror of forty-nine years of stuff has disappeared.

WES
Thank you.

Wes announced a break. The assignment for the break: get a partner and complete your experience of the exercise.

The Forum adjourned for a break at 4:00 pm.

SESSION TWO INTERVAL

The Forgetting of Being, Part Four of Eight: The Pre-Socratics

Martin Heidegger's purpose as a philosopher was to think a way back to the greatness which was promised at the beginning of Western history, but which has remained unrealized due to the metaphysical tradition that has dominated human understanding.

Historically, the term *metaphysics* has referred to the branch of philosophy that dealt with questions about the nature of things, about ultimate causes and that which does not change—questions, that is, about the nature of Being. This area of philosophical inquiry is now generally designated as ontology. In the normal course of events, most people, aside from academics and theologians, give little or no thought to the subjects of metaphysics and ontology, or even to Being. But Heidegger proposes that whether or not we are aware of it, the metaphysical tradition is deeply embedded in the way we understand the world. In our everyday lives, he says, this metaphysical understanding constrains our ability to be.

We remind the reader again as we begin this Interval that we are engaged in an inquiry into something that is *not* something—that is, it does not fall within the range of phenomena that are readily available for us to think about. In his writing, Heidegger was persistent in his efforts to indicate this mysterious aspect; for example, in the text of one of his later books (*The Event*) the word "Being" was repeatedly printed with a strikethrough. Here, the authors suggest that whenever the word "Being" (in its capitalized form) occurs in our writing, it might usefully be thought of as accompanied by a parenthetical question mark.

From the beginning of his career, Martin Heidegger's work as a philosopher was driven by the question of the human relationship to this mystery. According to Hubert Dreyfus, a scholar with whom Werner Erhard consulted while creating The Forum, Heidegger at some point had an experience of Being similar to the one elicited by Erhard's work, and he "struggled all his life to find an adequate language to express it without falling, as he put it, into the ruts of metaphysics" (Assessment 2). Over the years, his articulation of the being/Being relationship evolved significantly, but his single-minded commitment to the question never wavered. At the heart of the inquiry was his sense that modern human beings are out of touch with this aspect of existence. It is as if, as Western culture has developed, *Being has fled,* and a critical element of human experience has been lost.

The "ruts of metaphysics" mark the road Western thinking has traveled during the millennia since the time of Plato. The word itself is derived from the Greek *meta ta phusika,* which indicates a realm *over beyond what naturally is.* In the metaphysical understanding of things that has developed in the West, Being has been severed from its original relationship with beings, and has been relegated to the *over beyond*, a lofty transcendental realm to which access is mysterious and, for contemporary thinking, no longer even desirable. For the most part, human beings are unaware that anything is missing. For us, says Heidegger, the "word 'Being' is then finally just an empty word. It means nothing actual, tangible, real. Its meaning is an unreal vapor" (*IM* 39–40).

From the inception of his work, Werner Erhard has engaged the public by calling attention to this absence of Being, as in this 1982 presentation that he delivered to some 20,000 people in audiences in nine cities:

 What I want to talk about is the gap between our expectations and reality. I say that you and I live inside that gap, that there's a chasm, a gap, between what you and I expect of life and what life really is. . . . I'm not talking about the gap between your dreams and reality. I'm talking about the gap between what you and I have a right to expect from life, and what we actually get from life. See, you and I have a right to expect our relationships to be deeply nurturing and really fulfilling, and for the most part they're not. . . . You and I have a right, when we go to work for an organization, when we move from an individual expression to an organizational expression, we have a right to expect our affiliation with that organization to empower us, to make an even bigger contribution than we could do as an individual. . . . You know, we've got a right to expect certain things from the government, and we don't get it. Not fantasies. We have a right to expect certain things from the practice of our religion, and for the most part people don't get it—what they have a right to expect. And it's all over the place. There is a gap. And it's a no-kidding gap. Something is missing. . . . And what [we—as the they-self—are] providing is not allowing it to show up. ("Taking a Stand for the Future")

In responding to Being's departure, both Heidegger and Erhard have focused their efforts on the design of a new *language.* Heidegger's most frequently quoted claim is that *language is the house of Being* ("LH" in *BW* 217). "In the word, in language," he said, "things first come to be and are" (*IM* 15). That is, the language of one's time and culture—the meanings, the values and standards, the art and the traditions, the metaphors—make available a particular way of understanding the world, and our lives are lived within the possibilities and limitations of that understanding. In our current understanding, made available by the metaphysical tradition, Being has been forgotten. In our world, there was no possibility of Being.

Therefore the work of both of these men was directed toward the creation of new terminology; and one of the terms that has been central for Erhard, and that has served the function of what might best be called "originary naming," is *languaging* (see the "Primordial Metaphor: Clearing" sidebar in Session Two of Day Four). While the word *language*, as a noun, indicates a formal structure of words and rules and the uses toward which they are commonly put within a given linguistic community, "languaging" as a verb form indicates an action that is not merely putting the words and rules of language to use. Languaging indicates the action of generating new meanings, thereby creating new ways of understanding the world. The creation of *distinctions*, which is the central element of The Forum, is a process of languaging new contexts or clearings for understanding, which make possible new ways of being and acting in the world.

For Heidegger, thinking a way to the presence of Being involved not only the creation of a new vocabulary for the human condition, but also a *thinking back into history* to discover how the earliest philosophers in Western culture languaged their understanding of the world, and why this understanding devolved into the ideas of the metaphysical tradition. Students of Western philosophy generally begin their studies with Socrates, Plato, and Aristotle; these philosophers are the most familiar to us because in their work we find the beginnings of our own tradition of thinking. But there was an earlier group of thinkers in ancient Greece whose ideas are in some ways at odds with that tradition, men in whose thinking a possibility emerged briefly that was never thought again, and has since been forgotten. It is in the writing of these men that Heidegger finds what he is seeking.

David Farrell Krell, in his introduction to Heidegger's *Basic Writings,* tells us that as a seventeen-year-old student, Heidegger read a German scholar's thesis (Franz Brentano) on Aristotle's understanding of Being. The experience provoked his thinking, and led him to seek out Aristotle's own *Metaphysics,* where he found the question that would guide him for the rest of his life: "The question that was raised in earliest times, that we raise today and that will always be raised and will always be a matter of perplexity [is]: *ti to on, What is being?*" (*Aristotle,* Metaphysics, VII, 3, 1028b, 2–4). Here Krell imagines Heidegger's perplexity:

> Had some Polonius asked the young man what he was reading in his two books on "being," he might well have answered, "words, words, words." German words from recent times trying to translate Latin words from a bygone age that were trying to translate Greek words from antiquity. *But what were the Greek words trying to translate?* (Krell, "Introduction," *BW* 5, emphasis added)

It was this mystery that ultimately led Heidegger to his etymological explorations of the earliest Greek philosophers. It puzzled him that although Aristotle's writing had been foundational in the development of almost every area of human intellectual activity, his most profound question, while it had generated two thousand years of scholarly disputation on the subject of ontology, seemed now to have lost its meaning.

Heidegger's focus in his quest was the work of those philosophers traditionally known as the pre-Socratics—particularly Heraclitus and Parmenides—who lived and wrote in the fifth and sixth centuries BCE. As Heidegger saw it, this brief historical period was a particularly explosive time in the evolution of human understanding. The pre-Socratics were not the first human beings to use language, but in Heidegger's view, they were the first to consider the difference it made that they, among all beings, were the language-users; and they left a written record of their thinking, of which only fragments remain.

As the first philosophers of the West, these early thinkers made decisions about the meaning of what they saw, and their decisions set Western culture on the path which eventually evolved into the metaphysical tradition. "[W]e constantly return to the Greek conception of Being," says Heidegger, "because this conception, though entirely flattened out and rendered unrecognizable, is the conception that still rules even today in the West—not only in the doctrines of philosophy but in the most everyday routines" (*IM* 64–65).

Therefore, to locate the source of this tradition and to discover how it might have been otherwise, Heidegger has turned to the writing of those philosophers. Their work survives only in brief fragments, but for Heidegger they provide evidence of a crucial moment in the history of the West. They speak of "what since ancient times is to-be-thought but is still unthought" (*EGT* 4). Here Krell, one of the translators of *Early Greek Thinking,* characterizes the fragments:

> **Each is a truncated monument of thinking. Like the torso of a river god or the temple of Poseidon at Sounion, each fragment conveys a sense of loss, of tragic withdrawal and absence; yet each is a remnant of an exhilarating presence. . . . (*EGT* 4)**

> **Only indirectly do the fragments indicate their subject matter. . . . These merest fragments seem to talk about *everything*, all *being*, whatever *is*. We moderns are convinced that this is nonsense. . . . (*EGT* 7)**

But Heidegger reads these words with the eyes of a man who is relentless in his commitment to hear the language of Being; and what he has found provides us with a new perspective on the way Western thought has understood the world for two millennia (*EGT* Intro 5).

Is Heidegger's understanding of pre-Socratic thinking credible? Is it persuasive? His reading challenges the traditional translations, and as Krell acknowledges, his interpretations are distressing, even violent:

> **Although Heidegger takes each word of the fragments seriously—rather *because* he does so—his thinking plies a dangerous, uncharted course which we are at pains to follow. . . . But it is the violence inherent in any attempt to cross over to that foreign shore, the violence by which we overcome inertia and translate ourselves to the matter of early Greek thinking. (*EGT* 11)**

As we have noted in the last Interval ("The Forgetting of Being, Part Three of Eight"), several scholars find Heidegger's etymologies controversial, including one of his recent translators, Richard Polt, who calls them idiosyncratic and often "fanciful," and wonders whether Heidegger is "so attracted to the pre-Socratics because they survive only in fragments whose interpretation can easily be skewed in a Heideggerian direction" (*HI* 133). But Polt nevertheless concludes that despite their idiosyncrasy (or perhaps because of it), his readings succeed in shedding new light on the tradition.

Heidegger reads the writing of the pre-Socratics to unconceal the language of Being. As we will see, what he finds has substantial relevance for our inquiry into the work of Werner Erhard.

When The Forum resumed at 4:30 pm, Kipp was on the platform. Erhard was present, seated on the platform's edge. Kipp asked participants to share what they had found out about their lives. A young man named Tony stood and said that he had sensed "the joke of it all."

TONY (*continuing*)
I remembered when I was six my mom took me to Taiwan and once I got off the plane there were all these children with missing fingers and hands and arms asking for money and I was terrified. And I saw that everybody is afraid of everybody and that's what's wrong with this world.

KIPP
When you got off the airplane, what happened at that moment?

TONY
I felt really bad.

ERHARD
The most important thing you said is that it's all a joke. That's what we've been heading for the past couple of days. All that stuff about rackets and being afraid and all that stuff—that's not important.

TONY
And I've been all afraid that "I'm not going to get what I came to get out of The Forum! I'm not going to be able to have what I want in my life."

ERHARD
You want to know what? You're not!

TONY (*laughing*)
And now that we got that cleared...

ERHARD
Yeah, well, once everybody gets that cleared we can all go home.

TONY
There really is nothing to get.

ERHARD
That's right.

TONY (*laughing*)
What the fuck am I doing in here?

FORUM DAY THREE:
SESSION THREE

ERHARD

Wait. Wait. See you just ruined it.

TONY

I'm just kidding.

ERHARD

You're like a block and a half ahead of everybody. We've got to get everybody caught up to you. That's why we got to discuss this now. There when you were a block and a half ahead of everybody, you made it mean something. "Then why am I here?" Well, where else would you be if you weren't here? You'd be some other stupid place. You're here because you're here. You want to start getting what he's saying. It's not really a soap opera. It's really a joke. You know what a joke is? A joke is when you think the soap opera's real. That's a joke. The joke is when you think you're going to get someplace. That's a joke. That's a joke.

TONY

That's a fix.

ERHARD

Exactly. And that thing about "that's why the world doesn't work"; no, the world works fine. It works just like this. And the idea that you're going to make the world work, whatever that means to you, is another joke. Look around you. That's the way it is. Just like this.

TONY

But we've gotten what the rest of the world hasn't gotten.

ERHARD

So what? The fucking walls are still the walls. The ceiling is still the ceiling. Life is still the way it is.

TONY

But by being different...

ERHARD

What do you mean by different?

TONY

By going through what we've just been through.

ERHARD

You're no different.

TONY

Okay.

ERHARD

Listen to me. You are exactly the way you are. You're not the way you were, you are the way you are.

(*interrupting Tony*)
Have you ever not been the way you are?

TONY

I think I've always been the way I am.

ERHARD

And you want to know what? It's going to be that way.

TONY

I'm just thinking that we're more powerful now.

ERHARD

You're more powerful than you were, so what? You're as powerful as you are. And you've always been as powerful as you are. That's part of that illusion, part of the fix. More powerful. I'm going to tell you how all this work started for me. I spent my whole life learning how to make it, or making it. I'm smart, and I worked real hard at it. I studied everything and did everything. And then one day I was sitting in the car, and I realized I was never going to make it. I looked back at my life, and it was a joke. I spent thirty-four years of my life climbing a ladder, got to the top, and found that the ladder didn't go to the top of the wall. I looked at all the other ladders and saw that they don't go over the wall either.

TONY

Why do they have to go up?

ERHARD

That's the way being human is: climbing ladders that don't go over the wall. That's the joke. That's what there is to get in here. *You are not going to make it.* You know what your life is about? You're not going to make it. Whatever it's about. I was real sad when I found that out, that I wasn't going to make it. I'd spent thirty-four years trying, thirty-four years of anguish, thirty-four years of trying to look good. Terrible not to make it. I realized I was never going to be intelligent enough or good enough, honest enough or contribute enough, anything enough.

TONY

Is it bullshit to think you can make a difference?

ERHARD

You make a difference if you do, you don't if you don't. And if you set up "making a difference" as over the wall, you'll never get over the wall. You're making "making a difference" the Holy Grail. No matter what you pick out, if you come through The Forum again three years later you'll see it's a joke. If you make it the Holy Grail, it'll turn into a fucking joke.

Erhard sat on the edge of the platform as he interacted with Tony, watching him intently.

TONY
Empowering others is what I want to do in life.

ERHARD
And when you do it, you do it, and when you don't, you don't. And that's the whole story.

TONY
I just want to keep doing it.

ERHARD (*raising his voice and standing up to approach Tony*)
You will if you do and you won't if you don't. And if you make it the Holy Grail you'll make it into a fucking joke.

TONY (*laughing*)
Okay...

ERHARD
You get it?

TONY
Okay, so I won't make it the Holy Grail.

ERHARD (*sitting down again*)
Yes you will. See, you just turned not making it into another making it. "I won't make it! That's the way I'll make it, by not making it. That's my new making it, that's what's going to get me over the wall."

TONY
I'm not ever thinking about the wall, I just want to do...

ERHARD
So what? You want, so what?

TONY
Okay.

ERHARD
The stars don't move for "you want."

TONY
I'm okay with that.

ERHARD
Almost. You're close to okay with that.

TONY
I just enjoy empowering others, and I discovered this recently...

ERHARD
So what? And you got hair.

TONY
Okay.

ERHARD
But you got it more than you got hair! You got it like some big goddamned thing.

TONY
Yeah I do.

ERHARD
No, it's a fart.

(*laughter*)

TONY
Look, I just discovered this for myself.

ERHARD
In about three minutes you're going to be real deep in this thing. With your foot nailed to the floor about empowering others.

TONY
I discovered that's what I want to do in life.

ERHARD
So what?

TONY
Okay, so what?

Choice

A chief quality that marks *Being and Time* as Heidegger's masterwork is that while it was written at an early point in his long career, and although in later years his thinking took some significant turns, *Being and Time* has nonetheless retained its stature. We see this as evidence for the presence of the Same in Heidegger's thinking over time—the single thought that lies at the heart of every thinker's thinking, and remains always unthought in that thinking (we will take up "The Same" in the sidebar of that title following "The Violence of Meaning," which follows this one).

As a narrative, *Being and Time* tells the story of Dasein, which arcs from inauthentic lostness in the "they" to authentic resoluteness. If, as Hubert Dreyfus suggests, we take Dasein to stand for human being, then as the being who understands, who interprets its self, Dasein must have a *self* that undergoes this adventure. But the self of Dasein, as Heidegger distinguishes it, is not the familiar ontic/psychological self—not the accumulation of experiences and preferences that is generally represented when one says "I." Rather: "Dasein's selfhood has been defined formally as a *way of existing*, and therefore not as an entity present-at-hand" (*BT* 312). The self of Dasein is not a being, but a way of Being. If there is no "I" to choose, how is choice, and the freedom it posits, even possible?

In its current manifestation, the specific way the self of Dasein occurs for itself is determined by the interests of the "they" (please see the last sidebar of Day Two Session One). The rules, the tasks, and the standards have been determined before Dasein was thrown into the game, to assure the survival of the "they," and that's the way the world is.

But the real issue in this situation is not that Dasein's choices are limited; the problem is that *they are not yet Dasein's choices.*

ERHARD

You think I'm saying "so what" like a put-down, but I'm not. I'm just saying "so what." Now you'll do that when you do and you won't when you don't. Just like you did before you discovered that. And then you'll go on to some other asshole thing. Really. You were in a very good place when you stood up at first. Stay there for a while. Really. Don't you understand? Thirty-four years of trying to make it, I found out I never was going to make it. I got really clear I was never going to make it. Never going to be anything enough. I found out I was a liar once. There was a time when my whole life was a lie. But there was a moment when I found out that everything that came out of my mouth was phony. I decided to stop lying. I almost didn't talk for a year, because I couldn't get anything to come out of my mouth that wasn't a lie. "Where's the toothbrush?" was about as close as I could get. Whatever I said, it was in-order-to, I was up to something, it was a con someplace at some level. What happened on that day this work began for me was I realized I was never going to be honest enough to make it. I was always going to be exactly as honest as I was. I was never going to be less honest or more honest than that. And if in three days I was going to be more honest, I was more honest, and if in three days I was going to be less honest, I was less honest. And however honest I was on that day, that's how honest I was.

TONY

What you're talking about is living in the present.

ERHARD

No, not quite. I don't like that hippie shit. That's horseshit for me.

TONY

I just got something.

ERHARD

What?

TONY

That my whole life I needed a mission in order to feel great about my life.

ERHARD

See, you've never done anything. I realized I knew nothing, because everything I knew, I knew *in order to*: I knew nothing as itself. Everything I knew was distorted, had a certain twist to it, a cast of color. It was never its own color. Everything I knew in-order-to—in order to make the world a better place, in order to get ahead, in order to look good, in order to get ahead—is all horseshit in your mouth, because it all has to do with looking good. So there's nothing ruthless about it Tony. None of it is itself. The tree is a tree: just a tree. It's a tree. It's not "in order to enjoy it." It's not "in order to" anything. It's a tree, like, a fucking tree. So I was real sad for a long time—about five minutes—then I started to laugh because I saw the joke of it all: the total joke. Because the realization was,

ERHARD (*continuing*)

"I can't *not* in-order-to." I didn't invent in-order-to; "Making it" invented me. They had that party and I got there late. And they said what it is to be a human being, the kind of being a human being is, is attempting to make it, to look good. That's what it is to be a human being. And everything you're going to do is going to be that. See, you started out this conversation in a great place and there have been a few changes since then. And when we're done with this conversation we're going to be in a great place and then go through even more changes. 'Cause you'll have a new kind of making it. For some people in this room, "making it" is not making it. They make it by not making it. It's a trap. It's a fucking trap. That's what it is to be human. The other side of it is, all those balls and chains I was carrying around for years, they all dropped. You know, I was sad for a while, but then I got the joke. It's all a joke. You're not going to make it. You know what? It isn't going to work out. *It is not going to work out.* You will never meditate enough, or work hard enough, or have your fortune told enough, or get enough information, or be smart enough, or be holy enough, or practice enough, or say your prayers enough, or be sexy enough, old enough, young enough, or think enough, or tough enough to make it. See, some people are trying to survive. That's also a joke. You're going to die and they're going to stick you in a hole in the ground and throw dirt in your face. It is not going to work out. That's how survival is going to work out. You're going to keep climbing the ladder and keep climbing the ladder and at the top of the ladder, there's going to be a hole there, and they're going to stick you in there and throw dirt in your face. And that's how survival is going to work out. It is not going to work out. It is not going to work out. You are never going to make enough of a difference to make a difference. You are always not going to have made a difference enough. It isn't going to turn out. This is the whole Forum, you might as well get it. The rest is just polish.

Erhard spoke very slowly and deliberately to the group at this point.

ERHARD (*continuing*)

It is not going to turn out. And you know why it's not going to turn out? Because it already turned out. *This* is how it turned out. Nobody notices that. You made it. This is it. It's not gonna turn out. It did turn out. This is the way it turned out. And you fucked it up. You're still struggling. What would it mean if you did make a difference? So what? You make a difference. Okay fine, so what?

TONY

It's "so what?" because…

ERHARD

No "because." Don't fuck it up with "because." It's "so what?" because this is what's so. That's why it's "so what?" It's just like this. This is how it turned out. You don't like that, do you? You didn't want it to turn out this way. It wasn't supposed to turn out like this, it was supposed to turn out some other way. Too bad. This is the way it turned out. It doesn't care that you don't like it.

TONY

There's still something up for me.

> The "they" has always kept Dasein from taking hold of these possibilities of Being. The "they" even hides the manner in which it has tacitly relieved Dasein of the burden of explicitly *choosing* these possibilities. It remains indefinite who has "really" done the choosing. So Dasein makes no choices, gets carried along by the nobody, and thus ensnares itself in inauthenticity. (*BT* 312)

The inauthenticity arises not from the situation, but from Dasein's way of being with this situation.

Choosing: Appropriating

And here we encounter one of Heidegger's most important reversals of everyday thinking, a move that has been central in Werner Erhard's rhetorical technology since its inception.

In our tradition, if one finds oneself stuck in a process generated by choices one did not make, the action indicated by the situation is clearly the making of new choices. But consider Heidegger's alternative and somewhat tricky perspective:

> This process can be reversed only if Dasein specifically brings itself back to itself from its lostness in the "they." But this bringing-back must have that kind of Being *by the neglect of which* Dasein has lost itself in inauthenticity. (*BT* 312–313)

What has Dasein neglected? It has *neglected to choose*; therefore, it must make up for not choosing. But "'making up' for not choosing signifies *choosing to make this choice*"—that is, choosing to make the choice not to choose. "In choosing to make this choice, Dasein *makes possible*, first and foremost, its authentic potentiality-for-Being" (*BT* 313).

While these passages are from Heidegger's early work, and the distinction *appropriation* became central in his later thinking, we propose that the unspoken Same can be heard in both cases. This intensely reflexive movement of thinking, called forth repeatedly throughout the four days of The Forum and culminating in Session Two of Day Four, is central to the achievement of its transformational outcome. It is also deeply embedded in Heidegger's distinction *appropriation,* a term which suggests the taking-ownership of something that is already at some level one's own. ■

ERHARD

You're a human being. There's always going to be something up for you. Your life is always going to be a soap opera. And it's always going to be a joke. And every once and a while you'll come back to me and get it again.

TONY

I just want to know one thing.

ERHARD

If we get this one thing it's going to change everything, right? It's not going to be the way it is, it'll be some other way if you get this. If you get this one thing answered, just this one thing.

TONY

Where does God fit into all this?

ERHARD

Remember I said I didn't discuss God with people who don't know their ass from a hole in the ground.

TONY

Yeah, believe me, there's a hole in the ground right over there. This is really big for me.

ERHARD

What?

TONY

Having God in my life, and that God makes a difference in other people's lives.

ERHARD

That's fine. Yeah, but you want to make that different than a fart.

TONY

Sure I do.

ERHARD

No, that's disgusting. If you got God in your life, you've got God in your life. That's all.

TONY

But if you have God in your life then you have purpose in your life.

ERHARD

Really? It's not going to end with you being put in the ground and dirt being thrown in your face?

TONY

It will end that way.

ERHARD

It will. And you want to know what? You'll be just like you are, whether or not you have God in your life. I didn't say there was something wrong with having God in your life. I didn't say there was something right with it. You want to turn this "God in my life" stuff into another fucking racket. You do. You don't like that idea.

TONY

If you have the concept of God you have to believe that there's a better place.

ERHARD

Who said that? The Pope?

TONY

Who the fuck is the Pope?

ERHARD

It's just you talking. I didn't say it wasn't true. I just don't want you to turn this into another fucking racket. God is not going to save your ass. Your ass is going into a hole.

TONY

It's already gone. Great. So if I have God in my life I have God in my life, if I don't I don't.

ERHARD

Exactly. That's the fucking truth isn't it?

TONY

That is the truth.

ERHARD

Right. You want to make some bullshit out of that.

TONY

Everybody does.

ERHARD

You want to make that mean something. I know everybody does, that's why I got a job.

(*applause*)

TONY

Yeah, well, I want your job.

ERHARD

You don't want my job: I'm a throwaway. You turn God into another racket, another way to be right and make others wrong, another way to avoid the domination of the responsibility to be human. They're going to put your ass in a hole in the ground and throw dirt in your face and that's the end of that story. Don't turn that into more bullshit. And don't do it because everybody else does. Tony, you kind of got there early. And it's important to go through all the parts of the conversation. We're going to do that. Stick around. Thanks

TONY

Thank you.

Participants continued to share their experiences from the day.

BETH

When I did the last session, I immediately felt ripped off, because my girlfriend took this last month. I already knew what was going to happen through the whole thing, and I…

ERHARD

Didn't make that much of a difference, though, knowing what was going to happen, did it?

BETH

Right. And it's because I didn't stop myself and a lot of times I stop myself. And so I thought, "okay, I'm going to do it," and so I closed my eyes, and I was… stuck. And I thought: "Okay, I want to get out of this" because I was thinking that this person was supposed to kill me and the person next to me was going to kill me and that was too far removed from me. And so I said okay, what other kind of fear do I have? And that kind of fear was the fear of intimacy.

(*crying*)
And that…

ERHARD

Slow down. Slow down. Go ahead.

BETH

That made me sad. But I felt good about being sad, because I was doing the process and I didn't stop myself and I still have the fear of intimacy. And I stop myself a lot of times by not taking risks.

ERHARD

And you made a soap opera out of it.

(*to the group*)
And you stopped yourself a lot of times and you don't take risks and that's sad and you tried and you struggled and then you gave up and figured the hell with it, and tried to be something

ERHARD (*continuing*)
else instead of trying to be intimate and then you found out that that was no good, and so then you went back to try to be intimate, and nah nah nah nah nah nah nah, nah nah nah nah nah, nah nah, nah nah nah nah nah.

BETH
Right.

ERHARD (*to the group*)
Now I'm talking about you, not her. She just happens to be standing up so we got some way to talk to you. You don't want to listen to her soap opera. You want to listen to your soap opera, your "what happened," and the sad, and the struggle, the effort, and the sacrifice that you have made, nah nah nah nah nah nah nah. Great, go on, you're doing a good job.

(*Beth remains silent*)
What does that mean that you avoid intimacy? I don't want to put words in your mouth if that's not the way you said it. Say it the way you said it. What does it mean?

BETH
That... I'm talking about a personal relationship...

ERHARD
I'm not asking you to explain it, I'm asking what it means. So what?

BETH
So what?

ERHARD
Yeah, so what? I asked you first.

BETH
You mean, what do I do?

ERHARD
No, so what?

BETH
Yeah.

ERHARD
I mean, so what?

BETH
I avoid intimacy.

ERHARD
Yeah.

BETH
That I don't take risks.

ERHARD
So what?

BETH
So what? I know...

ERHARD
I asked you first. So what "you avoid risks"?

BETH
Yeah.

ERHARD
You avoid risks. You made that into some kind of crummy meaning. You know what? You avoid risks. Okay. You turned it into a soap opera. You made it mean something. You put violins in the back, and turned it into some meaning. What does it mean that you avoid risks? It doesn't mean anything. Rocks are hard. You know what that means? Nothing. They're just hard. You avoid risks. What does that mean? Nothing. I'm getting older. What does that mean? Nothing. I didn't succeed in life. What does that mean? Nothing. I had a divorce. What does that mean? Nothing... but I had two divorces. What does that mean? Two nothings. But I'm not worthy. So what you're not worthy? You're going to make a federal case out of it? You're not worthy. I got that. Now what? You want to make something out of it. It does not mean anything! It's meaningless. Does it mean something that rocks are hard? What about the spirits-in the-rocks shit? More fucking voodoo.

(*laughter*)
Voodoo! You avoid risks. I got it. "Oh, but you don't understand." What you mean is, I don't get all the meaning and drama and turmoil and soap opera and the sadness and upset. You're right. I don't get that. That's your crap. What I get is that you avoid intimacy. I got that. Rocks are hard. Water's wet. And you avoid intimacy. And each one of those has an equal amount of significance. But you made a big deal out of avoiding intimacy. Turned it into a whole fucking soap opera. You know, it's back and forth. Sometimes Beth resists that and tries to be intimate. And sometimes she succumbs to it and gives up the attempt to be intimate. She changes so that she's more intimate. Is that getting clearer?

BETH
Yeah. I'm going to take a risk.

BETH (*to the group*)
All available men: see me at the break.

ERHARD
Very good trolling. Have them line up.

(*to the group*)
There was a little something you didn't get out of that.

Erhard held up his hands and stuck one index finger into the circled fingers of the other hand, making a gesture indicating the sex act.

ERHARD
This is very significant. God and that.

Erhard looked over at Angel, the participant who had shared the day before about being twice-divorced.

ERHARD
What are you doing over there, Angel?

ANGEL (*angrily*)
What do you mean nothing means anything?

ERHARD (*to Angel*)
I didn't say "nothing means anything."

(*making the sex-act gesture*)
I said this... means this. Stand up.

(*to the group*)
How would you like to carry around what she carries around?

ANGEL
You gave me something yesterday, and you just now took it away.

ERHARD
And you turned it into shit when I gave to you. And I didn't give it to you anyhow; you gave it to your self, but then you turned it into shit, because you made it mean something, and now you've got a new soap opera. The old soap opera was "I was divorced twice." Now you got a new soap opera. Can you not see that you're stuck and you have a conversation with Kipp and me to get unstuck? Then we bring up some new thing and then you get stuck again. You're a series of stucks, one after the other after the other after the other, making up stucks. Tell us your story here. What is it that's bothering you? Tell Kipp.

ANGEL
Nothing.

ERHARD
Oh bullshit.

KIPP
Try again. Stand up.

ERHARD
You're a long way from nothing. When he's done...

ANGEL (*angrily*)
So what?

ERHARD
When he's done with you, you may get to nothing. Right now you're something.

ANGEL
Why is it important for me to be nothing?

KIPP
Well, how is something treating you right now?

ANGEL
I don't know how to be nothing.

ERHARD (*interrupting Kipp to address the group*)
What you're watching, what this is designed to do, is to let you look down to the very foundation of what the already always being of human beings is. You're going to get to see whence you came. In this conversation—it's gonna take hours, and given how stupid you are, it's gonna take a lot of hours—and what you're going to see if you're watching, is whence you came. I mean you. What a "you" is, what an "I" is, what a "me" is. This is whence it comes. Remember what I said earlier about working backwards? We're going to get all the way down to the bottom, to the source of you. And this is the conversation in which we're going to do it. And if you watch here, and map this on to your own life, you'll get to see where you came from.

(*pausing*)
This is where you came from. You didn't come from your mother. You got your body from your mother. This is where you came from. Remember I told you the first half of The Forum was the already always being of human being? This is you "already always." She sat down yesterday beautifully unstuck. Now she's as stuck as she was yesterday. By the time we finish this conversation most of you will be unstuck. And by tomorrow you will be stuck again. Because

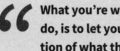

> **What you're watching, what this is designed to do, is to let you look down to the very foundation of what the already always being of human beings is.**

ERHARD (*continuing*)

that's what it is to be human. To be stuck. You don't like it, too bad. Stay in California. Then you can play stuck trying to get unstuck. You understand stuck trying to get unstuck?

(*very loudly*)
You are stuck trying to get unstuck, you asshole!

KIPP

So Angel, what did you give meaning to?

ANGEL

Life.

KIPP

No. You were going along fine, right?

ANGEL

I was going along great.

KIPP

That's right, you were going along great.

ERHARD

And you made going along great mean something, didn't you?

ANGEL

Yes.

ERHARD

Yeah, you turned it into a fucking soap opera. You want to get that, you want to get that real clear because you're going to do the same thing. You will do it. I'm not telling you about it so that you won't do it. That'll make a fool out of me. 'Cause you will do it. Remember I said "ride the horse in the direction it's going"? I walk out to the street and watch for which way the traffic is going. I point in the direction it's going. Someone says, "Jesus, that guy makes the traffic go in that direction. Look at that guy! He makes everything go the way he makes it go." I'm just telling you so that I'm pointing in the direction you're going anyhow. No sense pointing in the other direction. That's stupid.

KIPP

So, you made what mean something?

ANGEL

That I don't care.

The Violence of Meaning

Human beings are the animals with language. As a result, we awake daily into a meaningful understanding of the world. We assign meaning to everything that exists and everything that occurs; we are compelled to know what things mean, and cannot stand *not* to know.

To understand the depth of our attachment to meaning, consider Martin Heidegger's view: language was not a property that was somehow granted to human beings; it was only through language that human beings *became* human beings. The impulse to mean and know is *constitutive* of our being. It is so much the way we are that we cannot recognize its downside, which is that our death-grip on meaning is the source of most of our problems.

So in any deep exploration of human being, such as that conducted in The Forum, it is essential to consider the function of meaning, as well as the process by which meanings emerge in the world, and are—or are not—maintained there. How did the world occur; how did human beings occur? In the writing of the pre-Socratic Greek philosophers, Heidegger finds this perspective: the beings currently in the world are there because human beings spoke them into being. Further, in doing so, we were at the same time creating ourselves as human beings.

> **Man, insofar as he exists as man, has always already spoken out about *physis* [Being], about the prevailing whole to which he himself belongs. Man has done so not only through the fact and for the purpose of talking specifically *about* things; for to exist as man already means: *to make whatever prevails come to be spoken out*. (*FCM* 26, emphasis added)**

In order to be spoken about, beings must be spoken out. For the Greeks, "speaking is called *legein;* the prevailing that has been spoken out is the *logos*" (*FCM* 26). But Heidegger suggests a more original meaning for both words: *legein,* in its original meaning, was not *to speak,* but *to gather and collect,* or *to lay out; Logos,* as what is gathered and laid before us, was the primary gathering principle.

This "original" meaning of *logos,* then, draws our attention to whatever is there *before* it is articulated—before the emergence of judgment, the assertion of opinion, and the contradiction of perspectives. These are all of course inevitable. But the writing of the pre-Socratics suggests to Heidegger that at the dawn of humanity, something was available to human apprehension, a *logos,* which now escapes us.

For Heraclitus, it was the *logos,* the background of collectedness, the sway in the event of its emergence into the world. The meaninglessness from which beings emerge cannot maintain itself in a world of meaning, but for a moment in history, for those who were open to its emergence, it was glimpsed. Heraclitus suggests that it remains available, but that human beings as a whole—the *hoi polloi*—are unavailable for glimpsing it.

> **But while *logos* constantly remains itself, human beings behave as those who do not comprehend (*axunetoi*), both before they have heard and after they have heard. . . . Hence one must follow the Together in beings—that is, adhere to it; but whereas *logos* essentially unfolds as this Together in beings, the mass lives as if each had his own understanding (sense). (Heraclitus, fragments 1–2, in *IM* 140–141)**

KIPP
Yesterday you saw something about not caring.

ANGEL
I saw that it was okay to care sometimes and sometimes I don't.

KIPP
Right.

ANGEL
It's not okay to have life mean something sometimes and for sometimes life not to mean anything.

ERHARD
It never means anything. It doesn't mean something sometimes and not mean something at other times. Life is empty and meaningless.

ANGEL
Then why should I be alive? Then I shouldn't be alive. Dead.

KIPP
Then you would be dead.

ERHARD
You know what you just did? I said life is empty and meaningless and you made that mean something. I said life was empty and meaningless and you got sad about it. "Really? Ohh. We'll maybe I'll just lie down now and watch television."

ANGEL
And so just because you say life is meaningless I should believe it?

ERHARD
I didn't say to believe anything. Didn't I tell you up front not to believe anything I say?

ANGEL
Yes, I forgot.

ERHARD
The truth speaks for itself, it does not need me. At any rate, when I said "empty and meaningless," you said, "oh my God, oh that's terrible." You made empty and meaningless mean something. You're a drama queen.

ANGEL (*vehemently*)
Yes, I am.

ERHARD

All right. And proud of it.

ANGEL

And sometimes I'm not.

ERHARD

Where is the chip queen? I'm going to get you two together. You can have a meeting. That would be great. Talk about movies. That's real entertainment: the drama queen and the chip queen together. Angel, do you understand that I'm not trying to make you not be the way you are? I'm simply trying to shed some light where you stand. I don't want you to not be the way you are. I know you're a drama queen. You're always going to be into the drama. And I didn't say that's bad. But you want to make everything mean something. You screw yourself over every time because you make it mean something.

ANGEL

Isn't it human to make everything mean something?

ERHARD

That's what I said. We were going to reveal the already always nature of being for human beings.

ANGEL

So what I got was that I am a human being and I can't get away from being a human being. And I spent a lot of time and effort trying not to be a human being.

ERHARD

Very good, but now you've turned that into a sacred cow. You've turned being a human being into a sacred cow. "Now the son of a bitch wants to take away my new sacred cow from me."

ANGEL

And my new sacred cow is being a human being.

ERHARD

Yeah, you turned that into some kind of a story. Instead of just being a human being you turned that into a soap opera, a drama. Life doesn't mean anything, sweatheart. It doesn't mean a thing.

ANGEL

You don't know how upset that makes me.

ERHARD

I understand that it makes you upset. I told you, this is my second Forum. I told you when I found that out I was real upset.

ANGEL

But then what did you do with it?

Heidegger develops this distinction further:

> **Heraclitus wants to say: human beings do hear, and they hear words, but in this hearing they cannot "hearken" to, that is, follow, what is not audible like words, what is not *talk* but *logos*. . . . But genuine hearkening has nothing to do with the ear and the glib tongue, but instead means obediently following what *logos* is: the *gatheredness of beings themselves*.** (*IM* 142–143)

Logos, Being, the Together in beings, is the unspoken background that emerges to be glimpsed in the dialogue of The Forum.

If we are listening for the *logos*, we may hear the gathering in Heidegger's words of one of his most important and provocative hints: his persistent play at the fuzzy boundary between Being and beings. By teasing out, over a fifty-year career, the question of agency in the Being–being relation, Heidegger provided human thinking with an essentially reflexive quandary, one whose thinking through may catapult us into a leap and land us with a more liberated understanding of the world.

Heidegger's early take on this question, in *Being and Time*, was that Dasein achieves an authentic existence through the achievement of *resoluteness*, and the existential choices thereby made available. One of those choices is to stop fleeing one's reality and let it be, recognizing that its meanings are made up and malleable: "When Dasein is resolute, it takes over authentically in its existence the fact that it *is* the null basis of its own nullity" (*BT* 354). In The Forum, this authentic taking-over of existence is made possible by the distinction of nullity (life is empty and meaningless), and of oneself as the null basis of that nullity (it's empty and meaningless *that* it's empty and meaningless).

In his later rubrics, *releasement* and *appropriation*, Heidegger moved toward the more receptive side of the Being–being balance, bringing *letting* and *allowing* forward as moments in the attainment of authenticity. But the clearing opened through all of these articulations is the Same, emerging in the unspoken reverberations as the distinction is teased out. "Hints," said Heidegger, "need the widest sphere in which to swing" ("DL" in *OWL* 27). ■

ERHARD
I got over being upset. It not only doesn't mean anything...

(*pausing*)
Listen. Life is not only empty and meaningless, but it is empty and meaningless that it is empty and meaningless. See, some asshole in here is going to say, "Well, if it's empty and meaningless then I'm going home."

(*loudly*)
No! *You made it mean something!* You didn't get it. It's empty and meaningless and it's empty and meaningless that it's empty and meaningless. Life's not going anywhere. It's like this. You don't like this? Too bad. This is the way it is. Just like this, and that, and that. Tomorrow will be like it is tomorrow, and the day after will be like it is the day after tomorrow. And a year from now will be like it is a year from now: like it is today. A lot of you are hearing me insulting your practice. You know, insulting your practice, let's call it, your relationship with God, your meditation, whatever it is. I'm not insulting your practice. I'm insulting practicing *in-order-to*. You practice when you practice. Shut up. Just practice. It's not going to get you anywhere. If you're practicing in order to get somewhere, stop it because you're wasting your time. You're not going to get anywhere. You're always going to be right where you are. If you practice long enough, you'll find that out. Talk to Kipp some more, you're doing a good job.

KIPP
Now what?

ANGEL
That's a very good question.

ERHARD
Very good...

ANGEL
I like the fact that...

ERHARD
Remember when I said that you thought your fire would go out if you didn't have this drama?

ANGEL
Right.

ERHARD
Yes.

ANGEL
But I got fire from the possibility of having an empty canvas.

ERHARD

I know. You turned that into another fire: drama, meaning, significance. You take everything and turn it into shit. We create something called possibility and you turn it into some kind of fucking golden calf. Like "oh! That's going to save me. Man, am I glad I got here! I didn't know that was the answer." The answer is that there isn't any answer. That's the answer. No kidding. Like really. You can go anywhere in the universe you want to go to get the answer. And that's the answer. Whatever it is you're doing to make it, you're never going to do that enough to make it. It isn't going to turn out because it already turned out. And this is the way it turned out. Just like this. Tomorrow will be just like it is tomorrow. And when you die, they'll put you into a box and throw dirt on your face. And that's how it'll all turn out. It doesn't mean anything.

ANGEL

So now that I know that, why not throw dirt in my face right now?

ERHARD

That's making it mean something. And it's high drama meaning. You could have said, "I'll go watch television." You could have said that but it's not dramatic enough. There are people in here that are not high dramatists like you are. Some people say "I'll go home and watch the game." Yours is "I'll kill myself." It's just a matter of style. You watch. The world's going to change here. It's going to stop being the way it is.

KIPP

What now? Can you see how attached you are to having it mean something?

ANGEL

Yes. Yesterday I was attached to caring which meant it means something.

KIPP

Yeah, and so what you're attached to is being attached.

ERHARD

That's a little advanced for most of you.

ANGEL

So, if I'm not attached to it anymore, it doesn't mean it's not still there. It just means I'm not attached to it anymore.

ERHARD

No. That's some kind of Zen horseshit. You are not attached to it. You're not attached to it, and that's the end of that story.

ANGEL

If I'm not resisting it, then I'm not attached to it anymore.

Speaking out

Another aspect of this perspective: in speaking *out,* we are "outing" something that has already existed, in the background, as a possibility. Indeed: "If we conceive of this state of affairs in an elementary and originary way, we see that what is spoken out is already necessarily within *physis,* otherwise it could not be spoken from out of it" (*FCM* 26). Heidegger presses the point: everything that exists has been spoken out, and everything that has been spoken out was already there. So:

> **The question for us is: What does this *legein,* this speaking out accomplish? What occurs in the *logos*? Is it only a matter of the fact that what beings as a whole are is brought to a word, formulated, come to word? To come to word—what does that mean? (*FCM* 26–27)**

To understand the meaning of a term or concept, says Heidegger, it may be useful to consider its opposite. He finds in a fragment of Heraclitus the suggestion that the opposite of legein—that is, "not letting come to word"—was for the Greeks precisely understood as *concealment*:

> **From this it necessarily follows that the funda-mental function of *legein* is to take whatever prevails from concealment. . . . Revealing, 'tak-ing from concealment,' is that happening which occurs in the *logos.* In the *logos,* the prevailing of beings becomes revealed, becomes mani-fest. (*FCM* 27)**

This, then, is what is happening in our speaking out: we speak out from concealment; we unconceal a world of beings. How fortunate we are that we have the ability to create meanings, and can thereby live in a world of culture and technology, and reap their benefits.

But there is of course a qualifier to the promise in this situation, which Heidegger finds elsewhere in Heraclitus' writing:

> **[I]f prevailing is torn from concealment in the *logos*, then it must, as it were, try to conceal itself. The very same Heraclitus tells us in addition . . . why *physis* came to be revealed and torn from concealment explicitly in *legein*. In the collection of fragments one sentence stands alone which to this day has never been understood or comprehended in its profundity: "*The prevailing of things has in itself a striving to conceal itself.*" (*FCM* 27, emphasis added)**

Being loves to hide. *Why* this is so is a question for which Heidegger does not specify an answer, since the question must be left open. In the swinging of that open question, thinking may distinguish new paths into Being. For example, if The Forum is a conversation for the emergence of Being, and if Being strives to conceal itself, then interesting implications emerge about the nature of The Forum experience, which we continue to explore and unfold in these sidebars and intervals. ■

ERHARD
Zen bullshit.

ANGEL
I'm from California.

ERHARD
That's right. What was the last thing you said Kipp?

KIPP
You're attached to being attached.

ERHARD (*indicating Angel*)
It was you. An emerging bit of light here. Attached to meaning. That's what it was. He said you were attached to meaning, and you said yesterday I was attached to caring and that made it mean something. And today I've gotten down an even more fundamental level, "I'm attached to meaning."

ANGEL
Yeah.

ERHARD
Yeah. You are attached to meaning. That's what there is to get. You are stuck with meaning. You have no freedom. Everything's got to be made to mean something. Everything's got to be made significant. That's the drama queen.

ANGEL
I don't see what's left.

ERHARD
So I'm gonna tell you. You want to know what's left? Nothing. What's left is nothing. I told you we were going to work our way back to zero. This is zero.

ANGEL
I can't be with zero.

ERHARD
I know. I told you it made me real sad. It's not going to be all right. It's going to be the way it is. What there is to be with is that life is empty and meaningless. That's what there is to be with. It is not going to turn out. It is not going to be all right. It's going to be whatever fucking way it is. However it is.

ANGEL
No matter what I do?

ERHARD

Yeah, but see, there's something a little off in that, because you're only going to do what you're going to do. People don't do what they want to do; they do what they do. You always do what you do. And you don't always do what you want to do, do you? The only time you do what you wanted to do is when it's coincidentally what you did. You aren't doing what you wanted to do; you're doing what you do. And you got this God damned story about wants. People don't do what they want to do; they do what they do, always and only. "Want to" is a story. Like explaining illness with evil spirits. Voodoo. The stars will not move for what you want. You do what you do, and you don't do what you don't do. And all the rest of it is some cockeyed story that destroys the simplicity, the power, the sweetness of the way it is. Look, did you ever notice you are never ever fucking satisfied? *Ever!* It doesn't make any difference how good it is. It never makes a difference what you achieve. Ever. *Ever!* You just can't get that this is it. Kipp, tell them about the practice life. Do your thing about the playing cards.

KIPP

The playing cards of life...

Kipp held up a pad of paper—as if they were cards—up to his chest.

KIPP

What it is to be a human being is to hold on to your aces. Because you know, that one time in life when you gave away everything...

ERHARD

When you were a kid one time, you gave away your aces and you got smashed... Every one of you. And from then on, you became "I don't play my aces." It wasn't a decision merely or a thought merely, from then on you became "I don't play my aces."

KIPP

You became what is known as a smart person. What a smart person looks like is a person who walks around holding their aces. Then along came Einstein, and Einstein said the problems that we got are not going to be solved with the way that we think we got into those problems...

ERHARD (*interrupting Kipp*)

Hold on, don't fuck that quote up.

KIPP

You fuck it up.

(*laughter*)

ERHARD

The problems we have are not going to be solved at the level in which we created them. What does that mean? It's real simple. You got someplace in life. People have gotten someplace in

> ❝ People don't do what they want to do; they do what they do. You always do what you do. And you don't always do what you want to do, do you? The only time you do what you wanted to do is when it's coincidentally what you did.

> **If you use what you got to get where you are, it produces success and a certain set of problems. You cannot solve those problems with that with which you succeeded, because those problems are a product of that which you used to succeed.**

life. What got you there gives you the problems you got. It's not that you fucked something up on the way. It's that you succeeded. If you use what you got to get where you are, it produces success and a certain set of problems. You cannot solve those problems with that with which you succeeded, because those problems are a *product of that which you used to succeed*. Did you get that? Those problems are a product of getting here, and you can't solve those problems with what got you here. Because what got you here, got you here and gave you those problems. You can't solve the problems you have at the level at which you generated the problems.

KIPP
So what's required is a new level of thinking. Here's what that looks like: You want all my aces? Here!

Kipp threw forward the pieces of paper representing his aces.

KIPP
But you can't do that because if you did, you'd get used by life.

ERHARD
He's a little too funny. And you don't get it. You fucking assholes! You held on to your aces so you wouldn't get used. You're going to go to your grave holding your aces.

Kipp continued the bit, very flamboyantly demonstrating not giving aces away to this wife, this job, etc.

KIPP
See, I wasn't going to give my aces to my wife Christine, because she wasn't the one. You know what the one looks like. Tall, blonde, always rides the horse and never wears clothes. So anytime I would be at a party with Christine, I wouldn't stand too close to her in case the one came riding in on the horse, I could just jump on and ride off into the distance. How about that job? You're not going to give your aces to that job, that's just the practice job. What about your body? The question is: What is going to be written on your gravestone?

ERHARD
You get the point. This is not your real life. You're living your practice life. Nobody would be stupid enough to take their real life and do what you've done with it. Suppose you were married to your real wife–I mean like the *real* one. Man, you would give everything to her. Everything you've got. But the one you're married to now is your "practice wife." Here's how you can tell. If she were the one, the woman of your dreams, you wouldn't be like you are with her, and you know it. The same with your job. You don't give everything you've got to this job. This is just a practice job. You keep your aces for when the real one comes along. That's when you'll spend your life on your life, when the real one comes along, but not on this life.

ERHARD (*walking across the room, speaking softly*)

There's no real one. This is it. It's not going to get any better. It's not going to work out. The right one is not going to come along. The right job isn't going to come along. This is the only job there is, this is the only wife there is, this is the only life there is. This is not practice. You're bullshitting yourself. This is the game, and you're playing like you're in practice. You want to get that this is the game. The right circumstances in which to be happy are not going to come along. They're not. You're waiting for it to turn out. Life is not going to work out. And someday it's not going to be all better. Today is the way it is today and someday is the way someday is going to be. And in between it's going to be the way it is in between. And the ultimate beyond that will be the way it is there.

(*speaking forcefully, while walking among the group*)

This is not a practice life. Whatever you've got when you die, you're going to die with it. And you are going to die with your aces. You thought "asshole" was insulting. It's starting to make sense, isn't it? It was a bit of a compliment, wasn't it?

(*laughter*)

A participant named Jacob stood and took a microphone.

JACOB

Angel seems to be very concerned about the notion that nothing means anything.

ERHARD

No no. Nobody said "nothing means anything."

JACOB

Well, at any rate...

ERHARD

It means what it means.

JACOB

Well, at any rate...

ERHARD

A bowl is a bowl.

JACOB

Yeah.

ERHARD

It's not nothing. It's a bowl.

> " The right circumstances in which to be happy are not going to come along. They're not. You're waiting for it to turn out. Life is not going to work out. And someday it's not going to be all better. Today is the way it is today and someday is the way someday is going to be. And in between it's going to be the way it is in between. And the ultimate beyond that will be the way it is there.

JACOB

I was just thinking if you take the phrase "nothing means anything" in a positive way. The words are interchangeable. The word nothing means anything; anything is nothing. That might be the kind of hippy definition you don't like.

ERHARD

True.

JACOB

I know, I know. I don't like it either, but...

ERHARD

I'll tell you what I do like, though, is I like that you're engaged in the conversation. What I don't like is being facile about it. Do you know what I mean by the word facile? Live easy with it.

JACOB

Yeah.

ERHARD

You've got to be ballsy with it. You've got to get down with this. This is not some airy fairy crap. I didn't say you've got to talk bad like I do. You've got to get down in your own way, but you've got to get down. You've got to get out of that "whoooo" shit.

KIPP

And you've made it into that. Do you know that?

JACOB

Yeah. What I wanted to say a couple of days ago about doing what you can or can't do, I think it was Benjamin Franklin who said...

(*forgetting*)

ERHARD

I know what they said too, but I can never seem to remember it. We'll read you that Einstein quote we butchered later.

(*laughter*)

JACOB

I remember now. He had a good definition of the word character. To have character is to follow through with the decision after the emotion of making that decision has passed. I thought that's what Werner was saying about being facile.

KIPP

What he's saying is that the way you're listening to what's happening in the room is like a concept. You're doing the same thing Angel's doing, just a different meaning. Hers is "As the Turd Whirls," and yours is "Fireside Chat with" whatever your name is.

JACOB

Yeah, but the point is, if you don't change, then it's not...

KIPP

And this is more of it. This is more Angel coming out of you. Same thing!

JACOB

Yeah.

KIPP

Same thing. Different meaning, that's all. And you're attached to those quotes like she's attached to the soap opera.

JACOB

Okay, okay, okay.

KIPP

That's "shut up, shut up, shut up."

JACOB

I didn't mean that.

KIPP

Yes you did.

JACOB

I didn't mean for it.

KIPP

Yeah, that's the problem. That's what you're saying. You see, you don't want to be with that it's empty and meaningless. You've got a nice neat package, just like Angel's got a dramatic package.

JACOB

And the problem with that is that I'm attracted to that meaning.

KIPP

Attracted to it? You're addicted to it! That's all you got.

JACOB

No, no, no, I'm attracted to... I like the idea...

KIPP

So what if you like the idea? Why do you like it?

JACOB

Because it's light-hearted. Taking the drama out of it...

KIPP

It's like morning TV instead of afternoon TV. Doesn't matter.

JACOB

Yeah, I know, what I'm saying is because I like your philosophy, I'm going to have to try to make it meaningful...

KIPP

I don't have a philosophy.

JACOB

Then what were you talking about?

KIPP

What I was saying. You think this is a philosophy. No philosophy here. Or if it is, it's not The Forum. See, this is fireside chats with Jacob. This is your little place where you hang out. This is your meaning you're holding onto with your fingernails and your toes and everything else. It's all in a nice neat box, the same as Angel. And for everyone else here in the room, what you should get is that this is what yours sounds like too, just your version of it.

ERHARD

This is not a philosophy. This is not a view of life. This is not one of the many views. This is not another religion. That's not what this is. It doesn't replace or negate anything. It's more like dog shit than it is like philosophy—something to step in. If you treat it like philosophy, you'll fuck it up. If you're going to treat it like something, treat it like dog shit. Step in it.

KIPP

As you were saying, Jacob...

JACOB

I was just thinking that I should sit down because as long as I'm standing I'm going to want an answer to all this.

The Same

In suggesting that the experiences evoked in The Forum and in the *est* Training are at some level the same, we are venturing into important and precarious Heideggerian territory. Werner Erhard suggested the nature of this territory in a 1983 interview, when challenged to compare the *est* Training with other enlightenment systems, such as Zen:

 I think that discussions about enlightenment are useless, and I think making enlightenment sacred is even more futile. My question is, what's this conversation all about? . . . *We're not really talking about anything.* I don't know how else to respond to you. You can't ask, "Is *this* enlightenment like *that* enlightenment?" That's counting enlightenments. That's nuts! (*Network Review*, 1:4, September 1983, emphasis added)

KIPP
Then when you sit down you'll do whatever you do when you sit down. And that's all there is.

JACOB
What's the motivation then?

KIPP
Whatever it is. You are the kind of being that thinks there has to be a motivation. There is no motivation, because there's no place to get to. People who are addicted to motivation are addicted to trying to get somewhere. Can you see that that's the source of motivation? But there is no place to get to. You know why?

JACOB
Why?

KIPP
There's no place to get to because it's already turned out. This is the way it turned out. How do you like it?

JACOB
No.

KIPP
It doesn't matter. You turned out this way, right?

JACOB
Yeah, but, it's imperfect. I can live with it, but...

KIPP
What's imperfect?

JACOB
The world's imperfect.

KIPP
Where?

JACOB
Ethiopia.

KIPP
Ethiopia is Ethiopia.

One cannot compare enlightenment experiences, because one cannot compare nothing with nothing, since there is only one nothing. Or, as an alternative interpretation, there is no nothing; nothing is a nullity, its existence is self-nullified. There is nothing to be compared. And yet, I can say these sentences, so nothing *can* be talked about.

In Heidegger's words, "'there is given' [*es gibt*] the Nothing." He adds: "but we cannot, at present, determine more closely who or what gives the Nothing" (*BC* 45). That question must remain open to call forth thinking. So Heidegger moves on to another possible interpretation of the situation: "We can also say that the Nothing *presences [west],* in order to indicate that the Nothing is not merely the absence and lack of beings" (*BC* 45).

 The Nothing does not first need beings and a being in order to presence, as if it would presence only if beings were eliminated in advance. The Nothing is not the result of such an elimination. There is given the Nothing in spite of the fact that beings are. (*BC*** 45)**

We referred to this territory as precarious, not because the topic is subversive, but because the conversation can easily begin to sound silly. Sophomoric. Heidegger is not surprised that we may be thinking this:

Here we easily fall into the danger of playing with words. People make use of the justifiable indication of this danger in order to banish all thought "about" the Nothing as fatal. But the danger is no less that, because we seem to be merely playing around with words, we take the Nothing too lightly and fail to recognize that there is given the Nothing. (*BC*** 45–46)**

Our experience with the work of Werner Erhard has led us to the recognition that a transformational leap must pass through the domain of meaninglessness, and that an experience of Being requires a confrontation with non-Being. We will therefore endure (or enjoy) any silliness we encounter, and recognize that we are mining one of the richest veins of Heidegger's thought—perhaps his most essentially reflexive distinction, sometimes his most perplexing, but inevitably a ride we want to be along for.

A core rubric for this distinction is *the Same*; and since a distinction can only be hinted at, Heidegger approaches this one throughout his writing from various directions. In the 1941 lecture series published as *Basic Concepts,* it emerges in a section concerning Being's *uniqueness,* and its difference in that respect from beings:

> **Beings can always be compared with beings and placed into equivalence with one another. However, [B]eing is never merely what is equivalent in the manifold beings stone, plant, animal, man, God. For to be what is equivalent it would have to be multiple. Being, by contrast is everywhere *the same,* namely, itself. In order to be equivalent, something other and additional is required. To be the same, *only* uniqueness is needed. (*BC* 44)**

Heidegger's languaging in such writing trips up our thinking. It forces us to stop and double back, to be certain that what we understood was what was said. It pulls the rug from under us. Heidegger's next sentence gives a final yank to a rug already well-pulled:

> **As the same and unique, [B]eing is, of course, forever different in and from itself. (*BC* 44)**

Thinking and Being

In the 1954 collection of essays entitled *Early Greek Thinking,* Heidegger develops the distinction "the Same" in his exploration of two fragments by Parmenides. A central question for

JACOB
I want to change it. I know this sounds sappy...

KIPP
Not sappy. Just disempowering. You're the kind of guy that's going to make no difference because you're going to try to change Ethiopia. Where is the world imperfect?

JACOB
There's two kinds of perfect. There's what you strive for, which we are neglecting here, and then there is what already is.

WES (*standing on the platform*)
Let's deal with your life first. You haven't seen what you look like.

JACOB
Yeah.

WES
You're talking to Kipp like someone who hasn't seen what a human being looks like who follows what you're talking about. You're proposing a way of being and you haven't seen how absurd it is. When you see how absurd it is you'll give it up in a minute: The absurdity of the story that uses people's lives.

JACOB
Yeah, I was going to say that there's what happened, and then there's the story. It makes life interesting.

WES
What makes life interesting? Certainly not your story. You know what you're story looks like?

JACOB
Yeah, violins playing in the background.

WES
Yeah, good.

JACOB
But it's still interesting to me.

WES
No it isn't. It stinks. There's no possibility. This is what you look like. I'm going to demonstrate you.

Wes held a pen about a foot in front of his mouth, trying to bite it while continuing to hold it out of reach, and chasing it around the stage while complaining about his failure to reach it.

JACOB
Yeah, I could have told you that, though…

WES (*continuing to try to bite the carrot*)
I'll get there. Shit. I'll get a Ph.D. Shit. I'll get married. Shit…

At this moment a participant seated in the "no-video" section of the room called out angrily that the cameraman focused on Jacob was also including those seated in the "no-video" section. Kipp promised that it would be handled and it was.

JACOB (*returning to the conversation*)
I get that. I'm like a stupid donkey tied to a cart chasing a carrot, trying to get it. But I see that I'm just a little bit hungry and that's leading me toward perfection.

WES
No, that's bullshit.

JACOB
Okay, why?

WES
Because it is.

JACOB
Okay, can I do a demonstration of you?

WES
No.

JACOB
Why not?

WES
Because I said so.

JACOB
Dick.

Heidegger—an important subordinate question to his overarching question of Being—concerns the relation between Being and thinking. What is the nature of that relation? How intimately do the two phenomena belong together?

One of these Parmenidean fragments has traditionally been translated, "For thinking and Being are the Same." Here Heidegger interrogates that translation:

 Does this word give us an answer to the question of how thinking belongs to Being, in that it says both are "the Same"? The word gives no answer. In the first place, because the determination "the Same" precludes any question about "belonging together," which can only exist between things that are different. In the second place, because the word "the Same" says nothing at all about the point of view from which, and for what reason, difference passes over into sameness. Thus *to auto*, the Same, remains the enigmatic key word for both fragments—if not for the whole of Parmenides' thought. (*EGT* 88)

Heidegger leaves us in the dark here, because he wants us to place that enigmatic term in question. He wants us to recognize our tendency to gloss challenging ideas with easy and familiar interpretations:

 Of course if we are of the opinion that the word *to auto*, the Same, means "identical," and if we accept "identity" completely as the most transparent presupposition for the thinkability of whatever is thinkable, then by this opinion we become progressively more deaf to the key word, assuming that we have ever heard its call. It is sufficient, however, to keep the word in our hearing in its thought-provoking character. In doing so we remain listeners. . . . (*EGT* 88)

We have suggested that an essential relationship exists between the experience evoked in the *est* Training and that made available in The Forum; and we have said that neither experience is captured in the spoken words of the conversations, but that both are communicated in the *unspoken context* of those words. Heidegger likewise directs us to consider the character of the context. If modern human beings are to engage in a thoughtful dialogue with the writing of the pre-Socratics—and Heidegger sees such a dialogue as critical for this moment in history—then we must begin to apprehend in our thinking "the unified totality of the manifold" (EGT 22).

 Dialogue with early Greek thinking will be fruitful only when such listening occurs. It is proper to dialogue that its conversation speak of the same thing; indeed that it speak out of participation in the Same. (*EGT* 22)

Over the vast chasm of time and language, can what we hear be the same as what the Greek thinkers are saying? To develop this question, Heidegger places a passage from the pre-Socratic thinker Parmenides alongside one from the thinking of a modern philosopher, Nietzsche, and makes this observation regarding the juxtaposition:

 The ancient fragment of early Western thinking and the late fragment of recent Western thinking bring the Same to language, but what they say is not identical. However, where we can speak of the Same in terms of things which are not identical, the fundamental condition of a thoughtful dialogue between recent and early times is automatically fulfilled. . . . [G]ranting the differences between these epochs, we are together with the early thinkers in the realm of the Same. (*EGT* 23)

WES

You're doing whatever you're doing, and you're adding this story that it's leading me toward perfection. But it's leading you toward a hole in the ground, and they're going to throw you in it, and they're going to throw dirt in your face. Think about that.

JACOB

Yeah, yeah. That's what happened.

WES

No, that's what will happen.

JACOB

Yeah, when I get there that will be what happened. I don't mind adding a story to my life, just to make it interesting, or entertaining. I don't mind tinting my life with fiction. Just to make it interesting.

ERHARD

You were doing fine until you added the "just to make it interesting."

JACOB

Or entertaining.

ERHARD

Or "just to make it entertaining." The story "in order to be entertained." That's terrible.

JACOB

Yeah, yeah.

ERHARD

The purpose to the story is the story.

JACOB

Yeah, yeah.

ERHARD

What's more entertaining than a tree? Nothing. Standing in front of a tree: nothing can be more entertaining than standing in front of a tree.

JACOB

So when you take what happened then there should be automatic meaning added to it without having to play violins...

ERHARD

There's no meaning to it. The tree doesn't mean anything. It's just a tree.

JACOB
Rather than meaning, there's a plot to it.

ERHARD
There's no plot to it. You add the plot. And you're not doing it to entertain yourself. You're doing it because you're doing it. You justify doing it in here when we get you to see that you're doing it by saying I'm doing it in order to entertain myself. But you're not doing it. And you're not doing it to entertain yourself.

JACOB
But what if it does entertain me?

ERHAD
Then it does. But you don't do it in order to entertain yourself.

JACOB
Yeah. You don't do anything in order to anything.

ERHARD
Exactly. You do what you do and you don't do what you don't do. And you got all the justification that you add to that.

JACOB
I do what I like.

ERHARD
You don't do what you like.

JACOB
That would be an in-order-to.

ERHARD
Right. Nobody ever does what they like. They do what they do. Have you ever done anything you didn't do?

JACOB
No.

ERHARD
Have you ever done anything you didn't like to do?

JACOB
Yeah.

Thus we can say, in the sense that Heidegger is distinguishing here, that the *est* Training and The Forum are the Same but not identical. Further, we can likewise say that the Same relationship exists between the "single thought" of Heidegger's thinking and the transformational experience evoked in The Forum.

The logos

Heidegger further teases out the distinction "the Same" in a discussion of *the Logos*, the site where beings, emerging into the world of meaning, are gathered and sheltered. Although in the West *logos* is traditionally translated as *discourse* or spoken language—and for Heidegger, of course, language is the realm of Being—the root term, *legein,* does not primarily indicate speaking, but means *to lay down, to lay before.*

 To say is *legein.* This sentence, if well thought, now sloughs off everything facile, trite, and vacuous. It names the inexhaustible mystery that the speaking of language comes to pass from the unconcealment of what is present. (*EGT* 64)

Saying and talking occur essentially as the letting-lie-together-before of everything which, laid in unconcealment, comes to presence. (*EGT* 63)

A central question for Heidegger concerns the truth of a being—the Being of the being—at the point of its emergence into the world. How can we perceive the thing itself, *physis* in the moment of its first flowering into meaning, but before its deflowering by the distortions of opinion and perspective? At the heart of the matter, says Heidegger in this intensely reflexive passage, is the possibility of openness to *letting*, and to the Same:

 Such a letting-lie establishes whatever lies before us as lying-before. It establishes this as itself. It lays one and the Same in one. It lays one as the Same. Such *legein* lays one and the same, the *omon.* Such *legein* is *omologein*: One as the Same, i.e., a letting-lie-before of what does lie before us, gathered in the self-sameness of its lying-before. (*EGT* 66)

Heidegger's languaging here may occur as tortured or as poppycock, unless we keep in mind the enigmatic nature of hints, which always beckon us *away* from that toward which they simultaneously point us; and of reflexive languaging, which creates perplexities to liberate our thinking. Under the rubric of the Same, Heidegger is distinguishing a way of listening for the world, and he invites us to follow:

 To think is surely a peculiar affair. The word of thinkers has no authority. The word of thinkers knows no authors, in the sense of writers. The word of thinking is not picturesque; it is without charm. The word of thinking rests in the sobering quality of what it says. Just the same, thinking changes the world. It changes it in the ever darker depths of a riddle, depths which as they grow darker offer promise of a greater brightness. (*EGT* 78)

We read in this passage an iteration of The Forum's rhetorical process, which takes participants down one level at a time to confront the empty depths of the Nothing, before lighting the opening that has thereby been unconcealed.

ERHARD

You do what you do, and coincidentally it sometimes matches the story you've got about what you like to do. And what makes you stupid is to say, "When I'm good I do what I like to do and when I'm bad I do what I don't like to do." No. When you're bad you're bad and when you're good you're good. And don't fuck it up with all that philosophical horseshit. That's what he means by fireside chat. That's your racket Jacob. I know you think that's the way to be. I know you think that's the right way to be.

JACOB

No, it's a way to be.

ERHARD

No, it's not even a way to be. That's just the way you are.

JACOB

And if I do it another way, it'll be another way.

ERHARD

But you won't do it another way. You'll do it the way you do it. That conversation is nonsensical. It gets you into trouble. Things are the way they are, and they are always not the way they're not. And what you do is say that you do it to make life interesting; and not because that's the right thing to say, but because that's what you do.

JACOB

But the one thing that I can control is...

ERHARD

But here's the thing. You're not getting the point, Jacob. You're too engaged in the conversation. Listen to what's not being said. There's something to get out of the conversation and I'm not going to say it and you're not going to say it. It's going to be unsaid. And that's what there is to get here. Otherwise you're paying 625 dollars to pass on your philosophy to a guy who couldn't care less. You paid him to pass on your philosophy.

JACOB

I paid 625 dollars to hear your philosophy.

ERHARD

No, I don't have any philosophy. All I have is dog shit.

JACOB

How about my philosophy through you?

ERHARD

That's horseshit. I don't like philosophies. That's more nah nah nah nah nah. Philosophies.

JACOB
Okay.

ERHARD
You're up there and this is The Forum. It's not like I picked you out. Why am I staying in this conversation with you? The Forum is for you and I to engage in this until what you're not saying and what I'm not saying is there for you to hear. There's something to hear that neither of us is going to say. That's the name of this game. It's underneath all that wisdom you got. I'm not denigrating your wisdom. Your wisdom's pretty good. I like it. And if we were out having a drink I would listen to it and discuss it. I would. I like that stuff too. But that's not The Forum. The Forum is to get what's underneath that. And what there is to get here is that it's empty and meaningless. Now you're a pretty sharp guy and you got some of that. But now you're going to turn that into a philosophy. Don't do that. Just get it. It's empty and meaningless, and it's empty and meaningless that it's empty and meaningless. And life is not going to turn out.

JACOB
It's the part that it is empty and meaningless that gets me, because that has a little bit of meaning to it.

ERHARD
No. It has no meaning to it. That's why I said it is empty and meaningless that it is empty and...

JACOB
I guess it was because I was thinking "because."

ERHARD
Beautiful. Exactly. You got it. You can't get "because" in there at all. Zero. If you add "because," you're above zero. At zero it's just empty and meaningless and it's empty and meaningless that it's empty and meaningless. It's not your life that's empty and meaningless. It's a rainstorm. Life is empty and meaningless and you showed up in that, and got wet in it. It's not your particular little crappy life that's empty and meaningless. It's that *life* is empty and meaningless. That's what we showed up in.

Erhard stood close to Jacob and spoke intimately.

ERHARD
Jacob, you want to listen up here. Some people I don't identify with. I can get them because I'm trained to get them. I can identify with you. And you're sharp enough to fuck yourself. I know you can do it because I did it. I got the answers very early, and I developed them really well, but I got them as answers.

JACOB
Yes, I've got this bucket of answers I carry around with me.

> " **The Forum is for you and I to engage in this until what you're not saying and what I'm not saying is there for you to hear. There's something to hear that neither of us is going to say. That's the name of this game.**

Heidegger on Thinking the Same

> **Every thinker thinks one only thought. Here, too, thinking differs essentially from science. The researcher needs constantly new discoveries and inspirations, else science will bog down and fall into error. The thinker needs one thought only. And for the thinker the difficulty is to hold fast to this one only thought as the one and only thing that he must think; to think this One as the Same; and to tell of this Same in a fitting manner. But we speak of the Same in the manner that befits it only if we always say the same about it, in such a way that we ourselves are claimed by the Self-same. *The limitlessness of the Same is the sharpest limit set to thinking.* (WCT 50, emphasis added)**

It is a job of The Forum leader to see that the conversation of The Forum always speaks the Same. ∎

ERHARD
You play the game right you'll end up with a mountain of answers. Yes. I had a mountain of answers. I had a trailer behind the car. I had answers from the best places.

JACOB
Yeah, but they weren't *the* answers. It seems like there should only be one.

ERHARD
Yeah there is one. I already gave it to you. There is no answer. See, you want to build a pile of answers and find out one day that it's a pile of shit and not a pile of answers?

JACOB
It sounds like you have all these answers that you've rendered meaningless.

ERHARD
They were *the* answers. I stood on top of that pile of answers, finely honed, hard earned, and recognized that the answer was: there is no answer.

JACOB
It sounds like what you're saying is that you read a book one day, maybe Freud, and that's what happened, but you kept it and made it mean something out of it.

ERHARD
Not something out of it, I made the answer out of it, and I had a mountain of answers. And look, I could do you real easy. "I could look at it this way and that way, and there's no one real way to look at it—the way to look at it—there are many ways to look at it." This week, this year, this era of your life: *the* answer. Not "the answer is that there isn't any answer, there are many answers." That's an answer. You get that that's an answer?

JACOB
Yeah.

ERHARD
Yeah, but if you've got an answer, then that isn't the answer: The answer is there isn't any answer. And if you turn that into an answer, that isn't it either.

JACOB
That's a vicious circle.

ERHARD
That's right. This whole thing is a vicious circle. And the only way to get to break the vicious circle is that there isn't any answer, and that life isn't going to turn out, it isn't going to work out, and someday isn't going to turn out so that you can play your aces.

JACOB
When you say "it," I get that you mean life, but something is going to work out.

ERHARD
Really?

JACOB
Yeah.

ERHARD
Are you the Pope?

JACOB
I anticipate that something's going to happen.

ERHARD
Yeah and evil spirits are going to come down and invade people's bodies and make them sick.

JACOB
And I'll go home and not get enough sleep to come back here tomorrow.

ERHARD
And you know what? You will if you do and you won't if you don't. And your anticipation is meaningless because it's going to be just the way it is.

JACOB
Yeah, anticipation means that there's going to be a stupid story attached to what happened.

ERHARD
Sure. And you're going to anticipate anyhow. See, it's a perfect trap, Jacob. That's the thing Californians don't understand. The attempt to get out of the trap constricts the bars of the prison. The attempt to get beyond the "this-is-all-there-is" keeps you in the trap. Trying to get out of the prison keeps you in the prison. And *not* trying to get out of the prison keeps you in the prison. Everybody's got a form of making it. Even not making it for some people is a form of making it. Either way is an attempt to get out of the trap and that keeps you in the trap. There is no outside the prison. Outside the prison is inside the prison.

JACOB
It's the spot you are in.

ERHARD
Yes. You're only going to be in the spot you're in.

> **The attempt to get beyond the "this-is-all-there-is" keeps you in the trap. Trying to get out of the prison keeps you in the prison. And not trying to get out of the prison keeps you in the prison.**

JACOB
So is that the perfect spot?

ERHARD
No. That's adding meaning to it. That's a Jacobism, that last one. That's the best one you did because you can see it in that one. See, you're trying to make it all right! That's what it means to turn it into a philosophy. You're doing a "fireside talk." It's a trap. But it's all right that it's a trap.

JACOB
That's what I'm saying.

ERHARD
But that's what ruins it. It's not all right. It's not not all right either. It's just like this.

JACOB
Okay.

ERHARD
You got it. Well done, thank you.

(*applause*)

KIPP
Patsy, you win the prize, and a large bicep. Holding your hand up for forty minutes straight.

PATSY
Aerobics!

KIPP
Exactly.

PATSY
It's taken me three days to get up and talk, and I love to talk...

KIPP
When should you have gotten up to talk?

PATSY
I said something the first day...

KIPP
You said it took you three days to get up.

PATSY
Now it's perfect that I'm up talking.

ERHARD
Certainly, if you'd gotten up earlier it would have been bad, right?

PATSY
No it would have been perfect at the time.

ERHARD
Because whatever happens is perfect, right?

PATSY
Absolutely.

ERHARD (*speaking with dramatic forcefulness*)
Wrong! Whatever happens is not perfect! That's fucking California crap! Whatever happens is whatever happens! You fucking Californians: you're disgusting! Goddamned platitudes.

(*calmly*)
At any rate: you're up.

PATSY
I really got what you said about the aces, I really got it, and as I listened to it and watched the demonstration, all of a sudden a conflict appeared. And that is: how many times do you throw your aces out and you get stepped on, kicked, shit on, and you say okay, and then do it again, and again, and the result that you wanted doesn't happen.

KIPP
What knocked you over is the last thing you said. "The result that you wanted doesn't happen." Because what always happens?

PATSY
What happens.

KIPP
So when you throw your aces out, you throw your aces out. And you don't when you don't.

PATSY
Right, but given that you are human...

KIPP
If you are...

PATSY

Sometimes, but when you keep throwing those aces out to the same person for fifteen years, for instance...

KIPP

Okay, roll 'em. Bring out the props. Okay...

PATSY

Angel's my roommate!

The room broke out into prolonged laughter as Kipp made a sweeping motion as if operating a giant projector.

KIPP

Okay! Roll 'em and weep!

PATSY

I keep doing it and there comes a point where I want to make a choice that I don't want that anymore.

WES

It's not a choice, by the way. If we ever get this across—which is not looking good at this point—we'll get to choice.

Wes imitated various possible internal dialogues participants might be having at this point in the proceedings, including, "Well, what about that multiple orgasm I had that time? Was that empty and meaningless?"

WES

That's what you sound like... an internal dialogue machine. The way to blow the circuits on that is actually getting for yourself that this is empty and meaningless, and this is it.

PATSY

It sounds real simple.

WES

Too simple for complicated minds. You want to see what the complication of your life is, and the story, and the drama. And this concern you have for giving away your crummy aces. Like you don't get it. It's the giving of yourself away in which life occurs. All the rest is a drama. It's all made up. It's absurd. You're absurd. But that's okay, because they're still going to throw dirt in your face whether you're absurd or not. Do you think in a hundred years people will be discussing your relationships?

PATSY

No.

Erhard left the room at this point. Wes was on the platform, Kipp down among the group.

WES
You sure about that? Because you and your roommate discuss it a lot, right?

PATSY
Only at work.

(*laughter*)

WES
I see, so it keeps you from working. I can understand it.

PATSY
While I'm here being human, I want it to be good for me. I want to like what I'm doing.

Wes produced a clipping from a South Korean newspaper.

WES (*referring to the newspaper clipping*)
This is your life. This is how your life could be with a little more significance. Here's the title: "Wife is late with the lunch, kills herself."

He read aloud the account, which concerned a woman who had forgotten that daylight savings time was being instituted for the first time. As a result, she had prepared her husband's lunch late. She then killed herself.

WES
You think she was dealing with some kind of meaning there?

PATSY
No, not a meaning that I know or recognize, or acknowledge.

(*laughter*)

WES
That's meaning. A person kills herself because she served lunch an hour late. That's the possibility of a human being's commitment to having things be significant. You have an analogy to that in your life. Really. No kidding.

Erhard had re-entered the room.

ERHARD
Did you not get that your story, read by a person in a different culture, would sound like that story sounded to you?

PATSY
Yes.

ERHARD
Serving lunch late to your husband is serving lunch late to your husband. That's all it is. And that woman hung herself. Can you see that you hung yourself? Isn't it silly to hang yourself because someone got a divorce? It's a joke, and you guys don't get the joke. Life is a joke. Are you getting that?

PATSY (*grimly*)
Yes. Very clear.

ERHARD
Yes, you are getting that. And you're having the appropriate response to it at the moment. And you're not all the way through it yet. Good.

(*applause*)

She sat. A participant named Beverly stood.

BEVERLY
I want to know, "now what?" I'm looking for a new possibility, a new language so I can relate to people, to work for both of... And now I'm hearing that I've been transformed, and...

ERHARD
And you don't like it. You don't like "transformed."

BEVERLY
No, because they have to be transformed again. Go to a new level.

ERHARD
There are no levels. This is all there is.

BEVERLY
As far as each individual is concerned there are levels.

ERHARD
Who told you that? Did you speak to the Pope personally? This is a product of your infinite wisdom?

BEVERLY
People differ from person to person.

ERHARD

So what? Each rock is different from each other. So what? There's some mythology going on here with this levels stuff. Tell me about levels.

BEVERLY

I don't know about levels. I'm just hearing that people are transformed.

ERHARD

Who?

BEVERLY

Friends and those that are here...

ERHARD

Do you know what it is to be transformed?

BEVERLY

No.

ERHARD

What it is to be transformed is to know that life is empty and meaningless—and I don't mean know like hear and understand, I mean know like "be." When you *are* that life is empty and meaningless, and you're not making anything out of that, and you're not doing anything with it, and it's not a justification, and it's not an explanation, and there's no prescription, and it doesn't give you a prescription, then you're transformed. When you are that life is empty and meaningless, and when that doesn't give you anything—in other words, when you *are* that life is empty and meaningless and that doesn't give you a prescription for living, and it doesn't explain everything, it'll give you light. It'll light up everything. In that moment I got it, when I got that everything was in order to make it, the universe lit up. I didn't need to know anything. I didn't need to know that there was a floor down there holding me up. It was just there. So what it is to be transformed is to be that life is empty and meaningless, and to be that it's empty and meaningless that it's empty and meaningless: To be that life is not going to work out. And you are not someday going to have a relationship into which you put your heart and soul.

BEVERLY

I want life to be easy.

ERHARD

Life is not going to be easier. You're not going to find an answer. It's going to be just like it is. And you can bank on that. Life's been around for a long time. It's always only been like it is. And tomorrow it's going to be like it is tomorrow. But you're not living there. You live for it to be easy, which means you haven't lived yet.

> **When you *are* that life is empty and meaningless, and you're not making anything out of that, and you're not doing anything with it, and it's not a justification, and it's not an explanation, and there's no prescription, and it doesn't give you a prescription, then you're transformed.**

BEVERLY
I'm at one point today and I'll be at another point tomorrow.

ERHARD
And another point the day after that. And after that you'll be in another point. On and on until there are no more points and they'll throw dirt in your face.

BEVERLY
I want to make it easier for me to get to points faster.

ERHARD
No. You won't get there any faster.

BEVERLY
Then where am I going?

ERHARD
Nowhere. There's nowhere to go. You already got there.

(*loudly*)
There's no place to go! You already got there! You don't like it now that you're there? That is too fucking bad.

BEVERLY
I think there's another way of looking at it.

(*laughter*)

ERHARD
Beverly, there are always other ways of looking at it and all of them are unenlightened.

BEVERLY
Why did I pay $625?

ERHARD
You paid $625 to *be* that life is empty and meaningless, and that it's meaningless that life is empty and meaningless. You paid $625 to find out that life isn't going to be different. Like it's always been: it is like it is. You don't live life like it is what it is. You live life like "it's going to be different." And that makes you an asshole. It's not a bad thing to be, just a thing to be, like a fart. All the stuff we did… everything we've done up to now was to get to the point where we could have this discussion. I told you up front that we were going to keep moving back until we got to zero. Empty and meaningless is as zero as you can get.

BEVERLY
And so now we're going to progress somewhere?

(*laughter*)

ERHARD
No no. See, if we progress somewhere then we'd have to get back to zero again.

BEVERLY
And so we're going in a circle to get back to zero.

ERHARD
No, we're going to be at zero.

BEVERLY
And then we'll be happy.

ERHARD
I don't know. But I am certain that you will if you are. You'll never be happy waiting for it to turn out. You're never going to be happy trying to get it to move faster. Listen carefully. You're never going to be happy waiting for the right tool, or the right answer with which to be related. If you're going to be related, you're going to have to be related like this. Just like this. This is not a practice session for the real relationship. This is the real relationship. That's what you want to get. This is it. It's not going to work out because it has already worked out. This is what you got to be related in and this is all you're ever going to have. You're always only going to have what you got. You're never gonna have what you don't got and are waiting for. If you get that, that should give you a very powerful sense of freedom. And take a great big burden there and let you be with the relationship you already have.

Erhard had been sitting on the platform edge, talking very directly to Beverly, who stood about seven rows back. He was very focused and deliberate throughout the exchange.

ERHARD
Is that a little clearer?

BEVERLY
Yes.

(*applause*)

RICHARD
Last night someone I was staying with in the room told me that I snored. I stayed up late last night, trying to make sure that... I told them I wouldn't snore and I stayed up most of the night to make sure I wouldn't snore. So it's not quite a divorce and not quite a divorcee's roommate. I

got that because I wrote my letter yesterday before I went to bed. And I didn't have to wake up to get there. If someone asked me what I would give up, if I snored, I could give up the idea if I could stop myself from snoring.

KIPP
You only snore if you snore.

RICHARD
Well, there's more to the story. I only snore in hotels.

KIPP
Got it.

RICHARD
I learned to snore in hotels. I lived in them for a year and a half.

KIPP
Clear.

ERHARD
What there is to get out of Richard's share is that life is made up of trying to be. It's made up of trying not to be, and of trying to be. Is there any being in trying not to be or trying to be?

(*Richard sits down and another participant stands*)

MOLLY (*in tears*)
I came to The Forum on a mission from God to save WE & A. It's actually not a joke. I mean: it is a joke on me... What I found out is that my racket is being abandoned. And I found out that I play my racket with God.

ERHARD
I don't talk about God a lot, because I don't have a license to talk about God. You didn't pay me to talk about God, so if somebody brings it up, I do what I can to avoid it, and if I can't avoid it, I say as little as I can. I don't like talking to you about God because God's a racket for you and that's disgusting. You need to listen to what Molly is saying because she knows both sides of the coin...now. So we're not going to have a lot of discussions about this. We'll have this discussion with Molly for everybody else. Go on.

MOLLY
I told my husband that when I was meditating that God told me to take The Forum, and he said, "so how are you going to get in this time, 'cause they rejected you last time." I said I would play it their way. On the form I wrote what was so, but not the real so. It was the "how to get in" so.

ERHARD

And the other "so" was in order to something else.

MOLLY

Well the whole thing was an in-order-to.

ERHARD

Yeah, good. Do you have any idea how sacrilegious that is? God in-order-to.

MOLLY

Every time someone called me from The Forum I ripped them off, because I was this holy person. I wasn't there for them, because I was on a religious path. I faked it. When I got to The Forum, I looked around to check out how tough a job it would be for God. And what I found out was, that when I was four years old I could remember back, and I did this through the process of completing with my parents.

(*addressing Erhard*)

I saw that I could trust you. And you said that the bonus points came with completing with your parents. I saw that I'd never done that. I tried everything. I threw everything out. I saw that I had paid $625... when you said that I had paid for it, and that if I was going to give it back for free that I was a sucker... Whatever I heard that got me here was for me. I saw that I came to The Forum to get The Forum. And you have to save your own soul.

(*laughter and applause*)

The room became very still as Molly spoke. Erhard sat on the platform in front of her, with Kipp and Wes seated nearby.

MOLLY (*continuing to cry*)

I called my parents. I didn't know how to do it. I was just standing there. They were both social workers, retired. I didn't know how to say this. And what I felt was that all they'd ever done for me is love me. That was it. No matter what, it was love. It was like Eden. Somehow I was back in Eden. Everything was everything. They asked what was wrong. I said there was nothing to worry about. I told them I loved them and knew they loved me. "I've been hurt by all this stuff that happened, but I get that everything you've done was done out of love." And they started telling me their stories, and doing their social worker stuff. What I got is that I didn't know much about them.

ERHARD

People love all that process stuff. That's why they're offended that The Forum is four days and one night. It's not long enough. There's not enough agony to it. When you can be with the story, you don't get stuck with it. And if you can't be with the story, they're going to keep telling it over and over and over and over because you can't be with it.

MOLLY

And then we got to the deeper part of the story. My father told me how much I didn't appreciate what he gave me, and my mother said that I abandoned them when I went to college...

ERHARD

Hold on, I want everyone to get this.

(*loudly*)
They've got a big fucking story too! They got their story. Can you imagine the story my mother's got? My mother doesn't have any story. She could have a story. So. You were noticing that they have a story.

MOLLY

I've been terrified all my life of anger. And I would do anything I can to avoid anger. I do that with my husband. Standing on this ledge on the phone with them. The anger would pull me down to the valley. I would become comatose.

ERHARD

Right, you became comatose once to survive being with your parents.

MOLLY

I was comatose.

ERHARD

When you are that it's empty and meaningless and it's empty and meaningless that it's empty and meaningless, and you can be with another's story no matter what it is, you're fearless. Without fear you don't have need for courage.

MOLLY

My father's anger didn't frighten me for a change. I loved him.

ERHARD

It's not that you like or endorse his being angry. He's angry, that's all. And when you can be with his anger it disappears. When you got to try to do something to get him from being angry, or get him to stop being angry, or some other ploy, the anger persists no matter how good the ploy is. I know this because I talk to your kids. They forgive but they don't forget, until you can be with whatever it is that they're remembering.

MOLLY

I didn't have to prove anything.

ERHARD

Because it's horseshit. What is this more or less love, to start with? "You either love me or you don't".

MOLLY

My mother shifted. She talked about how she'd made a lot of mistakes. And how her parents were different. They weren't taught how to be with their kids.

ERHARD

You made mistakes raising your children means you made mistakes raising your children, it doesn't mean "bad mother," even though that's what you got it to mean.

MOLLY

And then she said: "How can we get from here to there?"

ERHARD

Nobody wants to be there. They want to get there. But you can't get there. You can only be there. That's the joke. Nothing is going to make you happy. Nothing. Nothing is going to make you happy. That happens to be literally true, by the way, but never mind that. You're going to spend the rest of your life trying to get what is going to make you happy, except that nothing's going to get you happy. You've gotta *be* happy, you can't get happy. Getting is anathema to happiness. The pursuit of happiness is the single most effective barrier to happiness. Nothing is more certain to deprive you of happiness than the pursuit of happiness. This is another form of that answer that there is no answer.

MOLLY

I said to my parents: "Didn't something shift? We're here now." And they laughed. And it was tender.

ERHARD

That's really living—that laugh. Is there anything more to complete about this?

MOLLY

After the phone call to my parents, talking to my husband, I remembered an incident when I was four years old. I was jumping on the couch and I hit the window and cracked open my forehead. 18 stitches. I was given a washcloth and there was all this blood. We went to the hospital. In the operating room, all I could see was a huge light, and this disembodied doctor's voice told my mother to leave. She left. She went away and left me there. My whole life has been about that. I've been stuck with that abandonment all my life.

ERHARD

Yeah, and stuck with that bright light.

(laughter)
You can't say anything more important than "that's what my life has been about ever since." That gets you to the source of your whole life. That gets you to zero. All the way back, at nothing.

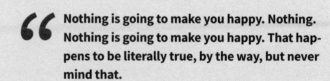

> **Nothing is going to make you happy. Nothing. Nothing is going to make you happy. That happens to be literally true, by the way, but never mind that.**

God

Here, Erhard is assuring that the "trap" that The Forum sets for participants—the trap of the current paradigm, in which Forum participants must find themselves hopelessly ensnared before they can access the liberation of transformation—is experienced as inescapable. Even God, for many still the most sacred of values, must finally fall victim to the demands of standing-reserve. As perceived through the metaphysical-technological lens of Western thought, God is inevitably burdened with the entailments of that paradigm. First, "He" becomes an unattainable ideality (the Creator who, in Heidegger's view, is an extension of the Platonic notion of ideal form); and, at the same time, "He" is placed in standing-reserve, along with everything else in the technological clearing, and thus can be loved and worshiped only in-order-to—that is, for salvation, forgiveness, eternal reward, and so forth. ■

MOLLY

What I got about my relationship with God? Well, my racket is that everyone abandoned me, including God. You have to buy love. And I was told you had to serve God to make God happy so he'd love you.

ERHARD (*to the group*)

Somehow, way back in history when all this God stuff got started, God got turned into a story. I invite you to consider the possibility that the story somehow served the transmission process in those primitive times. This notion rings very hollow for me. Nevertheless, for people like you and me to be living those stories is disgusting and sacrilegious. To reduce an infinite possibility into some crap story... That's the end of my sermon.

MOLLY

I've spent a lot of years serving.

ERHARD

The only time serving is nurturing is when you're serving to serve, not serving in-order-to.

MOLLY

What I saw was that everybody was getting served except me, and I was getting exhausted.

ERHARD

I don't know that being stuck with God is a good thing. *Free to* might be a more appropriate relationship to God than *have to*.

(*to Molly*)

But that's your business. My business is dog shit.

MOLLY

Apparently mine is too.

(*laughter*)

So when I saw that I had taken on this job to make God happy...

ERHARD (*laughing*)

Isn't that ridiculous? This is a very good discussion. Go ahead.

MOLLY

And when I saw how ridiculous it was and how tired I was getting...

ERHARD

I got tired making God happy. It's a new book. Look, you understand that Molly's probably produced more freedom in people's relationship with God in the last fifteen minutes than she has in her whole life? She's giving some room to be by sharing. She did it by sharing herself, not her fucking platitudes, not her beliefs.

MOLLY

I saw that I wanted to end hunger to make God happy. And I saw that God was sufficient. I mean, God was just doing fine.

(*laughter and applause*)

And it was a tremendous relief. I didn't have to make God happy. I could do what I did just for the joy of it.

ERHARD

Good.

WES

Got it. Congratulations.

Molly sat down.

WES

Here's what I got from Molly: God's happy. What's your problem?

(*laughter*)

We're going to dinner. That doesn't change empty and meaningless. Let me point out the places people are at at this point in The Forum. For some the possibility is very clear. Some don't know exactly what is happening. Some are very sure they're not in tune with what's happening. Recognize places you are in.

ERHARD

He means possibility like an opening, like freedom, not like an answer... You want to get that real clear in here, because I know you've been hearing possibility like an answer. We do not mean possibility as an answer, but a clearing in which life can happen. You can't dance with answers. You dance with freedom. You can't paint knowing how to paint, knowing the answers. You've got to have an openness, room.

WES

So you're in different places with regard to the conversation. I invite you to go to dinner in a group.

ERHARD (*regarding the approaching dinner break*)

You notice you're a little less frenzied about dinner? Like dinner might be just dinner, rather than a chance to get away.

WES

At dinner, have a conversation about where you are in The Forum. Not your opinions, ideas, and notions: something about where you are and what you see in your life. Continue to stand in this conversation. You don't need to go anywhere. Let it unfold for you. With regard to your experience at the moment, some people at this point are high. Some people are angry. Some people are sad. Some people are "What's the big deal?"

Wes had those in each category raise their hands. On the video each time Wes asked for hands, very few went up until the last one: "What's the big deal?"

WES
It doesn't mean anything. You can almost be assured that by the time dinner is over you'll be in a different experience anyway. It doesn't mean anything.

ERHARD
Who in here knew that it was empty and meaningless? For a long time knew it?

(*several participants raise their hands*)
You have it like an answer, which is different from how we are saying it here. It's not a solution to a problem, so you smart-asses didn't get it.

WES
Let yourself be where you are. The other assignment: see if you have any questions about the seminar program.

ERHARD
Up till now we've talked about dog shit. Now we're going to talk about the truth. The truth about the truth is that it doesn't mean anything. It's just the truth. People do occasionally stumble into the truth. Sometimes they fall over the truth. But they invariably suck the power out of it, the truth-value out of it and turn it into an empty shell. And they do that by trying to make the truth useful. The truth is useless. I mean that the truth does not justify anything. If you stumble across the truth, or had a flash of insight, and you use it to explain something, if it was true, it's now not true, because you've taken the truth out of the context in which it exists, which context is useless, and put it into a context in which it cannot exist as the truth, which is "use." The truth is useless. It gives no prescriptions. None. It's never the basis for a rule, never the basis for a prescription. The truth is useless. So anything you're doing based on the truth is based on bullshit. You don't use the truth; the truth uses you. If you want to have a relationship with the truth, be a place for the truth to go to work. Don't try to use it, because when you try to use it in any way, it loses its truth-value. If you want some evidence for that, look around the world, and the places where you'll find the greatest destruction, the most evil—those things were done in the name of the truth. Don't fuck with the truth. Let it be. Let it use you. Let it be and let it use you. Don't try to use it. Because if you got lucky and you stumbled over the truth and then tried to use it, you sucked all the truth-value that it had; all the power it had as the truth is gone.*

> **"** If you stumble across the truth, or had a flash of insight, and you use it to explain something, if it was true, it's now not true, because you've taken the truth out of the context in which it exists, which context is useless, and put it into a context in which it cannot exist as the truth, which is "use."

---

*▶ **NOTE:** Please see the sidebar entitled "The Three Levels of Truth" in Session Two of Day Four.

WES

Later you will have an opportunity to ask about the seminar, or about the visitor evening tomorrow.

KIPP

How many of you have invited people to come tomorrow night at 9 pm? Use the dinner break to invite those people.

WES

There are plenty of people there that you could complete with, that you could get off it with. Bonus category. Use the dinner break for that.

The Forum broke for dinner at 8:00 pm.

SESSION THREE INTERVAL

The Forgetting of Being, Part Five of Eight: *Physis*

To gain insight into the elusive nature of transformation, we are tracing the history of Being, as unearthed by Heidegger in his reading of the Pre-Socratic Greek philosophers. When Heidegger speaks of the Pre-Socratics, he often says simply "the Greeks"; however, as we will show, the level of insight achieved by these thinkers was not likely shared by the *hoi polloi,* the Greek population as a whole.

One of the tasks required by Heidegger's project was to distinguish the original meanings of words which, for the Greeks, *said Being.* Discerning these meanings was an extraordinary challenge. According to Heidegger, the great thinking of these philosophers was *non-conceptual thinking*, and therefore radically different from our current practice of reasoning, that is, comparing and contrasting propositions that each state some relationship between a subject and its predicate. Subjects and predicates are always and already generalized abstractions drawn from the particularities of lived experience.

> **Concept and system alike are alien to Greek thinking. [...] The interpretation of Greek thinking that is guided by modern conceptual thinking not only remains inappropriate for Greek thinking; it also keeps us from hearing the appeal of the problematic of Greek thinking, and thus from being held to a constantly more urgent summons to go on questioning. (*WCT* 213)**

Keep in mind that when we talk about a new way of thinking, we are introducing a topic that cannot be brought to mind in our current way of thinking. So whatever you thought when you read that phrase isn't it.

Of the words used by the Pre-Socratics, none is more challenging than *physis* (pronounced *foo'-sis*). What was said in this word, for the Greeks, was what Heidegger calls *the power that emerges.* The original force of the word has been lost to us; and it is the judgment of the scholar Charles E. Scott that if we can think *physis* as the Greeks did, we will "find ourselves in an original dimension of our history," one that has been lost almost since its inception (*A Companion to Heidegger's Introduction to Metaphysics* 26).

But to translate the Greek terms successfully, Heidegger insists, we must first *translate ourselves to the source of what comes to language in their saying.* Since in each pre-Socratic fragment the background from which it speaks is spoken as well, we must "seek the opportunity which will let us cross over to that source first of all

outside the fragment itself; it must be an opportunity which will let us experience what *ta onta* [beings], thought in Greek, says" (*EGT* 28, emphasis added).

This book proposes that the transformational experience made available in The Forum provides that opportunity. We show in this book that The Forum experience is consistent in significant ways with the experience in language that Heidegger aimed to evoke in his thinking. Further, since Heidegger is analogizing his understanding of Being with the experience of the Pre-Socratics, we invoke the principle of transitive equality and propose that The Forum, through its intentional dialogic transactions, provides the opportunity called for in the passage above—it allows us to experience, outside the Greek fragments themselves, the meaning of *physis* and *ta onta*.

Blossoming Emergence

Heidegger summarizes the complexity of *physis* here:

> **Now what does the word *physis* say? It says what emerges from itself (for example, the emergence, the blossoming, of a rose), the unfolding that opens itself up, the coming-into-appearance in such unfolding, and holding itself and persisting in appearance—in short, the emerging-abiding sway. . . . *Physis* is the event of *standing forth*, arising from the concealed and thus enabling the concealed to take its stand for the first time. (*IM* 15-16)**

This short but dense passage suggests the dynamic of *physis*—emerging, unfolding, standing forth—as well as its complications. The word at once designates a process (*blossoming*), the entity that emerges in that process (the *rose*), and finally the phenomenon that comprises both the emergence and the rose itself, which is named here the emerging-abiding *sway*. Note further that as the rose (the being) emerges into unconcealment (the world), it brings with it *the concealed from which it has emerged*—the sway, the Being of the emergent being—and thereby brings what has been concealed to stand "for the first time" in the world of meaning.

The word *sway* is a translation of Heidegger's German word *Walten*. This is sway in the sense of *holding sway,* by exercising rule or dominance over some realm. But the term inevitably sounds overtones of persistent, back-and-forth vacillation, a quality appropriate to any discussion of Being. In his writing about the Greeks, Heidegger uses both *physis* and sway as designations for the realm of Being, and sometimes he seems to be using them interchangeably. More often, however, the terms serve to distinguish Being *in two different contexts, or stages.* Of course, Being cannot have a context, or anything at all like stages; but to talk about a topic that cannot be talked about, one must tell some lies.

It may be helpful to consider the situation this way:

For the Pre-Socratic Greek thinkers, to whom a new level of world-awareness was becoming accessible, pre-phenomena presented themselves in a state of "originary unity"—an "overwhelming coming-to-presence that has not yet been surmounted in thinking" (*IM* 67), an upheaval of entities and forces not yet held in language, their boundaries uncertain, their natures and relationships not yet fully distinguished.

To use a phrase that is central in the work of both Erhard and Heidegger (a term further discussed at the Session Two Interval), we might say that these pre-phenomena lived as *possibilities for Being.* As undistinguished, however, they swam without limits in the realm of possibility. The *sway* designates that realm, a realm of Being which is not yet in-the-world but is on the verge. These pre-phenomena may also be usefully understood as possible *meanings,* or not-yet-meanings, and the sway may therefore be seen as a realm of meaninglessness (an experience of this realm—which Heidegger refers to as the Nothing—will be seen to be a critical aspect of The Forum transformation). The not-yet-meanings, presumably, might include both physical and non-physical pre- phenomena that had not yet pressed forward to be named and distinguished as possibilities—such as microbes, sexual abuse, gravity, ethnicity, digital communication, homophobia, and egotism.

Heidegger has distinguished a mode of speaking he calls *Saying,* which has the force of *bringing forth,* rather than merely re-presenting. "The essential being of language," he says, "is Saying as Showing" (*OWL* 123). This is languaging that generates. In the speaking of the Greeks, which Heidegger calls *originative Saying,* a world was brought forth.

Physis, then, is: Being brought forth by originative Saying to stand in the world; as well as the beings brought forth and set into limits by the naming; as well as the process by which beings and Being emerge. *Physis* is the "event of *standing forth,* arising from the concealed and thus enabling the concealed to take its stand for the first time" (*IM* 16).

All of this, as we have said, is essentially talk about something that cannot be talked about, and here Heidegger scholar Susan Schoenbohm suggests the challenge we face in attempting to analyze this phenomenon:

 How, if at all, is it possible to render in words that which "is" previous to any being, word, or name? How to articulate the very coming-into-being of determination for the first time? [. . .] In its most originary meaning, *physis* means the emerging, for the first time, of something out of no determination at all . . . in other words, the process of something's coming-to-be-something

from nothing. (*A Companion to Heidegger's Introduction to Metaphysics.* **148**)

For the Pre-Socratics, not-yet-beings were becoming manifest as possibilities. The task for humans was to bring them forth, from a background of meaninglessness, to stand as beings in a world of meaning.

Emerging into the world as a possibility, a being enters a *lighting* "from which whatever lingers awhile in presence can be appropriately collected and brought forward by mortal *legein,*" by human naming (*EGT* 70). Naming for the Pre-Socratics was not merely providing a label; it was distinguishing a possibility of meaning, and therefore of Being. Here, in a passage from the second day of The Forum, Erhard describes the process:

 Distinction is an operation in language. In the normal course of events you and I think of language as something we use to report on something. . . . But now we're distinguishing a new kind of operation in language. It's an operation in language called *generating.* **It's as though I said "chair" and a chair fell out of my mouth. . . .** *What distinguishing is, is to take something like an undifferentiated mass and to bring forth from that mass a realm of possibility.* **Distinction gives existence. It makes existence possible.**

From the undifferentiated mass of the sway, the Pre-Socratics were distinguishing the possibilities of a world.

Heidegger describes the events of this time as a process of *strife,* "not war in the human sense" but "strife that *holds sway*" (*IM* 67, emphasis added). The Greeks were engaged in a struggle to bring *physis*—the turbulent sway, vacillating in its persistent emergence and withdrawal—to stand in the world, by naming and differentiating its elements as beings:

 As Heraclitus thinks it, struggle first and foremost allows what essentially unfolds to step apart from each other in opposition, first allows position and status and rank to establish themselves in coming to presence. In such a stepping apart, clefts, intervals, distances and joints open themselves up. In con-frontation, world comes to be. [. . .] This breaking forth, breaking up, capturing and subjugating is in itself the first opening of beings *as* **sea,** *as* **earth,** *as* **animal. (***IM* **67, 174)**

In Heidegger's imagining of this process as he finds it in the fragments of the Pre-Socratics, we find a saga of violent images and primal struggle, at "the dawn of early times in the land of evening" (*EGT* 18). He is not aiming to provide a record of events, since events of the time are necessarily shrouded in darkness. His tale, he says, must therefore be less natural science than mythology (*IM* 173). He is presenting an account of the forces that must have been at play as human beings, and their world, emerged into a crucial evolutionary phase, and the thinkers of the time struggled to engage that emergence. In Heidegger's account, the engagement is violent.

But where in the world are these violent events occurring? This is not, after all, a saga of nations in battle, but a story of thinkers thinking; and certainly it was on one level an intellectual event—a struggle of minds to engage and comprehend the new, an "internal" process of perception and deliberation. But that process was at the same time bringing forth a world *into the world* for the first time. This world was not "out there," waiting to be labeled; world arose (as it continues to arise) in its apprehension by human Being-in-the-world. These primordial events, then, were occurring at the wavering interface between looking and thinking and naming.

Further, in the process of naming, and thereby creating an order of rank and place in a world of meaning, Heidegger says that the Greeks were leaving the realm of mythology and *entering history*. They were the beings into whose evolutionary path had emerged the gift of language. Now they were recognizing the inescapable obligation of the gift: humans must unconceal beings and name them as the beings they are, opening them to existence and providing that existence with limits. This was the task of the Pre-Socratic thinkers, as well as the poets, statesmen, and artisans through whose work Greek culture developed: "Against the overwhelming sway, they throw the counterweight of their work and capture in this work the world that is thereby opened up" (*IM* 68).

> **The temple, in its standing there, first gives to things their look and to men their outlook on themselves. . . . It is the same with the sculpture of the god, votive offering of the victor in the athletic games. It is not a portrait whose purpose is to make it easier to realize how the god looks; rather, it is a work that lets the god himself be present and thus *is* the god himself. ("OWA" in *PLT* 43)**

Indeed, Heidegger writes, the "nature of art, on which both the art work and the artist depend, is the setting-itself-into-work of truth" ("OWA" in *PLT* 72). And in

responding to the demand of truth setting-itself-into-work, humanity was for the first time "coming to itself": "The selfhood of humanity means this: it has to transform the Being that opens itself up to it into history, and thus bring itself to a stand" (*IM* 160). And as the Greeks opened themselves into history, says Heidegger, the question about their own Being underwent a change from "What is humanity?" into the form "Who is humanity?" (*IM* 160).

Like many of the questions raised in Heidegger's thinking, this one leaves us thinking a precarious balance between human agency and evolutionary forces. At this distance we cannot conceptualize the situation; Heidegger hints at its nature:

> **the violence-doing of poetic saying, of thoughtful projection, of constructive building, of state-creating action, is not an application of faculties that the human being has, but is a disciplining and disposing of the violent forces by virtue of which beings disclose themselves as such, insofar as the human being enters into them. This disclosedness of beings is the violence that humanity has to conquer in order to be itself first of all, that is, to be historical in doing violence in the midst of beings. (*IM* 175)**

But Heidegger challenges

> **the opinion human beings cherish of themselves as those who have invented and who could have invented language and understanding, building and poetry. How is humanity ever supposed to have invented that . . . due to which humanity itself can *be* as humanity in the first place? (*IM* 174)**

> **The struggle meant here is originary struggle, for it allows those that struggle to originate as such in the first place. . . . (*IM* 68)**

This situation creates an interesting chicken-or-egg challenge for thinking: How did human beings create a world in language, when human beings themselves first came to be human beings through language? The scholar Charles Guignon has provided this useful observation of the quandary:

[B]ecause the meaning of a word is determined by its web of relations to other words as embedded in a set of linguistic practices, and because humans are, as the Greeks saw, the "language animal" (*zoon logon echon),* there is no way to suppose that humans first existed and then later invented first one word, then another, and so on. To see how language emerged, then, we need to make use of something like Wittgenstein's metaphor, "Light dawns gradually over the whole." This image of a dawning light seems to be what is implied by Heidegger's descriptions of the originary struggle that is prior to the appearance of humans and their explicit acts of naming. (*A Companion to Heidegger's Introduction to Metaphysics.* 41)

Heidegger might put it this way: just as the modern era is the technological age, in which human being is enframed in the service of technological devices, the age of the Pre-Socratics was the age of the dawning light, when for a brief historical moment a full experience of Being was made available to human Being-in-the-world.

The struggle for the Greeks, then, was to seize this moment, individuating beings into their meaningful places in the world while at the same time retaining their essential relation to the sway, and thus their fundamental orientation to Being. For Heidegger, the greatness of the Pre-Socratics consisted in their recognition of this challenge, and its articulation in their thinking. At the same time, the promise of this achievement for Western thinking has been lost. As we proceed in this series of intervals on the forgetting of Being, we will consider further the nature of this loss.

The Forum resumed at 10 pm, following the dinner break. The four TV monitors located at various points in the room have been turned on, so that the participants now have the option of watching the action on the monitors rather than directly. Erhard and Kipp began by interacting with participants' sharing.

KIPP
Who would like to share what's happening?

ANDY
I had a terrific time at dinner. And anything beyond "I'm here and I speak" is a joke. Well yeah because, nothing. It's great.

KIPP
When it is.

ANDY
Yeah.

KIPP
When it's great it's great, when it's not it's not. Thank you very much.

DON
I basically got tired of listening to people's shit. A lot of the observation I made was people fell back into story telling. And I stopped listening. I didn't enjoy it.

KIPP
Okay.

DON
I didn't enjoy that at all.

KIPP
So what?

DON
Well, yeah, right. I just like the meat and potatoes. That good stuff.

KIPP
But so what? You've got it that it should be some way.

DON
Right.

FORUM DAY THREE: SESSION FOUR

KIPP

As long as you've got some way you think it should be, that means it means something. And as long as it means something, that meaning has you.

DON

Exactly.

KIPP

Thank you.

(*Applause*)

SANFORD

I would like to share where I'm at right now and I'm just being.

KIPP

Great! Just being.

SANFORD

Yeah.

KIPP

And the only time you're being is when?

SANFORD

Right now.

KIPP

When you're being. And the only time I'm going to catch you not being is when? When you're not being.

SANFORD

Yeah.

KIPP

Thank you very much. Fred?

FRED

I finally got down to my big racket of rackets and that's being sad.

ERHARD

Listen up here. You may not be sad; you may be something else. What you always are or often are, that you don't want to be? That's a racket.

FRED

And at dinner I got to what the cost is, because when I see all the happiness around here, I just want to push it all down. And what I discovered about how I dominate is I don't want you to be happier than I am. So I come in with sad, and I really get sad and I get heavy with the sadness. But what I also discovered was this incredible disempowerment just all the way down. If I make a commitment and something happens like I don't want to fulfill that, then I go into sadness, and then I don't want to do anything, like the whole bottom falls out. So any joy in my relationship with my wife? Well I don't want her to be quite that much happier than I am. I take away all that joy…

ERHARD

Because if you don't have sadness, and sadness is the way you dominate and avoid domination… If you don't have sadness you lose your weapon. You can't be happy except tentatively. Just for a little while maybe. Very good. Continue.

FRED

So also what I've looked at: I've been talking about having a television show for two years. To have teenagers and parents interact in a powerful way to get over all this stuff about clean rooms. And whenever I get up to speed about that I get sad. And I don't want to do that. I'm avoiding the domination of being powerful and making that kind of contribution to the world.

ERHARD

That's hard to hear—avoid the domination of being powerful. It's hard to hear.

FRED

I don't want that domination. I want to be free just in my relationship with my wife. I don't want to be dominated by my commitment to her. I want to be away from that. I've dominated with anger, and with depression, and now with sadness.

KIPP

There's no freedom in wanting to be free. It sounds free but it is the trap. Whatever you can't be with has you.

FRED

I found what this was all covering up. I just don't accept myself. I don't accept who I am. I have a tremendous fear of just being with, being with who I am.

KIPP

Yeah but that tremendous fear is what comes with being a human being. You don't make it up; it makes you up.

ERHARD

I don't like the term fear here. I'd like to be a little more precise. It's really a threat in the form of the domination. The fear is just a part of it. In other words, your emotional system is going to be consistent with what your racket is up to. So you're going to have emotions appropriate to what your racket is up to. If what your racket is up to is avoiding domination, for you Fred, given the way you've got it structured, it's going to produce a bit of fear. The fear is not the source of it. The source of it is avoiding the domination of the responsibility for being powerful and able.

FRED
Thank you...

ERHARD
See if you weren't frightened, you couldn't justify avoiding. If you weren't sad you wouldn't have a reason.

(*to Kipp*)
We didn't deal with reasons yet have we?

KIPP
No.

ERHARD (*jokingly*)
Why are we so far behind?

KIPP
That's one of my issues.

(*laughter*)

ERHARD
Comes up particularly around me, right? Otherwise he's fine. Around me he's got this issue.

(*returning to the topic*)
Very important to get this. I want to cut out this crap of explaining your life on the basis of the way you feel... Fred is giving you the insight that the way you feel is a product of your racket, not the other way around. You are not molded by your fear. Your fears are there merely to be consistent with what your racket is up to, so you have got this kind of justification. You are not run by your emotions. That's the apparency. Underneath that, what's driving things is the racket.

FRED
Part of what I was looking at was also the inauthenticity/authenticity issue. I had it all wired that I was absolutely authentic. All I had to do was be around and I was authentic. And when I could accept the fact that I am inauthentic, not like guilt, or like mortal sin, or like confession...

ERHARD

Hold on. You want to get that. That conversation's come up in here a lot of times and it's still not flat. Being able to be what you're afraid you might be gives you power.

FRED

So when I finally looked at that I actually had a tremendous feeling of real freedom. I really got that I'm absolutely inauthentic, it's just how I am, it's like telling the truth for the first time, it gave me a whole playground where I could just be or express or create who I am. I had this thing tied up with the God issue the lady had brought up before, that I was here on earth to be the guardian of the playground...

(*laughter*)

But I couldn't play. My job was to be this superior, arrogant person who is going to guard and protect the playground, but I wasn't going to get to play. But I can't play. When I finally saw that I'm inauthentic, it was almost a celebration. It's great! I'm inauthentic. Now there's a place to start from to find out who I really am.

ERHARD

Don't misinterpret what Fred is saying. He means what he says but don't listen to it wrong. He's saying, "embracing what you're afraid you might be gives you power." He didn't say, "make being inauthentic right." He said he was able to embrace it. That he was able to be in the face of it. Whatever you can be with lets you be. Whatever you can't be with won't let you be.

FRED

So it's like a...

ERHARD

It's almost starting to get clear in here. It's like "yeah, yeah, I know that, why are you saying it again?"

FRED

And so it's like this whole new sense of freedom. You know before The Forum my wife was telling me, "Fred, you don't know who you are." That made me furious. And the truth is I don't know who I am. And to be able to get that I'm inauthentic, that's the most freedom I think I've ever had.

KIPP

It is the most freedom you've ever had.

FRED

I was looking at the issue of the empty and meaningless. I'm not sure that I have that like I have "inauthentic." And I want to interact for a moment to get it...

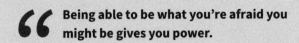

" Being able to be what you're afraid you might be gives you power.

ERHARD

Hold on a second. You notice he didn't say he was confused. You want to listen that he's saying the same things a lot of other people have said in here. Talking about not quite getting something yet. But he's talking about it, he has framed it, he's construed it, he's spoken it so that there's an opening for him to get it. Rather than a way that there is no opening for him to get it so that Kipp has to beat him up to get him to get it.

FRED

So what I was looking at, the possibility that empty and meaningless, if we had the opposite of that, if life was full and fulfilling there would be no space for me to come up, to express myself, to be fully blown as a human being, in the sense that I would be spending all my time trying to find out what's the meaning of life if it's already so full? I'm looking at empty and meaninglessness as a place to start from like it's empty, it's open.

ERHARD

Here's the problem in that. It's one of the problems Kipp and I have in leading The Forum. This empty and meaningless you've got to get just like it is. You can't get it as a place to start. If you're getting it like a place to start you're getting it in-order-to. You've got to *kill hope.* Otherwise your life is going to be full of hopelessness. See the one thing that goes away with hope... When you suffer the pain of getting rid of hope, the other thing that goes away with it is "hopeless." We're going to get a little deeper into this business about empty and meaningless and take a look at what the structure is. If it's all empty and meaningless then how did all this crap happen? Everyone's seen enough crap to be clear about the amount of crap there is? We don't need to do more crap in here?

Erhard stopped to acknowledge a participant for how different she looked from the first day.

ERHARD (*continuing*)

In Fred's straight talk about it, I want you to get that you've got to get it just to get it, not in-order-to. See if there's an iota of getting out of the trap in your getting it, you didn't get it. You gotta go through the despair, you gotta go through whatever emotion you have, or whatever mood you've got about it. You've got to get it cleanly. You can't get it knowing that there's going to be a way out, because the way out is the way in. See if you get it knowing there's going to be a way out, you didn't get it because you got it in a way that's going to keep you in. I had forgotten who I was talking to over here in the last session, what I said, that the attempt to get out of the trap... you know, what makes Californians silly is their attempt to get out of the trap, because the attempt to get out of the trap is being in the trap. What it is to be in the trap is to try to get out of the trap. You can't get out if you try, because trying to get out is part of the trap. You read the right books, and they tell you that. Okay, so you figure, I'm going to give up trying to get out of the trap. Well, that's part of the trap. See, you can't get out if you try, because trying to get out is being in the trap. And you can't get out if you don't try. There's no getting out of the trap. There's no way to win this game; you can't beat this one. You've got to be able to *be* in the trap. Every one of those words was chosen very carefully. You should listen to them very rigorously. Giving up, surrendering to the trap: won't work. All that'll do is leave you in the trap. Trying to

> **"When you suffer the pain of getting rid of hope, the other thing that goes away with it is 'hopeless.'"**

ERHARD (*continuing*)

get out of the trap won't work because the trap is constructed in such a way that the attempts to get out are the very bars of the trap. That's what keeps you in the trap. You can't get out if you try, and you can't get out if you don't try. You've got to be able to be in the trap. You know, you can't write that. That's oral. If you read it, it sounds like I said you've got to be able to *be* in the trap. No. I said you've got to be able to be in the trap. You've got to find freedom in the ropes: full, total, absolute freedom in the ropes. You've got to find freedom in your asshole-ness. Find freedom in the racket. Not avoiding the racket, not running the racket, not indulging yourself in the racket. "Okay, I'll just do my racket." That's trapped. You've just surrendered to it, given up to the racket. Trying not to do your racket will just be a new racket, even if you succeed at it, which you probably won't. Very, very rarely do people succeed at not doing their racket, and if you did succeed that would just be your new racket. Your new racket would be not doing your racket. Lots of people around here like that. They're Enlightened. You're the kind of people who fall in holes or get hit by busses. So, no in-order-to. It's empty and meaningless. And it's empty and meaningless that it's empty and meaningless. It doesn't mean anything that it doesn't mean anything. It just doesn't mean anything and it doesn't mean anything that it doesn't mean anything. And it isn't going to work out. It isn't going to work out because it already worked out. You think it's going to work out someday. The right woman is not going to come along someday, the one who's blonde and naked on a horse. You're gonna be stuck with the one you got. You aren't going to make it. There's no making it. And you got plenty of evidence for that already. A lot of people in this room have a lot of making it already. There are no failures in here. We could go down the street and find people whose lives are desperate due to their failures. Everyone in here is pretty successful in dealing with life. You're pretty stupid, but you're successful at dealing with life. We've made it this far despite our stupidity. Evidence that the stupid do make it... At any rate... So no cheating. You can't cheat your way out of this. You've got to lose and then be able to be.

FRED

It looks like... I don't know if that's as far as I can take it. That's what is. Like there's no supporting, no stuff around it.

ERHARD

Yeah. It's called the existential moment of truth: naked and without any support. You've got to be able to be there. You've got to be able to be with nothing underneath you. You won't make it. You won't make it in The Forum. It'll take years for you to get that. Fred and I have been working together a long time, pretty intensively. He's a real good guy. It's hard to tell when he talks about himself. You don't get it all when you open it up. We're opening it up in here. This is kindergarten. But it's started. This is an experience over which you will never get. You'll hear me talking for years. What you'll never get over is knowing that you've got a choice. I know you don't know what choice means yet, but you'll never get over that. No matter how fucked up you get, *that* you'll never get over. Still lots of work to do. And you'll do it if you see it as a privilege to do that work. If you can't see what an extraordinary opportunity it is to do this work, then you ought to complete The Forum and get every ounce of value you can get out of it, and there's plenty of value there to get, and you ought to go on your merry way. That's a fair deal. You paid for it. You're not obligated to do anything; you haven't joined anything because there's nothing to join.

> " Giving up, surrendering to the trap: won't work. All that'll do is leave you in the trap. Trying to get out of the trap won't work because the trap is constructed in such a way that the attempts to get out are the very bars of the trap. That's what keeps you in the trap. You can't get out if you try, and you can't get out if you don't try. You've got to be able to be in the trap.

FRED

When I made out my list of items for doing The Forum, I put down twenty-six individual, separate, items on the form I filled out for The Forum. And as I shared my detailed list with the lady I spoke to when I registered, she was aghast. What is driving me in the direction of twenty-six items that need to get handled otherwise my life isn't... Where is the value in me standing up here?

KIPP

Not in those twenty-six items.

FRED

Yeah, I got that far.

ERHARD

Who said there was any value? Who said there was supposed to be any value? Who said that life was about value?

FRED

Um, that if I accomplish those things, then I would be of value.

ERHARD

No you wouldn't. You'd be a guy walking around saying I accomplished those twenty-six things and now I have value. Nothing wrong with that.

FRED

Yeah.

ERHARD

Who said that those things were of value, was you.

FRED

Yeah, I did.

ERHARD

He made that up. It's okay with me that he made that up. But he's not the Pope, and the Pope doesn't say that. He said that. The only problem with it is if he believes in it, if he believes that it's true. If he believes that he said that and that's the game he's playing, that's wonderful. You don't have any value. You're nothing. Nothing and bullshit. No value. And you've got a mouth. And you can say, "I've got these twenty-six projects, twenty-six commitments, and accomplishing them gives me value, because I said so." Let me ask you a question. Is a ball in a hole at one end of a field more valuable than a ball on the top of a little stick at the other end of the field? Which is the more valuable condition? A ball in a hole? Or a ball on a stick? A lot of people think that God said that balls in holes are better than balls on sticks. They're called golfers. They think that it is that way, and not that someone made it up... If you forget

ERHARD (*continuing*)

that *you say so*, you do get nutty about it instead of having fun. So yeah, your twenty-six things: wonderful as long as they belong to you.

FRED

I just had the thought standing up here, that if I have so many things going on then I can avoid domination. Because I could always say "I'm too busy. I've got this meeting to go to so I can't go to this other meeting."

ERHARD

Lots of people too busy to do anything. Who in here is too busy to do anything? "I don't get to accomplish anything because I'm too busy."

FRED

I gave up the twenty-six items and I saw that there's no satisfaction in them. I'm driven to them, and there's no sense of empowerment. So I'm actually looking at the wonder of complacency. That it might be just wonderful to go home and watch TV, have a beer and forget about my twenty-six items. There might be more authenticity in relaxing, watching TV with a beer than scrambling after my twenty-six items.

ERHARD

Yeah, and neither one of them is going to get you anyplace.

(*pausing*)

And you're actually going to do what you're going to do anyhow, not what you contemplate doing. You haven't got much choice about it. In fact, none. You can only do what you do; you can't do what you don't do. As soon as I find someone who has done what they didn't do, we're going to stop doing The Forum because it'll be bullshit. So far, looking through half a million people, we haven't found anybody who did what they didn't do. Everyone's only done what they did.

(*to another participant sitting*)

Get that? You ever do anything you didn't do? You only do what you do, right?

PARTICIPANT

I do what I want to do.

ERHARD

You do what you want to do?

PARTICIPANT

Always.

ERHARD

Always?

(*to another participant sitting next to the participant who said she does what she wants to do*)
Sit on her lap, or hold her arms down, or something.

(*the other participant sits on the first participant's lap*)
Now: want to stand up.

(*the participant cannot stand up*)
So, you don't always do what you want to do. And you don't do what you like to do. You do what you do. That's all you ever do. You've always done what you did, and sometimes coincidentally, from time to time it happens to be what you wanted to do.

PARTICIPANT
That's nonsense.

ERHARD
It is nonsensical.

PARTICIPANT
Then why do The Forum?

ERHARD
That's what I said. We're going to stop doing The Forum as soon as I find someone who did something they didn't do.

A participant named Kevin stood, who, during Erhard's conversation with Jacob in the previous session, had complained that the camera pointing at Jacob was also pointing at people in the "no-video" section.

KEVIN
I came to The Forum very skeptical of the whole thing. My feeling was that I would probably get something out of it. I was sure I was going to have to go through so much bullshit I wasn't sure I was going to last it out. As it turned out that was partially true, because I, like a bunch of other people, I sense, I felt like we were being sold the next session at every opportunity. But at this point in the game I'm willing to accept that too. It wasn't as bad as I thought it was going to be. I didn't really start to get into this until yesterday, or maybe it was today. In searching for my racket, I just couldn't seem to find my racket. But during the sharing, I had the feeling that every single person who stood, everyone's racket seemed to be my racket. I couldn't believe it. Today I guess I made a breakthrough.

WES
Hold on. I want to complete this stuff about "I guess I had a breakthrough." I don't mean even the "guess" part. Where are you looking to declare a breakthrough? Where does breakthrough occur?

KEVIN
I felt like I discovered something I didn't know before.

WES (*pointing to his mouth*)
This is where the breakthrough happens. Right here.

ERHARD (*coming forward*)
Wait a second, this is something we need to handle here. Kevin, did you know that you are stingy?

KEVIN
Well, that's kind of a surprise.

ERHARD
I want you to wake up to that. You are stingy, my friend. You think you're precise and careful, but you're actually stingy. You mistake precision and care—which are laudable—for being stingy. You're ungenerous. Not big. It does not enroll people into your view. It alienates people. They don't fuck with you because you're too careful and precise. But they don't like you. It's unattractive and it disempowers you. You've probably got something to give, but nobody will get it from you. People won't "get" from stingy people. I don't require that you discuss that with me.

KEVIN
I don't mind discussing it with you, I just can't really find in my mind where I'm stingy because I don't think that other people feel that I'm stingy. I've got other problems, but I'm searching to find where I'm stingy and I don't see it.

ERHARD
And that's what I want you to do. I want you to stay in the question tonight about being stingy. Are you married?

KEVIN
Yes.

ERHARD
Ask your wife.

(*laughter*)
I don't mean stingy with money. I mean stingy with forwarding the action, stingy with contributing aliveness, stingy with empowerment. Ask your wife, or ask the people that work for you. Okay, please go on. I don't mean to cut you off on that, I just think that it's more useful for you to take a look at it overnight, and if you're wanting to discuss it further I am willing to do that tomorrow. Is that all right with you?

KEVIN
Sure.

ERHARD
Thanks.

KEVIN
Where was I? I was going to share my breakthrough.

ERHARD
You were going to share your "guess" breakthrough.

KEVIN
Now I'm not even sure what a breakthrough is. In any case, I feel like something happened. I don't know.

WES
I don't want to hear that. You're either going to say there was a breakthrough, or you're going to say there wasn't a breakthrough. But there's no guessing. There's no maybe. There's no place to look.

KEVIN
I had a breakthrough because something new and different was happening to me that I hadn't experienced before.

WES
No, you had a breakthrough because you say so.

ERHARD
Kevin, breakthrough is a declaration phenomenon. Do you know the meaning of assertion? The commonplace meaning of assertion?

KEVIN
Yes.

ERHARD.
Breakthrough is not an assertion.

KEVIN
Okay.

ERHARD
It's a declaration.

KEVIN
Okay.

ERHARD
It's a stand one takes in the matter. That's what Wes is discussing with you, to put it in more technical language.

KEVIN
Okay.

ERHARD
That's what he means when he says "It's whatever you say it is."

KEVIN
Okay.

ERHARD
Like a declaration.

KEVIN.
My breakthrough was my racket, finding my racket, which was standing right in front of me all the time, was that I have to do everything: Every goddamned thing in the world for everybody. I even have to run this Forum for you.

(*laughter*)
Now there's going to be some people laughing, but as The Forum went along, I realized that I was running The Forum because The Forum wasn't working out the right way for me, so I was having to make adjustments in The Forum so it was working out right for me. And so I made those adjustments. When I wanted to go to the bathroom, I went to the bathroom. And I tried to come on time, but I was late a couple of times, so I guess that means that I didn't really try.

WES
No it means you were late.

KEVIN (*laughing*)
Sorry I said that.

ERHARD
You did try.

KEVIN
Okay. I have to do everything because everybody around me is ineffective. And I am very good at it. I can do anything. Fix this, make sure everything gets done, and I can't let anybody do anything for me. And I was aware of this, but I never saw this was such a dominant feature of my life as I did until today. At that point it leaves my mind blank.

ERHARD
Kevin, what was the last thing you just said?

KEVIN
I'm afraid to repeat anything I said you might have found interesting.

(*laughter*)
No, I said "At that point it leaves my mind blank."

ERHARD
Got it.

WES
Let me give you some way to look at...

ERHARD
By the way, you're not afraid of me, you're afraid of looking bad.

KEVIN
I'm not afraid of you...

ERHARD
That's right. You're afraid of looking bad.

KEVIN
I'm a little bit afraid of you.

(*laughter*)

ERHARD
I'm going to leave you with that delusion.

(*laughter*)

WES
Inside of what you've said, I'll give you another way of looking at it, or an aspect of it--
something to hang out with tonight along with Werner's comment about your stinginess: you've
been resisting being in a coaching conversation.

KEVIN
Yes.

WES

You're going to do it your way. Now you're not the only one in this room that's going to do it his way or her way. That's human being. And that's the absurdity of human being. Because you've done it all your way and it took you to where you are now—no, sorry—it took you to where you were before The Forum. So if you tell the truth now about where you were before The Forum, you'll see the effectiveness of doing life your way. The planet is full of people doing life their way.

KEVIN

But I've done it more so than anybody else in this room.

WES

Always.

KEVIN

No, I'm dead sure of that. See I have evidence. There's only a few people here who wouldn't allow themselves to be taped. And I've already talked to the other people. I didn't seek them out after that stupid incident here. And I'm getting blocked here.

WES

You're doing great. You're actually getting off it. If I hear you right: you're willing to tell one on yourself, right?

KEVIN

Yeah.

WES

A person who resists a coaching conversation never gets coached. That's got its...

KEVIN

You're a great coach but, excuse me, I'll... I'll only take from you whatever I'm going to take. Everything comes through some sort of filter, and I only take whatever I think is okay for me, and the rest of it I think, for the most part you're on the ball, but where you're a little screwed up there, I'm not going to accept that.

WES

Right, of course. I'm not saying "believe everything." That's not the other side of what I'm saying. But it's not going along with it. We're talking about a coaching conversation.

KEVIN

It's all right. I won't let myself. I'm afraid to put myself in the hands of somebody else completely. Trust somebody completely.

WES
Okay.

KEVIN
I always have to back it up, in every way I can, so that if they screw up I'll have a way to get myself out of the situation.

WES (*shifting back and forth*)
Yeah. So you're like this. One foot kinda in, one foot kinda out? In coaching, right?

KEVIN
Professionally I've been very effective. Been very successful. So why am I here, well because this doesn't work in other aspects of my life.

WES
It may not even work in the area you think it does work.

KEVIN
Well I think there's certain objective evidence there that...

WES
Oh, I know you're successful and all that stuff, but you have no idea of what could have been possible.

KEVIN
Oh yeah, I agree, now, looking back, I can see what I could have done better, if I...

WES
Yeah, not even taking into account who you could be in life.

KEVIN
Right.

WES
Rather than just successful, but who you could be.

(*to the group*)
Kevin's sharing something powerful in telling one on himself. Remember: people resist being coached, so we're not really open to other people's contribution. And to the degree you do that you miss the contribution that's available. Now you can start to see that. You'll always come up with a story that justifies it; there's always a story that justifies it: "I didn't like this"; "they're selling me this"; "they said that"; etc. That's human being.

KEVIN
Oh, I've got a lot of those stories.

WES

And there's another possibility outside the story. And what you got to do to step into it is like you're saying, "surrender into something." I don't like the word... give something up to get in there. To be a willingness to be contributed to, to be generous, to be big, to forward the action...

KEVIN

I feel like I need to risk something.

WES

Yes.

KEVIN

And a... I'm going to have to risk something that is really, really important to me, and I'm not even sure what that's going to be at this point. That's going to be really tough. That's going to be real tough because I don't risk anything.

KIPP

Keeping yourself that closed up, that's what's been tough. Couldn't be any tougher than you are doing now.

KEVIN

Well, I don't think I have a story beyond that.

WES

Here's what I'm asking. Look at this conversation about being generous, about being big, about being coachable, look at this thing about what you're willing to risk. Tonight. And come back and share it tomorrow.

KEVIN

Okay.

KIPP

What is this thing you have about being video- taped?

KEVIN

Well, I'm really surprised that more people don't want to be videotaped. I don't trust you. I'm not willing to be videotaped because I don't trust the organization, WE & A. Because I think you'll fuck it up, one way or the other. And once it's on tape, there it is, there's a lot that you can do with it. A lot can happen to it. I lose control of it. So I don't want to lose control again. So I don't see why I should be videotaped, that's for your benefit. It's not helping me. I came here to help me.

KIPP

And to be clear I am not advocating that you should be videotaped. Just between you and me I couldn't quite get what it was all about. So I needn't find out.

Waiting for the Leap

Central to a dialogue for the presencing of Being, says Heidegger, is the abandonment of a "thirst for knowledge and greed for explanations"; we must, instead, be willing to *wait*, and to "abide in hope before what is worthy of thought" ("DL" in *OWL* 13). Therefore it is of interest that, at one point in his dialogue with the Japanese scholar, even Heidegger expresses impatience with his partner's enigmatic hesitation: "I shall not hide from you that you are throwing me into a state of great agitation," says Heidegger, "especially because all my efforts to get an answer to my question from language experts and linguistic scholars of language have so far been in vain" ("DL" in *OWL* 28).

Heidegger's agitation may give comfort to those of us who, thrown to the efficient formulation of definitions and concepts, nevertheless aspire to true philosophic dialogue—conversations that in the vernacular allow for "deep thinking." Such dialogue, which thinks its way into the unknown and trusts the dialogue itself to find a way out, is a challenging undertaking, especially as a form of pedagogical inquiry.

The balance of mutuality and directedness in ontological dialogue is one of the distinctions developed in the unspoken background of The Forum, and of this book.

The intention that generates ontological dialogue is the thinking of the unthought, and ultimately the unthinkable. Paradoxically, such thinking occurs both slowly and suddenly. As Werner Erhard has put it, you don't get it and you don't get it and you don't get it—for a long time—and then you get it, all at once. This is the moment of insight that Heidegger calls *Augenblick*—a moment of vision—and he says it occurs as a *leap*:

> **There is no bridge here—only the leap. [. . .] The leap alone takes us into the neighborhood where thinking resides. [. . .] In contrast to a steady progress, where we move unawares from one thing to the next and everything remains alike, the leap takes us abruptly to where everything is different, so different that it strikes us as strange. [. . .] Though we may not founder in such a leap, what the leap takes us to will confound us. (*WCT* 8, 12)**

On the other hand, he cautions:

> **Leap and vision require long, slow preparation. . . . (*WCT* 233)**
> **Nobody can in just one single leap take distance from the predominant circle of ideas, especially not if he is dealing with the well-worn tracks of traditional thinking—tracks that fade into realms where they can hardly be seen. ("DL" in *OWL* 36)**
> **Only one who takes the right running start can leap. Everything is decided by this run, for it means that we ourselves actually *ask* the questions again, and that we, in these questions, first create the perspectives. (*IM* 196)**

Yet it is important to remember, again, that while we are on the way to language and thinking, we are always *within* language and thinking. Therefore the paradox and reflexivity continues, once we have made that leap:

KEVIN
What the reaction was all about?

KIPP
No, exactly what you said, that you didn't trust. The way you got trust, trust isn't available. Trust to you is accounting.

KEVIN
Right.

KIPP
So when you're bored, you get this big accounting sheet with everybody's name on it.

Kipp did an entertaining demonstration of Kevin's view of trust: as a matter of accounting, using a list he carried with him crossing people off whom he did not trust.

KIPP (*continuing*)
And you walk down the path of life, with your little pad with everybody's name on it, and "you remember twelve years ago we were working on that thing, I wanted to do that thing, but you got to and I didn't?"

(*crossing off that person's name on an imagined list*)
"Seventeen years ago, that company picnic, you walked over to the boss and started talking to him? And he stopped talking to me?"

(*crossing off another person's name; pointing at another person*)
"You didn't do anything but someone with a beard like that did."

(*crossing yet another name off the list, to laughter*)
That's what you call trust.

KEVIN
But my list is way longer.

KIPP
There's no trust there, just adding up and keeping track.

KEVIN
That's right.

KIPP
Trust. I'm inviting you to consider that maybe, trust is simply, "I trust you."

KEVIN

But I don't.

KIPP

That's right. I didn't say to. I'm not manipulating you into trusting. I'm not advocating it…

ERHARD

He's not going to get that because he still doesn't get the distinction between assertion and declaration. Kevin, did you know that you did your whole number in your response to Kipp? You did "stingy"; you did "don't risk"; you did "nobody does it right."

KEVIN

Yeah.

ERHARD

Like counting down. That was totally automatic.

KEVIN

Yeah.

ERHARD

Not one thing you said had a shred of intelligence in it. I want you to listen to what I'm saying. It was not an expression of your intelligence. It was not an expression of your common sense. It was an expression of your act—limited completely to your act. You had no choice in the matter. It was not some product of an intelligent choice or a commonsensical choice.

KEVIN

I'll accept that.

WES

So you got the assignment?

KEVIN

Yes.

WES

I just want to acknowledge your willingness to be in this conversation.

KEVIN

I just wanted to say to everyone else in the auditorium, that I'm safe to be around. It's not that bad.

 And where have we leapt? Perhaps into an abyss? No! Rather, onto some firm soil. Some? No! But on that soil upon which we live and die, if we are honest with ourselves. A curious, indeed unearthly thing that *we must first leap onto the soil on which we really stand.* (WCT 41, emphasis added)

In distinguishing the leap, Heidegger continues the reflexivity that characterizes his thought: we leap to where we already are.

In *Being and Time*, he says that Dasein "*is* existentially that which, in its potentiality-for-Being, it is *not yet*. . . . [O]nly because it *is* what it becomes (or alternatively, does not become), can it say to itself 'Become what you are' and say this with understanding" (*BT* 185–186). Scholar Joan Stambaugh calls this movement of thinking an "ongoing reaching that belongs to what it reaches" (*ID* 14).

As we have noted elsewhere, such reflexivity is central to the thinking of Zen, as Erhard has observed: "In Zen, one is working toward enlightenment from and in a context of already being enlightened" (Bartley 125). ∎

(*applause*)

At this point Jane raised her hand. When she stood, her appearance was strikingly different, and the participants applauded.

> **ERHARD** (*to Jane*)
> Do you know what they're clapping about?

> **JANE**
> No.

(*laughter*)

> **ERHARD**
> People don't clap for ugly worthless people, do they?

> **JANE**
> No.

> **ERHARD**
> So you know what they're clapping about?

> **JANE**
> Yeah.

> **ERHARD**
> They're clapping in part due to your attractiveness, which comes from your being a big, generous person.

> **JANE**
> Hmm hhmmm.

(*laughter*)

> **ERHARD**
> You got that didn't you? You've been big and generous in our conversations, haven't you?

> **JANE**
> Yeah.

> **ERHARD**
> Good. Nothing to be embarrassed about there. Nothing to be caught in. They're also clapping for another kind of generosity and that's the generosity that they think they see and that I think I see in your beginning to get off it. Like getting off your act about being worthless. All those other things.

JANE
Yeah.

ERHARD
You think you're getting off that? Being ugly and worthless?

JANE
In some ways, but it'll probably still be with me.

ERHARD
You're saying that you're getting off it but that in some ways it'll probably still be with you?

JANE
Yeah.

ERHARD
Couple things. First off, there's the difference between apes and you and me: you and me have "probablys." The ape doesn't have any probablys, because the ape doesn't have—listen up here—don't get sucked in by her attractiveness...

(*laughter*)
The ape doesn't have any "probablys" because the ape doesn't have any language. Only you and I have probablys. And we invent those probablys with our mouths. We don't know that. We think we're inventing probablys by extrapolating the past into the future. You understand the word "extrapolate"?

JANE
No.

ERHARD
Extending the past into the future? You know you take a line that goes like this...

(*drawing a line in the air*)
And then it goes like that. You're extending the line from the past into the future.

JANE
Yeah.

ERHARD
So, you and I think that we say probably based on this mental operation called extending the past into the future. And that's why you said "probably" to me, is it not?

JANE
Yeah.

ERHARD
Because given your past you're probably not going to get off it entirely, are you?

JANE
Yes.

ERHARD
And that's sensible and intelligent dealing with the future as an extension of the past. Did you follow what I said?

JANE
A little.

ERHARD
When you said "I probably wouldn't get off it entirely," I said that was an intelligent, sensible extension of your past into the future.

JANE
Okay.

ERHARD
Good. Now there's a particular discussion I want to have with you now. Our previous discussions have been for your benefit. This one I'm having for the benefit of the group. I think you have something to contribute here; that you will be an example that will illustrate what I want people to be able to see as powerfully as anybody else in The Forum could illustrate it. I want to be straight with you and tell you that so that I can find out if you're willing to have this discussion with me. And you won't know what that discussion is; you'll have to take a chance. I'm not saying you won't get any value out of it, because you may. I suspect you will. Probably.

(*Jane smiles*)
Anybody see her smile like that before? Okay, so, you with me? Ready to do this?

JANE
Yeah.

ERHARD
Earlier we talked about when you were four, five, or six, and what it looked like for someone of that age for your mother to be taken away... you get that it would look that way for a child that age, that "my mother left me, or abandoned me, or she was taken away"? By the way, it doesn't make any difference that she can't remember that. Remember you told me you couldn't remember that very clearly? But we know it happened and that somebody either told you or you figured it out. It's not something you remember directly, right?

JANE
Yeah.

ERHARD
Right. That's there more powerfully than what she remembers. Is there anybody who doesn't understand what I just said? Stand up.

(*a participant standing up*)
I said, what's there when it's not recognized—I hate this word but I'm going to use it because it's getting late and I want people to understand—what's there and unconscious is there more powerfully in terms of its ability to shape your behavior and your feelings and thoughts than what's there and is conscious. You got that?

PARTICIPANT
Yeah, I got it.

ERHARD
Okay, so that's there whether she remembers it or not. And then there was this woman who came in and broke the bond, which was your haven, with your father.

JANE
Yes.

ERHARD
Good. And I said that... I first asked if you made any decisions. You remember that?

(*many participants replying "yes"*)

Whatever it was, she made some decision. And I said this was a critical point, this was something that everybody's got to get. I said: "we talk about it like 'I decided,' and maybe you did, but what really happened is that you became huh huh huh huh huh... You *became* that 'I'm worthless.' It's not merely 'I decided.' That's not forceful enough. It's: you *became* 'I'm worthless.'" You remember that, vaguely?

JANE
A little.

ERHARD
Okay, good.

ERHARD (*to the group*)
You remember that?

(*many responding "yes"*)

Remember I said "you become something." You *are* worthless. Or to say it with a little bit more rigor: You now *are* that you are worthless. Everybody got that? Anybody didn't get that? Okay good. Now what we're going to look at is where did all this mess get generated? Why would anybody be stupid enough to generate the kind of mess you got? Anybody not clear there's a mess here? Do we need to get more mess up for you? Everybody's got a mess. People in here are in good shape to start with, and still we've got a mess. Can you imagine what it would be like for somebody who is in bad shape? We screen out people who are in bad shape. We only let people in here who are in good shape. Most people who have participated in our programs are above average in their adjustment to life; they are able to handle life on average. What we're going to look at here is where did this mess come from?

(*pausing*)

Now you've got to get back to where Jane was. I said I want you to be standing in being a four-, five-, six-year-old and I want you to tell me—I want to know-what it looked like from there. So you want to get there in order to get this. You've got to be a little girl whose mother is gone. Either abandoned her or taken away from her, whose only place of belonging is in her relationship with her father. And that bond that represents for her the only place of belonging, which represents for her "home"—I don't mean a building with a family in it—I mean a home, like *being* home, home. Being home, home. And that bond, which represents being home: home is broken. And so what do you suppose you decide when that happens? You got any idea what you decided when things got to be that rotten?

JANE

I think I decided not to love her and ignore her.

ERHARD

Yeah. Very good. And you've been working over on top of that trying to be good about, trying to love her and trying to respect her? Yes?

JANE

Yes. But I can't do it.

ERHARD

Yeah. That's what you decided about the situation. What did you decide about life? Can you remember? Take a look.

JANE

I would try to outdo her so my dad would like me more than her.

ERHARD

Yeah. That's great. So that's looking into the situation. You decided that about the situation with your stepmom. What I want to know and what I want you to look at Jane is if you can see what you decided about life itself. Take a look and see what you decided about life itself.

ERHARD (*to the group*)

And what you want to be doing is being a four-, five-, six-year-old girl whose mother was taken away or abandoned her and whose only place of belonging, her only place to be, like be at home, was her father and that just got smashed. What did you decide about life? You see, you made all those decisions like she made about herself and about her stepmother, and about how she was gonna deal with her stepmother, and all that stuff. What I want to know now is what you decided about life.

(*to a participant with raised hand*)

I don't want an answer; I want you to think.

(*indicating Jane*)

She'll answer: you think.

(*to Jane*)

Remember what you decided about life? "I decided..."

JANE

Not to be worthless.

ERHARD

You mean, try to overcome being worthless.

JANE

Yeah.

ERHARD

That's what you decided about yourself. What did you decide about life?

JANE

I don't know.

ERHARD

Okay good.

(*to the group*)

So I'm going to tell you what you decided about life, because you've got one of those. You may have been three when you made that decision, or ten, or eleven, or twelve, but everybody in the room made the same decision in some circumstance similar to that which Jane just described. The only obvious decision such a child could possibly make... And that decision is *there is something wrong here*. Where? Where is there something wrong? Not you. That's the part you already told us about. There's something wrong here: in life! *There's something wrong here. Something is off.* There's something wrong! Can you see that would be an inevitable conclusion for some eleven-on-down-year-old person? You think about it for a second. If I get you as a

A Violent Way

"The word 'way,'" says Heidegger, "probably is an ancient primary word that speaks to the reflective mind of man" ("NL" in *OWL* 92). The central notion behind Heidegger's use of "way" to designate his process of thinking calls for action and vigilance to maintain ground gained:

> To clear a way, for instance across a snow-covered field, is in the Alemannic-Swabian dialect still called *wëgen* even today. This verb, used transitively, means: to form a way and, forming it, to keep it ready. Way-making understood in this sense no longer means to move something up and down a path which is already there. It means to bring the way. . . forth first of all, and thus to *be* the way. ("WL" in *OWL* 129–30)

One *is* the way oneself, since until one advances there is no way.

This perspective of his own work emerged early on in Heidegger's career as a professor of philosophy. Here he describes his development of this perspective, as it occurred for him during a course he taught early in his career:

> **. . . the course was most imperfect. Yet there was quickening in it the attempt to walk a path of which I did not know where it would lead. I knew only the most immediate short-range perspectives along that path, because they beckoned to me unceasingly, while the horizon shifted and darkened more than once.**
> **("DL" in *OWL* 6)**

This is the first of three points that we want to stress here about Heidegger's *way*: that in entering upon the way to Being, one is jumping off into the unknown. This is necessary because the thinking of Being cannot be understood in advance of its being thought. Therefore its undertaking is *necessarily* an advance into what is not known. But it is important to note that this advance into the unknown is *not* simply thinking about some thought content which we do not yet understand, something that we know we don't know. That would be equivalent to examining new territory using a map; but Heidegger has no map. Werner Erhard has made this point about his own work: in such thinking, we are not merely traveling in uncharted waters, but in water that does not always act like water ("Heart of the Matter").

This is an important point for Heidegger: to be on the way we must free ourselves from our subservience to the "common comprehension," which is "convinced it was born comprehending everything" (*WCT* 77). We must give up judging each new thought on the basis of whether it is consistent with our old thoughts, a tendency which is pernicious in our current mode of thinking.

big, tough, mature, intelligent adult, and I get you into a bad enough set of circumstances, you ever remember saying to yourself, "life is fucked"? You see how easy that conclusion is for a three-year-old, four-year-old, five-year-old? What would it take to come to that conclusion for a three-, four-, or five-year-old? Nobody comes to your party. Your mother's mean to you. Almost anything, right? Real easy, right? Not only easy, it's inevitable. And it's not merely inevitable circumstantially. I'm not going to demonstrate this part to you, I'm just going to tell you. So I'm not asking you to accept it or believe it: It's the already always being of human beings—that there is something wrong. If you're a human being, you are that there's something wrong waiting to happen. Now forget that, because I'm not going to give you enough evidence of that to make it clear. But I just want you to hear it. What I want you to get is that it's inevitable circumstantially. When you were growing up you had a circumstance in which the inevitable conclusion was, would have to be, "there is something *wrong* here!" There's something wrong innately, profoundly, deeply, at the foundation, there's something wrong! Life is constituted—you don't think in these terms, but—life is constituted as something wrong. Something's wrong! And you don't make that decision. You *are* that there's something wrong. Now, you don't get that yet; you're not supposed to get that yet. You're supposed to follow what I'm saying.

(*posturing as the voice in a participant's "head"*)
"Gee, I don't know. I don't think that I'm 'that there's something wrong.' I see what you're saying Werner, I see that it's logical that I would have to have come to that conclusion in my childhood, like a way of being. But gee I don't get that 'there's something wrong.' I mean, I actually think there's a lot of right things. I mean, I don't live my life out of 'there's something wrong.'"

(*returning to his own voice*)
That's what you should be saying to yourself, unless it's already obvious to you that who you are is that there's something wrong. For most of you that won't be obvious yet. What I said will be obvious: that there is in your childhood and in your early childhood the circumstances in which you as a child would have to come to the inevitable conclusion that there is something wrong in life. That part I know you can see. The part you can't see yet is how to fit that into today. So we're going to fit that into today for you now. Jane, so, what I said made sense? Like you decided there was something wrong?

JANE
Yes.

ERHARD
You answered the question I asked: Did it make sense?

JANE
Yes.

ERHARD
You got any recollection of having made that kind of decision?

JANE
No, I don't.

ERHARD
Okay, thank you. You can sit down now if you want.

(*applause as Jane sits*)

ERHARD
You became that there's something wrong. The question is: What did you do about it? The answer is that from there on out, everything you did, everything you are, most particularly what you're really good at, was a response to, a way of dealing with, that there's something wrong! Your best moments, what you're best at, what you're most confident at, the best things in your life... You got married—listen up!—you got married because there's something wrong. It was a way to deal with that there's something wrong. No shit. I didn't say your marriage wasn't wonderful. Your marriage may be the greatest thing that ever happened, but you got married because there's something wrong. You had kids because there's something wrong. You chose your profession because there's something wrong. You live your life because there's something wrong. And you developed the answers—that you got to what to do about the fact that there's something wrong—to a very high level. You're really good at a lot of things, aren't you? Really! There are things you are really good at. The things you're really good at—listen up. I know you don't get it yet—the things you're really good at started out, had their genesis, are at the source a way of dealing with that there's something wrong. Here's the evidence for my assertion: nothing satisfies you. Nothing satisfies you. The things that you're good at don't satisfy, don't nurture you, don't fulfill you, don't leave you full of joy. They gratify you, because they make up for the fact that something's wrong. But they don't fulfill you, don't leave you full of joy, don't leave you fulfilled. They don't leave you complete. Did you ever notice, you're never complete? Never. No matter what you accomplish. No matter what you build, no matter what you create, no matter what pleasure or accomplishment or satisfaction there is in your life, it's never enough.

(*Erhard moves around the room, speaking very loudly and forcefully*)

And it's never enough because you're never going to be anything enough. You see, this is the other side of the coin. We were talking about the bad stuff before. I'm talking about the good stuff. I'm talking about the good stuff in your life: you know, your marriage, your romance, your love affair, the job that you're very good at, that you've really developed your real skills in. The stuff in life that people can really count on you for. Your contributions to other people, the difference you've made in life: that's also only in the service of making up for the fact that you *are* that there's something wrong. The evidence for that assertion is that even the things that you're the best at, even the things that are the finest part of you, like your contributions to other people, like the difference you've made for other people, like the sacrifices you've made for the benefit of other people—you know, you raised children all your life and you've done a great job at it, and it's still fucking not enough. You know you gave, gave, gave, and after a while you stop giving, because it's not enough to make up for "there's something wrong here." Yeah. Nothing. Nothing. Nothing's good enough for you, because nothing is *for* being good enough. Nothing is

Clearly, in a thinking that requires our familiar way of thinking to be put under the possibility of deconstruction or erasure, one is inherently at *risk*. This point was made repeatedly by Heidegger, and is central to the rhetorical strategy of Werner Erhard. The identity, the subject, the *cogito*, which is presently dominating the clearing and thus confounding the appearing of Being, *does not want to be displaced*. In clearing our "there," in unconcealing the clearing, we render our subjectivity homeless: this is essential, since in our being "put out of the home in this way, the home first discloses itself as such." Thus the event of unconcealment is also "the happening through which human beings become homeless" (*IM* 186). Always on the way, we have no home. No wonder we resist.

In *Being and Time*, in a passage which Erhard has quoted, Heidegger states that any attempt to analyze Being "constantly has the character of *doing violence*, whether to the claims of the everyday interpretation, or to its complacency and its tranquilized obviousness" (*BT* 359; quoted in "Heart of the Matter"). Heidegger has further expressed this violent characteristic by describing the opening for Being, not as a sylvan and tranquil clearing, but as the turbulent battleground of a breach: "Historical humanity's Being-here means: Being-posited as the breach into which the excessive violence of Being breaks in its appearing, so that this breach itself shatters against Being" (*IM* 181). The sense of "historical" here is not that of mere facts and trivia; rather, it has to do with the making of history that occurs in moments when the way in which a human being understands itself transforms, leaps from identifying with what Erhard has termed the "story" to Being-in-the-world as a new possibility for Being. Any transformation threatens what is already there—held in place as it is by the "they" self who seeks to reduce, or level down, Being to accommodate the averageness of the everyday.

Thus, this fundamentally threatening nature of unconcealment produces in Dasein what Heidegger calls the "will to conquer that at the same time shrinks back" (*IM* 196). The task at hand is forbidding: to be on the way, Dasein must engage in a violent struggle to wrest Being from unconcealment, and in the struggle must risk itself essentially. "Here," writes Heidegger,

> **the uncanniest possibility of Dasein shows itself: to break the excessive violence of Being through Dasein's ultimate act of violence against itself. Dasein does not have this possibility as an empty way out, but it *is* this possibility insofar as it is; for as Dasein, it must indeed shatter against Being in every act of violence. (*IM* 197)**

As we show in our series of sidebars on Technology (during the third and final session of Day Four), The Forum provides an opportunity for Dasein's calculative machinations to be seen for what they are, and the game is up. Yet only through this struggle can Dasein *become* itself, and serve its constitutive role as the site for the disclosure of Being: the struggle is "an act of violence *against* the overwhelming, but at the same time always and only *for* it" (*IM* 196).

Heidegger has at times described this ongoing struggle in oppressive terminology:

> **Dasein is the constant urgency of defeat and of the renewed resurgence of the act of violence against Being, in such a way that the almighty sway of Being violates Dasein (in the literal sense), makes Dasein into the site of its appearing, envelops and pervades Dasein in its sway, and thereby holds it within Being. (*IM* 198)**

In his later work, it must be noted, Heidegger's languaging of unconcealment is less violent: it is articulated more gently as a turning-toward Being, a *releasement* of and into Being. However, we emphasize the element of resistance here (as has Heidegger) because such resistance characterizes much of the dialogue in The Forum (as well as many discussions of Erhard himself). Erhard does not attempt to minimize this resistance; in fact, he acts strategically to *unconceal* it. For instance, early on Day One of The Forum, after confronting the participant Bill concerning being pressured to be in The Forum, Erhard asked, "Why was I bad with

for being complete. Everything is *for* making up for that there's something wrong here. What gives you your life—more accurately, sorry, more accurately—what gives you your self, what gives you your identity, the person you've built yourself into being, was built in response to

(*speaking each syllable with equally intense emphasis*)
that there is some-thing pro-found-ly wrong. Now if you need evidence, what you've got to use for evidence is "what is it that's left you full of joy?" What is it? Look, there are eight hundred people in here in this room. There's got to be some pretty remarkable accomplishments in this room. People of remarkable accomplishment; there's got to be people in here who have made ridiculous contributions. There's got to be people in here who have saved people's lives, there's got to be people in here who have nurtured people's lives, there's got to be people in here who have impacted whole communities, there may be people here who have made important, significant contributions to countries, and there's not one person in here satisfied. Not one person in here truly, completely, wholly fulfilled. Not one person in here full of joy. That's my evidence.

(*calling on a participant*)

PARTICIPANT (*Forum leader 8*)
I've done some looking at this and I have a question and we can use me as a case in point. When I was in the third or fourth grade, a few things happened close together, where I got really embarrassed, and I decided that no one was going to embarrass me that way again. No one is ever going to laugh at me again. Out of that I became a master student, head of the class, straight A's all the way through college. Awards, degrees, all sorts of honors and no satisfaction. My first wife made a fool of me and so in my second marriage I married someone that would never leave me. It's all a solution to "no one is ever going to make a fool of me again."

ERHARD
Right.

PARTICIPANT (*Forum leader 8*)
So all the things you're saying I can really see in my life, where what could really be accomplishments are I'm making a point and I'm making sure there's no satisfaction.

ERHARD
Right because there's no satisfaction in compensating for being "there's something profoundly wrong here." All you do is what? Reinforce down there at the bottom that there's something wrong here.

(*asking a participant to stand up; Erhard pushes against his shoulders*)
It's kind of like this: whatever you're pushing up against, you're attached to. I'm attached to him, just as surely if he held me close to him. In fact I'm more attached to him than if he held me close to him because he doesn't have to do any of the work; I do all the work.

ERHARD (*continuing*)
(*participant sits down*)
So if your accomplishments are there as an answer to that there's something wrong, to make up for that there's something wrong, to deal with that there's something wrong, then the more you accomplish the more powerfully the context—listen!—the more powerfully the context that there's something wrong is established. See look...

(*moving to the chalk board.*)
Remember the two circles, "tall" in two contexts? Suppose the context is "there is something wrong." The more content you build, the more achievement, the more accomplishment, the more content builds, the more fulfilled the context becomes. Anybody who can't see that?

SUZANNE
I don't understand.

ERHARD
Okay, thank you.

SUZANNE
I don't understand the statement that the more achievement one has, that there's something wrong.

ERHARD
Good. Did you see that she asked the question very precisely? Real big opening to get the answer. What I said was that "that there's something wrong" becomes—you become that there's something wrong; you are that there is something wrong. In other words, "that there is something wrong" is the clearing in which life happens now. It's the opening for life to occur. It's the space in which everything arises. You clear about that statement so far? That's not the answer yet, but are you clear about that so far?

SUZANNE
Is it, "that there's something wrong," is it the cause and the achievement is the effect? Or...

ERHARD
Not quite, no. Sorry. The answer is no, and it's like that, but it's not that. It's "that there's something wrong" is the context, and the achievement is the content in that context.

SUZANNE
So, the achievement is not an effect of "there's something wrong." It's a context.

ERHARD
It is a content of the context "there is something wrong." See hold on for a second. This business about cause and effect you and I understand, and are very comfortable with. You don't have to think that, you have those thoughts. You think in a cause/effect world. But the world of

you just now? Because I want to get this story up. There's a lot of people with that story here and I want to get that story killed." This unconcealing clears the way for the *appropriation* of the resistance: participants in the dialogue, by recognizing, allowing, and owning their resistance, *become who they are*, in preparation for the disclosure of their possibility.

Lest the view of Dasein as scene-of-violent-unconcealment be taken as unduly negative, Heidegger adds an important point:

 This [talk of violence] looks like pessimism. But it would be preposterous to label Greek Dasein with this term—not because the Greeks were somehow optimists at bottom after all, but because these assessments miss Greek Dasein altogether. The Greeks were, to be sure, more pessimistic than a pessimist can ever be. They were also more optimistic than any optimist. Their historical Dasein had not yet entered the realm of pessimism and optimism. (*IM* 197–198)

This way of thinking, in which relatedness with Being allows the transcendence of subjective value dualities, appears to come into play within Heidegger's and Erhard's ethics. While the results of The Forum, to whatever degree they manifest themselves in participants' lives, are certainly played out in the moral arena, morals (and their contemporary variation, "values") are an ontic issue, and the *essential* content of The Forum is ontological.

Here we think Joseph J. Kockelmans, synthesizing Heidegger, expresses Erhard's view as well: "Every *valuing*, even if it values in a positive manner, is and remains a subjectivizing; it does not let beings be. To call God the highest value is to degrade the true essence of God" (*On the Truth of Being* 258). Being is not moral. Being "is" not anything except Being.

The rhetorical conversation of The Forum, rather than taking morality as its content, approaches morality indirectly, by way of Being. Here, we wish to underline Heidegger's point: that the violence of the act of unconcealing Being is the "flip side" of the attainment of the clearing of *aletheia* (please see the sidebar "The Three Levels of Truth" in Session Two of Day Four). Both positive and negative, emergence and concealment, violence and *aletheia*, are constitutive of Being. This idea is worked out most fully in Heidegger's conception of the "Nothing." ■

being is not like that quite. There's causality too, but there's a more subtle relationship, one of context and content. Contexts don't *cause* contents. The relationship is not one of causality. It's a different relationship. But it's like cause and effect, but not the same.

SUZANNE

I'm equating achievement as power.

ERHARD

I don't have any problem with that. However, achievement, even as power, in the context "there's something wrong," each achievement reinforces the context: the more achievement, the stronger, more forceful the context. As you build content, you validate the context. So for example, if I say two, and three, they're content in the context called numbers. You follow that?

SUZANNE

Yes I follow that.

ERHARD

Very good. If I go on to seventy-four, ninety-nine, one third, and three point one four, I've expanded the amount of content, and by doing so I've validated the context called numbers. The context called numbers has gotten stronger and stronger. Even if the content is empowering, nevertheless the context is more and more validated. Clear?

SUZANNE

There is an aspect in that logic on what's wrong: that area I'd like to explore.

ERHARD

Please.

SUZANNE

I don't see... I still don't understand that statement. I'd like to go deeper. But then, not that I'm confused. I got an equation of the earlier, I never, I don't want to share. But this particular premise strikes me because of achievement, the word achievement I equate with power.

ERHARD

First off, you've got your foot nailed to the floor about achievement a little bit—like some of you had your foot nailed to the floor about God and some of you had your foot nailed to the floor about sincerity—it's kind of like you have idolized accomplishment a bit. Accomplishment is kind of like the Holy Grail for you. A little bit, and so it makes the conversation a little bit hard for you to hear. A little bit it sounds like I'm denigrating accomplishment. I'm actually not denigrating accomplishment, but never mind, it sounds like I am. Does it not?

SUZANNE

It did at the beginning.

ERHARD

Sure. So it makes the conversation a bit hard for you to hear. But now that we've said that let's do what you asked to have done and take a deeper look.

SUZANNE

Yes.

ERHARD

So, did it make sense—was it valid for you—what I said that you and I and everybody else, as little girls or boys, had experiences in which it's entirely logically, so powerfully logical, so predictable that we're going to conclude that there's something wrong, that we could all accept that at some point in our childhood we did conclude that there's something wrong here? Or was that the logic you were questioning?

SUZANNE

I'm not going to add to that statement. That's a period. There's something wrong here. But in addendum you said "there's something wrong here and the achievement is there." That premise is correct.

ERHARD

Okay good, I'm just trying to find out where the sticking point is.

SUZANNE

I agree with that premise.

ERHARD

So then I said that it's not a mere conclusion, I said that you *become* that there is something wrong. You are that there is something wrong. You know, you're a four-year-old, a five-year-old, and *become* that there's something wrong and it becomes the shaping ground of being for everything you built. See, you built a Suzanne, and I built a Werner, and he built whoever he is. And I did it over years. I had a certain aspect of me built by the time I was five. I had another aspect of myself built by the time I was nine. By the time I was seventeen I was pretty much built. Everything I've done since I was seventeen has been additive. I've gotten a little better, or a lot better at those things I was good at, or the things I could be good at. In any case, around that age, seventeen or twenty, they've built their persona, they've built an identity, they've built a self. Okay, I said that that self that I built was built in response to the ground of being called there is something wrong here.

SUZANNE

For this moment I will accept that and think about it.

ERHARD

Okay. Let me just give you one thing. That's an assertion. And an assertion deserves evidence, because an assertion is a promise that I've got evidence. So I'm going to give you my evidence.

My evidence is that your best and my best moments, my talents, the "what I'm good at," the "what I can be counted on"—including getting married, a good moment; having children, raising children, a good moment; doing well in my job, a good moment: I'm talking about the stuff... I use to generate achievement. The exercise of *that* does not leave me full, whole, complete, full of joy. It's gratifying. God knows that whenever I have an accomplishment, I feel great: a couple of moments, a couple of hours, a couple of days, a couple of weeks, maybe even a year. But at some point I'm back to: that wasn't enough.

SUZANNE

So where is the satisfaction?

ERHARD

The level of satisfaction is that there's *no* full satisfaction. There's no being complete with life. One is always incomplete. It's the conversation we had earlier about someday. See, someday, someday I'm going to contribute enough, achieve enough, to have made it. No. Because every accomplishment makes the context—there's something wrong here—bigger, more stronger, more valid, all that below the level of awareness. See up at the level of awareness I'm developing myself and being a decent human being and making some sort of contribution, and taking care of myself and taking care of the people around me. That's all content, that's all foreground. The context, the background, which is reinforced by every achievement, is "there is something wrong here." What that leads to is never being satisfied. Ever. Never being full of joy. Never. Never being complete never being whole. Life is always incomplete. And life is lived as a struggle to be complete, to finally be satisfied. So that's my evidence. It doesn't prove what I said, because you can't prove an assertion. But it does validate it.

SUZANNE

So it's best to assume that in anything we do we have that, we don't get satisfied. There's more. I should assume that there should be more.

ERHARD

I'm not saying you should assume that, I'm saying we live like that. You and I and the other eight hundred people sitting in this room and the other half a million people that I've worked with.

SUZANNE

So that follows the logic that life is meaningless and empty, and therefore if life is meaningless and empty, it is zero. Zero.

ERHARD

I don't want to make the conclusion you made. Yes, what we are saying here is entirely harmonic with that life is meaningless and empty. You see it got to be pretty clear that everybody's soap opera was bullshit, meaningless and empty, now I want to get it clear that the rest of it is bullshit: the good parts. I want you to see where they come from. So that you get that the whole thing is meaningless and empty. It's not that I want it to be that way. It is that way.

SUZANNE
Yes. I get you.

ERHARD
Thank you very much.

(*returning to The Forum leader who had shared about living life in order not to be embarrassed*)
What did you say to get us started down this conversation with Suzanne? Is there anybody left that doesn't get that as you built the content called accomplishment and contribution, you are reinforcing the context for that contribution, which context is "there's something wrong." Is that clear for everybody?

PARTICIPANT (*Forum leader 8*)
So I wouldn't be so foolish as to ask how to get out of this predicament.

ERHARD
Yeah, because you don't.

PARTICIPANT (*Forum Leader 8*)
I'm too smart I guess.

ERHARD
You see: What do you do about being dead?

(*laughter*)
Nothing. See it's not a bad thing to know that you're dead when you're dead. You lie down. You know that there are some dead people in the room? There are actually some dead people in here–walking around bolt upright, dead though. There are people in here who have killed themselves. They didn't kill their bodies, they killed their selves. Their bodies walk around but they are dead. There are dead people in here. You might even find out that you were dead. That would be good news because then you could lie down and relax.

(*laughter*)

PARTICIPANT (*Forum leader 9*)
So one of the surprises for me in this Forum is that yesterday I saw that my racket is that I'm a victim...

ERHARD
This is very surprising to hear from a guy like this. Very accomplished, very able guy.

PARTICIPANT (*Forum leader 9*)
And I've always disliked victims. So other than, so tonight for dinner, after the series of meetings I ended up that there was nobody to go to dinner with, and the violins begin to come

out. And true to what you said yesterday it occurred to me that this was me running my victim racket. I laughed at myself for a moment. And then I went to find some people to go have dinner with.

ERHARD

See, hold on a second. He's a little bit ahead of us. I almost wish he didn't say that because now he's leaked out the truth, and you'll latch on to that real fast. That'll be the new prison bars. When you get that it's empty and meaningless you see things you've never seen before. As long as you're stuck with your soap opera you can't see those things. For instance, if who you are is that people are unable, you can't see the opportunities to develop their ability. And you can't see their ability. As soon as you get that that's your racket, as soon as you get that whole soap opera that you've got to do everything your self because there's nobody around able enough to do it, you begin to see things you didn't see before. Now, I shouldn't have told you that, you see, because you'll spend the whole night trying to figure out how to get out of the trap. And you'll come in here tomorrow all stuck in the trap again. We'll have to spend the whole day getting you out of the trap. And then we'll have to do an extra day of The Forum with you all. Go ahead.

PARTICIPANT (*Forum leader 9*)

So I'm actually not going to ask the question now. But what I have gotten, and just to share, one is that some people's coaching for me recently is to take myself a little less seriously and I can hear the room to be that way now. Secondly, is I've been able to share myself with people, Werner, not like something happened.

ERHARD

To speak himself. Not in-order-to.

PARTICIPANT (*Forum leader 9*)

I can see as a graduate, staff member, and Forum leader candidate, that that's probably something for all of us to take on, the sharing in-order-to business.

ERHARD

Good. Thank you.

(*applause*)

ALEX

What about a child who's been told everything's right?

ERHARD

That's called Skinner's "glass box," and Skinner already demonstrated that it doesn't work. Did you get my answer?

ALEX

Yes.

> For instance, if who you are is that people are unable, you can't see the opportunities to develop their ability. And you can't see their ability. As soon as you get that that's your racket, as soon as you get that whole soap opera that you've got to do everything your self because there's nobody around able enough to do it, you begin to see things you didn't see before.

ERHARD

The other answer is that you don't actually get that from what happens, you're already always that as a human being. In other words, you are "there is something wrong here" waiting to happen. See listen, if we had the time, and we don't—that's another program—I would get up enough people in here whose experience was almost always what you and I would call positive. The athletic kids, the successful kids, the right kind of families. And you would find out that they had somehow fucked that up. It's amazing. Hard to believe. There are people in here like those kids we grew up with that we thought had it all. People like that in here. And if they stood up and shared with you, they would tell you that it was bad.

ALEX

Yeah.

ERHARD

So there's no way to escape it. Even if you're told "you're wonderful," "you can have anything you want," "life is great." Now, that is preferable over being told that you're shit. No question about that.

ALEX

That is my question. Is that preferable?

ERHARD

Oh sure. It's kind of like carrying less baggage. You're still going to carry the baggage. You're still going to get into the trap. You can't keep your kids out of the trap.

ALEX

The kid is told "You can do anything you want to," or the parent gets that child in as much difficulty as to tell the child they're worthless. Is it in the same elevator shaft, or is it different?

ERHARD

That's correct. I've looked at it as far as I can see it, and yes. But it's too long of a conversation to have right now.

LUCY

Two things. One I found this conversation the most powerful for me personally. The experiences that I heard are very applicable to me.

ERHARD

One will hear oneself in other's sharing.

LUCY

I think I understand why I don't get a sense of fulfillment out of the many things that I...

ERHARD
Sure because you're an accomplished person.

LUCY
I am trying to avoid something, that feeling that something is wrong. But the next question that comes to mind is what is the strategy to fix that? And you said you don't fix it.

ERHARD
No you don't.

LUCY
But I don't agree with that.

ERHARD
It's not that you don't agree with that. You are addicted to fixing it.

LUCY
That's true.

ERHARD
You have to have an answer.

LUCY
Not an answer, but to find a way to fix it, and then fix it.

ERHARD
Yeah. You and Suzanne ought to get together. These are two achievement nuts. You can't fix it.

LUCY
Why not?

ERHARD
Well, you tell me how to fix being dead and I'll tell you how to fix it.

LUCY
Well a lot of things are one's frame of mind and how you think things...

ERHARD
That's not true. A lot of things are explained using the terminology of the frame through which you look at things. Like positive thinking. Good stuff. What kind of a person would need to think positively?

LUCY
Somebody who's kind of negative.

ERHARD

Yeah. Every time you think positively, that is the content. The context is negative, that you are a negative person. Life is negative. No kidding. I've done that whole achievement thing for quite a while. Made a lot of money doing that. Lot of money. That whole business about being successful and achieving, and positive thinking. You name it I did it. And it works. The problem is that it's never enough. Never fulfilled, never whole. What you're asking me is how to get out of the trap and the answer is that the attempt to get out of the trap is what keeps you in the trap. I want you to think about this tonight. This is hard to get. Because getting out is supposed to get you out. In this case getting out keeps you in. This is a very strange kind of prison. The bars are not made of iron. They are made out of the attempt to get out of the prison. So Lucy, tonight, I want you to see if you can come to accept that you're going to have to live the rest of your life in this prison.

LUCY

I have another question. The concept... life is empty and...

ERHARD

I don't talk in concepts. Distinctions.

LUCY

I'm trying to relate how we can apply it to our lives.

ERHARD

You cannot apply it. Worthless, useless information.

LUCY

Then what's the purpose in knowing that? Or accepting that?

ERHARD

Because it's the truth.

LUCY

But how can knowing that or accepting that create personal power for us?

ERHARD

So wonderful. Hold on one second, I'll be right back.

(*to the group*)

Lucy and I are going to demonstrate terminally that you are addicted to the answer, that you are addicted to getting out, to getting the answer. That no matter how many times I'm going to tell you that the attempt to get out is the bars of the prison, you're going to spend the rest of your life trying to get out. She's going to demonstrate the very thing I'm talking about; she's going to demonstrate that she's going to spend the rest of her life trying to get out. And nothing I tell her is going to stop her. There are no answers. You don't get out. It's not going to work out. It's not

> **...the truth has a power that, if you're only looking for what you can use, you can't see.**

going to be all right. You know how it's going to be? Just like this. Yeah, it's not gonna be all right. It's going to be like this. You're either going to make it like this or you aren't going to make it. You're either going to learn to *be* in prison or you're just going to be unhappy. You're going to be in prison one way or the other. So, why did we talk about empty and meaningless if it isn't going to be useful? Because the truth has power not predicated on being useful. The truth has power, which most people can't see. You want to get this because Lucy's question opens this up. The truth has power, which you can't see, because you're only looking for what's useful. You're not looking for power, you're looking to exploit, to use, to consume. So you can't see the power of the truth. So Lucy, what I said was, that the truth has a power that, if you're only looking for what you can use, you can't see. That's why we had that whole thing about empty and meaningless.

LUCY
I can think of a way that "life being empty and meaningless" can be of use to us and giving us power.

ERHARD (*to the group*)
Am I demonstrating my point?

LUCY
One of the many alternatives I can think of...

ERHARD (*to the group*)
You want to listen to this.

LUCY
I think it revolves around the issue of performance versus expectation and if we tell ourselves often enough that life is empty and meaningless, our expectations as a consequence would be set lower over time, potentially...

ERHARD
No.

LUCY
And performance of life relative to expectations, could make us...

ERHARD
That's wonderful. You ought to do a seminar on that. People would buy that. Look, they bought thinking positive big. Yeah, I expect there to be a seminar—if you don't do it, somebody will. So you ought to do it: The Empty and Meaningless seminar, the purpose of which is to lower your expectations far enough down that anything feels like winning.

(*applause and laughter*)
You're actually having fun with me, aren't you? She doesn't mean this, she's only joking with me. She's kidding me. She's not looking for the answer. She knows there's no answer. She's only kidding with me.

LUCY
Well, I disagree. I really do. Because I think everything is a state of mind.

ERHARD
Oh absolutely. You go out and tell the bus that. Lucy, you've been in too many success seminars. Everything is not a state of mind. Buses are not a state of mind. I don't care what anybody has told you. And the evidence is all on my side.

(*responding to a participant not on camera*)
Excuse me?

(*repeating thoughtfully what the participant said*)
A new suit of clothes for the king. Yes. My tongue's way more tied than yours is; you can't out tongue tie me. Yeah, I understand what you said. I was just trying to get it. Yeah, what about it?

(*repeating what the participant said—who does not have a microphone*)
Is that all in the mind?

(*addressing himself out loud*)
Let's see, am I going to give him the truth or just shut him up?

(*laughter*)
It's all in the mind.

(*laughter. Then seriously*)
To stop being a smart-ass about this, I will respond to you. Yes, it is what you and I ordinarily call "in the mind," but if we look a little closer, it is not in the mind, it was in the mouth. A suit of clothes is a conversation, not a mental image. But that is a fine point and your point is valid. Buses are not a suit of clothes, right? It's not all in the mind. A lot of people think buses are in the mind. And they look like they've been hit by buses.

(*to Lucy*)
You all done?

LUCY
Yes, I'm done.

ERHARD
Okay great!

(*applause as Lucy sits*)

ERHARD

Okay, there's a certain part of The Forum for which you need to be less tired. I didn't say not tired. I said less tired, less tired than you're going to be if I answer all your questions!

(*laughter*)

So we're not going to answer any more questions tonight. Tonight we're going to...

(*after a participant shouted out: "Let's vote."*)

Does it really make you feel good to vote?

(*laughter*)

What about "The rug is red? Yeah!"

(*laughter*)

If you like voting why don't you vote on stuff like that? "Yeah! This rug is red! Yeah!"

(*clapping with everyone else joining in*)

So, we're not going to keep you up with answering questions, we're going to keep you up with an assignment. Stay up at home.

KIPP

Between tonight and tomorrow morning your assignment is to get clear that life is empty and meaningless. So what you're going to come up against between tonight and tomorrow morning is all those places that you say have...

(*the group shouts back: "meaning"*)

And you're going to inquire into those to see that they are...

(*the group shouts: "meaningless"*)

ERHARD

One other thing is to look at where they've made it mean something that life is empty and meaningless. Particularly add that in there.

KIPP

The second part: what you've made it mean that life is empty and meaningless. Therefore... There is also an invitation: to share what's been opening up for you with people in your life. Get clear that life is empty and meaningless. And what have you made it mean that life is empty and meaningless?

The third day of The Forum concluded.

END OF DAY THREE INTERVAL

The Forgetting of Being, Part Six of Eight: Saying Nothing

The bundle of concepts associated with non-Being and the negative—emptiness, meaninglessness, nothingness, nihilism—are of central significance in understanding the rhetorical movement of The Forum. They are likewise fundamental in the work of Martin Heidegger; and are deeply embedded in the perspective of Zen, another major influence on Werner Erhard's thinking. According to the Japanese scholar Masao Abe, who has written extensively about the relationship of Zen to Western thinking, "Martin Heidegger takes the issue of 'nothingness' not only with utmost seriousness, but perhaps with the most profundity in Western history" (Maseo Abe, *Zen and Western Thought* 134). For both Heidegger and Erhard, a transformative ontological event—an experience of Being (of what it means "to be")—demands an authentic encounter with Being's other side; and a conversation that aims to evoke such an encounter makes special demands, since, says Heidegger, "there is, after all, something peculiar about Nothing" (*IM* 30).

We cannot overstate the importance of this element in Erhard's work. Central to his achievement has been the development of a rhetorical structure—manifested in both the *est* Training and The Forum—that consistently provides participants with an experience of nothingness as a liberating context for their lives. The experience is evoked by a progression of ontological distinctions, generated in speaking by the Forum leader and developed dialogically with the participants. What is made present in the dialogue—heard, though unsaid—is Being; and its presencing occurs in a particularly dramatic way. One of Heidegger's central claims is that an experience of Being must be preceded by an experience of Being's other side, *nonbeing*, which Heidegger called *the Nothing.* Human existence, he says, means "being held out into the nothing" ("WM" in *BW* 103). This requires that one open oneself to an experience of *meaninglessness*, an experience that one may encounter in moments of anxiety, despair, or profound boredom—moments when the meaning of life drops away, and one confronts existence nakedly, without the familiar comforts of one's personal identity. Human beings, says Erhard, are addicted to their identities, and an addiction cannot be dealt with effectively until the addict has "hit bottom." But for Forum participants, most of whom have achieved a comfortable level of personal and professional success, such an experience may never arise—*without assistance.* Therefore the function of The Forum is to "raise the bottom" so that participants hit it; and where this happens is in the confrontation with the Nothing, as the conversation's penultimate distinction.

In Heidegger's work, of course, the distinctions are presented in writing. While many of his published works were originally delivered as lectures, and although he is reported to have been exceptionally dynamic in their delivery, there is little evidence that dialogue was an element of his pedagogy; and in the cultural context in which he worked, certainly nothing like the personal interactions of The Forum would have been possible (see the sidebar "Heidegger's Pedagogy," in Session Two of Day Two).

But consider: while Heidegger's collected works include 102 volumes, he is generally acknowledged to have been single-minded in his exploration of one question: the question of Being and its meaning. As he wrote in 1947, "To think is to confine yourself to a single thought that one day stands still like a star in the world's sky" ("TP" in *PLT* 4). Significantly, a few pages later we find: "What is spoken is never, and in no language, what is said" ("TP" in *PLT* 11).

In Heidegger's writing, then, the distinctions that he created to *speak Being* are generated and communicated *in the unspoken/unwritten background.* There is, we propose, a *central encompassing distinction*—the Distinction—that is hinted at by all of the distinctions, a "single thought" that remains unspoken and the Same through all of the turns and evolutions of his thinking. The rubrics for the various distinctions that comprise the Distinction, such as *the Same, the they-self,* and *the Nothing,* occur repeatedly throughout his work as he opens new ways into the distinctions, beginning from different originating terms. In an essay from a collection entitled *Holzwege* ("Woodpaths"), Heidegger wrote this:

 "Wood" is an old name for forest. In the wood are paths that mostly wind along until they end quite suddenly in an impenetrable thicket. They are called woodpaths. Each goes its particular way, but in the same forest. Often it seems as though one were identical to another. Yet it only seems so. Woodcutters and foresters are familiar with these paths. They know what it means to be on a woodpath. (Quoted in Krell, "Introduction," *BW* 34)

For the authors of this book, our experience of Werner Erhard's work has enabled us in negotiating the "impenetrable thickets" of Heidegger's writing—if not with the skill of woodcutters, at least with the sense that we are always on a way.

Krell comments that in Germany, "to be on a woodpath" means to be in a *cul-de-sac,* a path that leads nowhere and has no exit. As an analogy for the rhetorical strategies we find in the work of Werner Erhard, the "no exit" image is of interest.

Throughout this book, we are proposing that both Heidegger and Erhard make important use of *reflexive languaging*—ideas presented in such a way that they turn thinking back upon itself, pulling the rug out from under the reader or the listener (e.g., "This statement is false"). We suggest that the reflexive impulse (reflex, reflection, self-referentiality, getting the joke) pervades the thinking and the languaging of both men, most dramatically when they are saying the Nothing. These reflexive processes share a particular affinity with the movement of thinking that makes available an experience of Being, and one view is that they evoke a *cul-de-sac.*

At a debriefing meeting between sessions of the 1989 Forum, Erhard told The Forum leaders that the "critical condition of satisfaction" for doing The Forum is that for the participants it must be *inescapable*. That is, in Heidegger's terms, all exits by which the they-self might escape an authentic confrontation with its own thrownness must be closed. To this end, a *cul-de-sac* may be a useful model; and The Forum's culminating distinction (as well as the final process of the *est* Training) may be seen as effective speaking of that form.

The French existentialist Jean-Paul Sartre evoked the *cul-de-sac* image in the title of his play, *No Exit;* and one of Heidegger's most important essays, published in 1947 as the "Letter On Humanism," was written, in part, as a response to an essay by Sartre. A comparison of Sartre's thinking with Heidegger's is beyond the scope of this book, but we will gloss the difference in this way: for neither man is there an exit from the trap of the human situation; but for Heidegger, the appropriation of that situation—the appropriation of entrapment—creates the possibility of authentic entrapment. The situation becomes the Situation, which gives releasement. ■

When the final day of The Forum began at 9:00 am, Kipp was at the front of the room. As soon as participants were seated, Kevin, the man who Erhard accused of being stingy, recommending that he ask his wife about that, walked up onto the platform and handed a piece of paper to Kipp, who then read it to the group. It was a signed video release form. The participants stood to applaud at length.

KIPP

That's exactly what's going to be required in your lives, to have something beyond what the past has given you to happen. What you just saw was an act of something beyond being stingy, something beyond what the past has given him. And like Kevin, you're attached. It doesn't take much to get you deeply rooted in what you are attached to. I think what just struck a chord for you was to see someone go beyond what life has given them. That's what it's going to take to go beyond what life has given you: all day every day. That's the choice you're going to have.

(*to Kevin*)
Kevin, I appreciate your courage.

(*to the group*)
Sharing about the empty and meaninglessness that life is, or the meaning that you made of empty and meaningless.

MARGARET

The only place where empty and meaningless is meaningful, is where it coincides with my racket, the only hitch is in there... This morning I called someone I'm engaged to...

KIPP (*interrupting*)

That was a quick sentence: "the only place where empty and meaningless means something is where it coincides with my racket"—that's the part you got to get. You see, where your racket is, no one dares to tread.

(*laughter; to Margaret*)
Yes?

MARGARET

My racket is: "I can't quite have it... I can't quite have it all." It's a joke. It's such a joke. But I do run it with a real verve and panache and other words that go with it. I called a former... well I was engaged to marry him for a year and a half...

KIPP

So it's perfect. Someone who "can't quite have it all" gets engaged for a year and a half...

(*laughter*)
And not married.

SPEAKING BEING

DAY FOUR

FORUM DAY FOUR:

SESSION ONE

MARGARET (*continuing to laugh*)

...and I shared my racket with him and I said "and furthermore, it's your racket, too!" It was so freeing. I mean it was so great to be straight with him. I said "You keep me around. Our sex wasn't that great, so you keep me massaging your racket every now and again. You liked that better than me massaging your penis." I mean I was able to be so straight with him. "You want me to massage your case and you didn't want anything else. And same with me: I have you buy me off every once and a while. You buy me wonderful gifts. It's exactly what we've always wanted!"

(*laughter*)

So that was that on that, and I just noticed...

(*more laughter*)

And he said, "You mean behind that, I don't really want a relationship?" and I said, "You should move to California to be with me..."

(*laughter*)

There was no hook to it anymore. But I run it with everybody, that my life isn't quite right. I started dating some great guys about four months ago. Really great guys, but it can't be that great. I'm a runner and hurt my leg, and so I've gained a little weight, and so now I've got that schtick going: I can't not have a schtick about things not being quite right. It's disgusting! You know, I never have to be responsible for producing at the level of who I am for my job, ever. Someone can't stab into me because they know how much I've already sacrificed.

KIPP

This is an important part because: some of you are successful and the success keeps the wolves off your back. The results are part of the racket, and that's why there's no satisfaction in them. The results are there to avoid the domination; they are not results that leave you satisfied, no, they are there to avoid the responsibility of ever really being responsible. "Don't touch me, because I'm the best you've got."

MARGARET

Right. It's horrible. Yeah, and I see the only way to do it is to state that I'm full of it, and "You can hold me to account, whether I don't like it, whether I get snarly, hold me to account." You know, my life is brilliant, it works, I've got the best life there could be. I really do. And yet I run this racket as good as anyone. Better.

(*laughter*)

And then I noticed, where are the miracles? Well, this morning I went for a run and it was effortless! I should have been late with all that I did this morning, but I was on time. I stopped eating last night when I was full. I even made my deep, profound commitment to ending hunger on the planet into an in-order-to, an in-order-to be liked, to make it, and to sacrifice: "oh woe is me." And that's ridiculous.

KIPP (*applause as Margaret sits*)

Thank you very much.

Being-in-the-World: World

The Forum promises participants a transformed perspective on their lives, which is to say their Being-in-the-world. Martin Heidegger hyphenated this phrase in his writing to indicate that the phenomenon must be seen as a whole, as a unitary structure. However, he said, its parts could be considered separately for emphasis. Previously, in Session One of Day One, we examined *Being-in*, and in Session One of Day Two, *Being-with*. Here we consider Heidegger's view of *world*.

Inside/Outside

In the Cartesian model of reality, the model that for the most part determines the way contemporary human beings understand our relation to the world, knowledge arises from an encounter between subject and object: the "I"—the human subject, the being that knows—encounters and comes to know the objects, and thus the world.

Martin Heidegger's model of human being as Dasein challenges this tradition: Dasein and its world do not correspond to subject and object (*BT* 87). Knowledge, in the sense that Dasein knows the world, does not result from a human subject's coming to understand an objective world separate from itself.

For Heidegger, the assumptions of the Cartesian model were problematic. That model presupposes that reality consists of an "outer" realm (that which becomes known, Nature, the objective world), and a separate "inner" realm of subjectivity that does the knowing. This inner realm is in some way distinct from the outer realm that contains everything else; but it is somehow able to escape its inner realm so that it can get outside and, well, *know*.

The problem of inner and outer, and the search for a proof of the "Dasein of things outside me," has concerned philosophy since Descartes. But, says Heidegger, if there is such a problem, it lies with the question itself.

> " The 'scandal of philosophy' is not that this proof has yet to be given, but that *such proofs are expected and attempted again and again.* [. . .] If Dasein is understood correctly, it defies such proofs, because, in its Being, it already *is* what subsequent proofs deem necessary to demonstrate for it. (*BT* 249)

That is, one always knows the world from the position of *already being out there in it*.

> " When Dasein directs itself toward something and grasps it, it does not somehow first get out of an inner sphere in which it has been proximally encapsulated, but its primary kind of Being is such that *it is always 'outside' alongside entities which it encounters* and which belong to a world already discovered. (*BT* 89, emphasis added)

On the other hand, there is certainly a sense in which we are inside:

> " [E]ven in this 'being-outside' alongside the object, Dasein is still 'inside,' if we understand this in the correct sense; that is to say, it is itself 'inside' as a Being-in-the-world which knows. And furthermore, the perceiving of what is known is not a process of returning with one's booty to the 'cabinet' of consciousness after one has gone out and grasped it; even in perceiving, retaining, and preserving, the Dasein which knows *remains outside,* and does so *as Dasein.* (*BT* 89)

So the inside/outside dilemma is a false problem. Human beings know their world through existing in it and coping with it.

ELYSE

I started to feel sick yesterday, and I wondered what was wrong with me that I was sick, and I'm not supposed to be sick. I could hardly sit in the room last night. During the break last night we went out for dinner, and I thought "I better go lay down for a while, otherwise I'm not going to be able to make it, I'm not going to be able to pay attention to what's happening, I'm not going to be able to do it." And I couldn't see what I couldn't be with, and finally it struck me. What I couldn't be with is—because I'd been thinking: "what's my racket?" I thought that my racket was that I couldn't be with how much people loved me because I was afraid that people didn't love me, and I saw that that wasn't my racket at all. My racket is that I've had no capacity to be with how much I love people and express that. I've said it like a concept, and I have to do things in order to express my love for people rather than "be" my love for people. And I still feel sick, and I have an incredible life and I can hardly be with that.

KIPP

Well, it makes you wrong.

MARGARET

Yes, absolutely. It's amazing. I wake up every morning and I think, "this isn't my life, this is someone else's life. Somebody's going to find out about me and they're going to pull the rug, and it's not going to be there anymore, and it's all going to be fucked."

KIPP

Well, it already is.

(*laughter*)
See, if you recall the conversation we started having last night, the clearing that it is to be a human being that you live in: "there's something wrong."

MARGARET

There is. Absolutely.

KIPP

Yeah. And it's not conceptual. You *are* "there's something wrong." You've also made that mean something. Not only is something wrong, it means something that there's something wrong.

MARGARET

It shouldn't be that way.

KIPP

What else?

MARGARET

Well I can see that it doesn't mean anything and then I woke up this morning and I thought, well then I shouldn't be upset that I didn't feel good, or that my throat hurts, or that my head hurts.

KIPP

This is very good now. This is the giving meaning to no meaning. See "If it doesn't mean anything, therefore, in order to..."

MARGARET

Or if I really got it, I wouldn't be sick.

KIPP

Right.

MARGARET

I don't even know if I'm sick. Truth is, I don't even know.

KIPP

Right. Well, for sure you'd be some other way than you are.

MARGARET

I'm kind of like backed into a corner. I can't talk about it, so now I should feel a different way than I feel physically. Which is crazy.

KIPP

No it's not crazy, it's called normal. This is normal.

MARGARET

I got it.

KIPP

This is what everybody walks around in every day.

MARGARET

And I also see: I've designed my entire life to be protected from anyone finding out that that's so about me. I'll produce great, unbelievable results; I'll create great things around me so that people won't find out. It's so fucking elaborate! People won't find out about me that all I'm petrified of is that people don't love me.

KIPP

You know, I think that we think it's elaborate. We walk around every day with these signs on telling everybody exactly the way it is with us.

Circumspection

Heidegger also points out that this antecedent understanding of the world has a particular quality. The things with which we concern ourselves in our everyday world are the things that we use in the business of living. Encountered this way, they are the material of a *phenomenological* knowing—a knowing that grows out of Being (*BT* 95). This knowing may or may not be explicit in our awareness:

> **How do the beings with which we dwell show themselves to us primarily and for the most part? Sitting here in the auditorium we do not in fact apprehend walls—not unless we are getting bored. Nevertheless, the walls are already present before we think them as objects. (*BPP* 163)**

Before they are objects for us, the walls are present as a part of the *equipmental context.* In a knowing that arises from Being, I am not immediately present to the things in my world in the role of contemplator, one who seeks to understand and describe them. Rather I encounter and *use* them in the business of living:

> **The *nearest things* that surround us we call equipment. There is always already a manifold of equipment: equipment for working, for traveling, for measuring, and in general things with which we have to do. (*BPP* 163)**

How do I understand these things?

> **The view in which the equipmental contexture stands at first, completely unobtrusive and unthought, is the view and sight of practical *circumspection,* of our practical everyday orientation. "Unthought" means that it is not thematically apprehended for deliberate thinking about things; instead, in circumspection we find our bearings in regard to them. Circumspection uncovers and understands things primarily as equipment. [. . .] We say that an equipmental contexture environs us. (*BPP* 163, emphasis added)**

I can of course assume a detached role in relation to the world, taking on understanding as a science, or an intellectual task to be accomplished. But this always happens against the background of the world I already know from being in it. The background understanding comes first.

> **World is not something subsequent that we calculate as a result from the sum of all beings. The world comes not afterward but beforehand, in the strict sense of the word. [. . .] The world as already unveiled in advance is such that we do not in fact specifically occupy ourselves with it, or apprehend it, but instead it is so self-evident, so much a matter of course, that we are completely oblivious to it. (*BPP* 165)**

It is, in a metaphor often employed by Werner Erhard, like water to a fish: fundamental to existence, yet unavailable to our purview. We see the beings within that purview—they occur as *extant,* which for Heidegger means that they occur as substantial *things* in the world.

MARGARET

That obvious, right?

KIPP

It's that obvious for everybody, isn't it, except you walk around like it's not that obvious.

MARGARET

Well, for me it's never lived like that. It's always been that I've had to make sure it was flawless, to cover all the little seams up, so people wouldn't find out.

KIPP

Wouldn't find out?

MARGARET

That I was afraid that people wouldn't love me, and the one I was hiding most from is me, or that I love people. It sounds like such a stupid thing to say. That I walked around like I was a machine. I've been like a machine.

KIPP

What do you mean by that?

MARGARET

Well, like... the easiest way I can say it is I had no right to be. I was always trying to get somewhere or do something.

KIPP

Yeah, but what I'm saying is that's a little conceptual... I don't hear you sharing yet.

MARGARET (*after a long pause*)

Okay. I called my mother. I was very upset with my mother, because I just got married a month ago. She didn't want to come to my wedding.

KIPP

No no. She didn't want to come to the wedding or she didn't come to the wedding.

MARGARET

She didn't come to the wedding. But I had it that she didn't want to come to my wedding and it meant all these things.

KIPP

It meant?

MARGARET

She didn't love me. "What's wrong with me that she didn't want to come to my wedding? How could that be?" And you know it was funny because when she first told me—that she wasn't coming to my wedding—it was fine. At first I got it, and then I had it mean something.

KIPP

So what it means that your mother wasn't coming to your wedding is...

MARGARET

She wasn't coming to my wedding.

KIPP

"My mother's not coming to my wedding."

MARGARET

And then I had it mean something.

KIPP

You had it mean what?

MARGARET

First it meant that there was something wrong with me that she wasn't coming to my wedding. If I wasn't the way I was, she would come to my wedding. There was something wrong with me. And then I had it mean that she didn't love me.

KIPP

Which means that there's something wrong with her.

MARGARET

Right.

KIPP

Everybody know that's the next step after there's something wrong with you? There's something wrong with them.

MARGARET

And then um, you know, I called her during the couple months before I got married and I would talk to her, and I could see that when I started to have that she wasn't coming to my wedding means something, all I could do was talk to her as an in-order-to: in order to get her to come to my wedding; in order to get her to love me. I even went from, "if she's not going to come to my wedding, the least she could do was tell me that she loves me." And it was just... It's funny, because I just called her up, two days ago during a break, and I said to her, "I just called

But the world itself is of a different order of being. The world itself occurs as Dasein does; and Da-Sein, remember, is both Being-there and, for Heidegger Being-a-clearing. The phenomenon is like nothing we are accustomed to thinking; thus Heidegger's presentation of the situation is provocative:

> **The world is not the sum total of extant entities. It is, quite generally, not extant at all. It is a determination of [B]eing-in-the-world, a moment in the structure of the Dasein's mode of being. The world is something Dasein-ish, It is not extant like things but it *is da,* there-here, like the *Dasein,* the being-da [das Da-sein] which we ourselves are: that is to say, it exists. (*BPP* 166)**

The world, then, may be seen as a clearing where things can occur meaningfully. This is also a working definition of human being: the clearing in the world for meaning. Both definitions direct us to a distinction, a distinction that hints at the unspoken realm of world.

> **World-understanding as Dasein-understanding is self-understanding. Self and world belong together in the single entity, the Dasein. Self and world are not two beings, like subject and object, or like I and thou, but self and world are the basic determination of the Dasein itself in the unity of the structure of [B]eing-in-the-world. (*BPP* 297)**

The transformational power of The Forum arises from its evocation of that unity. ∎

to let you know that...I just called to say hello." We just kind of talked. And she told me what was going on with her. I told her that our wedding was great and that I got back great pictures from the photographer, that I couldn't wait to show them to her, that I really love her. She said to me, well, I said to her that I don't know how to create a relationship, or how to have a kind of relationship that works for you. I keep trying to do something and I haven't been doing anything that's really worked. "All I've done is figured out what was wrong with you or what was wrong with me and try to tell you that, and make you do something different." And she said to me, "just be yourself." You know, it was really remarkable. Because whatever she's going through she's going through. And my father just died and she told me that, you know, she just shared with me a little bit about that...

KIPP

She said?

MARGARET

She said: "It's tough and I don't know how I'm going to get over it and what I'm going to do." And I also saw... My mother and my brothers have been saying to me: "You don't live in the same city we do, you can't have the same kind of relationship we have with each other." And I saw that she's upset that I don't live where she lives. I've never heard it like that before. So we just had a conversation where there was no sting anymore. There was no more me trying to get her to do something. It was a conversation where we were actually talking to each other instead of me trying to get her to do something. And it's a beginning. And I also said to her that all I was committed to was that she really, you know, have her life work for her. And I had no idea what that was going to be and she didn't either. It was really a beginning, a place to talk to each other from. And I saw I wasn't trying to get her to do something. So however I hung up the phone, I was satisfied, and however way I've been operating never left me satisfied in talking to her.

KIPP

Anything else?

MARGARET

One of the things I came to The Forum to get is a way of working with the people I work with that I don't live like some special unique human being, but really able to contribute whatever distinctions are clear to me to them so that they can get done whatever I can get done. And I can see, who I'd have... I have no idea how to do it and actually live like a possibility for me, inside my relationship with the people I work with, rather than something I'm supposed to do, someway I have to be in order to make it. And how I've been... when I couldn't be with something I didn't know how to do, or continuing to stand in the face of not knowing how to deliver on all the work that we've got, not knowing how to do that. What I do is I use force instead of being able to be with whatever's happening.

Erhard entered at the side of the room, wearing a brown sweater-vest and gray-brown slacks. He stood in the back, listening, looking around the room, occasionally greeting and touching a participant.

KIPP

That's a big one. See, when you can't be with what's happening, what you're always left with is force, no power.

MARGARET

That's it.

KIPP

Okay. Thank you very much.

(*applause*)
Clear on the empty and meaninglessness that life is, or the meaning you've given to the empty and meaningless. One of those two.

JEB

I woke this morning and realized I am the sum total of my likes and dislikes, that's all I am. I am the sum total of my likes and dislikes, no more than that.

KIPP

Yes, so, if you take a person's life, and you put all their opinions in a jar, and you stick them in the jar with it, that's their life. What they like and what they don't like; what they agree with and what they don't agree with; what they think is good, and what they think is bad; what they think is right and what they think is wrong.

ERHARD

Is it possible to get some insight into how stupid that is? The significance with which we have given to what we like and don't like, with what you agree and don't agree with, with what you want and don't want? Is it possible to get some insight into how trivial and trivializing that is to your life? I told you I would tell you about the spiritual exercise. You have to do the spiritual exercise at night, because it has to be dark out, and it has to be clear out so that you can see the stars. Here in San Francisco that isn't always easy, but sometimes. Go down to the beach at about two or three in the morning when there's nobody there, and look up at the sky, at the stars. When you get over the awe—and we always do, don't we?—as soon as you get over the awe, what you do is you watch the stars very, very, very carefully. You have to watch them very carefully. Watch the stars very carefully while you tell the stars your opinions, what you don't like and what you do like, what you agree with and what you don't agree with, and particularly tell them what you want and what you don't want. If you've watched them very carefully, at the end of that exercise, you will be in touch with, you will have a deep insight into the profound indifference the universe has for your opinion.

(*laughter*)

And then you can do something else with your life instead of figuring out what you agree with and what you don't agree with. That would give you a lot of time, because right now you are spending a lot of time figuring out what you agree with and what you don't agree with, and what you like and what you don't like, and what you want and what you don't want. Very important to know that the stars won't move for your opinions. They will not move. They'll move for something, but not for your opinion. And you're pretty stuck with your opinion. You know, with what you think is right and what you think is wrong, and which way you think it ought to be done and which way you don't think it ought to be done. You watch the stars carefully, like I said, you will have a profound insight into the awesome indifference with which the universe holds your opinion. Then you can use your life for something else. The stars will move, but not for your opinion. Very good what you said. Thank you for letting me interrupt you. Please go on.

JEB

It gave me an opportunity to observe myself doing it because it came in the context of empty and meaningless, and so I could retrace the steps. Like this: "Life is empty and meaningless. Okay I could see the value in that. It gives you the freedom you spoke of, all of those things. I can like that idea." So what I saw happen was, I could incorporate that without challenging the structure of my life. I could make that something I like, give it that meaning without upsetting the way I do business.

KIPP

You see what he's saying? It can be absorbed into the conventional wisdom. It would be an extension of what you already knew. If you put this as an extension of what you already know, it will be more of what you already know. Very powerful what Jeb is saying. "Oh, yeah, I agree that it's empty and meaningless. And of course, when I don't agree with it, it won't be." See, you don't have any wants. You *are* your wants. Somebody tries to take your wants away from you, you will act like they are trying to take you away from you. Yes?

WALKER

I got that I am complete with my mother but not with my father. And I began to look at that and I saw that I thought that my father owed me something. Who I'd been being with my father was that he owed me something. I called him up during the meal break last night, and just apologized for being somebody who thought that he owed me something. And he said, "Well what is it you thought I owed you." And I said that I couldn't even think of it, but that I just wanted to apologize for that. He said: "apology accepted." And that was that, and afterwards I began to see that the other side of that is that if who I've been being is that he owes me something... the other side of that is that I've been being someone who owes somebody something. I have something to complete with you, Werner. In 1974, I couldn't say it then, but what I got was what my life could be about. Everything since then has been about how I could pay you back,

The Uncanny

Approaching the final stages of writing this book, the authors also were faced with another "end": in January of 2015, Bruce Hyde, the senior author, was diagnosed with a recurring and aggressive cancer. A new urgency emerged, as the very existence of our project was called into question. The "end" itself was addressing us, calling us, summoning forth a whole new clearing for partnership and activity, and in that clearing this book in its entirety emerged with the senior author free to complete the remainder of the sidebars and intervals, doing so before he was unable to participate any longer.

WALKER (*continuing*)

like in order to pay you back for this gift you've given me. And what I got yesterday is that I don't owe you anything. I owe you nothing. And you've always told me "you owe me nothing." But I couldn't quite get that without this piece of it. And now I'm wholly complete with that I owe you nothing. And I am complete that I am participating in this work to pay you back for something or in order to something...

ERHARD

You can't give when you owe. Paying back is not a very powerful expression. Giving is a more powerful expression than paying back.

WALKER

So we're even.

ERHARD (*to laughter*)

Deal. By the way I didn't say I owed you nothing. I said I promised you nothing. It's a throwaway.

WALKER

In a very real way, who you have been being for me is my father. Like trying to get something from you, trying to pay something back to you. So I want to thank you for the opportunity to be in The Forum and the opportunity to complete that.

ERHARD

Thank you.

KIPP

See, participation begins when you have no reason to participate. What you call participation has always been in-order-to... That's not participation. That's some kind of entanglement. Some kind of a deal, strategy, tactic—not participation: Can you even imagine participating for no reason?

ERHARD

You can't imagine anything for no reason. You really can't imagine anything for no reason. You know it sounds like we keep insulting you, like when I told somebody they haven't lived yet. Insulting, right? Except everything in the world for you is in-order-to, and nothing is for itself: that's not to have lived yet. If everything is in-order-to, you've never gotten anything for itself, you know, the thing itself, as itself. Like another person as that other person; not the other person in-order-to. It's a very different context. Remember what we said about "tall" and the context in which "tall" shows up? Other people in-order-to don't look like other people as them-selves. Even a tree in-order-to does not look like a tree as a tree. Love in-order-to is not love, it's something else: It's called love in-order-to. It's not love. People who only know love in-order-to, do not know what love is.

In *Being and Time*, Heidegger has shed light on this phenomenon, which has gained special significance given our recent encounter with the most implacable of limits. For Heidegger, this call reaches Dasein and turns it toward its end, toward the possibility of its impossibility, the Nothing. Anxiety then is the correlative attunement in which the call is heard—at that moment when we find our limit. It is in this attunement that Being-in-the-world is disclosed as entirely unrecognizable within any familiar rubric. Thus, the call of conscience cannot be said. It comes from a strange, unrecognizable domain. The call, when heard, is uncanny (*Unheimlich*).

What is the Uncanny?

For Heidegger, uncanniness refers to the human relation to death, to the possibility of our non-existence, and our tendency to flee from an authentic confrontation with Being-towards-the-end. This tendency to flee is not surprising, given "the everyday publicness of the 'they,' which brings tranquillized self-assurance—'Being-at-home,' with all its obviousness—into the average everydayness of Dasein" (*BT* 233). In an authentic confrontation, for instance, here in Session One of Day Four of The Forum, even "as Dasein falls, anxiety brings it back from its absorption in the 'world.' Everyday familiarity collapses. Dasein has been individualized, but individualized *as* Being-in-the-world" (*BT* 233). Everything that had heretofore supported the self-understood existence that constituted our self falls away. There is no "you" there, nor is there an "I"; only Being-in-the-world. "This is it" says Erhard. "You wanted to know how it was going to turn out. Well this is it. This is how it turned out" ("Heart of the Matter"). Inevitably, Being-in-the-world "enters into the existential 'mode' of the '*not-at-home*'" (*BT* 233). This sense of not-at-homeness is what is referred to as the uncanny.

Over the last several months, as the senior author has become more open in his thinking, as well as in conversation, to his own death as something impending, he has begun to experience this uncanniness. And while letting go to this confrontation has certainly included a quality of danger—the discomfort of being on the edge, of jumping off the high diving board, of being ungrounded—there has also been an experience of great liberation regarding the tendency to flee given by the "rainstorm" of the "they" self, which "*does not permit us the courage for anxiety in the face of death*" (*BT* 298). Heidegger continues:

> **As falling, everyday Being-towards-death is a constant *fleeing in the face of death*. Being-towards-the-end has the mode of *evasion in the face of it*—giving new explanations for it, understanding it inauthentically, and concealing it. Factically one's own Dasein is always dying already; that is to say, it is in a Being-towards-its-end. And it hides this Fact from itself by recoining "death" as just a "case of death" in Others—an everyday occurrence which, if need be, gives us the assurance still more plainly that 'oneself' is still 'living.'**
> **(*BT* 298)**

One might read in Heidegger's words a degree of disparagement toward the everyday way of Being-in-the-world endemic to the "they" self. Perhaps Heidegger is attempting to lay bare everydayness such that his readers might hear the call of conscience that itself brings us to face a profound lack present in the tranquil life dictated by the "they":

(*to Kipp*)
Did you ever get to reasonableness?

KIPP

No.

ERHARD

Were you planning on doing that today?

KIPP

Exactly.

ERHARD

Great. Raphaela?

RAPHAELA

When I was thinking of standing up, I was wanting to participate in-order-to. And life is meaningless to me is really... I'm stuck. I want this coaching, I want to accept that, but if it's meaningless to me then what does that mean? I keep going in that circle.

ERHARD

Yeah, what does it mean that it's meaningless and empty?

RAPHEAELA

Exactly. But for me to say that, I don't... I'm still not accepting it. So, so what?

KIPP

You've made not accepting it mean something also. You know, like you should accept it.

RAPHAELA

Well, I follow what you're saying...

KIPP

You mean you can see that accepting and not accepting are both meaningless. They both mean the same thing. One means accepting and the other means not accepting.

RAPHAELA

Yeah. But at the same time I feel my racket coming up saying "I can't accept that."

ERHARD

What's your racket?

RAPHAELA

My racket is that I won't make a decision. So, to work that racket I make a decision for me and I make a decision for everyone else and the decision I'm making is that I can't accept that. And I'm standing up here now because I have been participating "in-order-to," so it's not participating, it's not sharing: Whatever I say, it's coming out as in-order-to.

ERHARD

Like you can't get out of that, can you? Everything you do is in-order-to; you can't get out of the trap. You try to get out of the trap, it gets you in the trap because trying to get out of the trap... you're doing what you're doing to get out of the trap. And if you succumb to the trap, you're stuck in the trap. There's no way out of the trap. It's called being human. There's no way out of being human. The only thing you've got is to accept it; not accept like give in, but accept like own, like be responsible for, like embrace. It's called embracing yourself. You read it in books: It's called loving yourself or accepting yourself. Nobody knows what that means. People think "loving yourself" is some *zzzzzt* thing. No. It's what we're talking about in here. We've kind of got it flayed open so you can see it. It's owning that you're always in-order-to; that every time you operate you're operating out of your racket; and any attempt to operate with something other than your racket is another racket. It's rackets all the way down... to the bottom. At the bottom you get to empty and meaningless. That's not a racket. Empty and meaningless is worthless. It's not good for anything. Empty and meaningless doesn't make you right and it doesn't make anything wrong, and it doesn't help you to dominate anything or avoid domination. It doesn't justify anything. And on top of that, all there is, is rackets and in-order-tos. And that's why it doesn't make any difference whether you accept it or not. So you don't accept that it's empty and meaningless? So what? It's still empty and meaningless—except that it's empty and meaningless that it's empty and meaningless. Doesn't make any difference. Still doesn't mean anything that it's empty and meaningless. And if you did accept it, so what? Still empty and meaningless. Doesn't help when you accept it. Doesn't go away. Doesn't get fixed. Still empty and meaningless and it's still empty and meaningless that it is empty and meaningless. You see? Like that. What else?

RAPHAELA

Yesterday when we went through the fear experience...

ERHARD

That wasn't fear, that was the danger exercise. You all will call it fear. That's what you call it; we call it the danger exercise.

(to Kipp)
Did you call it fear?

KIPP

Absolutely not.

> The "they" gives its approval, and aggravates the *temptation* to cover up from oneself one's ownmost Being-towards-death. This evasive concealment in the face of death dominates everydayness so stubbornly that, in Being with one another, the 'neighbors' often still keep talking the 'dying person' into the belief that he will escape death and soon return to the tranquillized everydayness of the world of his concern. Such 'solicitude' is meant to 'console' him. [. . .] In this manner the "they" provides a *constant tranquillization about death*. At bottom, however, this is a tranquillization not only for him who is 'dying' but just as much for those who 'console' him. (*BT* 297–298)

Following the familiar flight away from the nothing, and listening away to the "they" self, we might easily conclude that people don't die. They pass. Yes, the euphemism is apt; certainly death is a passage. At the same time, more openness and authenticity in this realm is a worthy goal. Uncanny conversation is not morbid; it only reveals that we are in an essential state of lack. We are to our core striving to live practice lives designed to allow us to escape, designed to relieve us of the anxiety that calls out from the Nothing, reminding us that we are thrown to be what we already and always are, human beings, meaning making machines, an existence and facticity—the trap—from which there is no escape other than to be in the trap. ■

(*laughter*)

ERHARD

Okay good. Raphaela?

RAPHAELA

That's my story, when we went through the fear process: I found myself angry because all these people were acting the way they were and then I saw that I was going through this process of I couldn't be whatever it was I was going to be because I was angry with these people for making these really fucking weird noises. Distracting me: "Come on, shut up and let me be who I am," you know.

(*laughing*)

ERHARD

Why are they laughing? Do you know?

RAPHAELA

It's really silly.

ERHARD

And also there's a certain recognition. People laugh when they recognize themselves in other people. Like when you said the king has no clothes, everybody laughed, right? Because they saw it all along but nobody had said it.

RAPHAELA

So right now I'm working on trying to understand the not having meaning in my life, because for so long it's been "there has to be a meaning," "there has to be a purpose," you know, you do things in-order-to. And it's really hard for me to get off that because, my story is that's what my parents have taught me. And the real truth is that they raised me, they fed me, and they loved me, but I get...

KIPP

The truth is you're a human being, and that's what you get with being human. That's what you get when you get here and the party's over. You get the kind of being that gives everything meaning. And what you're doing is thrashing around inside the trap. Flailing around. Well if it doesn't mean anything, what does that mean?

RAPHAELA

Well, I now say... I hear that it doesn't mean anything, so how do I get out of that trap, which is a trap in itself?

At 9:45, Wes entered and joined Kipp in this interaction.

WES (*to Raphaela*)

Did you ever see Chinese handcuffs? You stick your fingers in them.

RAPHAELA

No.

WES

So imagine this gadget where you put your index fingers on either side of it, and then you go to pull your fingers out. You know what happens?

(*to the group*)
What happens?

(*many answer together: "it tightens up"*)
See, that's your problem! You never stuck your fingers in a Chinese handcuff!

(*laughter*)
So you're going to have to make this up. You stick your fingers in this thing. You pull on it and then it tightens. Can you get that?

RAPHAELA

Yeah.

WES

And then you pull on it more and it tightens. And the harder you pull to get your fingers out, the tighter it gets. Can you get that? That's what's happening right now. You are in a giant Chinese handcuff. How do you like it? It's called your life.

RAPHAELA

I don't like it.

WES

Good. That's the first recognition. If that makes any difference.

RAPHAELA

I don't like to be wrong and for me being in a Chinese handcuff is being able to be right.

WES

Yeah, it's not a matter of being wrong. It's just a matter of it doesn't work. Not for someone who wants to live their life. Either way you're going to die, so it's just a conversation right now. But someday you'll be dead and they'll put on your tombstone: "lived her life fully," or they'll put there something like "tried to get out of the trap, and died…"

KIPP

..."in the trap."

WES

So you want to know how you get out of the trap?

RAPHAELA

Well, I think...

WES

Do you want to know how to get out of the trap?

RAPHAELA

No.

WES

That's the problem. So you should sit down with the understanding that you don't want to get out of the trap and then that's at least clear between us. And you won't complain about it. The rest of your life, when you notice it's not working and it's trapped and your trapped and things are kind of dead, and you're not getting off on things, and you're bitching and moaning about complaining about things and the people around you are bitchers and moaners and complainers—all friends—then that'll be okay with you because you took a stand in The Forum that you prefer that.

(*long pause*)

RAPHAELA

My racket prefers that, I think, because who I am is not...

WES

Do you want to get out of the trap?

RAPHAELA

Yes.

WES

Let me tell you how to get out of the trap. Are you willing to listen?

RAPHAELA

I'm willing to listen.

WES

Great. Stop trying to get out of the trap. That's how you get out of the trap. You stop trying to get out of the trap; just stay in the trap. You accept the trap. Then your relationship to the trap transforms. Look: Stay with this because this is important for everybody else. See the floor? Okay.

(*pacing back and forth*)

I'm just doing whatever I'm doing right now, right? And in terms of my ability to go through reality right now, there's no problem, right? But there's a floor there, okay? I want you to imagine that I had an argument with the floor being there. Okay? I'm going to show you what that's like.

(*looking back and forth down at the floor*)

What the hell is that floor doing down there? This is the stupidest floor I've ever seen. My mother doesn't like this floor. I don't like it. It should be a foot higher. Who was the stupid person who put this floor here? They've got to change this right now.

(*to Raphaela*)

You see where I am in relation to this floor? I'm stuck with it. I'm in an argument and a complaint about this floor. I'm not accepting the floor. This floor is wrong. Not okay. It ought to be different. I should change it. It's a problem and I'm totally stuck with the stupid floor. What it takes to transform my relationship with the floor is to let it be the floor as it is. And then the floor and I get along perfectly well. And nothing's changed. The floor is still there. So that's an analogy to your relationship to your racket. You know, if you can let your racket be, it'll give you some possibility of being. The way you let your racket be is you realize that it's empty and meaningless. Your racket's designed to add meaning to everything. It doesn't mean anything.

RAPHAELA

I got that.

WES

Good. You're now up to date with The Forum. Congratulations.

After the applause, Kipp called on a participant named Kenneth.

KENNETH

I thought I had a lot of this figured out because I took the training. I also thought I had it figured out that there's no meaning because I gave up religion. I'm a native Californian.

(*laughter*)

I've had a lot of attachments to the way things ought to be. My karma is like my religion. I didn't even see that. I thought I was really clear with things. I have a huge trap. I have a savior complex. In my line of work I've seen a lot of people with savior complexes. That's my schtick.

Probably a lot of people here can identify with that. I've noticed a lot of tears. I've been identifying and commiserating with a lot of people. What I tell myself is that I'm crying for me. I'm very selfish. And what I thought I heard Werner say yesterday was "Get off it." And that really scares me.

KIPP

What does that mean, it really scares you to get off it?

KENNETH

Well I just lost my job. I'm about to lose my marriage. I think I just lost the house I was going to buy.

KIPP

You mean you got fired?

KENNETH

Yes.

KIPP

You don't lose jobs. You lose keys, right?

KENNETH (*laughter*)

Right. My story is I got laid off. I really got fired.

KIPP

Got it.

KENNETH

It feels good to say that. I've got a long history of "poor me" and boy that's fucking me.

KIPP

No, it's poor me-ing you. Poor me is poor me; not poor me is not poor me. They both mean the same thing: nothing.

KENNETH

Yes. I almost got to the point where I can laugh about that.

KIPP

Careful, don't. It'll be a shock to your system.

KENNETH

Right. And when I was looking at...

KIPP

You are truly a heavy guy, aren't you?

KENNETH

Yes. And I've lost a lot of vitality in the last...

There was laughter from the participants, because the absence of vitality was so apparent.

KIPP

You're also a master of understatement.

KENNETH (*laughing*)

And to have a certain façade that really I thought worked.

KIPP

And you have to keep that whole heavy and significant thing in place!

KENNETH

Right. And then to find out it doesn't mean shit.

KIPP

Right.

KENNETH

Wooo!

KIPP

What it means is being heavy and significant, and whatever else you say, that's what it means.

KENNETH

Just before dinner last night I got light.

KIPP

Yeah, and it scared the shit out of you. You see it's risky. See, what you already are is familiar. Being scared, sad, upset. That's what you call "you." Anything else is unfamiliar. Unfamiliar is awkward, embarrassing, so you'll take anything that's familiar, even if it's destroying your life.

KENNETH

Yeah, at dinnertime I felt great, like maybe I could get off this schtick. I had a real sense there of lightness and then I got heavy.

KIPP

And that's the way it's going to be for you. How many of you have noticed things opening up and closing, opening up and closing, opening up and closing, opening up and closing?

(*many hands go up*)
Put your hands down. Now, how many of you would like it to stay open forever?

(*many hands go up*)
And that's what makes you stupid.

KENNETH

Whooo!

KIPP (*loudly*)

Because as soon as it opens up you make opening up mean something. That's the way life should be now!

KENNETH

Yeah, that's what I did.

KIPP

Yeah, you want an event. You don't want to live; you want an event.

KENNETH

Yeah. I want a drama around the event.

KIPP

And so you'll have drama around the event. Everybody wants an event, an easy answer, so they don't ever have to inquire again, or think again... Did you share with people?

KENNETH

Yeah.

KIPP

What happened? Who did you share with?

KENNETH

I shared with several people.

KIPP

What did you share? "I said..."

KENNETH

I shared about losing my job, about poor Kenneth, about why I feel there's a poor Kenneth there. I got relatively clear on that during the training why I have a poor Kenneth thing, what that's doing to my life. I didn't get to the tears that I've been experiencing here. That's new. I didn't have that in the training. I feel like my life the past two years has been going upside down and it's scaring the shit out of me.

KIPP

No, what happened is, you got laid off, and your marriage is...

KENNETH

My marriage is about to terminate.

KIPP

It's about to terminate. You sound like it's a computer turning off.

(*laughter*)

KENNETH

Really. Okay.

KIPP

And something about your house.

KENNETH

Right.

KIPP

Anything else?

KENNETH

I have a new relationship.

KIPP

Are you always this excited about that or is this a breakthrough?

(*laughter*)

KENNETH

That's great, yeah. Pardon my schtick.

KIPP

You understand that enthusiasm is a threat to your survival? Joy is a threat to your survival? Self-expression is a threat to your survival? I'm not saying any of those are good, or the way you should be, and the way you are isn't the way you should be. I'm not saying that; it's easy to hear that. I'm just saying that you're locked out of most of life. One's not better than the other. But right now you have no choice.

KENNETH

It would be nice to have a choice.

KIPP

It would give you freedom to have a choice.

KENNETH

Yeah, which is what I felt for a little bit last night.

KIPP

Yeah, and rigorously speaking, it wasn't a feeling.

KENNETH

That's what I saw last night.

KIPP

Yeah. Your feelings are a product of your racket, or the context of whatever you give your feelings to occur in. So far your feelings have had the space of your racket.

KENNETH

Yes.

KIPP

Anything else?

KENNETH

Thank you.

(*applause as Kenneth sat*)

KIPP

Well done!

SARAH

Where do I start? Let me find a place... I got my racket, and saw, last night, the terror of it.

KIPP

Of what?

SARAH

My racket is "I'm an incompetent parent." And as the people I had dinner with me last night would tell you, you get anywhere close to that and like, it's survival, this is war. It's like, you know...

KIPP

What are you talking about? What's war? What's survival?

SARAH

It's like I... my racket is "I'm an incompetent parent."

KIPP

You're an incompetent parent.

SARAH

Right.

KIPP

And if somebody says...

SARAH

And if somebody even gets even pretty close to that...

KIPP

And questions you as a parent?

SARAH

They don't even have to get that close. You know...

KIPP

Okay.

SARAH

So, last night, um, I was looking at some other always...already always beings, and I saw them as, you know, there was no meaning there for them. I looked at my past. I'm from the South, and I looked at some of these southern things we have; and I really got it: You can jump into that game, or you don't, you know, it's there. And I looked at my "I'm an incompetent parent" and the terror, and I really felt the terror, and I couldn't get to no meaning, to empty and meaningless. I couldn't get it; I had that terror all night long. And I understood the person who stood up and said "when I was a little kid I was embarrassed, and I'm never embarrassed." He's

The Call of Conscience

As we have shown, for both Martin Heidegger and Werner Erhard, the current experience of human being is fundamentally missing something. Heidegger located the source of this absence in the assumptions of the metaphysical tradition, whose understanding of the world does not include the background realm that he calls Being. At this point in development of that tradition, that anything is missing has also been forgotten; and beyond the next forgottenness is oblivion (see the last sidebar of Session Three of Day Four). "Being," says Heidegger, "is still waiting for the time when it will become thought-provoking to man" ("LH" in *BW* 227). Thus a central task of The Forum is to make present this deficiency in such a way that it transforms into a new possibility for Being.

However, human beings, when listening away to the "they" self, avoid confronting any deficiency by embracing distraction, losing themselves in the ways of the world into which they have been thrown. The Self of Dasein, remember, is a *way of existing,* and the way we exist is to fall into the arms of the possibilities we find open to us—the arms of the "they," a world of curiosity, idle chatter, and ambiguity, which constitute the groundless public discourse that is always right, and for whom nothing is new. But in thus falling, we remain lost, wherein "Dasein makes no choices, gets carried along by the nobody [the "they" self, or as Erhard sometimes calls it, the "anybody" self] and thus ensnares itself in inauthenticity" (*BT* 312). Such a life may be easy, interesting, and pleasant; but it is never one's own.

And yet: since this is the only mode of existence we have experienced, how could we know that any other mode is available? What is needed is a hint, a prod, a direction: "In terms of its *possibility*," says Heidegger, "Dasein *is* already a potentiality-for-Being-its-Self, but it needs to have this possibility *attested*" (*BT* 313, emphasis added). For this purpose, we are introduced here to an old friend whom we have undoubtedly encountered before:

> **[Because] Dasein is *lost* in the "they," it must first *find* itself. In order to find *itself* at all, it must be 'shown' to itself in its possible authenticity. . . .this potentiality [-for-Being-its-Self] is attested by that which, in Dasein's everyday interpretation of itself, is familiar to us as the "*voice of conscience*" [*Stimme des Gewissens*]. (*BT* 313)**

But precisely because the conscience is such a familiar element of our moral/psychological/theological mythology—one that has been assessed, disputed, and interpreted in manifold ways—it is likely to occur here as a tired concept reduced to ambiguity in the idle talk of the "they." So Heidegger emphasizes that he is positing the voice of conscience as an *existential* phenomenon. That is, like our attunements, which cannot be ascertained without being inhabited, the voice of conscience is there, waiting to happen, and so is only heard when Dasein, attuned in anxiety, *wants* a conscience. Thus, it is never factual, only factical.

> **As a phenomenon of Dasein, conscience is not just a fact which occurs and is occasionally present-at-hand. It 'is' only in Dasein's kind of Being, and makes itself known as a Fact only with factical existence and in it. (*BT* 313)**

got, maybe, the terror there. And the terror was there. I couldn't get out of it. I have a beautiful concept of it. And I can tell you metaphors about it, but it was there. I got up this morning, and it's like... my son came in and he sits down on the bed. He said "Mom, tell me about this thing you're doing." Before I tell you that, let me tell you a little bit about my son. He spent five years in a mental hospital. He's thirteen now. And I said "Wll, we're talking about how we are as human beings. And we've been talking about how we have these things that exist for us from when we were really little, and he said "You mean those things we know from the time we were born?" Shit.

(*laughter*)

So I say "Yeah." So anyway, and we go on and we're talking, and he's following me, and I say "Yeah, I've been looking at the way I am, and this thing I've got about being an incompetent parent, and the terror I have with it. And he says, "Mom, you're an incompetent parent," and then he laughed—

(*she demonstrates the laughter*)

"Mom, we're related!"

(*applause*)

And I'm blown away, laughing and crying at the same time, really, and he's standing there and says "Mom, I don't understand you're laughing and crying, but don't look, I'm crying." It was like... Later on in the morning he was sitting on the bed and terrorizing the cat. So I says "now what would you do if somebody came in and was terrorizing the cat the way you're terrorizing the cat?" "Well I would shoot 'em." And I said, "I just don't know what to do about it." And he says "well you're an incompetent parent!"

(*laughter*)

I said "I got it. If I were terrorizing the cat, what would you do?" And he said "I'd tell you to stop it." And I said "Well, stop terrorizing the cat." And he did.

KIPP

A lot of work.

SARAH

Yeah.

KIPP

It's been this drama. And this tragedy, and how to work it out, and what to do...

SARAH

"How do I do it to you to make you stop terrorizing the cat?"

KIPP

Yeah, building a strategy and looking for the options.

SARAH

Yeah, well that was it and it was like, it's "I'm an incompetent parent."

WES

Someone is willing to say what's so, rather than give a reason for it or try to explain what it all means, deal with the significance of it...

SARAH

And it was real clear to him, "you're still my mother. You're my mother!" He said that! And in all the discussing about The Forum with people in my life it never occurred to me to talk to him.

WES

Yeah, it only occurred to you to talk to yourself.

SARAH

Oh, I love that one.

(*laughter*)

Yeah, he talked to me. He got up early to come talk to me. I left him—maybe I shouldn't say this—we were out of kitty litter. The cat pooped on the carpet and I told him to clean it up and go buy more kitty litter. It's not like I have to do it for him. Yeah.

(*applause*)

KIPP

Thank you Sarah.

WES (*to the group*)

Your whole life has been lived inside of meanings, explanations, reasons, and justifications. The lowest level in which human beings can live their life... I'm now going to give you a name for that. You're at a place where you can begin to recognize it. Before you were too much in it to be able to recognize it. You know, like the fish cannot recognize water. The fish cannot discern water; it's everywhere. You're like a flying fish, for the moment. You jumped out of the water, and you looked back to see the water. And when you discern the water, you can take that back into the water: That's possible. It's an analogy for what is occurring in the room: When you get stuck with anything, it sheds a little light on it. So when you jump out of the water and you see the water that human beings swim their life in, that water is called *reasonableness*.

(*pausing*)

The *reasons* for people are more important than the *results* in their life. Human beings care more about reasons than they do about results. And when you ask people about what happened and why it happened and how come, you get drawn into a conversation for all your reasons. People trade in reasons. They pretend to care about results, but all they really care about

The call is not something that occurs from time to time in such a way that lends itself to inductive empirical study, for "the Fact of conscience cannot present itself at all" (*BT* 314). Rather than search for empirical instances, to encounter the call, to "hear" it, requires before all else a transformation in the listener, a shift from listening away to the "they" to a listening that is altogether different.

 Dasein fails to hear itself, and listens away to the "they"; and this listening-away gets broken by the call if that call, in accordance with its character as such, arouses another kind of hearing, which, in relationship to the hearing that is lost, has a character in every way opposite. If in this lost hearing, one has been fascinated with the 'hubbub' of the manifold ambiguity which idle talk possesses in its everyday "newness", then the call must do its calling without any hubbub and unambiguously, leaving no foothold for curiosity. *That which, by calling in this manner, gives us to understand, is the conscience.* **(*BT* 316)**

First Dasein must find itself *as* having failed to hear itself, which refers to the dominant self-reflexive trope of The Forum: being authentic about one's own inauthenticity, which necessitates finding oneself to be inauthentic, that is, to be living a life not one's own, all the while pretending one is. This finding of oneself as inauthentic is the lack that the conscience reveals, the charge of "Guilty!" which the voice of conscience calls Dasein to own up to. "To be" means to be falling, to have lost touch with Being because Being loves to hide. We are left with words that become dead, as mere transparent husks. But how can we get those husks to come forward and speak Being? ∎

is reasons. "Well I really tried to produce that result. And you know I tried this and I did that, and this happened and this happened." "Oh, I understand: Well, as long as you really tried; as long as you really meant it; you really were sincere." "I understand" often means, "Okay, I'll give you that one as long as you put up with my bullshit for not producing the result I said I would produce. You'll accept that then, too, right?" See you're either at The Forum on time or you're not. You're either on the airplane when it leaves or you're not. The airplane does not care about the traffic jam you got into. It just leaves, and you stand there like a jerk watching it leave, complaining about the unfairness of life. You either keep your word or you don't, with regard to life. Life is not fair. Children think life should be fair. Some people—most people—never grow out of that, and they argue about the fairness or unfairness of life, and their reasons for what they have done and why they did it, and why it should have been this way, and their story, and it's all stuck together; and people are asleep, and what keeps them asleep is reasonableness. And by the way, it is very real when you're discussing it. The basis for your reasonableness ultimately is your commitment to your story. But the level of living your life we're discussing now is called reasonableness, and it stinks. You know, like, we invite you to participate in something and you will deal with "why are we doing that?" and "should I be doing that?" and "how come we're doing that?" and "what's really happening?" And you'll never deal with the offer and the possibility of the offer. So one way to listen to Sarah's sharing is: Somebody who's willing to give up reasons in her relationship with her son, and relate to him, like straight, like "here's what I say and I'll take what you say and out of what we say to each other, we'll be committed to it as itself and not deal with all the story about it that's not being communicated." So, she can acknowledge being an incompetent parent, which by the way is only a conversation anyway—which I know you know—but it opens something up. That conversation opens something up. She doesn't have to explain it, and justify it, and make her son wrong, like he's the reason for her incompetence. He doesn't have to deal with her reasons. He can just deal with her self, and they can deal with each other. See: That's a breakthrough. That's what's possible in terms of participating in life when you can step out of your story, and let the floor be there, let life be there, let your self be there, embrace it, and play with it. But you have to give something up. You have to give up your significance and your commitment to reasonableness. You need to know what it looks like, really. What you look like—your story, and your reasons for it, and the justifications for it—really are absurd. Time for another newspaper article. I'm going to show you what a life looks like, carried to the extreme, when someone's commited to some meaning, some significance, some reasons and justifications for their life.

Here Wes read a newspaper article which demonstrated reasonableness carried to an extreme. It was the obituary, from the *Los Angeles Times,* of the musician Billy Tipton, who had died earlier in 1989. It was headed "Death reveals musician who lived as man to be woman." At her death at the age of 74, it was revealed to friends and family that Tipton, who had lived as a man, had been in reality a woman. Tipton died poor, said Wes, and tired of keeping her secret.

WES

There you go. Aren't you tired? Of keeping the secret? Think it's worth giving the secret up? You think it's worth giving up what you've been withholding from life? You know what you've been withholding from life? Your self. What you've been giving to life is your secret; what

WES (*continuing*)

you've been withholding from life is your self. And you put the two together and you look at life from the possibility that you're going to die: What's the point? I mean really, what is the point? Why not just give it up? Where's Kevin? I wasn't in the room earlier. I hear you turned in your video release today. Congratulations. That's giving something up. I invited you last night to confront what it costs, the risk... you want to share about that?

KEVIN

Kind of funny, because after I got my standing ovation from everyone, I sat here thinking, "I don't want to put my hand up, because I've already received too much attention. So I'll just sit here." And it took me about, I don't know, a half an hour before I finally realized "I could put my hand up and they could choose me whenever they wanted. I wasn't in control..."

(*laughter*)

WES

That's very good.

KEVIN

Yeah, I got a lot...

WES

Wait, let me just use that, because a number of people have been coming up to me demanding I call on them to share. You ought to get what Kevin is saying. You either will or you won't and you'll know it at the end of The Forum if you've been called on. Don't worry about it because it doesn't mean anything anyway.

KEVIN

And you're not going to get any more out of it if you're called on.

WES

You want to listen. That's when you get something out of The Forum. The Forum takes place in your listening.

KEVIN

And I know that because as I was sitting here, I was thinking about that, "well, it doesn't matter if I get called on, if I get called on, that's fine, I get called on."

ERHARD

It's not even fine. You get called on, you get called on.

KEVIN

You're right.

ERHARD

And if you don't get called on, you don't get called on.

KEVIN

You're right.

ERHARD

And that's the way that it is. And you could make a great big drama out of that. "Wes doesn't like me. Kipp doesn't like me even more. Nobody likes me. They're trying to torture me. I really got something to say that's important. I gotta get up here, nah nah nah nah nah nah nah nah nah nah." Very good Kevin. Go on.

KEVIN

I was like that. Is it okay if I say something to somebody else in the group?

ERHARD

Not usually. But in your case we'll make an exception. Go ahead.

(*laughter*)
I appreciate your asking.

KEVIN

Well I'd like to talk to someone in the group but I'm not quite sure how to handle it, but I'll count on you to stop me if I get out of line. I heard myself, as I told you before, I had everybody's racket so maybe I'm a good person to talk to everybody because I've got everybody's racket. But maybe everybody here has everybody's racket... But there was a young person last night that really got to me because I saw myself in that young person, maybe twenty, thirty years ago, and I really wish I could talk to that young person but I don't think I'll be able to talk to that young person because I got a feeling that that young person probably isn't listening to me right now.

WES

Actually I think they are. I think everybody is. I don't believe what you... I don't accept what you're saying. So let me tell you what you are saying: The future needs to be just like the past; nobody can learn from anything. Everybody has to go through the same mistakes. It's bullshit. Something's happening in the room in the conversation where the person twenty years younger than you, Kevin, is getting you. And the benefit of the twenty years you screwed your life up.

KEVIN

I'm sorry, but I think that's completely wrong, because I think that person's sitting there thinking "I can't possibly learn anything from this old fart," and...

ERHARD

They do say that but it doesn't make any difference anyhow.

(*applause*)
And let me tell you what they learn from you, Kevin. Young people don't learn from our preaching. They learn from who we are. You know, you can't miss your magnanimity. You cannot miss it; it can't be missed.

KEVIN

My magnanimity?

ERHARD

Yes, your magnanimity.

KEVIN

I'll have to work on that a little later. If I can get that together with my stinginess, that's gonna take a lot of work.

ERHARD

Remember one thing. Stinginess is not a quality inside you. It's a product of your actions. And magnanimity is the same thing. You give yourself being big when you get off it. When you're being moved in here by other people's sharing, you can't help it. I suppose you might be able to do it, but it would be very difficult to be in here and not be moved by people. And what moves us is not their story. That may entertain us but it isn't what moves us. What moves us is their magnanimity. Magnanimity arises in action, like the act of getting off it. That's real magnanimity. We don't have a good way of talking about it because I have to say "you have to be big," and it sounds like some quality inside. There are no qualities inside people. Qualities arise in action. And yes, yesterday you were being stingy, and you're a bit thrown to being stingy, and what you said last night gave you a possibility beyond being stingy. You know, you bit the bullet. You spoke straight. And anytime somebody bites the bullet and talks straight a possibility beyond their inauthenticity arises. And you gave yourself a new possibility last night. You want to listen up because I'm putting this in words that you might find a bit hard to, you know, a bit hard to deal with.

KEVIN

I'm dealing with them.

ERHARD

Okay very good. So, last night in speaking straight and speaking yourself and being authentic about your inauthenticity, you created a possibility beyond your inauthenticity, and today you acted in that possibility...

> **And what moves us is not their story. That may entertain us but it isn't what moves us. What moves us is their magnanimity. Magnanimity arises in action, like the act of getting off it.**

(referring to the video form)
and in that action there was magnanimity. There was being big. And it's extraordinarily attractive. I mean extraordinarily attractive, and I don't mean it looks good, Kevin.

KEVIN

No. The nice thing about it is that I don't even need it now.

ERHARD

Exactly.

KEVIN

Now that I got it I don't need it.

ERHARD

Now, let's get that one last thing straight for everybody. That's right. Nobody pays any attention to your opinion. Nobody pays any attention to your expression of what you agree or disagree with. Particularly young people don't pay much attention to it. They're organized not to pay any attention to it. They need not to pay any attention to it. They're struggling to establish themselves. And they cannot get away from the message delivered by *who* you are. That makes a difference for them no matter what their stance in the matter is. Okay, please go on.

KEVIN

Well this person I saw as me twenty or thirty years ago. I don't even know how many characteristics of this person I want to describe... but there was a lot of defiance in the statement that was made.

ERHARD

Defiance?

KEVIN

Defiance, defying you. And when I first came here I still had some of that defiance. I'm sure that...

(laughing)
I know why they're laughing.

ERHARD

And the smile on your face is an expression of being able to be with their laughing, which is a lot more powerful than being insulted by it or wondering why they are laughing.

KEVIN

So I think I probably had a pretty good need to take you on. And I probably wouldn't have taken you on because I understand how stupid it is to take you on, even if I wanted to take you

KEVIN (*continuing*)

on, because I'm playing on your field and you're going to win. There's no question about that, even if I'm as good as you are. By last night I didn't have the need to take you on anymore. I didn't care if I took you on. And I didn't care if I won. And I didn't care if I lost if I took you on. It didn't make any difference. So that was really good. So, back to the young person I am trying to get to. I don't know why: There's some reason I'm trying to get to this person and I don't understand what that is. Somebody came up to me last night after I finished and said that must have really been hard to do. Last night was not hard to do. Today is hard to do.

ERHARD

Stingy is easy. Magnanimous is not easy.

KEVIN

So, to this person, I came in here and I'm a person who has spent their whole life—I'm 56 years old—I spent my whole life, I don't think, ever trying to look into my head, until just recently, and so I'm new at this game. I'm not a head looker. I've been busy being successful and all that and so I'm looking at this young person. Not a real young person. Just getting a little beyond young, but really defiant, really pissed off about something. I wanted to say to that person "Hey look boy, I'm the biggest case of all," which I'm sure a lot of you are saying "No, I am." But I know I am the biggest case of all, that came into here thinking "Boy, I'm going to have to put up with a lot of bullshit," but I think there must be something to this thing, and I'm clever enough that I can get around the bullshit, and sort that out, do it my way and control it, and figure out whether there was really anything good in this and I'll extract out what I think is good in this and I'll let the bullshit slide by my ear. And the reason that I think I'm able to get something out of this: I'm lucky I guess. I came into this, well, the only way I can get something out of this is if I just really say "okay, push those thoughts out of your mind, and get something out of this. I'm gonna get something out of this. I'm going to get into this." And I've really gotten into it, and last night was a hell of a night, because I went to bed and it was a long time before I went to sleep, thinking. My head was exploding going through all these things, my assignment and everything else, and boy, did I make progress. I'm not sure... Something happened, I've had so many breakthroughs...

ERHARD

Let's get clear. It's not progress, it's dropping stuff.

KEVIN

I've dropped a load they must have heard...

(*laughter*)
At least four or five floors down.

ERHARD

That's generous Kevin. That's generous. That's generosity. Sharing "winning" is generosity.

KEVIN

So to this young person who doesn't have much time left to get something out of this Forum.

ERHARD

Never mind the editorial.

KEVIN

This person is looking forward to really getting the job done at the next event, because this person's talking about the next event, where this person's going to get the job done. And I don't think this person's going to get the job done in the next event unless they start right now getting the job done at this event. That's what I have to say.

(*applause*)

WES

Kevin, I appreciate your generosity, so I'm gonna share a poem with you.

Here Wes read the e e cummings poem, "What gets you is nothing."

WES (*completing the poem*)

So you've been gotten, and what got you is nothing. It is inescapable. What there is to be gotten by—to be used by—in The Forum is nothing. If that now sounds like possibility to you, if now you hear that communication as possibility—you don't understand it...

KEVIN

I feel like I understand it.

WES

Maybe you do. I'm saying, even if you don't. If it just has that sense of possibility to it, raise your hand.

(*most of the participants raising their hands*)
How many don't?

(*a few raising their hands*)
Okay. So are you complete Kevin?

KEVIN

No. I still have my homework assignment.

WES

Those who don't: Your job is to transform the conversation we're having now, somehow, into possibility. You notice that a lot of people in the room have done that. That's your job now. Your job. That's where the value of your money occurs.

KEVIN (*almost crying now*)

I did my assignment; I almost didn't do it. I called my wife this morning. I had forgotten that I was supposed to ask her if I was selfish. So I asked her if I'm selfish. Her first response was to laugh.

(*laughter*)

It wasn't a big laugh.

(*bigger laughter*)

I really mean that, I wasn't trying to be cute I don't think. But it was a genuine laugh. And I wasn't quite sure what that was going to be followed by. And she paused for a minute and was thinking. And then she said, "Well, you do have to have control." And so I was sitting there dealing with that. And then she said "But you've got a lot of good qualities to offset it." I'm not trying not to cry. I don't know what I'm trying to do. I've certainly never cried in front of a group like this.

ERHARD

Let me tell you something. Anytime you actually meet yourself, it'll move you to tears.

KEVIN

Well I'm not worried about crying. In some respects I wish I could cry.

ERHARD

That's close enough. What you're doing is fine.

KEVIN

So I told her I loved her and she told me she loved me and that was the end. I'm complete. Thanks.

ERHARD

Good.

(*long applause*)

WES

Just because we're committed to you, we're going to give those of you who raised your hand, those of you who didn't get possibility yet, we're going to give you one more shot at waking the fuck up.

(*laughter*)

ERHARD (*lightly*)

No scatological language, Wes, please.

What is Said When Conscience Calls?

The call of conscience is a calling to listen past the hubbub and to be brought back to one's Self, but the "they" is not entirely circumvented; one cannot leap over what it means to be human. Rather, the "they" self plays an essential role:

 But the fact that the call *passes over* both the "they" and the manner in which Dasein has been publicly interpreted, does not by any means signify that the "they" is not *reached too*. Precisely *in passing over* the "they" (keen as it is for public repute) the call pushes it into insignificance. But the Self, which the appeal has robbed of this lodgment and hiding-place, gets brought to itself by the call. (*BT* 317)

In the language of The Forum, the concern for looking good and being right, inauthentic to the core, gets revealed as empty, as lacking any ultimate ground, as utterly without meaning. That is, the "they" self is not some inner self enclosed within the frame of the external world; rather, it "is" only by virtue of Being-in-the-world.

But if conscience occurs as a call, as a summons that passes over the "they" self, what form does it take? What is said in the call? The call is not vocal utterance; nevertheless, as calling, it *is* a mode of discourse:

> **But how are we to determine *what is said in the talk* that belongs to this kind of discourse? *What* does the conscience call to him to whom it appeals? Taken strictly, nothing. The call asserts nothing, gives no information about world-events, has nothing to tell. Least of all does it try to set going a 'soliloquy' in the Self to which it has appealed. 'Nothing' gets called *to* this Self, but it has been *summoned* to itself—that is, to its ownmost potentiality-for-Being. (*BT* 318)**

The call of conscience, says Heidegger, is discourse in the mode of silence, and its message is unequivocal: it says *nothing*: the call speaks through what is left unsaid. Any misunderstanding of this message is due not to its mis-calling, but to interference from the soliloquy through which the "they" self (i.e., the socially constructed identity) interprets the call (*BT* 318–19). Thus the "nothing," revealed in anxiety through the call of conscience, holds the possibility of authentic self-revelation.

Throughout Heidegger's thought we find the essentiality of non-Being as the other side of Being; and Heidegger takes full advantage of the rhetorical possibilities of the nothing, recognizing the opportunities for paradox and reflexion which arise in discussing a "something" which is "nothing." We mean "rhetorical" in two related senses. The first is its essential sense as the use of language for the primal assignment of meaning as

Kipp asked those who did not see possibility in empty and meaningless to stand. About fifteen people stood; one of them received a microphone.

WES

There's just one last little piece stuck to it, a little piece of meaning stuck to it keeps possibility from occurring.

Kipp confirmed with those standing that they are yet to be "clear" about life being empty and meaningless and that it is empty and meaningless that it's empty and meaningless.

ERHARD

Hold on. Is it that you don't get it or you don't like it? Which is it with you?

ANABETH

I don't see either. I thought the question was: "do we see possibility?"

ERHARD

We're restating the question. The question is: Did you *get* that it is empty and meaningless, and that it's empty and meaningless that it's empty and meaningless? Did you get that?

ANABETH

Yes.

ERHARD

Good, then we apologize for misleading you. You're welcome to sit down now.

(*several participants sitting down*)
The only people who should be standing are those who didn't get that it's empty and meaningless and that it's empty and meaningless that it's empty and meaningless. So that's what you didn't get.

BRADLEY

I don't think so.

ERHARD

Who should I ask?

(*to a seated participant*)
Did he get that?

(laughter)
Should I ask him? Who should I ask?

BRADLEY

Me.

ERHARD

Did you get that?

BRADLEY

No, I'm still attaching meaning to it.

ERHARD

I'm not asking whether you are attaching meaning or not attaching meaning. You're always going to attach meaning.

BRADLEY

I will?

ERHARD

You are a machine that attaches meaning. As long as you're functioning you will attach meaning. However, it's possible to attach meaning in the context that it's empty and meaningless. It's possible to get that it's empty and meaningless and attach meaning to it. See, this is not a conversation for convincing you of something. This is a conversation for leaving you dwelling in the truth. Dwelling in the truth, you can't use the truth. So the question is, did you get—and by "get" I mean: "dwelling in" that it's empty and meaningless? By "get" I mean: Are you "coming from" that it's empty and meaningless? Not: Are you attaching meaning to things?

BRADLEY

Yes.

ERHARD

Then you are welcome to sit down.

(*addressing Jacob, standing*)
You didn't get it, right? You got it partly and partly you didn't get it?

JACOB

Well I understand that, um, that a lot of times we try to take things for more than their face value, which is what happened, and add a stupid story to it and try to give it meaning. But I was wondering about your wording. When you say that it's empty, is that where potential comes from, or possibility?

ERHARD

Is that where what?

primordial metaphor (see the sidebar "Primordial Metaphor" in the Second Session of Day Four)—or, in this case, the radical undermining of meaning, since to bring Being (originative meaning) to language we must also bring nothing to language, and not merely ontically: the ontological saying of the nothing is primal rhetoric.

The second sense of "rhetoric" is closer to the Aristotelian tradition: that is, Heidegger, and especially Erhard, use the language of nothing *strategically*, exploiting its paradoxical possibilities to reorient the audience by revealing to that audience its true relation to nothing and thus to Being. ∎

> Life is like a rainstorm. It does not rain in order to water the little flowers. It just fucking rains and life is like that. Life is just like it is. Life is just that way. It's not that way for a reason. It's just that way. It's just the way it is, and it's just devoid of meaning and significance, except to the degree that you bring some meaning and significance to it. And the meaning and significance that people bring to it does what you saw in here over the last three days.

JACOB

Is that where possibility comes from, being empty?

ERHARD

It may or may not, but, in my answering you in the context in which you are asking me, that isn't going to make any difference for you, because you're asking me in order to understand. If you do this exercise... the way we know you did the exercise is because possibility arises. Now I didn't ask that question yet, we're going to ask that question in a little while because we need to get this other thing flat first. What we want to get flat is not did you figure this out, and does it fit with everything you know. But rather, did you get that life is empty and meaningless and it's empty and meaningless that it's empty and meaningless? It has no inherent meaning, no inherent significance. Life is like a rainstorm. It does not rain in order to water the little flowers. It just fucking rains and life is like that. Life is just like it is. Life is just that way. It's not that way for a reason. It's just that way. It's just the way it is, and it's just devoid of meaning and significance, except to the degree that you bring some meaning and significance to it. And the meaning and significance that people bring to it does what you saw in here over the last three days. So that's what there is to get. What there is to get is that life is empty and meaningless and it's empty and meaningless that it's empty and meaningless. That is to say, it's not only empty and meaningless but you can't make something out of that without getting into trouble. Is that clear?

JACOB

Yeah. But...

ERHARD

You're going to screw it up trying to make up a conclusion out of it.

JACOB

Yeah I am.

ERHARD

Don't do that. Stop that.

JACOB

Okay.

(*applause*)

ERHARD

It's very important what Jacob just illustrated for you. I heard you say it goes in and out and in and out and in and out. It goes in and out and in and out because you try to make a conclusion. I told you the truth has no use. It's use-less. Worth-less. What is "worth"? Worth is what makes

ERHARD (*continuing*)

you right. That's the only thing that's worth anything. Something that makes you right; that's worth something. Something that makes somebody or something else wrong; that's worth something. Something with which you can dominate; that's worth something. Something with which you can avoid domination; that's worth something. Something you can justify yourself with or invalidate others; that's worth something.

(*loudly*)

The truth isn't worth anything. It's worthless because you can't use it. And the instant you try to draw a conclusion from it, you make a "therefore"; you put a "therefore" behind the truth and it sucks all the truth out of it. It's no longer true; it is now more bullshit. You stumble across the truth, you happen to bump into it, leave it alone. By leave it alone I don't mean walk away from it, or ignore it, I mean: let it be. Is that clear? You want to take that page out of Jacob's book, and it will move things forward here more rapidly. And we won't still be here Monday morning.

(*Jacob sits as Erhard addresses another standing participant*)

You did not get that it's empty and meaningless?

DENNIS

I want to believe that I'm getting it, but I'm not getting it.

ERHARD

What is it that you're not getting?

DENNIS

That life is empty and meaningless.

ERHARD

Okay. What is the meaning of life?

DENNIS

I don't know. That's what I'm here for.

WES

I'm now going to tell you. You want to know the meaning of life? Let me tell you the meaning of life, and then you'll know the meaning of life and you'll see the difference it makes in your life.

Wes got a dictionary from the table and read from it the definition of "life": "The property or quality that distinguishes living organisms from dead organisms...etc."

ERHARD

It's all clear now, isn't it? It's all clear now. Absolutely. That cleared it all up, now didn't it? Go on Wes.

(after much laughter, Wes continues to read several definitions of "life")
It's all clear now isn't it?

DENNIS

No it's not...

ERHARD

Listen up. You've got a hidden standard for getting it. Did you hear what I said? You've got a hidden standard for getting it. It's kind of like, when I hear the angels trumpet then I'll know I got it. So you want to get that standard up on the mat in order to be able to get it. What's the standard? How are you going to know when you got it?

DENNIS

I guess when I hear my bells ring.

KIPP

He wants the bells. We'll give him the bells.

ERHARD

Listen, now. This is it.

KIPP

We're going to demonstrate something so that every time you give significance to your life, you can see what life really means.

Kipp opened a dictionary and balanced it on his head. Then he held a chalkboard eraser in each hand and walked around the room through the group, very solemnly clapping the two erasers together and dispensing eraser dust like the incense in a church processional. He approached Dennis and clapped the erasers directly in front of him, as if dispensing a blessing. The room broke out into extended applause and laughter.

ERHARD *(to the group)*

You understand he was illustrating you all; you're just covert about it. That's what you look like when you stand in the truth. Is that silly enough? Think you'll remember that? When you're pontificating, you want to remember that's what you look like.

(to Dennis)
See: You're wanting to make some significance out of getting it.

DENNIS

That's correct.

ERHARD

And getting it is to get that there is no significance. So there can't be any significance in getting it. You want to know where you've got your foot nailed to the floor? When you were younger somebody told you some bullshit about what it was to get it. What were you told when you were young about what it was to be enlightened, to get it?

DENNIS

I was brought up believing that one should be successful and make things happen for yourself, to be in control.

ERHARD

Yeah, and you know that was the product of the culture in which you were brought up, and family in which you were brought up, and the time of history in which you were brought up. And you know, there are cultures in which success is looked down upon, in which you have to hide your success. You know that, right?

DENNIS

Sure.

ERHARD

Sure. So what's the significance of that? I mean, which is right? Which is the right way to go? Is the right way to go and devote your life to success, or to devote your life to something else? Which is the right way to go? Do you see that the question is insane? You go the way you go. The question whether it is right or wrong is irrelevant, stupid, is stupefying. Look at how stupid it made you. That was not an insult. It was just a report. Look at the stupidity that you've revealed in your own lives. You know, the "at the heart of it" stupidity. Yeah there's nothing wrong with being oriented around and regarding being successful or accomplishment highly.

DENNIS

Yeah but, I feel like... I don't consider myself overly successful, but somewhat successful, like you said...

ERHARD

Here's how successful you are. I've seen your bank account: You're as successful as you are. That's how successful you are and it'll probably remain like that. No matter how much you accomplish, you will only be as successful as you are, and you will not be as successful as you aren't. And that's the way it's going to be for the rest of your life. Right? It's like "who's buried in Grant's tomb?"

DENNIS

Sure I can buy that.

ERHARD

Grant is buried in Grant's tomb, and that's about how complex this whole thing is. Things are the way they are and things are not the way that they are not, and they are always like that and they don't change.

DENNIS

See, I have a hard time... I want to believe, Werner...

ERHARD

I appreciate that...

DENNIS

...but it's like, I came here with some conceptions that... "Okay, I am here, because I feel fine. I am successful. There are certain things wrong I would like to fix." Sitting here, wanting to believe, but I'm hearing, "let it be."

ERHARD

I never said "let it be." That's somebody else's horseshit. I never said "let it be," because you can't do anything *but* let it be--and pretend that you're doing something else. What I said is "what is, is, and what isn't, isn't." That's mine. That's pretty goddamned safe. I'll take on anybody who wants to attack me on that one.

DENNIS

No, I'm not trying to attack you...

ERHARD

No, no, I know you're not trying to attack me. I did not mean to imply that, and I'm sorry if it sounded like I did.

DENNIS

No, I'm just trying...

ERHARD

You're trying to hear bells. All you're going to hear is simplicity.

DENNIS

Yeah, I guess I came here thinking that four days and three hours on the fifth day is going to make a difference in my life. I just can't go home and quit and say the rest will be history. You have to go back to your life.

ERHARD

Nobody said "quit." Okay go on.

DENNIS

Right, I know. When I try to make sense out of believing there is no meaning...

ERHARD

No, I don't want you to believe that there's no meaning; that would make you crazy.

DENNIS

Yeah, if I went home and said that life doesn't make any sense, it doesn't mean anything...

ERHARD

I didn't say it doesn't make any sense. I said it's empty and meaningless, and it's empty and meaningless that it's empty and meaningless. That's all I've said. And if you went home and said it's empty and meaningless and it's empty and meaningless that it's empty and meaningless, you would get into trouble. See, just like I would get into trouble if I said that to people who didn't pay me $625. And I don't say it to people who don't pay me $625, and then I don't say it until the third day. Don't tell people life is empty and meaningless, because they can't hear you. They can't hear that because it's all the way down at the bottom. Where are they? They're all the way up at the top. They're floating on all that soap opera and drama, all those rackets and all that act. They can't see down through the murk that it's empty and meaningless. What you've been through is designed to take you down one layer at a time, until you can get far enough down so that you can see that all the way down it's empty and meaningless. And it's very, very difficult to get down there because you can't use that. And that's kind of what you're complaining about. It didn't leave you feeling wonderful. It didn't leave you free and easy and wonderful, and it never does until you get there. The secret is perfectly hidden. That's why almost nobody gets it. It's why it took three days, four days of hammering to get you close to getting it. And you may not get it. But I want you to know something: That's all there is to get here. What there is to get for your $625, and the four days and three hours crushing your backside, is that life is empty and meaningless, and that it's empty and meaningless that it's empty and meaningless. And that the soap opera you've made out of your life is a very bad joke. It's a bad joke. You've made everything significant and meaningful and it's caused you to suffer. And not only the bad things, but you suffer the good things, because the good things don't leave you fulfilled and whole and complete. They don't leave you full of joy and satisfied. So you not only suffer the bad things, you suffer the good things as well. Your life is nothing but suffering. And the source of suffering is a lie. There's only one source of suffering. The source of suffering is a lie. Stop lying and you'll stop suffering. And the fundamental lie is that it all means something, that it's going to work out, that you're going to make it someday, that you're going to get there, that someday the fairy prince is going to come along, or the fairy princess is going to come along, or someday the right job, or someday the right life, or someday the right body. That's the lie that keeps the suffering in place. When you get to empty and meaningless you get that there's no more suffering. All there is, is possibility. Freedom. Openness. But you

 Your life is nothing but suffering. And the source of suffering is a lie. There's only one source of suffering. The source of suffering is a lie. Stop lying and you'll stop suffering. And the fundamental lie is that it all means something, that it's going to work out, that you're going to make it someday, that you're going to get there, that someday the fairy prince is going to come along, or the fairy princess is going to come along, or someday the right job, or someday the right life, or someday the right body. That's the lie that keeps the suffering in place.

can't get to empty and meaningless in-order-to. And every time you turn it into an in-order-to, you lose that it's empty and meaningless, because the truth is sucked out of it, and it becomes a mere platitude.

DENNIS

I just want to end with saying that I will leave here with the thought that life is empty and meaningless and that opens up a possibility.

ERHARD

I don't want you to leave with "it opens up a possibility." That ruins it.

DENNIS

Is that an in-order-to?

ERHARD

Yeah. See, you're a real in-order-to guy. That's not bad. That's not an insult. That's highly valued in this culture. We place a lot of value in this culture in in-order-to.

DENNIS

Thank you.

ERHARD

Yep. Very good. Thank you.

(*applause*)

(*turning to another participant*)
What is your story?

JOYCE

My story is that I get it and I reject it.

ERHARD

Okay. Don't do that. What are you crying about? Do you know? Yeah, you know, what are you crying about?

JOYCE

Because I came to make a change in my life and I don't see it happening.

ERHARD

Yes. I understand. So, you wanted to make a change in your life because there's a little suffering there, yes? Yeah. The way to perpetuate the suffering is to try to change your life. You stop changing your life, the suffering will go away. Is that clear?

JOYCE

Yes. It's clear.

ERHARD

So, don't do that anymore. Cut that out. Stop rejecting it. Stop trying to get better. Stop trying to change your life. What is it you want out of life, that's so goddamned important that you want to change your life? What is it that's bothering you because it's missing?

JOYCE

I want to like myself. I don't like myself.

ERHARD

Okay. Now. Start not liking yourself. Do that right now. Don't like yourself right now.

(*Joyce laughing*)
What are you smiling about? I thought you said you didn't like yourself.

(*laughter*)
Don't like yourself some more. This is pretty good. Now don't like yourself even more. You notice everything changed. Now like yourself. Like yourself.

JOYCE

It's not different.

ERHARD

It's no fucking different is it?

(*laughter*)
Liking yourself and not liking yourself are the same thing: It's all bullshit.

(*raising his voice to a pitch*)
What is this goddamned fantasy about liking yourself? What in the fuck is that? That's crazy! That's like walking around saying "Don't look! Don't look! Oh my God there's a man back there following me with a knife with blood dripping down." Bullshit people made up: liking your-self/not liking yourself. You know what not liking yourself is? It's a conversation you have with yourself. Bullshit people made up, this "liking yourself/not liking yourself." You know what not liking yourself is? It's a conversation you have with yourself.

JOYCE

It's a conversation I constantly have with myself.

ERHARD

Yeah, but stop it then. This is craziness. What is the significance of liking yourself or not liking yourself? Does it change a hair on your head?

JOYCE

It doesn't change anything externally.

ERHARD

It doesn't change anything. It doesn't change any little thing. It changes absolutely nothing. It's a bullshit conversation. It's like talking about "Which way is left?"

(to Joyce)
Which way is left?

(she points to her left)
No, that's right.

JOYCE

No, it's not right.

ERHARD

It is so right!

JOYCE

To you.

ERHARD

But do you see how nonsensical this conversation is between you and me now?

JOYCE

Yes.

ERHARD

Liking yourself and not liking yourself is just as nonsensical. You got conned into some bullshit conversation.

JOYCE

Yeah.

ERHARD

Did you ever hear people on drugs talking? They're like, nutty. Like myself/don't like myself is the same crap. "Whoa. Sha? Go man! Jack Damn!" What does all that shit mean?

(laughter)
It's all drama, drama. You ever been to the movies?

JOYCE

Yeah.

ERHARD

People are acting up there. It's not for real. This is your act, not liking yourself. It's your act.

JOYCE

I get that. I get that I put on an act.

ERHARD

There's nothing to like or not like. What does that mean: like or don't like? You are the way you are. That's the whole story, isn't it?

JOYCE

Yeah.

ERHARD

And you're always going to be the way you are. And you're going to be the way you are when you are the way you are. Today you are the way you are today. Tomorrow you'll be like the way you'll be tomorrow. And the day after that you'll be like you are the day after that. And that's going to be true for the rest of your life. What is this conversation like or don't like yourself? What does this mean? This is insane this conversation I like, I don't like. And you ought to be able to begin to see the insanity of it. It's like really insane. What is it about, for God's sake? What is the point? The point is drama, like soap opera. You know, you use life to make a soap opera: that's disgusting. Life is empty and meaningless. It's just like that.

JOYCE

I see that. It doesn't make any difference whether I like myself or not. But I'm stuck. I want to like myself.

ERHARD

But no. Let me ask you something. Listen up you all! What happens when you raise the issue of liking yourself? What *has to* go with the issue of liking yourself? Must. What is it that has to be there in order for you to like yourself? There's only one thing that has got to be there for you to have the issue of liking yourself.

JOYCE

What would have to go with it?

ERHARD

Yeah. What is it that has to be there in order for you to like yourself? There's only one thing that's got to be there.

JOYCE

Not liking yourself?

ERHARD

Yeah. Obvious, huh? You can't have liking yourself without not liking yourself. Get rid of both of them. It's a bullshit conversation. There's nothing in there. It's pure drama.

JOYCE

It's arguing with yourself.

ERHARD

It's like arguing if you're blue or green. Are you blue or green?

JOYCE

I'm neither.

ERHARD

Absolutely. It's like, are you likable or unlikable? It's like asking you if you're blue or green. It's the same kind of question. Are you blue or green? It's nonsense. It's garbage, and if you ask garbage questions you get garbage answers. Every time someone likes theirself, what gets reinforced?

JOYCE

I don't know.

ERHARD

Not liking theirself. Don't you see that you can't have a lot of liking yourself and just a little bit of not liking yourself? They got to be exactly even, because you can't build liking yourself except in contrast to not liking yourself.

JOYCE

You're saying to throw both of them away.

ERHARD

Yeah. This is a garbage question liking yourself/not liking yourself. Cut that out. Hold some-body's hand; look up at the sky; go make something happen: But don't waste your time with the question of liking yourself or not liking yourself. That's your racket.

JOYCE *(weeping)*

One of my rackets...

ERHARD

Right: and a significant racket for you. What you have to get to is that it's empty and meaningless. Underneath your racket is all empty and meaningless. If I take away liking yourself and not liking yourself, what are you left with? Nothing. There's where we want to leave you: with nothing. Is that clearer?

JOYCE

Yeah, but I don't want to be left with nothing.

ERHARD

I know, because there's a payoff in not liking yourself. You're getting something out of it. You're a racketeer. You're in it for the payoff.

JOYCE

Yes, I am.

ERHARD

Yeah. You like the payoff, be my guest.

JOYCE

No I don't like it.

ERHARD

Then cut it out. And if you can't cut it out, where you need to get to is that underneath the racket is empty and meaningless. You have to see that your racket's a joke. You're not going to get rid of your racket, ever. You get rid of one, you'll find another one under that. It's endless. It's rackets all the way down, I told you. It's like peeling an onion. You take off one racket, you get another racket. You take off another racket, you get another racket. You know what's at the center of an onion? Nothing. When you pull the last layer off, what's left? Nothing. Sorry for the cheap metaphor. Life is empty and meaningless and it doesn't mean anything that life is empty and meaningless. Did you get it? I didn't say "did you feel good?" I said "did you get it?"

JOYCE

Life is empty and meaningless that life is empty and meaningless means nothing.

ERHARD

No. It's life is empty and meaningless and that doesn't mean anything. Don't give any meaning to that. See, you're trying to make that mean something. Like, "Well, then I shouldn't have to bother!" No. It doesn't mean anything; you can't make meaning out of it, otherwise you destroy it. And as soon as you do make it mean something you take the truth power out of it; you take the truth value out of it. Then it becomes some stupid platitude that you bother people with. "Don't you know that life is empty and meaningless?" People don't want to hear that shit.

(*laughter*)

Don't go around telling people life is empty and meaningless. Live your life from it. Don't tell people that. So what there is to get is that life is empty and meaningless and that that doesn't have any meaning. That is to say: the fact that life is empty and meaningless is empty and meaningless. It's just empty and meaningless.

JOYCE

I get that.

ERHARD

Okay, that's all there is to get for the moment. I didn't say you have to feel good.

Erhard continued working one by one with the people who had stood because they did not get that life is empty and meaningless.

ERHARD (*to another participant*)

What is your problem?

SALLY

I'm having a hard time with life being empty and meaningless that life is empty and meaningless.

ERHARD

Let me make it easy for you. Life is empty and meaningless: Did you get that part?

SALLY

Yes.

ERHARD

What does that mean? What is the significance of that statement?

SALLY

That it's empty and meaningless, but I'm sitting here thinking, "Fuck it! Who cares?"

ERHARD

No, you just made it mean something. You didn't get it because you made it mean something. You said, "well if it's empty and meaningless then…" See, once you said "then," you didn't get it; you ruined it. Is that clear what I just said?

SALLY

Yeah, then it becomes something. Then it means something.

ERHARD

What it means is, "Then fuck it!" So you've got to get, not only that it's empty and meaningless, but also that it's empty and meaningless that it's empty and meaningless.

SALLY

Well, I want to do something with it…

ERHARD

I understand.

SALLY

But there's nothing to do.

ERHARD

That's right. There's nothing to do. Anything you do ruins it. You want to make a prescription out of it, Sally. You want it to tell you what to do. And like I said yesterday, the truth never gives any prescription. And if you get any prescription out of the truth, you suck the truth value out of it. It becomes devoid of any truth value. All you can do with this is get it. It's not worth anything; it's worth nothing; it's worthless: Because you can't use it. It doesn't help you to win; it doesn't help you to avoid losing; it doesn't help you to be right… see, if only it would tell you what to do with your life, then you would be happy. See, you would all be happy if we put on a presentation here, skillfully enough so that you actually believed that you knew what you were supposed to do with your life. So listen up. If we had a real scam … and Wes and Kipp and I are smart enough to put one together—make a note—it's maybe worth doing.

(laughter)

But I want you to listen. What would people say if you did The Forum and it left you knowing clearly what you were supposed to do with your life? People would really love that, wouldn't they?

SALLY

It would be a lot easier to sign up.

ERHARD

Yeah, it would be a lot easier to sign up, and we could charge more.

(laughter)

I want you to see how silly you are. If The Forum… You'd really have to believe it, wouldn't you? Otherwise it would be bullshit. Suppose after The Forum was all over, you had no doubt—none—it was crystal clear to you that you had found out what you were supposed to do with your life, really supposed to do. You would be very happy. Very happy. If you knew exactly what you were supposed to do, what you're really supposed to do, you'd be real happy, because you'd have the answer. Julie?

Nothing: Beyond Nihilism

In *An Introduction to Metaphysics*, Heidegger points out that if the fundamental question of metaphysics were to be put simply as "Why are there beings?" then we would be starting from an assumption of the being's *is*-ness, its givenness as a being. But, says Heidegger, with the addition of a second clause—"Why are there beings at all instead of nothing?"—the givenness of the being is thrown into question, and the being itself is held out "into the possibility of not-being," and thus begins "to waver" (*IM* 31). Until we have confronted this possibility of non-Being, and have thus opened ourselves to the other side of Being, we have not appropriated our true nature: "Da-sein means: being held out into the nothing" ("WM" in *BW* 103).

The event of *nihilation* is an essential element of Being: "Being nihilates—as Being" ("LH" in *BW* 261). However, this statement should not be heard as justifying charges that Heidegger's thinking is *nihilism*:

 But where is the real nihilism at work? Where one clings to current beings and believes it is enough to take beings, as before, just as the beings that they are. But with this, one rejects the question of Being and treats Being as a nothing (*nihil*), which in a certain way it even "is," insofar as it essentially unfolds. Merely to chase after beings in the midst of the oblivion of Being—that is nihilism. . . . *In contrast*, to go expressly up to the limit of Nothing in the *question* about Being, and to take Nothing into the question of Being—this is the first and only fruitful step toward the true overcoming of nihilism. (*IM* 226)

Thus nihilism consists in the *avoidance* of the nothing, since by avoiding nothingness, we in fact avoid the full disclosure of Being. Thereby, we retain an incomplete apprehension of our possibility as beings. Nevertheless, Heidegger does not deny that the "Nothing" speaks something fundamentally disturbing:

 The nothing itself does not attract; it is essentially repelling. But this repulsion is itself as such a parting gesture toward beings that are submerging as a whole. This wholly repelling gesture toward beings that are in retreat as a whole, which is the action of the nothing that oppresses Dasein in anxiety, is the essence of the nothing: nihilation. It is neither an annihilation of beings nor does it spring from a negation. Nihilation will not submit to calculation in terms of annihilation and negation. The nothing itself nihilates. ("WM" in *BW* **103)**

As Being and beings move apart, as Being withdraws into its always-potential concealment, the everyday meaning of beings is ongoingly subject to nihilation. Revealing and concealing, Being gives and nothing nihilates. This is the way of the world. And in the nihilating of the nothing lies the possibility of the clearing:

 In the clear night of the nothing of anxiety the original openness of beings as such arises: that they are beings—and not nothing. [...] The essence of the originally nihilating nothing lies in this, that it brings Da-sein for the first time before beings as such. Only on the ground of the original revelation of the nothing can human existence approach and penetrate beings. ("WM" in *BW* **103)**

JULIE

And then I would start bitching.

ERHARD

Exactly. This is a wise woman. How does she know "then I would start bitching"? Because you always bitch. That's like shooting fish in a barrel, that kind of a prediction. I told you about the Boy Scouts. It didn't make any difference: "Today we're going on a hike"; "Today we're going swimming." "Oh no!" Everything was "oh no!" So, you can't get anything out of this. I told you the truth. You don't use the truth; the truth uses you.

SALLY

Where I keep... I guess where I keep getting stuck is I want to get it so that possibility opens up.

ERHARD

That's an in-order-to. That's called a "rice Christian": That's when you go to church to get rice. Getting paid. Most of you go to church in-order-to, don't you? Sure you do. Don't bullshit me. I know why you go to church. You go to church in-order-to. It's sacrilegious.

(*asking a participant to stand up; turning back to Sally*)
So you've just got to get rid of the in-order-tos: Whether you do or not is up to you, not up to me.

SALLY

But aren't they just going to keep coming back?

ERHARD

Sure, they're going to keep coming back; that's why you've got to be able to dwell in that it's empty and meaningless, and that it's empty and meaningless that it's empty and meaningless. Dwell in; not believe, not understand, not remember. That's why we don't speak in concepts in here, because concepts are things people remember and forget. Distinctions remember you. You don't remember them; they remember you. You don't use them; they use you. That's why we've got this funny language. It's the language of distinction, not the language of conceptualization.

(*to Sally*)
What else?

SALLY

I'm going to sit down, because I don't know what there is I have to do.

ERHARD

There's nothing you have to do.

SALLY

So then I'm going to sit down.

ERHARD

No. You're only going to sit down if you do. You're not going to sit down because there's nothing to do; you're going to sit down if you sit down. And if you don't sit down, you don't sit down. You're not going to sit down "because." You're still trying to find something to save you. There's no life rings in here. This is the place where we take all the life rings away. There's nothing to stand on. I want you to stand on nothing. I want you to stand on empty and meaningless. Meet life with no foundation, with no background, with no learning. Yeah of course you have all the learning and all the experience, but you're not stuck with it. You're not stuck with what you know; you're not stuck with your condition; you're not stuck with your past.

SALLY

I have a question. So, if what I'm making it mean is that it's hopeless: Are you saying that I don't have to make it mean that?

ERHARD

If what you're making it mean is that it's hopeless, what you want to do is to see that *you are making it mean* that it's hopeless. You're doing that. Now, by the way: It is hopeless. And the reason it's hopeless is because of what you have to have if you're going to have hope. There's only one thing you've got to have. Hope cannot exist without hopelessness. And the stronger you get your hopes up, the more down in the swamp, down at the bottom of the Valley of the Shadow of Death, down in the swamp there, is hopelessness. So the more hope you've got, the more green slimy monsters there are down in the Valley of the Shadow of Death. Hopelessness. It lives down in the swamp at the bottom of the Valley of the Shadow of Death, with all your hope up there at the top, except the green slimy monsters keep you from ever being satisfied, from ever being full of joy. Look, you make a drama up out of being tired. You should have seen you the first night. A true drama out of being tired; you make a fucking drama out of death. That's right, death is so nasty because you made a drama out of it. Death is nothing but dying. It's not a drama. Who said death was bad? You did. Okay fine: Pope. One thing. People worry about death, right? What is there to worry about? Let me explain something to you: You are going to die. Don't worry. You are. You are going to die. And so is everybody else. Everybody you love and care about, they're all going to die. Don't worry. They will.

(a participant objects)

You're a bit nutty about this. You get up every time I talk about dying. And you know what? You won't die one minute before you do. And you want to know what? You won't live one minute longer when you're dead. You don't have to worry about that. It's all taken care of. You're not going to die before you do and you're not going to live after you die. Now you can worry about something else. So that business about hope and hopelessness: It's the same conversation about liking yourself. What is this hope crap? What does that change? What does that do? What does that make? What is the value of hope? If you hope it's going to turn out all right, that

This is an essential element of the approach to Being which is taken in the dialogue of The Forum. To reach Being, one must travel by way of the nothing. To discover possibility, one must confront the facticity, the trap, of no-possibility. Further, what Heidegger calls "authentic Being-towards-death," or "freedom towards death," may be seen as consistent with these other views: to experience the authentic possibility of one's life, one must confront one's essential nullity. Conscience calls Dasein— fallen into the untruth of the "they" self—to "appropriate untruth authentically" (*BT* 345), to bring authenticity to one's inauthenticity, to *be* in the trap.

It is of the utmost importance, however, to stress again this point: to "confront" means to experience an *ontological encounter*, not merely an ontical or conceptual realization. For instance, the merely ontic recognition that we all die is of course commonplace. On the other hand, the *ontological experience* of the death of one's self as identity, and the deep realization of the possibility of one's self as an opening, with all the ramifications of anxiety and homelessness which that experience entails, is far from commonplace. This is the revelation of the nothing, the call of conscience, which Heidegger posits as the ground for authentic existence, and this is the encounter for which the rhetorical structure of The Forum is designed.

Authentic inquiry into Being is likely to arouse resistance, and this resistance may be located precisely at the juncture where Being's other side, the Nothing, must be confronted. Here is the true challenge of Heidegger's thinking, which Caputo calls "the danger of Heidegger's path": at this juncture "there are no assurances," and "in this darkness and uncertainty lies one of the largest difficulties with Heidegger's work" (The *Mystical* Element in Heidegger's Thought 245). Caputo quotes Paul Huhnerfeld, who has compared Heidegger's way with religious paths to transformation, such as that of the Christian mystic Meister Eckhart: "Meister Eckhart would never have taken the mystical step if he had believed that he was leaping into Nothingness instead of into the arms of God" (245).

Caputo finds in this aspect of Heidegger's thought a "serious difficulty": "It does not seem to me that many of Heidegger's excited and enthusiastic followers, who speak like Heidegger, as though they have experienced what Heidegger experienced, have recognized the austerity of Heidegger's path or acknowledged the danger which lies along this path" (252–253). The danger of the path, says Caputo, lies in the powerlessness of human beings who travel it, and in their inability to find secure ground and comfort in the mysterious realm of Being, whose apparently arbitrary nature Heidegger has described here, explicating Fragment 52 of Heraclitus, as "play":

> **The "because" withers away in the play. The play is without "why." It plays since it plays. It simply remains a play: the most elevated and the most profound. But this "simply" is everything, the one, the only. Nothing *is* without *ground/reason*. Being and ground/reason: the same. Being, as what grounds, has no ground; as the abyss it plays the play that, as *Geschick* [destiny], passes [B]eing and ground/reason to us. The question remains whether and how we, hearing the movements of this play, play along and accommodate ourselves to the play. (*PR* 113)**

Thus, for Caputo, Heidegger's thought moves "close to the edge of despair. For he makes us dependent upon the outcome of a 'game' upon which our very essence is staked, a game in which thinking may lend a hand but in which it has no final say" (251–252).

> **The difficulty with Heidegger is not that he is a mystic, but that he is *not*. His thought is so radically worldly and secular and drained of absolute and divine assurances that it can at best assist in a world-play; for the kingdom is in the hands of a child. (252)**

makes it turn out all right, right? Or it's going to turn out wrong if you hope it's going to turn out so you don't dare hope. It's voodoo. That's nuts. That's a guy following me with a knife with blood dripping down from it: "Don't look! But you can't see him anyhow, only I can see him."

(laughter)

Look, what are you hoping for? You're hoping it'll all be all right, huh?

SALLY

Yeah.

ERHARD

But it won't be all right. It'll be the way it is. It won't be any different from the way it is. That's the way it will be. It'll be the way that it is. And all you're doing is making a drama out of it. Is that clear?

SALLY

Yes.

ERHARD

If you like making dramas out of it go ahead. What you do with your life is none of my business. That's not my business, that's your business.

SALLY

So there's no good or bad, there's just the way it is.

Erhard's manner is very relaxed and casual at this point, ranging freely in volume from loud to intimate.

ERHARD

There *is* good and bad. Go out there and shoot someone; then you'll find out how bad it is.

SALLY

All right, that's where I'm stuck then, because...

ERHARD

I know you're stuck. I know how you were brought up.

(laughter)

Yeah, there is good and bad, but not inherently. Inherently there's nothing. Was there goodness in the rainstorm when the flood came from the rain that killed people? Don't you see that that's insane? The rainstorm isn't good or bad it's a goddamn rainstorm. Where does good and bad exist? In a conversation. And that conversation has a lot of force to it. You exist in a particular culture; a particular religious culture, a particular ethnic culture, a particular national culture, a particular family culture, and that's where good and bad arose from. It's a phenomenon

ERHARD (*continuing*)

which arises only in language. There is no good or bad outside of language. Now good and bad is very real stuff. But it's a phenomenon that only exists in language.

(*loudly*)

Listen up, goddamn it! You've stopped thinking again. You think you've got it so you don't have to think. The floor as an object exists independent of language. That clear? For whom is that not clear? Put your hand up if that isn't clear?

(*looking around the room*)

The existence of the floor as an object doesn't require language. Is that clear?

(*pausing*)

Good. Is there any such thing as art independent of language? Where there is no language, is there art? No, because art is a phenomenon that arises only in language. Now you assholes think I said art's not real and floors are. I didn't say that. Art is very real. It alters the course of history, has a profound impact on the culture, changes people's lives, brings things into people's lives that would not be there were it not for art. It's very real stuff. It's real, and it does not exist independent of language. Art is a phenomenon that only arises in language. Is that clear? There's no such thing as beauty independent of language. Beauty is a phenomenon which only arises in language. There's no such thing as beauty independent of language. Beauty is real, and it does not exist independent of language. You need to start thinking and stop believing. You believe too much. There is no such thing as art or beauty or design, no such thing as love and happiness. None of the things that are important to you in life exist independent of language. Birds don't build homes. Nests are hard-wired into birds. You don't understand that then don't get engaged in the conversation. That part of the conversation. Only agents with language, only people build homes. Homes are a phenomenon that only arises, only in language. So there's no such thing as beauty or art. Here's what you want to get out of this. Not beauty or art: This is not a course on aesthetics. What you want to get out of it is that there are certain phenomena that arise only in language. Over where your dog is, nothing is bad. You know where bad is for your dog? Where you are. That's where bad arises to the dog, because bad is a phenomenon that only exists in language. Independent of language there is no bad. There is no bad in an earthquake *for the earthquake*. There's only bad for people with language...sorry: entities with language. And that's the same thing about good. But it's very real stuff. It's not unreal. Now, language comes out of silence, which is a form of empty and meaningless. Good and bad come out of nothing. It doesn't come out of inherent good or bad. It's not like you can ignore it. It's not like it isn't true. It's real stuff, and it arises only in language. You can't report that something is good. You can't give a report that something is bad. Good and bad only arise in language. You can't talk about something being good: Now you do, don't you? That's because you're stupid. You talk about things being good and bad. You talk in ignorance that what you're talking about when you talk about good and bad is talking. That's like talking about talking, you understand? When you talk about good and bad you're talking about talking.

(*to Sally*)

You were saying?

Caputo's point is important, and is central to a consideration of the path which Heidegger is inviting us to follow. The authors of this book are certainly among those whom Caputo has described as "excited and enthusiastic" about the possibilities of Heidegger's thinking. However, we do not claim to have "experienced what Heidegger experienced": we do feel an affinity for that realm of experience about which he speaks; that affinity is due, at least in part, to our participation in the work of Werner Erhard. Thus, in the face of Caputo's challenge, we must ask ourselves whether we have truly confronted the "austerity and danger" of Heidegger's path.

This is a question that must be asked persistently—a question which must be stood within, rather than answered—since Being must be continually wrested from, and contextualized by, non-Being. The nihilation of the nothing must be ongoing. But the original encounter is fraught with *agon*, that is, with contest: human resistance to confronting the Nothing is fundamental. The Nothing's enormity so violates our everyday identity that we instinctively close ourselves to the possibility which it contains. Heidegger states:

> **We are so finite that we cannot even bring ourselves originally before the [N]othing through our own decision and will. So profoundly does finitude entrench itself in existence that our most proper and deepest limitation refuses to yield to our freedom. ("WM" in *BW* 106)**

Therefore, the struggle to provide an authentic confrontation with the austerity of the Nothing, and to overcome the resistance to its realization, is a central element of The Forum.

The important questions to be considered in comparing Heidegger with religious models of transformation, such as Meister Eckhart, are these: what might be the transformative power of a leap into the truly unknown rather than into the arms of a comforting and fatherly God? Might not the "danger" of Heidegger's thinking, that abysmal lack of certainty which characterizes his leap, in fact constitute its possibility? Might not the transformation of human being arise in that very surrender of human control to the unpredictable play of Being, the surrender to the mutuality of the event of appropriation? The following passage, in which Heidegger is thinking through a Parmenidean fragment, suggests the essential and continual uncertainty constitutive of the three-fold path he posits, "that of Being, that of not-Being, and that of seeming":

 Superior knowing [. . .] is granted only to one who has experienced the sweeping storm on the way of Being, to whom the terror of the second way to the abyss of Nothing has not remained foreign, and who has still taken over the third way, the way of seeming, as a constant and urgent need. To this knowing belongs what the Greeks in their great age called *tolma*: to dare everything with Being, not-Being, and seeming all at once—that is, to raise Dasein above itself into the de-cision about Being, not-Being, and seeming. (*IM* 125) ■

SALLY

I got what you were saying up until you were talking about talking.

ERHARD

Good and bad is talking. When you talk about good and bad you're talking about talking.

SALLY

Okay, I got it.

ERHARD

Did you sort it out?

SALLY

Yeah, there's just one more thing I want to ask.

ERHARD

Sure.

SALLY

So this morning, we got into a fight, my whole family...

ERHARD

Right. Families do that, don't they?

SALLY

Yeah, all the time.

ERHARD

No: They do it when they do it and they don't do it when they don't do it.

SALLY

Right.

ERHARD

"All the time" is a story.

SALLY

Right. So we got in a fight this morning, and so I said "It doesn't mean anything, so leave me the fuck alone."

ERHARD

Right. How many people have done that already: "It doesn't mean anything, therefore..."

ERHARD (*continuing; participants raising hands*)
You're scum, I know that.

(*laughter*)
We told you not to do that and you did it right away, and if you haven't yet, you will. Sleazy.

SALLY

I've also found myself wanting to do the same thing with them. It's only bad if you make it mean something bad.

ERHARD

No, it's bad because it's bad. But you have to understand whence bad arises, or bad disempowers you. You can't avoid bad. Bad's there. Like I said, go out and do something illegal, and you'll find out about what bad is.

SALLY

So what if I don't think something's bad but my dad does?

ERHARD

Who pays the food bills in your house?

SALLY (*laughing*)

He does. So it doesn't matter if I think something's bad or not.

ERHARD

Sure it matters if you think it's bad. But look, what you've got is not the same kind of authority that your father has because you don't pay the bills. So if you're going to deal with the way you see things and the way he sees things, you're going to have to deal with it in a different method than he does. He deals with it like he pays the bills. You can't deal with it like that, because you don't pay the bills. You've got to find another way to deal with it. Did you hear what I said?

SALLY

I think so. What I do costs him money, so...

ERHARD

No, what I mean is, he's got authority. You don't have authority. You're not the boss in his house, he is, right?

SALLY

Yeah.

ERHARD

And that's the way that is. And you know you can bitch and moan and complain, and all the stuff about that, or you can get that that is where the door is. A lot of people want to go out there, and they go over and start kicking on the wall. Because they want to go out there! Fine, the door is over there. You want to have your way, what you got to get is where the door is. And where the door is, is that your father's the boss. That's how to get what you want is "my father's the boss." If you try to get what you want through "my father's the boss," you go through the door, instead of kicking your way through the wall. You have a much better chance getting to what's on the other side of the wall going through the door than kicking your way through the wall. Yeah, you'll get through the wall every once in a while, but you'll also be left bloody. Yeah, and the other thing is that it isn't fair. Gravity isn't fair. Shouldn't old people get a break from gravity? That's what you sound like with that "life isn't fair" shit. Okay fine. That's where the door is: The door is, "life isn't fair." You want to get where you're going, you've got to go through the door. Continuing to kick the wall is saying "life isn't fair." What is this conversation "Life isn't fair"? What is it? What is the point? It's another goddamned drama. Life isn't fair. Your father's the boss, and you live with another adult. You ought to be equal. Too bad. That's not the way it turned out. Your father's the boss, and you can get what you want—not that you can always get what you want—but you got some power to get what you want, as long as you go through the door. If you don't go through the door you're going to have to use force. You're going to have to make your father wrong, or run away, or fuck something up…

SALLY

Even if I'm going through the door, but I'm being covert about it then I'm kicking down the wall.

ERHARD

Exactly. And I didn't say you shouldn't use your wiles. Nothing wrong with buttering up the old man.

(laughter)
You don't want to define everything. "Okay, now we're going to do foreplay, are you ready?" It's not a good approach. So yeah, covert is one thing, and playing the game is another thing. You're allowed to play the game and that will work.

SALLY

Being covert won't work?

ERHARD

No. Being covert doesn't work. That's like trying to put one over on somebody. But playing with people works. Particularly with fathers with their daughters. Fathers are easy with their daughters, except when the daughter tries to kick through the wall, right? Okay, you can sit down.

GLORIA

I keep trying to bring morality into this.

ERHARD

The drama of morality...

GLORIA

Like what she said: If life is empty and meaningless, why produce?

ERHARD

Why produce if life is empty and meaningless?

GLORIA

Not if...

ERHARD

Given that life is empty and meaningless, why produce? There is no reason to produce. Except for one thing, Gloria: You did not hear that life was empty and meaningless. You've been in a conversation with other people and not with me. See, "life is empty and meaningless" does not tell you what to do with your life. It gives you no guidance at all, none. My "empty and meaningless" is worthless. Your "empty and meaningless" gives you guidance. So your "empty and meaningless" tells you that going on is worthless. My "empty and meaningless" tells me nothing, gives no prescriptions, explains nothing, justifies nothing. That's the "empty and meaningless" we're talking about here. The "empty and meaningless" you're talking about is not the one I'm talking about. Out of your "empty and meaningless" you get a meaning about what you should do, you get a prescription for what you should do for your life. My "empty and meaningless" has no prescriptions in it. You went to the seminar on the other side of the wall. Over there they got a seminar about empty and meaningless and it tells you what to do with your life.

GLORIA

I can understand it intellectually.

ERHARD

What does that mean "intellectually"? I don't understand "intellectually."

GLORIA

I understand it makes sense.

ERHARD

You understand it with the understanding you have, I get that. You understand it. Period. Now what is it that's missing?

GLORIA

It makes me feel like shit.

ERHARD

Yeah, you don't like it. The man did not say you would like the truth. As a matter of fact, the first thing the truth will do is piss you off. Didn't you notice people in here?

GLORIA *(laughing)*

I almost got into a fight last night because of that.

ERHARD

Because of the truth?

GLORIA

Because of it was empty and meaningless. She was a Forum staff person so it made me really want to punch her.

ERHARD

This is turning the truth into shit. How could empty and meaningless generate anything?

GLORIA *(referring to Sally)*

What she said about "fuck it."

ERHARD

But that's not the empty and meaningless that you got in here. That's the empty and meaningless you got in the seminar on the other side of the wall. The one you paid $625 for, you didn't get that one. You got the cheap one, you got the one that doesn't cost anything. The $625 one does not give you any prescriptions, it does not justify anything. See, you want to use it to justify something. Right?

GLORIA

Yeah.

ERHARD

You think it justifies doing nothing, but that's not the empty and meaningless we're talking about in here. The empty and meaningless we're talking about in here justifies nothing. And what bothers you is it's going to invalidate your whole life because you're a "rice Christian." You didn't work to work.

GLORIA

I don't go to church.

ERHARD

Yeah, you're a "rice Christian." I don't care whether you go to church or not, you're a "rice Christian." You don't work to work. You work in-order-to. That makes you a slave.

GLORIA

That's human. We're all human.

ERHARD

Horseshit, human. It's crap. See, you just used the truth to justify something. You took all of the truth out of it. Yes, it is quite human and it justifies nothing, it explains nothing, and if it does justify or explain something it is no longer the truth. It's just some stupid justification.

GLORIA

I can't get any possibility out of it.

ERHARD

No, because you haven't gotten it yet.

GLORIA

Okay.

ERHARD

You've got to go through that feeling bad, Gloria. You get to feeling bad and stop. You've got to go all the way through the feeling bad. Did you get that? You've got to go all the way through it. You still have got something there. You haven't gotten to empty and meaningless yet. You've gotten to "empty and meaningless and that's bad." That's not all the way through it. Clear?

GLORIA

Yeah.

ERHARD

Good for you.

(*applause*)
Jake?

On the first day of The Forum, Jake, an architect, was the participant who was "hustle waiting to happen," and who also had his "foot nailed to the floor" in regard to sincerity and inauthenticity.

JAKE

I was going to ask about the truth, but you already answered that question. But I wanted to also share a little about my racket. I wanted to thank you. It sounds like you knew a little bit more about me than I expected. I appreciate that.

ERHARD

I know about being human.

JAKE

It sounds to me that you know what my profession is. I have an attractive profession. It makes me more attractive.

ERHARD

I have a profound respect for your profession. And I probably have more respect for it than most of the people who do it. I see it as a very, very, very important opening for humanity. And I know there are also people in your profession who also see your profession in that way, but not a lot of them. There's something very important in there that humanity has yet to explore. I have a deep respect for design. A deep respect. And it's a mystery I don't get. But your particular profession would not be a bad place to explore the mystery of design. But exploring the mystery of design is different than just doing design.

JAKE

And that's what I would want to do, but having it as a racket just fucks it all up. And I chose the profession because it was an attractive profession. I chose it because I needed a job. I come from a highly educated family, and there's one time I thought I was going to be a bum.

ERHARD

And you decided against that.

JAKE

Yeah, I decided against that, so I went to school. I got a career: a degree and a license. And I was lucky enough to pick a profession, which I now find exciting, but it's really fucked the way—it could be a lot more exciting if I get this other shit out of the way.

ERHARD

Exactly. That's very good. Jake and I have had enough interactions for something useful to happen here. See I know it sounds in the beginning in particular—and for some of you it still sounds like—that everything I say is an insult, everything I say is a put-down. I know that some of you will describe this to people as "they called me bad names"; "they beat me up"; "They wouldn't let me use the bathroom"; "He said 'fuck' and went like this."

ERHARD (*to laughter, making a gesture with his hands indicating the sex act*)
I actually acknowledged that when Jake and I first began to speak, that there's a lot of accomplishment in this room. I didn't call you an asshole because I didn't know you were accomplished. I knew you were accomplished and I called you an asshole. Like Jake said: There's a lot of satisfaction in what he does and there's the possibility of a lot more satisfaction in what he does. That is what the asshole was about. It was not meant to denigrate you. It was said in full knowledge of your accomplishment. It was way more insulting than you thought, but it was not meant to denigrate. It was said in full knowledge that you're accomplished and there's a lot more there could be.

JAKE

This has been a great experience. I stole a lot of the microphone—talking is another racket. I've got every racket in this room. And I think everybody else in this room have all the rackets...

ERHARD

Yeah: because they're not your rackets. The racket is not yours. You are the rackets. The racket owns you; you don't own the racket.

JAKE

I came in with a chip on my shoulder too. You invited us to speak there at the beginning. I thought I would ask a question that would really throw this guy about guests for the evening session, and the money. This experience was a genuine experience and I owe you an apology for that.

ERHARD

The apology is: You made this work for you.

JAKE

I did.

ERHARD

That makes us even.

(*applause*)

KIPP

Okay, we're about to go on a break. Standing in the empty and meaninglessness of life, see if a conversation for possibility, for participating in life...

ERHARD

Let's not give them an assignment at this point. Just stay with the empty and meaningless, we'll talk about the rest of it when you get back.

Kipp handled a few logistical items (*handing out seminar schedules for those who had received an erroneous schedule, etc.*). The course supervisor followed Kipp upon the stage to deliver several announcements.

At 12:15 pm, The Forum adjourned for a break.

SESSION ONE INTERVAL

The Forgetting of Being, Part Seven of Eight: *Logos*

Are humans missing out on an important element of existence? How would we know? How did this come about? Further, if this element is the experience of Being that is available in The Forum, why does that experience occur as elusive—that is, as something you get and lose and get and lose? To shed some light on these questions, we are following Heidegger's history of Being.

As we proceed here, we invite you to read from the perspective that while Heidegger's project was supremely intellectual in its approach, it was not epistemological in nature: he did not want to help us know more about Being, or to achieve what we generally call a greater understanding. Rather, he wanted to create, through thinking, a clearing for the presence of Being in the world. In his reading of the existing fragments of their writing, he finds evidence that the pre-Socratics experienced this presence.

The Unconcealment of Being

The fifth and sixth centuries BCE were an extraordinary period in human evolution, giving rise to "a development in the art of philosophical inquiry that is quite unparalleled in world history" (Wheelwright, *The Presocratics* 1). Language, by some estimates, had entered our evolutionary path a million years earlier; and by the fifth century, complex aspects of existence were emerging to be named, and dealt with. There was a new level of demand for humans to understand themselves, and their place in the world. The decisions made at this point, Heidegger says, have proven to be decisive.

We have seen that for the Greeks, Being occurred as *physis,* the *sway*, an "overwhelming coming-to-presence" of emerging possibilities. In a process of languaging that Heidegger calls *originary naming*, the Greeks were engaged in a struggle to create a world: "[T]his sway first steps forth from concealment—that is, in Greek, *aletheia* (unconcealment) happens—insofar as the sway struggles itself forth as a world. Through world, beings first come into being" (*IM* 67).

Physis, emerging as world, stands in the world in *aletheia*. *Aletheia*—unconcealment—was for the Greeks *self-blossoming appearance.* Heidegger sometimes translated the word *aletheia* as "truth," but at other times he was emphatic that *aletheia* for the Greeks bore no relation to our usual notion of truth as the correspondence of a proposition with its object. *Aletheia,* for the pre-Socratics, was

the truth of a being at its inception. To think *aletheia,* we must imagine an existential moment—a moment of virginal emergence when a being is first available to be seen, and thus first opened to being apprehended in the world before multiple perspectives of its appearance have given rise to multiple propositions regarding its nature:

> **For the Greek essence of truth is possible only together with the Greek essence of Being as *physis*. On the grounds of the unique essential relationship between *physis* and *aletheia,* the Greeks could say: beings as beings are true. The true as such is in being. . . *Truth belongs to the essence of Being*. (*IM* 112)**

The idea challenges our thinking, immersed as we are in a persistent cacophony of conflicting truth claims. But the view that beings *as beings* are essentially true was grounded in a particular ontological/historical context: for the pre-Socratic thinkers, *physis* was Being brought to stand in the world with beings, and in that context the unconcealed beings stood in truth. The truth of beings was the truth of Being. We cannot grasp that notion of truth—cannot imagine it, cannot bring it to thought—because we have lost the requisite orientation to Being.

Truth as Freedom

Fundamental to that orientation, says Heidegger, is that the essence of its truth is *freedom*. But this understanding of the situation calls for a shift in what our Western tradition has considered to be the relation of freedom to truth. In that tradition, freedom is a property of human beings, and consists in our freedom to say, and in saying to judge what is true. This is the Cartesian model, with the balance of power weighted on the side of the subject.

But now the emphasis in Heidegger's view is the freedom that arises in *aletheia*—in unconcealment, the freedom of the openness of the open region in which beings are first revealed. This shift—from the freedom of the human sayer to speak truth, to the freedom for *beings to be the true things they are*—is a central movement in Heidegger's later thinking: "Freedom now reveals itself as letting beings be" ("OET" in *BW* 125). But this is not letting-be in the sense of neglecting, or letting things alone. Here it means the opposite: "To let be is to engage oneself with beings," not by managing or planning but by an alert attunement to the open region "into which every being comes to stand, bringing that openness, as it were, along with itself" ("OET" in *BW* 125).

Heidegger is distinguishing a delicate balance—a way of relating to the world in which we neither impose ourselves upon, nor surrender to and lose ourselves in, beings. Rather, we withdraw somewhat, so that "they might reveal themselves with respect to what and how they are," and so that we might find their truth in the event of their unconcealment ("OET" in *BW* 125). In *aletheia*, Being appears in undistorted emerging: "Considered in regard to the essence of truth, the essence of freedom manifests itself as exposure to the disclosedness of beings" ("OET" in *BW* 126). *Aletheia*, says Heidegger, is "Revealing as the order at the start" (*EP* 65).

The Truth of Integrity

We note here that Werner Erhard has consistently avoided truth claims for his work, emphasizing repeatedly that he does not know the truth. We propose, however, that an experience of the truth of Being is a fundamental element of The Forum (see the first sidebar in the next session, "The Three Levels of Truth"). It is hinted at throughout the dialogue in the unspoken realm of the conversation, and culminates with the evocation of the Nothing; but perhaps its most pertinent articulation is Erhard's distinction of *integrity,* which begins with this definition: integrity is "*the state of being whole, complete, unbroken, unimpaired, sound, in perfect condition*" (Erhard and Jensen, "Putting Integrity into Finance: A Purely Positive Approach" 6).

This understanding of integrity is harmonic with *phua,* the root of the word *physis,* which according to Heidegger means "what one originally and authentically already is: that which essentially unfolds as having been, in contrast to the subsequently forced and enforced contrivances and fabrications" (*IM* 111). In the context of their fundamental orientation to Being, beings were seen by the pre-Socratics as *originally true,* a truth arising in the moment of their free emergence. Distortions of their truth were subsequent to their unconcealment. This sense of Being as *what one originally and authentically is,* we assert, is consistent with Erhard's understanding of integrity, and the distinction of integrity is a fundamental element of the transformation that The Forum makes available.

Logos: Primal Gathering

Emerging into the truth of unconcealment, *physis* is gathered in *logos*. According to Heidegger, just as the original power of the Greek term *physis* has been lost, so has the meaning of *logos* devolved over time. The traditional academic conception of this term is that it concerns *discourse* of some kind—generally reason, assertion, or logic. In Aristotle's *Rhetoric,* for example, *logos* designated that category of evidence in which a speaker uses evidence conducive to a given audience's ability to reason, making an argument persuasive to that audience.

But these interpretations are later derivations, since the fundamental meaning of the term for the pre-Socratics had "no immediate relation to language" (*IM* 137). Instead, *logos*, as *legein,* a form of the verb *lego,* meant originally to *lay, to gather* or *collect. Legein* is to lay down, to lay before; *logos* signified the *primal gathering principle*.

As beings emerged from the sway and into the world, embryonic in their meaning, fragile in their truth, the task to be undertaken was to preserve them in their unconcealment and in their fundamental orientation to Being: "To be human," writes Heidegger, "means to gather, to gather and apprehend the Being of beings" (*IM* 194). Naming is not something that follows the event of emergence. Rather, naming, as originary saying, allows "the Being of beings" to be "opened up in the structure of its gatheredness… Human beings, as those who stand and act in logos, in gathering, are the gatherers" (*IM* 191). How can we think this idea of humans as gatherers? As we read and listen, we gather letters to make words, gather words to make sentences, and gather ideas to make sense. As we go through our lives we gather the hours to make a day, and through time we gather days and years and events to make a life. In so doing, we order these phenomena—the events of our lives—arranging them in our understanding to create narratives, stories filled with meaning, that serve to leave us looking good and being right. Likewise, for the pre-Socratics, the gathering of *logos* brought order to the upsurge of the sway: "Being as logos is originary gathering, not a heap or a pile where everything counts just as much and just as little—and for this reason, rank and dominance belong to Being" (*IM* 147). In *logos*, phenomena were arrayed as a world, with differences, limits, and degrees of importance.

But for the Greeks, there was an element in the gathering that we today have difficulty comprehending: as "the originally gathering gatheredness that constantly holds sway in itself," *logos* "is constant gathering, the gatheredness of beings that *stands in itself, that is, Being*" (*IM* 141, 145 emphasis added). The Greeks were not merely gathering beings into the world, but were struggling to do so in a way that retained each being's origin: Being, the sway, the background in which it had been concealed and out of which it had emerged in unconcealment.

Legein for the Greeks gathered the unconcealed into the world *as it was unconcealed.* Only in this way can *logos* as authentic speaking be possible. It is the letting-be of what is unconcealed in the open region of its unconcealment; and in distinguishing this fragile phenomenon, Heidegger employs (as he often does) languaging whose poetic character respects its fragility:

> The saying and talking of mortals comes to pass from early on as *legein,* laying. Saying and talking occur essentially as the letting-lie-together-before of everything which, laid in unconcealment, comes to presence. (*EGT* 63)

> [. . .] Such a letting-lie establishes whatever lies before us as lying-before. It establishes this as itself., i.e., a letting-lie-before of what does lie before us, gathered in the selfsameness of its lying-before [. . .]. This exceptional laying is the *legein* which comes to pass as the *logos.* (*EGT* 66)

This was the challenge for the first philosophers: to bring Being—the realm of meaninglessness and possibility from which the meanings and possibilities were made distinct—to stand in the world: "*Physis and logos* are the same. *Logos* characterizes Being in a new and yet old respect: that which is in being, which stands straight and prominently in itself, is gathered in itself and from itself, and holds itself in such gathering" (*IM* 145).

When participants returned from the break at 1 pm, Wes and Kipp were on the platform.

WES (*referring to a minor earthquake that happened during the break*)
Did you notice that coming from empty and meaningless, an earthquake is just an earthquake?

(*some participants raising their hands*)

Okay. Wait a second. We're going to extend an invitation to you that makes sense when you can come from dwelling in empty and meaningless. We invite you to a campaign, a campaign against reasonableness. We're inviting you into a campaign to destroy reasonableness in your life.

(*applause*)

So we have a question for you so you can confront what the campaign would mean and what it would look like in your life. Look now at the reasons you have for not participating in life. So you're looking through the areas of your life where there has been no participation, and instead of participation, there have been reasons for not. You have to actually start going through your life. When you are looking from where we are in The Forum now, you can see things you didn't see before. And you're looking at where there could have been participation, and there wasn't and isn't. And all there is are reasons for not. What new openings are there for participation?

Preston, who spoke at length at the beginning of Session Two of Day Three, stood and took a microphone.

PRESTON
I knew before I got here that I was not going to be allowed to take notes.

KIPP
Right.

PRESTON
This is like: I don't know of a greater threat to me.

KIPP
An enormous threat.

PRESTON
I'm running my racket, but I'm running it like a coyote through the back roads. And I noticed on the first day that no one had said, "no notes." We hadn't gotten to the promises, so we were in the pre-promised land, and I'm making my notes. You know, nugget following nugget, which I can eventually read later when my brain will at least serve me for that because I don't trust my brain. So I'm suddenly confronted with the fact that I really haven't promised that I'll keep the promises, but I've been keeping them so far because that's what I'm doing so far.

FORUM DAY FOUR:
SESSION TWO

KIPP

You mean you're not taking notes, so far.

PRESTON

I made a few notes in pen on my wrist when I just couldn't bear it.

(*laughter*)

KIPP

Really? You made notes on your wrist? Really?

PRESTON

And then I go out on the break and wash it very carefully.

(*laughter*)

It was a little bit like smoking dope as a kid in the bathroom, where you have to clear it out with the spray, but everybody knows you can't make such a sweet smell when you're taking a shit.

(*laughter*)

But I'm here to keep my promises and I haven't been taking notes. And I realize this is what I've been running in my life up until now. One of the elements of structure here is how I've survived, totally by taking notes: I have notebooks; I have reference books in my notebooks, but I probably can't find them because I haven't labeled them properly. So I noticed in a passing thought that I've kept all these notes but I can't access any of them very well. That's not story, that's a fact. So I have given up what has kept me afloat. And by yesterday I was willing to do it. I've only made one note, just three words, which I washed off before looking at it.

(*laughter*)

And from what Werner said this morning, that is my apology. So I've been looking at what I haven't been able to keep myself in, now that I haven't got any notes, and feeling that something is—there is a piece that hasn't been coming together for me yet, like many others here. I was able to get my finger on the piece because I wasn't taking notes about it. And the piece was "boxes," and I was helped by one of the people on staff who said to me after the last session, "Structure is a great supporter of promises." When you have structure, it helps you to stay on purpose with your promise. I began to see that the boxes are where you apply structure, where I apply structure. I went out and had a look at my life and looked at the cracks in the pavement, because that's my way, and I saw a sign over a parking lot that said "validation." It winks on twice and then goes black. I wondered how far the energy of this room extends?

(*laughter*)

I realized that the stronger my stand in emptiness and absence of meaning; the stronger my stand in that place, the more I'll be able to utilize structure.

The Three Levels of Truth

Martin Heidegger's purpose as a philosopher was to bring the truth of Being to presence in the human experience. It is difficult to imagine just what that would look like, or what it might make possible, since it has for the most part been missing for us; and when it has shown up, it has not stuck around for long. Why?

KIPP

The more you come from life being empty and meaningless.

PRESTON

Yes. It's a total paradox. All you can do is what Werner seems to do, is just repeat it over and over and over again. And three people get up and he repeats it over and over again. I'm walking along and this thing goes: "validation." And I see that there's something for me inside that space I'm trying to stand in now, that I've been instructed to stand in, rather than doing an exercise. And what I find in it is something in my own terminology, because I love language as distinction—that is where I cross humbly with Werner's path: that's my martial art, my practice. And I found that there was something already in that emptiness that didn't leave it somehow and maybe it could stay with me and help me bridge my way back to that part of myself—it's what I would call trust and innocence, and what I mean by innocence for myself is not naïve, it's just readiness—kind of a readiness state—a trust I also reached yesterday. So in a way I've pulled the floor up under my feet another few inches by being with structure, by being willing to be boxed, by boxing myself. And it occurred to me—since that is something that hadn't been brought up a lot in the talk—maybe it was something because of the time squeeze and the pressures and what goes on could have had on another occasion, in another format, a little more time to it. And I thought that if that was what was missing for me and I could fit it in, then I could guess what Werner was going to do next.

KIPP

The danger of the conversation, Preston—I'm not saying the conversation is dangerous the way you are saying it, but the danger is you making that into an answer.

PRESTON

I would say it was just a thought. It was what happened in my head as I was watching the "validating" sign. I don't take any of this personally.

KIPP

Or like an answer.

PRESTON

No, it's just what is happening as I am doing some thinking rather than being thought.

KIPP

Very nice. Okay.

PRESTON

And the last thought about this. What had happened to me was a set of distinctions. I had made choice after choice after choice so it seems the place I'm at in my Forum is being with choice. Not making choice an answer even...

Heidegger says that Being comes to presence as *Augenblick,* a moment of vision—an all-at-once gestalt switch in which we leap suddenly onto new ground, where everything is different. But the gift of Being comes with non-negotiable conditions. First, the leap cannot be accomplished unless the appropriate time and space are created for the necessary run-up. Second, the new ground will be revealed as the old ground, the familiar ground upon which we have been standing all along, but will be apprehended in a profoundly new light. Third, in this new light, the ground is not solid in the way we have always counted on ground to be; therefore we must open ourselves to a new level of uncertainty, which also means a new level of ontological freedom. The action of the run-up is always the teasing-open of old ground, so that a background can be revealed.

For Heidegger then, and likewise for Werner Erhard, transformed human existence already *is;* its freedom has always already been available to us. But we rarely experience its power because we have not appropriated it—that is, we have not authentically accepted and taken ownership of our existence. "Being" is a fuzzy concept for us; it is not a distinct realm. Therefore the run-up occurs as a gradual process in which we distinguish the old ground—our current Being-in-the-world—*as itself,* so that we can own it for what it is. This is the essential first step in achieving transformation, and the process occupies the first three days of The Forum.

A fundamental distinction in this process is the distinction of *distinction* itself. In this section we will cut another path into that clearing.

Aletheia

One of the terms by which Heidegger distinguished the ontological dimension is the Greek word *Aletheia,* or unconcealment. This word, for Heidegger and for the pre-Socratics, says the free openness in which beings are first revealed. The term has often been understood as denoting *truth;* but this is not to be mistaken as the "truth" of our current everyday understanding, as the correspondence of an assertion with its object; that kind of truth is at best a shadow of what is meant by this ancient Greek word.

When we are there with a being in the moment of its undistorted emerging, prior to assertions—that begins to get at what is meant by *Aletheia*: a free way of encountering beings that allows them to be the things they are.

However, according to Thomas Sheehan, in his book *Making Sense of Heidegger*, there are not just two, but three ways in which Heidegger treats *Aletheia*, which will prove useful in an analysis of The Forum's methodology. We remind the reader, as we have done throughout this book, that we are talking about a realm that has no levels. When talking about the realm of Being, Werner Erhard has said, all we can do is lie ("All I Can Do Is Lie."). But that does not mean we should stop talking, and Thomas Sheehan has opened some interesting possibilities for thinking. Sheehan proposes that *Aletheia* may be thought of as having three levels—that is, that there are three ways of understanding what Heidegger meant when dealing with the "truth":

Aletheia 1, Aletheia 2, and *Aletheia 3.*

Aletheia 3 refers to the correctness of a statement—the correspondence of a proposition with the state of affairs to which it refers. This definition glosses many aspects of evaluation and judgment, of course, but it is what we generally mean when we use the word "truth" in our everyday conversations. *Aletheia 3* also indicates the average level of truth we expect in our everyday coping in the world, and it is the kind of truth that operates within our "stories."

Aletheia 2 is the pre-propositional meaningful presence of things in the world, the realm of inescapable meaning in which we live our lives. For human beings, everything means something, that is, can be understood *as* something. *Aletheia 2* is the kind of truth that emerges when participants distinguish "what happened" as distinct from their story about what happened.

Aletheia 1 is existential openness, the realm of unspoken meaninglessness. This is the context for the other two realms, and Sheehan calls this context the "unique presence-*by-absence* of the thrown-open clearing" (Thomas Sheehan, *Making Sense of Heidegger* 75). This is the groundless ground of our humanity, Being's gift: the Nothing.

KIPP
Yeah.

PRESTON
But being with it so that I can operate from the box I call choice.

KIPP
When we get to this conversation about choice, being with choice, we'll come back to that one. Okay. Anything more for you, Preston?

PRESTON
No.

KIPP
Thank you.

(applause)

KIPP
So, we're asking you to look at where in your life you have had reasons for not participating, that's the question at hand. And we're distinguishing this distinction called *reasonableness.*

BARRY
It's been entirely reasonable for me to keep myself distinct from people. Separate, not distinct.

KIPP
Yeah, separate.

BARRY
There's a sense of being protected, of protecting myself. I feel like I'm not going to get sucked into things that I don't want to get sucked into. I choose the game; I choose the way it's played.

KIPP
By the way, you don't choose it.

BARRY
I decide what game to play...

KIPP
You use the evidence that's given to you by your racket, and examine that evidence, and the product of that evidence has you do what you do. And the product of that evidence is "lots of reasons."

BARRY

Loads of them.

KIPP

Yes.

BARRY

And I noticed yesterday in the danger process that I took from that, that my experience of that, what I created was that my experience was shallow, that I was shallow, my emotional states in both directions were. And...

KIPP

You don't have much range of participation for yourself?

BARRY

Yes, I inherently limit that. And the idea of terror, although I know it's true, I didn't even have a direct experience of that, so I had an experience of not having an experience of that.

KIPP

In place of a reason for not having it...

BARRY

Well, up to that point, yes. And even at that point. I said "Okay, that's a reason. And this is me, and this is now, and here I am, and let that be for the first time." And a big part of the story of the racket had been that I just don't feel deep emotions.

KIPP

Yeah, "you know me. I just don't feel them. Some people got 'em, some people don't."

BARRY

And I don't like it but it's safer than having them. So I got to "Okay that's where I am." And kind of cooked along in it and noticed that for me my thoughts are like one of those signs that gives you the news while you're standing in line at the deli, that makes you dizzy when you watch it too long.

KIPP

It's not limited to you, by the way.

BARRY

And I noticed there was really no difference as they were coming by as they did, and by not ascribing significance to any of those thoughts and letting them be there, I just noticed that

Erhard's methodology of inquiry, a strategic recursive practice iterated in each conversation with each participant, discloses the Being of human being beyond the everyday propositional level (*Aletheia 3*). In order to accomplish this, the level of "truth" called *Aletheia 3* must first be distinguished *as itself*—as the level of un-committed understandings of the world: the justifications, reasons, explanations, and prescriptions regarding the circumstances of one's life and the strategies enacted to deal with those circumstances, what in The Forum is distinguished as one's *story*. It is to this level of truth that Erhard refers when he declares that he does not know the truth, as any statement taken as an assertion to be used in some way in-order-to already has lost any of its truth value.

In the process of distinguishing *Aletheia 3* as *Aletheia 3*, *as* story, a further background becomes accessible as the background from which *Aletheia 3* is disclosed. This further background is *Aletheia 2*, which in the conversation of The Forum is the *what happened*. As the smokescreen of our crystallized stories dissipates, *Aletheia 2* becomes distinguished from the "truth" of *Aletheia 3*, the level of truth in which "what happened" has heretofore been held. What was formerly the "truth" becomes disclosed *as* an interpretation forgotten as such, an interpretation that can never reach the "what happened." At this new level of truth, *what happened* becomes opened up *as* what happened, and now unhinged, so to speak, from the narrow meaning the story had framed it within. Thereby whatever happened becomes open to be taken a multitude of ways; it becomes possible to see that there could be many ways to make "what happened" meaningful, and to see that we will never be able to speak a single truth concerning what happened.

What makes distinguishing *Aletheia 3* and *Aletheia 2* possible is the background of the unspoken realm of Being, *Aletheia 1*, the background of meaninglessness, of Nothing, in which our world of meaning arises. That is to say, the reiterative acts of distinguishing in language "story" and "what happened" already and always evokes "life is empty and meaningless, and it is empty and meaningless that life is empty and meaningless" as the background context, or clearing for meaningful presence. We cannot grasp the nature of a truth except from a perspective beyond that truth, and that perspective must be created and discovered for oneself as one *lives within* the rhetorical dialogue of The Forum as it unfolds. Participants of The Forum are called, again and again, to stand in another perspective given by a level of truth altogether different from the level from which life is ordinarily understood—as story, as *Aletheia* 3. However, when someone speaks Being, names the primordial clearing that we are, it can only be done at the level of "you do what you do and you don't do what you don't do." The continuing creation and expansion of this perspective—of unconcealment—is the work of Werner Erhard since the inception of the *est* Training.

But how does this unconcealment happen in The Forum?

We call attention to the environment of *authenticity* that has been created in The Forum room over the past three days—first, through disclosing the fundamental inauthenticity of human beings through the discursive acts of distinguishing story and what happened, racket, and so on; second, through disclosing *sharing* as a particular way of communicating; and third, through the authentic sharing itself that has emerged in the participants' interactions with Erhard and the other Forum leaders.

In this environment, a new level of unconcealment becomes possible as stories begin to be heard as stories—even by the individuals telling them, those whose lives have been shaped and limited by the "truth" of their stories. Too angry and afraid to reveal it, Marsha had maintained the deception of having it all together, which began to "make her thin"; Angel decided as a child that she would be the most caring person in the world as a way to overcome her fear of not really caring at all; Mike became stupid and in need of the help of others as a response to experiencing himself as incompetent; Jane hides out to avoid experiencing the embarrassment of rejection due to being worthless. These are disclosures, openings only possible from a point of view from which story and what happened are distinct and uncollapsed. Thus, as the shaping power of the stories begins to waver, the presence of the underlying circumstances emerges with a new clarity; simultaneously, a new freedom to be emerges.

without saying anything, or directly about it, that I felt more intimate with the people that were sharing in the group and that emotions were starting to well right up out of me. And I know I can take that and be reasonable and say "Oh, that's great, I'll do this now all the time and I'll have these emotions and everything will be fixed." And hey, I'm feeling it.

KIPP
When you do.

BARRY
I am right now. I may not tonight or I may not tomorrow. Now I am.

KIPP
You always will when you do.

BARRY
I'm there.

KIPP
Thank you very much.

(*applause*)

So, we're distinguishing this distinction called reasonableness. Is it so that in life you either have the results or the reasons for not having them? And is it also so that as a human being, the way it is to be a human being, is if you give yourself a sufficient reason that you also give equal weight to that? That's enough reason for not having this result. So if the result doesn't occur, where do you immediately look? At the reason why it didn't. So we're asking where in your life do you have reasons for not participating. Please...

SANFORD
Well, sharing is one of them. For the first day and a half in here I was sitting on a lot of shares, I had lots of reasons, you know, the golden share, the whole bit. So now I have reasons for sharing, so there's really no way of getting away from either one. But beyond that, I've had reasons for not choosing a career, for not living into the full possibility of what life could be for me. Reasons for not keeping promises—made some promises to people back in Seattle about being in communication with people in The Forum about various things around the work, and just everywhere, everywhere I look. There are reasons for doing things and not doing it. When I produce results I have reasons for getting the results. If I don't get the results I have reasons for not getting them, but if I get results I have reasons for getting them.

KIPP
Okay. Anything else?

SANFORD

Yeah. The question was reasons for not participating. I have a lot of reasons for not participating in the assisting program.

KIPP

Everybody know he's referring to the people who have been running microphones and managing this entire program? Those are assistants in a program. You'll have an opportunity to acknowledge them later. Thank you. Go ahead.

SANFORD

So, I'm not sure there's a lot of value going into what those reasons are, but the cost of having those reasons instead of assisting is that, number one, I don't have available to me whatever would be there for me out of assisting and I'm ripping everybody else off from what I could contribute by doing that.

KIPP

Yeah. What you've got is your reasons.

SANFORD

Yeah. And if I continue to indulge myself in that, at the end of my life that's what I'll have is all the reasons for what I did and what I didn't do instead of powerful results.

KIPP

And that's what most people got.

SANFORD

Yeah. Probably what everybody's got; possibly what everybody's got.

KIPP

Yeah, well, you talk to a lot of people and pretty much this is what people tell you about their life: "I would have, *if*..."

SANFORD

Yeah, that's my story for sure.

KIPP

Sanford, thank you. Anabeth?

(*applause*)

ANABETH

The reasons for not participating go back a long way. So I can see that now. Earlier when Werner was talking about when we were six or five or four, whenever that happened, and my reaction

Fallenness

Nevertheless, stories have power. The meaningfulness of these interpretations has provided the practical understanding by which we have coped with the circumstances in our lives. As Erhard puts it in Session Three of Day Four, our actions are always in a dance with the way the world occurs. But while we remain immersed in the oblivion of *Aletheia 3,* the dance is inauthentic. We do not own the reality we are living because we have not chosen it; nor have we chosen *not* to choose it. We have merely fallen into the drift of the dance that has been thrown-open for us; and rather than confront the situation, we flee into the tranquillizing distractions of the "they."

The inevitable forgetfulness of the "they" self—the forgetting of Being that follows the unconcealment of one's story as a story—is what Heidegger termed "fallenness." Thomas Sheehan in *Making Sense of Heidegger* writes that fallenness is a kind of forgetting that results from focusing on what is meaningful to us: "the more I focus on the meaningful, the more I forget that I am the thrown-open clearing that makes meaning possible and necessary" (116): we forget *Aletheia 1 and Aletheia* 2 and devolve to the order of truth given by fallenness, that is, by *Aletheia* 3. The conversation of The Forum is designed to bring the participants to Nothing, the thrown-open clearing of *Aletheia 1*, which is possible only through undergoing the experience of the dialogue for oneself as it moves backwards from truth as *Aletheia 3* to *Aletheia 2*, which already brings to presence *Aletheia 1*. Again and again and again.

For instance, during his conversation with Jodie during Session Two of Day Two, Erhard brought Jodie and all the participants to *think* and *experience for themselves* these three levels. To Jodie's recognition of her story as a story—that boys did not like her when she was a little girl—Erhard said, "a story *is* just a story"—a point of view of *Aletheia 3* only granted us when "standing in" or "coming from" *Aletheia 2*. When Erhard continues to say that "The 'what happened' is what's true or not. It did or it didn't," he is speaking from the point of view of the thrown-open clearing given by *Aletheia 1* as it regards *Aletheia 2* and *Aletheia 3*. Erhard continued:

> **If your listening is that somebody doesn't like you, everything they say is an expression of not liking you [*Aletheia* 3]. If we pushed Jodie hard enough she could go back and remember that "oh yeah, one of them was trying to be nice to me once" [*Aletheia* 2].**

Aletheia 2, then, is the meaningfulness we attend to, where something or someone occurs *as* meaningful in some way *to us*, which in turn gives us our way to be with that something or someone. Forgetting the *as* locks us into the fallenness of *Aletheia* 3: *as* becomes *is*. Remembering the *as* transforms the *is*. *This* is the work of The Forum: the disclosure of truth as unconcealment, and in the clearing granted by Nothing the generation of a new possibility of Being for human beings becomes available. ■

to that was: "Oh we have to do this again? I have to go back to when I was six-years-old?" But it didn't take very long for me to see that that's where I was, for a long time. And I always have a reason for why I'm not there. But I really am there. So it goes back to an incident that happened, not when I was six, but when I was like twelve or thirteen, and I just wasn't there for my sister. I just wasn't there and I had wonderful reasons for it. The best reasons. I was always the best kid, the best sister; so I never got anything for it: I just wasn't there.

KIPP

You lived inside a story called "I'm the best kid," which gave you a justification for anything that happened that was inconsistent with that.

ANABETH

Right. So yesterday, I called my son, who is twenty-one. I have four children, but he's the only one I called because I got that he could listen to it, because he's had an experience somewhat like The Forum.

KIPP

This is another reason by the way. More crap, right?

ANABETH

The reason I called Johnny?

KIPP

"Well, you know Johnny, he's like that."

ANABETH

No, no, no. That's not it.

KIPP

Okay.

ANABETH

I called Johnny because I wanted to tell him that I was proud of him. And when I couldn't reach him, I thought well, "I'll call one of my other kids."

KIPP

Is it true that you couldn't reach him or that you didn't reach him?

ANABETH

I did not reach him. He was not on the other end of the phone call. He was out. So I called another number where he was supposed to be, and he was out at that number too. So I just kept calling all day long until I finally got him woken up to come to the phone. I called him: I could tell him how proud I was of him, and for calling me and telling me about how he learned about his act,

ANABETH (*continuing*)

and I didn't know what that was then, but I know what it is now. And that I don't think I was there for him, when I was divorced, and all the time from when he was three until he was fourteen, I don't think I was there for him, and I just wanted to tell him that. And he got it. He just got it. He said, "I'm glad you know that." And I have a lot of reasons that I could give you for why I wasn't there for him. But the fact of the matter is I just wasn't there for him. I just didn't participate. The list is a mile long.

KIPP

It's called your life.

ANABETH

Right, all the things I didn't participate in. So now I have a question. Can I ask you a question?

KIPP

Sure.

ANABETH

The question is: So if you know that you were a six-year-old for all this time, but... and you've worked with that and stayed with that...

KIPP

In other words, you can see your racket.

ANABETH

You can see your racket, and so you don't have that anymore, so then... but you have something...

KIPP (*responding to several participants laughing*)

By the way—I think someone was laughing in the background, when you said, "you don't have that anymore."

ANABETH

You have it.

KIPP

It's still there...

ANABETH

It's still there.

KIPP

...at all times and under all circumstances, ready to use your life.

ANABETH
So it's just there.

KIPP
Yeah, it's just there, and sometimes it uses your life.

ANABETH
Well yeah, that's the answer.

KIPP
What's missing for you is any choice about it.

ANABETH (*pausing thoughtfully*)
What's missing for me is any choice about it.

KIPP
Yeah, so far in your life, your life has not been a chronicle of choosing whether you're going to do your racket or not. Your racket used you, without choice.

ANABETH
Right. I did not choose. Right.

KIPP
So, what's missing for you is a distinction called "choice." See, when you come from empty and meaningless, into life, you're left with a choice. But we haven't distinguished choice yet; we're still working on reasonableness. Can you see that that's missing for you?

ANABETH
Yes. Okay.

KIPP
Anabeth: thank you very much.

(*applause*)

CLAUDIA
I saw that what stops me from participating is the fear that I have of all you people, which...

KIPP

It's not fear. Remember, fear is inside the box of the racket. Fear is the emotion consistent with the racket. It's not the fear. It's the racket. And the racket has those emotions. It has the feelings consistent with that racket. Yeah.

CLAUDIA

What I saw in the danger process yesterday was that the reason I was afraid of other people, I was afraid of everybody looking at me. One of my rackets is handling everything so that in my relationships or at my job, everything is so set that people aren't looking at me.

KIPP

What do you mean "looking at you"?

CLAUDIA

I mean looking at me with your eyes.

KIPP

You're afraid of people looking at you.

CLAUDIA

Yes.

KIPP

Got it.

CLAUDIA

So, that has really stopped me from participating. This year I had lots of opportunities to speak in front of people, and although one on one people have told me that I am articulate, and sometimes entertaining, I thought I would be good at speaking in front of groups of people and I was miserable at it. I didn't do very well and they criticized me in feedback.

KIPP

Or: You did what you did.

CLAUDIA

I did what I did. I didn't enjoy it...

KIPP

You did what you did and people said what they said. The problem is you listened to them.

CLAUDIA

Right. So I realized that I stayed away from things that would cause me to stand up in front of people to speak.

KIPP

Do you understand what she's saying? She says your life is designed by your case, by your racket. You get a life inside your case. And that's your life. You don't do things that are inconsistent with your racket.

CLAUDIA

Right, and the other thing... The reason that I don't want anybody to look at me is because, um, can I say "I'm afraid"? I'm afraid of being unattractive. And so I'm always unattractive from the context of being attractive or unattractive...

KIPP

Is that how you say it to yourself, is that "you're unattractive," or what?

CLAUDIA

No. I don't want anyone to look at me because they're going to notice or judge and decide whether they find me attractive or not.

KIPP

Well, what do you think? Are you attractive?

CLAUDIA

Well, seeing that life is empty and meaningless...

(*laughter*)

KIPP

Good. See all the service those people paid to let her speak like this?

CLAUDIA

So, I attract people when I attract people and I don't when I don't.

KIPP

Yeah.

(*applause*)

CLAUDIA

And the other thing that it has cost me from participating in, and what I've been noticing here is...

WES

Notice how the significance of all that has disappeared: this whole thing about attraction. Most relationships... how significant can a relationship really be when most relationships are like two slot machines face-to-face waiting for a simultaneous jackpot?

(*laughter*)

CLAUDIA
So the other way I didn't participate, because I had being unattractive and attracting people caught up with one aspect of being female, of being a woman I should say.

KIPP
Aren't they the same thing?

CLAUDIA
Female is more scientific for me.

KIPP
That's fine. You've got to educate me. I'm stupid.

CLAUDIA
So it stopped me from enjoying certain aspects of being a woman.

KIPP
Yes, this is the important part.

CLAUDIA
And now it kind of unhooked a lot of those experiences from being an attractive woman. I could just be a woman, be a person, enjoy those pleasures of...

KIPP
Well, you're not going to use that conversation to not participate in your own life is what I hear.

CLAUDIA
Yeah.

KIPP
Well done, Claudia. Thank you very much.

(*applause*)

KIPP
See, where this is really going to be evident for you is in your conversations with other people. If you notice, if this strikes true, then put it on: that a lot of your conversations with other people are, that you get people to buy your reasons. What you call your friends, your pals, are people that buy your reasons. So when you don't do what you say you're going to

do, then you have your pals there, and you go up to them and you say, "you know that thing I said I was going to do? Well I didn't do it, but you know what happened? You know how my mother... and I was busy, I got real afraid, and I didn't feel real good, either. You understand, right?" And of course my pal's job—if he's my friend, my buddy—his job is to buy my reasons. Why? So when he doesn't do what he said he was going to do, he's got his mark all set up. So he comes to me and says "Hey Kipp, remember that thing I said I was going to do? Well I didn't do it because..." What a lot of your friendships are based on is buying each other's reasons—interlocking conspiracies of disloyalty. That's what you call your friends: people who buy your crap. See, if somebody comes along and sticks your crap back in your face, you get offended. Those are the people who are going to make some kind of difference in your life. The ones that are straight with you. You've got the people in your life trained to not be straight with you. You better find some people in life to be straight with you—they aren't going to be so reasonable.

WES

One of the things you can count on in the seminar program is the conversations you're going to have there are going to be very unreasonable.

(*shifting*)

So, we're practicing a new conversation that involves the destruction of reasons and the creation of participation. I want you to turn to the person next to you and practice this conversation. So get a partner...

Participants organized themselves into pairs with Wes assisting them.

WES

Here's what you're going to say: "In this part of my life I didn't participate, and these are the reasons I've used." And while saying this, see if you're willing to give up these reasons, and if you are, then create some way of saying how you're now going to participate there. You're creating a commitment to participate. You'll notice you don't even need to give a reason for it. You're just sort of saying you will and you're confronting the reasons for not. Listen for the possibility of participating in life rather than to the reasons for not. Pick who will go first. Ready? Begin.

Participants shared with each other for several minutes. Wes directed participants to provide feedback, then to switch roles. Wes then gave the participants another opportunity to share once again with their partners, after having reiterated the instructions, emphasizing the requirement to clearly state what the reasons were for not participating in life ("why you shouldn't, wouldn't, or couldn't..."), and to express willingness to give up the reasons.

WES

Stop. Please acknowledge the person who shared with you. We've begun a conversation for participating in life. One of the things we want to deal with is where people get stuck in their

WES (*continuing*)

lives, how they get stuck in their lives, and a way of shifting that. The fundamental place where people get stuck is in their problems. You know the problems you have in life? You can have a breakthrough in the matter of your problems. Parts of the conversation will be fairly abstract. You want to give up your considerations about abstractions. To get a sense of what your problems are, look at places in your life where you are stuck. You'll notice that that's a place you never would in a million years find it possible to participate. There's a real problem there. Get up some of your real problems for yourself. What are some synonyms for problems? Looking at a real problem in life?

Participants shouted out various answers: difficulty, stopped, upset, stuck, barrier, worries, suffering, concerns, burden, hassle.

WES

Fundamentally what a problem is, is something is stopped: Something is stuck. The way in which you are dealing with it is: There is a stuckness. There's not movement. When you're moving, you're not stuck. You may be dealing with something. It may be difficult to deal with but it doesn't occur as a problem. Problems are places you are ineffective. And you are ineffective, obviously, because of circumstances, reasons, situations, and so forth. The first thing to look at is where problems occur. You can't be effective with something if you don't know its location. So if I try to move the chair and I think the chair is here...

(*indicating a location on the stage in which there is not a chair*)

...the chair's not going to be moved. So we have to get where problems occur. A problem seems to occur in the world, doesn't it? Think of your problems: Somehow the problem is out there. And that's what makes it so difficult to deal with: It's out of your control. And out there where it lives is very big. And fundamentally that's the thing that makes people ineffective with problems, because problems don't occur out there. There are no problems, as problems, out there. "I've got cancer. It's in my body." The cancer may be in your body, but the problem you've got with the cancer isn't in your body. "My car is a piece of crap. That's a real problem for me." There's no problem with your car. The cancer as a problem, your car as a problem, your children as a problem, are not out there. Problems don't occur in the world as problems. Rocks don't have problems, even the ones that get kicked and fall down the hill. That is not a problem for the rock. See if you can point at where problems are. Take a shot.

(*indicating his mouth*)

I didn't say there are no problems. There are problems. They just don't occur out there. They occur over here. They are in your speaking and your listening. Or more rigorously, problems are in languaging. No languaging, no problems. The home of problems is languaging. The home of reality, for life for human beings, is in languaging. The occurrence "problems" occurs in languaging. Rocks don't speak and listen, and so don't have the problems human beings have as problems.

PAULA

Is languaging and distinguishing the same thing? What about signing?

WES

They are close enough for now. People who sign are participating in languaging. Here's what I'm including in languaging: picturing, signing, speaking, music-ing: that whole range of human activities in which communication takes place. The easiest thing for us to talk about is speaking and listening.

PAULA

What about touching?

WES

What about touching?

PAULA

To me, touching can be communicating.

WES

It can be, and it may not be…

PAULA

Are you including it…?

WES

…if it's an intentional communication.

PAULA

Okay.

(*sits down*)

WES

Okay, so problems occur in languaging. Is there anyone who cannot see that? Clear enough. Close enough… for government work.

(*laughter*)

DAVID

I'm not really clear that the problem is in languaging.

WES

Yeah. Where is it? Give me a problem you got?

DAVID

Fully participating in the projects that I do. Getting excited by the projects.

WES

There are two things there: fully participating and getting excited.

DAVID

Getting really excited about the projects I'm involved in.

WES

"I do projects. I'm not excited. That's a problem for me." Is that how it goes?

DAVID

Yes.

WES

See the languaging there?

DAVID

Yes.

WES

That's where the problem is.

DAVID

Thank you.

WES

You're welcome.

(laughter; David sits)

So now that we've put it into the domain of languaging, we have some access to them. If you can locate problems where they are, that is to say, in languaging, you now have an access to dealing with problems that will allow for a breakthrough in problems. We're now going to deal with the real breakthrough in problems. This is what you all need to get is the next thing I deal with. I deal with a little bit more, but this is it. You want to find the specific box... I want you to imagine: Languaging has many boxes. Make believe: Many boxes in languaging; many possibilities for things to occur in within languaging. We want to find the specific box that problems occur in. Problems occur in one box only for human beings. It doesn't show up as a box, because people think their problems are "out there," shows up like "out there." But now that you know that it shows up in a box in languaging, we have to find the box. Knowing the box will give us some power with regard to our problems. It'll actually blow the whole thing open.

Wes moved to the chalkboard, drew a square, and wrote "problems" inside it.

So, here are problems. Whatever problem you got occurs here, in languaging. What is the name of the box that problems come in?

PARTICIPANT
Declaration.

WES
No. Ultimately, yes, okay? But you're a little too advanced for us. I want to know the specific kind of declaration that problems occur in.

(referring to participants with yellow name tags, who are there taking The Forum for the first time)
I want some yellows to answer this. I don't want anybody "remembering" this.

A participant named Paul stood, the participant who, like Jake, had his "foot nailed to the floor" concerning inauthenticity in a dialogue with Erhard in Session Two of Day One.

PAUL
You talked about being a problem. We talked about it being an obstacle before. What first occurs to me as the name of the box that problems come in is the problem box.

WES
No. Well, yes, but not useful.

PAUL
But what is the problem is really what the problem is and the problem is trying to label it. I would think that it's an obstacle and all the other things people would say it is.

WES
It's not a box that shows itself to you. You remember we did that discussion? You remember that "danger interaction"? The thing we did yesterday?

PAUL
How could I forget?

WES
Remember, we had a lot of stuff go on the board. Then I proposed the possibility that there was a frame around all of it, that all of it was variations of, like a meme, of "Life is dangerous for human beings." We're looking for some statement like that. What is the statement that...

PAUL
You are the problem. You become the problem. Within that framework that's...

WES

Yeah. Okay. That's not how problems occur. Problems don't occur for people "I am the problem."

PAUL

Okay.

WES

When my car is broken, the car is the problem. And there's a way my conversation occurs, my relationship to all of that.

PAUL

Okay.

WES

You can just keep looking. You got it started well, though.

PAUL

Um, so you're saying that the box in which problem occurs has a name to it...

WES

A statement in which it occurs has a particular name to it. The conversation occurs in "human being." It's the already always conversation. You know, you're born into languaging, and languaging gives you your life, reality, and problems: Once a problem comes your way, there's an already always way it occurs for you. That's the box: the already always way it occurs for you. You have nothing to do with it. You didn't choose it...

PAUL

It's the rainstorm.

WES

It's the rainstorm. We want to get a sense of the already always way it occurs for you. This is one of those "too simple for complicated minds..."

PAUL (*laughs*)

Okay, then maybe the problem is your racket.

WES

No, that's an explanation of it maybe. We're looking for the statement.

PAUL

The statement that contains the problem...

WES
That tells them the occurrence. That gives them the occurrence.

PAUL
Them?

WES
Whatever problems you've got.

PAUL
I don't know.

WES
That's a good place to be right now. We'll call on someone else.

NICOLE
Through definition...

WES
No, no, no, this is all too descriptive. There is a statement...

NICOLE
This is a problem.

WES
Okay. That's not how problems occur. You got a problem? Give me a problem: a good one.

NICOLE
My thesis.

WES
Is a problem? There's no movement on it?

NICOLE
Correct.

WES
You're dealing with all the "hunnahunnahunna." "What am I gonna do?"

NICOLE
Right. Nine years.

WES
Nine years, yes.

(*laughter*)

So Nicole. "My thesis not getting done" does not occur like: "It's a problem, my thesis isn't getting done." Right?

NICOLE
Right.

WES
Yeah. It occurs some way. How does it occur?

NICOLE
Through being stuck.

WES
No, you just explained it. Not bad. But explained it. I want the occurrence. What's your relationship to the thesis not getting done? Talk to me about it. Tell me... what goes on with you about it?

NICOLE
Oh I use a lot of reasons.

WES
Right. You've got reasons. And lying. What else?

NICOLE
And disbelief.

WES
And why is that going on with you? Why do you have to give all those reasons for it and lies about it and disbeliefs about it?

NICOLE
So it won't get done.

WES
No.

NICOLE
Ask the question again?

WES
Yeah. You give reasons for not doing it.

NICOLE
Yes.

WES
And lies about it. Right?

(*Nicole nods*)
And there's other things that you're not doing that you don't feel the need to give reasons for and lies about.

NICOLE
Yes.

WES
How come you feel the need to do it in this thing, which is a problem and not in the other thing?

NICOLE
Because it has to get done.

WES
Close. Close. "It has to get done" has got some quality in it. It's like that. Now, see, there's some things that have to get done and they're getting done. This other thing has to get done, and it's not getting done. And what's your relationship to that?

NICOLE
I make myself wrong.

WES
Yeah. Now it's closer. Someone or something is being made wrong. You see that?

NICOLE
Yeah.

WES
That's at the source of a problem. The box that problems come in is called shouldn't be.

(*writing "shouldn't be" above the square on the chalkboard*)
"I'm not getting my thesis done": that shouldn't be. "There's something wrong here." "I should be thin; I keep eating. That shouldn't be." It's not like, "hey, I'm fat, dig it." It's not like "Hey stupid-ass thesis.

Primordial Metaphor: Clearing

Earth—the planet—existed prior to the emergence of human beings. The *world* as clearing did not "exist," however, since "world" is a meaningful phenomenon, and meaning emerged on the planet concurrently with human beings.

One interesting view of the way the world came into being was proposed by the eighteenth-century Italian philosopher

WES (*continuing*)
I'll just keep lying to people so that they keep giving me grant money. I don't care." But no, that's not your relationship to your thesis, but it could be. You wouldn't have a problem: You'd have a scam.

(*laughter*)
What turns it into a problem is "it shouldn't be." "I should be doing this thing and I'm not getting it done." "Not getting it done" shouldn't be. The box that problems occur in is "shouldn't be." It's kind of obvious, right?

NICOLE
Yeah.

WES
You're waiting for the heavens to part. They're not going to part; you just may get a powerful and profound insight that may let you get your damn thesis done.

NICOLE
True.

WES
Can you see that the occurrence "not getting thesis done" occurs "shouldn't be"? That whole thing?

NICOLE
Yeah.

WES
Great. And where does "shouldn't be" occur? Does "shouldn't be" occur in the thesis?

NICOLE
No.

WES
Does "shouldn't be" occur in the ceiling?

NICOLE
No.

WES
No. "Shouldn't be" occurs where?

(*Nicole points to her mouth*)
Very good Nicole. Thanks.

Giambattista Vico. Like Martin Heidegger, Vico perceived a lost power in the thinking of the ancients. His interest in the thinking of the "first men," those who shaped the early use of language, anticipated Heidegger's persistent attempt to reconstruct the understanding of the pre-Socratic Greek thinkers. Like Heidegger, Vico understood that he was entering shadowy territory: it is beyond our power, he said, "to enter into the vast imagination of those first men, whose minds were not in the least abstract, refined, or spiritualized, because they were entirely immersed in the senses, buffeted by the passions, buried in the body" (*The New Science* 118).

But his exploration of this realm led him to develop a theory of *primordial metaphor* that resonates with Heidegger's distinction of *originary naming*. Metaphor, for Vico, was based in *identity* rather than similarity (James M. Edie, *Speaking and Meaning: The Phenomenology of Language* 166). It was a theory of *first thought*; according to the scholar Donald Phillip Verene, Vico proposed that the mind's cardinal act was "a transference or bearing of meaning from sensation as placeless, momentary flux to the fixation of sensation as a god." Thus, through metaphor, the beings were brought into Being. Says Verene: "Metaphor can be understood as likeness or similarity only if we ignore its role in relation to the *is*. To regard the constructive power of metaphor as based on its analogical capacity is also to presuppose its primordial power to construct the *is*" (*Vico's Science of Imagination* 174).

There was, then, a moment at the dawn of time when humans brought forth beings through the creation of metaphors. On this view, whether we recognize it or not, we are already always thinking and speaking from within the metaphors that have been constructed and then passed down in our tradition, metaphors that generate assumptions about what is possible in being human. The philosopher Richard Rorty has proposed that what we should be doing as thinking beings is using up the metaphors that we have inherited, and creating new ones. Not to do so, says Rorty, is to worship the dead metaphors of our ancestors (*Contingency, Irony, and Solidarity* 20). The work of Martin Heidegger and Werner Erhard may be seen as the creation of new metaphors.

An important Heideggerian metaphor that Erhard has adapted for use in his own work is the term *clearing*. "Clearing" is a metaphor for human being, a *constitutive designation* for the Being-in-the-world of Dasein. Such metaphors, introduced into a tradition, shape the way we understand ourselves and our world. In the Cartesian model that has dominated our Western tradition for several centuries, Dasein is the self-certain thinking *subject*—the *cogito* of "*Cogito, ergo sum*"—and the opening for the world (and for Being) is as an "object," or *cogitatum*. If Dasein is that specific development of subjective self-consciousness referred to as an *identity*, the opening for Being is whatever is allowed by that particular identity's value and truth structure.

In these perspectives, what is determinative is that Dasein itself—as *cogito*, or subject, or identity—"'gets into the picture' in precedence over whatever is." Whatever is, is forced "back into this relationship to oneself as the normative realm" ("AWP" in *QCT* 129). The world becomes my "picture" of it, and Being is cut to fit that picture. The world, in other words, is all about me.

In contrast to these perspectives, Heidegger proposes the metaphor *clearing*, a metaphor which, as Michael E. Zimmerman points out, has been implicit in the Cartesian model all along: "Modern philosophy posits a gap between subject and object because it has failed to notice that a temporal *clearing* (transcendence) is needed for subject and object to present themselves in the first place" (*Eclipse of the Self* 25, emphasis added). In Heidegger's model, absent the normative self-referring subject, there is simply the clearing itself, and the *lighting* of whatever is:

> " In the midst of beings as a whole an open place occurs. There is a clearing, a lighting. Thought of in reference to what is, to beings, this clearing is in a greater degree than are beings. This open center is therefore not surrounded by what is; rather, the lighting center itself encircles all that is, like the Nothing which we scarcely know. That which is can only be, as a being, if it stands within and stands out within what is lighted in this clearing. [. . .] The nature of truth is, in itself, the primal conflict in which that open center is won. . . . ("OWA" in *PLT* 53, 55)

(*applause*)

"Shouldn't be" is the box that problems come in for human beings. The already always existing box you're given when you're born—you're born and they slap you on the ass and they hand you a box "this shouldn't be." Yeah, that's the party. Someone's good idea. I don't know. And now you've got this box and you put some of your junk in it, and the question is, "how come you love that box?" Yeah, you were given the box, but you really love it. Like you have some fascination and addiction to "shouldn't be." Do you have any sense that it may relate to your racket?

(*laughter*)

Think about it. Rackets love problems and problems love rackets. They're natural. They're a fit. They're a couple. Rackets and problems fit together: a marriage made in heaven. Do you think a racket would be any good without some juicy problems in which to make somebody wrong? You think a racket would stay around without any problems? She has a racket with her thesis. Her racket loves the thesis. You're fat and you want to lose weight and you don't have a racket about it, you lose weight. Or you say "the hell with it" and just accept being overweight. There's no problem having no money, unless it "shouldn't be." Some people give away all their money so that they can be free. They make money "shouldn't be." Your problems are a function of "shouldn't be," and you get to say what "shouldn't be." The availability "shouldn't be" comes with languaging, but the specific use of it: That's you. It nails your foot to the floor, and then you don't have to be responsible for going anywhere, so that's kind of good.

(*walking in a circle as if his foot is "nailed to the floor"*)

"Oh God! My car won't start. I can't get to work. I'll never get promoted. I'm a failure. My mother was right. She's always right, the bitch. I was right to make her wrong. She didn't lend me the money for the car I really need. Don't you understand?" People love their problems. When people get attached to their problems they carry them around forever, like this:

(*Wes holds onto one of the director's chairs and drags it as he walks slowly across the stage*)

They bring them to parties. "How's it going?"

(*laughter*)

People never know what to talk about when they're confronted by being, so they talk about their problems. "Hey, did I tell you about my problem?"

(*laughter*)

Some people become PhDs in their problem. "Oh, I've finally understood it." Some people find a therapist they pay to listen. Therapists love people who love their problems. Then they analyze it.

(*examining an imaginary object*)

"Well, this particular one I've got is gray."

WES (*continuing; laughter*)

And they never get that this "understanding it," and "analyzing it," and this "studying it," has only one problem to it: They've still got "it." So, how to let the problem go? Have it disappear? How to let the problem disappear? That's where the discussion is headed. Wake up! We're coming to a good part. I promise. Well, if problems occur in languaging, and the specific languaging that problems occur in is "shouldn't be," how about trying out a new languaging? How about creating? You know this is already given, so you'll have to confront it ongoingly. Your racket will continue on after The Forum, I promise. And its love for problems will continue on after The Forum, I promise. And your fascination with problems stuck to your racket will continue on after The Forum, I promise. But here's the possibility in what I am saying. You can confront it: In the presence of it, you can take your problem, and transform it by confronting the box it already comes in, and allowing a new box—putting it into a new box—intentionally putting it into a new box. So I'm going to give you a name of a new box you could put your problem in. This is not the truth. Problems "shouldn't be"? Here's the question you have to confront: Who made you the judge? God's happy, what's your problem? Who made you the judge, the ultimate decider of what shouldn't be in life? Not a lot of power in that. So try this one on. Put a new conversation around the actual problems that you've got, like a possibility. And the conversation I'm inviting you to put around them is: In life there are problems.

Wes erased "shouldn't be" and wrote "in life there are problems" over the top of the box with the word "problems" inside it.

WES (*continuing*)

Simple enough. In life there are problems. Not: Life's about no problems. When problems shouldn't be, the conclusion is that a great life is a life without problems. That's nonsense! A life without problems is a lousy life. It's a stinky life. You want a life without problems? We have a little operation we can perform on you; you would have to do it in Mexico, though. We'll remove all your internal organs and suspend you in tepid water. That's a life without problems. Powerful people are judged by their problems. The problem with you is, your problems are small and crappy—and the same ones over and over. You're boring. She's been dealing with this crummy thesis for nine years. Imagine listening to her for nine years about it?

(*laughter*)

She should get some big problems and she'll finish the darn thing. And then take on a job that's a real problem for her, and do great with that until she takes on more responsibility, runs a university and has a lot of problems. Then you'd be interesting to talk to. That's the problem. You're resisting the very thing that gives life its whole excitement—problems—because they "shouldn't be." So the way to transform that is to confront each of your problems and the whole distinction "problem" and put them in a box called "in life there are problems." Okay. Any questions? Any "yeah but"s and "how about"s?

DONALD

So I take a problem, in my case, say, my weight. And in life there are problems. I've got a problem that I'm sixty pounds more than I want to be, or sixty pounds more than healthy.

As we have shown elsewhere, this is the clearing that Heidegger saw manifested in the thinking of the pre-Socratics, the site of the primal struggle by which they brought Being to stand, thereby brought forth the world, and won the clearing for the emergence of truth. A human being is a clearing in the world for things to be the things they are.

For both Heidegger and Erhard, this is a central point: generative thinking, thinking that wants to unconceal the truth of Being and thereby light beings, can do so *only if there is first created a clearing for the lighting*: "Light can stream into the clearing," says Heidegger; but light itself never *creates* the clearing. "Rather, light presupposes it" ("EP&TT" in *BW* 442). According to the scholar William Lovitt, Heidegger has expressed a preference that the *da* in Da-sein, be translated as *openness,* rather than the traditional *there* (Intro to *QCT*, xxxv). A human being is fundamentally *Being-openness*.

"The *lumen naturale*," says Heidegger, "the light of reason, throws light only on the open" ("EP&TT" in *BW* 443). But it is important to note that while Dasein is the clearing for the light, Dasein *is the light*, as well. In *Being and Time*, Heidegger pointed out that the figurative expression, *lumen naturale*, denotes the existential-ontological structure of Dasein itself. The light is a constituent of Dasein, and begins to shine when Dasein "*is* in such a way as to be its 'there'" (*BT* 171). In becoming the opening of the clearing, we become simultaneously the light which illuminates the clearing.

The dialogue of The Forum may be seen as a process for clearing the opening that The Forum participants are, thereby enabling them to know themselves as a "there" for the lighting of Being. The first step in the process is the deconstruction of participants' normative subjectivities, the primal struggle that responds to the first question of The Forum: What is the Being of human beings? This clears the opening for the second question: What is the *possibility* of Being for human beings? It is through this second question that the clearing is lighted. ■

WES

But there's no problem yet. See "I'm sixty pounds more that I want to be" is not a problem. That's "sixty pounds more than I want to be."

DONALD

That's right. I spoke that. I languaged that. So if I wanted to weigh 235 pounds, and I weighed 235 pounds, I'd be happy, because that's how much I wanted to weigh.

WES

No. I don't know that you'd be happy.

DONALD

Because I said so.

WES

No. That's just how much you would weigh.

DONALD

There wouldn't be a problem there.

WES

Not yet. If you weighed what you weighed, there's no problem.

DONALD

It's a problem...

WES

If you weigh what you weigh and you shouldn't weigh that, then there's a problem. Or you're on a diet and it's not working fast enough and that shouldn't be. Or you try and it doesn't work and it should have worked.

DONALD

But if I wanted to weigh 235 pounds and I weigh 235 pounds...

WES

The first step is to say to your problem called "your weight" that "in life there are problems," not "the problem about my weight shouldn't be. I shouldn't have a problem with my weight."

DONALD

That's what I'm saying: "I shouldn't have a problem about my weight."

WES

No it's more like "I shouldn't have the problem 'weight.'"

DONALD

I shouldn't have the problem "weight," I should be more like Ron.

(*indicating person sitting next to him who looks more fit than Donald*)

WES

No.

(*laughter*)

That you have problems, is wrong. You'd be better off without your problems, right Donald?

DONALD

Yeah.

WES

That's what we're dealing with.

DONALD

Oh, I've got it.

WES

You wouldn't be better off without your problems, because if have life, you'll have problems.

DONALD

I got it.

WES

The whole group "problems" has opened up. We haven't dealt with the specific problem called weight.

DONALD

I got it.

WES

You can stand with your problems like "acceptance," or even more than acceptance.

DONALD

Recognition.

WES

Recognition that that is part of the deal.

DONALD

Right and that's part of the deal of being human, not part of my deal, not part of Ron's deal. The gorilla doesn't have the problem "weight." The gorilla is just the gorilla. Because we're human and we show up in this culture of human, and we've got languaging then we've got a weight problem.

WES

No, we've got problems that shouldn't be problems.

DONALD

We've got problems that shouldn't be problems. Yeah. To me, when you put up there that in life there are problems, that seemed very flippant. Like "Huh, in life there are problems." Like there's no weight to them, there's no...

WES

No, you should have the problems that you have. Sorry. The problems that you have are appropriate. And they are part of your being alive.

DONALD

Not just my being alive.

WES

Right, being alive. So there's an appropriateness to problems. There's not a "shouldn't be" to problems. It's part of living.

DONALD

Oh, in life there are problems.

WES

Exactly. Yeah. So you have started to shift your relationship to problems.

DONALD

So it's not a problem that I have a problem. It's in life that I have a problem.

WES

Yeah. It's not a problem that you have a problem.

DONALD

Right. Like everybody else doesn't.

WES
Like the people over there who've really got it made have less problems than you do.

DONALD
But... they do.

(*laughter*)

WES
No, they don't. I promise you they don't. They have more problems than you.

DONALD
So it's something like the relationship with the problems?

WES
Yeah. They are able to relate to problems as part of the game.

DONALD
Instead of that it shouldn't be.

WES
Exactly.

DONALD
Oh, I got it. Earlier someone said that problems are a declaration. You said no. But they are a declaration...

WES
We're a little ahead of ourselves. "In life there are problems" is ultimately a declaration. And "In life, problems shouldn't be" is ultimately a declaration.

DONALD
We just don't know that.

WES
Right.

DONALD
So, would the declaration that problems show up in be a complaint declaration?

WES
Yeah.

DONALD (*sitting*)

Okay I'm done.

TIM

The difficulty I'm having is to get the baggage away from the problem I carry because of the culture and my own experiences, because when I hear the word "problem," whether it "shouldn't be" or "in life there are problems," there are invitations to certain kinds of action around the word problem, like "solve it," or "do something about it."

WES

Very good. Yeah.

TIM

Or "remedy."

WES

Sure, we haven't gotten there yet. "Shouldn't be": What is the response to something that shouldn't be?

TIM

You get rid of it...

WES

Get rid of it. Do something about it. Solve it. Fix it. Change it. Right?

TIM

Right. Find the solution.

WES

Find the solution. Solve it! See we never notice something. Let me tell you something about this conversation. We're doing different dimensions. It isn't like you have to get everything on the same dimension. But you have to get the dimensions to get the conversations. We did this on the first day, right? In geometry we learned about three axes.

Wes drew a diagram on the board representing the x, y, and z axes.

WES (*continuing*)

You know you can't collapse those. That's the very nature of them, that they are distinct axes; they etch out different dimensions. What people try to do to figure things out—because figuring out has to have things in a linear fashion—is they try to fit everything on a single axis. What they don't see is that there's power in creating in a conversation a group of dimensions, which when you get them all, you get the picture. You can't put a sphere on one dimension, can you?

WES *(continuing)*

You can't even put a circle in one dimension. Before you can have a circle you have to create the two dimensions. So we're creating different dimensions in this conversation. Okay, so we'll jump dimensions somewhat.

TIM

So, your invitation to me is to look at the possibility that the word "problem" can exist in a different dimension than with "solution."

WES

Yeah: a different context in which you will not be immediately moved to solve it.

TIM

Got it.

WES

Hold on a second. What you're bringing up is great. This whole thing about problem/solution: Here's one thing that people almost always never get.

Wes walked over to a the chalkboard on stage right and erased "Right/wrong; dominate/avoid domination; justifies itself/invalidates others."

WES *(continuing)*

Take a look at any problem that you've had and look at what you've done with it. What you've done with it is: solved it in some way. The way people solve problems is they do something about it, and if that didn't work, they do something more, and if that didn't work, they do something better, and if that didn't work, they do something different. They are led to dealing with it, solving it.

(drawing a "P" on the board and then encircling it)
You've got a problem, and then you solve it. What happens with regard to the solution to the problem?

TIM

It becomes a truth, or something right, the right thing to do.

WES

Yes. But it's worse than that. You have to actually look at a problem that you've had that you've solved and then look at the solution to see what happened to it. Take a look at a problem that you had.

TIM

I'm thinking: Some solutions become problems.

WES

Yes, exactly! The solution becomes your next problem.

TIM
Some.

WES
No, all of them! When they're solutions. Take a look. It's a very nasty trap. What's a very big problem for somebody in high school?

TIM
Zits.

(*laughter*)

WES
Yeah but only because zits mean something: That's the real problem.

TIM
Yes.

WES
If all the models had zits, zits would be good. What does that mean?

TIM
Looking good.

WES
Getting a boyfriend, getting a girlfriend, and getting laid. Have you forgotten?

(*laughter*)

Grades too, but we'll talk about getting laid because it's more fun.

(*laughter*)

So that's the big problem. Look back at your life and look at teenagers and see what it's all about. It was about getting a girlfriend, getting a boyfriend, and getting laid, and also getting laid with the right one. So, many people immediately solved that problem right out of high school. What did they do?

TIM
They get married. And then they've got a new problem.

WES
That becomes the next problem. Aren't marriages that solve problems the next problem? I didn't say marriages are a problem. Listen carefully. Marriage is not a problem. Marriage is marriage.

WES (*continuing*)

But when marriage is a solution to a problem, it becomes the next problem. This is the way it is for most people: For most people a relationship is a solution to a problem. What do you think that does to the relationship? It turns it into a thing, with a group of expectations. It becomes part of your racket. That's not relating. You turn someone else into a solution to your problem. That's what you're relating with and that's not relating. That's making it a problem. How many people found it difficult at some point in The Forum, for them?

(*a large number of people raising their hands*)

You know how some people solved that problem? There are people for whom that's a real problem. When they experience something, that's a real problem; they don't like something, it's a real problem. You know how they solve that? Some people? They leave. That's their solution to the problem. Not a lot of people; a couple people. You think that ends up as a problem for them? What about the relationships that you've left? Look at a relationship. And it was a problem and the way you dealt with it is you left it. You will drag that crummy relationship around with you forever. That's this whole thing about being incomplete with your parents: That's at the source of it.

TIM

Okay I understand it in the examples you used and it makes real sense that solutions become problems.

WES

Well, it's part of the quote that Kipp butchered. Where is Kipp? I'll read it to you exactly: "The world that we have made as a result of the level of thinking we have done thus far creates problems that we cannot solve at the same level we created them at." Because if we solve them at the same level we created them at, we are in worse shape.

TIM

Well that still doesn't address the issue though of needing to be solved.

WES

No, no, no, no, you're trying to go too fast. You're trying to solve the problem called "solving doesn't work."

TIM

Yeah, that you solve it at a different level. That's the invitation of Einstein anyway: to solve it at a different level.

WES

We're going to give you a different level. And it won't be the level... the level that you deal with problems, what you call solutions...

TIM

The "shouldn't be..."

WES (*drawing larger circles around the first circle around the "P"*)

...becomes the next problem, which you then solve, which becomes the next problem. So you've got to solve that one, which becomes the next problem. On and on and on: which is all racket, by the way, and leaves you looking like this.

(*hunching over*)

TIM

It seems that there are problems.

WES

It says up here "In life there are problems" that occur in languaging.

TIM

There are problems with solutions that don't become problems.

WES

Really? Give me one.

TIM

I left my wallet where I bought a gift. And I came and sat down and realized I left my wallet. I sat there and thought, "Gee, I don't remember putting my wallet away." I got up and went to check my coat and my wallet wasn't there. So I left and went to the store...

WES

But this is a story. I don't hear any problem in this.

TIM

So you're defining that losing a wallet is not a problem.

WES

No, not necessarily a problem.

TIM

Unless you say "it shouldn't be."

WES

Exactly. Losing a wallet is losing a wallet. Having cancer is having cancer. People are going to die. "Those people with cancer are going to die!" You are going to die.

TIM

What are the problems that are in life? Give me a problem in life?

The Drift

The work of both Erhard and Heidegger is the generation and development (the teasing out) of primordial metaphors, which may be held, for the purpose of this discussion, as what Erhard has called *distinctions* (and more recently, "linguistic abstractions"), the distinguishing of which unconceals new possibilities for Being-in-the-world.

WES

Any one you got, they belong here, because they belong in life.

TIM

Not because they shouldn't be but because they are there. So saying "shouldn't be" doesn't make them a problem.

WES

No: "Shouldn't be" is the source of your problems and the solutions to your problems that are attached to your rackets. Now we're going to look at problems outside your racket to see what you can do with them. What would you have to give up to have the problems that you have—not changing them—but to have the problems that you have and just have them? You'd have to give up a lot.

(*indicating Nicole, and her unfinished thesis*)

She'd have to give up a lot with the thesis: a lot of story, and "something's wrong," "something's wrong with me," or "something's wrong with it," or "my mother..." She'd have to give that all up. Then she'd have a problem. "I need to get my thesis done and I'm not getting it done." That's the name of that tune. If she would be with it like that she'd have to give up all the "shouldn't be"s around that, right?

TIM

Yes.

WES

She's solved that problem about the thesis a lot. She gave some explanations about it as a way to solve it. She lied about it as a way to solve it. See how those solutions are building the problem?

TIM

I think I'm getting it. So a problem can exist out of the context of "shouldn't be..."

WES

But not out of the context of languaging.

TIM

In life... They are there... Period.

WES

Yeah. Problems will occur in languaging one way or the other, because that's all there is for human beings.

TIM

They are a rainstorm.

The development of a distinction begins with positing what at first appears to be a definition or premise—a "hint"—that participants then "try on," and from which they are to "stand" and then "look out" at their everyday lives, and fill in for themselves what is hinted at in the hint. In dialogue with Erhard and the other course leaders—in combination with witnessing such dialogues—participants share what they see, and in the authentic space of this sharing, the distinction continues to emerge in the background, in what is unsaid in the conversation that directs our attention to a way of seeing and Being-in-the-world—a world that is itself being called out into unconcealment by the series of hints. The very act of undergoing a dialogue in which a distinction is distinguished *gives* Being-in-the-world.

Calling a distinction by a descriptive title, then, such as "story," or "what happened," or "concern," or "distinction," or "racket," or "empty and meaningless" can only ever be a hint, a piece of a whole that cannot ever be fully represented adequately as a descriptive statement. Thus, these "hints" function rhetorically as metaphors, language that on the surface is familiar, but once we take up the language and follow its movement, it "turns" us away toward something utterly different from itself. What makes these metaphors "primordial" is that speaking them, and following them, brings forth Being-in-the-world from nothing. What makes the work of Erhard so *distinctive* is precisely this approach.

Through his encounter with Heidegger's thinking, Erhard has said, new specifications for the communication of his work became available—ways to say things more pointedly, increasing the work's value to participants (Erhard, interview with the authors). The fundamental dynamic of Erhard's work—its all-encompassing generative distinction—has remained consistent since its inception as the *est* Training, and throughout its iteration as The Forum. At the same time, new languagings have been added to its vocabulary, creating other paths into the generative distinction. But just as Heidegger's language evolved significantly over the course of his career, Erhard has consistently experimented with other new primordial metaphors.

Experimentation is essential if such a methodology of language is to retain its generative power. An ontological distinction is communicated in the unspoken background as concepts are generated in the foreground of a conversation; but the distinction maintains its force *only while* those concepts are being generated. In this relevant passage, Heidegger distinguishes two ways in which beings (including ideas and concepts) can be brought to appear in the world:

> **Considered in terms of the essence of space, the difference between the two types of appearing is this: appearing in the first and authentic sense, as the gathered bringing-it-self-to-stand, takes space in; it first conquers space; as standing-there, it creates space for itself; it brings about everything that belongs to it, while it itself is not imitated.**

> **Appearing in the second sense merely steps forth from an already prepared space, and it is viewed by a looking-at within the already fixed dimensions of this space. The aspect offered by the thing, and no longer the thing itself, now becomes what is decisive. Appearing in the first sense *rips space open*. Appearing in the second sense simply gives space an *outline* and measures the space that has been opened up. (*IM* 203–204, emphasis and paragraphing added)**

In the initial saying of a primordial metaphor, then, the space of a distinction is ripped open. Subsequently, with each new and onto-logically consonant languaging of that distinction—or with each re iteration of the dialogic unfolding of the series of hints—the space that has been created expands.

But this demands that the space be *opened newly* in each occurrence. Erhard is emphatic on this point: "I never repeat material," he told an audience in 1989, "and I mean that quite literally. Every time I deal with something, I deal with it anew, like something to make present between you and me" ("Beyond the Winning Formula").

Two categories of distinctions are suggested by the two guiding questions of The Forum. The first category includes our current but concealed ways of being human—our "blind spots." These are

WES
No, there is languaging.

TIM
Languaging creates the rainstorm.

WES
Languaging creates everything.

TIM
Yeah. Including problems.

WES
Including problems. And you are given an already way of relating to problems. We're giving you a new way to relate to problems: to let them be.

TIM
Okay.

WES
For the moment. In order to deal with something powerfully, you have to be able to let it be. I can change the floor if I could let it be. If I'm arguing about the floor all day I'll never get around to changing it. From complaining about the floor all day I'll never get to deal with it.

TIM
Thank you.

WES
We've got "problems are in languaging," and we've got a way where we can let them be. It's okay to have a problem. They occur in languaging. We want to look at a specific problem to see what access we have to the problem when we let it be. Now I'm going to share my one real problem—the problem of all The Forum leaders who live in California. My problem is "I want to go to the beach but I don't have time. I'm always in The Forum." Whatever your problem is, it fits in that form. Something... but something.

On the chalkboard Wes wrote "I want to go to the beach but I don't have time" on the chalkboard.

(continuing)
You need to take one of your problems and put it in that form. Get the conflicting things. The way you get something stuck is you get one force opposed by an equal and opposite force. They have to be equal and opposite or you won't get stuck. If one force is bigger than the other, there will be movement. Anybody who can't see that? That's the nature of a problem.

WES (*continuing*)

Problems in life are presented as two equal but opposite forces in which you get stuck. Get a problem up for yourself and see that they are constructed by equal but opposite forces. The only problem with this is that there are some lies up here. What's a lie up here?

GRACE

It's the word "but" and it implies that there is no solution or no way out, or that you're stuck.

WES

Okay. Here is what "but" means, and why it's a problem: Problems are created by buts...

(*laughter*)

Welcome to the fourth day of The Forum. Problems are created by buts, because "but" means what follows it—this is the logic of linguistics here, okay—what follows "but" negates what precedes it, like an equal and opposite force to it. "I want to go to the beach" is stopped by the equal and opposite force "I don't have enough time," because of "but." You see that?

GRACE

Say "and"?

WES

Why would we want to say "and"?

GRACE

If you say "and" you have two things to look at and you can do something if you want to.

WES

That's close. Here's the question. "But" says this is an equal and opposite force to that. Is it really?

GRACE

No. They are two separate issues!

WES

What's the equal and opposite force to "I don't have time"?

GRACE

"I have time."

WES

"I do have time," right? "I do have time" is the equal and opposite force to "I don't have time," so that's what's really equal and opposite. And "I don't want to go to the beach" is the equal and opposite force to "I want to go to the beach."

the things about ourselves and our behavior that "we don't know that we don't know," which emerge within the question: "What is the Being of human beings?" In the second category are the new possibilities of Being, which can be distinguished only when the blind spots have been discovered and chosen, and the background of meaninglessness revealed as it is within the question: "What is the possibility of Being for human beings?"

This categorization is certainly valid at the levels of affect and value—the "bad" behaviors we want to change versus the improved versions we want to create—but considered ontologically, the difference is only apparent. The distinctions in both categories assign meaning to the meaningless. But, it may be argued, were not the behaviors being distinguished in the first category—such as my racket—already there, albeit unrecognized?

Heidegger responds that they have *always been available as possibilities.* "What is spoken out is already necessarily within *physis* (Being), otherwise it could not be spoken from out of it" (*FCM* 26). This is why its emergence into the world clicks for us even as it blows us away, occurring as something that at some level we already knew; and thus its showing up is accompanied by "the ring of truth," as shown in this brilliant passage from *Being and Time:*

> **Before Newton's laws were discovered, they were not 'true'; it does not follow that they were false, or even that they would become false if ontically no discoveredness were any longer possible. [. . .] To say that before Newton his laws were neither true nor false, cannot signify that before him there were no such entities as have been uncovered and pointed out by those laws. Through Newton the laws became true and with them, entities became accessible in themselves to Dasein. *Once entities have been uncovered, they show themselves precisely as entities which beforehand already were. Such uncovering is the kind of Being which belongs to 'truth.'* (*BT* 269, emphasis added)**

The ring of truth signals not only "Of course! That's true!" but also, embedded in its reverberations, "It's been true all along."

¥

In the early- to mid-1980s, during the period when the *est* Training was being retired and The Forum was being generated, Erhard's organization produced a series of audiotapes. In them, we hear Erhard developing distinctions, often in dialogic sessions with seminar participants. In some, the influence of Heidegger's vocabulary may be heard. In others, we observe Erhard exploring other articulations. As with Heidegger, Erhard's work is generated from a central distinction, which may be approached from an abundance of starting points.

One such starting point is *the drift,* a distinction developed on the 1985 audiotape, "Effective Action and Accomplishment." This distinction opens a way to Erhard's central transformational distinction; we suggest that the dynamic of this distinction may be analogized to several that Heidegger hints at throughout his work, with rubrics such as *thrownness, the "they,"* and *the play of Being.* To use a Heideggerian term, the two men are saying the Same (see the sidebar entitled "The Same" in Session Three of Day Three).

In this 1985 seminar, the distinction is teased out collaboratively in the interactions between Erhard and the seminar participants, all of whom have had previous experience of The Forum and are familiar with Erhard's basic vocabulary of distinctions and the rhetorical dialogue in which they get distinguished. In what follows here, we provide brief excerpts (elisions are not shown).

Erhard opens the seminar with the image of a "boat in the water with no rudder and no sails":

 Now when you put a boat in the water it doesn't stay still. It moves. And some ninny on the shore might say, "Boy, there's a lot of intention in that boat." But really what there is in the boat is *drift.* **So I want to invent this distinction for ourselves called the drift. You and I are drifting. Life is drifting. The world is drifting. Humanity is drifting. The United States is drifting. . . . There's a certain drift. And there's** *no distinction* **called the drift.**

WES (*indicating both independent clauses of the sentence on the board*)

These two are not equal and opposite forces: That's the lie. It's possible to have both of those and no conflict. They are not inherently conflicting. The "but" makes them conflicting. So, we change "but" to "and." If we say, "I want to go to the beach and I don't have time," we'd be telling the truth about the two forces operating on us. "I want to go to the beach," and "I don't have time." But is there a problem? Does "I want to go to the beach and I don't have time" occur as a problem?

GRACE

Yes, it occurs as a problem because you're dealing with two opposing forces.

WES

No, they are not opposing.

GRACE

They're separate and distinct.

WES

You're the one who said so a moment ago.

GRACE

Right. What next?

WES

So: "I am here in The Forum and I want to eat." Is that a problem?

GRACE

Not unless there's a "but" in there.

WES

Do you hear a problem there?

GRACE

No.

WES

But: "I'm here in The Forum, but I'm starving to death." Do you hear a problem?

GRACE

Yes.

WES

Taking the same forces and I've presented them to create a conflict, at which I am at the effect and stuck with. And it comes from, not from life, because in reality there are no problems, it

WES (*continuing*)

comes from me and my speaking. So here's what there is to get: all your problems as stucknesses are lies. All your problems as stucknesses are lies. All the presentation of the stuff there, that's not a lie. "I want to go to the beach and I don't have time": That's not a lie and it's not a problem.

GRACE

Right.

WES

Any time you find yourself stuck. Not moving. That's bullshit. You've lied. Wake up! The stuck is the lie. It comes from the—not the use of the word "but"—this is not about take every "but" out of your language—this is about: Appreciate what you're presenting in the problem, with "but," or whatever you use. Whenever you try to make things opposing and put yourself at the effect of them, there's a lie there and you're doing it, and the lie is that you're not doing it. The lie is: You're not doing it when you really are. That's the lie. Nothing is inherently stuck in life. Life's moving along fine. You see that?

GRACE

Yes.

As Grace sat Donald raised his hand and stood up again.

DONALD

So if I say "I want to lose weight, but I hate dieting," there's a lie there. It's like saying "I want to lose weight and you're wearing a black vest." Or "I want to lose weight and Vaclav Havel is the president of Yugoslavia."

WES

Yeah, it's that crazy, really. Why would anybody be so crazy as to do that?

DONALD

To be a victim.

WES

Not just victim, but to be a racketeer.

DONALD

So if I say "I'm overweight because my mother used to make fritters," that's the same lie.

WES

Yeah.

DONALD

Like "I'm overweight because you're wearing a black sweater." But the reason I blame my mother, say, when I don't like dieting, is because I've...

> So there's this enormous body of superstition about accomplishment and failure which has nothing whatsoever to do with accomplishment or failure. It's merely the drift. . . . I want you to see that in many ways you are a drift for yourself. You have a certain drift. The tide comes in, you go this way; the tide goes out, you go that way. So in many ways, you yourself are a part of the drift for you yourself.

> Now if this one drifts into the other one, they impact each other. But that's all part of the drift, yes? Your relationships drift. They've got a life of their own. Projects drift, they've got a life of their own. When I'm considering the distinction "accomplishment," my question is, what impacts the drift?

The distinction is teased out in the subsequent dialogue between Erhard and the seminar participants. Some of what appears here in embryonic form would later be developed in the Being a Leader Course (http://beingaleader.net) Erhard has developed together with Michael Jensen (Professor Emeritus of Economics at the Harvard Business School), Steve Zaffron (CEO of the Vanto Group), Kari Granger (Fellow, Center For Character and Leadership Development, United States Air Force Academy), and Jeri Echeverria (Professor and Provost Emerita for the California State University, Fresno). The next sidebar presents an excerpt from the pre-course readings for the Being a Leader Course (from 2015). ■

WES

You've gotta have something be wrong.

DONALD

It's fun to be stuck in "I'm fat and my mother..." There's more juice in the being stuck than in just going ahead and losing weight. What's that about?

WES

It's called "racket." That's what it's about.

DONALD

Okay, so I've got a racket.

WES

You are a racket. And your whole "fat" story is part of your racket. All your problems about "fat" are part of your racket, and all your solutions to those problems are part of the racket. And all your not-solutions to those problems are part of the racket...

DONALD

If it's a racket then there's some payoff holding it in place.

WES

Absolutely.

DONALD

I thought it happened the other way around. The costs... I got the costs... There's some payoff in holding onto my little problem here. So I've got some payoff...

WES

You want to be looking at what Donald is looking at: your problems and their relationships to your racket, and your payoffs and your costs. That's what the conversation—that's what makes the difference in the conversation; that's what you want to be looking at. There should be an opening into the problems that compose your life. Now—"That harmonizes with the rest of The Forum?"—that's what you want to be looking at.

DONALD

So I've got a racket called—I have, I've manufactured, I've created a racket called "I'm fat and I want to lose weight," right? This is a racket. I can see the costs. The costs are real clear: it's health, it's aliveness, vitality.

WES

No your racket is, "I want to lose weight but I can't."

DONALD

Right, okay. That's it.

WES

"And my mother's the one who did it to me." Was it your mother?

DONALD

Yeah. As a matter of fact.

(*laughter*)

WES

You love to make your mother wrong! You really do. He can do it on a daily basis. He can live now... Here's how he solved the problem of how to make his mother wrong on a continual basis. He has a problem with his weight. So every time he looks in the mirror his mother's wrong. Think about how accessible that is to him now. He doesn't even need to call her up on the phone. It's just: Look in the mirror. That's the payoff. Making her wrong is the payoff. You love it. People love to make people wrong. There's nothing like it: It's the spice of life.

DONALD

Wes, I saw some people in New York a couple of weeks ago and they said, "Donald, you've gained a lot of weight since moving to California." I said "well, the relationship I moved out here for didn't work out."

WES

Oh, so you made that relationship wrong.

DONALD

Got it.

WES (*to the group*)

Donald is learning something. His mother was the teacher—no, his need to make his mother wrong is the teacher. He can make people wrong by gaining weight. It works every time. And they did it to him. And they're creeps, just like his mother, the original weight giver.

(*laughter*)

By the way, your problems are like that. They repeat themselves. They're repetitive in nature. So that's an insight.

DONALD

My mother...

WES

And your solutions to problems, as rackets, are repetitive.

DONALD

I got another repetition. My mother never graduated from high school. She went to work instead. She wanted us to go to university. It was a big thing in our family to go to university. My mother really wanted all eleven of us to go to university, and I made my mother wrong by dropping out. And so I get to be uneducated, to continue to make my mother wrong, and Dad in there too. And so when she writes me letters... and tells me about my sister's grades—like I don't give a shit about my sister—I wish she'd stop reminding me of her being about education, because really she's wrong. I really didn't need to do that... So does that mean that in every problem that I have, I can see where I'm making someone wrong?

WES

Yeah.

DONALD

And if something happens, like if I lose my wallet, that's not a problem and there's no charge on it, I could just go back to the store where I lost my wallet and get it back. So when something's there, there always has to be a lie for there to be stuckness...

WES

And whenever you lie, you lie for a purpose, to make someone or something wrong, to avoid the domination of, to win, or to justify something: That's why you lie. You lie to avoid the domination of something, someone, make someone wrong or make yourself right, win, avoid losing and justify yourself and invalidating others. That's why people lie. That's the whole point of it.

DONALD

I caught myself lying on Wednesday, on Day One of this Forum, and I forget what process we were sharing about, but I was saying that the airlines had messed up my flight, but what happened was more like a dance with the changing schedules.

WES

You were more committed to moving through the stops than you were to making something wrong. If you were more committed to making something wrong, then that is what you would have been engaged in, and you would have ended up with the problems that most people have.

DONALD

I was so committed to having it work that I called the office here in San Francisco to get the address to send my bags here in case the flight got canceled again. I was committed to just have it work. But then at the same time, I lied about it on the phone, complaining to someone that I was stuck in Denver for three hours.

WES

Yeah, there's nothing like a little sympathy along the way.

DONALD

You know the thing that I didn't want to stand up and talk about was my weight because I didn't want to have eight hundred people come up and give me suggestions now.

(*laughter*)

I think there's like a stuckness that that creates.

WES (*to the group*)

Don't give Donald suggestions.

DONALD

Okay, thanks, Wes. That's it.

WES

Very good. Thank you.

(*Donald sits to applause as Illiana stands*)

What you want to be doing is looking at your problems and the payoffs to them.

ILLIANA

I'm trying to figure it out.

WES

Bad deal. Wrong deal.

ILLIANA

Okay. Just a second. My racket is that I want attention.

WES

What problem allows you to run the racket?

ILLIANA

Asking for attention.

WES

Is that the problem? Asking for attention?

ILLIANA

I have many different problems on that basis.

"Way of Being" and the "Nature of Being for Human Beings"

The following is an excerpt from the Pre-Course Reading Assignment #5 from the Being a Leader Course (http://beingaleader.net) as of fall 2015. In the manner in which this pedagogical document opens up a way to distinguish the difference between "way of being" for human beings, and the "fundamental and essential nature of Being for human beings," the authors find a further development of Erhard's work in The Forum (circa 1989) that both continues to resonate with Heidegger's thinking while experimenting with new languagings of primordial metaphors.

What is Meant by "Way of Being"

In speaking about another person's *way of being* you or I might say, "She's in a good mood," or "That made him sad," or "She's always cheerful," or "He is an extrovert." We also sometimes similarly think about our own *way of being*.

Our *way of being* is some combination of our mental state, emotional state, bodily state, and our thoughts and thought processes, and memories. Or saying the same thing in more experiential terms, our *way of being* is some combination of our attitude or state of mind, and our feelings or emotions, plus our body sensations, and our thoughts and memories. For short, our way of being is *what is going on with us internally* in a given moment or in a given situation.

Note that the temporality of our *way of being* is what is going on with us in *a given moment* or in *a given situation*. Even if a certain way of being could be said to be our general or characteristic way of being, none of us is always only the way we generally or characteristically are.

Once you have checked out in your own experience what we have said so far about *way of being* (and you should certainly do that), what we have said becomes pretty obvious. But, there are two facts about our *way of being* that are at first perhaps not so obvious:

Fact One

Our *actions* from moment to moment are generally *consistent* with our *way of being* in those moments. This is true for any *way of being,* such as annoyed, or sad, or loving, and the like. For example, when we are *being* angry we are also likely to find ourselves *acting* angrily, and when we are *being* confident we are likely to be *acting* confidently. It is clear that when we are *being* angry, or confident, or annoyed, or sad or loving, our *actions* are likely to be *consistent* with that *way of being*.

Note that we have said that our *actions* are virtually always *consistent* with our *way of being* (what is going on with us internally). And that is all that can be verified in our experience (in our consciousness). We can have theories about some additional connection or relation between our *way of being* and our *actions,* but there is no proof (evidence) of any further connection or relation between our way of being and our way of acting other than that they are *consistent* with each other.

However, we must note that most people go through life and act in life as though what is going on with them internally (some combination of their mental state, emotional state, bodily state, and their thoughts and memories) *causes* their actions. But there is no scientific evidence for believing in such a causal connection. All we can say about the relationship between our way of being and acting is that they are mutually arising or co-arising. In fact, during the course we will present neuroscience research (Clancey 1993; Libet 1999; Hawkins 2004; Soon 2008; Haggard 2009; Kandel 2009; Bode 2011; Wolpert 2011; Zimmer 2013 and Buckner 2013) that is contrary to the belief that what is going on with you internally causes your actions. For now, the following quotes from neuroscientist Sam Harris (2012) summarize in everyday language the research about the connection between *what is going on with you internally* (in this case, your decision or intention) and your *action*:

WES

Right: With this person and with that person…

ILLAINA

Yes.

WES

"I want attention from him but he's not giving me any attention," and so you develop a whole story about what kind of person he is, and she's had this problem before with other people, and none of it should be, it's all wrong and she's less-than, and you're into this whole crummy story and somebody's wrong. And somebody's right. Of course she's right and something else is wrong.

ILLIANA

From that I developed asking attention in different ways.

WES

Right: as a solution. But they never really work, do they?

ILLIANA

No. Until today. I don't get what I want.

WES

Yeah.

ILLIANA

Now, you said to bring up the problem, okay? The problem that I came up with was… I'm dealing now in my life with a… working with a new company, trying to do something that I don't believe I can do. And what I really want is their attention, to know that I can do it.

WES

Yeah, and that'll make everything lousy, with no satisfaction. She's doing it to get attention, not to produce results. There will be no accomplishment, and she'll never get enough attention, so she'll be driven, and it's a racket. And she'll also conclude about it that it shouldn't be. The whole situation "shouldn't be," and you shouldn't be this way. However it turns out, "it shouldn't be." And you'll have a problem again, and that shouldn't be. And so now you can stand in empty and meaningless and see the absurdity of that. The absurdity of the problem called "needing attention." You want attention?

ILLIANA

Yeah.

WES

Great. Take what you get and call that "attention." That would be a possibility, right? From empty and meaningless?

ILLIANA

You mean, whatever comes?

WES

Yeah. Take what you get and call that "attention." Someone looks over at me, "great. That's attention." And then get along with my work. Not like "They didn't look long enough. That must mean I'm not okay." Swirling around in your racket. Who cares if you didn't get attention? Produce some results. And then you'll die.

(*laughter*)

ILLIANA

I want to ask a question. I would like to fit my racket with what you are saying.

WES

Where is the "unfit"?

(*after Illiana asks Wes to read the board once more*)
"I want to go the beach, but I don't have any time." That's a problem.

ILLIANA

So that's the "but": "I want to get attention, but I don't want to ask for it."

WES

Great. That's a problem, right?

ILLIANA

Right.

WES

Let's shift it: It's a lie. It's a racket.

ILLAINA

Okay.

WES

Tell the truth about it. "I want to get attention and I'm afraid to ask for it."

ILLIANA (*smiling*)

And I'm afraid to ask for it. So the "but" is creating the problem.

 Some moments before you are aware of what you will do next—a time in which you subjectively appear to have complete freedom to behave however you please—your brain has already determined what you will do. You then become conscious of this "decision" and believe that you are in the process of making it. (9)

The intention to do one thing and not another does not originate in consciousness—rather, it *appears* in consciousness. . . . (8)

In summary, our *actions* are merely *consistent* with our *way of being*—that is, our actions are likely consistent with *some combination* of our mental state, emotional state, bodily state, and our thoughts and memories; but our actions are not *caused* by these aspects of what is going on with us internally.

Fact Two

And, perhaps even less obvious is that both *our way of being and our actions* (arising together consistent with each other) is *correlated* with—is naturally, necessarily, closely connected with; or more poetically, in-a-dance-with—the way in which what we are dealing with *occurs* or *shows up* for us. In short, *our way of being and acting* is a *natural correlate* of (in-a-dance-with) the way what we are dealing with *occurs* for us. For example, if the way a situation we are dealing with *occurs* or *shows up* for us as threatening, *our way of being and acting* is likely to be a *natural correlate* of (in-a-dance-with) the situation *occurring* or *showing up* for us as threatening. On the other hand, if the way a situation we are dealing with *occurs* or *shows up* for us as an opportunity to excel, *our way of being and acting* is likely to be *correlated* with the situation *occurring* for us as an opportunity to excel.

You can confirm facts 1 and 2 for yourself by checking them out in your own experience. Regarding fact 1: Is your *way of being* at this moment—that is, some combination of your attitude, and your feelings, plus your body sensations, and your thoughts and memories regarding what you are dealing with—*consistent* with *your way of acting* in this moment? Or more pointedly, is your way of being and way of acting consistent with each other, virtually arising as one thing?

And then, fact 2: Is your way of *being and acting* (arising as though one thing) *correlated with* (closely connected with) the way what you are dealing with *occurs* or *shows up* for you? And, has that been essentially true in situations you have dealt with in the past? (For those of you who are tempted to do so, don't stop at understanding the text of what we said; rather, take the time to actually check it out in your own *as-lived* experience.)

In summary: Our *way of being and acting* is *correlated* with (naturally, necessarily, closely connected with; in-a-dance-with) the way in which what we are dealing with *occurs* for us.

During the course everything in this section will be gone over and made clear for you so that you can confirm its validity in your own *lived experience*. In addition, the critical importance for being a leader and the effective exercise of leadership of what has been covered in this section will be dealt with in depth during the in-class sessions of the course.

A Fact about the Way in which what we are Dealing With *Occurs* for us

When we go through life such that who we are is whatever we are referring to when we say "I" or "me" (which is the way we usually do go through life), there is a *background* for the way in which life, living, and self *occur* for us. That is, when who we are for ourselves is what we are referring to when we say "I" or "me," this background (or we could say "environment") for the way in which life,

WES
You see that?

ILLIANA (*nodding and smiling*)
Yes.

WES
Yeah. This is a woman who just got the lie in her life. Why you're driven to the "but" is your racket. You'll find yourself taking things and putting "but" between them. Opposing them from your racket. You'll have to train yourself in telling the truth.

ILLIANA
The "but" makes it fighting. "And" is making peace.

WES
Yes! Very good!

ILLIANA
Thank you.

(*applause*)

Paul stood up again, the participant who can speak several languages and who struggled to get the distinction "being inauthentic" during Session Two of Day One.

PAUL
I see something now about having my foot nailed to the floor. When you were going around there: I saw myself one day going around in my living room in a circle, and it just cracked me up that I did that. What's come out of it, I sat there wanting to go into real estate, and wanting to have a career in real estate, but I don't know if I should because I... "I'm not really good at this, I don't understand it. I really should go to school. But school takes a lot of money and I don't have a lot of money and I hate my job. And I hate my job because I can't make a lot of money." It just kept going and going and going. What's funny is that it led to me coming here, because I got that everything, this all is going to collapse and I'll be dead. If I don't do something about it, or do something, it'll be the end of me. Not only that, I can see how I've done this with other things I love in my life, like music, that I've completely talked myself right out of it. It's something I wanted to do but I started too late. I'm not a great technician and I don't have all these things. And I eventually lost sight of the fact that I just like making music. Instead of just being in that making music I've gotten tangled up in all the little piddly details and it became a racket after a while. And it kept me from dealing with the fact that I have to practice if I want to make it, and I didn't want to. Now it is so easy to see it. Now I'd like to get home and play.

WES

Right. It opens up participation. Your problems are stops to participation.

PAUL

It's not this big tragedy anymore, like "I've got to commit myself to this!" Just do it.

WES

Great. Thanks.

DOREL

I've been sitting here thinking about my problems, and there's a lot of them.

KIPP

All the problems you have in your languaging.

DOREL

In my languaging.

KIPP

You see the difference between those? There are no problems in your life, are there?

DOREL

I think I see what you're saying, it's just that I created...

KIPP

Be careful about this creation business. They live in the conversation you are. There are no problems out there. Your dog never has any problems. And when you say you have a lot of problems in your life, you're saying there's this "life" someplace that contains these problems; the problems are in your conversations. Languaging.

DOREL

One of the things I got was that I get easily upset and angry.

KIPP

You're kidding. How did you get in here? He gets easily upset? Angry?

(*laughter*)

DOREL

I think a big source of that is I want to make others wrong.

living, and self *occur* for us, *colors and shapes* that occurring. We term this background or environment for the way life, living, and self occur: "mood." The *occurring* is in the *foreground* and the *mood* is in the *background* coloring and shaping the *occurring* in the *foreground*. During the in-class sessions of the course we will clarify and fully deal with what is introduced in this paragraph. At this point, the only thing there is to get about what is said in this paragraph is that there is this something called "mood," and *mood* is distinct from and different than what is meant by "*clearing*," a term you will encounter in the next section.

The "Fundamental and Essential Nature and Function of Being for Human Beings" in Contrast to One's "Way of Being"

There is a difference between the *fundamental and essential* nature of "being" for human beings, and any person's individual *moment-to-moment* particular "way of being."

We are sometimes aware of our particular moment-to-moment *way of being*, but we human beings so take for granted that we *exist* (that we *are*), that we give no thought to the actual nature and function of *being* for us human beings (unless it is to think about the time when we won't be at all). As a result, getting clear about the fundamental and essential nature and function of *being* for human beings (as contrasted with our individual moment-to-moment *way of being*) will be somewhat challenging.

Being for human beings (that is, the fundamental and essential nature of *being* for human beings) is "being the *clearing*" (the possibility, or something like, the emptiness or nothingness) in which life, living, and self *occur* or *show up* for us. What shows up in the *clearing that we are* is all of it, the entire "state of the world." All of it, our entire "state of the world"—includes physical objects and non-physical entities of every kind (and their properties and in various relationships), other people (and their properties and in various relationships), and we ourselves (and our properties and in various relationships), along with the spatiality of here and there, and the temporality of the past, the present, and the future.

The "ourselves" that shows up in the clearing that we are, is that to which we refer when we say "I" or "me"—that is, our particular way of being in this or that moment, or our sense of ourselves (our identity or persona). You can confirm this by noticing that you (as the clearing you are) are capable of being aware of yourself as whatever it is that you are referring to when you say "I" or "me," and the at-the-moment way of being of that "I" or "me." In other words, what you refer to when you say "I" or "me" shows up for you in the *clearing* that you fundamentally and essentially are.

We note here that a drawback with the phrase the *clearing that we are* is that it seems to imply subjectivity, and it is definitely *not* meant in that way. We will clarify and fully develop this during the in-class sessions of the course.

Saying all this in other words: *Being* for human beings (the fundamental and essential nature of *being* for human beings) is always and only, as philosopher Martin Heidegger so brilliantly nailed it, "being in the world" (*Being and Time*). While we generally think of *being* as something located "in here," if you take a careful look you will see that you are always being *with* something or being *about* something, that is, always being in the world (even if the part of the world you are being with is that thing you refer to when you say "I" or "me" or the way of being of "I" or "me").

You can confirm for yourself that *being* for you is being in the world, that you are so to speak a clearing for it all, in that when you are conscious, you are always conscious of something or conscious about something (even if what you are conscious of in a given moment is being conscious). In other words, for human beings what it is to *be* is for the world, all of it (our entire "state of the world") to *show up* (to occur).

Our moment to moment *way of being* is *not* the fundamental and essential nature of *being* for us human beings. When we are being the *clearing* for life to show up, and our "I" or "me" self is

KIPP

Right. That's accurate terminology. Wants are part of the structure of being a human being. The truth is: You've got to make people wrong in order to be right.

DOREL

The first night I left here I got lost, because I don't live here.

KIPP

No, you got lost.

DOREL

I got lost.

KIPP

You hear the difference? You got lost. You just got lost.

DOREL

And I got so damn angry at my brother-in-law who was supposed to leave me with a map and directions and everything, but he didn't. He just called me the night before everything started.

KIPP

You were lost and angry. Before you were just lost. Now you got lost and angry. A stupid person, right?

DOREL (*laughing*)

Right.

KIPP

You could have just been lost.

(*laughter*)

Except you had to screw it up and put anger in there.

DOREL

That's right. And in a way I enjoy that.

KIPP

It's familiar. Kick the walls. Spit on the floor. Exactly.

DOREL

The following night I had to get mad at the parking lot attendant.

KIPP
Yeah. He was there.

(*laughter*)
Right. What the hell is he there for? That's his job.

DOREL
The following night, I didn't get angry. So what if it takes fifteen minutes to let one car go.

KIPP
Right. If it takes fifteen minutes, then it takes fifteen minutes. And that's the whole story. Get your car. Life is hard. And then you die. They throw dirt over your face, and that happens whether you get your car or not, whether you get it in two or fifteen minutes.

DOREL (*smiling*)
I am just a goddamned bitcher and complainer in life. I get upset and angry and I bitch and bitch and bitch and bitch.

KIPP
That's right.

DOREL
So that's the thing with me.

KIPP
Yeah. It's interesting. You're so honest in your speaking, it contributes to everybody in the room a lot, Dorel. Your authenticity is powerfully contributing. It's real. Makes a big difference for people. I was leading The Forum in London, and during the evening session after the four days, a man stood and shared that his younger son came to him: "Daddy Daddy, Johnny hit me." "Uh huh." "But Daddy, you don't understand, he hit me in the same place as before, where it really hurt!" "Uh huh." "But Daddy, Johnny's older and you said before he should know better not to hit me." "Uh huh." "Daddy, I don't want you to go back to that seminar anymore because it makes you stupid!"

(*laughter*)

DOREL (*laughing*)
Am I going to be stupid?

KIPP
Yes. What's going to be stupid is: It's going to take fifteen minutes to get your car when it takes fifteen minutes. And when you're lost, you'll be lost. And that's life, yes? You don't have to add

simply one of the things that shows up in the clearing, that leaves us free to be and free to act in life—free to be and free to act with whatever we are dealing with in any situation. This is critical for being a leader and exercising leadership effectively *as one's natural self-expression*; and during the in-class sessions of the course *access* to this fundamental and essential nature of *being* for us human beings will be made available to you.

As was the case with the previous section (Section 2), during the course everything in this section will be gone over and made clear for you so that you can confirm its validity for yourself in your own lived experience. In addition, the critical importance of what has been covered in this section for being a leader and the effective exercise of leadership *as your natural self-expression* will be dealt with in depth during the in-class sessions of the course. ∎

all that other stuff to it. As a matter of fact, when you're lost, you could discover something. But when you're lost and angry, you're too busy being angry to find out anything beyond being lost and angry. Anything else?

DOREL
No. Thank you.

KIPP
Well done. Thank you very much.

WES
Wait a second, Kipp. Just to complete this: You have to deal with your own listening to this conversation. Consider the possibility that you are listening to the conversation about problems like it would help you solve them. See that? It's listening to this like "Oh, here's new stuff to help me solve my problems." That's more of the same. This conversation is intended to create a new clearing for problems, which clearing will alter you and the problems in life. That's the intention. If you were looking at Illiana's face, she got a new clearing for this whole thing about attention. She still needs attention. She still has a racket. Still has the same job. But the occurrence "attention" occurs in a new clearing. This clearing will give her the opportunity to make new requests. See, she's never tried out being straight with people about giving her attention. Like...

(*to Illiana, who is sitting*)

"Would you give me some attention? Let's stop for five minutes. I'm producing great results. I want you to listen to what happened to me today. Would you be willing to do that?" The racket is to do it and have a problem with doing it. Now you can just do it. By the way, this attention thing has something else behind it.

(*to the group*)

The point is that there's a possibility for you and your problems to relate differently. A new clearing. You don't have to remember any of this. No, there's one thing you have to remember: Your problems are part of your racket and your racket stinks. That's all you need to remember. That'll create a new clearing for you.

At 3:30, Kipp asked participants to stand up and stretch and then sit back down.

KIPP
When you come into life from empty and meaningless, and you're able to be with your racket, what opens up for you is choice. However, you don't know anything about choice. So we're going to spend some time distinguishing choice as choice. So when you say you're going to do something and you want to do it, you say what? You go out and make a what? A decision, yes? You say something like "I made a decision to do this." First of all, we want to get choice and decision distinct. The word "decide" comes from the same family as suicide, matricide, and

KIPP (*continuing*)

patricide and all the cides—meaning to kill. Decide means to kill or murder the alternative. So when you decide something you are destroying the alternative. "I've decided to do that!" That's a decision—based on something. "I'm deciding this because..." It's always based on something. What gives a decision is it's based on something. Choice is not based on something. It's based on no thing or nothing. Choice is to select freely and after consideration, not limited by whatever the evidence that you have to give for a decision. The first thing we need to do is to get a decision to be a decision and a choice to be a choice so that they can live distinctly for you. When you say choose, what you mean for the most part is decide. What you're actually saying is decide. We're going to do a little demonstration with someone to distinguish a choice from a decision, so you can see it clearly for yourself, so you can see a choice in action.

Kipp asked for a volunteer who has not taken The Forum before, nor seen the demonstration. The participant chosen was Bill, the young man who had interacted so combatively with Erhard during Session One of Day One of The Forum.

KIPP (*continuing*)

Are you willing to do this demonstration, to stay with it all the way through, keep participating, even if it looks like it might be frustrating for you and you might not get it, and go right to the end and keep on playing?

BILL (*smiling*)

Couldn't look any worse than I did on the first day. So yeah, I'm willing.

KIPP

That's true.

(*laughter: to the group*)

Okay, so. All right. Now, your job is not to coach Bill. A lot of the time when you are sitting in your chair and you don't have whatever it is that you have when you're standing there attempting to get it sorted out for yourself, where it's sometimes a little more difficult to see, so don't say it out loud, or coach him in some way. Let him struggle with it because it's the inquiry into the distinction, the struggle that will bring forth the distinction. We're not defining a distinction; we're not explaining a distinction. We're not describing choice. We want to see choice as a distinction in action. So Bill, I'm going to ask you to make a simple choice, and each time I ask you to make a choice, you'll say to me, "I choose..." whatever you chose, "because..." And you'll fill in whatever comes after that for you, okay? You clear how to respond? Okay ready?

BILL

Yeah.

Kipp held out two hands as if he had an ice cream cone in each one.

KIPP (*to Bill*)
Chocolate or vanilla: Choose.

BILL (*pointing at the hand representing chocolate*)
I choose chocolate... because I prefer the flavor.

KIPP
Perfect. Okay, so, "I chose chocolate because I prefer the flavor." That's a perfect decision, because what selected the chocolate was what? What did the selecting?

BILL
I did.

KIPP
Well, if you really look at it, the reason, the thought, the consideration—"because I prefer the flavor better"—came along, right?

BILL
Yeah.

KIPP (*pulling a tissue out of a tissue box*)
Like this little thought—peep!—comes along...

(*dangling the tissue in the air*)
"I prefer the flavor of chocolate better."

(*pointing at the tissue*)
And that reason, that consideration, that thought, selected the chocolate, didn't it? Not you. That's what the selection was based on, wasn't it?

BILL
Yeah.

KIPP
That's a decision because it's based on something. Perfect! That's what your job is up here, so everybody can see a decision as a decision, and a choice as a choice. Okay, ready?

(*holding out his hands again to Bill*)
Chocolate or vanilla: Choose.

BILL
Chocolate.

KIPP
Perfect! Now why'd you choose chocolate?

BILL (*after a long pause*)
I chose chocolate...

KIPP
Because...

BILL
If I put a because in there it'll be a decision...

KIPP
We did this before, it works...

(*laughter*)
"I chose chocolate because..."

BILL
I chose chocolate... because it's black. I don't know.

KIPP
Perfect! So, along came this thought...Peep!

(*pulling another tissue from the box and dangling it*)
"Because it's black." And what did the selecting was the reason, the feeling, the thought, the consideration, the evidence, the something did the selecting, not you. So that's a clear-cut decision.

BILL
How do I get out of this?

KIPP
You keep inquiring, just like you're doing. You're doing perfectly. Okay? Ready to go again?

BILL
Yeah.

KIPP
Chocolate or vanilla: Choose.

BILL
Vanilla.

KIPP
Vanilla! Perfect! Why did you choose vanilla? "I chose..."

BILL (*to laughter*)
Can you give me a hint?

KIPP
A choice is to select freely and after consideration... "I chose..."

BILL
I chose vanilla because I want to experiment with a new taste.

KIPP
Perfect! So along came a thought—peep!...

(*pulling another tissue out of the box*)
"because I want to experiment with a new taste," right? And "because I want to experiment with a new taste" selected vanilla, and not you: That's a clear-cut decision because it's based on the reason, the feeling, the consideration, the thought...

(*holding many tissues*)
See we're starting to get "the mind" built here. This is what the mind is made up of, all those things, those thoughts, those feelings, those considerations. And you're doing great, training everyone in the room in these distinctions. I know it may not feel that way to you, but you're doing great. Ready?

The demonstration continued, with Bill selecting a flavor after Kipp presented the choice: because he only had two choices; because it's there; because he decided to, etc. At each juncture Bill reiterated his complaint that he knew the problem (how to make a choice using the word because, when using because leads to making a decision) but that he didn't know how to get out of it.

BILL
I chose because I exhausted all my reasons.

KIPP
So the reason—peep!

KIPP (*pulling another tissue out of the box*)

"I've exhausted all my reasons" is a reason. It doesn't sound like a reason, but it's a reason. And so the selection of chocolate was once again based on a reason. It was based on something; a choice is based on nothing, except you saying so. Chocolate, vanilla: choose!

BILL

Vanilla.

KIPP

Perfect! Why did you choose vanilla?

BILL

I chose vanilla because I decided to...

(*Kipp pulls out another tissue, wafting it will a string of "peeps"*)
Because I chose to.

KIPP

Okay, okay. Let's check it out again. Chocolate or vanilla: choose!

BILL

Chocolate.

KIPP

Perfect! Why did you choose chocolate?

BILL (*hesitating*)

I have to use because?

KIPP

Yes.

BILL (*to laughter*)

I don't see any way to develop from this.

KIPP

Right. You're distinctioning something. You're distinguishing something, and you're doing great. Chocolate or vanilla: choose!

BILL

Chocolate.

KIPP

Perfect! Why did you choose chocolate?

BILL

I chose chocolate... because I enjoy choosing chocolate.

KIPP (*pulling out another tissue to a elongated "peep!"*)

"I enjoy" is like a feeling, a thought, a consideration, a reason, isn't it? It's based on your enjoyment. That reason came along and selected it again.

BILL

I do not know how to make a choice without... with using the word because. I must have missed something.

KIPP

You didn't miss anything. They are real glad it's you up here, not them.

(*applause*)

When you come from life is empty and meaningless and you're able to be with your racket, choice opens up for you, but you don't know anything about choice. Why we are working this way is to distinguish something called choice, and a choice is based on nothing: It's a pure choice, simply because you choose. Chocolate/Vanilla: choose!

BILL (*finally*)

I choose chocolate simply because I choose... chocolate.

The participants erupted in applause.

KIPP

The important thing is all his reasons, thoughts, feelings considerations, are still there, weren't they? See, you think you have to get rid of these...

(*holding up all the tissues he had pulled out of the box*)

In order to make a choice. No. They are all still there, except his choice isn't based on these. He has his reasons, his thoughts, his feelings, his considerations, but he's not being those. He's being his choice. You think you have to get rid of all these, then you can make a choice. Yes?

BILL

I thought that way. I think that way.

KIPP

So far that's what's been available for you, is you thinking that this is what you got for your life, yes? If you can get enough of these lined up in one way or the other, it will give you the action that you want.

BILL

Yes.

KIPP

Exactly. What's been missing for you is the distinction choice, for you "Bill," and for you "human being." It doesn't come with being human. You don't come equipped with that one. You've got to invent that one. You want to test this now to make sure you and everybody else is clear about it?

BILL

Sure.

KIPP

Bill, why is the floor down there?

BILL (*looking down*)

It's just there?

KIPP

It's where? The floor is down there because...?

BILL (*laughing*)

It doesn't choose to be there. That's for sure.

KIPP

Good, Bill. So...?

BILL

Because it's there.

KIPP

Where? The floor is down there because...?

BILL

Because the floor is down there.

KIPP

Let's check this out a bit more.

KIPP (*pointing up*)
Bill, why is the ceiling up there?

BILL
Because it's up there.

KIPP (*pointing at a participant*)
But Bill, why is Ashley like that?

BILL
Because Ashley's like that.

KIPP (*pointing at another participant*)
Wait a second Bill, why is John like that?

BILL
Because John is like that.

KIPP
Yeah, but Bill, what is the sound of one hand clapping?

BILL (*to laughter*)
I've heard this one before...

He took a long time mulling over this, trying various answers: "it's nonexistent," "there is no sound," etc. Kipp repeated the prompts for the floor and the ceiling, and then returning to the sound of one hand clapping.

BILL (*to laughter*)
It can't manifest a sound. It must have something to do with the floor and the ceiling.

KIPP
Human beings love logic. It's all got to be logical. Right? What is the sound of one hand clapping?

BILL
There is no sound.

KIPP
Where you are looking there is no sound. But the sound of one hand clapping is what? It's simply what?

BILL

Simply, it's nonexistent.

KIPP

Or: The floor is down there because...

BILL

There's no "because" to the floor being down there.

KIPP

The floor is down there because...

BILL

There's no reason for it to be down there.

KIPP

And the floor is down there because...

BILL (*laughing*)

It doesn't have a because. Because somebody built it and stuck it there.

KIPP

The floor is down there because...

BILL

I shouldn't have volunteered to continue with this. I seem to be losing it.

KIPP

That's fine. That's the difference between a distinction and a definition. You can't get a distinction by defining it, or exampling it; you can only get it by creating it... So the floor is down there because... Okay, forget about the floor, but the ceiling's up there because...

BILL (*looking up*)

Because it's there.

KIPP

Where? Up there, right? The ceiling's up there because it's up there.

BILL

...because the ceiling's up there. Is that correct?

KIPP

I don't know if it's correct or not, but the ceiling's up there because the ceiling is up there, isn't it? And Ashley is the way that Ashley is, and the floor is down there because the floor is down there, and the ceiling is up there because the ceiling is up there, and the sound of one hand clapping is... What's the sound of one hand clapping?

BILL

There is no sound.

KIPP

That's one interpretation. What's another one?

BILL

It doesn't make any sense.

KIPP

Right. And what does make sense is your reasons. Choice doesn't make sense. It just is. So the sound of one hand clapping is...

(*Bill swings his left hand back and forth*)
What is that?

BILL (*to applause and laughter*)
It's the sound of one hand clapping.

KIPP

They got it, but I don't know if you got it. The sound of one hand clapping is the...

BILL (*smiling and to applause*)
Sound of one hand clapping.

KIPP

The sound of one hand clapping is always the sound of one hand clapping, isn't it?

BILL

Right.

KIPP

You cannot answer what they call in Zen a koan—a little riddle given by a Zen master to someone studying Zen—you cannot answer that koan in your mind. You've got to be out of your mind.

KIPP *(continuing)*

And all you've had so far to operate from in life is your mind. All you've had is your reasons, your thoughts, your feelings, your considerations, for action. It's all you've been given by human being to do something: You've had to decide and have a reason for your actions. But as you have demonstrated for us, we can distinguish that choice is based on what? It's based on...

BILL

Your choice.

KIPP

Exactly. It's simply your choice. Now which is more risky? A decision or a choice?

BILL

Choice.

KIPP

Exactly. Because as long as you have your reasons, if it doesn't go well, if it goes a way it shouldn't have gone, you can always say "See, it didn't work out! Why?" That's why people get married. "Let's see. I'll get married because you're nice looking, and we get along, and you want to live in the same city I do, and all that other stuff, and then, when something happens and the reasons for doing something stop being present in your life, well then, you question your marriage, because your marriage isn't based on you, you never got married. What got married was your reasons. That's not called a marriage, that's called an entanglement. You see, you've never chosen to work where you work. You wonder why you have no power where you work? Because you're not there. What's got you there are your reasons. No power here, just force: just trying to move around the reasons.

(to Bill)

Bill, you did an extraordinary job. And why you did an extraordinary job is because you were absolutely authentic about it.

BILL

Thank you.

KIPP

Why I appreciate it and why everyone in the room appreciates it is because you never stopped looking and inquiring. Most people, when they don't see it right away...

(referring to the quote Erhard read from On the Way to Language)

Heidegger says that the kind of beings that human beings are, we're born thinking that we comprehend everything, you know, everything is comprehendible. And so if something is not comprehendible, the best we can do is be offended by it. We're offended by what we don't comprehend versus being willing to think. In order to create that distinction, Bill, and if you were sitting in your chair doing the demonstration, you had to think. It wasn't given by thoughts; you had to really think. So I'm asking you to start thinking that thinking and distinguishing are synonymous—not perfectly, not neatly. But you have to think to get a distinction, to bring forth distinction.

(*to Bill*)
And that's what you were willing to do. And you were big about it. And we appreciate it.

Bill returned to his seat as the group applauded. Another participant, Joan, raised her hand and stood.

JOAN
I feel really stupid. I didn't get it.

KIPP
Okay. What didn't you get?

JOAN (*in tears*)
I don't understand how to make a choice without a reason.

KIPP
The reasons are still there, aren't they? They don't go away.

JOAN
No they don't. I have a zillion of them.

KIPP
What's a current choice you need to make?

JOAN
Figuring out what I want to do with my life. It sounds really stupid. What I want to do for a job.

KIPP
Okay. "What I want to do for a job." You have a couple different ideas?

JOAN
Yes.

KIPP
Okay good. What are the ideas?

JOAN
Start my own business.

KIPP
Okay.

JOAN
Or work for a small company.

KIPP
Let's take those two for an example, Okay? Start your own business, work for a small company: choose!

JOAN (*laughing*)
Start my own company.

KIPP
Perfect! Now why are you going to start your own company? "I'm going to start my own company because..."

JOAN
Because my father did.

KIPP
Perfect reason! That's an example of a decision. What has you now starting your own company is your father did that: That's not you making a choice, is it? It's your father, so if it doesn't work out, you can kick the shit out of your father.

(*laughter*)

Decisions get you off the hook, don't they? Because the reason "because my father did" has you starting your own company, not you. When you make a choice, you're the chooser. You can still have all the thoughts; you can still carefully consider it all. I'm not saying to throw out the analysis. But if what you do is based on your analysis, I promise you a future determined by the past. Because analysis is always looking where? What's already happened! And so far, that's where you look in your life. You go:

(*contorting his body to look behind him*)
"Let's see what's possible in my life."

JOAN (*laughing*)
Yes I do that.

KIPP (*to the group*)

And everything we're starting to distinguish—you didn't come equipped with this. You've got to invent it. We're beginning to invent a body of distinctions beyond what you got when you became a human being. You're not used to this; it's going to take real thinking. This is what Einstein was talking about: The problems that we've got are not going to be solved at the level of thinking that created them. What's required is a new level of thinking. Choice requires thinking.

(*to Joan*)

Start your own business or work for a small company: choose!

JOAN

Start my own business.

KIPP

Great! And why did you make that choice? "I'm going to start my own company because..."

JOAN

...because if I don't do it in my life, I'm going to be really disappointed.

KIPP

Perfect decision! The reason "because I'll really be disappointed"—that's what's getting you going again, that reason. Choice isn't based on that, it's to select freely: You are the chooser. You simply choose because you choose. You can still look at all that stuff. Look at this part of it and that part of it, but when it comes to a choice it's you choosing. Ready? Start your own business, work for a small company: choose!

JOAN

I choose starting my own company because it's what I want to do.

KIPP

That's a wonderful want.

JOAN

Because I think I should do it.

KIPP

And your wants and shoulds, which are totally a product of your past, now have you starting your own small business and what you're going to be given—see the important thing is—if that's what gets her into that game, she's going to have whatever she's got from her past. Everything she needs for that is going to be given by the past because she's not there starting her own small business; it's the past starting her own small business, and she'll have whatever power, ability, excellence, and all that other stuff she's got from her past, and not "you," because you

KIPP *(continuing)*

haven't started your own business yet; the past is: all the reasons for doing it, right? Now, start your own business, work for a small company: choose!

JOAN

Start my own company.

KIPP

Good. Now why are you going to start your own company?

JOAN

Because it sounds like fun.

KIPP

Good. Then when it's not fun, you're going to go: "Well, this really wasn't fun! I really thought it was going to be fun, but now it's not, so now I'm not going to do it anymore." Do you understand? Are you hearing your own reasons?

JOAN

Here are my reasons...

KIPP

By the way, they aren't even your reasons. They are reasons given to you by being human.

JOAN

Does choosing have anything to do with looking forward with nothing out there and not looking behind you?

KIPP *(now face-to-face with Joan)*

It's got to do with you saying so. You being the chooser. When you make a choice, you're the chooser. When you make a decision, the reasons are doing the deciding, not you.

JOAN

Okay.

KIPP

Start your own business, work for a small company: choose!

JOAN

I'll choose working for a small company.

KIPP

Okay. Fine. And why are you going to do that? Neither one is better than the other. That's fine. We're just distinguishing choice. "I choose to work for a small company because..."

JOAN
Because I'm into suffering.

KIPP
Okay good! Can you hear that that's a decision?

JOAN
Yeah.

KIPP
And it's a decision because the reason "I'm into suffering" is doing the selecting, not you. You're the chooser. When you make a choice it's based on nothing except you saying so. You are the chooser. This is why it's so difficult, because your entire life has been used to reduce the risk. Choice is going to put you fully into risk. You make the choice, you're at risk, with no back door. Start your own business, work for a small company: choose!

JOAN
My own company.

KIPP
Good. "I choose to start my own company because..."

JOAN (*to applause*)
Because I chose it.

KIPP
Because you choose it, yeah. And she messed up a little bit because she said she "chose" it. Choice is never in the past. It's only right now and right now and right now and right now. And you wonder why the aliveness, the enthusiasm, the possibility starts disappearing from those choices you've made in your life, it's because you've stopped choosing. See you chose once...

(*brushing hands together*)
"I chose fifteen years ago! What do you want?" No, a choice is right now and right now and right now and right now. Risky, huh?

JOAN
Yeah, that's what I've been looking at the whole four days here, is that risk.

KIPP
Which risk?

JOAN
Choosing. Choosing to be out there.

KIPP
Right. That is the risk. That's what everybody here is up against. Nobody here is interested in living their lives; they are very interested in having their reasons design their life—their thoughts, their feelings, their considerations, not them, "not me! Then I couldn't complain!" See, if you choose, you can't complain. It's what everybody in here is up against. And what it is to be a human being is to avoid responsibility. You cannot make somebody else responsible. You've already tried doing that. You can't even make yourself responsible. You can only choose to be responsible. But we haven't distinguished responsibility yet. Choice equals freedom because it's you choosing, not some reason. I didn't say reasons were bad. They just don't give you: you!

JOAN
I got it.

KIPP
Thanks for staying with it.

Another participant stood.

ROSS
Somewhere along the line I got stuck in that you have to choose yes, and that if you choose no, it's not a real choice.

KIPP
No, no, no, they are both the same. A choice is a choice. So "I choose no because I choose no."

ROSS
Whenever I'm presented with a choice...

KIPP
Notice how you said that: as if it is an edict. "Whenever I'm presented with a choice, at all times..."

ROSS
Sometimes when I am presented with a choice, I choose yes because, who would say no?

KIPP
But that's not a choice then. That's the reason: "Why would somebody say no?" That's a decision, not a choice. A choice is a choice. You choosing for no reason, simply because you say so.

ROSS

I had this distinction of choice at some point, and then I made a choice called "no" when I really wanted to say "yes," and now I can't say no anymore. So when faced with big things, real choices, I say yes, and then look around and say "what did I get myself into?"

KIPP

Consider that you lost the distinction "choice." It got folded back into reasons and thoughts and feelings. What's going to empower you in the matter is to work with this choice business, to actually see: "Oh I see, choice is simply a choice. Me choosing. I choose whatever because I choose whatever. You stopped being the chooser. You called a decision a choice and got them muddled up again.

ROSS (*hesitant*)
Yeah...

At this point Wes rejoined the conversation.

WES

We're not saying choice is right. We're saying choice is choice. We're not saying decision is wrong. We're saying decision is decision. They're different games. You don't want to play one game and call it the other. That's pretty silly. Mixing them up is like dressing up to play football and then walking out onto the baseball field, and the pitcher throws the ball to the catcher and you tackle the catcher.

(*laughter*)
Does that look like your life Ross?

ROSS

Exactly. I really got that because sometimes the circumstances are really overwhelming and I give into them, and instead of saying that I gave in to the circumstances and made a decision, I say "Oh, I chose that."

WES

You should decide when deciding is the game you want to play and be responsible for the process called decision. Choosing is distinguishing a way of being with life. And there are appropriate times for deciding.

ROSS

Or at least be clear when you decided or when you chose. At least you're on the right ball field and can play that game.

WES

In your game—you're a physician, right?—you better make decisions.

ROSS
Sure. Lidocaine, epinephrine...

WES (*to laughter*)
Well, "I did the operation because I chose to." You get in a lot of trouble that way. That's not responsible. Choice puts you into a certain relationship to life like "responsible for." It shifts your relationship to what is. So now we need to do the real choice demo, right? So, all that stuff we did? That wasn't it. We're close. We did the "getting up to this place" choice demonstration. We haven't done the real one yet. There's an illusion in the one we just did, which we are going to handle.

KIPP
So we want to distinguish choice as choice. Okay, ready?

(*holding out one hand to a participant, Andy*)
Chocolate. Choose.

ANDY
Chocolate.

KIPP
Chocolate: How come you chose chocolate?

ANDY
Because I chose chocolate.

KIPP
Yeah. And what else was there?

ANDY
No choice at all...

KIPP
Was there anything else other than chocolate?

ANDY
Yes.

KIPP
Where? Chocolate: choose!

ANDY
I choose chocolate.

KIPP
Yeah. Was there anything else?

ANDY
There was a choice not to choose chocolate.

KIPP
Where was the "not choose chocolate"? Chocolate: choose! Where did you get the "not choice"? There was no "not choice." Chocolate: choose!

ANDY
I choose chocolate.

KIPP
Right and that's all that was there, right?

(*laughter*)
Don't you think that choice is selecting options?

ANDY
Yes.

KIPP
When you come down to it, you are that choice is selecting options. Choice is not selecting options. Choice is choosing what you've got. Chocolate: choose! And you go "Where's the strawberry?"

(*laughter*)
What strawberry? What "not choice"? What vanilla? Chocolate: choose! This business called being? There's no such thing as being in here.

(*pointing to his chest*)
Being is giving being. What is giving being? Giving being is very much like choosing chocolate when what you've got is chocolate. And it's operationally true that whatever you can grant being to, allows you to be. It works in operation that whatever you can grant being to, allows you to be. What happened? Chocolate: choose! Can you grant being, can you choose chocolate? Life is presenting you, moment by moment by moment by moment everything that it presents you. And what do you keep doing? Well, "not that! Not that! Not that! Not that!" And the moment you say "Not that!" The moment you don't choose: no being. Being is granting, or giving, being. And granting or giving being is very much like choosing chocolate when what you've got is chocolate. What's the difference between the ordinary quarterback and an extraordinary quarterback? They both do the same things: The ordinary quarterback goes to the sidelines and talks to the coach about what the defense is going to run. They walk out on the field...

KIPP *(continuing)*

(grabbing a dictionary from the podium)

The ordinary quarterback walks out on the field and goes "Ready! Hike!" And the defense doesn't do what he thought it was going to do. So the ordinary quarterback goes "Ready! Hike!"

(Throwing the dictionary down on the ground and walks away from it, to laughter and applause, and then walks back and snatches up the dictionary)

The extraordinary quarterback goes to the sidelines and talks to the coach about what the defense is going to run. The extraordinary quarterback walks out on the field and goes "Ready! Hike!" And when the defense doesn't do what he thought it was going to do, he steps back into the pocket and gets the ball down the field. He's not waiting for life to be any other way than it is. He chooses whatever's happening as it's happening. He can be with life. That's choice. Choice is being with whatever is there, whatever life presents you with. The first thing you've got to be willing to be with is your own racket. It's taken you three days of hard work to be with the racket you've got. Pretty powerful. I've had the privilege of leading The Forum when—at this point—a gentleman in a wheelchair came forward and took the microphone and said "Cerebral Palsy: choose!" Or in a Forum for prisoners, where someone comes up and says "Jackson Prison: choose!" Because at that moment they stop serving time and time starts serving them, because they choose what they've got. Are you willing to choose what you've got? I didn't say succumb. I didn't say submit. I said choose. Grant being. Give being like "chocolate: choose!" So far in life you've been trained to—"Chocolate: choose!" "No! What the hell are you giving me this chocolate for?!"

(laughter)

"Why do I have to be fat? That person's racket is that they're lonely. Why can't I have lonely as a racket?"

(laughter)

What's going to have you be powerful in life is your choosing moment to moment. Choice isn't selecting options. It's granting being, giving being and granting being is very much like choosing chocolate when what you've got is chocolate. The moment you can be with it, something opens up. Andy, thank you very much for that work.

(Andy sits to applause)

In a moment we're going to go on a meal break. During the meal break, I'm asking you to continue to inquire into this distinction of choice, and to see how much you're willing to choose. So far in life you've got this little teeny-weeny opening for yourself. You know, if you say that and they say that; and life acts like that and it doesn't act like that, "that I'm willing to grant being to." See, what the rest of your life is going to be about is, if you take this on, what mastery is about, is simply opening up and opening up and opening up and opening up what you're willing to be with. When you're only willing to be with a tiny part of life, you'll only have a tiny life. Be willing to open up with what you're willing to open up to, to be with. It's easy in here, and when you go out there it isn't so easy. You'll be sitting there, choosing, and someone across from you will be eating with their mouth open and you'll want to stick a fork in their forehead.

(laughter)

Because you can't choose mouth open with food in it. "Not that! No, not that!" You've got no mastery yet. You've got no muscles for living your life yet. You've got a lot of muscles for persisting and a lot of muscles for surviving, but no muscles for living, and the rest of the Forum is committed to bringing forth a body of distinctions to give you those muscles. To begin to: It's not over in just four days. You're not going to get a PhD in four days. It's a beginning. A breakthrough. An opening. I'm inviting you during the meal break to inquire into this distinction choice. To notice what you're willing to choose and mostly what you are not willing to choose. Not like you're bad, not like you're wrong: just like you've cut out most of life for yourself. So far your life has had to be consistent with your racket and that's all that's been available to you. I'm inviting you to open that up for yourself.

Kipp announced that an opportunity to register into the seminar would occur after the meal break. The Forum supervisor announced a dinner break at 4:35 pm, and that The Forum would begin again at 6:35 pm.

SESSION TWO INTERVAL

The Forgetting of Being, Part Eight of Eight: The Heart of the Matter

A significant moment in the development of Western thinking, for Martin Heidegger, was that point in ancient Greek history that he calls the "the inceptive end of the great inception" (*IM* 200). The great inception was the new possibility for Being-in-the-world that emerged in the thinking of the pre-Socratics; and this possibility reached its end with Plato. The end of a great possibility, however, does not occur as the culmination of a decline:

> **The great begins great, sustains itself only through the free recurrence of greatness, and if it is great, also comes to an end in greatness. So it is with the philosophy of the Greeks. It came to an end in greatness with Aristotle. (*IM* 17)**

This process, which Heidegger calls "the play of Being," has proceeded in such a way that "this 'inception' also covered up the inceptive inception" (*IM* 200). This is why current students of Western philosophy begin their studies with Plato and Aristotle: the great inception of the pre-Socratics has been subsumed by the metaphysical tradition of Western thinking, which has demonstrated its own greatness, and has created the circumstances of its own end.

Plato's role in this development lay in his reinterpretation of *physis*—which for the pre-Socratics was the self-blossoming emergence of beings into the world—as *eidos, or idea*. Here Heidegger suggests the implications of this move:

> **We can easily assess the distance between the two intepretations if we pay attention to the difference between the perspectives in which these essential determinations of Being, *physis* and *idea,* move. *Physis* is the emerging sway, the standing-there-in-itself, constancy. *Idea,* the look as what is seen, is a determination of the constant *insofar as, and only insofar as, it stands opposed to a seeing.* (*IM* 203, emphasis added)**

For Platonic thinking, then, the term *idea* had quite specific implications: "The word *idea* means what is seen in the visible, the view that something offers. What is offered is the current look or *eidos* of whatever we encounter" (*IM* 201). Emergence has been captured in appearance.

As this development has played itself out, therefore, the visible and substantial outcome of unconcealment (i.e., the being that is unconcealed) has come to subsume in understanding the process by and through which that being has emerged. *Idea, the "whatness" of beings, becomes the definitive interpretation of Being.* Eventually, when Greek terms were translated into Latin by the Romans, *physis* became *natura.* Nature, the manifestation of *physis* which is most visible and accessible to us, in time came to represent Being.

Being was thereby enshrined in language *as beings.* But an element has gone missing in that enshrinement, says Heidegger, since "to be the Being *of* beings is the matter of Being" (*EGT* 50). Thus a puzzle arose, a puzzle in the languaging of Be-ing; and the puzzle lay in the unobtrusive but critical word "of":

> **The grammatical form of this enigmatic, ambiguous genitive ["of"] indicates a genesis, the emergence of what is present from presencing. Yet the essence of this emergence remains concealed along with the essence of these two words ["Being" and "beings"]. Not only that, but the very relation between presencing and what is present remains unthought. (*EGT* 50)**

The thinking of both Heidegger and Werner Erhard is designed to distinguish this relation between Being and beings, and to retrieve this relation from oblivion.

Subsequent to the oblivion of this relation, the question of Being, now understood as a higher being, had to look *beyond* other beings in an attempt to find its subject. For the Greeks, the tradition which placed Being beyond nature became *meta ta physika.* Furthermore, this *metaphysical separation* of essence from existence was set firmly in place for the Western tradition by the thinking of Plato:

> **...Being as *idea* was elevated to a suprasensory realm. The chasm, *khorismos,* was torn open between the merely apparent beings here below and the real Being somewhere up there. Christian doctrine then established itself in this chasm, while at the same time reinterpreting the Below as the created and the Above as the creator [. . .]. And so Nietzsche is right to say that Christianity is Platonism for the people. (*IM* 116)**

We are approaching the heart of the matter with regard to the question which has generated this inquiry: Why does the transformational experience that is made available in The Forum occur as elusive, evasive, as a get-it-and-lose-it phenomenon?

It is the authors' policy, consistent with the thinking we are exploring, to allow questions to remain open, and if possible to open them further. We therefore propose this response that opens up a new line of inquiry: *it is the nature of Being to withdraw.*

> **[T]his concealing of its essence and of its essential origin is characteristic of Being' s primordial self-illumination. . . . The being itself does not step into this light of Being. The unconcealment of beings, the brightness granted them, obscures the light of Being. As it reveals itself in beings, Being withdraws. [. . .]** *Man's inability to see himself corresponds to the self-concealing of the lighting of Being.* **(*EGT* 26, emphasis added)**

Being is always the context of meaninglessness from which the meanings have emerged, the everything/nothing of the sway from which the Greeks struggled to bring forth beings. Not-Being is Being's flipside, and must remain its persistent orientation, as Heidegger finds in this passage from the pre-Socratic thinker Heraclitus (Fragment 123):

> *Physis kryptesthai philei:* **Being [emerging appearance] intrinsically inclines toward self-concealment. Being means: to appear in emerging, to step forth out of concealment—and for this very reason,** *concealment and the provenance from concealment essentially belong to Being.* **Such provenance lies in the essence of Being, of what appears as such.** *Being remains inclined toward concealment,* **whether in great veiling and silence, or in the most superficial distorting and obscuring. (*IM* 126, emphases added)**

It is essential to recognize, then, that the emergence of *physis* into the world, and the unconcealment of Being's truth that is manifested in such emergence, is never a once-and-for-all event.

It is the power of *logos* to hold together what tends apart, maintaining the oppositional tendencies of that which it gathers in "the highest acuteness of its tension" (*IM* 149). But this is not achieved without human participation in the struggle: "*Where struggle ceases, beings indeed do not disappear, but world turns away*" (*IM* 68, emphases added).

The mystery of Being, for the fortunate among us, may cease for a moment to be a mystery. That moment may be a minute, a month, or even a year. But inevitably the mystery becomes again a mystery, a puzzlement. Finding one's way back into the heart of the mystery is the adventure of emergence returning to concealment and emerging and returning to concealment. It is the ongoing challenge of transformation.

When The Forum resumed at 6:35 pm, following the dinner break, Wes and Kipp were on the platform. Kipp began the session requesting that participants share what they had seen about "choice." The first to respond was Mac, the man in a wheelchair who had previously complained on the morning of Day Two about the late ending time of the first day.

MAC
You'll have to indulge me because I have a need to thank your organization for going out of their way for me. It was generous. It was done with love and caring. Good stuff.

KIPP
You're worth it.

MAC
Thanks.

KIPP
Thank you very much.

(*applause*)

MAC
I also have a need to share with you a progression. I came here and some of you remember that I was kind of angry. The first thing I said was "Goddamn it, what the hell are you keeping us up for, to one o'clock, we need our sleep." Someone I was carpooling with asked what I thought, and I said, "Werner Erhard: He's an asshole." That's how I started this. A lot of anger. The next day they asked me, and I said, "You know, he's not bad." Today I am convinced he is a genius. And all you guys really know your stuff, and really care about people, how to get the most for people. I want to thank you because it has made a big difference in my life. I thought I knew a lot of stuff, and I really don't. I've discovered it doesn't matter that I don't know very much. What the hell's the difference? What is, is. That's what I've discovered here today. I was having dinner and someone asked what are we going to tell people what we got out of this and what it is all about? We'll tell them "Why don't you go and experience it. It's a hell of an experience. Period." Because I don't know how to describe in words what has happened to me.

KIPP
You *are* in the sharing of yourself. Your sharing is the opening for action for people.

MAC
I get it.

KIPP
See, when you share like you just shared, Mac, people want to participate. Whatever opened up for you in your life, the way you said it, is consistent with who people are. You just share your self.

MAC

That is what we plan to do. And other issues have come up. For example, I told my wife, "You know, we have a lot of tension around getting lost here in the Bay Area." And we've gotten lost a lot! You know, getting lost is like a way of life for us! So who I'm going to be the next time we get lost, is lost. I'm going to let myself be lost and enjoy some new lost area!

(*applause*)

It's genuine. It's how I'm going to live! I'm amazed at the difference this is in my life! And how did I get here? I've resisted this for something like ten years. I belong to a men's group. Six of us. Very intimate. Met twice a month. Five were involved with your program. I was not. I fought it. I didn't need it and I thought it was a bunch of shit. Okay? About six months ago my son called me. He said "Dad, you know what? I just experienced something. I was at a Forum and I think you ought to go." I paused and listened to him. I was still resisting. And then he went and did other programs and kept saying simply, "Dad, I think you ought to go." And now I am going to call him to thank him for the wonderful gift he has given me.

(*long applause with many people standing*)

KIPP

Thank you very much. What occurred to me when you were standing, acknowledging Mac, you know, what brings tears to your eyes is being in the presence of your own magnificence. As Mac spoke, what he opened up for you is being in the presence of your magnificence. He was astounding as he is in his speaking and his generosity, but what's present in the room is *who* you are. And by the way, if you're not that way right now—some of you are at the other level of the roller coaster and you think you should be where the other people are standing and cheering for Mac—don't get sucked into that. Wherever you are is where you are.

WES

The other thing you want to get is how shitty you were before The Forum.

(*laughter*)

It might be useful for you to confront what you were like for those people who shared The Forum with you, and who you were like for others in your life. Regardless of whether they shared with you skillfully or not, they were committed to something. And that's a lot more than most people are up to. And you couldn't help but be in the presence of the work when Mac shared. This is a big person, and you remember he and I had that conversation about the ending time the other day. Same person. And this is who Mac is now. I had to confront the same thing when I did The Forum. I'm inviting you to confront it: who you have been for other people and who you can be. And as you step out of The Forum into your life... you know, I know that Mac will share The Forum with people, and he'll do it as well as he does, and he'll learn and he'll do it better—sounds pretty good right now—and no matter how great Mac will be, there will be people unwilling to get what he's really committed to, who will turn it into something. And the question will be whether Mac will stop being committed to whatever he's committed to in sharing The Forum, or will he continue on in the face of that.

Kipp asked participants to raise hands to indicate how many guests (who had invited the current participants to take The Forum) were coming at 9 pm, so that enough chairs could be set up to accommodate them.

MAUREEN

When you said, "Chocolate: choose!" I started to cry, because I have this big trauma drama that has taken me forever to get over, that if I told it to you, I could make you cry, and I could write a whole soap opera about my childhood, I mean it is so good, right? And it always felt like I never had a choice, and I worked through that stuff, and I could never like really be with it, and it was like when you said "chocolate: choose!" I had that choice to choose it, and I didn't, I resisted it, I made people wrong, and ran my rackets on them, did a lot of crazy stuff, and I just sat back there and cried because I got that you said that for me. You gave me a gift. Thank you for giving me that.

KIPP

You're welcome. Good work!

(*applause*)

The gift, the satisfaction, is in the creating of the distinctions. There was something inherently satisfying in the creating of the distinction, which gave her freedom. Like *The Karate Kid*, washing cars, waxing cars: wax on, wax off. Wax on, wax off didn't seem like freedom to the karate kid until he got out on the court and played, and he was left in the presence of karate. Coaching doesn't look like what you think it should.

JORIE

I just came back from dinner and I was talking to my brother—he is also in The Forum—and I have been struggling with The Forum. I was grieving over the relationship with my parents, because I realized I didn't really know them, with their stories and my stories. And my brother helped me. He said, at the same time I was grieving, instead of having to grieve, those times I was, I could have accepted the possibility that now I can be friends with them and just accept them, and find out who they are instead of grieving about who they were, and being sad about all the stories that they have. And also, this is my first time to share. This is just the beginning, like everybody said, and I cannot tell you how much freedom it has given me. Talking about choice and decision, in every part of my life, and especially my job. I just wanted to share that.

KIPP

Sharing it empowers you. The more you share it and make it real for yourself, the more it's you. Fabulous. Thank you very much.

(*applause*)

VINNY

People who know me: I'm a very significant guy. Very serious. I saw a racket of mine and how it ties in during the choice exercise I wanted to share with everybody. What I do with people is I make them authority figures. I don't care who they are. Started off with my first wife. I made her the boss: She was a couple years older than me. That was easy. Then I made my second wife the boss. She was eleven years younger than me. That was a little harder. It took longer but I turned her into an authority figure. And if you're over twenty I'll do that to you.

(*laughter*)

Somehow I'll make you boss. If you're under twenty, I'll have an edge for a little while. I didn't see the cost; didn't see the racket very plainly until this Forum. And I saw that I did it at my job. Also, I own a company. I've got three other partners, and one isn't even an equal partner, he's got ten percent of the company. Two are younger than I am and I've turned them all into my bosses. I made one into the president and I call him the boss. I'll do that. You can count on that.

KIPP

It's a great way to avoid the responsibility of your own power.

VINNY

Exactly, not to be dominated by my own power, and the cost is everywhere. But the choice, to choose, the ability to choose that that's that: That's my racket. And to choose that—there's a tremendous freedom in that, tremendous possibility to actually not have to be run by the racket. So thank you.

KIPP

Thank you!

MONTY (*to laughter*)

Thanks for calling on me, finally! It's my first share! I did the training in '78 and I didn't share, a couple of seminars and I didn't share. And when we were dealing with that fear thing the other night, I couldn't see my fear, but there was sadness. That was the feeling I got up. And I get a lot of tears, through you and through everybody's stories. But I can't contact my fear. I'm up to being scared shitless. That's why I got up here to share; I always find a way not to. And I'm standing and it's okay. Fear runs me. That's my major racket. It makes it possible for me to be invisible; it's okay to be invisible and not count. Every mealtime I go through a panic, who am I going to eat with? Am I going to be alone? Can I just walk off into the city and avoid being with anybody? Everyone's been so generous to me. People gave me a ride back home. I've met more people here in these days than I've met and been with.

(*choking up*)

I'm overwhelmed. I don't know what this thing's about, but the people in this room are available to me.

KIPP

That's what it's about.

MONTY

I'm really getting that. And I'm so pissed off that I've let myself be run by this fear thing, that I have to be alone with no friends. It's all horseshit. And so choosing that is kind of a challenge for me.

KIPP

Moment by moment by moment by moment choosing that.

MONTY

Right. In and out of, and I'm sure, I get I'm real excited about what I've realized and then it's gone.

KIPP

You have no muscles in this area yet. You have teeny-weeny baby muscles in this area. What this work is about, what the seminar's about is the Nautilus of Possibility.

(*laughter*)

It's true! You have no muscles for this. You cannot stay unhooked for more than five minutes. Somebody who looks like your mother walks by, and you're three years old: You're gone! It's not bad to be weak. It's just stupid to lie about it if you are. That's what's been disempowering you. Not your weakness. It's been your *act* of saying that you're not. The moment you get to be weak, you can start building some muscle. It's going to take everything you got in your life. You've got to have people around you that are more committed to you than you are.

MONTY

That's what it is. The people I've met here are more committed to me than I've ever been committed to myself in my whole life.

KIPP

The conversation that comes with being a human being is not on your side. On my pillow in the morning, the conversation that's never there—I never wake up into: "Why don't you get up and jog?"

(*laughter*)

Never, it's always a committee about how many times I've done it already this week, what the weather's like, why I really shouldn't today because I need my rest. It's never on my side; it's always telling me: "Slow down. What are you doing this to yourself for? No jogging. What you need to do for yourself is get up and go to the fridge, pull out that piece of chocolate cake you didn't eat last night, bring it back to your bed, eat it in bed, and then sleep some more."

MONTY

It's real easy for me to make, like you and Wes and Werner, and other people, like not... not be like that. And therefore...

KIPP

We're not like that? That's true. Yeah, you can be like us someday.

(*Monty laughs and so does Kipp*)

He's not sure!

MONTY (*to laughter*)
I'm lost.

KIPP
Right. Yeah, it's easy to make somebody else not be like that, therefore you can sell out. Because if somebody has some quality, like leadership, or ability, or talent, or whatever that is, and you don't have that quality, that property, you get to say, "If I had that property, I would be great like them, but since I don't, I won't."

MONTY
Yeah.

KIPP
I don't mind the interpretation "leadership," you know, if there's this stuff called leadership, except what I've noticed is, if you don't have it, you're out of luck. As long as there's this stuff called leadership, or skill, or talent, or ability, you've got to get it somewhere.

MONTY
Well that's what I came here for.

KIPP
Exactly, or if leadership is a conversation, you've got access to it, don't you? You have access to a conversation?

MONTY
Yeah.

KIPP
Exactly. So I'm inviting you to consider that leadership or whatever it is that you see that calls you to be is a conversation. And the conversation that you have been listening to is not worth your life. That's the one you've been honoring.

MONTY
Yeah. Good. Thanks.

PARTICIPANT (*Forum leader 10*)
When Werner was talking yesterday, or you were talking, and he talked about, if this work "calls" to you in some way... When I participated in this work for the first time thirteen years ago, this work called to me. You know, I can remember sitting in that room in New York City, present to that this was somehow how I knew life could be, like a possibility, really. Whether I liked it or didn't like it, or whether I felt like I belonged, or whether I felt like I didn't belong, I was called to that. It spoke to me. So I said "yes" to whatever was in front of me, and I kept saying "yes," and I kept saying "yes," and I kept saying "yes." And I'm left with a couple of things out of this Forum for myself, and one is that...you know, I lead The Forum almost

PARTICIPANT (*Forum leader 10, continuing*)

every weekend, like you do, and I'm never not brought to my knees, like knocked out, by what happens for people in The Forum, or really what The Forum is for people. And these four days, sitting in this chair, in different parts of the room, I saw that I had no idea what the possibility of this Forum was, at all, in being a participant. Who walked in here four days ago was, you know, "Yeah" to what life brings. But who's walking out four days later is "Yes!" to life. I don't care what life brings me, I'm a "yes" to that. To be grateful, to be thankful, to be blessed... I don't know what the words are for that, but to be "yes," to be able to be a "yes" to life, that is the greatest gift. Thank you.

KIPP

Avril.

AVRIL

That's what I wanted to talk about: choice.

KIPP

Good.

AVRIL

I definitely have my foot nailed to the floor in the area of choice. I've been trying to find satisfaction in my marriage. I've kind of tried all kinds of things, hoping about it, creating it. I created it for about two weeks and that didn't work. And about two years ago what I realized is that what I keep doing is trying to do all this stuff on top of "no." And so it's like, "oh!..."

KIPP

The clearing that you are in life is "no." That's what you're saying?

AVRIL

Yes. It's like "no" has me. And all the other stuff is on top of that. And so then I finally thought, "Okay, I got it. The choice is no!" So, I separated from my husband, and we're both here to see what to do about our marriage. I've got all the reasons to get divorced and all the reasons why not to, and it seems like my choice is "no, I don't want to be married."

KIPP

These are two different things. "My choice is no" and "I don't want to be married" are distinct. One's a decision and one's a choice.

AVRIL (*weeping*)

My choice is no, and I have this huge "should."

KIPP

Yeah, that's right.

AVRIL

And I think that's where I get mucked up, you know, the risk: The "should" is so huge that I keep getting back into the mud with it.

KIPP

That's why nobody wants choice. It leaves them being responsible. It's much easier to be used by whatever life gives you.

AVRIL

Where I feel confused is, when you say "take what you got." What I got is my husband, so then I think that...

KIPP

You don't have your husband.

AVRIL

I have this marriage, this entanglement.

KIPP

What you've got is this question about your marriage. That's what you've got.

AVRIL

That's what I need to choose.

KIPP

That's what you've got right now, right? This question about your marriage.

AVRIL

Right. I feel like I've had that for twelve years.

KIPP

That's your drama, though. You're pretty dramatic about the whole thing. I'm not trying to reduce what it is to be married, to love somebody and not have it go according to your dreams, and what comes along with that, but we've had a pretty straight conversation for four days, and we can kind of cut the drama pretty easily now: to get on with your life. If you didn't have this question, this entanglement, what would you get on with? What's the big payoff in your life for all these histrionics?

AVRIL

I feel like I've gotten on with it in every other area of my life except this one, and the payoff is that I don't count, or rather, that's the racket.

KIPP

You getting on with every other area except this one is not getting on at all.

(*holding out both hands like the vanilla or chocolate choosing exercise*)
Marriage, no marriage, choose. Choose!

AVRIL

No marriage.

KIPP

Okay, now what are we going to do? That's complete.

AVRIL

Yeah, okay. I was great when I had that...

KIPP

What do you mean when you have that? You just chose it!

AVRIL

Right, but then I thought, but somehow, he doesn't mean, that's not what they mean by choice, because that's what I got two years ago. And I got lit up about it...

KIPP

But then you got sucked right back into it.

AVRIL

Right, and then my husband comes back with, "You've got the marriage you've got, so stick with it." And we've been going around and around for two years.

KIPP

The whole question is what are you willing to be responsible for in your life? Isn't that it? You don't quite want to be responsible for it.

(*referring to Vinny*)
It's like, he doesn't want to be responsible for his own power, so he turns everybody else into an authority figure. Nobody wants to be responsible. It doesn't come with being a human being. So you have to go on with this crap about your marriage. You're either going to be married to him or not. Both of you are going to die, be buried in a box and have dirt thrown on your face. What's all the racket about? What being a human being is about is generating sympathy. You're going to get everybody sucked into your sympathy. Sympathy is between shit and syphilis in the dictionary.

(*laughter*)
But that's what you sound like. Did you ever see puppies born? Kittens?

AVRIL
Yeah.

KIPP
How would you feel about the runt of the litter unable to get to the mother's milk?

AVRIL
I would feel sad.

KIPP
Well, that's you. That's your life.

(*making a sound like a puppy whining while trying to break into the litter; laughter erupts*)
This will be on your gravestone: "I couldn't quite figure out what to do enough," right?

AVRIL
Right.

KIPP
Some of you might be listening, "Well, it's all right to be divorced"; "It's all right to be married": It's all the same. Simply choose and that leaves you responsible, and what goes along with that. Now the consequences for what you are doing don't seem to be nurturing you. Yes?

AVRIL
Right.

KIPP
My litmus test is always: What empowers you? What leaves you empowered?

AVRIL
Thanks.

KIPP
Thank you very much.

(*applause*)

PARTICIPANT (*Forum leader 11*)
I discovered in this Forum that I decided to get married. I didn't choose.

KIPP
Something got you married, not you.

PARTICIPANT (*Forum leader 11*)

Exactly. And my wife also saw this. Our marriage was a decision, and not a choice. I am now the possibility to choose to be married. I am choosing to be married.

KIPP

Which transforms the past. You can choose into the past and transform the past.

PARTICIPANT (*Forum leader 11*)

Thank you!

KIPP

Thank you very much.

(*applause*)

PARTICIPANT (*Forum leader 12*)

I was walking outside and I turned to someone and I said, "Man that 'problems' talk was a bitch. I really had a lot of problems with going unconscious, it was really difficult for me." And she said "that's because you make everything a problem." And I said "What do you mean I make everything a problem?" And I saw right there that my response to some issue coming up, some problem is "this shouldn't be. I don't want this. This is crap." And that's the way I would literally be about anything unexpected or that I didn't want to have happen, when I'm at home, I don't want this. And what I saw in the choice distinction that I haven't somehow had come together so I could see this: what it is a conversation. That's all a problem is, is a conversation. There's no problem out here. There's only a conversation. It isn't anything else. There's no problem out here. It is a conversation. And what it means to choose it is to choose *that* conversation right there. So that conversation is called "I don't want to be in that relationship right now." Or if it's a conversation called "My car!" or whatever the conversation is. I would have that conversation, whatever it was, with myself. And the problem would linger as a private personal conversation that I kept going on with myself. But I would never choose the conversation. I wouldn't choose that private conversation. And what I saw was that in my relationship, or that in any problem, it's that moment I choose that conversation right there and externalize that, get that out here in our relationship, make it public.

KIPP (*to the group*)

Watch out for listening to this like a formula, or for the seven easy steps for relating. It's a distinction he's sharing.

PARTICIPANT (*Forum leader 12*)

Yes. And that's what there is to choose, not what's out there but what is right here, and to communicate what's right here. All of a sudden I got freedom, I had release, I was awake again. It wasn't something I couldn't do. "Choose that" had always been to me: "submit to it," or "give in to it," or "suppress what you don't like about it." That's what choice was about. Rather than, "If I'm having a conversation called 'I don't like that,' choose that conversation 'I don't like

PARTICIPANT (*Forum leader 12, continuing*)
that.'" And if it's appropriate you communicate that, and that has the thing moving. And the other thing I saw about problems is, just like you said, it's stuck, it's not moving, and when the conversation is out here, it's moving then, and it begins to work its way through whatever's stuck.

KIPP (*to the group*)
What you want to notice here is that even if you don't quite understand what he is saying, you can be with him distinguishing something. What's enlivening is this business of learning and growing. That's what's attractive to you, it's his life that he's inquiring into here. The guy's so turned on he can barely stand it.

PARTICIPANT (*Forum leader 12*)
That's the last thing I want to say. I've been doing this for a long time...

KIPP
That's why this Forum is special. You've got the old timers in this room. You find out what it's like to live this stuff for seventeen years. Doesn't get less. Not like something you did seventeen years ago.

PARTICIPANT (*Forum leader 12*)
I remember when I read *Zen Mind, Beginner's Mind*. The biggest pitfall is that you think you know Zen, is that you "got it." There was a part of this Forum when I was listening, "yeah I got that." And then there was another moment when I saw that I'd had the conversation fifty times and a lot of people have gotten value out of that, but my life sucks in that area. I'm so good at working with all these people making a difference, but what about me and problems?

KIPP
That's the difference between leading The Forum and being The Forum.

PARTICIPANT (*Forum leader 12*)
Exactly. And all of a sudden, at that moment, I got all excited about The Forum and the work, and participating in it again, and learning, and growing and it was all brand-new for me.

KIPP
Thank you.

(*applause*)
It's going to take everything you've got to be unreasonable with yourself to keep it opened up.

WANDA (*whose mother is also a participant in The Forum*)
I completed my relationship with my mother, I'm thrilled to say, and I actually didn't think that I needed to. But then yesterday when someone was sharing, I just started to cry a lot, and I didn't know what she had just said that made me cry.

KIPP

She said what she said. You cried. She did not make you cry.

WANDA

All right. What I did notice was I didn't want her to see me crying. What I saw was two things my mother said to me as a little girl that had been driving my life. She said that the way to make her happy was that she'd be happy if I was happy.

KIPP

A lot of you withhold that from your parents. A lot of you don't want to be well, alive, happy: You've got to keep being a little bit screwed up so that they're not quite sure they did it all right.

WANDA

The second thing she said about how to make her happy was that whatever I did was that I would do my best, be the best that I could be. I saw early on that I could not deliver on the first point, I couldn't make her happy by me being happy because growing up, my mother was beat up a lot and I was miserable in that situation. I was telling her this whole thing over dinner and she didn't want to hear that part. It was too painful. It brought up that I wasn't supposed to share all of the sadness that I had. I was only allowed to share the good things. So I made that decision that I couldn't deliver on that promise. I did deliver on the arrangement that I would be the best I could be at what I chose to be. I went on to gather a lot of credentials and accomplishments, so that my mother would be happy. I told her that I have been living her life for her because she also told me when I was little that she had her artwork as a teenager featured in the Brussels World Fair and I said "Why didn't you pursue that?" She said, "I went to career day and went into the room for commercial artists and it was all men." And the man leading the event said to her that she had the wrong room. "The typing room is down the hall."

KIPP

You all got sucked into that one. That's how much strength you've got. One little thing and you go...

(*to laughter, Kipp imitates again a runt trying to break into the litter to feed from*)

WANDA

When she had shared that with me, that she didn't get to pursue her career I made a decision that I would for her. I've been living her life for her. I would carry that torch...

KIPP

It's not a torch; it's an anvil around your neck.

WANDA (*to laughter*)

Right. Right. And then I asked her why she didn't pursue it later and she said, "Well, I got married and had sixteen children."

(*laughter*)

KIPP (*to the group*)
Are you starting to see how much room you have in life to be? Every conversation, you're gone. You are a Velcro ball.

WANDA
I'm sharing this to see the decisions I've made and how they have run me. And what I decided at that point was to never allow my family to stop me in my career. I was sharing this with her during dinner and she said, "This is too painful, I don't want to talk about this." My point in sharing this is that without this Forum we wouldn't have had the breakthrough we did have. At one point I finally said, "Mom, the only way you and I and the rest of the children will be freed is to talk about it like 'that's what's so,' rather than to suppress it."

KIPP
Think back to the conversation we were just having a few minutes ago. In the real-life sense, these are the conversations he was talking about choosing, like those, the ones that are there to talk about.

WANDA
So at that point she asked me for some coaching—she'd never asked for that before...

KIPP
You had not been available for that before. It's not that she never asked you: You've never been there, available.

WANDA
So we started sharing about the experience. She acknowledged that the experience was painful for her. The first time she had ever acknowledged that and that it might have been painful for us as children growing up around that. She had not been willing to confront that with us.

KIPP (*correcting her*)
She hadn't *said* that.

WANDA
Right. Well, I hadn't been willing to confront it either...

KIPP (*correcting again, getting her out of the story into the what happened*)
You hadn't *said* that...

WANDA
We did share it. It looked like what was coming across was that she didn't do a good job.

KIPP
It looked like that's what you were saying?

WANDA
Yeah. I was sitting across the table and I got up and went around and I said "Mom, I want you to know that all of the accomplishments are a result of the incredible support and love and training that you gave me in growing up and that anything that has not worked is a result of my racket, I am the source of all of that. You did a great job. We all turned out." She had this great big smile on her face. I said "Being able to talk about this, we may be able to laugh about it now." She said, "well, maybe." We hugged and kissed. We went our separate ways but then ran into each other in the bathroom. She comes up to me and whispers in my ear, "Wanda, I want you to know that I am so proud of you, for all your accomplishments, even though it was kind of hard growing up, wasn't it?" And she started to laugh. This kind of communication would never have occurred if it hadn't been for The Forum. I now have a relationship with my mother I've never had before. And now I can open up with her and even share the rough times as well as the wonderful times.

KIPP (*to the group*)
Get these things captured in your conversation. When you're sharing this week, you will want to stop, because you're not used to sharing. But people in your life are worth this conversation.

WANDA
Something else opened up out of this conversation. One of the things I've been struggling with today is my relationship to my manager, looking at some resistance I've had and all of a sudden realizing, as I walked in, this great sense of freedom, I've not been willing to let my manager manage me, to get close enough to me to manage me and coach me. I've been afraid of him discovering all this stuff underneath what I'm hiding, all the things that I've had with my mom that I've carried around with me everywhere. An incredible opening and insight!

KIPP
Thank you!

(*applause*)
You need to see that you're going to need that campaign to stamp out reasonableness in your life, to keep this happening in your life.

TRUMAN
Thank you for calling on me. Yesterday I had decided I wanted to share. And I didn't get called on when I had my hand up, and then I was getting pissed off. I said, "Wait a minute. I'm black..."

(*laughter*)
"...you're supposed to call on me now. I'm ready!" I knew I had a black act but didn't know I had such a chip on my shoulder. How I go about it is I get close to people and as soon as I get

enough responsibility, and somebody'll try to get close to me, and I'll sit down. I'll go on strike, I'll dare them to do whatever...

(*breaking out into extended laughter*)
A lot of people I've worked with—I've not allowed them to support me. I never realized that I was just being my act about it. It never dawned on me that it was about being black and being right. How it occurred for me is that they didn't really care about me; that they were out for their stuff. It wasn't just who they are and who I am playing a game together. If I allowed in what this work does for people; that would destroy my racket.

KIPP
And it would allow them to get the most out of you.

(*laughter*)

TRUMAN
Get the most out of me?

KIPP
Yeah. If this work gets the most out of people, it'll get the most out of you.

TRUMAN (*laughing*)
Right, and I'm not interested in that.

(*laughter*)
I was sitting here. It was so funny. You were saying "Chocolate, choose." And then it got funnier when I was thinking "Chocolate chip, choose."

(*laughter*)

KIPP
You all understand that all people are doing is sharing? All that's happening is that people are sharing. And you're so excited; you're peeing in your pants here. This is really more than you ever bargained for in life. You never thought you could be a big enough person so that you could hear people and let people this deeply into your lives. Thank you.

DARRELL
My whole act has been kind of being afraid of people, and then when I realized I got into the conversation and saw that everybody is about as afraid of me as I am of them—that was a bright light for me. I've been Mr. Aloof, sitting back like I know it all, and just wouldn't talk to anybody. I'll just sit here looking like I'm in deep thought with myself and everyone will leave me alone.

KIPP

And you are in deep thought with yourself.

DARRELL

But what does it mean? It doesn't mean anything.

KIPP

Right.

DARRELL

In these four days I've been talking about myself to people I don't even know. It was useful. It feels good. I feel that I don't have to go around with this act. I don't have to keep myself separate because I'm afraid people will find out who I really am. I'm happy with that. Thank you!

(*applause*)

KIPP

Well done. Thank you!

HARRIET

I'm feeling tremendous energy that it is to choose to take the microphone and to be willing to engage in the conversation, and not know anything about being right, and what the in-order-to is. Just feeling the energy of the danger and the danger of the energy be used by power and all that. Now I feel stupid.

KIPP

Now you're just here.

HARRIET

I'm just here. And I've been afraid to engage in conversation, wanting to be right in the conversation, wanting to be reasonable, wanting to wait for just the right moment to share the right thing.

KIPP

It's a very big one, that business of waiting for the right moment, the right thing, the right way to do it, that's a killer.

HARRIET

It has a lot to do with significance. I have to make everything extremely significant and extremely important.

KIPP

Everything has to be extremely significant and extremely important?

HARRIET
Yeah. Really carrying it to absurd degrees.

KIPP
Like what?

HARRIET
For example, Thursday, I parked my car, got out of my car: I stepped in shit, literal shit.

(*laughter*)
"What does this mean?" And I started thinking that I wasn't in harmony with the universe, or I wouldn't have stepped in shit. So I wipe it off.

KIPP (*to laughter*)
That is so great! You step in shit: You're out of harmony with the universe...

HARRIET
Ah, but wait! But then yesterday when Werner was talking about stepping in dogshit I thought, "Wow! I'm really doing it right."

KIPP (*to laughter*)
Wow! You're on the leading edge of shit! Nothing could ever just happen!

HARRIET (*laughing*)
That's my life!

KIPP
Stepping in shit and having it be in harmony with the universe. Anything else Harriet?

HARRIET
I choose whatever is in front of me.

KIPP (*to laughter*)
Or underneath you.

HARRIET
Yup! And I'm still making it real significant.

KIPP
That's right. It all can be significant as hell.

HARRIET
Right. Yeah.

KIPP

Well done. Thank you very much!

KAREN

On my way down from Washington to do The Forum, the bus driver had heard of this work and he suggested to me that it was brainwashing and I shouldn't do it. The first day, I had that thought just a bit. I mean, brainwashing does happen.

KIPP

Yes. Rub a dub dub.

(*laughter*)

KAREN (*becoming moved as she speaks*)

Then I listened to the sharing, and I saw that if the work can call forth this kind of authenticity, and recognize that authenticity, then it's got to be authentic. And it's got to all be authentic. All of it. I want all of you who have stood up to share to get that it's been such a huge contribution to see people having that kind of courage and willingness to step out and it really is profoundly moving to see people come up against pain and grief and fear and push through when they never thought they could, it's extraordinary, and people are magnificent. I came to America to have adventures, and love and joy were not two things that were especially present in my life before coming here, and that's what I got here.

KIPP

Thank you.

(*applause*)

PARTICIPANT (*Forum leader 13*)

I've been participating in this work since 1975—that's about half my life—and this is the greatest thing I ever did... the first minute I was in the original program I knew I'd never seen anything like this, and I knew I'd be around this for a long, long time, and through the fourteen or fifteen years that I've been participating, I've seen a lot of people get to that kind of moment where they lost touch with life or, sometimes we call it an incident, I've seen probably a hundred thousand people get to what it was for them, and I've never ever had a sense of what mine was, until today. I figured there was something wrong with me, after fourteen years you'd figure it would pass by, but it never came up, and I'd like to share it if I could. When people stand up and share about having a horrible childhood, and having these terrible things happen to them, I didn't have anything like that. I had the greatest childhood in the world, the greatest parents, they told me they loved me all the time, they sent me to the best schools. When I was about four years old, I was in the first grade because I could read and write, I was a really smart little kid, and I got great grades, I got on the honor roll all the time, and I got merit badges and merit pins, and awards, and I didn't even know half the time what they were giving them to me for. It wasn't like I was working hard, or like I did anything, I just went to school and I loved God and I did what my parents told me to do, and it worked. It was kind of like that for a few years. I remember starting third grade, and the first day—and I always sat in the front row, I loved to participate—the teacher kept asking all these questions and I kept raising my hand, participating and answering the questions and was giving all the right answers, and the teacher said "You are going to be my best student." She went on and asked another question, and I gave my answer and I got it wrong. And she looked at me and said "That was really stupid." And that was it! That was it! I just said "Okay! Fine! We'll do it your way" and it's been that way ever since. And the funny thing is, I really got that's definitely the point at which I started to withdraw. It started to become about me. Up to that point there wasn't me, there was just participating and I felt like life was a privilege all the time...

KIPP

There's something in there, a bit clouded. You might not have seen it. Up until that point there was just participation. Not me. When you're really participating, you're not even there. You know, when you're really dancing, or really cooking, or really involved in something in life that you love—that's happening, not you.

PARTICIPANT (*Forum leader 13*)

So when she said "You're going to be my best student," or whatever the hell she said to me, well I had never thought about that, I never thought that there was a best or a worst or anything like that. I started thinking, "Well, I'm going to be the best!" And the next stupid thing out of my mouth was the exact wrong thing to say, and I decided that...

KIPP

The next stupid thing out of your mouth was the next thing out of your mouth.

PARTICIPANT (*Forum leader 13, laughing*)

I don't even remember what it was, and when I got in touch with it today, I was like, "ahh yeah! I finally got my incident!" And it made absolutely no difference to know what it was. None!

KIPP (*to applause*)

Thank you very much. You know, there's a story in science called evolution. In that story, sometime, a long time ago, there was a little bit of something that became life in the water. It started to evolve over eons of time. And then in a moment, a fish walked out of the water onto land. That's no longer evolution. It's the evolution of evolution. That's transformation. What the past four days have been about was providing you a clearing to walk out on the land. And the truth is you are not equipped for the land. What the seminars are about is equipping you to create a new possibility of growth and learning and extraordinary results on the land. And if you apply the rules of the water to see if you're going to be in a seminar or not, they're not going to work. I invite you to choose to be in a seminar. Don't concern yourself with which seminar to be in. If the seminar reserved for you works, do that. If that night doesn't work, pick another one. Some of you are saying, first I've got to digest The Forum. I invite you to consider what you digest turns into. You are invited to participate. And you have the right to decline... ...When

KIPP (*continuing*)

I first started doing this work I'd get up in front of people and they'd send me up notes saying, "You are a disgusting person. Get off it." But I didn't know how. And two things allowed me to get off it. I gave my word to be a Forum leader. And the people in this room didn't give up on me. They were more committed to me than I was.

Kipp then set up for the seminar enrollment. A number of people in The Forum group—many of them WE&A staff and Forum leaders—stood and moved to the enrolment tables that were placed around the room. There followed a period of about 45 minutes during which participants could register for a seminar series.

At the conclusion of the enrollment period, participants returned to their seats. It was 9:00 pm. Werner Erhard was on the platform.

ERHARD

Okay, as you know, we're at the second half of The Forum now. Everybody clear about that? We've done enough going backwards; we're starting to move forward. Nick?

NICK

You know this thing about mucking around in the swamp at the bottom of the Valley of the Shadow of Death: I've been swimming there for the past couple of months. The thing that I came face to face with was that I was afraid that I was a nobody. But it was more than being afraid, it was actually being a nobody. Last night we were driving home and I was sharing with...

ERHARD

Whatever you're afraid you might be, you are, by virtue of being afraid that you might be. Not like you are for real. Whatever it is that you can't *be* owns you.

NICK

When I was a kid, I had a great childhood, and I had a great friend. My memory of it was... like it was telepathy. We were completely, totally, absolutely related to each other. One time we both wore shorts, we both got cowboy boots for Christmas, and we walked around with them on the wrong feet, and had the best time, always together. We were almost never not together. I ate dinner at his house, he ate dinner at my house. And then one day during the summer between kindergarten and first grade, his mother told me they were going to move and I was never going to see him again. I didn't quite understand what that meant. One day they loaded everything up in a truck and a station wagon, and he got in the car and they pulled away and I never saw him again. In this work on rackets I was looking for this decision that I made, and it wasn't a decision like something I could see happening. It was more like pulling out a tablecloth from under everything on the table. Everything was the same but it was suddenly different. Completely different. I knew there was something wrong. But it wasn't like there was something wrong. There was something *wrong*.

ERHARD

Nick has told this clearly enough that you can get it. I don't know if you can picture it or not, but the scenery is all the same. All the scenery is the same except there's something wrong.

NICK

I'm not sure that that has something to do with being a nobody, but I think it has something to do with being a nobody, because when I looked at the alternative to being a nobody, it wasn't being somebody, because I created nobody to be somebody. And I know that sounds weird, but a nobody is a somebody; it's not a nothing. And yesterday working through our rackets that's what I was present to, and this afternoon talking about choice, the thing that I saw that I got out of all that was that I got to avoid the domination of being responsible for my life. Because, at that moment, if I could re-create it the way it looked, was... the choice was either to be, was not either to be nobody or to be somebody, the choice was to be nobody or to have to create it ongoingly.

ERHARD

You want to get that last thing you said, Nick. That's a critical point. Say it again.

NICK

The choice wasn't between being somebody and nobody. The choice was really between being a somebody called a nobody, or nothing. And that just looked like absolute domination.

ERHARD

The domination of the responsibility to create yourself. Better to be a nobody and avoid the domination of the responsibility to generate yourself.

NICK

Anything that is an opportunity to be somebody is a hook for me. Anything. And I am like an addict for...

ERHARD

You understand that Nick sharing this with you takes the air out of it for him to some degree. That you can't quite ever do that like you used to once you've shared it with people. You can't quite get away with it anymore. You know, it's become a public conversation. And you can't get away with it as much anymore. You know Nick will try, because he's thrown to that. And you and I will try what we are thrown to. But once you've made it public, you can never... it never quite has the grip on you that it used to. It never quite has the ability to own you that it used to.

NICK

I really have to laugh at myself, because...

ERHARD

That's the place you want to get to about your racket.

NICK

There's really two pieces to that. If you're a nobody trying to be a somebody: That's crazy. I mean, that's crazy.

ERHARD

Can you hear the craziness in that? If you're a nobody trying to be somebody, every action to be a somebody reinforces that you're nobody. Every time you succeed in being somebody, it reinforces that you're nobody. Only people who are nobody try to be somebody. It's the whole thing I told you in that short piece I did with you about empty and meaningless: Even the accomplishments are empty and meaningless, because Nick's accomplishments are all in order to be somebody, and each accomplishment simply reinforces that he's nobody. Only nobody tries to be somebody. A somebody doesn't try to be somebody. They *are* somebody. You're not trying to be somebody. Only people who are nobody are trying to be somebody.

NICK

And that is the thing I was going to say. I've got a list of accomplishments that, I mean, I've got a good list of accomplishments. And the way that lives for me is that the past invalidates right now. And the future, like my dreams or my—nothing highfalutin like a vision—like the thing Wes was chasing around yesterday, the carrot, all that invalidates right now. It's not only robbed me of satisfaction: I was looking at the cost, and clearly happiness is a cost. It also costs me vitality. I never saw that before. I'm tired all the time.

ERHARD

Sit in the chair and try real hard for about five minutes. It's a big strain trying. Being is no strain at all. Trying is very stressful. Work is not stressful. Trying is stressful.

NICK

That was one side of the sword. The other side is I don't know what makes a somebody somebody, but whatever the measure is that someone could come up with, I'm somebody. The other side of the insanity is denying who I am and what that cuts off is my self-expression. So by not being myself, and having...

ERHARD

So what you want to get is that the whole conversation is crazy. Being nobody trying to be somebody and denying that he's somebody.

NICK

This is the insanity wrapped in the craziness. Werner, I just thank you for the profound privilege of participating in this work. I can see that who I have been is wanting to be anywhere but here. The only thing that's different is me.

ERHARD

By the way, for those of you who were in Beyond the Winning Formula, this is the other side of "and yet." One side is the experience of "I've accomplished this, and yet..." This is, "I didn't accomplish this, and yet..."

A Substance Ontology

Today, as we gather and order the phenomena in our world, we take for granted that *they are.* Beyond that, their Being is a matter with which we don't concern ourselves.

That we don't, according to Heidegger, is an outcome of developments in Greek thinking, and ultimately Western understanding, beginning with the thinking of the pre-Socratics. For Heidegger, this period has brought forth the beginning of philosophy—"one of the few great things of humanity" (*IM* 17)— and also the beginning of its end. It bears repeating that "The great begins great, sustains itself through the free recurrence of greatness, and if it is great, also comes to an end in greatness. So it is with the philosophy of the Greeks" (*IM* 17).

Greek thinking began as "the first and definitive unfolding of Western philosophy . . . when questioning about beings as such and as a whole received its true inception" (*IM* 15). But on Heidegger's view, it "came to an end in greatness with Aristotle" (*IM* 17). Within two centuries, Greek philosophy had already begun digging the "ruts of metaphysics."

What happened? For Heidegger, the evolution of Western thinking was an evolution in language; and here he turns specifically to the complex of terms that cluster around the Greek word *on.* Simply put, this is the noun-form derived from the verb *to be* (i.e., being; the plural is *onta*). But for Heidegger's purposes, putting it simply is not an option, which he explains here:

> **Thus *on* says "being" in the sense of *to be* a being; at the same time it names a *being* which is. In the duality of the participial significance of *on* the distinction between "to be" and "a being" lies concealed. What is here set forth, which at first may be taken for grammatical hair-splitting, is in truth the riddle of Being. (*EGT* 32–33)**

Even in contemporary English usage, we can identify examples of the ambiguity Heidegger is pointing out here. If I tell a friend, "You *are* stingy," that friendship may be at risk. But if my friend takes an action that I find inconsistent with her generally generous behavior, I may say to her, "You *are* being stingy." In the first case, my statement suggests a defect in the *being she is;* in the second case, I am pointing out an unpleasant way she is presently *be-ing that being.* The verbal difference is slight, but the difference in implication is significant.

By the time of Plato and Aristotle, says Heidegger, *on* and *onta* had become *conceptual*—that is, they had become representations of already-thought ideas. They appear for us today as the roots of the words *ontic* and *ontological.* But for the pre-Socratics, who were for the first time raising questions about existence itself, the distinction between the event of be-ing—that is, emerging into unconcealment—and the entity which emerged and persisted, had never been thought before.

Beings as Substance

As we have seen, *physis* is an ambiguous term with a complex of meanings, including both the *event* of a being's emergence into unconcealment, as well as *the being that has thereby emerged* into unconcealment. The early Greek thinkers experienced this phenomenon in its entirety, says Heidegger. Their world was grounded in what the scholar Charles Guignon has called an "event ontology" (*A Companion to Heidegger's Introduction to Metaphysics.* 36)—that is, they experienced not only the beings in the world, but their emerging and presencing as well.

They experienced the *logos* as gathering. But they experienced it, says Heidegger, "without question" (*IM* 66).

> " In the thinking of Heraclitus the Being (presencing) of being appeared as *logos,* as the Laying that gathers. But this lightning-flash remains forgotten. [. . .] In fact, the Greeks *dwelt* in this essential determination of language. But they never *thought* it—Heraclitus included. [. . .] Nowhere do we find a trace of the Greeks having thought the essence of language directly from the essence of Being. (*EGT* 76–77)

NICK

What I wanted to ask, you know, I'm standing at the threshold of not what I used to call possibility, but of nothing—like, really nothing.

ERHARD

There is no possibility for an authentic conversation for possibility until you are standing on nothing. And Nick's gotten us to the right place because that's where we are going. We need to demonstrate something. You have to watch that The Forum gives you a platform to stand on, and then The Forum is designed to pull the platform out from under you. So remember that whenever you get set, we're going to pull the platform out from underneath you. "Oh now I got that! I got my racket!" Now we're not interested in rackets. That's horseshit. What is this rackets crap? Don't get stuck back yesterday. Be with today. It's a new ball game.

(pausing)

The question is: What is the source of action? Why do I act the way I act? I'm defining action broadly. Normally we think of action as just some kind of moving. Consider that your feelings are a kind of action, a kind of action in the world, and that your thoughts are a kind of action in the world. And so we're asking in a broad sense, what is the source of action? Why do you and I act the way we act? Now there's a standard answer, isn't there? There's an everybody-knows answer; there's an everybody-knows answer, isn't there? If I ask you "Why did you do that?" There's an everybody-knows answer, and the answer that everybody knows is "I did it because I figured out that it was the right thing to do," or "I did it because I have this thing in me that makes me act automatically, or I did it out of my experience, or my intelligence, or I did it out of my training." It's like that. Why are some people more effective in their actions than others? Tell me why. Why are some people more effective in their actions than others? Well some people have more talent than others, right? So we've got this notion that there's something inside of us whence springs action. We look at someone and say that person has more talent than me and so they act more effectively than I do. Or he has more experience. Or she has more training than I have. Or he is more intelligent than I am and so he figures it out better than I can. We have an idea it's talent, experience, training. I want to get you oriented because it's not a question anybody asks. Nobody ever asks you *what is the source of action?* They ask why did you do that and you come up with that stupid reason, which doesn't have any access to the source of action. But if you stop to ask the question... so I want you dwelling in the question, and I want you dwelling in the answer you dwell in. Let's get this "dwelling" straightened out. You don't *think* that the source of action is something inside you. You *are* that the source of action is something inside you. You don't need to think it. Everybody get that? It's not merely something you think. Without thinking you and I *are* that the source of action is something inside of people: either a quality you have, or an experience you have, or knowledge you have, or something of the sort. And I want you to see that you and I go through life and deal with life and deal with ourselves dwelling in that the source of action is something inside of ourselves. Anybody who can't see that? Get your hand up.

SHERYL

I don't see it.

ERHARD

Do you play tennis?

SHERYL

Sometimes.

ERHARD

Are there people who are better than you at tennis?

SHERYL

Yes.

ERHARD

How do you explain their being better?

SHERYL

They play more.

ERHARD

And by playing more what do you mean? It's not just a matter of playing more, it's that they have something inside themselves...

SHERYL

They've developed the skill...

ERHARD

Yeah, they've developed the skill. They have the experience, but they also carry that around inside themselves, don't they?

SHERYL

Yes.

ERHARD

In other words, if they played every day but it didn't change their insides, they wouldn't be better than you are, would they?

SHERYL

Yes, that's true.

ERHARD

You and I *are* that the guy who can play tennis better than you or I might be able to do, can do so because of something inside of him or her. You get the point?

In the terminology of Heidegger's *Being and Time,* the pre-Socratic understanding of their experience was *pre-ontological* (*BT* 32). In Guignon's words, they never thematized the insight of their experience (*A Companion to Heidegger's Introduction to Metaphysics.* 37). If they had, says Heidegger, the world would undoubtedly be quite different:

> **Language would be saying. Language would be the gathering letting-lie-before of what is present in its presencing. [...] Nothing less than this: the Greeks would have thought the essence of language directly from the essence of Being.... (*EGT* 77)**

But human thinking took a different path, and "Greek philosophy never returned to this ground of Being."

Instead, the focus shifted to "the foreground of *that which comes to presence...*" (*IM* 66, emphasis added). With this shift, Western thinking began its evolution toward the metaphysical model—what Guignon calls a "substance ontology" (*A Companion to Heidegger's Introduction to Metaphysics.* 36). Being as the happening of unconcealment was forgotten, and the ground of reality became the constant presence of what has been unconcealed—beings as present-to-hand substance: beings as things.

In his reading of the Anaximander fragment—the oldest existing fragment of Western thinking—Heidegger finds a further clue to this evolution of Western thinking into the metaphysical tradition. The etymological path by which he arrives at this conclusion is complex and undoubtedly idiosyncratic, but we quote the passage at length because it resonates at a number of points with the languaging of Werner Erhard.

> **From early on [in the thinking of the Greeks] it seems as though presencing and what is present were each something for itself. Presencing itself unnoticeably becomes something present. Represented in the manner of something present, it is elevated above whatever else is**

present and so becomes the highest being present. [. . .] Ultimately, presencing as such is not
distinguished from what is present: it is taken
merely as the most universal or the highest of
present beings, thereby becoming one among
such beings. The essence of presencing, and
with it the distinction between presencing and
what is present, remains forgotten. *The oblivion
of Being is oblivion of the distinction between
Being and beings.* (*EGT* 50)

But Heidegger hastens to add:

> However, oblivion of the distinction is by no
> means the consequence of a forgetfulness
> of thinking. *Oblivion of Being belongs to the
> self-veiling essence of Being.* [. . .] This means
> that the history of Being begins with the
> oblivion of Being, since Being—together with
> its essence, its distinction from beings—keeps
> to itself. The distinction collapses. It remains
> forgotten. (*EGT* 50)

Here, some light is shed into the clearing of our question: why does
the experience of transformation that is made available in The Forum
occur as perpetually elusive?

What gradually became forgotten was Being's other aspect:
its nature as emerging, its presencing and withdrawal, the not-
Being which is always the other side of Being. Beings became
understood as permanent presence; lost was the recognition
that the maintenance of the originary power of Being depended
upon the persistence of the struggle, so that the event is
continuously regenerated. Unconcealment is not a once-and-for-all
accomplishment:

SHERYL
Yes.

ERHARD
That's the point.

ERHARD
You and I dwell in, you and I come from, you and I *are* that the source of action is something
inside of people. Is that clear? Like I said before, this is a corollary, a harmonic, an "also." I'm
going to tell you what I said before because it's an "also": That there's a world out there that is a
certain way and that my job is to get the representation of the world in here...

(*pointing both hands at his head*)
...which is accurate because I act out of the representation in here on what's out there. And if
my representation is accurate I will be effective in acting with what's out there. Is that clear?
You don't think that; you don't need to: You *are* that. You *are* that there's a world out there, like
an *is* world: The world is like this. And it isn't like that. And my job is to get the representation
in here or here,

(*pointing to his head and then his heart*)
or wherever you think representations are, and my job is to get it out in the world out there
accurately. And some people have more wisdom and more knowledge and more insight than
others. And there are those of us who are arrogant enough to think that we have a special
perspective on the world that allows *us* to see it rightly: "Those other fools who have just got
it wrong because they've got the wrong perspective. Now I've got it right, you see?" At any
rate, it's all the same thing. It's all that my actions are a product of what I know, or of my
experience, but something inside of me, or the qualities I have. You know, smart, talented,
whatever it is; or stupid, clumsy. You see, clumsy is a quality inside people, isn't it? They walk
around with it. It's ready to put to use whenever they need it. That's the way you and I *are*
that it is. You and I are that it is like that. Is everybody clear about that now? And then the
corollary: There's a world out there that is a certain way—what I call an *is* world—can you
hear "*is* world"?—an is world rather than a made-up world. There's an *is* world; it is a certain
way—and my job is to get a representation in here that's accurate because I *act* out of what's
in here. If what's in here is accurate then I'll be effective with what's out there. Does anybody
not get that?

(*pausing*)
So now we're going to do a demonstration to look at the source of action, and we're going to
find out that the source of action is not in here. So I say that the source of action is *not* in here,
that you don't have any qualities in you at all. All you've got is entrails. Guts. Goop. That's
what's inside. Now that's affronting, isn't it? That's affronting to who you are, because you
are that there's something inside called qualities and experience and talent and know-how
and intelligence: because that's the standard interpretation which you are. So I'm saying this

ERHARD (*continuing*)

counter—commonsensical, counter—"what everybody knows" thing: I'm saying "no, that's not the source of action." We're going to do a demonstration to see if we can actually get some insight into the true source of action. What we need is somebody who's clumsy.

Erhard called on a participant named Ellen, who then mounted the platform.

ERHARD

Thank you. You've got to be a little brave to be clumsy, because clumsy is not in.

ELLEN

That's my racket.

ERHARD

We're going to play catch in order to demonstrate clumsy, okay?

Erhard and Ellen stood at opposite ends of the platform. Erhard began to toss her a tennis ball. She caught it several times.

ERHARD

I'm going to make it a little bit harder, because you're less clumsy than you thought. And they need to see "clumsy," so I'm going to bounce the ball in front of you.

Erhard bounced the ball in front of her, and after a few times, she failed to catch the ball to laughter from the group.

(*continuing*)

Wait, wait, wait. Missing the ball is not "clumsy." That's just missing the ball. The way you deal with the ball, that's where clumsy is... Now we're going to stop playing catch. We're going to play a new game called "Which way is the ball spinning?" So you're going to tell me which way the ball is spinning, and it doesn't make any difference whether you catch the ball this time or not.

Erhard threw the ball repeatedly. Ellen caught it some of the time and missed it some. Each time she reported which way the ball had been spinning, and then tossed it back each time.

(*continuing*)

So you did that demonstration perfectly. Thank you, you're wonderful.

Ellen returned to her seat, and Erhard addressed the group.

(*continuing*)

I started to throw the ball in places that were uncomfortable for her. She also started to use her body, and to step back to make it easier to catch, instead of stepping forward, which is an inappropriate reaction but a natural one for someone to whom the ball appears uncatchable.

> **Struggle as such not only allows for arising and standing-forth; it alone also preserves beings in their constancy. Where struggle ceases, beings indeed do not disappear, but world turns away. . . . Beings now become just something one comes across; they are findings. [. . .] To be sure, beings are still given. The motley mass of beings is given more noisily and broadly than ever before; but Being has deserted them. (*IM* 68-69)**

Language is the house of Being, so language is the site of the struggle. Being deserts beings when their Saying becomes only talking, a speaking "in which no world is worlding any more. . . That which originally holds sway, *physis,* now degenerates into a prototype for reproduction and copying" (*IM* 68-69).

Here Heidegger distinguishes two ways in which *appearing* may be understood, which we examined in "The Drift" sidebar in Session Two of Day Four, and which we repeat here in an attempt to open up the space newly: "First, appearing denotes the self-gathering *event* of bringing-itself-to-stand and thus standing in gatheredness. But then, appearing also means: as something that is *already standing there*, to proffer a foreground, a surface, a look as an offering to be looked at" (*IM* 203, emphasis added). Appearing, in its first and "authentic" sense, "rips space open. . . it first conquers space; as standing there, it creates space for itself." Appearing in the second sense "merely steps forth from an already prepared space, and it is viewed by a looking-at within the already fixed dimensions of this space" (*IM* 203-204). Appearing in the second sense may be characterized as dogma, or received wisdom, or relating to the self or others as possessing "qualities," such as being "stingy" or being "big." In Werner Erhard's work, this distinction is also developed in the term *sharing:* to share one's self in communication is to conquer the space—to create context as one speaks, and in such a way that shifts the way the world occurs, with which our actions are correlated.

But here is the tricky part of this distinction: appearing that rips space open is *always* ripping space open. Otherwise it would become appearing in the second sense: an already prepared space. Presence as an event of coming-to-presence is *always* coming-to-presence, or it becomes constant presence.

To be always coming to presence, a being must be always withdrawing. If a being's existence in the world occurs as an event, then each occurrence of the event must end with a return to the state from which the event begins. The state from which an event of Being begins is non-Being; therefore the happening of Being must include non-Being as the context to which it can return and from which it can begin.

This was the nature of the sway, where unconcealment always returned to concealment, and meaninglessness was always the context for meanings. In bringing the sway to stand in the world, the pre-Socratics were creating a world in which beings did not attain a state of constant presence, but were always wavering, always "held out in a questioning manner into the possibility of not-Being" (*IM* 31).

This wavering has been forgotten. Heidegger's purpose, and that of The Forum, is its recovery. ■

Nobody told her to do that: How did her actions change? What happened is this: Ellen's actions are perfectly correlated to the ball. They're not perfectly correlated to the "is" ball; they're perfectly correlated to the *occurring* ball. See, you watch where the ball goes, and you're sitting out there observing, so the ball looks like it's more or less difficult to catch, it's going more or less fast, or whatever it's doing, but that's not what Ellen's watching. What Ellen was watching was the occurring ball. You get the difference between the two? At first the ball occurred as fast and small, and her actions were perfectly correlated with a small and fast ball. Later, after she got oriented, the ball got bigger and slower. Instead of being up there like a threat, it was floating up there, and she could reach up and catch the ball. Now I'm going to make the point more clearly for you.

Erhard walked to the back of the podium to the table there to get a dictionary.

(*walking back holding the dictionary*)
So you can tell what the source of action is, we're going to handle it with the dictionary. So you've got to watch!

Erhard suddenly tossed it off to one side into the audience. A participant caught it and then tossed it back. This process was repeated several times.

ERHARD
Do you see any talent down there? Do you see any experience down there? Do you see any know-how down there? No: just dictionaries flying and people's hands moving. See how that happens? No talent; no experience: just the dictionary and people's hands moving. Is that clear? *Action is a correlate of the occurring.* However the ball occurs, your actions will be perfectly correlated. You get a truly uncoordinated person, or a person who calls themselves uncoordinated, and you lob the ball at them… it doesn't look like that. It looks like a pea traveling at supersonic speed. You want to see a true athlete dealing with a pea traveling at supersonic speed? I'll show you how clumsy they look.

Erhard then called for someone who was athletic to come up. Erhard began tossing the ball to this participant, but threw it widely, to a point where he was unable to catch it. Erhard pointed out to the group how "clumsy" the athletic participant looked.

(*continuing*)
That's how the ball looks to somebody "clumsy," where the ball occurs as uncatchable. He acts like Ellen acts, like the occurring "uncatchable ball." Actions are correlated to the ball as occurring. Correlate is a difficult word for people because we think in terms of "because," or "cause and effect." Correlation is not cause and effect. His actions are perfectly correlated to the ball as an occurring ball. Ellen's actions are exactly the same: perfectly correlated to the ball as occurring. Your actions in life, what you do at work, the way you act with your wife or husband, the way you act with your friends, the way you act with things, are a correlate of the occurring.

ERHARD (*continuing*)

There's no such thing as action, there's only *action-in-the-world; "world"* as an occurring and "action" are correlates of one another. That ball looked uncatchable to you. That's how the ball looks to somebody called "clumsy." It looks uncatchable, and their actions are those of anybody else, athletic or not, their actions are the same, because the actions are not a product of a property inside one's self called "athletic." People's actions are a correlate of the way the world occurs for them. Anybody didn't get that?

JERRY

I didn't get it.

ERHARD

What didn't you get? Did you get that we are talking about the source of action?

JERRY

I heard it.

ERHARD

There's a difference between hearing and getting. Did you get that we're talking about the source of action? Is that clear to you?

JERRY

Yes.

ERHARD

So what didn't you get? "I didn't get…"

JERRY

I didn't get that it's the same thing when you throw the ball over there to him as when you throw it to her and she doesn't catch it.

ERHARD

That's good. That's clear. Now we can have a forwarding discussion. So, his actions down here are correlated to an uncatchable ball, yes?

JERRY

Correlated to me means "goes along with."

ERHARD

That's close enough for the moment, yes. His actions are consistent with—go along with—an uncatchable ball, yes?

JERRY

Yes.

ERHARD

Now, you think that the ball is uncatchable or isn't uncatchable. I'm telling you that his actions are not correlated to an "*is* uncatchable." His actions are correlated with an "occurs as uncatchable." Occurs. You get the difference?

JERRY

I get the second, what was the first...?

ERHARD (*throwing the ball to a participant in another part of the room from Jerry*)
Let me ask you something: Was that ball uncatchable for you?

JERRY

Yes.

ERHARD

No, because there's a possibility of your catching the ball.

(*throwing the ball the same way again*)
Catch that ball. What happened?

JERRY

I didn't catch it.

ERHARD

Because it occurred as uncatchable for you.

JERRY

Right.

ERHARD

Is that clear for you?

JERRY

Yes.

ERHARD

And if I'm a certain way, and the ball goes like that,

(*throwing the ball again*)
the ball occurs as uncatchable for me. If I threw the ball and it occurred as uncatchable for you, you wouldn't have put your hand up like that, you would have acted "clumsy." So your actions, and her actions, and my actions, and his actions are all a correlate of the ball as an occurring, not the ball as an is. That ball is going a certain rate of speed and it is within a certain number of inches from your body.

Event Ontology

To begin, try this: imagine that the phenomena in the world around you—people, trees, dogs, the sky—do not merely exist, but are at every moment *coming into existence*. Imagine that when you look at a tree, you aren't observing a thing that is just there, but an *event*. The tree is *occurring*. Instead of just a tree, like a thing, you are in the presence of a happening: *treeing*. The happening is ongoing, as the tree withdraws from the world and emerges—its emergence and withdrawal so correlated in time that they are perceived only as a quality of aliveness. You *sense* the withdrawal,

JERRY

I hear you. I'm worried that I'm missing what "is" means.

ERHARD.

Good. Listen up. You told me what you didn't get. We would say, you and I, because of the way you and I are, that the ball *is* going at a certain speed, and it *is* arriving at a certain proximity to your body at a certain place. So we would say it is catchable depending on how fast it's going and on how far it was when it started coming at you...

JERRY

I have a problem concentrating on what you're saying. I'm sorry. It's like you're talking too fast or I'm thinking too slow.

ERHARD

I understand: We're talking in a place where you have your foot nailed to the floor. It's all right. You're doing great. Just tell me to slow down.

JERRY

Thank you. Please slow down.

ERHARD

We're contrasting an "*is*" ball and an "*occurring*" ball.

JERRY

I understand an occurring ball, I don't understand an "*is*" ball.

ERHARD

The ball *is* going at a certain speed, yes? And the ball *is* in your range of vision for a certain amount of time.

JERRY

Okay.

ERHARD

That's what is, you and I would say. It is going at a certain speed. And it is in your range of vision for a certain amount of time. And you and I would say if it *is* going in this envelope of speed—not faster than this, but in this envelope of speed—and if you have that much time to watch the ball going at that speed, the ball is catchable.

JERRY

Right. I got it.

ERHARD

So that's an *is* catchable ball. But you and I do not act on "*is* ball"; you and I act on "*occur* ball." It doesn't make any difference how fast the ball is going. Your actions are correlated to how fast the ball

and the absence, as a persisting background that contextualizes your experience of the presence. In the presence of something, you sense the possibility of nothing.

Heidegger scholar Susan Schoenbaum has proposed an interesting analogy as a clue to this world of emergence and withdrawal: the way the differentiation between *foreground and background* occurs for us in our visual consciousness:

> **In this differentiation, the background is determined as receding into indetermination as the foreground becomes more or less determinate. The phenomenal movement of foregrounding and backgrounding, the coming to be background and the coming to be determinate foreground, all occur simultaneously. This complex movement of determination is *originary* in the sense that it makes simultaneously possible (a) the determination of background (however indeterminate) as background and foreground as foreground, (b) the consequent appearing of determinate beings that appear (in the foreground), and (c) the coming into being of the entire constellation as context or world, including background, foreground, and the determinate movements of differentiation. All these aspects belong to an originary event of differentiation of background and foreground. (*A Companion to Heidegger's Introduction to Metaphysics*, 149–150, emphasis added)**

In other words, there is much going on in our perception of the world that happens below the level of awareness even as it shapes that awareness.

Imagine now that this is the nature of reality: that we live in a world of be-ings, rather than merely beings, a world that is renewing itself in each instant. And imagine further that you, as a being in that world, are likewise emerging newly in every moment. Imagine that "you" are not a fixed phenomenon, but that, like the tree, you *occur*, for yourself and for others, and withdraw, and occur, a new being in each occurrence. Imagine that a human being is an *event*—an event with language, and therefore very different from trees, but nevertheless a happening, like all of the other beings in the world, where absence is always the background accompaniment to presence. Nonexistence is the background for your existence.

According to Heidegger scholar Charles Guignon, such a world is what Heidegger was aiming to retrieve for human beings. Guignon calls it an *event ontology*, an alternative to the *substance ontology* that has dominated Western thinking, in which the world is just a collection of things. Such a world of events may sound tenuous and risky; but consider: might you, reborn anew in every moment of now, be more alive to existence? Might such a world be more vivid, more challenging, more engaging? Might living in that world keep you on your toes, or on the edge of your seat?

Heidegger proposes that the reality we have imagined here was what the world was like for the early Greeks. This is also the nature of the transformation that occurs in The Forum, where participants get Nothing as a liberating context for their lives. ■

occurs as going. See you and I think that the guy who hits the ball over the net in tennis all the time has skill. No. That's a guy for whom the ball comes over the net very slowly and very big. That's the difference between him and me. He does not have some property inside himself that I don't have.

JERRY
So you're using "occurs" as the way the ball is perceived? The way the ball is seen or perceived?

ERHARD
Yeah, I don't like that and it'll get you into trouble if you push it too far, but yes, that's a correct understanding. It's not mere perception. It's not mere seeing. It's an ontological phenomenon, not a physiological phenomenon. It's the way the ball occurs. So here's what I've said so far. Your actions are not a correlate of "is." Your actions and her actions and my actions and his actions are all perfectly correlated to the occurring ball. And why some people look clumsy to us is because we don't realize their actions are correlated to the occurring ball; we think their actions are correlated with the *is* ball. It *is* going a certain speed. It is in their sights for a certain amount of time.

JERRY (*laughing*)
This sounds pretty simple to me now.

ERHARD
Yeah, it is.

JERRY
Everybody else have that?

ERHARD
Yeah, they got it listening to you.

JERRY
I guess my problem was I didn't know what you meant by occurring and what you meant by is.

ERHARD
You and I don't dwell in the distinction called "occurring." You and I dwell in the distinction called "is."

JERRY
Why not?

ERHARD
A thing called stupidity.

JERRY
Kids dwell in occurring, don't they?

ERHARD
They dwell in "is" too. Nobody coaches occurring. They coach is. They tell you how to hold the racket.

JERRY
How about the guy who wrote the book Inner Tennis. He coaches occurring, right?

ERHARD (*walking toward Jerry and then standing right in front of him*)
He doesn't talk about it that way, but he does "occurring." What makes Tim Gallwey's coaching effective—Tim coaches a shift in the occurring; he's not trying to change the behavior. No matter how much I know how to behave, I'm going to behave as a correlate of the occurring. I'm not going to behave like I know how to behave. That's true about you because you didn't always behave the way your mother told you to behave. By the time I was five years old, my mother told me everything I needed to know about how to be a decent human being. I had all the knowledge I needed. Didn't make a damn bit of difference. I was a rat. You too. You tell yourself what to do, but you don't do it, do you?

JERRY
Sometimes.

ERHARD
Yeah. Sometimes. But you always, your actions are always correlated with the occurring of the world. That dictionary flies through the air, your hands will move in a dance with that dictionary, because your hands are correlated with the occurring of the world.

JERRY
Yeah, I believe that, but it sounds like I missed something.

ERHARD
Don't believe. I want you to get it.

JERRY
Well it feels like I'm missing something, because you're saying it like it's a big deal.

ERHARD
Yeah, it is a big deal. I'll tell you what the big deal about it is: Stop trying to change yourself. Stop trying to put properties inside of yourself. Stop trying to get yourself to do the right thing. Alter the way the world occurs for you, and your actions will naturally alter. You get that?

JERRY
Yeah, I believe I get it.

ERHARD

Good. It's simple. I understand. Took you a long time to get that simplicity, yes? Anything is simple. It just takes a long time because we've got to get all the garbage out of the way. You didn't get what I said even when you felt that you got what I said.

JERRY

I felt I wasn't listening. I had the problem that I didn't hear what you said. I wasn't listening.

ERHARD

I understand. You didn't hear me because you were listening to your barriers to hearing what I was saying. And the barriers to hearing what I was saying were provoked by what I was saying. We've been doing that for four days here. We say stuff that we don't expect you to get. We say stuff designed to drive the barriers up in front of your face. Then we keep dealing with the barriers. Then you start to drop the barriers. Then all of a sudden it's empty and meaningless, and then it's like "well, obviously it's empty and meaningless. Why didn't you just say that in the beginning?"

(*laughter*)
Clear? Give me my ball back. Thanks.

(*applause*)
Let me say it all over again. Here's what I want you to get out of this. Your actions are not the actions you want, or the actions you decide. They're not a product of your past; your actions are a correlate of the world as an occurring, not the world as an *is* world, but the world as an occurring world. Your actions are perfectly correlated to the way the world occurs for you. If the world occurred for you like it occurs for the person you most despise, you would act like the person you most despise. No shit. Really. I know you think you've got goodness and all that bullshit inside you. Go to the doctor and have him open you up so you can see. Cut that noise out. Your actions are a correlate of the world as an occurring. You want me to throw the dictionary a couple more times so you can see? Now the question is, "Well, what generates this occurring?" We're going to get to that, but not until you get... see you're almost as stupid as you were when you came in here, because you're sitting out there trying to decide whether you agree with this or not.

(*laughter*)
"Is that right? Do I agree with that? I practiced tennis for ten years, and that practice really made me a good player. And I remember learning buh buh buh, and that made me better at that." Wrong! The practice and the learning alters the occurring. Staying in the conversation Jerry and I were having: you know, you train an athlete. Most people train athletes like they're grooving in behavior, so you do it repetitively, that's what training is, right? Repetition. So you do it over and over and over again so you can do it automatically. Horseshit. Anything you do automatically lacks skill, lacks power. You wouldn't want an athlete who acted automatically. You want an athlete free to act with the world he or she has to act within. What happens is,

> Your actions are not the actions you want, or the actions you decide. They're not a product of your past; your actions are a correlate of the world as an occurring, not the world as an is world, but the world as an occurring world.

ERHARD (*continuing*)

you take behavior out when you train an athlete with repetition. You take behavior out, not add behavior. He has to do this. You don't want him to do that. Let him keep doing *that* and he'll stop doing that if the training's any good, and he'll be free to do anything. When he's free to do anything, he'll deal with the ball effectively. You don't need to tell people "step back when the ball bounces in front of you." Because you're never going to be effective when you're trying to remember what to do when the ball bounces in front of you. When the ball bounces in front of you as catchable, you step back, because stepping back is perfectly correlated with the ball that bounces in front of you and is catchable. Stepping forward is what you do when the ball bounces in front of you and it's not catchable.

(*pausing*)

Is it starting to get through? Not "do you agree with it?": Are you able to stand in the possibility that my actions in life are not a product of internal properties? My actions in life aren't a product of anything. My actions in life are a correlate of something. What they are a correlate of is the world as an occurring. For example, if the world occurs as threatening, your actions will be perfectly correlated with a threatening world. The question is not: "Is the world threatening?" The question is: "Does the world occur as threatening?" It's not that one person is strong and the other person weak. You think you're strong, let me put you in a set of circumstances that occur sufficiently threatening and you will cower. People who cower are not weaklings. The world occurs for them as overwhelmingly threatening. People who are musical: Music occurs for them in a way that it doesn't for those of us who are not very musical. The keyboard does not look like it does to you and me to a pianist. Totally different. I did an experiment driving a racecar for a year. Didn't know anything about racing cars when I started. Didn't even drive for the most part when I started. I had a license. I hadn't been in a gas station for something like ten years. When I started out, the car went very *fast*. Really fast! I mean overwhelmingly fast. Except for the guy on the sidelines who had the stopwatch. For him it was going very slow. But the slower the car went for me, the faster my times were. I could see divots in the roadway a quarter of an inch deep and put the edge of my tire in that divot. The car got real slow. Real easy to drive a car slowly. You get into a race car and drive it slowly, it's easy. Takes no talent, no ability, which was very good in my case. The slower the car goes the faster the times are, because action is a correlate of the occurring. How many people in here manage other people?

(*several participants raising their hands*)

How many other people in the room raise children? That's managing people, by the way.

(*more raising their hands*)

Good. Put your hands down. You want to know why your kids act like they do? Because the world occurs for them in such a way that their actions are a perfect correlate. They do not do what you tell them to do. No shit. And if you think they're doing what you tell them to do, you're wrong. Their actions are a correlate of the way the world occurs for them. People murder not because they are bad people. Nobody has ever found bad inside anybody. People murder because murder is a perfect correlate to a certain kind of occurring. The law recognizes that by recognizing self-defense. Never mind how they explain it. Ellen is not clumsy. Her actions are perfectly correlated with the way objects occur for her. She's

Technology

 So long as we do not, through thinking, experience what is, we can never belong to what will be. (**Martin Heidegger, "TT" in** *QCT* **49**)

While Martin Heidegger's thinking was consistent in its focus on the question of Being, his philosophical inquiry led him along a number of paths within this domain. None is of greater relevance to our current cultural situation than his perspective on technology, a subject central in his thinking during the last forty years of his career (Zimmerman, *"Beyond 'Humanism'"* 219). In this light then, it is significant for our inquiry that Werner Erhard has chosen the name "technology of transformation" for his own project ("The Heart of the Matter" 1985). In these series of sidebars concerning technology, we will show how Erhard's choice of this term indicates, paradoxically, both a crucial intersection of his work with Heidegger's thought, and at the same time, Erhard's contrast with what we might call Heidegger's "racket"—a persistent complaint with a fixed way of being—concerning modern technology.

Regarding technology, Heidegger is emphatic on two points. First, we have misunderstood its nature; and second, as a consequence of this misunderstanding, we have underestimated its role and influence in the current human condition. Our problems with technology—which might include overuse, inadequate mastery, overreliance, and addiction—do not arise because of some incorrect understanding of technology, for instance, as a human contrivance, as an instrument for our use, or as a means to serve our ends. Rather, our problems with technology have arisen in an epoch in which we can no longer grasp that "the merely correct is not yet the true" ("QCT" in *BW* 313). Our instrumental understanding, wherein anything worthy of understanding must be able to be put to use, fails to reach deeply enough to capture technology's essential impulse. Here Heidegger develops that particular point:

 Everywhere we remain unfree and chained to technology, whether we passionately affirm or deny it. But we are delivered over to it in the worst possible way when we regard it as something neutral; for this conception of it, to which today we particularly like to pay homage, makes us utterly blind to the essence of technology. ("QCT" in *BW* 311–312)

not clumsy. There's no quality called clumsy. Put your hands down for a second. The only hands I want to see are those who can say "I didn't get that." Not an "I have a question" hand, but an "I didn't get that" hand.

Seven people stood. Erhard moved to work with Art, and requested of the others that if they got it when Art got it, they should sit down.

ART
I'm trying to come up with answers. The occurring for life... That's just how they see it.

ERHARD
It's not quite right, and what's not quite right about it is that it's not a physiological phenomenon; it's an *ontological* phenomenon. The ball exists as slow or fast. It's not seeing. It's not perceiving. The ball exists as slow or fast. It's not "I see the ball." The ball is, like existence, slow or fast.

ART
I'm trying to put that into my life. I used to ride motorcycles and I could ride really fast and I can see little things in the road at ninety miles an hour.

ERHARD
Because the bike is occurring as slow for you.

ART
Well I'm with the bike, I know how to do that.

ERHARD
No. That's your explanation. You do not know shit about how to do it. As a matter of fact, go out on your bike and try to ride it out of what you know. Try it. You race your bike?

ART
Yes.

ERHARD
Try racing your bike out of what you know.

ART
I'd pop the clutch and it would shut off.

ERHARD
Yeah, exactly. You don't race out of what you know. You race out of the occurring. So let me ask you...

(*getting the dictionary and then tossing it at Art*)
what does your behaving have to do with what you know?

ART (*having caught the dictionary*)
I just reacted.

ERHARD
That's your explanation. There wasn't any reaction. There was a dictionary and hands. You made up "reaction." That's your story about what happened. All that happened was a dictionary flying and your hands moving.

ART
Yes.

ERHARD
You didn't say to yourself, "Oh, put the microphone under my arm, reach out my hands…" None of that happened. None of your athletic experience there either. Not one bit of it was there, was it?

ART
No.

ERHARD
No. Nothing. What was there was flying dictionary and moving hands; because your hands— the motion of your hands—are a correlate of the dictionary as an occurring. Suppose the dictionary… give me my dictionary back.
(*laughter as Erhard receives the dictionary back from Art*)
If I throw the dictionary at you so you can't catch it, what are you going to do? You're going to go like this, aren't you?

(*flinching*)
Not like you did the last time. Why? Because you're not athletic? No, because the dictionary occurs as uncatchable, and your actions are perfectly correlated with an uncatchable dictionary. Got it?

ART
Yes, but it just seems foggy. Like I'm always trying to come up with an answer for everything. I don't want to use the wrong words here. I can understand but I want to come up with an answer for it.

ERHARD
No, you want to put it to use. You mean, "Shit, I can't figure out a way to use this yet."

ART
Well, I don't see how to apply it to my life.

And in *What Is Called Thinking* he posits that

> …the essence of technology is not anything human. The essence of technology is above all not anything technological. The essence of technology lies in what from the beginning and before all else gives food for thought. It might then be advisable, at least for the time being, to talk and write less about technology, and give more thought to where its essence lies, so that we might first find a way to it. The essence of technology pervades our existence in a way which we have barely noticed so far. (*WCT* 22)

Heidegger concludes this thought with a reversal: "Our age is not a technological age because it is the age of the machine, it is an age of the machine because it is the technological age" (*WCT* 24). We are reminded of one of the central rhetorical figures Erhard employs throughout The Forum, in many instances, wherein the commonplace understanding we have of ourselves as conscious agents of our lives is thrown into question: "You don't think it; it thinks you." As our thinking enters into this antithetical "figure of thought"—which rhetoricians term *chiasmus*—again and again during the course of The Forum, this *way* of thinking, as a *technology of transformation*, opens us toward new possibilities to *be*.

But if we hold this figure of thought at a distance, refusing to follow its course, it loses any of its transformational power. As scholar Hubert Dreyfus observes, Heidegger's position with regard to technology is easily misunderstood *as a position*, when it is more appropriate to follow it as a movement. Dreyfus writes that Heidegger's "view is so radical that one is tempted to translate it into conventional platitudes about the evils of technology, so Heidegger's ontological concerns are mistakenly assimilated to ontic humanistic threats about the devastation of nature, the atomic threat, the media, consumerism, et cetera" ("Gaining a

Free Relationship to Technology"). But Heidegger's focus is a less apparent threat, namely, the threat posed by "the technological understanding of Being" (ibid). Technology, for Heidegger, is a manifestation of a particular way of Being; and it is that way of Being, rather than technology itself, that poses the real danger. ■

ERHARD
You can't apply this in your life. It applies you; you don't apply it. Weren't you here earlier to hear about the truth?

ART
Yes.

ERHARD
All you've got to do is get it. It will use you.

ART
And once I try to do it that's when I screw it up.

ERHARD
Exactly. But that's a little off too because that's another answer.

ART
Right.

ERHARD
Don't turn it into an answer. All there is to do is to get it. Here's what there is to get: My actions, my way of being, my feeling, my thoughts, my self, are a correlate of the world as occurring. You get that?

ART
Yes.

ERHARD
Good. Sit down. Very well done.

BOBBY
What I got is that you're talking about "muscle memory."

ERHARD
What is muscle memory? What's the difference between muscle memory and muscle spirits?

(*laughter*)
One is in vogue and the other one is not in vogue. "The catching God moved my hands." What's the difference between that and muscle memory? They are both explanatory principles. They both explain what happened. And the only other difference is that one is in vogue and the other is not in vogue. Neither one of them has anything to do with having any access to your behavior. What does muscle memory have to do with having access to your behavior?

BOBBY

Well then I don't get it. I thought that's what you were talking about.

ERHARD

That's not what we're talking about. You heard me say muscle memory?

BOBBY

That's how I translated it.

ERHARD

Yeah: Don't translate me. I speak perfectly what I mean. If you translate it, you don't get it. What I said was, your actions are a correlate of the world as an occurring. Your actions are not a product of properties inside you including something called muscle memory. You get that?

BOBBY

I heard you.

ERHARD

Did you get it?

BOBBY

Well, I'd have to translate it to get it.

ERHARD

Don't translate it. Just get it. My actions—the way I act—are a correlate of the world as an occurring. That's what there is to get. I don't act like I act because I'm stupid, or because I'm smart, or because I'm ambitious, or because I got drive, or because I think positively. They're all explanatory principles. They have nothing to do with the source of action. They explain action beautifully. You could say that you're possessed by a certain kind of spirit. That explains it perfectly, doesn't it? Some people are possessed by good spirits, some are possessed by bad spirits. Doesn't that explain action? You don't like that explanation. But doesn't it explain action? Does it not? What's the difference between that explanation and the explanation that I act because of properties inside me? The only difference is that one is in vogue and the other is now out of vogue. This is a conversation for gaining access to action, not for explaining action. Remember I told you the first day? Remember that X thing? This side you get explanation, this side you get access to the source of the action. We're talking about the source of action, not the explanation for action. Somebody asks you why you act the way you do, you tell them properties because what they're looking for is understanding. You want something to say about your actions, start dwelling in the possibility, the distinctions, that your actions are a correlate of the world as an occurring. Is that clear?

BOBBY

It sounds like reaction, but I know that's not what you mean.

ERHARD

That's quite right, it's not reaction. Is the back of my hand reacting to the front of my hand? No. It's correlated to the front of my hand, isn't it?

BOBBY

Right.

ERHARD

Another word for correlation is something like dancing. You and I dance together; you don't move because I move. I don't move because you move. We move in correlation with one another. Our motion is correlated. That's what correlated is: It's like dancing. You need a poetic understanding of correlation. Like dancing. Clear?

BOBBY

I don't understand how catching the dictionary is like dancing.

ERHARD

It's exactly like dancing. And what you're dancing with is a flying dictionary. And Ellen dances with the ball as uncatchable sometimes and at other times she dances with the ball as catchable. In both cases, Bobby, her actions are perfectly correlated to the ball.

BOBBY

No thinking.

ERHARD

It's not a matter of "no thinking." There may be thinking as well. That's not the point. The point is that her actions are perfectly correlated to the ball when she's graceful and perfectly correlated to the ball when she's clumsy. That's why I got someone who was athletic up, because he looks clumsy when I throw the ball to him in a way that he can't catch it. That's pretty clumsy. When I throw the ball to him so that it looks catchable to him, he's very graceful in his dealing with it. Clear?

BOBBY

Yeah.

ERHARD

Thank you.

(*addressing another participant*)
What's your problem?

(*laughter*)

BECKY

I don't get that when I'm driving fast it occurs slow. I'm not even sure I said that accurately.

ERHARD

Do you remember how hard it was to steer the car when you first started to learn to steer the car?

BECKY

Yeah.

ERHARD

You had to steer it.

BECKY

Yeah.

ERHARD

You don't have to steer the car anymore, do you?

BECKY

No, right, I don't.

ERHARD

The road steers the car. You don't steer the car. The road steers the car. Because when you first got into the car your actions were a correlate of what you were told to do. That's all that was there for you. "Oh, let's see, he said to do this! Oh, he said to do that! Don't do this, do that!" Your actions were correlated to the telling because that was occurring. There wasn't any road out there. The road was just frightening. Now there's nothing between you and the road. The road does the steering. You don't say "Curve. Turn slowly." Your actions are perfectly correlated with the road as an occurring.

BECKY

Is it that the steering goes out of existence at some point?

ERHARD

Not quite and that's a different conversation that'll get you into trouble. That's the transparency conversation. That's not a part of The Forum. That's another course. You have to pay more money to get into that conversation.

(*laughter*)
Yeah, but nevertheless the steering becomes transparent and the instructions become transparent. Not that there's no steering wheel. It's still there. You know for a great typist, there's no typewriter.

BECKY

Right.

ERHARD

There's the finished paper. Whatever he or she is typing from and the finished paper. The rest of it is transparent. There's no typewriter. If you're working on a typewriter, you're not working fast. You've got to produce paper with type on it.

BECKY

I understand all that. I'm going to be very stupid. I am very stupid here.

ERHARD

You're being very smart. It would be stupid to sit down when you're not getting something.

BECKY

I have not stood up many times in this Forum when I've not understood something.

ERHARD

Don't editorialize anymore. This is the fourth day.

BECKY

Okay. I don't get: "I'm in a racing car. I'm going a hundred miles an hour…"

ERHARD

But a hundred miles an hour is an *is* speed, read off of a dial. It's not an occurring speed. See, I went fast when a hundred miles an hour was slow. I went slow when a hundred miles an hour was fast.

BECKY

Well what shifted it for you?

ERHARD

You're into the next question. The next question is going to be "What access do I have to the occurring?" We're not up to that question yet.

BECKY

But you're talking about the end result of the shift without telling me…

ERHARD

Yes that's right, it's horrible, isn't it?

BECKY (*laughing*)

Yes, I'm frustrated.

ERHARD

I understand. That's because I want you to have a question. The question I want you to have is: "How do you gain access to the occurring? I want to alter my behavior. I know I can't alter my

ERHARD (*continuing*)

behavior by telling myself to alter my behavior. I now see I can alter my behavior by altering the way the world occurs for me. How do I gain access to the occurring?"

BECKY

Got it. Thanks.

ERHARD (*to the last standing participant*)

This better be really fucking original.

(*laughter*)

MIKE (*the participant who had the "stupid" racket*)

I don't understand. You threw a ball over there, with the gentleman standing over here. He can't catch it.

ERHARD

No. You say he can't catch it. There are athletes who could catch that ball. If that was an ape, the ape would have caught it. The ball is catchable, but the ball occurs as uncatchable. How close does the ball have to be to you to be catchable?

MIKE

It depends on how fast the ball is coming...

ERHARD

At a given speed, how close does it have to be?

MIKE

A ball at a given speed?

ERHARD

Yeah, how close does it have to be to be catchable?

MIKE

I have to be able to run to it in time in order to be able to catch it.

ERHARD

And that depends on how fast the ball is moving.

MIKE

Correct.

ERHARD

Very good. And how fast the ball is moving is not determined by a radar gun. It's determined by the speed the ball occurs for you. Guys who play baseball for a living, play baseball with big, fat,

Techne

To develop the perspective on technology and the danger posed by the technological understanding of Being, Heidegger turns, as he often does, to etymology in order to explore the historical meanings deeply embedded in our language. "In the word, in language, things first come to be and are," he says (*IM* 15). Therefore the way the world occurs for us today can be traced to the way it was originally understood and put into language by the first Western thinkers, the pre-Socratics, who lived at a time when the increasing complexity of phenomena emerging from the flux required the development of a deeper understanding of things.

In their response to this challenge, so Heidegger's account runs, the Greeks unavoidably set a direction for Western thinking; and from that meaningful beginning, the "play of Being"—the evolution of human thinking and thus of human Being—can be traced through history, culminating in our current view of ourselves and our world. "What is Greek," says Heidegger, "is the dawn of that destiny in which Being illuminates itself in beings, and so propounds a certain essence of man; that essence unfolds as something fateful . . ." (*EGT* 25).

A central artifact in this archaeology of language is the Greek word *techne.* Heidegger notes that "the Greeks, who knew quite a bit about works of art, use the same word *techne* for craft and art and call the craftsman and the artist by the same name: *technites*" (*PLT* 59). Over time, *techne* came to mean the activities of the craftsman, primarily the work of making things; so its subsequent evolution as a term for the functioning of technical instruments is not surprising. But Heidegger asserts that this meaning is "oblique and superficial," and that the word *techne* "never means a kind of practical performance. The word *techne* denotes rather a mode of knowing" (*PLT* 59).

But it is knowing in a unique mode: *techne* is knowing that creates what is known. It reveals things by *bringing them forth* for the first time, a stage in the creative process that precedes the act of making. When a house or a ship is to be built, it is *revealed* before it is produced:

> **This revealing gathers together in advance the aspect and the matter of ship or house, with a view to the finished thing envisioned as completed, and from this gathering determines the manner of its construction. Thus what is decisive in *techne* does not at all lie in making and manipulating, nor in the using of means, but rather in the revealing. . . . It is as revealing, and not as manufacturing, that *techne* is a bringing-forth. [. . .] Technology is a mode of revealing. Technology comes to presence in the realm where revealing and unconcealment take place, where *aletheia*, truth, happens. ("QCT" in *BW* 319)**

For Heidegger, what is fundamental in *techne*, and therefore in technology, is not the tools and instruments it manifests, but that it is a way of disclosing entities *as* entities. Here we find a harmonic with Erhard's technology of transformation as the process of distinguishing distinctions, the distinguishing of which, entirely in language, discloses worlds within which human beings have access to acting on and fulfilling new possibilities for Being-in-the-world beyond what is already and always given for human beings to be: the in-order-to—the *techne*—of our technological age. *Techne* as the in-order-to discloses entities as raw material and resources that can then be used up to enhance power and security, and a correlative way of Being is brought forth in that disclosure, in that manifestation of the tools and instruments *techne* calls for, a technological way of Being that on Heidegger's view poses great danger to us.

slow, baseballs. Guys like you and me who play baseball once at the company picnic, we play with very small, supersonic bullets...

(*laughter*)

...and our behavior is correlated to uncatchable balls. See you were not a creep when you were sweeping up and missed those spots. The floor occurred as clean for you. And you stopped when it did, like anybody would, like your father would. The floor occurred as not clean for your father. Therefore, for your father you should have kept sweeping.

MIKE
So I could have caught that ball if I saw it big, and slow, over there?

ERHARD
Let me ask you a question. Forget that you can't reach it because there are people around you. If I threw the ball over there...

(*throwing the ball*)
...could you catch it?

MIKE
There's a possibility.

After receiving the ball back from another participant, Erhard threw the ball farther away from Mike.

ERHARD
If I threw it there could you catch it?

MIKE
No.

ERHARD
Who said so?

MIKE
I said so.

ERHARD
Because the ball occurs for you as uncatchable.

MIKE
So if it would occur for me as catchable I could catch it.

ERHARD

There would be the possibility of catching it and your actions would be consistent with catching it. Let me ask you a question: Have you ever seen a great athletic feat?

MIKE

Yes.

ERHARD

If you don't move, you don't catch. Did you hear what I said?

MIKE

If you don't move, you don't catch.

ERHARD

Yeah. So. Guys who move have the possibility of catching. And you see them do things you thought were impossible. You get that now? Is that clear? You don't move, you don't catch. And you only move when the ball occurs as catchable. These are not guys calling for superhuman effort from themselves. These are guys who because of certain ways they are trained see a ball as catchable like a possibility, which you don't see. You don't catch the ball every time I throw it right there, do you?

MIKE

No, not every time.

ERHARD

Exactly, but you don't move to catch the ball every time, when I throw it there.

MIKE

Right. The occurring.

ERHARD

Got it?

MIKE

The occurring I don't understand.

ERHARD

How fast was that ball moving?

MIKE

Feet per minute?

ERHARD

You have no idea, right?

MIKE
No I don't.

ERHARD
You've got to say slow or fast. Don't you.

MIKE
Right.

ERHARD
How fast does the baseball travel when the pitcher pitches?

MIKE
Maybe sixty miles an hour?

ERHARD
Is that fast?

MIKE
Yes.

ERHARD
Not for guys with high batting averages: That looks like a home run. A ball traveling that fast: That's a ball with home run written on it. That's like me picking up this ball off the floor for them. It occurs as a home-run pitch if it's traveling fast enough. And for me, I don't even see it. Right?

MIKE
Right.

ERHARD
Same ball traveling at the same speed according to the radar gun, occurs one way for one person and a different way for a different person.

MIKE
So state what you said about occurring? You mentioned something else...

ERHARD
I said that your actions are a correlate of the occurring. Your actions dance with the way the world occurs for you, not the way the world is. And not because of something inside you, Mike. You don't have properties inside you. You don't have skill or intelligence or stupidity or clumsiness inside of you. All you've got is your actions correlated with the world as an occurring.

ERHARD (*throwing the ball just out of Mike's reach*)
Why did you put your hand up there when I threw the ball?

MIKE
To catch the ball.

ERHARD
No you didn't. Did you say, "I'm going to catch this ball?"

MIKE
To myself I did.

ERHARD
Did you really?

MIKE
Yes I did.

ERHARD (*throwing the ball again out of Mike's range*)
What did you say then?

MIKE
I said...

ERHARD
You didn't say a goddamned thing! Nothing. Afterwards, in the moment afterwards, you might have said, "that's not catchable." If the ball was catchable for you, you would have reached over. And you may or may not have caught it, but you would have reached over. Are you athletic?

(*pausing*)
Stop thinking! Are you athletic or not?

MIKE
I'm neither.

ERHARD
You're a person for whom the ball is slow and fat. And I'm a person for whom the ball is very small and fast. And the slower the ball goes, the more athletic you look. Is that clear?

MIKE
Yes.

ERHARD
Very good. Thanks.

(*applause*)

ERHARD (*to another participant*)
You got it before. And now some gas has been introduced and now you don't get it, is that it?

(*laughter*)

MELINDA
I'll keep it short, okay? I have a friend, his son is brain-damaged. His brain works fine except for the part that controls his muscles. He can't walk. If somebody throws him the ball, it's uncatchable.

ERHARD
Sure. If I cut your arms off and throw you the ball, it's uncatchable.

(*laughter*)
Don't bring up this stupidity: It's going to make you look silly. I'm not talking about some kind of magic that if you were a rock and the ball occurred as catchable that you would reach up and catch the ball.

MELINDA
I'm trying to see where this occurrence is.

ERHARD
It's not in your muscles. Stick around. You're asking the next question. Look, do you think with your brain? You know that if we opened up your head and stuck a pencil in your brain you wouldn't feel it?

MELINDA
I'll accept that.

ERHARD
That's the case. You don't see with your brain. You see through your brain, maybe. It mediates seeing. You don't see with your eyes either. You know those things you didn't see and now you see? The eyes are a tube through which seeing comes, but not with what you see. And that's the case with the guy with brain damage.

MELINDA
You said it's an ontological event, but how could an ontological event occur...

ERHARD
Because the ontological event expresses itself through a physical tube. That's trivial.

MELINDA
That's what I don't get: That an ontological event could occur by cutting off someone's arms.

ERHARD

No, it does not. I said it can't. If you can't get it down the tube—if the tube's blocked—your brain, your nervous system, your muscles are just a tube to get it down. This is real simple. We're not talking about growing a third arm here. So it's a trivial conversation to get stuck in this muscles and bones and nerves thing. I'm willing to do it if we need to because I'm someone who can stay up all night. But that's not the conversation that you and I ought to be having when we're talking about your being able to behave effectively.

MELINDA

Okay.

ERHARD

Growing a third arm is a different conversation. It's true that your body is a tube down which this gets expressed, but it's only the tube. You know, I've worked with brain-damaged children. There's no less of a person there. There's less of a person expressed. No question about it. There are ways to get around the limits of the tubes. Blind people function with the same equipment I've got at a way higher level than I do. Your body is merely the tube down which this gets expressed. The tube is trivial.

(*Melinda sitting*)
About the occurring, and about access to the occurring... We now know that access to action is in the occurring. You don't gain access to action through decisions, and making up your mind, and all that other nonsense. That's a very weak access to your actions. If you checked and counted up how many times you made up your mind and then checked how many times you did what you made up your mind to do: very infrequently. It's a lousy access to action. Takes you forever to produce any effective action that way. Takes years of practice and discipline to produce any effective action that way. And it isn't the way to produce action, even taking years to do it. It's just a stupid way to behave and it's based on a stupid explanation; an ineffective way to behave based on a stupid explanation.

(*pausing to take a sip from a silver mug*)
Now here's another hard part. Where does the photographic image occur? Not on the paper! Because if the photographic image occurred on the paper, everybody who looked at the paper would see a photographic image. There are people who look at the paper and don't see any photographic image, that is to say, no photographic image occurs. Is that clear? Where does the photographic image occur? This is the question you should be asking: Where does the photographic image occur?

BARRY

When I'm shooting...

ERHARD

A photographic image is not shooting.

BARRY

I'm a photographer.

ERHARD

Oh, I apologize: I forgot you were a photographer. I don't want to know about taking pictures; I want to know where the photographic image occurs. So if you show me a photograph: Where does the image occur? It's not on the paper.

BARRY

It's the person who can recognize it there.

ERHARD

Where does that recognition happen?

BARRY

Through an association?

ERHARD

Not through association. The photographic image occurs in a medium called *the possibility of a photographic image*. Now, how long is it going to take you to get this? This is pretty simple. A photographic image occurs in a certain medium. The name of the medium is the possibility of a photographic image. To say it a bit more rigorously, a photographic image occurs in a medium called photographic image as a possibility. Photographic image as a presence, as an occurring, occurs, happens in a medium called photographic image as a possibility. Is that clear?

BARRY

No.

ERHARD

Then you're going to have to go home without that being clear then. Sorry. It's hard.

(*Barry sits*)

The medium of occurrence is possibility. Possibility shapes the occurring. What Ellen and I did was to shift the realm of possibility in which we were working. In one realm we were working on the possibility of catching the ball. That had a smaller possibility for Ellen. In the other realm we were working on the possibility of telling me which way the ball was spinning; that had a bigger possibility for Ellen. Hence, the ball traveling at the same *is* speed, alters its *occurring* speed, because occurring is a phenomenon which arises in a medium called possibility. Not possibility like you mean possibility, something that might, maybe could, maybe happen. Photographic image as a possibility is like—listen!—a *clearing* in which photographic images can happen. It's not a maybe, might. It's not made up of photographic images either. Photographic image as a possibility is not made up of photographic images, any more than "two" as a possibility is made up of examples of two. As a matter of fact, examples of two arise in the possibility "two." So, access to your action, access to your feeling:

Enframing

For Heidegger, our technological understanding of Being emerges in three stages: "challenging," "standing-reserve," and "enframing."

Challenging

"The revealing that rules in modern technology," Heidegger says first, "is a challenging (*Herausfordern*), which puts to nature the unreasonable demand that it supply energy which can be extracted and stored as such." Thus the "earth now reveals itself as a coal mining district, the soil as a mineral deposit." Heidegger protests this development as a significant change from the days of "the old windmill." While the windmill served human beings, the call for its service was left to the wind's blowing, since "the windmill does not unlock energy from the air currents in order to store it." Modern technology, on the other hand, "*sets upon* nature," always driving on toward "the maximum yield at the minimum expense" ("QCT"

ERHARD (*continuing*)

You've got no access to your feelings right now, do you? Yeah, you can't feel sad if you want to feel sad. You can't be happy if you want to be happy. The circumstances determine your happiness or your sadness. And all you got to deal with your feelings is fucking around with your circumstances. So you do what you think you need to do to create circumstances that will make you happy. And they don't. They gratify you for a little while, and then you're unhappy again. So, to gain access to your actions, to gain access to your feelings and thoughts, as actions so to speak, you need to see that your actions and thoughts and feelings are a correlate with the occurring. And the occurring arises, occurs, in a medium called possibility. So now the question is: "Well, how do I gain access to this possibility stuff?" Because if I can shift possibility, I can shift occurring; and if I can shift occurring, I can shift action. But you've got to get possibility like I'm saying it, not like something that might happen. That's an option. Something that might happen is an option. That's what Mike and I were talking about back there, options. "If the ball is over there, I might be able to catch it." That's an option. "And if it's over here, it's more likely that I'll catch it." That's a better option. These are options, not possibilities. Possibility doesn't limit. It opens up. It frees one, not limits one. So possibility is the medium of occurring, and occurring is the correlate of action. Does anybody not get that? You're starting to slide back into the first day. You're starting to wonder how to use this stuff. "I don't understand it." What you're really saying is "I don't see its applicability. I don't see how I'm going to apply it, or use it. I don't see how this is going to make me thinner, or richer, or younger, or sexier. So I don't understand it. If it isn't going to make me thinner, or richer, or younger, or sexier, then what is it?" So now the question is, "Where do I find possibility?" And the answer to that is in the ape never picking up the stick because he might find bananas hanging in the jungle clearing later on. Possibility arises in languaging. And I use the term languaging instead of language so you don't confuse what I'm talking about with vocabulary and syntax and grammar. You know, music is languaging, action is languaging when it speaks, and actions do speak don't they? And "in a glass," which is never said, and is yet present without being said by virtue of what is said, that's languaging too. And you want to know what? Sitting in a chair is languaging. A lot of people would look at a chair and never sit in it. It would look stupid to them: silly, uncomfortable, or nasty. Like sitting on two stakes sticking up. You look at two stakes sticking up—that doesn't look too comfortable to us. There are people who look at a chair and don't see it as a comfortable place to sit. It's something to stand on to get something in the cupboard that's up high. Not a place to sit. And the way it occurs to you is a product of languaging, not a product of what it is. Is a chair a chair? No, it's not an *is* chair, it's an occurring chair. In other cultures it occurs as something to stand on to get up to the cupboard that's up high. It's not an *is* chair; it's an occurring chair. And your actions with it are exactly like they are with the dictionary. Your actions are correlated to the object as an occurring. So we're sneaking up on a statement: *You do have something to say about your actions. You do have something to say about it*. And why you have something to say about it is because *possibility arises in language*.

At one point during this conversation, at about 10 pm, the doors to the room were opened and about two hundred people filed into the room and seated themselves in rows of chairs that had been placed at the sides and rear. These were friends of the participants who had previously taken The Forum, and who had been invited by them to join them, for this portion of the course.

in *BW* 320–321). As Michael E. Zimmerman has pointed out, this new way of revealing has now overtaken even the windmill: "Forty miles east of San Francisco in Livermore, California, thousands of turbo-driven windmills cover the hills as far as the eye can see. The wind's energy is, in fact, being harnessed and stored to produce electricity" (*Heidegger's Confrontation with Modernity* 216). However, what stands in the way of windmills being really useful as a power source is merely that no power can be generated when the wind isn't blowing. The solution, which is already likely at hand, will be to invent super batteries that could *store up the energy* for use and distribution when and where we need it. This would transform the "freely flowing" wind into something stored up, standing at the ready, in reserve.

Standing-Reserve

This situation reveals a second stage of the technological understanding of Being, which Heidegger calls *Bestand*, or *standing-reserve*. In this mode of revealing, says Heidegger, "everything is ordered to stand by, to be immediately on hand, indeed to stand there just so that it may be on call for a further ordering" ("QCT" in *BW* 322). This mode of revealing distorts the appearance of things: the airliner on the runway, for example, "conceals itself as to what and how it is."

 Revealed, it stands on the taxi strip only as standing-reserve, inasmuch as it is ordered to insure the possibility of transportation. For this it must be in its whole structure and in every one of its constituent parts itself on call for duty, i.e., ready for takeoff. ("QCT" in *BW* 322)

David Tabachnick has provided a useful contrast between the old and new ways of revealing, between the *techne* of the craftsman and the *techne* that we observe in current technology. For the craftsman, "'bringing-forth' describes a working in partnership or co-operation with the nature of materials to construct an artifact, such as a chair or a house, while the contemporary technologist is described as 'challenging-forth' or changing the nature of materials to make them stronger, more flexible, longer lasting, etc." Tabachnick continues, explaining that, for example,

> A doctor may "bring forth" the already available health of an individual through medicine, whereas cloning or genetic engineering "challenge" the natural bounds of the body, creating a wholly new "artifact" with different characteristics. As Heidegger details, earlier human inventions did not permanently impose a new form onto nature. Under normal conditions, because the material of an artifact was still bound by natural characteristics, nature would always "shine through" the imposition of the artist, craftsman or technician. A carpenter imposes the form of a chair onto wood, but once the chair is finished that wood still maintains its natural characteristics to rot and decompose in the same way a fallen tree rots and decomposes on the forest floor. In other words, the craftsman's chair is a site of openness for the revealing of nature. (Tabachnick 2004)

Tabachnick compares these earlier technologies with some that are representative of more recent developments, "technologies that do not co-operate with nature but attempt to replace it":

> A nuclear engineer can manipulate the structure of natural elements to produce artificial elements. Plutonium, for example, is designed to never abide by or return to the characteristics of the uranium from which it was derived. The character of plutonium (i.e., its level of radioactivity) is always artificial. Likewise, the genetically altered human is designed to never return to the natural characteristics of the material from which it was derived (e.g., a sick or weak body) and thus is always artificial. In turn, contemporary

Erhard called on Jane, the young woman with whom he had interacted with on Days Two and Three about her being "worthless" after having no one she invited come to her birthday party.

ERHARD

Jane and I were having a discussion when she was standing over there. And I said: "are you going to act out of being worthless and ugly?" And she said "not as much but probably some." Right? Something close to that?

JANE

Yeah.

ERHARD

Is that true or false? It's neither. The question is garbage. She has shaped the possibility for her future actions because she shaped the world as an occurring, by speaking a possibility. She said "my possibility is limited to this."

(*holding up both hands to eye level*)

This is how big the possibility is. It's that big because she said so. It's not that big because she believes it's that big, and not because it is that big, not because it's her opinion that it's that big. It's that big because she said so. Remember, languaging is not just what's coming out of your mouth. I don't say "in a glass," and yet it's there in languaging. I want to make sure nobody confuses what we are saying with "positive thinking." See, I'm not asking her to think positively. I don't like positive thinking. I'm an anti-positive thinker. I like honest thinking, not positive thinking. I like straight thinking, not positive thinking. I know that possibility is a product of languaging, but I don't like the word product: possibility arises in language... and that Jane can be a conversation for the possibility of anything she wants to be. See, where am I going to find "ugly"? Can I find anything ugly in somebody's face? This is not some nice platitudinal horseshit. Things are ugly, but they're ugly in people's mouths, not on people's faces. Ugly is not a phenomenon that arises independent of language. My dog looks at me and sees neither ugly, nor anything else about me, because ugly is a phenomenon that only arises in language. There's no ugly in anybody's face or body. Faces and bodies are just like they are. Ugly is a phenomenon that only arises in language. This doesn't sound very useful, does it? It sounds what you call abstract or conceptual. See, there's a difference between is ugly and occurs as ugly. What's the difference between *is* ugly and *occurs* as ugly? Something called plasticity, malleability, or something more aptly called possibility. If something is ugly you've got to adjust to it, don't you?

(*forcefully*)

It *is* ugly so you have to adjust to it. If it *occurs* as ugly there's the possibility of some malleability, some plasticity, you might be able to shape it in a new way if it *occurs* as ugly. I want you to begin to see that there's a lot of what you deal with that only arises in language. And because it only arises in language, you've got something to say about it. You've got something to say about being ugly—no shit—because ugly only arises in language. I've seen a lot of women whose features don't measure the perfect standard who are extraordinarily beautiful and so has every other man in this room. Beauty is not a matter of standard features.

ERHARD (*continuing*)

It's a way of being, not features. You know, it's nice to have good equipment, but too fucking bad, you've got the equipment you've got. Ugly is a conversation. That's all it is. You can't find ugly anyplace in the universe except in people's mouths. That's a metaphor. Now I'll say it rigorously. You can't find ugly anyplace but in languaging. And if you're listening to this like some platitude, then you are truly an asshole. This is hard stuff I'm taking about. Not "nice nice." And "worthless." Where am I going to find "worthless"?

JANE

In the conversation "worthless."

ERHARD

Yeah. Beautiful. See, you've got something to say about "worthless." You've got nothing to say about your feelings. You can't feel anything but what you're feeling. You've got nothing to say about how you feel. But you've got something to say about worthless and ugly. Because worthless and ugly are a conversation, that's all. One is a conversation for being worthless, or one is a conversation for being ugly. And that becomes the possibility in which life and the world and your own image occurs for you. You don't see yourself when you look in the mirror. You don't see yourself like an is, you see yourself like an *occur*; you see yourself as an occurring self, not an *is* self. And what occurs in the mirror is not in the mirror. It's in languaging, therefore, you have access to what occurs in the mirror: Like a conversation for the possibility of being beautiful. It's idiotic to walk around saying "I'm beautiful," especially if you look like me. You look like her, maybe, because there's some agreement for that. I didn't say I walk around speaking positively. I said it's possible for me to be engaged in the conversation for the possibility of being beautiful. I and you and the world will occur in the space, the clearing given by that conversation for possibility. And my actions, and my feelings, and my thoughts, will be a correlate of that occurring. And my actions, and my feelings, and my thoughts will work on the world. You getting this?

JANE

Yes.

ERHARD

And so you have something to say about this. What you say about it is none of my business. That's your business. We know why you said you were ugly and worthless, because you got something out of that, right? For the payoff. Remember the payoff conversation?

JANE

Yeah.

ERHARD

And so ugly and worthless was a racket for a payoff. But there's no payoff for the possibility of beauty. Beauty as an assertion, "I am beautiful," like describing yourself, like you are an object, there's a payoff in that. But there's no payoff in the possibility of beauty. As a matter of fact it puts you further at risk, because now you're at risk for being beautiful. When you're ugly you

technological artifacts do not disclose nature. And, because in a technological society so much of our world is filled with these "undisclosing artifacts," we are cut off from, become unaware of, or forget the essential movedness or transience of existence. (Ibid.)

We remind the reader that we are not advocating a universal return to wooden furniture; we do not regret advances in medical science that employ new materials. To do so would be tantamount to the demonstration Wes carried out during The Forum, earlier in Day Four, of arguing with the floor. At the same time we are not making an ethical statement concerning what the technological understanding of Being has done to human beings such that we might, as a matter of course, accept without question even radically dangerous technological advances. Here we are simply focusing on the view that we are already in a technological way of Being-in-the-world, and therefore, what is at issue is the way of being human that has emerged with these developments.

One principle way of being human that has emerged is one that Erhard himself has exemplified in his development of his technology of transformation: entrepreneurship. The term "entrepreneur" stems from the French term *entreprendre*, to undertake. An entrepreneur is an enterpriser. Far from accepting or even tolerating the way things already *are*, the entrepreneur envisions and *reveals*, through originary naming, new possibilities which alter the way the world occurs. With language we impact the occurring world and consequently, our Being, for our Being is always and already in a dance with the occurring world. We bring into Being what could never be without being *said* into Being: we speak Being.

The relationship to modern technology at work in Erhard's technology of transformation does not immediately square with Heidegger's persistent complaint that holds our technological way of being as presenting us with profound danger. The difference is subtle, and will require us to walk a thin line as both thinkers are nevertheless treading the same waters.

For instance, if we envision Heidegger's understanding of our technological way of being as harmonic with the in-order-to mechanism of the "they" self, the two thinkers appear side-by-side, but this is only a semblance. For Heidegger, one notable effect of understanding the world as a source of resources is that humans have surrendered their role as the self-certain ontologically centered subject. Since standing-reserve is an "inclusive rubric," it moves us beyond the Cartesian subject-object model in which we have come to conceptualize our relationship to things. Instead, says Dreyfus, "we are passing from the subject-object stage to the stage in which the culture is becoming, one might say, one big cybernetic system" ("Gaining"). Clearly, this is not the overcoming of Cartesian subjectivity that the early Heidegger of *Being and Time* and Erhard—from the *est* Training to the present—have been working toward. It is not the opening for a new possibility of Being for human beings. Instead:

> **As soon as what is unconcealed no longer concerns man even as object, but exclusively as standing-reserve, and man in the midst of objectlessness is nothing but the orderer of the standing-reserve, then he comes to the brink of a very precipitous fall, that is, *he comes to the point where he himself will have to be taken as standing-reserve.* ("QCT" in *BW* 332, emphasis added)**

This precipitous fall, we offer, has already taken place: this is the way of being human The Forum addresses in its participants from the very beginning. Those seeking to improve, to acquire the tips and techniques to overcome and change their lives for the better, who take any morsel of wisdom and put it to use, all the better to *order it*, but in the process they—we—unwittingly rob the truth, as unconcealment, of its power—this is the way of being that self-destructs against the bulwark of the Nothing the inquiry of The Forum brings to presence.

Enframing

And so, we arrive at the final stage in the way modern technology reveals the world: "the essence of modern technology," says Heidegger, "lies in enframing [*Gestell*]" ("QCT" in *BW* 328). This

don't have to risk much. You don't have to put your lines out when you're ugly. You all awake? If you're beautiful, you've got to put your lines out. You understand why?

JANE
Yeah.

ERHARD
Do you understand trolling?

JANE
Yeah.

(*laughter*)

ERHARD
Trolling is a game called being alive. And it's as meaningful as everything else in life. Zero. Therefore you're free to play. And there are certain agreements in society about playing. And society is weird, but that's too bad: That's what we got. I may not get a chance to talk to you again tonight, and I want you to know how deeply grateful I am for your contribution to this Forum. You're really beautiful.

JANE
Thank you.

She sat to long applause from the group.

Erhard moved to the chalkboard, and drew three circles. The first two he labeled "story" and "what happened."

ERHARD
Remember on the first day, we drew these two circles. One was your "story" and the other circle was "what happened." So there was what happened, and there was your story about what happened, and then we talked about the vicious circle where those two domains got collapsed, and you couldn't tell the difference between what happened and your story about what happened. And you began to think that your story about what happened *is* what happened. And that makes people suffer. Just like putting your hand on the gas stove makes you suffer. That's why you can't trust psychology, because all of the then-known facts in psychology had been established with experiments with rats and college sophomores, neither one of which might be human—I don't know about college sophomores, but I know that rats are not like human beings. And the difference between a rat and a human being is a rat will stop crawling into the oven if it gets burned, and human beings will keep crawling into the oven. Forever. Why? Because "it's the right fucking oven, and I believe in it." And then we got more sophisticated and said there were two realms of existence: that what existed, existed as a presence, and what existed, the same stuff, exists as a concept. These are two distinct realms of existence, domains of existence.

ERHARD (*indicating the "story" circle*)
In this realm there are things like explanations.

(*indicating the "what happened" circle*)
And in this realm there are things like experience. So one is the experience and the other is the explanation of the experience. This was the whole story at the time we discussed this earlier. We were going backwards. We got to zero, we got to empty and meaningless. Now we're seeing that there are two sides to The Forum. The first side is "What is the already always being of human beings?" And the other side is "*What is the possibility of being for human beings?*" Now you heard "*What is the possibility of being for human beings*" as the something maybe, could I, might be, maybe, like some stupid image you got of yourself as thin and sexy and young and rich, or whatever your silly notion is for your self. Holy. It fits in there. The same crap.

(*indicating the first two circles*)
That's what you got born with. That's what came with the package—those two domains. There's another domain.

(*drawing a new circle to the left of the "what happened" circle*)
It doesn't come with the package. You don't get it for free.

(*indicating the "story" circle*)
You can talk about that domain right here, but that's talking about it. That's like eating the menu.

(*indicating the third, still empty circle to the left of the "what happened" circle and of the "story" circle*)
A lot of people talking about this domain.

(*indicating the "what happened" circle*)
You can even have experiences of it. People who merely have the experience of it get weird. Lot a weird people in this room, by the way. They gravitate to California.

(*laughter*)
People with the experience of that other domain: Makes them weird. They can't get over it, so they stay weird. They've got no mastery of the domain. They don't dwell in the domain; they don't come from the domain. They don't dwell in it, but they've touched it experientially. Everybody in the room has had that experience. Everybody. Some of you haven't had enough of that experience to be weird yet, that's all. You know that experience where you don't have to eat, where you don't have to go to the bathroom, and you don't have a home, and there's nothing but what you're doing. You're not even there, right? It's like when you get out of the way, and there's that thing that happens when you're out of the way? By the way, when do you come back? When it goes bad. Right away you're right there: "Oh shit!"

is the culmination, the gathering of the challenging-forth and ordering, the box in which human beings as resources already find themselves at this juncture in our history. To employ the vernacular, the technological way of Being is a done deal: "The actual threat has already afflicted man in his essence. . . . Thus the question as to how we are to arrive at a relationship to the essence of technology, asked in this way, always comes too late" ("QCT" in *BW* 333, 329). In a 1966 interview with the German newsmagazine *Der Spiegel*, asked what was missing in the world when, after all, everything seemed to be functioning and production was at a peak, Heidegger replied: "*Everything is functioning*. This is exactly what is so uncanny, that everything is functioning and that the functioning drives us more and more to even further functioning, and that technology tears men loose from the earth and uproots them" (in Zimmerman's *Heidegger's Confrontation with Modernity* 199, emphasis added). Thus uprooted, says Dreyfus, human beings "become a resource to be used, and more importantly to be enhanced, just like any other resource" ("Gaining").

And yet, it is Erhard's technology of transformation that brings forth its participants to arrive at such a relationship to the essence of technology, right in the midst of being torn loose from the earth, used and enhanced as any resource would be, caught up in the relentless logic of the in-order-to. Rather than turn away from the technological way of being we are thrown to be, the inquiry of The Forum directs its participants to come face-to-face with it, to own up to it, to *be* in the trap that it is for human being. ∎

ERHARD (*continuing to laughter*)
That's you. You're "oh shit!" That's how we know when you got back.

(*laughter; indicating third empty circle*)
So a lot of what the second half of The Forum is about is access to this domain. And you and I are not going to do as good a job at access to that domain as you were getting to zero, because you all were a pain in the ass and it took too long to get to zero. If you didn't hear me making you wrong, I was just making you wrong.

(*laughter*)
The other side of that is that we haven't gotten our shit together to get The Forum to zero quickly enough to do a good job on the second half. That's making me wrong. You notice nothing changes, no matter who's wrong?

(*laughter and applause*)
The point is that we can't do very much more than open up the second half of The Forum. That's as much as we can get done, because you all need your beauty sleep.

(*laughter*)
Okay, so what is this domain? If it's not experiential, and it isn't; it's not conceptual, and it isn't: What is that domain?

(*writing "possibility" in the third circle*)
Simple. It's the *domain of possibility*. Not this possibility or that possibility,

(*indicating the "story" circle*)
...that's here. You could say that it's the possibility of possibility. But there's no such domain. No matter where you go to look for it you can't find it. You can't have it unless you *invent* it. You have to invent the possibility of possibility. You want to listen to that. People don't have possibility in their lives. They have options. Options are futures generated from the past. The past could work out like this, or it could work out like that. You know, common conversation between people. Things could work out like this, or they could work out like that. "They're likely to work out like this, but oh boy would I love them to work out like that, but that is not very likely." That is not possibility; that is "options." Options are conceptual. And your experience—listen up—your experience will mostly be limited to the options that you give yourself to experience. It's the vicious circle all over again.

(*indicating the "story" circle*)
The options are here. Why do I call them options? Because they're derived from your past experiences! The options shape your future experience. And the option-shaped experiences reinforce the options. So now you finally got yourself figured out so you don't need to get up in the morning anymore, because there's nowhere to go. Why bother? You already know how it's going to be, so why bother? The only reason why most of you get up is because you

ERHARD (*continuing*)

like suffering. That's a psychiatric problem called masochism. Go to a psychiatrist to get that handled. We don't handle that in here. But most of you get up because you like suffering. I mean, you must like suffering: That's what you do. And you know you're going to do it. No, what gets you up is hoping, hoping you're going to make it, hoping it's all going to work out, hoping it's somehow going to be different, hoping you're going to get the answer. What's that?

(*in response to a participant calling out, Erhard repeats*)

Yeah. You suffer hoping. Exactly. Hoping keeps you suffering. Why would you bother getting up in the morning if you know what it's going to be like?

(*walking back to the chalkboard to indicate the "possibility" circle*)

At any rate, you've got something to say here. You've got nothing to say about experience—you can only report on it more or less accurately.

(*indicating the "story" circle*)

And you're limited to what you say here reporting on experience. This is reporting on that.

(*indicating the "possibility" circle*)

Here you are free. Now, there's one little catch. A pipe dream is not a possibility. Pipe dreams and possibility are not the same thing. Possibility is the future. You could say that the past could have possibly been like this. But in the future, we might learn that the past was really different than what we thought. Possibility is *always future*. It's got that kind of temporality: future. And you're going to have pipe dreams and call them possibility. I'll tell you how to tell the difference between a pipe dream and possibility. There is no future, which will ever be realized, which is not an extension of the past when it happens. All futures will be an extension of the past. There are no discontinuous futures. Not in your lifetime, because all futures, *when* realized, have a continuity with the past. There is nothing that ever happened that was inconsistent with the past. If necessary, the past is rewritten. On the basis of Columbus and Einstein, the past was rewritten. See, it *was true* the world was flat, until someone did something inconsistent with that. Then we said, oh, it wasn't flat. How the hell do you know it wasn't flat? The point is that you're free to create possibilities for your life and you want to ground those possibilities by bringing the possibility back into the present. Like standing in the future to create a future. And then you tease it back to the present, so there's a structure to fulfill that possibility. But that's too technical, and we don't have the time to go into all the technicalities tonight. All I'm going to tell you is this: If you live with possibility, you live with both risk and power. None of this works; it's only empowering. None of this is the answer, and it is empowering. Life is authentically risky. You got the wrong idea about life. You think life is about reducing the risk with finding the answers. You want to cheat. If you want to reduce the risk, play tennis with three-year-olds. You win all the time. Makes you feel great.

(*laughter*)

If winning all the time makes you feel great then you like playing tennis with three-year-olds. Winning doesn't make people feel great. Being powerful and able and playing and dancing, that makes people feel great. And to do that you've got to have power, and that's what we're

> " All I'm going to tell you is this: If you live with possibility, you live with both risk and power. None of this works; it's only empowering. None of this is the answer, and it is empowering. Life is authentically risky.

talking about here: What we're talking about here is empowering yourself, not reducing the risk. We're not talking about giving you the answers so that you know how to beat people; it just reduces life and people to a three-year-old. That's silly. If the point was getting to the top of Mount Everest, some goddamn entrepreneur would put an elevator on it. The question is: How powerful and how able can you be in the face of the risk called Mount Everest?

(pausing)
Okay. So we're almost home. We've got two more definite steps. And the first step is a step called *responsibility*. Remember the choice exercise? You discovered something about choice that was inconsistent with the interpretation you already had that choice was, and that there's a certain power to distinguishing choice the way you distinguished it during the exercise. Same thing about responsibility. The first thing you want to get is, responsibility is not blame or guilt or fault. When I say I'm responsible, I'm not saying I did it, or I am to blame or that I'm guilty. When I say I'm responsible, what I mean is that I stand for being cause in the matter. Not "I caused it." It's a stand for being cause in the matter.

(indicating the "possibility" circle)
And you can't take a stand without this domain. Without this domain, your stand is a mere position. Some position you've taken on the matter. I don't know if you've been watching this over the past four days, but your positions have gotten you into a lot of hot water. Your positions have ruined your life a little bit. Or a whole lot.

(pausing)
Without this domain... See, a possibility is established by taking a stand for something as a possibility. A position is established by setting something up as something toward which you are working. Possibility is something you are free to realize, which is different than something you are working towards. It's like you're free to realize whatever it is that you're willing to stand for. That's different from working towards something. Can you imagine: Working toward hitting the ball over the net in tennis does not make great tennis? Or working toward dancing. My mother only made one mistake in raising me. She sent me to the Bala Cynwyd Women's Club to learn to dance. This was a big mistake.

(laughter)
Knowing where to put your feet is not dancing. I didn't know that for a long time.

(indicating the "possibility" circle)
The action in this realm is declaration.

(indicating the "story" circle)
The action in this realm is assertion.

(indicating the "what happened" circle)
The action here is expressives. These are Speech Acts, but that'll get too complicated. To understand declaration, you have to go to an umpire convention.

> " See, a possibility is established by taking a stand for something as a possibility. A position is established by setting something up as something toward which you are working. Possibility is something you are free to realize, which is different than something you are working towards. It's like you're free to realize whatever it is that you're willing to stand for. That's different from working towards something.

Here Erhard told the story about the three umpires: the rookie umpire who said he "calls them like they are," the experienced umpire who said he calls them "like I see them," and the master umpire, who said "They ain't anything until I call them something."

ERHARD

That's declaration. See, the umpire's got the power of declaration. What is it? If President Carter wakes up in the middle of the night, says "to hell with glasnost, I'm sending the bombs out," what does Rosalynn say? "Shut up, Jimmy, go to sleep." But if President Bush does it, Barbara runs for the bomb shelter. Actually, the president doesn't do that, but never mind; it ruins the story if I go into that. This power of declaration: That's what it takes to be responsible, because being responsible is merely a declaration. It is the declaration that one is cause in the matter. It's not a description of the case. It's not a report on the facts: It's a place to stand in life regarding what you care about. When I'm in India, I say the people who are hungry are responsible for their hunger. And the bleeding hearts have a problem with that. But I'll tell you, if you are responsible for your hunger you're a lot more powerful than if you're a victim of being hungry. It's quite clear to me that the hungry do not want to be hungry, and the hungry would not have it that way if they had the opportunity to do something about it. It's quite clear to me that it takes more courage to live one day there than it takes for me to live ten years. But treating people as if they have no responsibility is disempowering to people. Now you can't argue that you're responsible, because that's not a declaration, is it? That's an assertion, an argument. A declaration has to be done freely, not coerced. You've got to have the power of declaration, and the power of declaration is a product of freedom. It's a privilege to be responsible, not a burden to be responsible. "I am cause in the matter" is a *stand* for giving yourself power, not a report on the facts or the circumstances. It's clear to me that I'm the cause in the matter of people's hunger. I make that declaration; it gives me power with regard to the issue of hunger. It's not a report on the fact that I did it. It's a place to stand from which one has power. If it's not my fault, if I didn't do it—but none of that interests me—whose fault is it? Somebody gets to be wrong and somebody gets to be right. That's the point.

(*indicating the "possibility" circle*)

The realm of possibility is also the realm of responsibility. Most people are never going to be responsible because that realm doesn't exist; you have to invent it. One of the things we haven't told you is what you're going to get out of being in The Forum. Listen up! What you're going to get out of The Forum—yeah you're going to get a lot of nice things and good things, but that's all chicken shit. What you're really going to get out of The Forum is whatever you're willing to stand for having gotten out of The Forum. You're not going to get out of The Forum what we gave you because we can't give you anything of value. You know, all these people are not here because we have something valuable to give to people. You can't get anything valuable from other people. Like "be given it." Chicken shit is what we get from one another. But you can give yourself something valuable. You can give yourself something extraordinarily valuable. You can give yourself something that will last the rest of your life. You can give yourself something that will make it that your life is never the same. So here's my promise: I promise that you can have anything out of The Forum you're willing to stand for having gotten. I also promise you

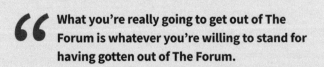

> **What you're really going to get out of The Forum is whatever you're willing to stand for having gotten out of The Forum.**

won't get anything else out of The Forum that's worth anything. What you'll get out of your participation in The Forum is what you're willing to stand for having gotten. You don't get what you're checking to see if you've gotten..." Let me see, what happened to me? Did my mind change? Did my feelings change? Did my eyesight change? Am I taller? Am I thinner? Do I feel better?" You can't have any of that. If you're willing to stand for having been empowered in here, you can walk out of here empowered. That's the truth. This isn't some airy-fairy crap. You are not the first people I have done this work with. This is grounded on a lot of evidence. You paid your $625. You bust your ass for four days, you still got one evening to go. Whatever possibility you're willing to stand for, whatever conversation for possibility you're willing to generate, that's what you will have gotten. Whatever possibility you're willing to stand for, that's what you can have. What you've done in here has given you the power to realize what you're willing to stand for, not like a formula, but like a possibility in which you can act and be. Not like a guaranteed outcome, not like playing tennis with a three-year-old; being fully at risk, but being fully empowered in the face of the risk. If you don't like risk, you don't like life. So we're up to the last thing now. Kind of. I say kind of because I never know what's really last. Who has any questions?

A participant raised his hand.

RICHARD

I got what I paid my money for. What has happened in the last few months is that my projects have become so successful that they're bigger than my possibility for them.

ERHARD

You hear what he said? He used up the world of possibility. The content has overwhelmed the context. He's created a possibility and has related to that possibility powerfully enough, with the power to fulfill the possibility such that the content is overwhelming the context. You know what a hero is? Not what you think a hero is. A hero is not some dashing figure, an extraordinary person. Only ordinary people can be heroes. A hero is an ordinary person who dares to recognize and accept the call of a possibility bigger than themselves. Real simple. A hero is an ordinary person who sees, who hears, who is open to, and accepts the call of a possibility bigger than themselves, or herself or himself.

CECILIA

I've accomplished a lot and I'm an artist and illustrator. I've done book publishing, and so all this work is sixty percent solitary at least, and I've been having this conversation for years that I ought to go participate with other people. And so once and a while I go do that from "ought to." I've done some good things but in the end I say "Jeez! That was a mistake. I wish I had done that by myself after all." I mean the nurturing is kind of awful out here and I've been doing this work for years going in and out of that. And what I finally got these last four days was that it's never going to work if I think I have to go and do it. It's like "Gee, I already like this thing I'm doing: painting. It's meaningless, so I'll just do it!" But I also got that I had killed off one of the main human attributes, which was love.

CECILIA (*continuing; breaking into tears*)

What I can do now is go out and be with you all from my love for you all, rather than because I think I ought to.

ERHARD

Very nice.

(*applause*)

HENRY

I'm speaking and listening and it's like the first time. I've been stingy and this is the first time that I'm not. I called my father and my mother. I told them that I loved them and they told me they loved me. I told them they were okay by me. My father said, "Well that's interesting!" I asked him if I was okay by him and he said "Sure you're okay by me." My relationships with my mother and father are complete. I say so.

ERHARD

By the way: They are if you say so. Not like you want to say so. You've got to be free to say so. You can't say so in-order-to. You've got to be standing where what you say is so. We'll talk about that in a moment. Please go on.

HENRY

Everything that I've accomplished in my thirty-two years of my life is empty and meaningless. I'm okay with that. My life is perfect. What's happened for me in the last several days is... I'm standing here trembling in awe and respect and gratitude for the incredible space of listening that you've created. I'm expressing myself for the first time. The parts of The Forum that have been difficult for me—I'm going through The Forum thinking I'm the only one going through this. But I've seen myself in everybody's share and it hasn't been difficult or painful. It's been great. I've gotten it: My back pain is gone, the stuffy nose is gone. I've got beyond the five-year-old. I was that "I can't remember beyond five-years-old." I don't know whether I'm remembering what happened or remembering the story, but I've started to remember when I was very young. And what that frees up for me: I couldn't own what was invisible to me. The racket, which came from incidents that were invisible to me and blocked out from me, kept coming up, and the incidents were so far back, way earlier than I've ever looked before. Even though I've done the training before, I've never experienced what I have now. I've always shared to look good, and now I'm sharing to contribute. I feel like the amount of time that people will listen to me is very short, and so I speak fast, cram it all in and nobody gets it. And I'm just worse off afterwards. It was an in-order-to.

ERHARD

Say what's there instead of talking about it. I didn't say, "say it fast," I said "say what's there." You may have already said what you stood up to say, which is "I love you. And I respect you. And I acknowledge you." If you've got something beyond that to say, say it. But get to the punch line. If you're going to talk, do it effectively.

The Oblivion of Oblivion

As we stated earlier, Heidegger's perspective on technology is an important element in the understanding of Werner Erhard's work that we are developing here. Dreyfus finds a useful summary of this perspective in the response of HAL, the computer/robot in

Stanley Kubrick's film *2001,* when he asked whether he is happy: "I'm using all my capacities to the maximum. What more could a rational entity want?" This, says Dreyfus, is "a brilliant expression of what anyone would say who is in touch with our current understanding of Being."

Of particular relevance is Dreyfus' observation that "the human potential movement perfectly expresses this technological understanding of Being" ("Gaining"). Werner Erhard's work, which Peter Marin has called "the logical extension of the whole human potential movement" ("The New Narcissism," *Harper's Magazine,* October 1975, 47), may therefore be considered as a *representative manifestation of our current technological understanding of Being*, especially to the degree that this logical extension is itself, paradoxically, *a denial* of the so-called human potential movement. This point is central to the conclusion we are moving toward here.

The situation: humans are always *subjected to* understandings of Being, and to the way they play themselves out over time. In Dreyfus' words, "We don't produce the clearing; The clearing produces us" ("Gaining"). Every historical epoch is characterized by a particular mode of unconcealment, a particular way in which Being shows itself, so that in each epoch humans are given a particular way to be. Through this epochal *self-revealing*, this *giving of itself* to humans, Being manifests its nature; and beings show up being that way, "the way they wound up being," as Erhard might say more recently.

But as Western thought has evolved over time, human beings have lost their awareness of Being, if ever they have even been aware of Being. Now, of the giver-giving-given event that is Being's gift, we see only the given, and we see it only as it is represented by beings. Being "withdraws in favor of the gift which It gives" (*OTB* 8).

When a giver withdraws and holds itself back, and gives only its gift, that giving is appropriately called *sending* (*OTB* 8). The gift is given, but the sender, crucially, is not present. So while an experience of Being is no longer available, the sending continues to shape human existence in every age. This is the process which Heidegger calls the *destining* of Being, and from this destining

HENRY

My promise is that the twenty-five year racket that I've lived—I'm giving that up and am now living out the distinction ecological health. I appreciate you very much, and I love you all.

ERHARD

Okay good. Thank you.

ZELDA

What do you mean: to stand for?

ERHARD

Declare the possibility of...; live out of the possibility of...; have as the context for living, the possibility of...; Generate a conversation for...; create a context for...

ZELDA

I understand that. It says to me to be generous.

ERHARD

I'm not asking you to be generous. You will be generous if you do that. I'm not asking you to be generous, because that would mean for you to have a quality inside yourself called generous. If you act on the offer to have anything out of The Forum you are willing to stand for having gotten... if you act on the offer you will be *being generous*. Generosity arises in an act of being. It's not a property inside of people that gets expressed in their actions. You get that?

ZELDA

Yes. Thank you.

(*applause*)

WALT

I say I'm not confused about what you've given us in the last hour, but it is a lot to hold.

ERHARD

Yes, precisely, so listen up here. This is good. I read something to you three days ago and I want you to hear it again. See if it occurs for you differently than it did then.

Here, he read again the passage from the Heidegger/Japanese dialogue in Heidegger's *On the Way to Language.*

ERHARD (*reading*)

"We Japanese do not think it strange if a dialogue leaves undefined what is really intended, or even restores it back to the keeping of the undefinable." ... "That is part of every dialogue that has turned out well among thinking beings. As if of its own accord it can take care that that undefinable something not only does not slip away, but displays its gathering power ever more

ERHARD (*continuing to read*)

luminously in the course of the dialogue." The Japanese inquirer said "Our dialogues with our teacher failed to turn out so well. Us younger men challenged him much too directly to satisfy our thirst for handy information." ... "Thirst for knowledge and greed for explanations never lead to a thinking inquiry. Curiosity is always the concealed arrogance of a self-consciousness that banks on a self-invented rationality."

(*to the group*)

You remember I told you that that means we treat anything worth knowing as something that merely extends from what we already know and that if we don't immediately understand something it must be bullshit.

(*continuing to read*)

"The *will* to know does not *will* to abide in hope before what is worthy of thought."

(*to the group*)

What you and I just spoke about in the last two hours is worth standing in front of. You may not get it all, which means you may not understand it all, which really means you may not be able to apply it all, and your applying it will only denigrate it anyhow. Much better to stand with it, to be with it.

WALT

So I'm way beyond what I understood before. I'm standing on a beach ball here, ready to lose my balance. But it's a good place to be. I understood you to tell us that the forwarding of this is in declaration, that declaration is the way to access this?

ERHARD

Declaration is the action out of which possibility is generated: the speech act out of which possibility is generated; it's the name of the speech act out of which possibility arises.

WALT

So that's what a person can do, in doing, to work with this.

ERHARD

Yeah, to generate a possibility. Precisely.

WALT

But the possibility, this possibility that's created, is itself not useful, or applicable, but it sounds "opportunity" somehow gets created.

ERHARD

There's an opening. A freedom. There's a freedom for that which you have declared possible. It doesn't mean you will—it means that there's a freedom for that which you've declared possible, that your actions may arise inside that possibility, and that your actions will arise inside that possibility. We're not done yet. We've got one last step to take.

"the essence of all history is determined" ("QCT" in *BW* 329). Here Dreyfus recounts the historical record:

> **In the Christian age, everything showed up as God's creation, and showed up in terms of its nearness or distance from God's own nature. In the modern age, everything showed up as either a subject with a deep essence, or an object with fixed properties. In the technological age, by contrast, everything shows up in light of what will allow us to put it to "the greatest possible use at the lowest expenditure." (*Companion to Heidegger* 13)**

Heidegger refers to this historical evolution of destining as the *play of Being*. Being holds itself back *in a particular way* in each epoch, and it is in the progress of the epochs that the play of Being is manifested. The order of that play defies human understanding and control: "The sequence of epochs in the destiny of Being is not accidental, nor can it be calculated as necessary" (*OTB* 9). *It plays.* Therefore enframing can be seen from one perspective as the essence of modern technology, while from another it is simply the particular clearing for unconcealment which the play of Being has sent at this moment in history.

At this point, the reader may notice herself thinking some version of "So what?" Yes, we can see the effects of technology in our world. We overuse our gadgets and texting while driving is dangerous and our interpersonal eye contact is suffering. But at the same time global communication and the conveniences of everyday living have improved exponentially, and marginalized groups around the globe have found a voice through social media that have also shaken the foundations of local, national, and world politics. Every advance brings its challenges. We can deal with it.

Perhaps. Certainly, the advantages are undeniable. But the threat embedded in technology's essence may make this *one* advance too far. With each development in the play of Being, we are moving farther and farther from the possibility of an originary experience of Being: "The epochs overlap each other in their sequence so that the original sending of Being as presence is more and more obscured in different ways" (*OTB* 9).

Therefore Heidegger makes his case in the strongest possible terms: it is not just that our technological way of being is distancing and impersonal. It is that once we lose ourselves in the system, we may not be able to find our way out. As the Cartesian subject, the self-certain lord of the earth, we encountered our subjective truth in every objective being. But enframed as resources for technology, "*precisely nowhere does man today any longer encounter himself*, i.e., *his essence*" ("QCT" in *BW* 332). We might begin to detect in Heidegger's discourse the hint of a persistent complaint reaching a fever pitch:

> **Enframing does not simply endanger man in his relationship to himself and to everything that is. As a destining, it banishes man into the kind of revealing that is an ordering. Where this ordering holds sway, it drives out every other possibility of revealing. [. . .]**
>
> **The rule of enframing threatens man with the possibility that it could be denied to him to enter into a more original revealing and hence to experience the call of a more primal truth. Thus where enframing reigns, there is *danger* in the highest sense. ("QCT" in BW 332–333)**

The culmination: what has been lost is forgotten.

> **Enframing disguises even this, its disguising, just as the forgetting of something forgets itself and is drawn away in the wake of forgetful oblivion. The coming-to-pass of oblivion not only lets fall from remembrance into concealment; but that falling itself falls simultaneously from remembrance into concealment, which itself also falls away in that falling. ("TT" in QCT 46)**

WALT

Okay. I'm just trying to handle the steps I've taken.

ERHARD

You're doing the right thing. Go ahead.

WALT

In the previous days here, I've been able to get outside of myself. The meaninglessness, and the meaninglessness of that, was a further push out of myself. And it's an exciting place to be for action. I have a concern that this will just remain potential. And I want to use it as soon as possible so that it does not remain potential, or just a memory.

ERHARD

Your actions will be consistent with it remaining a potential, and consistent with your avoiding that.

WALT

So I will not avoid that.

ERHARD

I don't know. I just said your actions would be consistent with the occurring you created.

WALT

Okay. So I say...

ERHARD

Relax. See, relax. All you got to do is be here. Real simple. All you got to do is be here. This stuff works. It actually works.

WALT

But it's too great just to let it sit.

ERHARD

No, it's so great you've got to let it sit. All you've got to do is take a stand for anything you want to get out of The Forum.

WALT

Yeah but me... get out of The Forum, it's puny compared to what you've put on the board.

ERHARD

I didn't say "you," like limiting it to you, like you, individually. "One can give..." Is that better?

WALT

It is... for me.

ERHARD

You have to free yourself, not limit yourself. You want to limit yourself: That's what you want to do—you want to limit yourself to be sure. You don't want to take the risk of letting yourself be free inside the possibilities you create. You want to limit your actions to make sure you realize your goal. That is not this course. That's a "Success" course.

WALT

So if I'm going to stay with it here, stay on board, really...

ERHARD

Give yourself some freedom. Create the possibility and then operate out of that possibility. Operate on what? Whatever the hell's in front of you, do whatever you do. Stop complicating it. You're back in the first day now. You're asking how to proceed. You're asking for the prescription. You go left and then you go right, that's how you get there; but the real way to get there is going wherever you're going. Do whatever you're doing. Don't do what you're not doing. It's real easy to follow that instruction.

WALT

And that's enough?

ERHARD

That's enough. Who would tell a guy like you that what you need to do is to box yourself in? The degree to which you need to be boxed in is the degree to which you need to be narrowed. You're going to handle that without any help from anybody. Don't you understand, Walt, I'm not going to tell you: "Walt, what has to happen is that the sun's gotta come up tomorrow morning!" That's going to happen anyhow. You don't need to take my time, and I don't need to take your time to have that discussion. You don't need to take our time to have the discussion you want to have, you're going to do that anyhow. You'll get enough of that mixed into the stew. You'll take care of that. You're thrown to that.

WALT

Yeah I am.

ERHARD

Yeah, you're thrown to that. We don't talk about what you're thrown to. It's not that we don't need what you're thrown to. We do, but why talk about it? We're going to get that anyhow.

WALT

I was trying to address something else. I was trying to address what you put out there.

At this point, for Heidegger, we let slip our own essential role as the beings with meaning, the beings for whom Being is an issue, the clearing in the world for beings to be the beings they are. "Being's coming to presence needs the coming to presence of man, in order to remain *kept safe* as Being. . ." ("TT" in QCT 38). But as enframing, we forfeit our role as safekeeper. Lost in the machinations of the cybernetic system, we not only let the truth of Being fall into oblivion, but we let fall into oblivion the knowledge that we have done so, until finally, oblivion itself is forgotten, and we forget that anything has been lost. "The most profound oblivion," says Heidegger, "is not-recollecting" (EP 63).

As evidence that this is already the condition in our world, we cite the difficulty that is inevitably encountered in any discussion of Being, for example, the recurring sense in reading this book of "What the hell are we talking about?" Being in our time, so goes Heidegger's persistent complaint, cannot be recollected, let alone spoken. ∎

ERHARD

You're trying to address what I put out there using *your* approach. And you need a little bit of your approach. But we don't need to discuss that; you'll come up with that with your genius in that quarter. You don't need to discuss that with me. What you need to do is create the possibility and to let yourself be free in the possibility. All the rest of it you're thrown to.

WALT

Okay, so create the possibility.

ERHARD

Yeah, that's what I said. You can have anything out of The Forum you can stand for having gotten. "Stand for having gotten" and "create the possibility" are synonymous.

WALT

And that's the declaration.

ERHARD

Yeah. That's: generate a conversation for.

WALT

So if I don't screw with that, it's going to be all right.

ERHARD

Yeah, just handle that... No, I don't know whether it's going to be all right. All I know is that you're going to have power in the face of the risk that life is. That's all I promised you. I didn't promise you things would be all right. I promised you the power and ability. I don't know about all right.

WALT

Thanks, Werner.

ERHARD

Yes, you're welcome.

(*applause*)
Bill? Stand up.

Bill stood, the participant from the chocolate/vanilla demonstration, who also confronted Erhard on the first day of The Forum concerning being pressured to be in the course.

(*continuing*)
It's called equal time, Bill. It's called "only fair."

BILL

I don't really have anything to discuss that I am confused about, but it's what has set me free that makes me feel a lot better about my experience here. For one thing, I want to thank you Werner for tolerating my controlling nature.

ERHARD

Yeah, and you and I needed to tolerate each other for it to work and so I want to thank you for tolerating my controlling nature, too.

BILL (*to laughter*)

I came in this Forum with somewhat of a chip on my shoulder,

(*laughter*)

...and I was kind of angry. I had a lot of rackets that I couldn't see until many of you stood up to discuss them.

ERHARD (*to the group*)

This is called being big. This is called magnanimous. And it's not that he *is* that. He gives *himself that* in this action.

BILL

Anyway, I found that for myself I have a tendency to try to analyze behavior and try to explain things on my terms in order for me to be in a controlling advantage. I don't like to be controlled at all. And at first I felt like I was being controlled.

ERHARD

The word's "dominated."

BILL

Exactly. But what I was shown is that I can't empower anybody. I lose love, lose self-expression, and I lose freedom.

ERHARD

And you lose power. When you dominate you lose power. Love is power. Happiness is power. Self-expression is power. Power is having your self realized in the world. That's power.

BILL

Right. I find that through letting that controlling element go and accepting myself for the way I am, recognizing that I'm always already being that way, and yet being able to accept myself more, and it was especially a release to find out that things I was putting a contingency on: My happiness is not contingent upon anything.

ERHARD

That's right. We're about to talk about your happiness. You're in the right place. Keep going.

BILL

For a great part of my life I've been doing things in-order-to. Very often in-order-to. I changed jobs in-order-to; I got a college degree in-order-to. Everything I've done has been in-order-to. I've been searching a lot to find out how to be happy just being. And coming here is a... I want to thank the people who compelled me to be here. Well, influenced me, empowered me...

ERHARD

People pressured you into being here. I understand. Go on.

(*laughter*)

BILL

They empowered me and they were very magnanimous in doing so. I recognize now that there's a lot of joy in just being.

ERHARD (*to the group*)

You want to hear that. You don't want to listen to that like it's some kind of platitude. Listen to it like it's a possibility into which to live your life. Joy in just being. That's different than running your racket just being.

BILL

I came here with a lot of things on the line.

(*holding back tears*)

I had a brother who lived with me who was just killed in an automobile accident, and...

ERHARD

And that's sad. Authentically so.

BILL

Yes.

ERHARD

Not racketedly so. Racketedly so it's bullshit. Authentically it's sad—to lose your brother.

BILL

But the way I was responding to it was I wanted to get out of my immediate environment and, as I said, I've always been putting reasons and contingencies on every move in my life.

ERHARD

Hold on for a second. We've gotten a lot of people up here so you could see yourself. And a lot of that was hard to see. Seeing some of the bullshit you are is hard to see. Now you got a guy being the other end of the spectrum. A guy standing up *being* possibility. Start seeing yourself there too. I don't hear Bill giving a report. I hear Bill making a declaration. I hear

ERHARD (*continuing*)

Bill standing for what he got out of his participation in The Forum. Bill's making all this up. There's not one bit of it that's not made up. Just like when the umpire says "strike": It's a strike because he said so. It's not a report on the man's internal state. That's not the way I listen it. I listen him declaring himself, saying who he is in the matter of his participation in The Forum.

BILL

I had called a friend that I had told I was moving to Germany. I had lived there previously and was looking forward to it. My experience is not that I am going there because of anything: I get now that I choose to go there.

ERHARD

Do you understand that's just a way of speaking? But it's not mere semantics as you would call it. "I'm going there because I've chosen to go there." It's just a way of speaking. He could say that he's going there because he already made the commitment, or that it would be inconvenient to get out of going there. Or I made the commitment when I wanted to get away from being reminded that my brother died. Which one is empowering? Which one's going to give Bill the most power? The most freedom to be?

BILL

I'd like to in the future use this experience to make choices for myself and not blame them on circumstances, and take complete responsibility for my life, and to experience the joy of each day, every day of my life: to look forward to each day with a possibility; to not have my happiness contingent upon anything I create or anything that I want in life. This is really giving me the framework for, the context...

ERHARD

Because you said so. It is because he said so. When he stops saying so it won't be. Brilliant, Bill. Absolutely brilliant. Thank you for your generosity.

(*applause*)

(*to the group*)

The last step is the answer to the question, why can't you say "I love you" to somebody? Because you're too sincere to do that. And you won't say "I love you" to somebody unless you really feel it, will you? I mean, that would be terrible, wouldn't it? Saying "I love you" to people you didn't feel love for, that would be insincere, wouldn't it? That's true insincerity. Saying "I love you" to people you don't feel love for. That would be insincerity, right? That's my proof for: You *are your feelings*. You get that? I just proved to you that you are your feelings. See, what you say isn't insincere unless it's an expression of your feelings. Which means you are that over which you've got no dominion. That's what you are... I'm accusing you of being your feelings. I'm accusing you of being something over which you have nothing to say. I'm accusing you of being sincere, which I find disgusting, because that's what sincere is, sincere is identifying with the way you feel and the way you think, and the way you see things, about which you've got nothing to say. Nothing. In fact the way you see things has to do with the way you were when you were a little girl or a little boy. Anybody not clear about that? I say you can't say "I love you" to somebody without checking your feelings, because if you say "I love you" to somebody and you didn't feel like it, that would be insincere, inauthentic for you; because your love is an expression of your feelings. Who you are is your feelings. Who you are is your internal state. Anybody not clear about the accusation? Good. Now I want to talk to you about a possibility beyond that accusation, which arises in getting clear about the accusation. Anybody want to tell me they're not clear about the accusation now that they know what the consequences are? Stand up.

RALPH

Can you repeat the accusation?

ERHARD

Sure. I said you can't say "I love you" to a guy you don't know—you can't walk up to someone you don't know and say "I love you," because it's not true! It's just a bunch of words. Unless you feel love for somebody you can't say "I love you" and have it be authentic. I say that that's incontrovertible, clear cut evidence that you are your feelings. That's who you are. You are your internal state: your feelings, and your thoughts, and your attitudes. That's who you are.

RALPH

Because you can say "I love you" without authenticity...

ERHARD

Because you can't say "I love you" without feeling it.

RALPH

And be authentic.

ERHARD

And be authentic. Precisely. But when you say "authentic," you mean say yourself "honestly," right?

RALPH

Yes.

ERHARD

And if you say "I love you" to somebody and you don't feel it, that's not saying yourself honestly. Therefore it must be true that you are your feelings.

RALPH

That's where I miss it. It's that connection I miss.

Transformation as Technology

In the face of this subjection to the technological way of Being, what is there for us to do? Certainly, any action can never have as its objective the "mastery" of technology. "That would mean, after all, that man was the master of Being" ("TT" in QCT 38). Besides, as Dreyfus observes, the more we try to master technology, the more

ERHARD

Look. I say "I love you." But it's just a bunch of words, because I don't feel it.

RALPH

But when you say "I love you" and you feel it, I don't understand why that means I am my feelings.

ERHARD

Because you can't say "I love you" without feeling it.

RALPH

So who you are is just the state of what is true for you, whatever that state is. Feelings or not feelings. When they are there.

ERHARD

When they're not there, then it's not there.

RALPH

Then who you say you are is a lie. So who you are is your feelings, only when who you are, who you are saying who you are is really the feeling.

ERHARD

No, you got it too complex. This has to do with thinking. Listen: "I assert that you are your feelings." And you should say "Okay, I heard your assertion; what evidence do you have to validate that assertion?" Then I say, "My evidence is: When you say 'I love you' to somebody, it's not authentic for you unless you feel it—hence the evidence there validating my assertion that you are your feelings. Because the 'I' which you're speaking is your feelings or it's not authentic. 'I love you': 'I' refers to my feelings."

RALPH

I got it.

ERHARD

Thank you. I assert "you are your feelings." And my evidence for that assertion is you can't say "I love you" to somebody and have it be authentic if you don't feel it. What you mean by "I" is feeling. "Feeling loves you. And I am my feelings, therefore I can say 'I love you' if I feel it. Because 'I' and feeling are one. I am my feelings." This is the age of sincerity. In an age of sincerity people identify with their feelings—I don't like "identify" because it's a psychological term and this is an ontological conversation. So I don't say people identify with their feelings, I say "you are your feelings," and their mood, and their attitude, and their state of mind, and the way they see things, and what they believe in—"believe" being something like feeling it, seeing it. You don't have a special "believe" organ. "Believe" is constituted of perceptions and thinking and feeling. So I'm accusing you of being your internal state. You are your internal state because this is the age of sincerity. In an age of sincerity, what you meant is what's really important.

technological we become ("Gaining"). During his conversation with Jacob in Session Three of Day Three, Erhard said, "The attempt to get out of the trap constricts the bars of the prison. The attempt to get beyond the 'this-is-all-there-is' keeps you in the trap. Trying to get out of the prison keeps you in the prison. And *not* trying to get out of the prison keeps you in the prison."

Having sounded the alarm, Heidegger has a suggestion—not an answer, but a hint, which also is echoed in Erhard's technology of transformation in the distinction "getting off it," where we are no longer constrained to entertain a given way of Being (an already and always way of listening). "In the normal course of events," said Erhard in Session Five of Day One, "if I found out my already always listening was disempowering I would try to stop it. He [the participant in dialogue with Erhard] didn't change it. That's the big secret. Because when you change it, nothing changes." Heidegger's suggestion comes from these lines from the German poet Hölderlin: "But where danger is, grows/The saving power also" ("QCT" in BW 333). That is, at its root, technology's danger is at the same time Being's gift. Therefore, Heidegger asks, "might not an adequate look into what enframing is, as a destining of revealing, bring the upsurgence of the saving power into appearance?" ("QCT" in BW 334). Here, he specifies the conditions for such an upsurgence:

 Because the essence of technology is nothing technological, essential reflection upon technology and decisive confrontation with it must happen in a realm that is, on the one hand, akin to the essence of technology, and, on the other, fundamentally different from it. ("QCT" in BW 340)

Being given by the technological way of Being, swept up into the in-order-to, we cannot but be given entirely by "its" aims. We don't run it; it runs us. But appropriating this lostness there at the precipice that Nothing brings us to face, at the very moment we can *be* in the trap of the in-order-to, the saving power surges up. That *is* Erhard's technology of transformation.

ERHARD (*continuing*)

For example, if I really meant to do it, that's just as good for you as if I did it. You can't even tell the difference. You don't relate to people out of what they produce, you relate to people out of their sincerity. No shit. So. There's another possibility. And the other possibility is *an Age of Integrity*. That's different than the age of sincerity. In the age of integrity *you are your word*. Real simple. You just got clear that who you are is your feelings, your attitudes, your states of mind, your internal state. In the age of integrity you are your word. That means you honor your word as yourself. You've got to get that, because if you don't you won't get the rest of what I'm going to say. You've got to get it abstractly. Not conceptually, but just the way I say it. You've got to create the possibility of actually being your word. Not the *idea* of being your word. Not the option of being my word. I am my word. I've got feelings, and I've got thoughts and attitudes and a state of mind, and I have a hand. I am not my hand. I take care of my hand, I enjoy my hand, I celebrate my hand, but I'm not my hand. And I have feelings. I take care of my feelings, I enjoy my feelings, I celebrate my feelings, but I'm not my feelings, or my states of mind, or my moods any more than I'm my hand. In an age of integrity you would *be* your word and you would honor your word as your self: You wouldn't honor your feelings as your self, you would honor your word as your self. You would be your word and you would *have* feelings. Not be your feelings. You be you word and have feelings like you have a hand. You would have feelings, and have thoughts, and have an attitude, and have a state of mind, and you wouldn't be that. So instead of your life being shaped by your thoughts and feelings and attitudes, your life would be shaped by your word. Because your word would be the context in which the world occurs, and your feelings and your actions and your thoughts would be a correlate of an occurring that arose in a world created by your word. So you would be able to love somebody just by saying so. See, if I am my word and I say "I love you," I love you. And it's got power that your feelings will never have. No different than feeling "I love you." See, if who you are is feeling, feeling "I love you" is the same as if who you are is your word saying "I love you." The same except that being your feelings will never have the power that being your word has, because you've got something to say about your word, and ain't got shit to say about what you feel. When you start to honor your word as yourself, live as your word, be your word, I don't mean some silly moral horseshit about keeping your word. You see this is only a possibility: You can't struggle toward this; you can't set this up as a goal; you can't try to achieve this; you can't pray for this. You've got to live in the possibility of this, because that's the only way it will work. To live in the possibility, to live from the possibility of being your word, and having your feelings, and your thoughts, and your state of mind, and having your attitude, et cetera. It gives you power to love people, rather than have love for them. It makes your word kind of sacred, and it gives you access to the sacred. Being happy is a sacred state. See, if you are your word, you can say "I am happy" and you are happy. And it ain't a bunch of fucking words: It's your self. It's no different than reporting on your internal state. If what you are is your internal state, then to say "I'm happy," you've got to have an internal state called happy. But if you're your word, you're happy because you say you're happy: I am happy." Your feelings and your attitudes and your state of mind and your thoughts and your hand start to line up with your word. I don't assess my feelings. I don't address my feelings to find out who I am. I don't look at my hand to find out who I am either. I also don't look at my nose or my feet to find out who I am. I don't look at my feelings to find out who I am. And my hand lines up with who I am and so do my feelings, and so do my thoughts. So I'm leaving you at this juncture of The Forum with the possibility of honoring your word as

> **In an age of integrity you would be your word and you would honor your word as your self: You wouldn't honor your feelings as your self, you would honor your word as your self. You would be your word and you would have feelings. Not be your feelings. You be you word and have feelings like you have a hand. You would have feelings, and have thoughts, and have an attitude, and have a state of mind, and you wouldn't be that. So instead of your life being shaped by your thoughts and feelings and attitudes, your life would be shaped by your word.**

ERHARD (*continuing*)

your self. Honoring your word as your self. Honoring your word as your self. Okay, speaking about one's word, and all the acknowledgments.

(*pausing*)

If I gave everyone in the room who's awake an opportunity to speak, we would all thank each other. The other people who participated in The Forum gave you an enormous gift, one of great generosity and magnanimity. You did not pay for The Forum. You did not. The Forum you just participated in was a gift from the people who assisted here—to you. Not to you as a personality because they didn't know you personally. It was a gift to the possibility that you are. This thing wouldn't exist without them. There were one hundred and twenty to one hundred and thirty people who volunteered their time and their intelligence and their ability and their energy and their humanity so that we could do this Forum together. They got here before you or I did, and were here after you and I left. You wouldn't have even gotten enrolled if it weren't for the assistants. And you know the kind of courage it took to enroll you. And the deep profound humanity that it took to put up with your shit. So I wanted to give you an opportunity to acknowledge the assistants.

(*long, loud standing ovation*)

Thirty-three staff members of WE&A from different centers put this together. If you get a chance to be around staff members, I recommend that you take that opportunity. Something rubs off. You know, they are ordinary people like you and me. They're not something extraordinary. But what they've chosen to do with their lives... what gives you your life—listen up—what gives you your life gives you: you. And what they've chosen to do with their lives gives them something, and you ought to get some of that. And the way to get some of that is be around them. One of the things you can do is nurture them and support them. That'd be all right. The other thing you could do is assist with them. Hang out and watch them. I'd like to give us an opportunity to acknowledge those thirty-three staff members who created this Forum for us.

(*long applause*)

Erhard at this point invited participants to go to church with him on New Years' Eve.

ERHARD

I'm inviting you to go to church tomorrow night, New Year's Eve. Some of you need to go to church on New Year's Eve.

(*laughter*)

It's an Episcopal church, but there will be a rabbi (a she), a priest, a Zen monk, whatever you're up to you'll be all right. You know, I spent a lot of time in church because my grandmother got me up on Sunday morning and made me go to church every Sunday. After a while I kind of liked it a little bit. I served on the alter and swung the incense. I wrote a little bit when I went to school, and got an award for something I wrote, and the best thing I wrote was about my experience in church. But let me tell you something: I've never had the kind of experience with church like I've had at the service I'm inviting you to. It's extraordinary. Whatever your experience has been, I promise this is worth doing, and I'm not hustling you to go to church, or I am, whatever you like. The last thing for me: Be at one of the seven evening sessions and get all that shit out of your head about my reasons for asking you. The other thing is that there is a lot of talk about me, and most of it is bullshit. I'm not worth all that talk, but there are some things I am worth.

Here Erhard told a story about an "award" he had received from a professor of English at the University of New Delhi—a Professor Manmohan—who had traveled with him in India. Normally, Manmohan was very quiet. But when he'd talk with Erhard about Erhard's work, he'd always ask when Erhard was going to bring it to India.

ERHARD
Eventually we did do the work in India, and Manmohan had participated in the first program we did. One of the things he got, he got the possibility of an extraordinary relationship with his father. Manmohan had a good relationship with his father, but particularly in the Indian culture, it doesn't matter how old you are, you are always your father's son. Manmohan took the train back to his father's village and they sat and talked for hours, and they cried together, and everything was wonderful, and opened up, and all that stuff. And Manmohan said, "Werner, my father asked me 'Son, what happened to you?' And he told him about the work, and his father said, 'Oh, I understand, son: you found a guru.'" By the way, "you found a guru" is not an insult in Indian culture. In this country it's an insult. You're in good shape if you found your guru in India. Manmohan said to me, "You know Werner, I had to think about it, because I had just finished being really straight with my father, and I really wanted to be straight with him and answer his question. I told my father 'No, father, I didn't find a guru. I found a friend.'" That's the most important award I've ever gotten. It's the only one I want. And what I can promise you is that I am your friend and I will always be here for you. I'll always be for the possibility you are, and if I never see you again, I'll still be your friend for the rest of our time. So, if somebody asks you: "You went to The Forum with Werner, who's he?" You say "He's a friend of mine" and you'll be telling them the truth. Thank you very much, and good night.

Erhard left the room through the opening in the curtains at the back of the platform, to a standing ovation.

KIPP (*walking up onto the platform*)
Okay. On we go, into the wee hours of the morning! Does anybody want to go home?

(*cheers of "no"*)
Okay. Let's welcome the visitors here in the room.

(*applause*)

Kipp then introduced himself to the visitors (those who have completed The Forum sometime in the past and who had shared that experience with those taking the current Forum), as well as Wes, and a long, standing ovation ensued.

KIPP

Thank you! I'd like to give some of you in The Forum an opportunity to say something to the people who came in to complete The Forum with us tonight.

Kipp proceeded to select a participant to stand and share, and selected new participants who had raised their hands as soon as one finished speaking.

SALLY (*moved*)

Thank you Roger, very very much, for sticking with me and being quite a person, a big person. And your contributions to me, I value them, they are very important. This experience has allowed me to get off it. Quite a bit. And you know I'm on it. That's a lot. That's a lot. Now I won't have to spend so much time defending myself. I know there's nothing to be afraid of. Thanks!

KIPP (*to applause*)

Well done. Thank you!

CIARLA

Ken introduced me to The Forum about five years ago, and at that time I didn't take the opportunity like I'm doing now. Thank you very much for having me participate in this work, and I want you to know that I love you. I'm looking very much forward—we just got engaged a couple months ago—and I'm very much looking forward to the rest of our lives together. Thanks!

KIPP (*to applause*)

Thank you!

PAUL

There are three woman in my life who are here, and I am madly in love with each of them: my mother, my future mother-in-law, and my fiancée. These three women stand for me, no matter what. They have a commitment to me being great, and I love them for it. I can say out of this work, and I've been participating for a while, I know my relationship with Becky will last forever out of just us saying so. Not out of how I feel, because I don't feel like it a lot. It's really just out of our commitment, and our stand together, the possibility of this work and the difference we can make, just like giving it away. And I just really want to say to you three that I love you, and thanks!

KIPP (*to applause*)

Very nice!

BERNICE (*very moved*)
This is the first time I've gotten up to share. I don't know if I can make it without crying. I want to acknowledge someone I haven't acknowledged in about ten years of my life. And that's my brother. I love you. He introduced me to The Forum and I fought him every step of the way. One of my rackets is that people are setting me up to fail, and I had thought: "If you set me up here, I will never forgive you!"

(*laughter*)
But you have given me more with this Forum, than I've ever gotten from anyone in my life. And I love you so much. I also want to acknowledge and thank Jane. Everything she said, I felt so deeply, and there are no words to describe my gratitude. But, I just want to say, I think you are a truly beautiful person, you have the courage to stand up and tell people, and I owe you for that. Thank you.

KIPP (*to applause*)
Very well said!

VICTOR
I don't know where they are in the room but my brother and my mother are here and I take my hat off to you, and I want to say that I love the both of you. You are my family, and are pretty much the most important thing in my life. I thank you for giving me the chance to see who I was, who the hell I really was. I love you. And I thank all the people that shared. I saw a little of my self in each and every one of you. And now I know who that is and I have to accept and be with that I'm a human being.

KIPP (*to applause*)
Well said! Thank you!

MIC
This is the first time I've gotten up to share, and I was pretty sure I'd get through the whole Forum without having to. I want to thank the people who I've had conversations with, each one is an exceptional person. And I want to thank my girlfriend, who was the first person to introduce me to The Forum and basically put up with all my shit. I just want to say thank you, and I love you, and I will tell you that in private, but right now I want everyone to hear that also. I love you.

KIPP
Beautiful!

ROB
I didn't expect you to call on me! I did est back in 1974, and it was great. A lot of things happened in between, and everybody has said what I want to say. I just feel at a loss for words. I want to express my gratitude for you Kipp. When you first came out, I thought, "who is this?"

KIPP (*to laughter*)

That's what I thought when I first came out.

ROB

After the second session, I was "this guy's incredible." Even though I've only talked to a few of you here, I love you all. I love who you are and I love who I am. I am comfortable in my own presence. Thank you!

KIPP

Thank you very much.

STEPHAN (*wearing clerical attire*)

I want to thank you Kipp, Wes, and Werner, of course, but you and Wes in a very special way, because you were with me in a very special way. I've been complete with my parents and my sister, who are dead now. And the completion I got is a great joy. And now out of this I get to pray to my parents. They are now with me, to empower me. That's an immense gift. The other gift I want to acknowledge for you out of the whole process of the empty and meaningless and being down in the shadow of the Valley of Death, you know, that's our territory...

(*laughter*)

I want you to know that I put on my meaning suit. This is a meaning suit, full of meaning. What I want to thank you for is being able to live again my priesthood. And I declare that I am a renewed priest, and available for the transformation of people everywhere, the people especially who are in religion, and if I can be selfish, in my own church, but for all people. God bless you and thank you for that.

KIPP (*to applause*)

Thank you very much!

(*walking back up to the platform*)

So, in the interest of sleep, we'll go on and what I'd like to get created a little bit for you is our Forum Evening Sessions coming up next week. And The Forum Evening Sessions are designed to complete The Forum, and there are two aspects of the completion of The Forum. One of the aspects is contributing this. As many of you said since being here, it took a lot to get you here, and it's now an opportunity for you to contribute the possibility of The Forum in everybody's life in your life. That's one aspect of The Forum Evening Session. And the other aspect of The Forum Evening Session is designed to create the third part of The Forum. The first part is about unconcealing the being of human being. The second part is about creating the possibility of being for human being, and the third part of The Forum is discovering your life as a commitment to possibility. So The Forum Evening Session could be said to be about the rest of your life. And it really is the completion of that.

Kipp proceeded to review the logistics and procedure of the evening, including a play-by-play recounting of what will happen, including having an opportunity to share during the evening session, right at the beginning, when The Forum Leader presents the opportunity to share.

KIPP (*continuing*)
...and I invite you to not hold back, to create for yourself and the people that you have there, having possibility in your life and in their lives... Now, I'm going to tell you everything you need to know to share The Forum effectively and have your friends and family do The Forum. It's very simple and it's very straightforward. So if you're committed to sharing The Forum and having people at your Forum Evening Session and having them register, the first thing is this: Do not sell The Forum. Simply be straight with the people in your lives. Say whatever The Forum is for you. Whether you think it's great or whether you're not sure, whether you're confused, or if you think it was stupid, or whether you are totally enthusiastic with a thousand breakthroughs. Whatever it truly is for you, authentically share that. Don't sell The Forum. Because what people listen to is not what you say. People listen to who you are being. The second thing is, it serves the people who you are bringing for them to know there will be an opportunity for them to register, so they should bring their schedules... and they should bring money with them. Be straight with people. That's what works. The last thing is this: When you walk out of here and share The Forum, that is, share your self, you will be speaking into the listening of the world. You already know what that listening is. When you share yourself, people will think it's a racket, it's a cult... When you speak, people will have those thoughts. Everybody clear? People will have those thoughts.

(*Kipp grabs a tissue and holds it up; laughter*)
Don't get stuck with their thoughts. Don't get stuck with your own. What there is to do is simple. Okay?

Kipp grabbed the dictionary from a table on the platform, and he asked a participant to stand up on the stage with him.

KIPP (*addressing the participant*)
When sharing The Forum with anyone, what's the worst thing they could say to you?

ED
"I think you're stupid and weird."

KIPP
So this dictionary represents "I think you're stupid and weird." Resist it.

Kipp light-heartedly attacks Ed over and over with the dictionary repeating "I think you're stupid and weird" with each attack, and Ed deflects each attack with upraised hands.

KIPP (*to the group*)
For the most part that's what you call communication.

(*laughter*)
Here is what to do when people say that stuff to you.

(*to Ed*)
This time take the dictionary.

(*as Kipp attacks once more*)
"I think you're stupid and weird."

(*Ed takes the dictionary away*)
That's your job. So when people say that stuff, your job is to be with them. Chocolate: choose. When you get a whole big pile of dictionaries, we turn around and put them down, and say, what else you got? Peacocks are these gorgeous birds. Do you know what peacocks eat? They eat poison off the ground. If you want to make a difference in people's lives, you've got to be willing to eat their poison. Thank you Ed.

(*Ed sits to applause*)
And, you're going to get stuck with some dictionaries. You're going to notice in the middle of a conversation with somebody, all of a sudden, you'll be resisting what they are saying. You notice that in the middle of a conversation, you can say, "I got hooked. Here's what I want to say." I invite you not to stop. You can make a real contribution to the people in your lives this weekend. Another thing: Whatever emergencies come up for you, whatever can normally stop you in life, don't get stopped. Be at your Forum Evening Session, and complete The Forum for yourself.

The fourth day of The Forum ended.

END OF DAY FOUR INTERVAL

CONCLUSION

Technology of Transformation

Two fundamental questions have guided our inquiry that has, at last, brought us to bring to language Erhard's technology of transformation as we have witnessed it in the dialogue of The Forum and in our ruminations that have brought Heidegger's and Erhard's thinking face-to-face: *What are the foundations of Erhard's rhetorical and ontological rhetoric? How does the dialogic rhetorical structure of The Forum achieve ontological transformation?*

First, *what are the foundations of Erhard's rhetorical and ontological rhetoric?*

We have sought to show that both Heidegger's philosophy and Erhard's rhetoric are founded upon the existence and nature of what Heidegger calls the *ontological difference*, the difference between beings and Being. Both projects attempt to span this difference and to develop a *language through which beings can speak and communicate Being*. The Forum may be seen as the practical, rhetorical development of Heidegger's thought in this area; Erhard appears to have taken certain difficult Heideggerian ideas and made them accessible in a profound way.

It is *not* our thesis, however, that Heidegger's thought is foundational to Erhard's work as a whole. According to Erhard, his project was generated by an experience of ontological transformation which he underwent in 1971; his subsequent work has been an evolving attempt to communicate that transformation experience. His use of Heideggerian terms and concepts in this effort began just a few years prior to the time The Forum replaced the *est* Training in 1985, and indeed, it may be argued that this encounter was crucial in this development of Erhard's work, which development continues to this day in Landmark Worldwide and in his new work with speaking the Being of leadership. In any event, while drawing upon Heidegger's ontological language to express his own transformation, Erhard has simultaneously extended the communicative possibilities of that Heideggerian language. That is, he has shown how a dialogue with Being might look in lived experience and what its effect might be for those who participate in such an unfolding ontological dialogue.

Thus the foundation of Erhard's rhetoric may be seen to be its relationship with Being, and that *where ontological language speaks from* determines its power: that in order to speak a language which communicates Being, one must speak *from an ontological location*, a clearing, which provides access to Being.

The second question asks: *how does the dialogic rhetorical structure of The Forum achieve ontological transformation?*

The Forum as an instance of *ontological rhetoric*—that is, *rhetoric which communicates strategically so as to produce a shift in its audience's way of Being*. What are the central functional characteristics of ontological rhetoric, as they have been developed in this book? Fundamental to ontological rhetoric is the communication of an *unsaid* element of language. That is, both Heidegger and Erhard hold that Being is a *region* or *horizon* which pervades and contextualizes language, but which cannot itself be articulated. Nevertheless, while Being must remain unspoken, it can nevertheless be brought to presence by means of a certain kind of speaking; Heidegger proposed that a *dialogue* which is conducted in a certain way can function to bring Being to presence for dialogic partners. Therefore, The Forum is an attempt to design and enact a dialogue which brings Being to presence *as an unspoken element of a spoken conversation*.

In order for Being to be brought to presence, an *ontological shift* must occur, a transformation in the way human beings *conceive* themselves. According to Heidegger, the presence of Being requires a *clearing*; in our current way of thinking and being, however, the clearing which human beings are is obscured by the normative self-structure which we call *identity*, or the "they" self and its current technological way of Being. Therefore, much of The Forum is devoted to the *deconstruction of identity and its in-order-to,* so that participants can begin to see themselves *as a different ontological entity*: a clearing for Being from which it becomes possible to appropriate one's inauthenticity. Furthermore, from this event new possibilities for Being arise, and as they are languaged, the world as it occurs transforms and takes us along with it. This process of ontological deconstruction and invention is posited in The Forum as a process that occurs entirely in language: The Forum is a dialogic enactment of Heidegger's thesis that "language is the house of Being." It creates the conditions for ontological transformation by engaging participants in the speaking of a *new language*, a language grounded in certain ontological assumptions (Erhard's *distinctions*, the figures of speech and thought which comprise his technology of transformation). During the four days of this 1989 Forum, as participants engage in the dialogue and speak its language, they gradually come to *dwell in* the ontological assumptions in which that language of distinctions is grounded, ontological assumptions which have become available as an *unsaid* element of the dialogue, and which produce the ontological shift which is The Forum's goal.

The strategic dialogue in which this process occurs is from time to time characterized by aggressiveness and intrusiveness on Erhard's part, and by frequent resistance on the part of his dialogic partners. Heidegger has pointed out that any attempt to analyze Being constantly has the character of doing violence to the complacency of the everyday interpretation. Thus what occurs in The Forum *is* the violation of the everyday interpretation, as identity (the "they" self) is deconstructed and Being is wrested from unconcealment. In the process, Erhard's rhetoric sometimes seems intrusive, and the dialogue which it stimulates is often combative; yet during the four days of The Forum the results of the dialogue are dramatic.

Central to Erhard's achievement is his rhetorical development of two Heideggerian ideas. The first is the complex and elusive notion of *appropriation*, which addresses the central paradox of the being-Being relationship: that human beings can attain ontological freedom only by recognizing and allowing their fundamental subservience to the play of Being. The second is the encounter with the *Nothing*, the emptiness and meaningless correlative to the mood of anxiety. Both of these ideas are communicated, in The Forum's persistent and reiterative ontological rhetoric, so that they can be apprehended as *ontological insights*: that is, so that they produce a result in the participants' way of Being by virtue of discovering it for themselves, rather than simply being understood conceptually. Through the reiterated dialogic communication of these ontological insights, participants in The Forum's dialogue come increasingly to *dwell in* the ontological assumptions given by those insights, and then act in their lives with freedom to be in the very circumstances that would otherwise appear as constraints.

Embedded in both of these Heideggerian ideas, and basic to The Forum's ontological rhetoric, is the figure of *reflexivity*. That is, for both Heidegger and Erhard, what is necessary for the creation of a clearing for Being is that human beings *turn around and see themselves as they are*. Thus The Forum is fundamentally the enactment of a reflexive turn, a rhetorical figure *par excellence*: participants in The Forum, by virtue of its technology of transformation, speak a language designed to reveal them as they are, so that what may be simultaneously revealed, within and beyond the way they are, is their own largest possibility.

We conclude that Erhard's work is both a *manifestation* of the metaphysical/technological tradition and a *new appropriation* of that tradition. Therefore, on the Heideggerian view, it is an appropriate venue for a reflexive thinking which can step back, and in taking such a step, to reach beyond the current technological paradigm by reaching *through* that paradigm. The technology of The Forum is putting-into-use putting itself to use in order to turn and see itself face-to-face. It is calculative, technological thinking calculating its own deconstruction, reflexion radicalized for the appropriation of its own essential nature. As a dialogic, rhetorical project, it extends the communicative possibilities of Heidegger's thinking, and makes the event of appropriation, and the freeing release which it occasions, available to an audience which Heidegger's work is likely never to reach.

AFTERWORD

WERNER ERHARD, MARTIN HEIDEGGER, AND THE POLITICS OF BEING

By Michael E. Zimmerman

Michael E. Zimmerman was a philosophy professor at Tulane University and the University of Colorado at Boulder before retiring in 2015. Author of four books, and more than a hundred articles and book chapters, Zimmerman's research interests include environmental philosophy, Heidegger, Nietzsche, Buddhism, and integral theory. His books include *Eclipse of the Self* (1981), *Heidegger's Confrontation with Modernity* (1990), *Contesting Earth's Future* (1994), and *Integral Ecology* (2009).

Reading Bruce Hyde and Drew Kopp's insightful book, *Speaking Being,* has been a remarkable journey, one that brings me back to the transformation I experienced when I took The *est* Training in December 1981. During the Training, I discovered a profound and wholly unanticipated connection between the work of Werner Erhard and that of Martin Heidegger. In spring 1982, I would find myself writing a philosophical appraisal of the Training at Erhard's request. This appraisal and related conversations were two of many factors that eventuated in The Forum, which rolled out in 1985.

Erhard developed the key elements of what would become The Forum (and later, The Landmark Forum) long before he knew anything about Heidegger. The point of *Speaking Being* is not to show that Erhard's ideas *derive* from Heidegger's, but rather that there is a remarkable affinity between ideas that the two thinkers arrived at *independently*. The first question I will explore at length is this: Do the remarkable parallels between the work of Erhard and Heidegger confirm the validity of their respective findings?

Some autobiographical comments will help to contextualize my answer. Although I eventually wrote two books and dozens of scholarly articles about Heidegger's philosophy, my first encounter with it was an abject failure. In spring 1968, as a senior philosophy major in college, I took a seminar on *Being and Time* (1927), Heidegger's most important work. I was feeling confident because the previous semester I had apparently managed to make a little sense of Alfred North Whitehead's *Process and Reality* (1927), a notoriously difficult text. The title of Heidegger's book attracted me, as did its cover, with large white letters standing against a black background. The seminar was over my head, although I was hardly alone in my confusion. Little secondary literature in English was available on *Being and Time*, which had been translated only a few years earlier. After struggling to about page 180, I realized that I had understood nothing about what was going on—especially not how important "nothing" was to prove in *Being and Time*.

As a graduate student at Tulane University, I gave *Being and Time* another try, this time in a seminar taught by Edward G. Ballard, who later became my dissertation director. In that seminar, I began to chip away at Heidegger's conceptual *massif*. Later, as a Fulbright-Hays Fellow in Belgium in 1972–73, I worked on my PhD dissertation, "The Concept of the Self in Heidegger's *Being and Time*." Ballard was enamored of Plato's thinking because it combined philosophical depth with the possibility of transformation for the one who engages wholeheartedly with the Platonic dialectic. Such a transformation, so Ballard maintained, is necessary to understand what Plato was pointing at.

Gradually, I concluded that the same was true for making sense of *Being and Time*.[1] (And later I found undergoing a transformative experience was also required to truly understand Erhard's *est* Training program and later The Forum program.) To understand the book meant doing more than writing intelligible sentences about its often difficult and controversial ideas. I needed to undergo the anxiety (*Angst*) that discloses human existence as neither a body nor even a mind, but instead as the temporal clearing or openness in which things can manifest themselves and in that sense can "be." Surrendering to the mood of anxiety, however, is akin to a death experience, from which we ordinarily flee. Heidegger's concept of authentic human existence, at least so I argued in *Eclipse of the Self,* amounts to the following.[2] One must own up to the fact that one has been thrown into the world as the mortal, temporal openness required for entities to reveal themselves in various ways. Anxiety invites us to suspend momentarily our absorption into the average, everyday way of existing (for Erhard, this includes what he would call "running one's racket"), so that otherwise hidden possibilities—specific to our own capacities and situations—can reveal themselves. Heidegger insisted, however, as does Erhard, that taking a stand upon one's own finite possibilities is not only unusual, but also difficult to sustain. We tend to fall back again and again into the tranquillizing mode of everyday life, in which there is supposedly nothing really new or important to be discovered.

One day in the early 1970s, while a grad student at Tulane, I had a full-blown anxiety moment that began as I was walking through the University Center. All of a sudden, the people, furniture, floor and ceiling began pulling away from me. Everyone and everything became utterly meaningless, insignificant, and pointless. My projects, self-understanding, goals and objectives—these, too, fell away, leaving only bare, unmotivated, directionless awareness. The world had become empty and meaningless. After a while, things started to regain their significance, such that I was able to find my way around once again. This experience confirmed for me much of what Heidegger had said about anxiety in *Being and Time* and elsewhere.

The occasion for another important insight occurred in early January 1978 on a dark and stormy night. At the time, I was suffering from the flu, which seemed like a symptom of my unhappy personal situation. Feeling miserable while holed up in my tiny apartment, I heard a knock at the door. A friend whom I rarely saw stood there, shielding himself from the rain. Presenting me with a book, he said: "Here, Michael. I think you should read this." With that, he departed, leaving me with a copy of Baba Ram Dass's book, *Be Here Now*.[3] Formerly Richard Alpert, a psychology professor at Harvard, Ram Dass (along with colleague Timothy Leary) had been dismissed from the university for turning students onto LSD. Traveling to India, where he found his guru, Ram Dass discovered that various meditative and yogic practices could generate the non-attachment and non-duality associated with enlightenment—without using drugs. *Be Here Now* was so influential because Ram Dass brilliantly explained major aspects of Indian teachings in ways that could resonate with Western readers.

Years earlier, I had seen *Be Here Now* at a bookstore, but I had dismissed it as pop psychology masquerading as Eastern religion. I had little patience for either, especially Asian thought to which my way was barred by a regrettable ethnocentrism. That this very book would appear unbidden in the midst of a personal crisis persuaded me to read it that very night. In the wee hours I experienced something like *kensho*, the Zen term for an initial awakening.[4] I realized with unprecedented conviction that my life was misguided, even though by the standards of most people, including academics, my life was successful. Gripped by fear, I had long tried to protect myself in ways that provoked unnecessary suffering in myself and in others. Attempting to satisfy various cravings, I had sometimes acted in ways that did not make me feel proud. Suddenly, Søren Kierkegaard's dictum, "The specific quality of despair is not knowing that one is desperate," struck me like a thunderbolt. That night, I resolved to become a Zen monk, thereby supposing that doing so would somehow bring me happiness.

First, of course, I needed to learn how to meditate. Asian traditions often speak of the tyranny of the "monkey mind," the relentless interior chatter that jumps from one topic to the next. My everyday experience was filled by neurotic chatter. All the time I was thinking that it was I who was thinking, even though perhaps it would be better to say that the thoughts were having me! After many years of meditation practice, I finally learned how to silence the interior voice upon command. In the summer of 1979, I spent five weeks as a guest student at Green Gulch Farm (near Muir Woods outside of San Francisco) and at Tassajara Zen Mountain Retreat Center, both of which were run by the San Francisco Zen Center. Arising at 4 am to meditate every day (except Sundays, when we could sleep in until 6!) was challenging, in part by the emotional torment provoked by being apart from my girlfriend, whom I eventually married. Clearly, I had a lot of work ahead of me.

In February 1980, I took part in a seven-day *sesshin* at the London Zen Center. This was very serious business. Run by a well-known Rinzai Zen monk from Kyoto, the *sesshin* required us to sit cross-legged for 40 minutes, *sixteen times per day.* Each day was divided into four sessions of four 40-minute sittings. During the evening of the third day, pain in my left knee had become so overwhelming that I was exhausted. There was no way out, of course, because if you *move your body* in a Zen *sesshin*, you might as well go home. Having held the pain at arm's length for as long as possible, I finally surrendered to it. My expectation was that I would be obliterated, leaving a smoking pile of rubble on the *zafu* (meditation cushion). Amazingly, however, the pain vanished, and was replaced by very intense sensations that had no pain valence, so long as I did not introduce any temporal distinctions, such as "This has lasted so long. . ." or "How many more minutes. . . ." Upon introducing such distinctions, the excruciating pain would return, only to abate when I dove ever more deeply into it, embracing and experiencing each subtle and not so subtle aspect of it. This was an astonishing discovery, which encouraged me to explore knee pain far earlier during a later ten-day meditation retreat in Barre, Massachusetts. By letting the sensations show up just as they occurred instant-by-instant, without telling a story about them or representing them in some other way, they showed up *as they were* rather than *as how I had been representing them*. By going ever more deeply into the source of pain, I eventually experienced the disappearance of self and even space/time, leaving nothing at all, which I later interpreted as what Heidegger called the "clearing," the no-thingness that allows all contents of awareness to reveal themselves. Those contents can include the multiple stories we make up about what shows up, but I discovered the difference between the sheer showing up (Being) of contents, on the one hand, and my representations/stories about them, on the other.

During the Zen *sesshin,* each of us had a nightly meeting with the Zen master, a remarkable human being. I was typically a basket case when climbing the stairs to his room, where he sat cross-legged. Usually, he just looked at me for a few moments—without saying a word—before ringing the dismissal bell. I hoped that the smile on his face was benevolent! Whatever shreds of self-assurance I may have had before climbing the steps—"After all, a man is justified in being tired after such rigorous meditation!"—were removed by his penetrating gaze. I had a long way to go before I could ever be like him. Nevertheless, his extraordinary mode of Being showed me *what is possible for a human being*. I didn't have to be this neurotic, self-absorbed, worried person.

In December 1981, I took the *est* Training in a suburb of New Orleans. Given the previous course of my life, which included writing about Heidegger's concept of authentic existence, practicing Zen meditation and hatha yoga, reading widely in Eastern and Western spiritual traditions, and above all still wallowing in ignorance, I was a prime candidate for what the Training had to offer. It allowed for the possibility of seeing that one's "personality" is deeply tied up with one's "racket," the particular way in which one defends one's identity by making oneself right and/or others wrong, or more generally, constantly justifying oneself. To experience being

free from my racket, I first had to become aware of its structure (that is, the "payoffs" and the gratification that seems to come from the payoffs of my racket, and on the other hand the "cost" of my rackets to the quality of my life), and second I had to identify with it, to embrace it (make it my own). Paradoxically, this move was a necessary condition for the next step, distinguishing myself *from* my racket. In doing so, a palpable sense of freedom spontaneously arose. What had been my subjectivity, my racket, now became a mere object in a wider awareness.

As the Training progressed, I began to conclude that this wider awareness is an instance of what Heidegger had in mind by the "clearing," the openness that constitutes human existence. For Heidegger, authentic human existing means letting this clearing disclose entities as they are, rather than as how they show up through one's projections, stories, and self-justifying assertions. At one point, in reply to the Trainer's query about what we were beginning to realize, I raised my hand to say: "Who we really are is no-thing! We are not things, not identities, not personalities, not emotions—we are the clearing in which all these can arise." Even the distinction that we are no-thing, so I came to realize, arises *within* the clearing. As Heidegger would put it, we don't own the clearing; instead, the clearing "owns" us so that things can show up and thus "be." I would later discover that while I was in that 1981 *est* Training, Werner Erhard was exploring some of the ways in which Heidegger's thought overlapped with and could grant greater force to the ideas embodied in the Training.

Not long ago, when I was conversing with Erhard, he referred to this famous phrase from Heidegger's essay "What Is Metaphysics?" (1929): We are "held out into the nothing."[5] Erhard maintains that The Forum is designed to allow for this experience, to be held out into the nothing, that is, into the *emptiness and meaninglessness* of existence. Without first-person experience of this emptiness, people continue to cling to the subjective narratives that give rise to their rackets, as well as other automatic instances of inauthenticity. Having become aware of their rackets and their narrative-based identities, participants can notice the clearing—understood not only as the open space needed for things to show up and thus "to be," but also as the opening for a possible future in which things might be *other* than what would otherwise be predictable; indeed, a possible future in which people at times might make choices *not* dictated by their rackets. The *experience* of being held out into the nothing, into meaninglessness, is necessary for disclosing the *ontological* event called the clearing.

In our conversation, Erhard affirmed that his profound encounter with the emptiness and meaninglessness of his own identity did not lead—contrary to expectation—to moral irresponsibility and nihilism. In fact, prior to that encounter, he had acted irresponsibly in ways that occasioned considerable suffering on the part of others, including members of his own family. He reported that by wiping away the significance of his story, he was left only with the *ontological* clearing. At this moment, what showed up was the mess that he had created, but without any story about it, as well as the authentic obligation to clean things up. Erhard told me that in cleaning things up with his family, he told them he was not apologizing to them, because that would somehow soften the raw fact of what he had done. So long as he *was* his story, his self-justifying interior narrative, the suffering he had provoked remained blunted. He could not *let others be* who they were; instead, they were reduced to pawns in his own game. Unthinking identification with his story stood in the way of allowing others to *be* beyond the limits imposed by their own narratives. This recognition contributed to his decision to initiate the *est* Training.

What it means to share in the est Training and The Forum

Most of the activity in the Training involved *sharing* by participants. Trainers (later, Forum leaders) were there to help participants recognize their rackets, their ways of manipulating self and others for ends that are often not understood. As Hyde and Kopp have demonstrated so well in their book, the inter-subjective component was crucial to the success of The Forum, as it was for the *est* Training. The centrality of sharing in the Training helps to explain why it could take people so far so fast, when compared to other avenues to transformation. Over the course of many hours, participants listen to each other describe a similar mode of Being-in-the-world: operating so as to promote survival often at the expense of others and their own quality of life. It is easier to recognize these inauthentic ways of being in others, but having done so leaves me with the possibility of seeing them in myself. The Training and later The Forum (and The Landmark Forum) allowed over two million people to reliably experience liberation from their rackets, from the compulsion to be right (often at the expense of others) and from the need to constantly self-justify.

In the Training that I took—and as in the 1989 Forum recounted in this book—the dialogue opened up, and soon revealed that the participants were frustrated, suffering, confused, and hiding their pettiness, all because of what the Forum leader called their "rackets." At first most people scoffed at the idea that *they* were running (or were run by) a racket. Instead, they were amazed at the ridiculous things that *other* apparently accomplished people were saying about conducting their lives. Gradually, however, the courage exhibited by certain participants in their honest

sharing shifted the mood in the room to one of utmost seriousness regarding what was being disclosed. Increasingly, we began to support one another in the sharing process. We came to recognize that, perhaps for the first time, we were speaking frankly with others about what really matters in life, and about the obstacles that we had placed in the path of living aligned with what really matters.

I recall one particular moment when I experienced this for myself. It was on the Saturday afternoon of the second weekend of the Training that I took in 1981, when participants were asked to take part in a "milling" exercise (which is not found in The Forum or The Landmark Forum). The ballroom had been cleared of chairs. In the large open space, we were asked to walk slowly around, making eye contact with others, but not engaging in conversation. We were simply to witness each other. By this point, many of us had already shared our stories. Otherwise successful, educated, and capable people had started to "come clean" about their rackets. We were in touch with the vast pain, heartache, sorrow, and frustration brought about by our treachery, lying, cowardice, and perhaps above all self-deception. Even as I write about this, I am brought back into that extraordinary moment, when waves of compassion began arising within me. I had never experienced anything like it. Finally understanding the mechanical, unavoidable aspect of so much human behavior, I also began to forgive others, and myself. We are thrown into a very difficult situation, we self-conscious human beings. Doing our best to survive and prosper, we sometimes act in ways that later haunt us.

The courageous sharing that occurred in the Training allowed me and others to see the truth of the Hindu saying, *Tat tvam asi*, "That thou art." The poor devil breaking down across the room, the other person who had made such a mess of her life even while being so "successful"—now I could see *that person is me*, just running a different racket! One by one, people began to realize that we are all in this together. Run by fear, we employ survival strategies, often developed before we became self-conscious. By the time we are adults, we are deeply patterned to act in ways that protect us and that justify us, such that everything we do is "in order to" promote our self-defending project, whereas we experience little if anything in and for itself. People *want* to act nobly, generously, courageously, and honestly, but doing so is difficult and rare, which is why we admire people on those occasions when they *can* act in such ways. Seeing how compulsive the actions of other people are, participants gain insight into how circumscribed their own lives are as a result of fear and anxiety, and see that furthermore, no amount of achievement, success, sex, drugs, and rock and roll will "fix me." It is sometimes said that people are above all committed to "Being right and looking good," but in the Training invidious distinctions between self and other melted away, without any sense of boundary violation. There arose a higher level of "we-ness" that respected difference, but that no longer allowed difference to create an insuperable barrier to being together in the world.

The Forum hammers home the idea that there is no way to escape the racket that constitutes one's basic way of Being-in-the-world, and that people do what they do because they have little freedom in the matter. However, perhaps the greatest realization generated in The Forum, as in the Training, is that despite all this, people are *more* than their rackets, more than their fear-driven habitual stances and practices. Rather, we are the clearing for possibility, as Erhard suggests in the transcript of the 1989 Forum. What makes the clearing for possibility available is what Erhard calls "being authentic about one's inauthenticity," where we own up to—take responsibility for—the fact that we compulsively "run rackets." Such resolute embrace of my own inauthenticity unexpectedly allows for a taste of freedom, in which a new possibility for action can show up. Such action is motivated not "in order to" improve my standing, but instead arises solely for the sake of handling what a given situation calls for, as an end in itself.

During the 1970s and 1980s, some critics charged the Training with promoting narcissism, as in the "Me Generation," and encouraging successful selfishness. Although the actions of some Training graduates may have encouraged such critical evaluations, the Training itself revealed step by step that self-absorption—especially clinging to my "views" about this or that—is the source of suffering in my life and in the lives of others. Insight into our *shared* openness, the marvelous freedom with which we are mysteriously endowed, generates not selfishness but rather compassion and the question: "How can I help?" One of Erhard's favorite phrases goes like this: "If you forget who you really are, then be of service." Erhard's often-stated goal of creating a world that works for *everyone* stems from a deep realization that life is not just about me, it's about everyone. Like many of those who took the Training and later The Forum, I would not trade the insight it provided for anything in the world. No amount of money, fame, power, sex, drugs, or knowledge is comparable to what one spiritual tradition calls the "the pearl of great price."

Spirituality and its relationship to the est Training and The Forum

Those who are interested in spirituality and philosophy of religion, as I am, can find parallels between Zen Buddhism, Hinduism, and Christianity, on the one hand, and the Training, on the other. The Training and The Forum are best understood, however, as *ontological* rather than "spiritual" explorations. Unlike traditional spirituality, as typically experienced in church, synagogue, or mosque, and in other non-religious spiritual disciplines, the Training sought to disclose the ontological structure of human existence.

Erhard would agree that theologians can *draw upon* this ontological insight, as twentieth-century German theologian Rudolf Bultmann drew upon Heidegger's philosophy so as to "demythologize" Christian theology. Theology, however, interprets the transformational experience in accordance with religious concepts and narratives, some of which conflict with the Training's claim that everything is inherently "empty and meaningless," until *we* assign a meaning to something that occurs.[6] For Biblical theism, the universe was meaningful long before humans showed up, because God intentionally created it. Although informed by an evidence-based idea of human existence, the Trainers engaged in phenomenology, that is, instead of getting bogged down in discussion of the merits of this theory versus another one, Trainers focused on what actually discloses itself in the processes of sharing and interpreting that sharing. As the transcript of the 1989 Forum reveals, the number of shares supporting The Forum's basic assumptions—that we are the clearing in which things can show up and thus "be," and that we assign meanings to events that do not inherently contain such meaning—was overwhelming.[7]

In the 1989 Forum, Erhard engages briefly in God-talk, but primarily to dissuade people from using the idea of God to further their rackets. Doing so, he says at one point, amounts to blasphemy. "Blasphemy" may seem to be a curious term to use in a secular, ontological inquiry. Here is one way to make sense of that usage. The God-talk in the 1989 Forum is an instance of what Buddhists calls skillful means (*upaya*). Mahayana Buddhism, especially Zen, maintains that "salvation" does not lie in some far-off realm still to come, but instead is always already available here and now, in this very human body/mind. Depicting God as some sort of super entity controlling everything from up in heaven, while apart from human existence, impedes discovery of humankind's own mode of Being and the possibilities belonging to it. This is the point made by the shocking Mahayana Buddhist directive: "If you encounter the Buddha on the road, kill him!" You can't kill the Buddha, however, because he's not "out there." Instead, Buddha-nature lies within each human being, awaiting the possibility of awakening to itself.[8] Toward the end of The Forum, there typically arises what I call "the space of transformation," that extraordinary moment when most participants had the experience of shedding the burden of their rackets. Yes, the rackets will return, but for many people, never with the force that the rackets once had.

Critics sometimes charge that Erhard's seminars lack "spirituality," but most participants in the 1989 Forum experienced with joy the realization that they are not substances with certain properties, but instead the clearing that is open to *possibility*. What The Forum refuses to provide, and in fact cannot provide based on its own method of exploration, is some *story* about the ultimate "meaning of life." The three Western monotheisms provide such stories, which have inspired faith for many centuries. Instead of offering such a story, however, The Forum leaves to participants the task of establishing goals and organizing their lives to achieve them. The issue of an otherworldly, metaphysical *eschaton* does not come up, except when it is brought up by participants, and then The Forum leader typically brings the conversation back to the here and now, to what's right in front of the participant. And yet, according to Erhard, most clergy, be they priest, nun, rabbi, minister, or imam, have left the *est* Training or The Forum with a deeper relation to their particular practice of faith.

Deflecting and dismissing "metaphysical" concerns is a common practice among Zen masters. Having been knocked off a bridge into the water below by a Zen master exasperated by his student's persistent metaphysical questioning, for example, one Zen student finally "awakened." The key was finally realizing the futility of such questioning and the opportunity of existing fully in this life, moment by moment. Another anecdote reveals the inveterate tendency to "go metaphysical," as well as the opportunity to follow a different path. A famous Zen *koan* says: "Show me your original face before you were born!" I used to think that the answer to this koan had something to do with revealing who I was in the *bardo*, the realm in which one's "habit-energy" dwells before manifesting itself in a new body-mind. This is "going metaphysical" in a way suggested by some Buddhist discourse. Only recently did I arrive at a very different interpretation of the *koan*, one consistent with what I learned in the Training and later in The Forum. The key is what word to stress in the *koan*: "Show me your original face before YOU were born!" By "you," the *koan* has in mind the fear-driven, greedy, delusional being that I had turned myself into. I did not show up in the world like that, but gave birth to that unhappy self by decisions I made while growing up. Not long ago, when I asked Werner Erhard if he agreed with this interpretation of the *koan*, he said "Yes! That's it!"

Erhard, Heidegger, and The Forum

Around the time I took the Training, I had been reading psychiatrist Irvin D. Yalom's *Existential Therapy*, which argued that much human suffering arose from not allowing anxiety and ontological guilt to play the revelatory and transformative role they could play in human existence.[9] Citing authors such as Ernst Becker, author of *The Denial of Death*, Yalom remarked that we shrink from life, we hide ourselves away, in order to avoid paying the debt: death.[10] Finitude is essential to authentic existence.

Staying in touch with mortality encourages us to be present each moment, rather than fleeing into the myriad distractions now available.

I wrote to Yalom to see if I could study with him during a six-month sabbatical, which I planned to spend in the Bay Area in the first half of 1982. He suggested that I would benefit more by studying and teaching at the California School of Professional Psychology in Berkeley. (The work I did there led to my subsequent appointment as a clinical professor in the Psychiatry Department at Tulane University School of Medicine.) Shortly after arriving in Berkeley in early January, Hubert Dreyfus invited me to his house for dinner. Dreyfus was a leading interpreter of Heidegger's philosophy and later was professor emeritus for many years at the University of California at Berkeley. Soon, I discovered that he, too, had done the Training, that he had been blown away by it, that he knew Werner Erhard, and that he was co-director of the PhD dissertation of Fernando Flores, who combined elements of speech act theory, which he learned from Berkeley philosopher John Searle, with Heidegger's view of temporal-historical human existence, to develop a powerful vision of "conversation for action" in the "office of the future." Erhard, a brilliant man in his own right, quickly came to appreciate the role played by language in creating futures where none seemed possible. This is a story for another time, however.[11]

Even before meeting Flores and learning something about Heidegger's thought, Erhard and colleagues had been planning to redesign the Training. Erhard invited Dreyfus and me to develop philosophical critiques of the Training. We gladly consented to do so, because both of us had gained so much from it. Each of us sat in on Trainings given at different times and locations, then composed our assessments of what we witnessed.[12] In May 1982 I met with Erhard, Flores, and several of their colleagues to discuss my findings. The papers that Dreyfus and I wrote contributed to what would become The Forum, the first version of which was presented in San Francisco in 1985. It was a pleasure to attend that signal event. I am proud and happy to have made a contribution to the emergence of The Forum.

Not long ago, I re-read the 104-page transcript of the discussion about my critique of the Training. Doing so confirmed for me that Erhard had already come up with the key elements of the Training, later The Forum, *independently* of what he learned about Heidegger from Flores, Dreyfus, me, and others. Heidegger's ideas were remarkably similar to Erhard's in many ways, and Erhard learned some valuable distinctions from Heidegger, but they arrived at their major ideas on their own.

Heidegger's writings have had an enormous influence on twentieth-century philosophy in Europe, Latin America, and to a lesser extent in the United States. Perhaps his university teaching helped to evoke transformation experiences on the part of some students, but he created no seminars with that aim in mind. Erhard's work, in contrast, has been made available to more than two million people by way of the Training and later The Forum. Linguistic distinctions developed by Erhard and colleagues have had a vast if underappreciated influence on culture in the past forty years. Many distinctions that Erhard coined or used in new contexts have found their way into the larger culture without being attributed to Erhard. The present book is in part an effort to correct this situation.

Another difference between Erhard and Heidegger concerns compassion and forgiveness. Those familiar with Heidegger know that such ideas rarely appear in his early writings. In fact, his writings in the 1930s often emphasize steely resolution, authentic being-towards-death, and a kind of ruthless commitment to revolutionary change. Such discourse became particularly frequent and charged in the years when Heidegger was involved with National Socialism, beginning in 1932. Later on, Heidegger developed his famous discourse on *Gelassenheit*, or "releasement," the attitude of letting things be, which some have read as including compassion for others.

Let me now answer the question that I posed at the beginning of this first section of this Afterword, namely, "Do the remarkable parallels between the work of Erhard and Heidegger confirm the validity of their respective findings?" The fact that Heidegger and Erhard arrived independently at similar findings about human existence justifies taking the two views more seriously than either one alone. The remarkable confluence of their findings does not, of course, mean that they are true, such that other possible approaches to understanding human existence are excluded. Indeed, there are many alternatives, which are often incompatible with one another. As any student of Heidegger's work knows, it exhibits unusual depth and originality; likewise, the distinctions that Erhard deployed in the Training and The Forum have elicited from many thousands of people an experience of the clearing that is central to Heidegger's thinking. I hope that the book that Hyde and Kopp have written will be the first of many other investigations into the ontology of human existence and into how we can elicit experiential insight into that ontology.

The question concerning Heidegger's Politics

Let me now pose a *second* and final question: Do revelations about Heidegger's far-right-wing political views negate the value of all his work and disqualify him as a philosopher?

Martin Heidegger settled on a philosophical career only after health concerns

required him to end his Jesuit novitiate. He remained drawn to the mysticism of Meister Eckhart, avidly read the works of Luther, and was influenced by Gnosticism. In *Being and Time* Heidegger drew on such sources, and many others, in describing humankind as "thrown" and "fallen," fleeing from finite openness and from the concrete possibilities disclosed therein, embracing instead routinized everyday practices, and being seduced by countless distractions aimed at concealing who we really are. This book revolutionized twentieth-century European philosophy, and Heidegger had a dramatic effect on students, many of whom were Jews, such as Hannah Arendt, Herbert Marcuse, Helena Weiss, Hans Jonas, and Karl Löwith.

These students were understandably shocked when in 1933 Heidegger publicly announced his allegiance to National Socialism. Caught up in the ecstatic revolutionary moment, Heidegger used his own discourse of resolute authenticity to encourage others to join him in supporting Adolph Hitler. For a few years Heidegger was a devoted follower, but gradually became disenchanted with what one might call the "really existing" Nazi party, which he came to regard as another version of the same techno-industrial nihilism that in his perspective animated American capitalism and Soviet Marxism. Nevertheless, he remained attached to the idea that National Socialism had contained an "inner truth and greatness" that had been perverted by leaders who were not up to the task. Showing little sympathy for Heidegger's attempted self-justification, however, the Allies in charge of post-war de-Nazification hearings concluded that his complicity with the Nazi regime made him unfit for teaching. He was removed from his post at the University of Freiburg. Ever since then, controversy has raged about the extent to which the positive contributions of Heidegger's thought can be separated from his far-right-wing, arguably anti-Semitic views.

I had always been concerned about his Nazi affiliation, so much so that my first published article bears the title "Heidegger, Ethics, and National Socialism."[13] At that time, I tended to side with his supporters, who contended that one should distinguish between Heidegger the thinker and Heidegger the man, that is, the misguided political activist. Critics, on the other hand, charged that his philosophy had much in common with Nazi ideology. In the late 1980s publication of books demonstrating the affinity between important aspects of Heidegger's thought and Nazi ideology led me to rethink my attitude toward his philosophy, as I reported in my book, *Heidegger's Confrontation with Modernity: Technology, Politics, Art.*[14]

In that book, I argued that Heidegger's notion of the "history of being" had much in common with views promoted by various Nazi ideologues and pro-Nazi philosophers. According to Heidegger, modernity is the final stage in the long decline of

Western civilization from its grand beginning in ancient Greece. Techno-industrial modernity brings to a culmination the nihilistic history of the West. It is worth noting, as Berkeley philosopher Hans Sluga has pointed out, that Heidegger was only one of many German philosophers who became either outright Nazis or else fellow travellers.[15] Many academic humanists of the era—German, French, English, Spanish, Italian—agreed with Heidegger that modernity was a colossal misstep, which promoted the revolt of the masses. Of course, Heidegger's already elevated philosophical status meant that his conversion had greater significance at a time when the Nazi regime still sought cultural legitimation. It is also worth noting that much of what he says about techno-industrial modernity, namely, that it reduces nature to mere raw material and humankind to resources demanded by the power-seeking system, is remarkably similar to what was said around the same time by leading members of the left-wing Frankfurt School, including Theodor Adorno and Max Horkheimer.

Heidegger's view of Western history as leading to nihilism stands in stark contrast to progressive interpretations, initiated by French Enlightenment thinkers, as well as by G.W.F. Hegel, Marx, and many other nineteenth- and twentieth-century European and American political theorists, according to which history leads to emancipation from ignorance and unjust political authority, and to scientific knowledge that promises relief from human misery. Heidegger's anti-modernist attitudes were similar in some ways to those held by Nietzsche. Both thinkers became major influences on post-modern theory, which depicts modernity in ways that at times have much in common with anti-modernist views that prevailed in Germany in the late nineteenth and early twentieth centuries.

Despite his rejection of modernity and his embrace of the far-right Nazi party, Heidegger carefully avoided anti-Semitic statements in his published works. Subsequent historical research has showed, however, that while he was Rektor of the University of Freiburg (1933–34), he made such statements in official letters and engaged in some anti-Jewish activity.

The ongoing publication of the *Black Notebooks*, which Heidegger began to compose in the 1930s, brings the political controversy to a new stage. In these *Notebooks*, now appearing in his *Gesamtausgabe* (*Collected Works*), Heidegger writes that European Jewry played a significant role in the rise of "calculative" thinking, which he held responsible for modernity's disclosure of everything as mere means for enhancing power. At times, he suggested that the Jews were somehow responsible for the rise of such thinking, but at other times he indicated that the Jews were pawns in the process by which the Being of entities had concealed itself, with the result that entities (including humans) had been gradually reduced to sheer instrumentality.

For Heidegger, human existence opens up the clearing in which entities can manifest themselves and in this sense "be." Supposedly, the ancient Greeks were opened up in a way that allowed entities to stand forth, to reveal themselves in ways that gave rise to incomparable beauty and terrible violence. Gradually, however, the clearing that constitutes human existence began to become constricted, beginning already with Plato and Aristotle (!). Hence, the Being of entities could reveal itself in ever more limited ways. Instead of existing so as to let entities be manifest in their own ways, humankind asserted itself as the human subject, arrogating to itself the right to dominate the planet. Such violent self-assertion, according to Heidegger, results not from a merely human decision, but instead from effacement of the Being of entities. In addition to blaming the Jews for this outcome, he also assigns responsibility for it to the Catholic Church, American capitalism, Soviet Marxism, scientism, democracy, and other institutions. In some ways, Heidegger was an equal-opportunity denouncer.

Heidegger goes so far as to suggest that the death camps, however terrible their outcome was for Jews, were the products of the very same calculative, instrumental, power-driven thinking that they had promulgated. Today, we would call this "blaming the victims." That he held such a view helps to explain, at last, his silence about the Holocaust. We may be charitable in saying that he did not endorse the death camps, but he did not speak out against them, even after the war, much to the consternation of his Jewish students as well as many other philosophers who had learned from Heidegger's publications.

Anti-Semitism was widespread in Europe and America in the decades leading up to World War II. It became particularly ferocious in Germany for many different reasons, one of them being that emancipated Jews turned out to be exceptionally intelligent, capable, and hard-working, thereby winning positions of influence in academia, medicine, law, and business. These achievements, presumably unexpected by a German population still harboring anti-Semitic views, provoked widespread *ressentiment*, as Nietzsche put it. Germany's defeat in World War I, accusations of internal betrayal that led to that outcome, the punitive treaty at Versailles, the Great Inflation followed by Great Depression, widespread street fighting between Nazi Brownshirts and communists, and the perceived political gridlock arising from the democratic Weimar regime, helped to create the conditions that allowed for a charismatic demagogue like Hitler to seize power by blaming Jews for Germany's misery. Describing these social, political, and economic conditions, however, does not remove personal responsibility for Heidegger and others who chose to side with the Nazis and who tolerated the violence they wreaked on millions of innocent people.

There has already been a virtual tidal wave of commentary addressing the question of Heidegger's anti-Semitism, most recently as it appears in his *Black Notebooks*.[16] Some scholars conclude that Heidegger's should no longer be taught or studied, because it is allegedly "contaminated" with far-right-wing and anti-Semitic views. My own view is that Heidegger's philosophical gifts were so great that we would make a mistake to boot him out of the philosophical cannon, any more than we should exclude Wagner from the musical canon, even though his anti-Semitic attitudes may be discerned on occasion in some of his greatest operas, not to mention in his published essays. In both cases, we must read and listen with discernment, with recognition that even brilliant philosophical work and stirring musical compositions may contain dark and dangerous aspects.

Publication of the *Black Notebooks* ought to be an occasion for reflection about the anti-Semitic and racist views that characterized much of the Western world, especially in the nineteenth and twentieth centuries. Recent work on American slavery has demonstrated that this dreadful industrial regime provided the wealth needed for capitalism to get up a head of steam by the middle of the nineteenth century.[17] American and European colonialism, justified by white supremacist notions of "the white man's burdens," included practices that we should look back upon with horror. Heidegger belonged to a version of that white supremacist world, even though he adhered not to biological racism, but instead to a kind of metaphysical-linguistic racism focused on the exceptionalism of the ancient Greeks and the German *Volk*. Racist views, to be sure, were held by many, including those whom we otherwise revere. The recent controversy over public display of the Confederate flag in some Southern states demonstrates the cultural staying power of anti-modernism, including white supremacy.

Heidegger should continue to be studied and appreciated for his important philosophical contributions, especially work from the era of *Being and Time*, which proves most important for understanding the parallels between Erhard's work and Heidegger's. His later writings, including his powerful reflections on the nature of language, and his effort to understand the essence of modern technology, also merit attention, though they should be read while keeping in mind that they sometimes entwined themselves with his far-right-wing political views.

One of the things that struck some of Heidegger's students when reading *Being and Time* was this: What should be the *content* of decisions made within the light of resolute authenticity? I am resolved, but resolved to do what? Heidegger answered that question for himself in the early 1930s by becoming a Nazi. According to him, only the situation itself makes clear what is called for. For him, then, authenticity was consistent with being a Nazi, which for Heidegger also meant taking a stand against Soviet Marxism, which he regarded as a mortal threat to Western civilization. The inconceivable atrocities of the Holocaust seem to annul the validity of Heidegger's decision to support Nazism, even if his concern about Soviet Marxism may have been justified. Throughout history, people have committed violence when they felt duty-bound to fulfill some great task. There is no guarantee that anything we choose to do now, even in moments of apparent clarity, will later prove morally praiseworthy.[18] Heidegger joined a movement that provoked World War II and killed millions of people in concentration camps. Presumably, readers of this book would agree that at some point before he died, or even posthumously, Heidegger should have offered some expression of regret for his contributions to the Nazi movement. We can only speculate about why he refused to do so, but one reason may be his inability to tell the truth about his personal responsibility. Heidegger was a particular moral agent, not the spokesperson for the "history of Being."

Although Erhard's Forum is apolitical, it is not morally neutral. Those who took The Forum in the late 1980s, or The Landmark Forum up until the present, will recall its emphasis on making a difference by contributing to the community. When Erhard initiated the Hunger Project in the 1970s, his goal was to demonstrate that we could end the conversation that holds hunger to be inevitable. Instead, we can initiate a new conversation, according to which hunger can be ended. Despite being criticized in some circles, the Hunger Project was an important social, economic, and political intervention. It invited people to commit to this proposition: We do not have to put up with hunger. There is enough food, but we lack the conviction that hunger can be eliminated. By changing our attitude toward hunger, we can end it, thus helping to create a world that works for everyone. Or as Erhard would put it, by altering the way hunger *occurs* for us as inevitable, so that it can *occur* for us as *endable*, our behavior related to hunger would also be altered.

Erhard would agree that life is dangerous. In taking a stand, we may end up going astray, even though it made sense to take that stand at the moment. One of the reasons that The Forum's sharing is so important, however, is its revelation that most people really want to make a difference that contributes to human well being and—these days—to planetary well being, too. Creating and attempting to bring to fruition possible and desirable futures—these are risky endeavors. Not only can they fail, and usually will fail, but at times they will cause more harm than they attempted to prevent. Recognizing this is an invitation to heed what others have to say, especially those who are most critical about what we propose to do. Heedless confidence in your own way of being *the one* that will perfect the world, as was the case in totalitarian movements of the twentieth century, is almost certainly a recipe for disaster. New worlds must be built together with people from a wide variety of perspectives, pre-modern, modern, and post-modern.

★★★★★★★★

In the foregoing book, Hyde and Kopp have threaded the needle. They have showed that Heidegger's work has important parallels with ideas that Erhard arrived at on his own, and they have done so in a way that leaves no room for ascribing either far-right-wing or far-left-wing views to Erhard. Although he may be an existentialist, he is also a modernist, unlike Heidegger. I regard *Speaking Being* as an enormously important contribution to understanding Heidegger and Erhard. The latter has received far too little serious academic attention, and this book begins to make up for that lack. Moreover, the book's analysis of Heidegger's thought is among the best that I have ever read. I commend this book to all readers without reservation.

AFTERWORD: ENDNOTES

1   Martin Heidegger, *Being and Time*, trans. John Macquarrie and Edward Robinson (New York: Harper & Row, 1962).

2   Michael E. Zimmerman, *Eclipse of the Self: The Development of Heidegger's Concept of Authenticity* (Athens: Ohio University Press, 1981).

3   Baba Ram Dass, *Be Here Now* (New Mexico: Lama Foundation, 1971).

4   A distinction is made sometimes between *kensho* and *satori*. *Kensho* is a first taste of enlightenment, but one that must be continually cultivated and repeated. One transformation experience is enough to get one started on the journey, but Buddhism argues that many lifetimes are required to overcome the conditioning imposed by the three poisons, greed, aversion and delusion.

5   Conversation with Werner Erhard, November 24, 2015.

6   In *Heidegger and Theology* (London and New York: 2014), Judith Wolfe shows that even though Heidegger's philosophy arose in constant critical dialogue with theology, *Being and Time* analyzes finite human existence, without reference to God. Heidegger's contention that authentic existence involves Being-towards-death suggests an "eschatology without *eschaton*." In "The Facticity of Being God-Forsaken: The Young Heidegger and Luther's Theology of the Cross," *American Catholic Philosophical Quarterly*, 79, 2 (2005), 273–290, Sean J. McGrath argues that the task of phenomenology is to describe the Being of the fallen human, and also to depict the extent to which finite, fallen existence can be authentic. Theology's eschatological concern with salvation and a possibly eternal afterlife are not matters of concern to philosophy, Heidegger concluded.

7   Humans are very good at recognizing patterns and making distinctions, but for patterns to be experienced as *meaningful*, they must somehow *matter* to our Being-in-the-world. Our existence is always at stake for us, which is what Heidegger meant by saying that the very Being of humankind is care. Arguably, until computers exist in a clearing of their own, their distinction-making—no matter how much faster than human distinction-making—will have *no significance* for computers themselves. Computers are (not yet) at issue for themselves. See Michael E. Zimmerman, "Heidegger on Techno-Posthumanism: Revolt against Finitude? Or, Doing What Comes 'Naturally'?" in *Perfecting Human Futures: Technology, Secularization and Eschatology*, ed. J. Benjamin Hurlbut and Hava Tirosh-Samuelson (Dordrecht: Springer, 2015). In his books and many articles, Hubert Dreyfus has pioneered a Heideggerian critique of Artificial Intelligence.

8   Something similar is true for certain interpretations of Christianity. When Jesus called his followers "sons and daughters of God," he affirmed they were *always already* divine, although cloaked in sin (analogous in some ways to rackets). As German philosopher G.W.F. Hegel put it two centuries ago, in a controversial interpretation, Jesus was the first person to awaken to his own divinity.

9   Irvin D. Yalom, *Existential Psychotherapy* (New York: Basic Books, 1980). See my review in *The Review of Existential Psychology and Psychiatry*, XVI, Nos. 2 and 3 (1980–81), 259–264.

10 Ernst Becker, *The Denial of Death* (New York: Free Press, 1997 [originally published in 1974].)

11 Through Dreyfus's good offices, I met both Erhard and Flores, as a result of which the six months I spent in Berkeley proved to be extraordinary. Flores introduced Erhard to Heidegger's work, as well as to my book, *Eclipse of the Self*. In introducing me to a talk I was to give to some Trainers, Erhard said that he had read more of my book than any book since *Shogun*. Erhard has often acknowledged his debt to the Zen tradition. Heidegger was new to him, but not to the Japanese, who have produced at least five translations of Heidegger's *Being and Time*, because they sense a connection between *sunyata* and what Heidegger had in mind by nothingness (*das Nichts*) or the clearing that constitutes human existence.

12 My 1982 assessment of the Training can be found at: http://www.scribd.com/doc/72095792/Est-A-Philosophical-Appraisal-by-Michael-Zimmerman#scribd.

13 Michael E. Zimmerman, "Heidegger, Ethics, and National Socialism," *The Southwestern Journal of Philosophy*, V (Spring, 1974), 97–106.

14 Michael E. Zimmerman, *Heidegger's Confrontation with Modernity: Technology, Politics, Art* (Bloomington: Indiana University Press, 1991).

15 Hans Sluga, *Heidegger's Crisis: Philosophy and Politics in Nazi Germany, German Politics and Society* (Cambridge: Harvard University Press, 1993).

16 German editor of the *Black Notebooks* has asked to what extent Heidegger's thought has been contaminated by what some call his "ontological anti-Semitism."

17 See, for example, Edward E. Baptist, *The Half Has Never Been Told: Slavery and the Making of American Capitalism* (New York: Basic Books, 2014).

18 On this issue, see my essay, "Authenticity and Duty in *Do Androids Dream of Electric Sheep?*" in *The Horizons of Authenticity in Phenomenology Existentialism, and Moral Psychology*, eds. Hans Pedersen and Megan Altman,. Vol. 74 of *Contributions to Phenomenology* (Doredrecht and New York: Springer, 2015), 75–92.

REFERENCES: HEIDEGGER

Abbreviations: Source:

"AWP" in QCT: "Age of the World Picture." In The Question Concerning Technology and Other Essays. Trans. by William Lovitt. New York, NY: Harper & Row, 1977.

BC: *Basic Concepts*. Trans. by Gary E. Aylesworth. Bloomington: Indiana University Press, 1998.

BPP: *The Basic Problems of Phenomenology*. Revised ed. Trans. by Albert Hofstadter. Bloomington: Indiana University Press, 1988.

BW: *Basic Writings: Key Selections from Being and Time to the Task of Thinking* Revised and expanded edition. Ed. David Farrell Krell. London: Harper Perennial, 2008.

BT: *Being and Time*. Trans. John Macquarrie and Edward Robinson. San Francisco: Harper & Row, 1962.

BTT: *Being and Time: A Translation of Sein Und Zeit* (1927). Trans. Joan Stambaugh. Albany: State University of New York Press, 1996.

"BDT" in PLT: "Building, Dwelling, Thinking." In *Poetry, Language, Thought*. Trans. and Introduction by Albert Hofstadter. New York: Harper and Row, 1971.

Event: *Contributions to Philosophy (of the Event)*. Trans. Richard Rojcewicz and Daniela Vallega-Neu. Bloomington: Indiana University Press, 2012.

"DL" in OWL: "A Dialogue on Language." In *On the Way to Language*. Trans. Peter D. Hertz. New York: Harper and Row, 1971.

DT: *Discourse on Thinking*. Trans. John M. Anderson and E. Hans Freund. With an Introduction by John M. Anderson. New York: Harper and Row, 1966.

EGT: *Early Greek Thinking*. Trans. David Farrell Krell and Frank A. Capuzzi. New York: Harper and Row, 1975.

EP: *The End of Philosophy*. Trans. Joan Stambaugh. Chicago: University Press, 2003.

FCM: *The Fundamental Concepts of Metaphysics: World, Finitude, Solitude.*

Trans. William McNeill and Nicholas Walker. Bloomington: Indiana University Press, 1995.

"EP&TT" in BW: "The End of Philosophy and the Task of Thinking." In *Basic Writings: Key Selections from Being and Time to the Task of Thinking*. Revised and expanded edition. Ed. David Farrell Krell. London: Harper Perennial, 2008.

ID: *Identity and Difference*. Trans. Joan Stambaugh. Chicago: UP, 2002.

IM: *Introduction to Metaphysics*. Trans. by Gregory Fried and Richard Polt. 2nd Ed. New Haven: Yale University Press, 2014.

"L" in PLT: "Language." In *Poetry, Language, Thought*. Trans. and Introduction by Albert Hofstadter. New York: Harper and Row, 1971.

"LP" in OWL: "Language in the Poem." In *On the Way to Language*. Trans.

Peter D. Hertz. New York: Harper and Row, 1971.

"LH" in BW: "Letter on Humanism." In *Basic Writings: Key Selections from Being and Time to the Task of Thinking*. Revised and expanded edition. Ed. David Farrell Krell. London: Harper Perennial, 2008.

"NL" in OWL: "The Nature of Language." In *On the Way to Language*. Trans.

Peter D. Hertz. New York: Harper and Row, 1971.

"OET" in BW: "On the Essence of Truth." In *Basic Writings: Key Selections from Being and Time to the Task of Thinking*. Revised and expanded edition. Ed. David Farrell Krell. London: Harper Perennial, 2008.

OTB: Heidegger, Martin. *On Time and Being*. Trans. Joan Stambaugh. Chicago: University of Chicago Press, 2002.

OWL: *On the Way to Language*. Trans. Peter D. Hertz. New York: Harper and Row, 1971.

"OWA" in PLT: "The Origin of the Work of Art." In *Poetry, Language, Thought*. Trans. and Introduction by Albert Hofstadter. New York: Harper and Row, 1971.

PLT: *Poetry, Language, Thought*. Trans. and Introduction by Albert Hofstadter. New York: Harper and Row, 1971.

PR: *The Principle of Reason*. Trans. Reginald Lilly. Bloomington: Indiana University Press, 1996.

QCT: *The Question Concerning Technology and Other Essays*. Trans. William Lovitt. New York, NY: Harper & Row, 1977.

"QCT" in BW: "The Question Concerning Technology." In *Basic Writings: Key Selections from Being and Time to the Task of Thinking*. Revised and expanded ed. Ed. David Farrell Krell. London: Harper Perennial, 2008.

"TP" in PLT: "The Thinker as Poet." In *Poetry, Language, Thought*. Trans. and Introduction by Albert Hofstadter. New York: Harper and Row, 1971.

"TT" in QCT: "The Turning." In *The Question Concerning Technology and Other Essays*. Trans. William Lovitt. New York, NY: Harper & Row, 1977.

"WL" in OWL: "The Way to Language." In *On the Way to Language*. Trans. Peter D. Hertz. New York: Harper and Row, 1971.

WCT: *What Is Called Thinking?* Trans. and with an Introduction by J. Glenn Gray. New York: Harper and Row, 1968.

"WM" in BW: "What Is Metaphysics?" In *Basic Writings: Key Selections from Being and Time to the Task of Thinking*. Revised and expanded edition. Ed. David Farrell Krell. London: Harper Perennial, 2008.

REFERENCES: WERNER ERHARD

"All I Can Do Is Lie." Undated reprint. *East West Journal*, September 1974.

Erhard, Werner, and Michael C. Jensen. "Putting Integrity into Finance: A Purely Positive Approach." *Capitalism and Society*, 12.1, 2017.

"Beyond the Winning Formula," 1989.

"Effective Action and Accomplishment." 1985.

"The Heart of the Matter," 1985.

"Taking a Stand for the Future," 1983.

REFERENCES: SECONDARY SOURCES

Abe, Maseo. *Zen and Western Thought*. Ed. William R. LaFleur. Honolulu: University of Hawaii, 1989.

Bartley, William Warren III. *Werner Erhard, The Transformation of a Man: The Founding of est*. New York: Clarkson N. Potter, 1978.

Bode, Stefan, Anna Hanxi He, Chun Siong Soon, Robert Trampel, Robert Turner, John-Dylan Haynes. "Tracking the Unconscious Generation of Free Decisions Using Ultra-High Field fMRI," *PLoS ONE* 6, no. 6 (2011): e21612.

Boss, Medard. "Martin Heidegger's Zollikon Seminars." Trans. by Brian Kenny. In *Heidegger and Psychology*. (HP) Edited by Keith Hoeller. Special issue from the *Review of Existential Psychology & Psychiatry*, 1988. (7–20).

Bruns, Gerald L. *Heidegger's Estrangements: Language, Truth, and Poetry in the Later Writings*. New Haven: Yale University Press, 1989.

Bruzina, Ronald. "Heidegger on the Metaphor and Philosophy." In *Heidegger and Modern Philosophy*, ed. Michael Murray, 184–200. New Haven: Yale University Press, 1978.

Buckner, Randy L., and Fenna M. Krienen. "The Evolution of Distributed Association Networks in the Human Brain," *Trends in Cognitive Sciences* 17, no. 12 (2013): 648–665.

Caputo, John D. *The Mystical Element in Heidegger's Thought*. New York: Fordham University Press, 1986.

Cassin, Barbara, and Emily Apter. *Dictionary of Untranslatables: A Philosophical Lexicon*. Princeton: University Press, 2014.

Clancey, W.J. "Situated Action: A Neurophysiological Response to Vera and Simon," *Cognitive Science* 17 (1993): 87–116.

Dreyfus, Hubert L. "Assessment of the Philosophical Significance of the est Training," 1982 (https://www.scribd.com/doc/72095343/Assessment-of-the-Philosophical-Signifcance-of-The-est-Training).

—. *Being-in-the-World: a Commentary on Heidegger's* Being and Time, *Division I*, 1991. Cambridge: MIT Press, 1995.

—. "Gaining a Free Relationship to Technology." Paper presented at the Applied Heidegger Conference, University of California at Berkeley, September 1989.

— and Mark A. Wrathall. *Companion to Heidegger*. Malden, MA: Blackwell, 2007.

Edie, James M. *Speaking and Meaning: The Phenomenology of Language*. Bloomington, IA: Indiana University Press, 1976.

Gopnik, Adam. "Word Magic," *New Yorker*, May 26, 2014.

Guignon, Charles. "Being as Appearing: Retrieving the Greek Experience of *Phusis*." In *A Companion to Heidegger's Introduction to Metaphysics*, Eds. Richard Polt and Gregory Fried. New Haven: Yale University Press, 2001.

Haggard, Patrick. "Human Volition: Towards a Neuroscience of Will," *Nature Reviews: Neuroscience* 9 (2008): 934–946.

Hawkins, Jeff, and Sandra Blakeslee. *On Intelligence*. New York: Henry Holt , 2004.

Harris, Sam. *Free Will*. New York: Free Press, 2012.

Huhnerfeld, Paul. *The Heidegger Affair: An Essay Upon a German Genius* (Munchen: Paul List Verlag, 1961).

Johnstone Jr., Henry W. "Persuasion and Validity in Philosophy." In *Validity, Rhetoric, and Philosophical Argument: An Outlook in Transition*. University Park: The Dialogue Press of Man and World, 1978.

—. "Rhetoric and Communication in Philosophy." In *Validity, Rhetoric, and Philosophical Argument: An Outlook in Transition*. University Park: The Dialogue Press of Man and World, 1978.

—. "Truth, Communication, and Rhetoric in Philosophy." In *Validity, Rhetoric, and Philosophical Argument: An Outlook in Transition*. University Park: The Dialogue Press of Man and World, 1978.

Kandel, Eric, Daniel Wolpert, and Thomas Jessell. "The Acting Brain," *Charlie Rose Brain Series, 2009*. First broadcast December 22 by Bloomberg.

Kemman, Ansgar. "Heidegger as Rhetor." In *Heidegger and Rhetoric*. Eds. , Daniel M. Gross and Ansgar Kemmann. New York: State University U.P., 2005.

Kockelmans, Joseph J. *On the Truth of Being: Reflections on Heidegger's Later Philosophy*. Bloomington: Indiana University Press, 1984.

Kotoh, Tetsuaki. "Language and Silence: Self-inquiry in Heidegger and Zen." In *Heidegger and Asian Thought*, ed. Graham Parkes. Honolulu: University of Hawaii Press, 1987.

Libet, Benjamin. "How Does Conscious Experience Arise? The Neural Time Factor,". *Brain Research Bulletin* 50, no. 5/6 (1999): 339–340.

—. *Neurophysiology of Consciousness: Selected Papers and New Essays*. Boston, MA: Birkhauser, 1993.

Marin, Peter. "The New Narcissism, *Harper's*, 251, no.1505 (October 1975), 45.

Moreno, Jonathan D. *Impromptu Man: J.L. Moreno and the Origins of Psychodrama, Encounter Culture, and the Social Network*. New York: Bellevue Literary Press, 2014.

Network Review, 1, no. 4, September 1983.

Polt, Richard. *Heidegger: An Introduction*. Ithaca: Cornell University Press, 1999.

— and Gregory Fried, eds. *A Companion to Heidegger's Introduction to Metaphysics*. New Haven: Yale University Press, 2001.

Rorty, Richard. *Contingency, Irony, and Solidarity*. Cambridge: University Press, 1989.

Sacks, Oliver. *The Man Who Mistook His Wife for a Hat*. New York: Touchstone, 1998.

Schoenbohm, Susan. "Heidegger's Interpretation of *Phusis* in *Introduction to Metaphysics*." In *A Companion to Heidegger's Introduction to Metaphysics*, eds. Richard Polt and Gregory Fried. New Haven: Yale University Press, 2001.

Scott, Charles E. "The Appearance of Metaphysics." In *A Companion to Heidegger's Introduction to Metaphysics*, eds. Richard Polt and Gregory Fried. New Haven: Yale University Press, 2001.

Sheehan, Thomas. *Making Sense of Heidegger: A Paradigm Shift*. London: Rowman and Littlefield International, 2015.

Simon, Richard, ed. "Quarterbacks and Coaches: Tossing It Around with Werner Erhard," *Family Therapy Networker: Werner Erhard's Forum—Selling It Like It Is.* March–April 1986.

Soon, Chun Siong, Marcel Brass, Hans-Jochen Heinze, and John-Dylan Haynes. "Unconscious Determinants of Free Decisions in the Human Brain," *Nature Neuroscience* 11, no. 5 (2008): 543–545.

Steffney, John. "Transmetaphysical Thinking in Heidegger and Zen Buddhism," *Philosophy East and West*, Vol. 27, No. 3 (July 1977): 323–335.

Stewart, John. "Speech and Human Being: A Complement to Semiotics." *Quarterly Journal of Speech,* 72 (1986): 55–73.

Storey, David. "Zen in Heidegger's Way," *Journal of East–West Thought*, Vol. 2, No. 4 (2012): 113–137.

Tabachnick, David E., "Techne, Technology and Tragedy." In *Techne: Research in Philosophy and Technology*, 7:3 (Spring 2004).

Verene, Donald Phillip. *Vico's Science of Imagination*. Ithica: Cornell University Press, 1991.

Vico Giambattista. *The New Science of Giambattista Vico: Unabridged Translation of the Third Edition (1744) with the addition of "Practic of the New Science."* Trans. Thomas Goddard Bergin and Max Harold Fisch. Ithaca and London: Cornell University Press, 1968.

The New Science of Giambattista Vico: Unabridged Translation of the Third Edition (1744) with the addition of "Practic of the New Science." Trans. Thomas Goddard Bergin and Max Harold Fisch. Ithaca and London: Cornell University Press, 1968.

Wheelwright, Philip, ed. *The Presocratics*. New York: Odyssey P, 1966.

Wolpert, Daniel. "The Real Reason for Brains," *TED Video*, 19 (2011): 59. www.ted.com/talks/daniel_wolpert_the_real_reason_for_brains.

Zimmer, Carl. 2013. "In the Human Brain, Size Really Isn't Everything," *New York Times*, December 26, 2013. www.nytimes.com/2013/12/26/science/in-the-human-brain-size-really-isnt-everything.html.

Zimmerman, Michael E. "Beyond 'Humanism': Heidegger's Understanding of Technology." In *Heidegger: The Man and the Thinker* (HMT), ed. Thomas Sheehan (Chicago: Precedent Publishers, 1981).

—. *Eclipse of the Self: The Development of Heidegger's Concept of Authenticity*. Athens: Ohio University Press, 1981.

—. *Heidegger's Confrontation with Modernity: Technology, Politics, Art*. Bloomington: Indiana University Press, 1990.

—. "Heidegger and Heraclitus on Spiritual Practice." *Philosophy Today,* 27 (1983): 83–103.

Index

Page numbers in bold are from the transcript of The Forum sessions